D0253097

# "DAMAGE THEM ALL YOU CAN"

\* \* \* \* \* \* \* \* \* \* \* \* \* \* \* \* \* \* \* \* \* \* \* \*

# "DAMAGE THEM ALL YOU CAN"

\* \* \* \* \* \* \* \* \* \* \* \* \* \* \* \* \* \* \* \* \* \* \* \*

## ROBERT E. LEE'S ARMY OF NORTHERN VIRGINIA

### GEORGE WALSH

A TOM DOHERTY ASSOCIATES BOOK

NEW YORK

"DAMAGE THEM ALL YOU CAN":
ROBERT E. LEE'S ARMY OF NORTHERN VIRGINIA

This book is printed on acid-free paper.

Map by Mark Stein Studios

Book design by Mark Abrams

A Forge Book
Published by Tom Doherty Associates, LLC
175 Fifth Avenue
New York, NY 10010

www.tor.com

Forge® is a registered trademark of Tom Doherty Associates, LLC.

Library of Congress Cataloging-in-Publication Data

Walsh, George, 1931–
    "Damage them all you can" : Robert E. Lee's Army of Northern Virginia /
George Walsh.—1st ed.
        p.   cm.
    "A Tom Doherty Associates book."
    Includes bibliographical references (p. 445) and index (p. 477)
    ISBN 0-312-87445-6
    1. Confederate States of America. Army of Northern Virginia.   2. United States—
History—Civil War, 1861–1865—Regimental histories.   3. United States—
History—Civil War, 1861–1865—Campaigns.   4. Lee, Robert E. (Robert Edward),
1807–1870—Military leadership.   5. Generals—Confederate States of America—
History.   6. Generals—Confederate States of America—Biography.   7. Confederate
States of America. Army of Northern Virginia—Biography.   I. Title.

E470.2 .W36   2002
973.7'455—dc21
                                                                    2002026069

First Edition: November 2002

Printed in the United States of America

0  9  8  7  6  5  4  3  2  1

*For Joan*

# CONTENTS

# PREFACE

In researching and writing this book on the gallant but doomed Army of Northern Virginia, one question stayed uppermost in my mind: How could Lee's men have fought so bravely, so long and at such terrible cost to defend an institution as inherently evil as slavery? Particularly to a Northerner like myself, the question at first seemed unanswerable. I knew, of course, that in the antebellum South the labor of African Americans in the fields had made a relatively small group of plantation owners rich, and the work of house slaves made their everyday lives carefree and privileged. The mid–nineteenth century's demand for cotton, which today is rivaled only by the need for oil, created immense fortunes in the South, which then produced three-quarters of the world supply—almost all of it handpicked by slaves. But I also knew that only three thousand Southerners owned a hundred or more slaves in 1860, and the typical white slave owner possessed one or two. Most Southern whites—the small farmers, artisans, clerks and laborers who comprised the men in Lee's ranks—owned no slaves at all.

Even Lee's officers, many of whom did own slaves, were uncomfortable—or at least in denial—on the subject. They insisted they were fighting to uphold states' rights; preserving slavery was an afterthought. Just before he rejected Lincoln's offer to take command of Union forces and resigned from the old army to throw his lot with Virginia, Lee himself declared his decision had nothing to do with the slavery issue. "How can I draw my sword against Virginia?" he asked.

This then was the paradox: The officers and men of the Army of Northern

Virginia believed passionately in freedom—the independence hard-won from Great Britain in 1783—but not in freedom for African Americans. Gradually I came to understand that Lee and his men deeply believed in a Southern way of life—political, social and economic—that turned a blind eye to the slavery that the Founding Fathers—both North and South—likewise had been forced to ignore in order to achieve nationhood. The Army of Northern Virginia simply reflected the prevailing Southern way of life. It was composed of moral men fighting to preserve an immoral system. Of course the Confederates did not see it that way. Wrote one soldier to his wife: "We will have to fight like Washington did, but I hope that our people will never be reduced to distress & poverty as the people of that day [were], but if nothing else will give us our liberties I am willing for the time to come."

One after another in the decades after the Revolution the Northern states, with their growing industrial bases and abolitionist sentiments, had abolished slavery and then sought to curtail it in the border states and the territories. But the agrarian South with its four million slaves could not change. Its mindset was such that freeing the slaves—unless the process involved emancipating small numbers and transporting them to Africa—could not even be considered. Lincoln's election in 1860 lit the fires of rebellion. Though he initially sought only to preserve the Union and not interfere with slavery in the states where it existed, his sentiments were well known. Slavery was "an unqualified evil to the Negro, to the white man . . . and to the State," he had warned on many occasions. Truly the nation could no longer exist half slave and half free. One by one the South's states seceded, fervently citing states' rights and utterly convinced of the righteousness of their cause. It would take a Civil War to remove the cancer of slavery from the American body politic, and the deaths of hundreds of thousands, both Federals and Confederates.

In "Damage Them All You Can" I try to present, against the background of the great battles fought by the Army of Northern Virginia, the human side of that war—sketching the strengths and weaknesses of Lee and his men, their tender relations with wives and sweethearts in the midst of carnage, and their chilling acceptance of death. They valued honor above all mortal things, and were convinced that God would give them victory. Instead they went down to defeat and America, purified, emerged all the stronger from the cauldron of war.

Ulysses S. Grant, the Union commander who ultimately defeated Lee, left us with some poignant words on the surrender at Appomattox Courthouse. "What General Lee's feelings were I do not know," he said. "As he was a man of much dignity, with an impassible face, it was impossible to say whether he felt inwardly glad that the end had finally come, or felt sad over the result. . . ." Grant could be a hard man, but that day he felt curiously depressed. "I felt like anything rather than rejoicing at the downfall of a foe who had fought so long and valiantly, and had suffered so much for a cause, though that cause was, I believe, one of the worst for which a people ever fought. . . . I do not question, however, the sincerity of the great mass of those who were opposed to us."

Within twenty-four hours, officers of both sides were freely mingling. "Some of [my men] seemed to have a great desire to go inside the Confederate lines," said Grant. "They finally asked permission of Lee to do so for the purpose of seeing their old army friends. . . . They went over, had a very pleasant time with their old friends, and brought some of them back with them." Soon Union and Confederate officers flocked to Grant's headquarters, "and seemed to enjoy the meeting as much as though they had been friends separated for a long time while fighting battles under the same flag." The healing had begun.

While I have striven for accuracy and balance in writing this story, I realize there will be those who will disagree with me on points large and small, and doubtless with good reason. Longstreet's growing foot-dragging, for instance, will be challenged by experts who believe he was right after all, and that the attack the third day at Gettysburg never should have been made. In hindsight, of course, Pickett's Charge was reckless. However, if Longstreet had followed Lee's orders diligently, who is to say Cemetery Ridge would not have been taken the second day of the battle? My reliance on certain memoirs may also be criticized, particularly for those deemed to be self-serving. To these critics I say all memoirs, to some degree or another, present the writer in a favorable light. The point is this: Were the writers *there*, and do their accounts shed reasonable light on what they observed? Lastly, the numbers of troops involved in certain actions may be questioned. Here, after making myself familiar with standard reference sources, I have exercised my best judgment. Civil War data can be endlessly open to debate.

In my Notes I have cited only those books, memoirs and periodicals I have actually used in the narrative. Citing the hundreds of sources I have not used, but which have contributed to my thinking, serves no purpose but to encourage pedantry.

Key to my research have been the *War of the Rebellion, a Compilation of the Official Records of the Union and Confederate Armies* (128 vols.); the *Southern Historical Society Papers* (52 vols.); and *Battles and Leaders of the Civil War* (4 vols.). Also innumerable memoirs ranging from the fevered prose of John Gordon Brown to the measured pragmatism of Edward Porter Alexander. My special thanks to that magisterial writer, Douglas Southall Freeman, whose *Lee* (4 vols.) and *Lee's Lieutenants* (3 vols.), first published in the 1930s and 1940s, remain the landmark works on the subject. To all Civil War historians both past and present I owe a debt, and I gratefully acknowledge it in the endnotes.

New York City, September 3, 2001

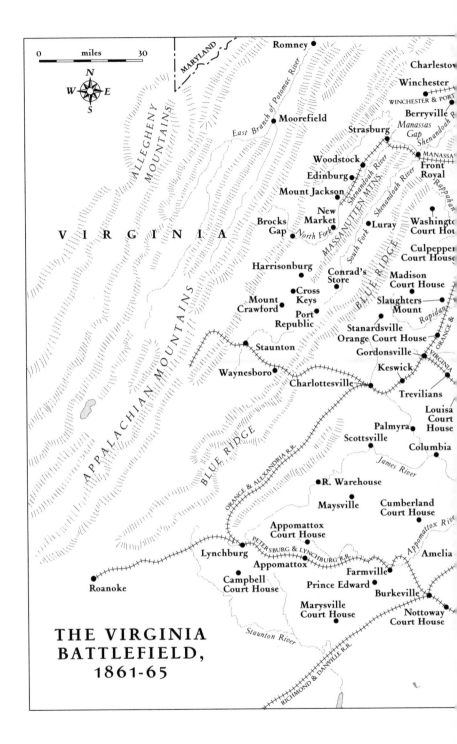

THE VIRGINIA
BATTLEFIELD,
1861-65

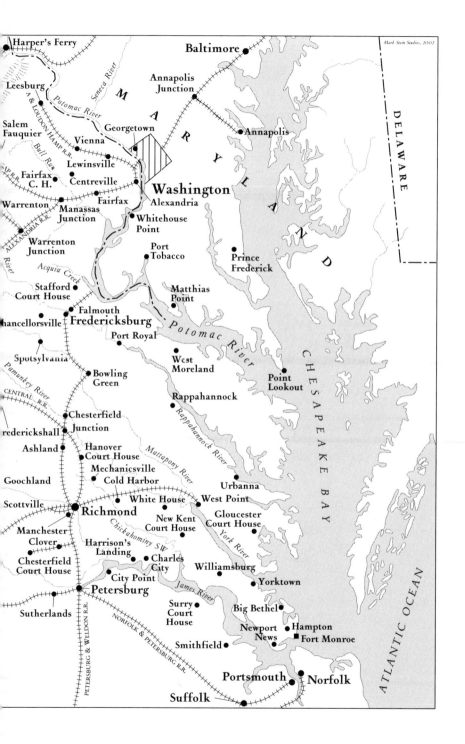

# "DAMAGE THEM ALL YOU CAN"

\* \* \* \* \* \* \* \* \* \* \* \* \* \* \* \* \* \* \* \* \* \* \* \*

# 1 8 6 1

ONE

\* \* \* \*

# THE  SOUTHERN  COMMANDERS

In both North and South the early months of 1861 clearly signaled the onset of the Civil War. Abraham Lincoln's election to the presidency, viewed as a decisive victory for the abolitionists on the slavery issue, had splintered the traditional political parties and divided the nation as never before. Emancipation had become a creed, states' rights a dogma. By February 1, all the states of the Deep South—South Carolina, Mississippi, Florida, Alabama, Georgia, Louisiana and Texas—had seceded, and soon would form the core of the Confederacy. Jefferson Davis of Mississippi, like many Southern leaders, vowed he would fight for secession if necessary. "I glory in Mississippi's star," he declared. "But before I would see it dishonored I would tear it from its place, to be set on the perilous ridge of battle as a sign around which her bravest and best shall meet the harvest home of death."[1] Yet as late as March 4, making his inaugural address, Lincoln pressed for reconciliation. "We are not enemies, but friends. We must not be enemies," he implored. "Though passion may have strained, it must not break our bonds of affection. The mystic chords of memory, stretching from every battlefield and patriot grave, to every living hearth and hearthstone all over this broad land will yet swell the chorus of the Union when again touched, as surely they will be, by the better angels of our nature."[2]

The shelling of Fort Sumter in Charleston, South Carolina, on April 12 changed all that. Davis, now president of the Confederacy, ordered Pierre Beauregard, newly named brigadier in its army, to make the attack when the North tried to reinforce its garrison. The seceded states had occupied most of the Federal property within their borders, but a few strongholds remained, and Fort Sumter was one of them. Its surrender escalated hostilities. When Lincoln called for 75,000 volunteers to put down the rebellion, Virginia and the states of the Upper South moved closer to secession themselves.

No one watched these developments with more concern than Colonel Robert E. Lee, called back to Washington that spring by 75-year-old Union General-in-Chief Winfield Scott, hero of the Mexican War and long his mentor. On April 18, Lee crossed the long bridge over the Potomac from Arlington to the capital and kept two fateful appointments. The first was with Francis Preston Blair Sr., former editor of the influential *Congressional Globe* and a power in Washington politics since the days of Andrew Jackson. Blair had already become a confidant of Lincoln, and had been authorized to offer Lee command of the force being mobilized to invade the South. "I told him what President Lincoln wanted him to do," he would say. "He wanted him to take command of the army."[3] After more than thirty years in service, inching his way up the promotional ladder, Lee must have been tempted; but he only shook his head. "If I owned the four million slaves of the South I would sacrifice then all to the Union," Blair would quote him as saying. "But how can I draw my sword against Virginia?"[4] Lee later affirmed the conversation, saying, "I declined the offer, stating as candidly and as courteously as I could, that though opposed to secession and deprecating war, I could take no part in an invasion of the Southern States."[5]

Lee's next call was on General Scott, who was awaiting news of his decision. Scott, a Virginian but a staunch Unionist, would have liked nothing better than for Lee to accept field command of the embryonic army and later to succeed him. Known as "Fuss and Feathers" because of his attention to detail, he was ailing and obese, and wanted the troops in good hands. "Lee, you have made the greatest mistake of your life," Scott said. "But I feared it would be so."[6]

Only after these interviews were over did Lee learn that the Virginia Convention, in closed session, had voted to secede. Arkansas, North Carolina and Tennessee would follow, while Kentucky and Missouri remained torn. On April 20 he resigned his commission in the U.S. Army. "My husband has wept tears of blood over this terrible war," Mary Custis Lee would write, "but as a man of honor and a Virginian, he must follow the destiny of his state."[7] Two days later Governor John Letcher named him commander of the military forces of Virginia, with the rank of major general, entrusting him to ready the state's militia for battle. This essential but thankless task would temporarily take Lee out of the war's mainstream. Regardless, he would do his duty. That was the way he had been raised.

Robert Edward Lee, a scion of the aristocracy, was born in Stratford, Virginia, on January 19, 1807, one of five children of Ann Hill Carter and Henry

("Light-Horse Harry") Lee, a gallant figure of the Revolutionary War and a favorite of George Washington. Henry Lee went on to become a governor of Virginia and a member of Congress, but a weakness for land speculation plagued his private life, and eventually plunged his family into near bankruptcy. Young Robert was only six when his father sailed for the West Indies, hoping to recoup his fortune. The boy never saw him again.

Though the numerous members of the Carter clan were wealthy, her husband's improvidence forced Ann Carter Lee to raise her own children in straitened circumstances. Money was always a concern. Robert and his siblings would visit or holiday with their many cousins, at their Stratford or Shirley plantations, but home for them was a small, modest house in Alexandria, just outside Washington. There his semi-invalid mother, honoring her husband's memory but conscious of his failings, imbued in her son the religious beliefs and moral convictions that stayed with him all his life. "Her unquestioning faith as transmitted to her son implanted in him that total acceptance . . . of working the best he could within the design of God," a commentator would say. "Whatever action duty assigned him, implicit in the duty was the *need* to do it the best he could. Nothing he wrote or any recorded word indicated that he ever presumed on any course of action, large or small, which did not assume its accordance with God's will. If his aim fell outside the divine design, then 'God's will be done.' Without articulating his attitude, it was as unreflectively assumed as breathing."[8]

Lee entered West Point in 1825, and during his four years of training compiled a distinguished record, finishing second in his class and never receiving a single demerit. "All his accomplishments . . . appeared natural to him," wrote Erasmus D. Keyes of Massachusetts, a fellow cadet who would become a Union general, "and he was free from the anxiety, distrust and awkwardness that attend a sense of inferiority."[9] Soon after his graduation Ann Carter Lee died, and the newly commissioned second lieutenant found himself in the Engineer Corps, building fortifications in Savannah, Georgia. But his leaves were spent back in Virginia, where he began courting Mary Custis, the only child of Mary Fitzhugh and George Washington Parke Custis, the adopted son of George Washington. Though Custis, the owner of a vast estate at Arlington, expressed reservations about Lee's ability to support his daughter, Mary and Robert were married in July 1831. She would bear him seven children, and continue to live at Arlington for long periods when, during the coming years, he would be assigned to posts outside Virginia.

For Lee, as for all the officers of his generation, the 1846–47 Mexican War was a testing ground. Southerners who fought in the conflict included Jefferson Davis, Pierre Beauregard, Joseph Johnston, Thomas ("Stonewall") Jackson, James Longstreet, Richard Ewell, Daniel Harvey Hill, Ambrose Powell Hill, Jubal Early and George Pickett. Northerners included George McClellan, John Pope, Ambrose Burnside, Joseph Hooker, George Meade and Ulysses S. Grant.

Captain Lee's most important service came in early 1847, when he landed with General Scott at Veracruz, beginning the drive on Mexico City. His aggressiveness, engineering skills and eye for terrain earned him Scott's high praise, several commendations and the brevet (temporary) rank of colonel. "His talent for topography was peculiar," said a fellow officer, "and he seemed to receive impressions intuitively, which it cost other men much labor to acquire."[10] From Scott he absorbed the belief that a commander should set overall strategy, then let his generals in the field handle the details. In years to come, this conviction would be sorely tested.

From 1852 to 1855, Lee served as superintendent at West Point, where he saw his eldest son, Custis, graduate first in his class, watched as his nephew Fitzhugh Lee was nearly dismissed for nighttime revelry, and himself became a mentor to a dashing cadet and tireless horseman named James Ewell Brown ("Jeb") Stuart. His youngest son, Robert, remembered him at the time as a quiet but firm disciplinarian. "I always knew it was impossible to disobey my father," he wrote. "I felt it in me, I never thought why, but was perfectly sure when he gave an order that it had to be obeyed."[11] Next came a posting to Texas, where he was sent as lieutenant colonel of the elite and newly formed 2nd U.S. Cavalry. There, with his own wife hundreds of miles away in Virginia, he gave some advice on courtship to a young officer named John Bell Hood, who he feared was feeling the loneliness of the frontier even more than he. "Never marry," he counseled Hood, "unless you can do so into a family that will enable your children to feel proud of both sides of the aisle."[12]

When his father-in-law died in 1857, leaving a complicated and messy estate, Lee as his executor was forced to ask the army for a series of protracted leaves. Custis, like Lee's own father, had incurred too much debt. Though he had lived lavishly he was land poor. Adding to Lee's sense of déjà vu was his wife's physical state. Mary Custis Lee had always been in delicate health but now, like his mother had been, was all but bedridden. "I almost dread him seeing my crippled state," she wrote a friend.[13] Month after month he labored on the problems of the Arlington estate—making needed repairs, paying down debt and juggling inheritances—all the while tending his wife. In October 1859 an urgent message from the War Department, brought by Lieutenant Stuart, broke the tedium. Lee was directed to nearby Harpers Ferry, where he took command of troops ordered to put down an antislavery insurrection led by John Brown, the Kansas abolitionist, who had seized an armory building and taken hostages. This he did with minimum bloodshed, capturing Brown and freeing the prisoners.

The next eighteen months passed swiftly. Lee briefly returned to duty in Texas, then answered Scott's summons to Washington. Now in April 1861 he was 54 years old, a handsome man in superb health, ruddy-faced, his black hair only tinged with gray, his eyes dark and compelling. His neck and torso were muscular, his hips narrow. Seen on horseback, his neck and shoulders made him seem much taller than his five feet, eleven inches. But it was his manner that most impressed those he met. Calm and patient, he was objective in his decisions, without pretense, and invariably considerate of others. Tact was inherent in his nature.

Nor was Lee self-serving. This was apparent from his first days as commander of the military forces of Virginia, when the state began integrating its troops with those of the Confederacy. Lee, a Virginia major general, might soon be taking orders from Confederate brigadiers, who at that time held the Confederacy's highest rank. Would this upset him? Recounted Vice President Alexander Stevens, who sounded Lee out on the problem: "He expressed himself as perfectly satisfied, and as being very desirous of having the alliance formed. . . . He did not wish anything connected with himself individually . . . to interfere in the slightest degree with the immediate consummation of that measure."[14] That Virginia would be the major battlefield of the war was a given. Washington and Richmond, soon to be the Rebel capital, were barely one hundred miles apart, and the state was the largest, most populous and richest in the Confederacy. It had more military-age whites (some 200,000) than any other Southern state, more slaves (some 500,000—although only one-quarter of the whites were slave owners), more industrial capacity and more railroads. To conquer Virginia was to win the war.

From April through June, Lee applied himself to creating an army. There was some early good news. Except for Fort Monroe at the tip of the Yorktown Peninsula, all Federal installations had been occupied. These included the armory with its small-arms machinery at Harpers Ferry, and the navy yard with its guns and dry docks at Norfolk. Thomas Jackson, whom Lee had not seen since their service in the Mexican War, was sent to Harpers Ferry and later superseded by Joseph Johnston, a West Point classmate of Lee and an old friend. John Bankhead Magruder and Benjamin Huger, two other regulars from the Old Army, took command respectively on the Peninsula and in Norfolk.

Organizing, arming and feeding the Virginia volunteers became an all-consuming task, but Lee's abilities were equal to the challenge. By June 8, regiments totaling 40,000 men had been integrated into the ranks of the Confederacy. What would come to be known as the Army of Northern Virginia, composed of units from all over the South, would always be one-quarter Virginian. Wrote Walter H. Taylor, Lee's longtime aide, "Under the direction of General Lee . . . the Virginia volunteers were in a wonderfully short time . . . equipped and sent to the front."[15]

The front was just south of the Potomac at the Manassas railroad junction. Not to give battle at this point would mean falling back 40 miles to the Rappahannock River, exposing a wide swath of northern Virginia to the enemy. Commanding the troops at Manassas was Pierre Beauregard, the hero of Fort Sumter.

Meanwhile, Lee had worked himself out of a job. The Virginia army was no more; the Confederate field commands were filled—with Johnston in the Shenandoah Valley and Beauregard on the Manassas line. President Davis, who had moved the capital to Richmond from Montgomery, Alabama, had high regard for Lee's military talents, but even higher regard for his own. The logical job for Lee would have been general-in-chief, but Davis, a West Pointer and former Secretary of War under President Franklin Pierce, was his own general-in-chief. At this point he kept Lee at his side as an all-purpose aide, giving him just enough but not too much authority. Explained his preeminent biographer: "Daily Lee's duties were enlarged, though they were not defined. Jealous as was President Davis of his prerogatives, and instant as was his resentment of all interference, he made the most of Lee's abilities. Soon Lee was in one sense an acting assistant Secretary of War and in another sense deputy chief of the general staff, to borrow a later military term. . . ."[16]

Jefferson Davis, a man alternately courtly and prickly, from the start of the war was intent on defending the whole South, dispersing his forces rather than concentrating them. Critics contended this was a mistake, and Davis on at least one occasion allowed that this might be so. "I acknowledge the error of my attempt to defend all of the frontier," he admitted.[17] But under the prevailing geographical and political conditions Davis had little choice. Out west in the interior, the Armies of Tennessee and the Trans-Mississippi played a vital role in protecting the Mississippi and keeping Union forces from dividing the Confederacy. Closer to home the governors of the seaboard states, driven by political concerns, adamantly kept substantial numbers of troops in their own jurisdictions. Even Virginia throughout the war retained some of its regiments far from the main lines of battle.

Considering the huge disparity between the North's resources and the Confederacy's, Davis managed the war quite well. In 1860 the North's population totaled some 22 million people, that of the eleven seceding states only 5.5 million whites. The North had 1.3 million industrial workers, the South 110,000. The North produced 97 percent of the nation's firearms, 94 percent of its cloth and more than 90 percent of its industrial output. Northern rail mileage, totaling some 20,000 miles of track, was more than twice that of the South. Draft animals in the North numbered some 800,000, those in the Confederacy only 300,000. The North's navy boasted 90 vessels; the South's was all but nonexistent.

Davis was used to battling the odds. Born in Kentucky on June 3, 1808, a son of Jane Cook and Samuel Davis, he was raised in Mississippi where his hardworking father, a Baptist and a Democrat in a state whose leaders were Episcopalians and Federalists, planted cotton alongside his slaves. Once, when young Jeff balked at going to school, Samuel put him to work in the fields. Two days under the broiling sun made book learning more attractive.

After his father's death, Davis's older brother Joseph persuaded him to enter West Point, which he did in 1824, a year before Lee. There he was a likeable cadet but a mediocre student who earned more than his share of demerits. Basically he subscribed to the carefree drinking song at Benny Haven's, a local tavern: "To our comrades who are fallen, one cup before we go / They poured their life blood freely out pro bono publico / No marble points the stranger to where they rest below / They lie neglected—far away from Benny Haven's, O!"[18]

Following graduation Davis began years of service on the frontier—scouting, fighting Indians and honing the skills of self-reliance. Those skills were never more apparent than in 1835 when he determinedly resigned from the army to marry, over her father's objections, 16-year-old Sarah Knox Taylor, daughter of Zachary ("Rough and Ready") Taylor, the colonel of his regiment. Later, in the Mexican War, Taylor would win fame second only to Winfield Scott, and in 1848 he was elected president. The young couple journeyed to Mississippi where Joseph Davis, who had become a wealthy planter, gifted them with an 800-acre plantation. Within months, however, Davis and his bride would be stricken with malarial fever. "Knoxie" would die, in her delirium singing lines from "Fairy Bells," a song she had learned in childhood. The groom would survive, gaunt and neuralgic, only to bury himself in almost ten years of seclusion, reading deeply in the law and the classics. In the process he became a learned, and perhaps rigid, man.

In 1844 his brother Joseph again influenced Davis's life, introducing him to Varina Howell, 17, a spirited young woman from Natchez, Mississippi. "I believe he is old," she wrote her mother, "for from what I hear he is only two years younger than you. . . . He impresses me as a remarkable kind of man, but of uncertain temper. . . ." Then she added, "Would you believe it, he is refined and cultivated, and yet he is a Democrat!"[19] They married the next year, and Varina would bear him six children. "She is as beautiful as Venus," enthused Joseph, adding: "As well as good looks, she has a mind that will fit her for any sphere that the man to whom she is married will . . . reach." Agreed Davis: "She is beautiful and she has a fine mind."[20]

When the Mexican War began, Davis was elected colonel of the Mississippi Rifles, a volunteer regiment. At Buena Vista, serving under his former father-in-law, he and his men saved the day, breaking a desperate Mexican cavalry charge. "My daughter, sir," Taylor told him, "was a better judge of men than I."[21] Returning home wounded and on crutches, Davis began a long political career that took him, beginning in 1847, to the U.S. Senate, President Pierce's cabinet and again to the Senate. There despite his neuralgia-racked body and easily ruffled temperament, he assumed the mantle of John C. Calhoun as the leading spokesman for Southern interests. The issue of states' rights, triggered by the bitter quarrel over slavery, loomed ever larger in his convictions. "We but tread in the paths of our fathers when we proclaim our independence," he declared in his January 1861 resignation speech, "not in hostility to others, not to injure any section of the country, not even for our own pecuniary benefit, but from the high and solemn motive of defending and protecting the rights we inherited, and which it is our duty to transmit unshorn to our children."[22]

Within weeks he was named president of the Confederacy. He spoke of his election, said Varina Davis, "as a man might speak of a sentence of death."[23] Regardless, he too would do his duty.

Joseph Eggleston Johnston, in command at Harpers Ferry since May 15, was the son of circuit judge Peter Johnston, who had served under "Light-Horse Harry" Lee during the Revolutionary War. Born on February 3, 1807, in Abingdon, Virginia, in the extreme southwestern corner of the state, Johnston's respected military career in the Old Army paralleled but never quite equaled Lee's. His rank in the West Point class of 1829 had been thirteenth (out of forty-six), but Lee's had been second. His conduct in the Mexican War earned him the brevet rank of major, but Lee's brought him the brevet rank of colonel. Both men in 1855 had been named lieutenant colonels of cavalry regiments, but Lee in 1861 had made full colonel. Though promoted to quartermaster general in 1860 with the staff rank of brigadier, Johnston held a permanent rank only of lieutenant colonel.

In 1845, he married Lydia McLane, 23, the daughter of a wealthy Maryland businessman who had been secretary of the treasury under President Andrew Jackson, thereby enhancing both his financial security and social status. Though they had no children, Lydia Johnston proved a devoted wife, dedicated to her husband's career. "If my Joseph is defeated I shall die," she told Varina Davis shortly before the first battle of Manassas. "Lydia, beware of ambition," Mrs. Davis replied.[24]

Johnston was small and slight, with a receding hairline, hollow cheeks and a wispy goatee. Extremely conscious of his reputation, he dreaded taking risks. One contemporary tells of the time Wade Hampton III, perhaps the wealthiest plantation owner in the South, invited Johnston to a hunting party: "He was a capital shot, better than Wade or I, but with Colonel Johnston . . . the bird flew too high or too low, the dogs were too far or too near. Things never did suit exactly. He was too fussy, too hard to please, too cautious, too much afraid to miss and risk his fine reputation for a crack shot."[25] Hampton and the others shot away, bringing down bird after bird. Johnston never shot at all. Explains one historian: "If he did not fight, at least then he could not lose, and to get him to fight or to make a movement that might prove unpopular, it appeared that first he had to be absolved of responsibility for the consequences. It was a shame, for Johnston possessed as much tactical skill as any general in the Confederacy."[26]

With the battle fast approaching and Federal troops already moving into

Arlington and Alexandria, this overly prudent soldier was the senior field commander of the Confederacy in Virginia. Soon he would abandon Harpers Ferry, moving his 12,000 men south up the Shenandoah to Winchester. Facing him was a Union army of 18,000 men under General Robert Patterson.

Junior to Johnston but commanding some 20,000 men on the Manassas line since June 3 was Pierre Gustave Toutant Beauregard, whose military instincts in sharp contrast to his chief's verged on the grandiose. If Johnston's forces were transferred from the Valley to *his* command, Beauregard wrote Davis, "we could by a bold and rapid movement forward retake Arlington Heights and Alexandria . . . which would have the effect of recalling all the enemy's forces . . . for the protection of Washington."[27] In rejecting the plan, Davis showed considerable restraint. He did not mention the obvious: that the Confederates still lacked the arms, ammunition and transport for such an ambitious assault. Instead he pointed out he had to keep Johnston's troops where they were, until it became apparent the enemy under Patterson would not be advancing up the Shenandoah to attack Beauregard in the rear. The hero of Fort Sumter, ever ready to push himself forward, had come to believe his newspaper clippings. "My troops are in fine spirits and anxious for a fight," he would say. "They seem to have the most unbounded confidence in me."[28]

Born on May 28, 1818, at Contreras Plantation just south of New Orleans, Beauregard was as proud of his patrician French Creole ancestry as he was fond of citing Napoleon's campaigns. His face was swarthy and mustachioed, his eyes dark and melancholy with heavily drooping lids. His manner was mild, even gracious, and he usually expressed his vitriol with his pen, writing lengthy reports and letters. Like Davis and Johnston, he could be quick to take offense, slow to admit error. He enjoyed champagne, gala balls and the company of pretty women. His sickly wife, Caroline Deslondes Beauregard, also a member of a prominent Creole family, remained in Louisiana. Commented a Richmond hostess: "Beauregard's wife is still in New Orleans and he gnashes his teeth. She will not leave a doctor who (only one in the world) understands her case."[29]

Beauregard graduated second in the West Point class of 1838, then spent more than two decades supervising U.S. Army engineering projects throughout the South. Named superintendent of West Point in 1860, he was dismissed within five days because of his secessionist views. He resigned his commission once Louisiana left the Union, expecting to be put in charge of the state's militia, but the post instead went to Braxton Bragg, another career soldier. Rescued from relative obscurity by his shelling of Fort Sumter, Beauregard now found himself in mid-July along a meandering creek named Bull Run, his line stretched out for eight miles, waiting for Union General Irvin McDowell's attack. His 20,000 men would soon be facing 35,000 Federals. Unless Johnston could reinforce him, the odds would be daunting.

# TWO

\* \* \* \*

# FIRST MANASSAS AND ITS AFTERMATH

Early morning of July 18 found Joseph Johnston at Winchester in the Valley, puzzled that over the last few days Union General Patterson had made little or no effort to engage him. Instead it appeared the Federal army actually was withdrawing, moving down the Shenandoah toward Harpers Ferry. What Johnston did not know was the 69-year-old Patterson, Scott's second-in-command in the Mexican War, had simply lost his nerve. When he was not grossly exaggerating Johnston's numbers, he was telling himself his men would not fight because their three-month enlistments were almost up. Even a telegram from Scott, explicitly ordering an attack on Johnston, did not stiffen his backbone. What, Patterson asked an aide, should he do? "I look upon that dispatch as a positive order from General Scott to attack Johnston wherever you can find him," the staff officer replied, "and if you do not do it I think you will be a ruined man."[1] The aide was right. One week later, Patterson was relieved of his command.

For Johnston, the Union army's withdrawal down the Valley was a godsend. Just the night before, in response to the news that McDowell was on the march, he had received urgent orders to reinforce Beauregard. Now with Jeb Stuart's 1st Virginia Cavalry screening his withdrawal he could send his four brigades through the Blue Ridge to Manassas without looking over his shoulder.

First to go, fittingly, was the 1st Brigade of Thomas Jonathan Jackson of Virginia, as devout a Christian as he was zealous a soldier. A West Point graduate in the class of 1846, he had received three brevets for bravery as an artillery officer in the Mexican War, rising from second lieutenant to major. "I don't know that I shall shake hands with Mr. Jackson," General Scott declared with mock sternness at an official reception. "If you can forgive yourself for the way you slaughtered those Mexicans with your guns, I am not sure that I can." Then he smilingly extended his hand.[2] Francis Bartow of Georgia, a Yale Law School graduate and prominent politician, followed with the 2nd Brigade. Barnard Bee of South Carolina and Edmund Kirby Smith of Florida, both West Pointers and professional soldiers, commanded the 3rd and 4th Brigades. Once across the mountains, Johnston loaded his men onto Manassas Gap Railroad cars at Piedmont Station and shuttled them to the battlefield. Jackson's would be the first brigade to arrive, Kirby Smith's the last. All during the early hours and into the morning and afternoon of Sunday, July 21, the movement would continue.

Still ignoring the fact he was the junior officer Beauregard had also been busy, taking advantage of Johnston's unfamiliarity with the field to push on him an ambitious plan to flank the advancing Federals. Five of Beauregard's own six brigades were led by experienced men, the exception being the 1st Brigade under the often abusive Milledge Bonham of South Carolina, a lawyer and politician who would soon resign from the army to become that state's governor. One of Bonham's aides wrote that for the general's behavior there was "no excuse, for a man capable to command others should be able to command himself."[3] All the other brigadiers were West Pointers. Bald, pop-eyed Richard Stoddert Ewell of Virginia, whose eccentricities were as pronounced as Jackson's and who would become his chief lieutenant, led the 2nd Brigade, while affable David Rumph ("Neighbor") Jones of South Carolina headed the 3rd Brigade. Burly James Longstreet, who daily impressed his colleagues with his attention to drill and detail, led the 4th Brigade. Patrician Philip St. George Cocke of South Carolina, who had resigned from the Old Army decades before to manage his plantations and write extensively on agriculture, commanded the 5th Brigade. Heading the 6th Brigade was the pugnacious Jubal Early of Virginia, who likewise had left the Old Army to pursue a career in law and politics.

Two other units would play important roles in the battle to come. One was the small brigade commanded by spindly-legged Nathan ("Shanks") Evans of South Carolina—comprised of his own 4th South Carolina Regiment and the 1st Louisiana Battalion. Evans, a storied Indian fighter on the frontier, "had the fiercest of black mustachios and small, restless eyes to match. His look was quick, cunning and contentious, as if he always were suspecting a Comanche ambush. It was only when a broad smile revealed glittering teeth that his martial mien softened."[4] Leading the 1st Louisiana, the unruly Zouaves called the "Tigers" who were recruited from the prisons and alleys of

New Orleans, was Major Roberdeau Wheat, a soldier of fortune and son of an Episcopal minister. Wheat, standing six-foot-four and weighing 275 pounds, was the only officer who could control the Tigers. "His men loved him—and they feared him," one soldier wrote. "The power or spell he had over [them] was truly wonderful."[5]

The second command was the Hampton Legion, a brigade of gentlemen volunteers raised and financed by Wade Hampton of South Carolina. This "Legion" consisted of a 600-man infantry regiment with its own cavalry and artillery, and some of the best-born men in the Palmetto State served as privates in its ranks. Hampton, 43, would become next to Stuart the army's foremost cavalryman. He did not reach Manassas on July 21 until the late morning hours. Without more than elemental military training, he instinctively marched his troops toward the sound of the guns.

Beauregard's plan to flank McDowell's oncoming army was both too complicated and too optimistic. The Confederate line still stretched for eight miles along the south bank of Bull Run, with Evans's small brigade anchoring the extreme left—at the Stone Bridge on the Warrenton Pike—and Cocke next to him. Bonham held the center at Mitchell's Ford, where Beauregard expected the main attack to come. He concentrated his other brigades on Bonham's right, hoping to strike the Federals just before they reached Bull Run, turning their left flank. Longstreet, Jones, Ewell, Early and the brigades from the Valley were placed there, as was the reserve brigade of Theophilus Holmes. "Ewell was to begin the movement on our right, crossing and sweeping to the left," explained Captain Edward Porter Alexander, Beauregard's chief engineer and signals' officer. "Then James Longstreet &c. in succession were to take up the movement as it came to them. But it turned out afterwards that the order sent Ewell . . . never reached him, & before this fact was discovered McDowell had gotten *his* attack at work so vigorously on our left flank that our proposed attack was given up. . . ."[6]

Beauregard had ignored the possibility that McDowell, a 43-year-old professional soldier, might make a turning movement of his own. He also had ignored the fact that Sudley Ford, upstream of Evans's position, could easily be crossed. Now his brigades were heavily concentrated on his right, while the enemy was assailing his left.

McDowell's intentions were not known, of course, when the battle began. The sound of skirmishing followed by Union artillery fire began as early as 5:30 A.M. on July 21, first involving Evans at the Stone Bridge, then slowly working its way downstream to Bonham at Mitchell's Ford. The Confederates at this point had no inkling McDowell was flanking them. But by 7:30 A.M. Evans was convinced that the Federals in his front, perhaps two brigades strong, were merely making a feint. "I perceived that it was not the intention of the enemy to attack me in my present position," he wrote.[7]

McDowell's army had begun the thirty-mile march from Washington on July 16, his men making excruciatingly slow progress in the stifling heat, and his original plan had been to turn the Confederate right. Nearing Bull Run, and learning that the downstream fords were treacherous, he instead sent two flanking divisions to the Confederate left. At 8:30 A.M. Captain Alexander was scanning the horizon with his glass when he caught the glint of sunlight off cannon at Sudley Ford. "Look out for your left. You are flanked," he immediately "wig-wagged" Evans. His follow-up note to Beauregard was more detailed: "I see a column crossing Bull Run about 2 miles above Stone Bridge. Head of it is in woods on this side; tail of it in woods on other side. About a quarter of a mile length of column visible in the opening. Artillery forms part of it."[8]

Evans acted decisively. Without waiting for orders, leaving only four companies behind at the Stone Bridge, he double-quicked his remaining 1,100 men and two guns upstream. There he took cover in a grove of trees atop Matthews Hill, opening a heavy fire on the approaching enemy and temporarily stopping the head of the column in its tracks. "If Nathan is the bravest and best General in the C. S., if not in the world," wrote one of his admirers, "he is at the same time the best drinker, the most eloquent swearer (I should say voluble) and the most magnificent bragger I ever saw."[9] Major Wheat did Evans one better, ignoring the odds and actually leading a charge. In the hand-to-hand combat that followed, many of the Tigers threw down their rifles to use their bowie knives. Wheat took a bullet in the chest, perforating one or perhaps both of his lungs. When his surgeon told him the wound was fatal, he replied, "I don't feel like dying yet." But, the man persisted, "there is no record of recovery from such a wound." Replied Wheat, "Then I will put my case upon record."[10] He would survive.

The South Carolina and Louisiana units took casualties, but they bought time. Bernard Bee rushed to Evans's support with the 2nd Mississippi and the 4th Alabama, followed by Francis Bartow and two of his Georgia regiments. Wade Hampton's infantrymen later reinforced them. Like Evans all three officers acted on their own initiative, without orders, throwing their men into the melee. Some 6,500 men were facing more than twice their number, the lead elements of two whole divisions. Taking severe casualties under the shot and shell, the Confederates slowly gave ground. By 11:30 A.M. the shattered survivors huddled on the crest of Henry Hill, where Thomas Jackson, knowing he was the last line of resistance, was massing his infantry and guns. There the legend of "Stonewall" Jackson was born. "General, they are beating us back!" a distraught Bee cried out. "Sir," replied Jackson, "we'll give them the bayonet!" Rallying the 4th Alabama, Bee reportedly shouted, "There is Jackson standing like a stone wall! Let us determine to die here, and we will conquer! Follow me!"[11]

Though Jackson's guns were outnumbered almost three to one, he grimly held the crest. "The contest that ensued was terrific," reported Captain John Imboden of the Staunton Artillery. "Jackson ordered me to go from battery to battery and see the guns were properly aimed and the fuses cut the right length. . . . His eyes fairly blazed. He had a way of throwing up his left hand with the open palm toward the person he was addressing. . . . The air was full of flying missiles, and as he spoke he jerked down his hand, and I saw that blood was streaming from it. I exclaimed, 'General, you are wounded.' He replied, 'Only a scratch. . . .' and galloped away along his line."[12] If the enemy infantry should charge, Jackson was ready. "When their heads are seen above the hill," he ordered, "let the whole line rise, move forward with a shout, and trust to the bayonet. I am tired of this long-range work."[13]

Beauregard and Johnston now were on Henry Hill, drawn from their command post on the Confederate right by the fury of the guns. Events had forced Beauregard to abandon his flanking manuever, but not his insistence on military protocol. With the battle in the balance, he respectfully but firmly suggested that Johnston, the senior officer, should leave the field, the better to facilitate the movements of the units coming up to reinforce Jackson. He, Beauregard, should conduct the actual fight on Henry Hill. With great reluctance, Johnston did just that. Whatever Beauregard's motives, his suggestion worked out well. Johnston from his rear vantage point skillfully moved up the reinforcements and Beauregard, who was not without ability as a tactician, placed them for maximum firepower.

From 2 to 4 P.M. the battle raged. McDowell at one point advanced two batteries with supporting infantry to the crest, some 300 yards to Jackson's left, where they poured fire on him. When some of the guns advanced still farther Colonel Jeb Stuart, concealed in the woods with his cavalry, saw his chance. "At them we went like an arrow from a bow," exulted one of his horsemen. "Half the distance was passed before they saw the avalanche coming upon them. . . . The tremendous impact of horses at full speed broke through and scattered their line. . . ."[14] Following up Stuart's charge with one of its own was the 33rd Virginia, led by Colonel Alfred Cummings, a Virginia Military Institute graduate, lawyer and farmer. "We were soon in possession of the guns, killed nearly all the horses, and a great portion of the men," wrote one of the men. ". . . and we were none too soon, for one minute more and four guns would have belched forth into our ranks, carrying death and destruction."[15] Cummings's men were brave, but they were also lucky. This early in the war, neither side had fully adopted the uniform of Union blue or Confederate butternut. The fact that the 33rd Virginia was wearing blue made the Yankee gunners hesitate just long enough to be their undoing.

Now the Confederate line was reinforced by elements of the Cocke and Bonham brigades, and much later by Kirby Smith's regiments. Still the Federals continued their assault, trying to envelop the Confederate left. General Bee was killed, as was Colonel Bartow. Kirby Smith was wounded, replaced by his senior colonel, Arnold Elzey. Then from the southwest, behind the Confederate line, came the sight of an advancing column. Were they Union troops, belatedly coming from Patterson's men in the Valley? Or were they reinforcements? Peering through his glass, Beauregard could not make out the column's colors. Then the first breeze of the long, hot day stirred the faraway flag. The newcomers were Early's men, coming up after an arduous three-hour march. Seeing them, the entire army was rejuvenated. Spirits soared; high-pitched rebel yells filled the air. By the time Early took his place on Elzey's left the Federals were already losing heart. Sensing this, Beauregard ordered a general charge. The Confederates rose as one, all along the line, driving the enemy back. Early was modest about his contribution to the victory. "It is an old saying that 'It is the last feather that breaks the camel's back,' " he wrote, "yet the last feather would do no harm but for the weight which precedes it. The *first* feather contributes as much as the last. . . ."[16]

About 4:30 P.M. the Federal withdrawal turned into a rout. "There were no fresh forces on the field to support or encourage them," one of McDowell's aides explained, "and the men seemed to be seized simultaneously by the conviction that it was no use to do anything more and they might as well start home."[17] With the occasional artillery shell keeping them company, the Federals hurried back toward Washington, jostling for space on the pike with the pleasure carriages and sightseers who had come down from the capital to see the fighting. The next day after thirty-two hours in the saddle McDowell dismounted at Arlington in a soaking rain, his six-day campaign a failure. Union casualties totaled some 3,000; Confederate, some 2,000.

Jackson's own losses were among the highest—about 525 men, or about 16 percent of his command. This pious Presbyterian, who ordinarily would not even write or read a letter on Sunday, had been forced by circumstances to fight a bloody battle on a day he normally devoted to prayer and contemplation. Twenty-four hours later he wrote his wife, Anna: "Yesterday we fought a great battle, and gained a great victory, for which all the glory is due to God alone . . . I only received one wound, the breaking of the largest finger of the left hand, but the doctor says the finger can be saved. . . . God made my brigade more instrumental than any other in repulsing the main attack. This is for your own information only—say nothing about it. Let another speak praise, not myself." When she wrote back, saying she saw little in the newspapers about him, but much about Johnston and Beauregard, he described his exploits in greater detail. "My brigade is not a brigade of newspaper correspondents. I know that the 1st Brigade was the first to meet and pass our retreating forces—to push on with no other aid than the smiles of

God; to boldly take its position with the artillery that was under my command—to arrest the victorious foe in his onward progress—to hold him in check until reinforcements arrived—and finally to charge bayonets and, thus advancing, pierce the enemy's center."[18]

Jackson had resigned from the army in 1851 to accept a position as professor of science and artillery at Virginia Military Institute in Lexington, Virginia Shortly thereafter, his first wife, Ellie, daughter of George Junkin of Virginia, a clergyman and president of Washington College, died in childbirth, the baby stillborn. Hearing the news Raleigh Colston, a V.M.I. colleague, went to the Junkin home to offer his condolences. "Sadly but calmly," he remembered, Jackson "led me to the chamber of death, and with unfaltering hand, removed the veil which covered the dead infant resting upon its dead mother's breast. . . . There were no tears, no quivering of the lips . . . and a casual observer would hardly have perceived the powerful emotions of his soul—kept down only by his indomitable will."[19]

Jackson remarried in 1857 at age 33, taking as his bride Mary Anna Morrison, five days shy of 26, a daughter of Robert Morrison of North Carolina, also a clergyman and president of Davidson College. His days in Lexington were as regular as the seasons. He rose early, prayed on his knees and took cold baths and brisk walks before breakfast. After his morning classes, he came home to study the Bible and prepare for the next day's recitations. Lunch was precisely at 1 P.M. Afternoons were largely devoted to Anna. They would talk, read together and go for walks. In the privacy of his home Jackson was a far different man from the stern, somewhat boring professor called "Tom Fool" by his cadets. He and his wife even would do a spirited polka, Jackson asserting the dance was not frivolous but good exercise. The only event marring their happiness was the loss of their first child, a daughter, who died of jaundice shortly after her birth in 1858. Wrote Anna about her husband: "No man could be more demonstrative, & he was almost invariably playful and cheerful & as confiding as possible. He commenced educating me . . . to be demonstrative as soon as we were married . . . & we rarely ever met alone without caresses & endearing epithets. I would almost always meet him on his return from the Institute, and his face would beam with happiness, & he would spend a few moments in petting me . . . & then go to his duties."[20]

On October 13, less than three months after Manassas, Jackson was named a major general and sent to the Shenandoah. Initially this meant leaving behind the Stonewall Brigade. "I shall never forget them," he told an aide. "In battle I shall always want them. I will not be satisfied until I get them."[21] The men demanded he address them one last time before leaving. "I shall look with great anxiety to your future movements," Jackson proclaimed in his high-pitched voice, "and I trust whenever I shall hear of the First Brigade . . . it will be of still nobler deeds achieved and higher reputation won." He paused, then raised his hand in farewell. "In the Army of the Shenandoah, you were the First Brigade! In the Army of the Potomac you were the First Brigade. In the Second Corps of this army you were the First Brigade! You are the First Brigade in the affections of your general, and I hope . . . you will be handed down to posterity as the First Brigade in this, our second War of Independence. Farewell!"[22] The cheers chorused through the air, but the leave-taking was short. Within weeks Jackson persuaded the War Department to let his men join him in the Valley. When General Johnston protested, he was promised twice the number to replace them.

Beauregard was also waxing eloquent, but in a different way. Though a grateful Davis, ignoring the fact he had totally misplaced his troops, had recommended his promotion to full general, he continued to aggrandize himself. The chain of events began with Beauregard telling some congressmen, "The want of food and transportation has made us lose the fruits of our victory. . . . Washington could have been taken up to the 24th instant by 20,000 men."[23] Implicit in this message was the idea that Davis had been holding Beauregard back, when in truth the army's hard-won victory had left it incapable of pursuit. "Enough was done for glory . . ." Davis mildly replied. "Let us rather show the untaught that their desires are unreasonable."[24] Simultaneously Beauregard sought through seemingly endless correspondence to perpetuate the fiction that his troops were a separate unit, operating in cooperation with but independently of Johnston. Even a blunt memo from the secretary of war that Beauregard was second to Johnston "in command of the whole Army of the Potomac and not first in command of half the army" could not shake him in this conviction.[25]

Next Beauregard leaked a draft of his battle report to the press stating he had been asking for Johnston's troops since July 13th, but Davis had not seen fit to send them until late on the 17th. This was at best a half-truth since all concerned knew Johnston had to stay in the Valley, holding off Patterson, until the last moment. Now vexed, Davis wrote Beauregard he was surprised by this claim, "because it seemed to be an attempt to exalt yourself at my expense. . . . The movement was postponed until the operations of the enemy rendered it necessary, and until it thereby became practicable to make it, with safety."[26]

Beauregard's self-created controversy reached a climax in November when he wrote a letter to the *Richmond Whig*, complaining that his report was being censored. "The president is the sole judge of when, and what parts of, the reports of a commanding officer should be made public . . ." he allowed. "Meanwhile I entreat my friends not to trouble themselves about refuting the slanders and calumnies aimed at me. . . . If certain minds cannot understand the difference between *patriotism*, the highest civic virtue, and *office-seeking*, the lowest civic occupation, I pity them from the bottom of my heart."[27] With this last cannonade Beauregard's service in northern Virginia effectively ended, although he would briefly reappear in 1864. Soon he would be transferred to duties in the West.

Johnston's relations with Davis were likewise becoming uneasy. Besides being fussy, Johnston was unpredictable. One moment he could be warm and attentive, the next moment cool and distant. Outwardly he looked every inch the unflinching soldier—admirers likened him to a gamecock. Inwardly he magnified all grievances. When Davis following Manassas sent to the Senate a list of five men to be confirmed as full generals, the ranking of the names enraged Johnston. He thought his name should lead the list. First instead was the 63-year-old Adjutant General Samuel Cooper, the staff officer who handled all the army's administrative details. Second came Albert Sidney Johnston of Kentucky, who would be mortally wounded the next year while serving in the West. Third was Robert E. Lee. Fourth and fifth, respectively, were Joseph Johnston and Beauregard.

"I will not affect to disguise the surprise and mortification produced in my mind by the action taken in this matter by the President and by Congress . . ." he wrote Davis. "I now and here declare my claims, that notwithstanding these nominations. . . . I still rightfully hold the rank of first general in the Armies of the Southern Confederacy." The president's action, Johnston went on, "seeks to tarnish my fair name as a soldier and a man, earned by more than thirty years of laborious and perilous service. I had but this, the scars of many wounds, all honorably taken in my front and in the front of battle, and my father's Revolutionary sword. It was delivered to me from his venerated hands, without a stain of dishonor. . . ." Now the president was "degrading one who has served laboriously from the commencement of the war on this frontier and borne a prominent part in the only great event of that war, for the benefit of persons neither of whom has yet struck a blow for this Confederacy."[28] This last was a slighting reference to Sidney Johnston and to Lee.

Ordinarily Davis wrote letters just as lengthy as any of Johnston's or Beauregard's, but this time he made his response brief and to the point. "Sir: I have just received and read your letter of the 12th instant," he replied. "Its language is, as you say, unusual; its arguments and statements utterly one-sided, and its insinuations as unfounded as they are unbecoming. I am, &c. Jeff'n Davis."[29] There the matter rested, never again discussed in public by either party.

Richard Taylor of Louisiana, son of Zachary Taylor and brother-in-law of Davis by his first marriage, soon to be a brilliant officer under Jackson in the Shenandoah Valley, worried about the rift between the two men but could do little to heal it. Johnston, wrote Taylor, "sincerely believed himself the Esau of the Government, grudgingly fed on bitter herbs, while a favored Jacob enjoyed the flesh-pots. . . . Having served under his command and studied his methods, I feel confident that his great abilities under happier conditions would have distinctly modified, if not changed, the current of events. Destiny willed that Davis and Johnston should be brought into collision, and the breach, once made, was never repaired. Each misjudged the other to the end."[30]

More mundane but equally heartfelt in the fall of 1861 was Davis's insistence on reorganizing the army. The president felt with good reason that regiments from different states, instead of being assigned at random to the various brigades, should be brought together and commanded by officers from the same state. The result would be a more cohesive unit, with more esprit de corps. Instead of placating Davis by explaining that he needed time to effect the changes, Johnston simply dragged his feet. When the president focused his concern on the scattered Mississippi regiments, Johnston continued to procrastinate. Worse, he allowed one of his subordinates, General W.H.C. Whiting, to reject Mississippi troops for his own command. Chase Whiting, a Mississippian himself who had graduated number one in the West Point class of 1845, had a way of being high-handed. He did not want to take strangers into his brigade, even if they were Mississippians, and have them replace men he already knew. "They are used to me and I to them, and accustomed to act together,"[31] he informed the War Office. Back, at Davis's direction, came a humiliating reply. Since there regretfully was no other brigade command available for Whiting, he was to report for duty at his fallback rank as major of engineers. Only after repeated apologies from both Johnston and Whiting was the latter's punishment revoked.

On the matter of reorganization, Davis prevailed. Regiments from the same state would soon be bundled together, and the result would be greatly improved morale. Four or so regiments, each numbering perhaps 800 men and commanded by a colonel, made up a brigade. Four or so brigades, each listing some 3,000 men and led by a brigadier, comprised a division. Each division, numbering some 12,000 men, was headed by a major general. These figures were theoretical, of course. From the beginning of the war regiments and brigades were fortunate if they were at 75 percent of strength, and as the conflict wore on 50 percent or less was common. Confederate brigades would become known, not by numerals, but by the names of their commanders. As brigadiers were promoted or became casualties, the unit names could be confusing. Dorsey Pender led Pender's brigade of North Carolinians until he became a major general; then Alfred Scales took over and the unit became Scales's brigade. Maxcy Gregg led Gregg's brigade of South Carolinians until he was mortally wounded at Fredericksburg; Samuel McGowan succeeded him, and the name was changed to McGowan's brigade. Jackson's 1st Virginia became known simply as the Stonewall Brigade—a fortunate description since it was commanded by seven different men, five of whom lost their lives in the war.

What of Lee in the aftermath of Manassas? Davis obviously valued his aide's counsel. He had kept him close at his side since coming to Richmond, and soon he would be naming him a full general. Lee had raised and organized one-quarter of the army that fought at Manassas. He had suggested concentrating there and forming the battle line along Bull Run. He had even monitored the timing of when to move Johnston to join Beauregard. Yet Davis continued to keep Lee in the background. Like many people who are sensitive about their own feelings, the president could be quite insensitive about the feelings of others. When the Federals were advancing on Manassas, Davis did not even invite Lee to the battlefield. No, he said, it is important you stay in Richmond.

Now, within days after the battle, Davis decided it equally important that Lee go to western Virginia. That area west of the Alleghenies had little in common with the rest of the state. The people there were unsympathetic to secession, few owned slaves, and in 1863 they would officially join the Union. Indeed Union General George McClellan had just defeated a Confederate army there. It would be Lee's job to reverse the momentum. This, it must be admitted, he did not do. His three months in western Virginia were the least distinguished in his military career. First he wasted precious weeks conciliating General William Loring, the well-connected commanding officer of the troops there, instead of giving him the choice of following orders or being relieved of command. This was Lee's most grievous fault as a commander—his unwillingness to have a confrontation. "All his life [he] had lived with gentle people," his biographer would say. "Now that he encountered surliness and jealousy, it repelled him, embarrassed him, and well-nigh bewildered him. Detesting a quarrel as undignified and unworthy of a gentleman, he showed himself willing . . . to go to almost any length, within the bounds of honor, to avoid a clash."[32]

Then Lee gave his trust, with disastrous results, to an officer he barely knew. He was Colonel Albert Rust of the 3rd Arkansas and the place was Cheat Mountain Pass, where the Federals held the high ground, protecting their army in the valley below. Lee's plan was to take the pass and then fall on the main body of the enemy, and it depended on surprise. On September 12 he advanced three columns of some 10,000 men simultaneously, with one column designated to flank Cheat Mountain from the east and touch off the assault. Colonel Rust's force of 2,000 was that column. Rust never did give the signal to attack, fearing he was outnumbered when the defenders totaled no more than a few hundred men. The enemy was alerted, and the opportunity lost. "With great effort the troops intended for the surprise had reached their destination," Lee wrote, "having traversed twenty miles of steep, rugged mountain-paths, and the last day through a terrible storm. . . . When morning broke I could see the enemy's tents. . . . We waited for the attack on Cheat

Mountain . . . *but the signal did not come* . . . The provisions of the men had been destroyed. . . . They had had nothing to eat . . . could not hold out for another day, and were obliged to be withdrawn."[33]

Frustrated at Cheat Mountain, Lee proceeded to the Kanawha Valley in the southwest, ordering Loring to follow. There two political generals, Henry A. Wise and John B. Floyd, both former governors of Virginia, were fighting with themselves as much as with the enemy. On September 21, when Lee arrived at their camps, he found them entrenched in separate positions, each stubbornly refusing to join the other. "General Lee perceived at a glance that Little Sewell (Wise's position) was the most favorable point to make a stand . . ." recounted his aide. "General Floyd was therefore at once ordered to move forward to Little Sewell. The bitter feeling which had been engendered between the two commanders had imparted itself, in some degree, to the troops, and seriously threatened to impair their efficiency."[34] Within days Davis settled the rivalry by relieving Wise of command.

With the arrival of Loring, Lee now had a fairly large force—perhaps as many as 14,000 men. But he still faced considerable problems: a hostile populace, torrential rains, a lack of food and supplies. He was in no position to oust the Federals from the area. The best he could do was keep them from advancing into the Shenandoah Valley, with its rich bounty of crops and livestock. For this he received no credit. Instead the public, egged on by the newspapers, perceived him as a timid officer. Before he left the Alleghenies Lee grew the beard he would keep throughout the war. Though his hair was still dark, the beard came in gray.

In November Davis sent Lee to Charleston, charging him with the responsibility of improving the coastal defenses of South Carolina, Georgia and Florida. Before going Lee put aside his usual reticence and asked the extent of his authority. Davis assured him that he had the total support of the administration. Relieved, Lee threw himself into his work. Some 300 miles of coastline, crisscrossed by scores of rivers and waterways up which the North might send its gunboats, had to be evaluated. Some of the coast was defensible; some was not. Dealing with the governors of the states involved, Lee was his usual tactful self, so much so that they helped him raise 25,000 more volunteers. Dealing with subordinates, he showed far more forcefulness than he had heretofore. For the rest of the year and into the spring he built up the defenses around Charleston and Savannah, abandoned some outlying areas, obstructed waterways and dug some formidable interior lines. If the public did not know what he was accomplishing, the professionals did.

From South Carolina he wrote to his wife in Virginia on Christmas Day: "I cannot let this day of grateful rejoicing pass, dear Mary, without some communion with you. I am thankful for the many among the past that I have passed with you, & the remembrance of them fills me with pleasure. . . ." Knowing his wife was distraught over the loss of Arlington, the Custis estate the Union army had occupied since the summer, he tried to console her. "With the number of troops encamped around it . . . & all the dire necessities of war," he said, "it is vain to think of its being in a habitable condition. I fear too books, furniture & the relics of Mount Vernon will be gone. It is better to make up our minds to a general loss. They cannot take away the remembrances of the spot, & the memories of those that to us rendered it sacred. That will remain to us as long as life will last. . . ."[35]

This was Robert E. Lee in December of 1861. The man who had been offered command of the Union army. The man who had mobilized Virginia. The man who was selflessly serving as Davis's aide. Soon he would move to the foreground, showing fierceness in battle that belied his nature. "You allow these people to get away," he would berate one of his commanders in the aftermath of one fight. "Go after them, and damage them all you can!"[36] Before 1862 was over he would lead his army in four epic battles—on the Peninsula, at Manassas again, at Antietam and at Fredericksburg—and his fame would resonate throughout the South.

# THREE

\* \* \* \*

# OFFICERS TO WATCH

Let us now look at some men who will figure prominently in the upcoming campaigns, and whose strengths clearly outweigh their faults. James Longstreet, the son of Mary Ann Dent and James Longstreet, was born on January 8, 1821, in Edgefield District, South Carolina, at the home of his maternal grandparents. His first nine years were spent on the family farm near Gainesville, Georgia, and then he was sent to Augusta, where he lived with his Uncle Augustus, a noted lawyer and judge, and attended school. Soon thereafter his father died, his mother moved to Alabama, and his uncle became his de facto guardian. James matured into a six-foot-two, heavily muscled young man, and an expert rider and marksman. His uncle, though a Methodist minister, saw nothing wrong with occasional whiskey-drinking and card-playing, and young James followed his lead. Reared in the Deep South, Longstreet did not *seem* Southern. "He was serious and stolid," said a commentator, "not romantic as proper Southerners of that age were, more materialistic than idealistic. Perhaps ancestry had something to do with it . . . Langestraat is the name originally, and there is something Dutchlike in Longstreet's physical massiveness and excessive stubbornness."[1]

He entered West Point in 1838. There "Pete" Longstreet was a popular but uninspiring cadet, being voted most handsome but ranking fifty-fourth out of a class of fifty-six. His best friend at the academy was the equally non-achieving Northerner Ulysses "Sam" Grant of Ohio, whom Longstreet would introduce to his cousin, Julia Dent, whom Grant would later marry. Following graduation Longstreet was posted to Jefferson Barracks, Missouri, where in

1844 he met Maria Louisa Garland of Virginia, 17, the daughter of Lieutenant Colonel John Garland, his regimental commander. They would marry four years later, and she would bear him ten children. Before the marriage took place, however, the Mexican War intervened. In the last stages of that conflict, as the American forces were assailing Chapultepec, the fortress guarding the capital, Longstreet carrying the regimental flag was in the forefront. A musket ball in the leg brought him down, and he passed on the colors to a fellow lieutenant, George Pickett of Virginia, who planted them on the heights. This would not be the last time the two men would face battle together.

Longstreet saw no action at Manassas, his brigade being positioned by Beauregard on the right, where the attack did not come. But late in the afternoon, as the Union forces began to flee toward Washington, Johnston sent orders to Longstreet and Milledge Bonham to chase them. "Longstreet, waiting for no man, was immediately in pursuit," recalled G. Moxley Sorrel, his chief of staff. "He was halted first by Bonham, who ranked him, to permit his brigade to take the lead. Then resuming the march hot-footed after the flying foe, we were again stopped, this time . . . with orders from Beauregard to attempt no pursuit. Painful was this order. We knew the Federals were in full flight, and we had only to show ourselves to bag the whole outfit. . . . I saw Longstreet in a fine rage. He dashed his hat furiously on the ground, stamped, and bitter words escaped him."[2]

Sorrel would describe Old Pete as ". . . a soldier every inch, and very handsome, tall and well proportioned, strong and active, a superb horseman and with an unsurpassed soldierly bearing, his features and expression fairly matched; eyes, glint steel blue, deep and piercing; a full brown beard, head well shaped and poised. The worst feature was the mouth, rather coarse; it was partially hidden, however, by his ample beard."[3] Thomas Goree, a young aide from Texas, had this to say about Longstreet's abilities: His strength as an officer "consists, I think, in the seeming ease with which he can handle and arrange large numbers of troops, as also with the confidence and enthusiasm with which he seems to inspire them. . . . If he is ever excited, he has a way of concealing it, and always appears as if he had the utmost confidence in his ability to command and in that of his troops to execute."[4] One of Stuart's cavalrymen was less taken with Longstreet. "He impressed me then as a man of limited capacity who acquired reputation for wisdom by never saying anything—the old story of the owl. I do not remember ever hearing him say half a dozen words, beyond 'yes' and 'no,' in a consecutive sentence. . . ."[5]

Later that summer, Longstreet's headquarters acquired a temporary but invaluable aide-de-camp, John W. Fairfax, a wealthy Virginian who owned Oak Hill, the former estate of James Monroe. "Major Fairfax was then of middle age, tall, courtly and rather impressive," explained Sorrel. "He had attached himself at once to Longstreet, and took charge of his mess. . . . He lacked nothing in courage; was brave and would go anywhere. But Fairfax had two distinctions—he was the most pious of churchmen and was a born bon vivant, knowing and liking good things. Whiskey later was hard to get, yet he managed to have always a good supply on hand. . . . We had great merriment and singing."[6] That fall Longstreet would be named a major general.

Then the merriment would stop. In January an epidemic of scarlet fever would break out in Richmond, where Longstreet's wife and children were staying. Within a week three of their children would die, even while he and Louisa nursed them through the long nights. The drinking and the card games were no more. "He was with them, and some weeks after resumed his command a changed man," wrote Sorrel. "He had become very serious and reserved and a consistent member of the Episcopal Church. His grief was very deep and he had all our sympathies. . . ."[7]

Daniel Harvey Hill was born on July 12, 1821, in York District, South Carolina, youngest of eleven children. The death of his father, Solomon, plunged the family into financial difficulties and his mother, Nancy, into fits of despondency. In later years Hill would hold his mother's moods accountable for the "dark traits" he saw in himself. "I have always had a strong perception of right and wrong," he said, "and when corrected from petulance or passion, I brooded over it, did not forget it, and I am afraid did not forgive it."[8] The boy grew up in a strict Presbyterian household, one devoted to both the letter and spirit of God's law. Bible reading was done aloud, and frequently. In 1838 the needy Hill entered tuition-free West Point. There his classmates included not only Longstreet, but Lafayette McLaws, Richard Heron Anderson and Gustavus W. Smith. He was a middling student, graduating twenty-eighth in a class of fifth-six.

Four years of garrison duty followed his graduation, but 1847 found him in the midst of the Mexican War, advancing on Chapultepec under Winfield Scott. When the fortress fell Hill and a handful of troopers raced up the road toward the capital, driving the retreating enemy before them. He called it "a sublime and exalted feeling . . . chasing some 5,000 men with little more than a dozen."[9] Then back down the road thundered 1,500 Mexican lancers, making a counterattack. Lieutenant Thomas Jackson and his two artillery pieces came up in support just in time. The lancers, forced to ride tightly together on the narrow road, were decimated by Jackson's guns. Hill's combativeness extended to friends as well as foes. In Mexico, receiving conflicting orders as to whether to advance or retreat, he followed the orders of his veteran colonel rather than his politically appointed general. Later, berated by the general in words Hill considered "harsh and insulting," the young lieutenant drew his sword, brandished it in the general's face and, in his words, "forbade him to use such language again."[10] Placed under arrest, he was released on his colonel's intercession. By the war's end, commendations for bravery had earned him the brevet rank of major.

In 1848 Hill courted and married Isabella Morrison, 24, oldest daughter of the Rev. Robert Morrison of North Carolina. She would give him nine children. Soon thereafter he resigned from the army. "I cannot contemplate without horror her entrance into one of our wretched garrisons," he said.[11] For the next six years he would teach mathematics at Washington College in Lexington, Virginia. Here he resumed his friendship with Jackson, whom he had recommended for the teaching position at V.M.I., and was then married to Ellie Junkin. So close was the relationship that once, when one of the Hill children came down with pneumonia and the parents had exhausted themselves caring for her, Jackson took up the vigil. All night he walked the floor with the little girl, nursing her back to health. In 1854 the Hills moved to North Carolina, where Harvey Hill accepted the chair of mathematics at Davidson College, and the friendship was interrupted. It resumed again in 1857, after Ellie's death, with Jackson's marriage to Mary Anna, Isabella's younger sister. Hill flourished at Davidson, publishing one book on algebra and two on religion and, just as important, bringing discipline and order to what had been a rowdy student body.

In June of 1861 Hill, the newly elected colonel of the 1st North Carolina Volunteers, fought the first land battle of the war—at Big Bethel Church, just south of Yorktown on the Peninsula. His brigade and John B. Magruder's brigade of Virginians, some 1,400 men, took on a Union reconnaissance force of 4,000 coming up from Fort Monroe to explore the Confederate defenses. In more of a skirmish than a battle, Hill soundly defeated the interlopers. Union casualties totaled 94; Confederate, 11. "They were all in high glee," he reported about his men, "and seemed to enjoy it as much as boys do rabbit-shooting."[12] More soberly he wrote his wife: "I have to thank God for a great and decided Victory, and that I escaped with a slight contusion on my knee. . . . It is a little singular that my first battle in this war should be at *Bethel*, the name of the church where I was baptised and worshipped until 16 years old. The Church of my mother, was she not a guardian spirit in the battle averting the ball and the shell. Oh God give us gratitude to Thee and may we never dishonor Thee by a weak faith."[13] In the aftermath of the skirmish, he was named a brigadier general.

Hill was not at First Manassas, spending the summer and early fall on the Peninsula and in North Carolina. By November, however, he was back in northern Virginia under Johnston's command. His letters home thereafter reveal his fundamentally decent but argumentative nature. To his children, whom he gave pet names, he was endearing: "Tell Eugenia she is my Comfort, Randoph my Hope, Nannie my Jewell, Harvey my Pet-Boy, Irwin my Bright-Star."[14] To Isabella, who suffered excruciating headaches worrying about his safety, he was demanding: "I am not sure that home has appreciated me, as much as I have appreciated it."[15] Of the possibility that Jackson, now a major general, might be patronizing him he seemed almost paranoid: "General Jackson's notes are strictly official," he wrote Isabella. "Well it is a funny world."[16] Responding to her suggestion he could be warmer toward her kin, Hill was dismissive: "God forgive me for all the wrong I have done," he said. "You are now distressed about my coldness to Anna and the General. Do you really think that I ought to seek a social correspondence with those, who entertain so contemptible an opinion of me? . . . This is a time of great events, and we ought not to worry about small matters. My dear wife, I try to do right, and I do not wish to wrong any one of your family in the least, the very least. Why then do you always suspect me and dwell upon things which are distressing to me. . . ."[17]

In March of 1862 Harvey Hill, doubtless much to Isabella's delight and relief, would himself be named a major general.

Ambrose Powell Hill was born on November 9, 1825, near the northern Virginia town of Culpeper, a son of Fannie Russell Baptist, a frail, quiet woman with a bent for hypochondria, and Thomas Hill, an extroverted, well-to-do merchant. Powell Hill's early education came at a private school where the headmaster, a devout Baptist, spouted both Latin epigrams and tobacco juice. Though the Hills were Episcopal, a Baptist revival movement swept through the area in 1840 and claimed Fannie Hill as a convert, with the result that dancing, card-playing and other such examples of untoward conduct were banned from the household. Mr. Hill's mint juleps, however, remained sacrosanct. Rebelling against his mother's strict beliefs, young Powell grew up suspicious of religion, and of people he considered overly devout. When he left for West Point in 1842, his father gave him a Bible, with the inscription, "Peruse this every day." His mother gave him a lucky piece—a tiny ham bone—and he kept it with him all his life.

Hill made friends easily at the academy. One exception was his relationship with Thomas Jackson, his opposite in every respect. Hill came from the gentry, was warm and outgoing, liked to carouse, had few problems with his studies, and little interest in religion. Jackson was a hardscrabble orphan, taciturn in manner, abstemious in all things, worried about his grades and earnest about his faith. Far more to Hill's liking was his roommate, the ebullient and charming George McClellan of Pennsylvania. Then came the great mischance of Hill's life: On September 9, 1844, he was admitted to the academy hospital "with gonorrhea contracted on furlough." Penicillin did not exist in those days. In most people gonorrhea cured itself; the burning pain ended after a few weeks and caused no further damage. In others the disease festered and infected the urinary tract. Hill was one of the unlucky ones; in years to come his prostatitis would intermittently flare up, causing bouts of intense and incapacitating pain.

Going to Mexico in the closing months of the war, Lieutenant Hill saw little action but fell victim to typhoid fever. Six weeks of vomiting, high fever and dehydration could only have aggravated his prostatitis, but his natural high spirits made light of his illness. " 'Twas a matter of toss up" whether or not he would "shuffle off this mortal coil," he wrote his father. "I am well now, and as every body must have an acclimating spell, I am glad mine is over," he told his sister. The family knew his recuperation was complete when he ruminated on Mexican women. "How would you relish a Mexican daughter-in-law? . . ." he asked his father. " 'Tis Sunday again, and the bells (belles) called me to my devotion."[18]

The years 1848 to 1854 found Hill on routine garrison duty in Florida, Texas and Florida again. "My God," he noted in his diary while in Florida, "will these mosquitoes never satiate their vampirean appetite for blood? . . . Mosquitoes were especially sent on earth as a torment for the wicked. Wonder if Noah had any in the ark with him!" One Sunday the homesick Hill visited the home of some locals. "Nearly split my throat yelling at the old woman who was deaf & shamed my eyes looking love to the daughter, who was confoundedly pretty. Wish to Heaven that old woman had been blind instead of deaf." Drinking was a way of coping. "The brandy bottle, a quart out, was full when I started," he said, describing a patrol through the Florida swamps, "but being so cold, wet, and thoroughly chilled, I drank all of it and came into camp and they tell me just rolled right off my horse."[19] Twice during this period he suffered exhausting bouts of yellow fever or prostatitis, or perhaps both.

Then in 1855, posted to Washington, D.C., with his health much improved, Hill met Ellen Marcy, 21, the daughter of Major Randolph B. Marcy of Massachusetts. "Miss Nelly" had no shortage of suitors, including George McClellan, whom her parents strongly favored as a son-in-law. Love temporarily prevailed, however; Hill proposed and Miss Nelly accepted. Her parents were irate. "Did my affection for you merit such a breach of confidence? . . ." wrote her father from Texas. "I forgive you, but I should at once expect that you abandon all communications with Mr. Hill."[20] Mrs. Marcy went further. Learning her daughter's suitor had been treated for gonorrhea, she spread the news. Now Hill, who truly believed he was cured, was irate. "I have heard from truthful lips and with delicacy," he wrote Major Marcy, "that Mrs. Marcy's objections . . . are that from certain youthful imprudences . . . my health and constitution had become so impaired, so weakened, that no mother could yield her daughter to me, unless to certain unhappiness. . . ."[21] Even McClellan was drawn into the debate. "I transmitted to Hill *none* of the remarks you made," he told Mrs. Marcy. "I thought that you would regret what you had written before the letter reached me—that reflection would convince you that . . . you had said unpleasant & bitter things to me in reference to one of my oldest & dearest friends."[22] Nonetheless the damage was done. By mid-1856 Miss Nelly broke off the engagement.

The next year, at a Washington party, Hill met the woman he would marry—vivacious Dolly Morgan McClung, 23, daughter of a prominent Kentucky family and widow of a well-off businessman. "You know that I am so constituted," he told his sister, "that to be in love with someone is as necessary to me as my dinner, and there is now a little siren who has thrown her net around me . . ."[23] To McClellan he wrote: "I'm afraid there is no mistake about it this time, old fellow, and please God, and Kentucky blue-grass, my bachelor life is about to end."[24] In July 1859 Dolly and Powell Hill were married at the Morgan home in Lexington, Kentucky. She would give him four children, all daughters. John Hunt Morgan, the brother of the bride and soon a storied Confederate cavalryman and raider, was best man. Ten months later, Ellen Marcy and George McClellan were married in New York City. Hill was a groomsman.

Joining the Confederacy just before First Manassas, Hill was named colonel of the 13th Virginia Infantry, part of Arnold Elzey's brigade. He drove his men hard, marching and drilling them through the days, knowing he had only weeks to mold them into soldiers. His efforts soon caught Joseph Johnston's attention, as did his dress. In an army of individualists, Hill's costume stood out: trousers tucked into thigh-high black boots, shirts of red calico sewn by Dolly, broad-cuffed buckskin gloves, all topped off by a broad-brimmed black felt hat.

Much to his chagrin he saw no action at Manassas. His regiment, detached from the brigade, was off on the right of the Bull Run line, guarding the lower fords. In the months of idleness thereafter he often functioned, in Elzey's absence, as temporary brigade commander. Commented a chaplain: Hill "so mingled rigid discipline and kind consideration for the command as to win the respect, admiration and love of the whole brigade, as he had of his own regiment."[25] Echoed an enlisted man from Maryland: he "came in and sat down with us, and talked to us in as friendly a way as if we had been his equals in rank."[26]

In February of 1862, Hill would be named a brigadier, taking over Longstreet's old command. Three months later, at age 36, he would be leading a division, the youngest major general in the army.

Born on February 6, 1833, in southwestern Patrick County, Virginia, James Ewell Brown Stuart was one of ten children of Elizabeth Pannill, who was fond of moralizing, and Archibald Stuart, who was fond of a good time—even if it adversely affected his career in law and politics. Elizabeth Stuart would ask each of her sons on his twelfth birthday to swear not to touch liquor. This young James did, and he would be a teetotaler all his life. Growing up, he was as physical as a boy could be—riding, hunting and using his fists if necessary. But he showed a sensitive side as well, and was openly fond of the splendors of nature and the delights of music and poetry. When he was fifteen he went off to Emory & Henry College, where he studied science and the classics and where, in the midst of a campus religious revival, he joined the Methodist Church.

Entering West Point in 1850, Stuart soon earned an endearing nickname. " 'Beauty Stuart,' he was then universally called," Fitzhugh Lee would say, ". . . his comrades bestowed that appellation upon him to express their idea of his personal comeliness in inverse ratio to the term employed."[27] Homely he might have been, but lacking in soldierly qualities he was not. By his senior year Stuart was second captain of the corps, and renowned for his horsemanship. "I well recall his distinguishing characteristics," Lee continued, "which were a strict attention to his military duties, an erect, soldierly bearing, an immediate and almost thankful acceptance of a challenge to fight from any cadet who might in any way feel himself aggrieved, and a clear, metallic, ringing voice."[28] Lee might also have mentioned Godliness, for Stuart was a dedicated Christian. "I expect that you . . . have come to the conclusion that I have renounced the cross," he wrote a friend while at the academy, "but I rejoice to say I still have evidence of a Savior's pardoning love. When I came here I had reason to expect that many and strong temptations would beset my path, but I relied on 'him whom to know is [life] everlasting' to deliver me from temptation, and prayed God to guide me in the right way and 'teach' me to walk as a Christian should. . . ."[29]

Upon graduation in 1854 Lieutenant Stuart first was posted to Texas, and then to Fort Leavenworth, Kansas, where he was assigned to the 1st Cavalry. There he met Flora Cooke, the 20-year-old daughter of Lieutenant Colonel Philip St. George Cooke of Virginia. Not only was Flora attractive and spirited, but she could ride and shoot. Stuart was entranced. They were married in November 1855, five months after they first met, and would have three children. Two years later, in an expedition against the Cheyenne, he suffered his first wound. It came during a skirmish at close quarters when, he wrote Flora, one of the Indians "fired his last barrel within a foot of me, the ball taking effect in the centre of the breast, but, by the mercy of God, glancing to the left, lodging near my left nipple, but so far inside that it cannot be felt. I rejoice to inform you that the wound is not regarded as dangerous. . . ."[30]

The year 1859 found the resourceful Stuart on leave in Washington, patenting a "saber hook" that let a cavalryman easily move his saber from his belt to his saddle, and selling the patent rights to the government. It was then that he brought Robert E. Lee the War Office message directing him to put down John Brown's insurrection. Stuart accompanied Lee to Harpers Ferry, and it was his signal that touched off the storming of the arsenal building. Wrote Stuart to his mother afterward: "I was deputed by Colonel Lee to read to the leader, then called *Smith*, a demand to surrender immediately; and I was instructed to leave the door after his refusal, which was expected, and wave my cap; at which signal the storming party was to advance . . . and capture the insurgents at the point of the bayonet. . . . I approached the door in the presence of perhaps two thousand spectators, and told Mr. *Smith* that I had a communication for him. . . . He opened the door about four inches, and placed his body against the crack, with a cocked carbine in his hand: hence his remark after his capture that he could have wiped me out like a mosquito. . . . When *Smith* first came to the door I recognized old *Osawatomie Brown*, who had given us so much trouble in Kansas. No one present but myself could have performed that service. I got his bowie-knife from his person, and have it yet."[31]

Stuart returned to frontier duty soon thereafter. But in 1861, with the secession of Virginia, he resigned his commission and offered his services to the Confederacy. By July he was colonel of the 1st Virginia Cavalry, turning some 500 riders into a disciplined command. One writer described Stuart's charisma: "Every trooper is watching the broad, erect soldier on the big bay hunter, who sits easy in his saddle, front and centre, and gives each man the impression that he, personally, is being examined in detail, from cap to boots. The Colonel has a dancing eye: they like that. There is more than the touch of the dandy about him, and they approve that, too. Gauntlets of snow white buckskin hide half the golden *galons* on his sleeves. . . ."[32] Echoed a comrade-in-arms: "He was so brave a man himself that he never seemed to attribute unworthy motives to his men, and this was one of the secrets of his great influence over them in action. They were ashamed to be anything but brave where he was."[33]

At First Manassas, determined to block the Federal effort to outflank the Confederates, Stuart late in the day borrowed an artillery battery under Lieutenant Robert Beckham from the infantry, ordered it far to the left beyond the infantry line and masked it behind trees and foliage. "Beckham soon got the range," a trooper explained, "and then worked his pieces as fast as he could load them, with terrific effect upon the dense masses so near. Their lines were enfiladed by this fire. . . ."[34] Declared Jubal Early: "The fact was that Stuart, who had been for some time in position beyond our extreme left watching the enemy's movements, had, by the judicious use of Beckham's guns on his right flank, kept the enemy in check, and prevented him from flanking Elzey. . . . But for his presence there . . . my brigade would have arrived too late to be of any service, as by falling upon the left and rear of Elzey's brigade, the enemy would probably have ended the battle before my brigade reached that point."[35]

Within weeks after the battle, the 28-year-old Stuart was named a brigadier, and placed in command of six regiments of cavalry—Joseph Johnston's entire mounted force. "He is a rare man," enthused Johnston, "wonderfully endowed by nature with the qualities necessary for an officer of light cavalry. Calm, firm, acute, active, and enterprising, I know of no one more competent than he to estimate the occurrences before him at their true value."[36]

Stuart in his personal life, meanwhile, was in a fury. His father-in-law had elected to stay with the Union, and in so doing, he felt, sullied the family's honor. "For our own & our children's sake," he told Flora, "let us determine to act well *our* parts & bear with the mistakes & errors of others . . . but by no means attempt justification of what must be condemned. . . . Be consoled . . . by the reflection that your husband & brothers will atone for the father's conduct." To her brother, Confederate officer John R. Cooke, he wrote of his father-in-law, "He will regret it but once, and that will be continually." Nor could he bear that his son, who had been named for his grandfather, "should keep any part of his previous Christian name." Philip St. George Cooke Stuart would henceforth be known as James Ewell Brown Stuart Jr.[37]

In the midst of the brouhaha, however, his love for Flora remained constant. She was his "second self." He yearned for the time they would have a home with "birds & flowers & books, the very best Society in the world. When 'war's dread commotion is over,' I would step quietly into such a home. . . ."[38] The war would last four more years, however, and many men would not survive it. Stuart, as realistic as he was romantic, made out his will and took out a $10,000 insurance policy on his life.

# 1862

## ONE

\* \* \* \*

## LINCOLN AND MCCLELLAN

Abraham Lincoln in January of 1862 was a troubled man. Immediately after the Manassas defeat he had named George McClellan, still not 35 years old and fresh from minor triumphs over Confederate forces in western Virginia, to replace Irvin McDowell, giving him a mandate to raise and train an army the South could not withstand. McClellan, a gifted organizer, had done just that. He had swelled the ranks of the Army of the Potomac to more than 160,000 men, more than three times the number under Johnston facing it across the river, and he had outfitted it superbly. But all during the fall and into the winter Lincoln, under intense pressure from radical Republicans, had been unable to persuade McClellan to launch an offensive or even reveal his plans. This even though he had also named him general-in-chief, replacing Winfield Scott, and given him dual responsibilities. Both Lincoln and Davis, it seems, were being served by less than aggressive field commanders. Now McClellan was sick with typhoid fever, and the prospects of taking Richmond in the near term seemed dimmer than ever. "Repaired to the President's house at eight o'clock, p.m.," wrote Major General McDowell, who had retained his rank, on January 10. "Found the President alone. Was taken into the small room in the north-east corner. Soon after we were joined by Brigadier General [William] Franklin; the Secretary of State, Governor [William] Seward; the Secretary of the Treasury, and the Assistant-Secretary of War. The President was greatly disturbed at the state of affairs . . . and as he had been to General McClellan's house, and the General did not ask to see him; and as he must talk to somebody, he had sent for General Franklin and myself to obtain our opinion as to the possibility of soon commencing operations. . . . To use his own expression, 'If something is not done soon, the bottom would be out of the whole affair; and if General McClellan did not want to use the army, he would like to borrow it, provided he could see how it could be made to do something.' "[1]

Two nights later the group met again, this time with the recuperating McClellan present. When one of the cabinet officers asked him what he intended to do, he was evasive. Wrote McDowell, ". . . he said he must say he was very unwilling to develop his plans, always believing that in military matters the fewer persons who were knowing them the better; that he would tell them if he was *ordered* to do so. The President then asked him if he counted upon any particular time; he did not ask what that time was, but had he in his own mind any particular time a movement could be commenced. He replied he had. Then, rejoined the President, I will adjourn this meeting."[2]

Congress was not as patient as Lincoln. The Committee on the Conduct of the War promptly hauled McClellan before its members, with two Republicans, Senators Zachariah Chandler of Michigan and Ben Wade of Ohio, doing most of the questioning. Why, Chandler wanted to know, wasn't the army advancing on the enemy? McClellan explained that the two narrow bridges leading across the Potomac to Alexandria were sufficient for an advance, but better lines of retreat were needed in the event he was driven back. "General McClellan," Chandler broke in. "If I understand you correctly, before you strike at the rebels you want to be sure of plenty of room so you can run in case they strike back." McClellan began elaborating, in a patronizing way, on lines of retreat and why they were as important as lines of communication and supply. "General," said Senator Wade, "you have all the troops you have called for, and if you haven't enough, you shall have more. . . . Is it really necessary for you to have more bridges over the Potomac before you move?" After McClellan had ended his testimony, Chandler complained to Wade, "I don't know much about war, but it seems to me this is infernal, unmitigated cowardice." As chairman of the committee, Wade then went to see Lincoln. When the president asked him whom he should name in McClellan's place, he shouted, "Anybody!" Replied Lincoln: "Wade, anybody will do for you, but I must have somebody."[3]

On January 27 the president, using his authority as commander-in-chief, issued General War Order No. 1, directing a forward movement of all military forces on February 22. He followed this up with Special Order No. 1, specifically telling the Army of the Potomac, on or before February 22, to occupy Manassas Junction, "all details to be in the discretion of the general-in-chief."[4]

McClellan was shocked. All along he had been counting on avoiding a frontal assault, and flanking the Confederates by putting his army on ships that would take it down the Potomac and up the Rappahannock, landing in the enemy's rear at Urbanna, fifteen miles upriver. Now he had no choice but to take Lincoln into his confidence. He did this in capsule form, but the president wanted more information. "You and I have two distinct, and different plans for a movement," Lincoln wrote him on February 3, "yours to be down the Chesapeake . . . mine to move directly to a point on the Railroad South West of Manassas. . . . Does not your plan involve a greatly larger expenditure of *time*, and *money* than mine? Wherein is a victory *more certain* by your plan than mine? Wherein is a victory *more valuable* by your plan than mine? Would it not be *less* valuable, in this, that it would break no great line of the enemie's communications, while mine would? In case of disaster, would not a safe retreat be more difficult by your plan than mine?"[5]

McClellan replied in detail. Going overland would involve a series of bloody assaults against well-entrenched positions, all the while stretching the Union supply lines. Flanking the enemy via the water would pull Johnston out of his defenses in order to protect Richmond, and allow the Union navy to protect the supply and communication lines and add its firepower to the assault. Lastly, McClellan maintained, the water-borne strategy offered flexibility: if Urbanna should prove unsuitable, the army could be disembarked at Fort Monroe at the tip of the Yorktown Peninsula, formed by the roughly parallel York and James Rivers.

Mollified, Lincoln agreed to consider McClellan's plan. February 22 came and went, and the Army of the Potomac did not move. Meanwhile Lincoln and his wife, Mary Todd Lincoln of Kentucky, suffered a personal tragedy. Willie, the middle son of three, came down with typhoid fever and died after a short illness. Mourned his father, "It is hard, hard, hard to see him die." Mrs. Lincoln was distraught to the point of madness. "She could not bear to look upon his picture," said her mulatto maid. "And after his death she never crossed the threshold of the Guest's Room in which he died, or the Green Room in which he was embalmed."[6] Adding to Lincoln's distress were the doubts about his wife's loyalty to the Union. Hers was a divided family: a brother and half sister chose to go with the North, a brother and three half brothers with the South. So strong were the rumors that the president one day walked unannounced into a meeting investigating them, declaring, "I, Abraham Lincoln, President of the United States, appear of my own volition before this committee of the Senate to say that I, of my own knowledge, know that it is untrue that any of my family hold treasonable communication with the enemy."[7]

March 8 brought many developments. First McClellan gathered together his twelve division commanders and told them of his Urbanna plan, asking them to vote on it. When they approved it, eight to four, he personally brought the president the news. Feeling he had little choice, Lincoln reluctantly endorsed the decision. The same day, however, he issued General War Order No. 2, promoting without McClellan's knowledge four of his division heads to corps command. They were McDowell, Samuel P. Heintzelman, Erasmus D. Keyes, and Edwin ("Bull Head") Sumner, all resolute Republicans.

Meanwhile at Hampton Roads, the great body of water lying between the Peninsula on the north and Norfolk on the south, a single ironclad Confederate warship, the C.S.S. *Virginia*, was wreaking havoc on the wooden-hulled Union fleet. When he got the news the next day, Secretary of War Edwin M. Stanton went into near hysteria. "To me," wrote Secretary of the Navy Gideon Welles, "there was . . . something inexpressibly ludicrous in the wild, frantic talk, action, and rage of Stanton as he ran from room to room . . . swung his arms, scolded, and raved."[8] He insisted on the readying of barges filled by rocks, to be sunk at the mouth of the Potomac to block the *Virginia* from shelling the capital. Weeks later, when the crisis had passed, Lincoln noted the unused barges and could not resist chiding Stanton. "Oh," he said, "that is Stanton's navy . . . as useless as the paps of a man to a suckling child. They may be some show to amuse the child, but they are for nothing for service."[9]

The C.S.S. *Virginia*, the warship that touched off Stanton's frenzy, has often been described as looking like a "floating barn roof." Confederate shipbuilders at Norfolk had raised the scuttled frigate U.S.S. *Merrimack*, cut it down to the waterline and topped it off with an iron superstructure that sloped at 35 degrees on all sides to help deflect cannonballs. She measured some 260 feet, carried 10 guns and a crew of 320 and had a 22-foot draft. Top-heavy and unstable, she was not suitable for the open sea. "Do you really think she will float?" Captain Sydney Lee, brother of Robert E. Lee, asked one of the builders.[10] Steaming into Hampton Roads on March 8, the *Virginia* headed straight for the blockading squadron. First to feel her sting was the 30-gun sloop-of-war U.S.S. *Cumberland*, whose broadsides bounced off her superstructure and whom she eventually rammed and sank. Next she set afire the 50-gun frigate U.S.S. *Congress*, forcing its surrender. Before darkness fell, helped by the receding tide, she drove three more frigates aground.

Now occurred one of those serendipitous events. Even while the *Virginia* was having her way with her wooden-hulled adversaries, a Union ironclad launched in New York some five weeks before was steaming down the coast. The next morning, when the *Virginia* came out of Norfolk to finish off the frigates, she found the U.S.S. *Monitor* waiting for her. "You can see surprise on a ship just the same as you can see it in a human being," said a *Monitor* crewman, "and there was surprise all over the *Merrimack*."[11] The Yankee warship was much smaller than the *Virginia*, carrying only two guns and a crew of fifty-eight, with a ten-and-one-half-foot draft. But she was just as odd-looking, and just as lethal. Only her pilothouse and nine-foot-high revolving gun turret showed above her flat deck, and people agreed she looked like a "tin can on a shingle." What ensued was a four-hour naval duel, with 180-pound cannonballs bouncing off iron plate, and crewmen of both vessels nearly deafened by the noise. The *Virginia* tried to ram her opponent but the

*Monitor*, faster and more maneuverable, flitted around her. Finally, just as the *Virginia*'s iron plate was beginning to crack, she delivered a shell at point-blank range against the *Monitor*'s pilothouse, blinding her captain. The engagement ended in deadlock, and the two ships never fought again. "They stood on the edge of the arena, each hesitating to advance, neither caring to retreat," said an observer. "Each commander accurately surmised the intentions of his opponent, and just as correctly refused to take the bait."[12]

Just as the duel at Hampton Roads was ending, Joseph Johnston, increasingly worried about the Union buildup, was pulling back from the Manassas line to the Rappahannock. Lincoln took the news as confirmation that McClellan, with any reasonable display of aggressiveness, could have overwhelmed him much earlier. On March 12 he issued General War Order No. 3, relieving McClellan as general-in-chief so he could, ostensibly, concentrate on taking Richmond. The demotion built a fire under the man his admirers called "Young Napoleon." The next day, with the *Virginia* neutralized, McClellan lost no time getting the support of his four new corps commanders for his water-borne assault. Disembarking now at Urbanna was not feasible, but landing at Fort Monroe was. Lincoln acquiesced, with the understanding the Washington garrison of 18,000 be supplemented with at least 25,000 more men.

To transport the army the War Department chartered every available vessel on the eastern seaboard. Hundreds of ships, large and small, began to gather along the loading wharves of the Potomac, most of them at Alexandria. They ranged from side-wheelers, clippers and excursion boats to barges, schooners and tugs. "I shall soon leave here on the wing for Richmond—which you may be sure I will take," McClellan assured a friend.[13]

How Lincoln got to the White House is, of course, the quintessential American success story. Born on February 12, 1809, in a one-room log cabin on the Kentucky frontier, he was the son of Nancy Hanks, an illiterate, and Thomas Lincoln, a carpenter and farmer. While the family was not impoverished, it was far from affluent. His mother died when he was nine but his stepmother, Sarah Bush Lincoln, encouraged the boy in his desire to educate himself. Spare hours were spent in a rustic schoolhouse, evenings voraciously reading well-thumbed books. He grew up in Illinois, doing manual labor like rail splitting, all the while intent on bettering himself. By the time he reached manhood he was six-foot-four and raw-boned, renowned locally for his homespun humor and already edging toward politics and the law.

Lincoln's only military experience came in 1832, when he joined a volunteer Illinois militia company to fight in the Black Hawk War, which pitted settlers against Indians. Though he saw no combat, he took deep satisfaction in the fact that his fellow volunteers elected him their captain. Two years later he won his first election, a seat in the state legislature, and in 1837 began practicing law in Springfield, the state capital. His silk stovepipe hat became his trademark. He was quite successful in his legal work, developing a reputation for reasoned arguments that stripped a case down to its essentials. Soon he was making as much as $1,500 a year, the same salary as a state governor. But he retained his folksy dress and manner. "He was still known as carelessly groomed," wrote a biographer, "his trousers mentioned as creeping to the ankles and higher, his hair rumpled, vest wrinkled, and at the end of a story putting his arms around his knees, raising his knees to his chin and rocking to and fro."[14] How much of his persona was a politician's ploy is open to debate. "The man that thinks that Lincoln sat calmly down . . . waiting for the people to call him, has a very erroneous knowledge of Lincoln," explained William H. Herndon, a former law partner. "He was always calculating, and always planning ahead. His ambition was a little engine that knew no rest."[15]

In 1842, after a troubled two-year engagement, Lincoln married Mary Todd of Lexington, Kentucky. From the beginning it was a marriage of opposites. His tall, gaunt frame accentuated her short, plump figure. His quiet, methodical manner clashed with her impulsive, imperious nature. He was a self-made man. She was the granddaughter of a Revolutionary War general, had gone to finishing school where she learned to speak French, read music and paint on china, and dearly loved pretty clothes. But for both the marriage had its positive side. "She was an excellent judge of human nature," admitted Herndon, ". . . quick to detect those who had designs upon and sought to use him. She was, in a good sense, a stimulant. She kept him from lagging. . . . Realizing that Lincoln's rise in the world would elevate and strengthen her, she strove in every way to promote his fortunes. . . ."[16] Mary Todd Lincoln would give her husband four sons, one of whom died before his presidency.

Other than one term in Congress in 1847, Lincoln spent most of the 1840s and 1850s practicing law in Illinois, dabbling in politics but largely out of the public eye. That would all change in 1856, when he ran against Stephen A. Douglas for the U.S. Senate. During their ensuing debates, which tens of thousands of spectators witnessed at seven different sites, he condemned slavery in ringing terms as "a moral, a social, and a political wrong," while Douglas skirted the moral issue. "You say [slavery] is wrong," Lincoln told him, "but don't you constantly . . . argue that this is not the right place to oppose it? You say it must not be opposed in the free States, because slavery is not here; it must not be opposed in the slave States, because it is there; it must not be opposed in politics, because that will make a fuss; it must not be opposed in the pulpit, because that is not religion. Then where is the place to oppose it?"[17] Lincoln narrowly lost the election, but now was a national figure.

Two years later, running on the six-year-old Republican Party's antislavery platform, he won the presidency. The Democratic Party divided its votes, Douglas getting 1.376 million in the North and John C. Breckinridge of Kentucky 849,000 in the South. The fading Whig Party's nominee, John Bell of Tennessee, received 588,000 votes. Lincoln triumphed with 1.866 million votes. He walked home alone from the Springfield Statehouse through the celebrating crowds and, with characteristic simplicity, told his wife, "Mary, we're elected."[18]

How the youthful George Brinton McClellan became, at this point, the Union's top general is another kind of success story. Precocious is the word generally used to describe him. Born in Philadelphia in 1826, the son of socially prominent parents, he was admitted to West Point before his sixteenth birthday, the age requirement being waived because of his superior physique and intellect. Though he was only five-foot-eight, McClellan's thick torso gave him great strength, while his self-confidence already projected an aura of authority. At the academy he graduated second in the class of 1846 and formed, as we have seen, his lifelong friendship with Powell Hill. Serving in the Mexican War he won two brevets for bravery, and in 1855 was thought so promising an officer that Secretary of War Davis sent him to Europe as an observer during the Crimean War. On his return McClellan wrote a well-received report, and also persuaded the army to adopt a new saddle of his own design. This so-called "McClellan saddle" was not universally popular, a British journalist writing that it "is adapted to a man who cannot ride: if a squadron so mounted were to attempt a ditch or fence, half of them would be ruptured or spilled."[19]

McClellan's courtship of Ellen Marcy lasted six years, both before and after her engagement to Hill. So far as the parents were concerned, McClellan and Miss Nelly would be an ideal match. "She is beautiful," his mother wrote him even before the two had met. Ellen's father, she continued, had praised him so highly to his daughter, "she was just ready to fall in love with you." Enthused Major Marcy: "He is generally regarded as one of the most brilliant men of his rank in the Army. . . . His family connections are unexceptionable and his staff position is such that his wife would always have a good and comfortable home." When the couple did first meet, in April of 1854, McClellan was instantly smitten. He proposed, only to be turned down. "I succeeded in making a very great blunder & doing a very foolish thing in the way of pushing too far & too quickly . . ." he told her mother. "Give Miss Nelly my warmest regards, or anything warmer you please. You can't make it too strong."[20] But Ellen was unmoved, and McClellan accepted her decision, not renewing his courtship even after she returned Hill's ring.

He resigned from the army with the rank of captain, taking a position as vice president and chief engineer of the Illinois Central Railroad. By 1859, however, he was writing to Ellen again, beginning a more propitious suit. "I hate to think of the future now—it seems so blank—no goal to reach, no object to strive for!" he entreated. "Was mortal man, *or* woman, ever contented? So life passes—we wish, and dream—build castles in the air—struggle for the unattainable."[21] That fall, after she accepted his second proposal, he pressed for an early marriage. "Don't talk to me about going East to 'prepare to be married.' As I've told you before I don't want any preparation. I want *you & you alone*. I want you just as you are, in the clear blue dress or any other. . . . I want Nelly Marcy just as she is."[22] In May of 1860 they were married at New York City's Calvary Episcopal Church. The bride was radiant, the groom triumphant, and the guest list read like a Who's Who of West Pointers North and South, moving the *New York Herald* to headline the event "Marriage Among the Elite."

In April of 1861, now president of the Ohio and Mississippi Railroad earning a munificent $10,000 a year, McClellan left his job to accept a major general's rank and command of all Ohio volunteers. Two months later, with Miss Nelly six months pregnant, he was leading an army of some 8,000 men in western Virginia. "Everything here needs the hand of the master," he grandly wrote his wife, "& is getting it fast."[23] On July 11 and July 13, his troops at Rich Mountain and Carrick's Ford routed much smaller Confederate forces, engagements that would have been little noted except for McClellan's hyperbole, which claimed that he had "annihilated two armies, commanded by educated and experienced soldiers, intrenched in mountain fastnesses fortified at their leisure." But the North was eager for good news, and took the dispatch as Gospel truth. "McClellan was the hero of the moment," explained Union General Jacob D. Cox, "and when, but a week later, his success was followed by the disaster to McDowell at Bull Run, he seemed pointed out by Providence as the ideal chieftain who could . . . lead our armies to certain victory. His personal intercourse with those around him was so kindly, and his bearing so modest, that his dispatches . . . are a psychological study, more puzzling to those who knew him well than to strangers. . . . In them he seems to be composing for stage effect."[24] Called to Washington immediately after Manassas, he took command of the Army of the Potomac before the week was out.

Initially McClellan could not have been more pleased. "Presdt., Cabinet, Genl Scott & all deferring to me—by some strange operation of magic I seem to have become *the* power of the land," he told his wife. "I almost think if I were to win some small success now I could become Dictator. . . ."[25] By August, however, he began to create hobgoblins for himself. In this he was abetted by private detective Alan Pinkerton, whom he hired to estimate the enemy's strength at Manassas. Pinkerton's guesses, for that is what they were, invariably came in at two to three times the real numbers, convincing McClellan that Johnston might attack him at any moment. Going into the fall his complaints became louder: the Union buildup was not progressing fast enough, and he was not getting sufficient cooperation. "The enemy have from

3 to 4 times my force," he wrote Ellen, "the Presdt is an idiot, the old General in his dotage—they cannot or will not see the true state of affairs."[26] When Scott asked for retirement, Lincoln on November 1 despite his reservations added the post of general-in-chief to McClellan's responsibilities. The honor did not ease the lack of rapport between the two men, with the subordinate's conduct only becoming more egregious. Once, when Lincoln scheduled a small conference in the White House, McClellan never showed up. The other participants were properly indignant, but the president seemed unruffled. "Never mind," he said. "I will hold McClellan's horse if he will only bring us success."[27] What Richard Taylor said about Davis and Johnston, that "each misjudged the other to the end," was equally true of Lincoln and McClellan.

Now in the spring of 1862 "Young Napoleon" was at last on the attack. By April 1 the ships transporting his army so crowded the waters off the Peninsula that, said one spectator, "It was impossible to count the vessels, though aided by a glass."[28] McClellan set up his headquarters at Fort Monroe, landing his force of perhaps 120,000 men for the march on Yorktown. Then came word that Lincoln, believing that McClellan had not kept his pledge to leave at least 40,000 troops to defend Washington, was keeping most of McDowell's 40,000-man corps from joining him.

What particularly concerned the president was Stonewall Jackson's activity in the Shenandoah Valley, where his 6,000 troops were managing to tie up some 35,000 Federals. Jackson had attacked Kernstown on March 23 and, though he had been repulsed, his aggressiveness was worrisome. "My explicit order that Washington, by the judgment of *all* the commanders of Army corps, be left entirely secure, had been neglected," Lincoln wrote McClellan. "It is precisely that that led me to detain McDowell." How many men *were* on the Peninsula, the president wanted to know. "There is a curious mystery about the *number* of troops now with you," he said. "When I telegraphed you . . . saying you had over 100,000 with you, I had just obtained from the Secretary of War, a statement, taken as he said, from your own returns, making 108,000 then with you, and en route to you. You now say you have but 85,000 when all en route to you shall have reached you. How can the discrepancy be accounted for?" Push forward, Lincoln told McClellan. "Once more let me tell you, it is indispensable to *you* that you strike a blow. *I* am powerless to help this."[29]

Lincoln's sense of urgency was understandable. "Moving this army from Washington by water," calculated one historian, "had required 113 steamers, 188 schooners, 88 barges, hauling for three weeks 121,500 men, 14,592 animals, 1,150 wagons, 44 batteries, 74 ambulances, besides pontoon bridges, telegraph materials, equipage, cattle, food, supplies." What was McClellan's reaction? "I have raised an awful row about McDowell's corps," he told Ellen.

"The President very coolly telegraphed me . . . that he thought I had better break the enemy's lines at once! I was much tempted to reply that he had better come and do it himself."[30]

On April 4 McClellan did advance five infantry divisions, some 60,000 men, the fifteen miles toward Yorktown, where Major General John Bankhead Magruder's some 13,000 defenders were entrenched, forming a ten-mile line along the Warwick River. But by the next morning, within sight of the enemy, two events conspired to discourage him. First there were the heavy rains, downpours that turned the roads into seas of mud and swelled the river, making the fortifications much harder to storm. Then there was the number of defenders, far greater than he had anticipated. "The way Magruder fooled them," said Lieutenant Robert H. Miller of the 14th Louisiana, "was to divide each body of his troops into two parts and keep them traveling all the time for twenty-four hours, till reinforcements came." His regiment marched from the York to the James and back six times. The 11th Alabama had a less strenuous but more dangerous assignment. Periodically it left the entrenchments and moved on the double through enemy fire, as Captain James H. McMath explained, "until we got out of sight just around the point of a hill. We were halted there some ½ hour, when we counter-marched over to the place we started from."[31] Spirited drum-rattling and bugle calls, the bellowing of orders and bursts of gunfire completed the tableau. Pinkerton's inflated estimates of the actual Confederate strength only alarmed McClellan all the more.

Such theatrics were nothing new for Magruder. Dubbed "Prince John" in the Old Army for his love of pageantry, the 52-year-old Virginian, who spoke with a lisp but sang in a clear tenor voice, had a well-deserved reputation as a bon vivant. At Fort Adams in Newport, Rhode Island, and then at Fort Leavenworth, Kansas, the entertainment he lavished on visitors was legendary. "Although in the West the brilliant show drills and dress parades were often only witnessed by a group of frontiersmen, or a squad of Indians from the plains," a fellow officer recounted, "he appeared as well satisfied as on similar occasions at Newport, when the spectators were the gay crowd of a fashionable watering place. The sequel to his military exercises was usually a dinner, provided with all the taste of a connoisseur."[32] Paying for these indulgences was difficult, however, particularly on a soldier's salary. Mrs. Magruder, the daughter of a wealthy Baltimore merchant, had long since tired of making the effort, and had decamped to Italy with their three children. Not that Magruder was not a skilled officer. His knowledge of artillery tactics and entrenching principles was first rate. It was only when he had to go on the attack that he faltered.

His deceptions stopped the Federals cold. With unusual speed McClellan decided that a frontal assault, despite his huge advantage in numbers, was not an option. "Our neighbors are in a very strong position," he advised the naval officer supporting him, whose primary responsibility was seeing to it that the *Monitor* continued to checkmate the *Virginia*. "I cannot turn Yorktown without a *battle*, in which I must use heavy artillery & go though the preliminary operations of a siege."[33] Positioning the siege guns, which were some seventy in number, would not be an easy task. Half of them could be moved on wheeled carriages, but only with great difficulty on the muddy roads. The remainder, seacoast guns and mortars weighing up to eight tons, would have to be floated by barges up to the front, using derricks to lift them onto stationary platforms. Once operational, outside the range of the smaller-bored Confederate artillery, they could hurl tons of metal a day at a helpless foe.

But the positioning took weeks, giving the South ample time to shift troops from the Rappahannock, and Magruder could take credit for a job well done. Within days his army swelled to 35,000 men. "Magruder did splendidly," Richmond diarist Mary Chestnut would write. "It was a wonderful thing, how he played his ten thousand before McClellan like fireflies and utterly deluded him—keeping him down there ever so long."[34] The Comte de Paris, a French military observer serving as one of McClellan's aides, agreed he was overcautious but praised him for the concern he had for his men. "General McClellan . . . deceived by appearances . . . did not dare to thrust his sword through the slight curtain which his able adversary had spread before his vision," he wrote. "A vigorous attack . . . would have had every chance of success. . . . The army needed a daring stroke. . . . But he would not compromise the young army entrusted to his care in an enterprise which he considered too hazardous."[35] To which we might riposte: You cannot fight without spilling blood.

# TWO

\* \* \* \*

# ON THE DEFENSIVE

In February of 1862, the Confederate forces throughout Virginia were far weaker than their foes in Washington could imagine. One problem was that the South's manpower pool, which had already produced its first wave of volunteers, was so much smaller than the North's that a conscription act would be needed to swell the ranks. Political pressures would delay the passage of such a bill for two more months. Then there was the continuing shortage of everything from weapons to food. Some equipment had been gleaned from the retreating foe after Manassas, but the South had not yet geared up to make the most of the resources it did possess. Last was the fact the Confederates were of necessity spread thin, facing threats in all directions. In the Shenandoah, Jackson at this point had no more than 6,000 men, while at the upper end of the Valley, Edward ("Allegheny") Johnson's small force of 3,000 guarded the roads from western Virginia. Joseph Johnston had less than 40,000 men at Manassas. Magruder had perhaps 13,000 troops at Yorktown, and Benjamin Huger another 13,000 at Norfolk. In all, the commands totaled some 70,000 men. Meanwhile McClellan's buildup in and around Washington had reached 160,000 and was increasing.

Summoned to Richmond on February 19 for an emergency cabinet meeting, Johnston convinced Davis the Manassas line might be overwhelmed or turned at any moment, and received permission to fall back. Left unresolved, however, was the question of how soon, since the muddy roads were still largely impassable for heavy transport, and how far. Johnston "declared himself ignorant of the topography of the country in his rear," Davis would say. "This confession was a great shock to my confidence in him. That a General should have selected a line that he himself considered untenable, and should not have ascertained the topography . . . in his rear was inexplicable on any other theory than that he had neglected the primary duty of a commander."[1]

Johnston's reports to Richmond were filled with pessimism. "The army is crippled and its discipline greatly impaired for want of general officers," he warned on February 25, "and besides, a Division of five Brigades is without generals; and at least half the field officers are absent—generally sick. The accumulation of subsistence stores at Manassas is now a great evil. The Commissary General was requested more than once to suspend those supplies. A very extensive meat-packing establishment at Thoroughfare [Gap] is also a great incumbrance. The great quantities of personal property in our camps is a still greater one."[2] Concerned as he was, Johnston still found time to feud with Secretary of War Judah P. Benjamin, the Yale-trained lawyer who would hold Davis's cabinet together and soon become his secretary of state. "The course of the Secretary of War," Johnston told the president, referring to what he believed was Benjamin's meddling in personnel decisions, "has not only impaired discipline, but deprived me of . . . influence in the army, without which there can be little hope of success."[3] Inured to Johnston's ways, Davis replied that Benjamin in turn "had complained that his orders were not executed, and I regret that he was able to present to me so many instances to justify that complaint, which were in nowise the invasion of your prerogative as a commander in the field."[4]

On March 5, Johnston overreacted to the news of unusual Federal activity at Dumfries on his right flank. Without informing the president he gave orders for a withdrawal over the next few days to the Rappahannock at Fredericksburg, some 55 miles equidistant from Washington and Richmond, and later to the Rapidan River. The orders were given piecemeal, creating considerable confusion. Because of the condition of the roads, tons of supplies and equipment had to be left behind, including most of the heavy guns. Worst of all, for an army chronically short of rations, more than one million pounds of meat were destroyed or abandoned. It was not until March 13 that Johnston gave Davis a grudging report on his movements. He explained away the loss of the guns and meat by insisting that the management of the Orange and Alexandria Railroad had denied him proper transport. Davis must have ground his teeth. ". . . Before the receipt of yours of the 13th," he replied, referring to the fact the enemy had not bothered to occupy Manassas until several days after the precipitous Confederate retreat, "I was as much in the dark as to your purposes, condition, and necessities as at the time of our conversation on the subject about a month hence . . . having heard of no cause for such a sudden movement, I was at a loss to believe it."[5]

In the midst of this confusion, the president suddenly ordered Robert E. Lee, still working on the coastal defenses from his base in Charleston, to rejoin him in Richmond. Davis made this move because he had been fighting a running battle with his critics in Congress over the need for a professional soldier to monitor the operations of the War Department. Recently they had passed a bill creating the post of general-in-chief, stating that its occupant had full authority to take command in the field if he thought it advisable. Still intent on being his own general-in-chief, Davis had vetoed the measure. To appease Congress, however, he had his adjutant general issue on March 13 the ambiguously worded General Order No. 14, declaring that Lee "is assigned to duty at the seat of government; and, under the direction of the President, is charged with the conduct of military operations in the armies of the Confederacy."[6] Lee now found himself in the same role he had been in the weeks leading up to Manassas—military advisor to the president. "I do not see either advantage or pleasure in my duties," he wrote his wife. "But I will not complain, but do my best."[7]

Lee's best would be good indeed. While it was true his days now were filled with the tedious details that ordinarily fell to adjutant generals and quartermasters, his position also gave him the opportunity to influence strategy. The antipathy Davis and Johnston felt for each other enabled him to step into the breach. Taking care to keep the preoccupied president informed and the rank-conscious Johnston appeased, Lee during the first days of April responded to McClellan's debarkation by arranging for elements of Johnston's army to leave the Rapidan and move eastward. When it was obvious McClellan's target was Richmond rather than Norfolk, they were able more quickly to reinforce Magruder. "By April 4," wrote his biographer, "[Lee] had called a total of three divisions from the line of the Rapidan-Rappahannock. It was done so quietly and so gradually that few protests were made."[8] Soon almost all of Johnston's army would be at Yorktown, bringing its defenders first to 35,000, then to 55,000 men.

Just as important, Lee began a correspondence with Stonewall Jackson in the Shenandoah Valley. If Jackson could go on the offensive, he suggested, perhaps by joining with Richard Ewell and Edward Johnson, the 70,000 Federals remaining in northern Virginia could be immobilized, keeping them from joining McClellan on the Peninsula. "If you can use Genl Ewell's division in an attack on Genl [Nathaniel] Banks and . . . drive him back, it will prove a great relief to the pressure on Fredericksburg," he said on April 21. "The blow wherever struck, must, to be successful, be sudden and heavy . . . I cannot pretend at this distance to direct operations . . ." he added four days later. "If you can strike an effective blow against the enemy west of Staunton it will be very advantageous. You might then avail yourself of your success to bring with you Genl Johnson's command . . . and move your army thus reinforced back to the Blue Ridge. Should your combined forces, with those of Genl Ewell prove strong enough to warrant an attack on Genl Banks, it might then be made . . ." he elaborated on May 1.[9] Jackson needed no more encouragement than this. His Valley campaign would exceed Lee's expectations.

Down on the Peninsula, McClellan's siege would last the entire month of April and beyond. Thousands of newly arrived Confederates found themselves cheek by jowl with their comrades in the rain and the mud and the muck, digging in under very difficult conditions. Georgia-born Robert Stiles, a Yale graduate whose family had moved to the North when he was twelve years old, had decided to return to his roots. Now he was serving with the Richmond Howitzers, which would become one of the war's best-known artillery units. The defensive lines, he observed, "were admirably adapted for the purpose for which General Magruder designed and located them; namely, to enable a small body of troops to hold the position—but for occupation by a large army they were simply execrable. There was scarcely solid ground enough accessible to afford standing, sleeping or living room for the men." Then there were the Federal sharpshooters. "Our positions were commanded by those on the other side," Stiles continued, "our earthworks were utterly insufficient, we were heavily outnumbered in guns, and the Federal sharpshooters were as audacious and deadly as I ever saw them."

Here he first met the men of the Texas Brigade. "The work of these worthies appeared little less than miraculous. They were apparently unconscious of danger and seemed to bear charmed lives. When the pressure of the . . . sharpshooters became intolerable, the Texans would pass the word that it was time to go out 'squirrel shooting.' Then they would get up, yawn and stretch a little, load their rifles and take to the water, disappearing from view in the brush. Then everything would be still a few minutes; then two or three shots, and the sputter of the sharpshooters would cease. After a while the Texans would straggle back, and report how many 'squirrels' they had got." Not every Confederate unit, however, could bear up under the pressure of the siege. "One of our detachments broke down utterly from nervous tension and lack of rest," Stiles admitted. "I went in as one of the relief party to bring them out and take their places. It was, of course, after nightfall, and some of these poor lads were sobbing in their broken sleep, like a crying child just before it sinks to rest. It was really pathetic. The men actually had to be supported to the ambulances sent down to bring them away."

Nightfall brought the greatest terrors. "Amongst the unpleasant experiences of these lines were the night attacks, or perhaps, to speak more accurately . . . the night alarms," he said. "Down in these swamps at night it was incredibly dark and musketry never roared and reverberated as terribly anywhere else. These exhibitions reached the dignity at least of fully developed 'alarms.' Especially was this the case when, one black night, a sudden outburst of fire . . . stampeded a working party of some two hundred Negroes who had just begun the much-needed strengthening of our very inadequate fortifications. The working party not only fled themselves, but the frantic fugitives actually swept away with them a part of our infantry support."[10]

On April 14, fresh from getting his first look at the Yorktown fortifications, Joseph Johnston and his key lieutenants Major Generals Gustavus W. Smith and Longstreet met in Richmond with Davis, Lee and George W. Randolph, the new secretary of war. The lantern-jawed Smith, a West Pointer from Kentucky who had resigned from the army to pursue a construction career, had been New York City's street commissioner before the war. Despite his robust appearance he suffered from a neurological condition that brought on sporadic bouts of semiparalysis, and he was untested as a field commander. Smith and Johnston insisted that Yorktown should be abandoned. They pointed out that McClellan's powerful seige guns could demolish the Southern batteries there, permitting his gunboats and transports to steam up the York River with impunity and turn the defenses. The two men called for withdrawing from the Peninsula and Norfolk, bringing up all the coastal troops from the Carolinas and Georgia to Richmond, and concentrating inland to fight one climactic battle. Longstreet contributed little to the discussion, other than remarking he believed McClellan so cautious he would not advance for weeks. "The President interrupted," Longstreet said, "and spoke of McClellan's high attainments and capacity in a style indicating that he did not care to hear anyone talk who did not have the same appreciation of our great adversary. McClellan had been a special favorite with Mr. Davis when he was Secretary of War. . . ."[11]

Lee and Randolph argued in turn that Yorktown should be held as long as possible, stressing that it was too soon to fight a climactic battle and that more time was needed to raise and arm more troops. Laws would be enacted within days conscripting able-bodied whites between the ages of 18 and 35 for a period of three years or the duration of the war. Even if a withdrawal became necessary, Lee maintained, it should not be all the way to Richmond. The Peninsula, with its network of rivers, creeks and swamps, offered numerous defensive positions. Based on his own experience, moreover, he was not at all certain the governors of the Carolinas and Georgia would divest their states of troops and send them to Virginia. Even if they did, the key ports of Charleston and Savannah might be lost. Last, evacuating Yorktown meant losing Norfolk and its navy yard, leaving the *Virginia* without a safe harbor and the South without a major facility for building warships.

The debate continued all day and into the night, with Johnston and Smith insisting a concentration on the Peninsula was foolish, and Lee and Randolph saying it was essential. Finally Davis made his decision. Johnston's entire army would be sent to the Peninsula, and Yorktown would be defended as long as feasible. "Though General J.E. Johnston did not agree with this decision,"

Davis would say, "he did not ask to be relieved, and I had no wish to separate him from troops . . . whose confidence I believed he deservedly possessed."[12]

Johnston left the meeting with no intention of fighting at Yorktown. "The belief that events . . . would soon compel the Confederate government to adopt my method of opposing the Federal army," he would write, "reconciled me somewhat to the necessity of obeying the President's order."[13] Soon he was bombarding Lee with dispatches indicating his true feelings. On April 22: "No one but McClellan could have hesitated to attack. The defensive line is far better for him than for us." On April 24: Future supplies should be held up: ". . . in the event of our being compelled to fall back from this point." On April 29: "Should the attack on Yorktown be made earnestly, we cannot prevent its fall; nor can we hold out more than a few hours."[14] On the night of May 3, he hurriedly evacuated his position, leaving behind all fifty-six of his heavy guns, fifty-three unspiked. Twenty-three brigades totaling some 55,000 men, organized into four infantry divisions led by Smith, Longstreet, Harvey Hill and David Rumph Jones (filling in for the ailing Magruder) and the cavalry brigade of Jeb Stuart, wended their way up the Peninsula. Other than fighting two rearguard actions, at Williamsburg and Eltham's Landing, they would not stop until they reached the capital.

Elements of Longstreet's and Harvey Hill's divisions would bear most of the burden at Williamsburg. The troops were a mixture of the old and the new, those who had served at Manassas and those who had not. Longstreet's brigades were six in number, and were led by Powell Hill, Richard Heron Anderson, George Pickett, Cadmus Marcellus Wilcox, Raleigh Colston and Roger A. Pryor. Powell Hill's background and personality we have seen in some detail. Dick Anderson of South Carolina, a well-born man from a planter family, graduated with Longstreet in the West Point class of 1842. Modest, amiable, unselfish are the words often used to describe him. A quiet pipe smoker, a determined fighter. George Pickett of Virginia, who finished last in his West Point class, was Longstreet's close friend. Both warrior and dandy, the man who gave his name to the last bloody charge at Gettysburg wore his hair in perfumed ringlets reaching down to his shoulders. He now led the brigade of the 52-year-old Philip St. George Cooke who, broken by the bloodshed he had seen, had taken his life the day after Christmas. Cadmus Wilcox, born in North Carolina and raised in Tennessee, like Pickett did poorly at the academy but returned to teach there and write what became the standard treatise on rifles and rifle practice. For Longstreet he would have no liking. Raleigh Colston, the former colleague of Jackson at the Virginia Military Institute, was born in Paris, the son of a wealthy doctor and expatriate. He returned to America to attend V.M.I., where he later taught military strategy, history and French. Roger Pryor of South Carolina, an ultra-secessionist, was a lawyer and former U.S. Congressman. He had no formal military training.

In Harvey Hill's division Jubal Early, Robert E. Rodes, Winfield Scott Featherston and Gabriel J. Rains led the principal commands. The arthritis-plagued Early, one of the heroes of Manassas, was as irritable and sharp-tongued as ever, and just as belligerent. Robert Rodes, a handsome and mustachioed V.M.I. graduate, had been a civil engineer before the war. Able and determined, perhaps his strongest quality was his coolness under fire. Stentorian-voiced Winfield Featherston of Mississippi, another lawyer and former U.S. Congressman, before his recent promotion had led the 17th Mississippi at Manassas. Gabriel Rains of North Carolina, a lieutenant colonel in the Old Army, primarily would become known for developing early versions of the land mine, shells with percussion caps buried in the roadbeds. Both sides thought them immoral and eventually banned them.

By the morning of May 5 most of the Confederates were beyond Williamsburg, with their Union pursuers at their heels. David Jones led the way, Smith was next, and Harvey Hill brought up the end of the column, leaving Longstreet's command as a rearguard. The Peninsula in front of the town was only seven miles wide and, with two waterways narrowing the terrain still further, the fight would be within a three-mile front. Longstreet during the night had placed Anderson's and Pryor's brigades with Anderson in charge at Fort Magruder, an earth-and-log redoubt built months before at the convergence of several key roads. Smaller redoubts flanked the fort to the right and to the left, and some of these Anderson's men also occupied. As the morning wore on, with rain and mist and limited visibility, Union General Joseph Hooker's division stepped up its attacks on the Confederate right. Longstreet sent Wilcox and Powell Hill back to reinforce Anderson, and later Pickett and Colston.

Rather than endure the pounding of the enemy's guns further, Anderson ordered his men to rise from their redoubts and take the fight to the foe. Here Powell Hill's brigade distinguished itself. "It was a fair and square stand-up infantry fight at close range, and most stubbornly contested," recalled Salem Dutcher, then serving as a private in the 7th Virginia. "For fully an hour the din kept up without cessation. Then the enemy's fire slackened, and we held up a little in turn. Then they reopened with fresh fury, and at it again we went, hammer and tongs. Those were the days, it will be remembered, of muzzle-loaders and the old-fashioned ball cartridge, the end of which you were obliged to tear off with your teeth. After heavy firing the guns would clog. . . . I had to stop, tear up my handkerchief and wipe her out." There was another letup, and then another advance. "It was evident they were putting in fresh men; our ammunition was running low, and General Hill ordered a charge," Dutcher continued. "We started with a yell and the firing ceased. It did not take us long to reach the enemy's position. The line of their formation did not need the double line of knapsacks piled behind it to mark where it had been. It was bloodily signified by prostate forms, many dead, others gasping. They lay in every direction, like a rail fence thrown down. . . . It was a wretched sight. We tried to give the wounded some water. . . ."

During a brief rest, Hill's men replenished their cartridge boxes from the bodies of the Federal fallen. Then they moved forward, emerging from some woods to engage the enemy anew. "Through the haze could be seen the long line of infantry, splendidly equipped and motionless as so many statues," Dutcher said, "the sombre blue of their uniforms relieved by . . . the gold blazonry of the regimental colors. . . . Our men at once settled down behind the logs, rested their muskets on the tree trunks and fired. . . . Stuart's horse artillery came up and unlimbered, and the guns at Fort Magruder began to play. Hooker put in his last man and so did Longstreet. . . . Our men began to fall. Ensconced as they were behind logs, when hit they would ordinarily be hit in the head or throat and killed. They dropped in all sorts of positions, some falling suddenly forward; others sliding gently backwards or sideways." Dutcher and his comrades had been in action now about seven hours, and the strain was intense. "Off on the right one fellow sprang up, dropped his gun . . . and made off back into the woods like a quarter-horse. The panic instantly spread, and up and down the line men took to their heels. To tell the honest truth, I gave leg-bail myself, but at the second or third bound a revered and gentle voice, now long silent, whispered reproach, and I wheeled about."

In the midst of the uproar Powell Hill proved his worth. Remembered Dutcher: "He stood bolt upright between the contending fires, looked around a while, then went off to the left, returned, looked once more intently into the timber as if to say this nest must be cleaned out. . . . Years afterward I stood by the grave of this valiant soldier . . . I saw him as he stood that day— erect, magnificent, the god of war himself, amid the smoke and the thunder." Again the order came to charge. "Of how we got up and went into and through that felled timber no man can tell. It was confusion worse confounded; now leaping from one tree trunk to another; now running along this, and then crawling under the other. But if it was hard for us to get in it was equally hard for the enemy to get out. Some rough work was done in there. . . . In every angle bodies were huddled. . . . After cleaning out the timber we had no more fighting. . . . The battle was over, and about dark we marched back into Williamsburg, and slept there that night."[15] Longstreet suffered some 1,000 casualties—dead, wounded and captured—the Federals, some 2,100.

Though the Confederates on the right bested their opponents, those on the left emphatically did not. About three or four in the afternoon, Union General Winfield Scott Hancock ended a circuitous flanking movement and placed his men and guns near an empty redoubt to the far left of Fort Magruder that no one had thought to occupy. From there they poured fire into the defenders.

Luckily Longstreet, sensing his left might be in danger, had previously asked Harvey Hill for reinforcements. Hill sent back his rearmost brigade, Jubal Early's, and then joined the unit himself. This force soon found itself near some dense woodland, on the other side of which the enemy guns could clearly be heard. Hill was just as aggressive as Early, and both were hungry for combat. In this instance, those traits led to a miscalculation.

Without proper reconnaissance, thinking they would fall directly on Hancock's guns when they emerged from the woods, the two men advanced the brigade in line of battle. Early led the leftmost regiments, the 24th and 38th Virginia; Harvey Hill led those on his right, the 23rd and 5th North Carolina. "They have left the field whence they started," then Major Richard Maury of the 24th Virginia would say of his men, "they have traversed the tangled woods down the hill, across a country road, into the forest again and up another slope . . . and still no foe is found, although half a mile and more has been passed. But now light appears ahead, the trees are thinner. . . . The enemy is seen. . . . His line faces rather to the southwest, while the advance is from the west. . . . The 24th alone sights the enemy, is much nearer to him. . . . But the wild advance, at such a foolish speed, and over such a heavy ground, had brought disorder on the line. The two middle regiments are not to be seen, and do not issue from the woods at all. . . . while the right regiment . . . does not reach the open until the 24th Virginia has been well engaged . . . Thus, as it leaves the woods, the 24th Virginia, alone and unsupported, with both flanks in the air, finds itself confronted by ten guns, defended by five regiments of infantry."

Instead of being on Hancock's flank, the 24th Virginia would be forced to make an oblique left turn to face him across some 300 yards of open wheat field. Here Early ordered a charge. "The leaden hail was fearful," Maury continued. "It poured in from the front and either flank. . . . The artillery, too, was well served, and soon both grape and canister were cutting through the wheat with a terribly suggestive sound, carrying down many a brave spirit. . . . Ten minutes—fifteen—have passed while they cross that field of blood, and every other man is down."[16] Now Hill emerged from the woods with the 5th North Carolina, the two other regiments having lost their way. Doubtless appalled by Early's rashness, he nonetheless ordered his men to his aid. Making its own oblique left turn to come up on Early's right, the 5th North Carolina had even farther to advance—perhaps 900 yards. But advance it did, until both units were closing with the enemy.

By this time Hill, who had been trying with indifferent success to re-form his two other regiments, realized the odds against the troops he did have engaged were too great. Some 1,200 Confederates and no guns were attacking 3,000 or more Federals and eight or ten artillery pieces. Early had been wounded, taking a minie ball in the shoulder, and dozens of other officers had gone down. Hill ordered a general withdrawal.

Early's men fell back without much further damage but the 5th North Carolina, because it was farthest from the protection of the woods, suffered fearsome losses. Close to the enemy, perhaps seventy-five yards from his lines, the terrain had sheltered them. Now their withdrawal, over hundreds of yards at an oblique angle, left them exceedingly vulnerable. "My regiment is now so reduced as to be inefficient," Colonel D.E. McRae later said with considerable understatement.[17] His command had 302 casualties, a rate of 68 percent. Early's brigade overall had 508 casualties; Hancock lost no more than a hundred men. What made the repulse all the more galling was that the Confederate attack need not have been made. Just before Early's charge, Hancock had been preparing to fall back. Longstreet handled the situation tactfully. "D.H. Hill arranged his forces for the attack with excellent judgment," he would report, "but in the hurry of bringing the troops into action some of the officers . . . exposed them to a fire that was not absolutely necessary. . . ." Early, he would confine himself to saying, "was severely wounded while leading an impetuous assault on the enemy's position."[18]

The second of the rearguard actions took place two days later, on May 7, at Eltham's Landing on the south shore of the York some twenty miles beyond Williamsburg. There General William B. Franklin, who had debarked his division under the protection of Federal gunboats, was a potential threat if he chose to move inland. General Johnston dispatched John Bell Hood and his Texas Brigade, together with assorted supporting regiments from Chase Whiting's command, with the admonition "to feel the enemy gently and fall back."

The 29-year-old Hood, a six-foot-two West Pointer, was a formidable fighter who led by example, at the head of his troops. This predilection, that day at Eltham's, nearly cut short his career. Hood had ordered his men to march with unloaded weapons, lest they fire on one another in the thick underbrush. Suddenly he encountered Union pickets. "I leaped from my horse," he wrote, "ran to the head of my column, then about fifteen paces in rear . . . and ordered the men to load. . . . Meanwhile a corporal of the enemy drew down his musket upon me as I stood in front of my line. John Deal, a private in Company A, Fourth Texas, had fortunately, in this instance, but contrary to orders, charged his rifle before leaving camp; he instantly killed the corporal, who fell within a few feet of me."[19]

Hood now pushed forward, and over the next couple of hours drove the enemy back one and one-half miles to the protection of its gunboats. He then called off the action. His casualties were less than 50, Franklin's about 200. Subsequently Johnston sternly queried him about the way he had interpreted his orders. "General Hood," he said, "have you given an illustration of the Texas idea of feeling an enemy gently and falling back? What would your Texans have done, sir, if I had ordered them to charge and drive back the enemy?" Hood gave the question some thought. "I suppose, General," he replied, "they would have driven them into the river, and tried to swim out and capture the gunboats."[20]

For the next three weeks Johnston continued to retreat. Meanwhile on May 9 Benjamin Huger, his command now reduced to some 9,000 men, evacuated Norfolk and headed north toward Petersburg. This left the *Virginia* without a home port. Efforts were made to lighten the ironclad's weight so that its reduced draft would let it maneuver up the James, thereby blocking Union gunboats from bombarding Richmond, but they came to naught. Two days later the ship was scuttled. "The hasty evacuation of the defenses below and the destruction of the *Virginia* hastens the coming of the enemy's gunboats," David wrote his wife. "I know not what to expect when so many failures are to be remembered."[21]

On May 15 at Drewry's Bluff, however, the Confederates achieved a considerable success. This cliff some 100 feet above the James and only seven miles below Richmond, located where the river takes a sharp turn, overlooked a mile-long stretch of water. Eight heavy guns had been installed on the bluff, also called Fort Darling, while tons of debris to impede navigation had been sunk in the river below. Early that morning five Union ships, led by the ironclads *Monitor* and *Galena*, steamed up the James to give battle. Three and one-half hours later, badly mauled, they turned back. Neither ironclad had been able to elevate its guns sufficiently to shell the fort, while the wooden-hulled ships were simply outclassed. The guns at Drewry's Bluff would protect Richmond from naval attack for the rest of the war.

By May 17 Johnston was within three miles of the capital, still keeping Lee and Davis uninformed about his strategy. "Your plan of operations, dependent upon circumstances perhaps yet to be developed," Lee prodded him on May 21, "may not be easily explained, nor may it be prudent to commit it to paper. I would therefore respectfully suggest you communicate your views . . . personally to the President. . . ."[22] Three days later Johnston did confer with Davis, but evidently to neither man's satisfaction. Finally on May 26, Lee rode out to Johnston's headquarters and there learned his intentions firsthand. Jeb Stuart's reconnaissance had made it clear that McDowell's 40,000-man corps was moving to join McClellan. Johnston intended to strike a blow within days, before this juncture could be made. McClellan had divided his army on either side of the Chickahominy River northeast of Richmond. Other than Jackson's small force in the Valley and Richard Ewell's division west of the Blue Ridge, Johnston could amass some 75,000 men. He proposed to hurl this entire force on May 29 against that part of the enemy north of the Chickahominy, overwhelming it before McClellan could move reinforcements across the rain-swollen river.

Then came further word from Stuart. McDowell was no longer marching eastward; in fact, he was heading back toward northern Virginia. Stonewall

Jackson's victories in the Valley, at Front Royal on May 23 and Winchester on May 25, had thrown Washington into panic. McDowell's men were again being kept back to defend the capital. Now Johnston revised his strategy. With no need to cut off the junction of McDowell and McClellan north of the Chickahominy, he would strike closer to home, on the south side of the river. The place would be Seven Pines, where the corps of Union General Erasmus D. Keyes was encamped, and the date May 31.

# THREE

\* \* \* \*

# SEVEN PINES

Johnston's plan was simple, and it could have been effective. Three principal roads led east from Richmond to Seven Pines. They were the Nine Mile and the Williamsburg Roads, each roughly parallel and only a couple of miles apart, and the circuitous Charles River Road, farther to the south. Longstreet was to advance on May 31 at daybreak on the Nine Mile, while Harvey Hill was to take the Williamsburg and Huger the Charles River Road. The divisions of Powell Hill and Magruder would be left behind, to screen the enemy along the Chickahominy. "On [the] Charles River Road . . . there were only pickets of either army," explained Major Edward Porter Alexander, now Johnston's acting chief of ordnance. "Huger's division was ordered to march down this road till abreast of Seven Pines, then sweep to the left through the woods & take the Seven Pines position in flank. As soon as Huger's attack developed D.H. Hill was to attack Seven Pines also, in front. Meanwhile, on Nine Mile Road Longstreet's division was to march down and pass through G.W. Smith's line & was then . . . to join in the assault . . . as soon as D.H. Hill's guns were heard."

Longstreet either misunderstood his orders, which Johnston gave him verbally, or decided to put more distance between himself and Johnston and Smith and give himself more independence. "Instead of marching straight down the Nine Mile Road & massing in front of G.W. Smith," Porter continued, "*he crosses over to the Williamsburg Road to get behind D.H. Hill. And in crossing over, his troops met & blocked the road of Huger's troops en route for the Charles City Road, where they were to open the ball. It is* said that when they met Huger asked Longstreet which of them was the older & ranking maj. Genl., & entitled to take precedence; & that Longstreet said he knew himself to be the senior, on which H. surrendered the road to him. It afterward turned out that Huger was the senior. . . . So it happened that Daniel Harvey Hill, listening for Huger's guns on the enemy's flank, & listening in vain from 8 A.M. to about 1 P.M., then decided to go it alone, & through all the mud and water attacked the enemy's fortified line in his front."[1]

Samuel Garland Jr., commanding the brigade of the wounded Early, led off Hill's assault on the left of the Williamsburg Road, pushing back the Federals under Generals Silas Casey and Darius Crouch. Soon Garland was joined by George B. Anderson, leading Featherston's brigade. "We drove the enemy before us out of the woods back into the abatis," said Garland. "Hurrying forward in person . . . I found that as the regiments emerged from the woods they overlapped each other as they deployed, and being thus in many places huddled together, were suffering terribly from the enemy's fire."[2] Wrote Leonidas Torrence of the 23rd North Carolina: "The balls were falling around us as thick as hail all the time. It did not look like there was any chance for a man to go through them without being hit."[3] Garland re-formed the regiments, and the advance continued. Eventually his brigade would suffer 740 casualties out of some 2,000 men; G.B. Anderson's, 866 out of some 2,000.

Robert Rodes and his men, coming up on the right side of the road, likewise came under murderous fire. "Lieutenant-colonel, major, adjutant, with their horses, were all dead, and I was left alone on horseback, with men dropping rapidly around me," recalled Colonel John B. Gordon of the 6th Alabama. "In both armies it was thought the surest way to demoralize troops was to shoot down the officers. Nearly or quite half the line officers of the twelve companies had by this time fallen. . . . General Rodes, the superb brigade-commander, had been disabled. Still I had marvelously escaped . . . I passed my young brother, only nineteen years old. . . . He had been shot through the lungs and was bleeding profusely. I did not stop. . . . There was no time . . . for anything except to move on and fire on. . . . McClellan's men were being pressed back into and through the Chickahominy swamp . . . but at almost every step they were pouring terrific volleys into my lines."[4] Gordon's brother would survive. Rodes's brigade would lose more than half its 2,000 men. Gordon's regiment would lose 370 of 630 men.

Gabriel Rains's brigade, supporting Rodes and Gordon, now managed to flank the enemy, who retreated to a second defensive line. "Rodes . . . moved up his brigade in beautiful order and took possession of the redoubt and rifle-pits," Hill said.[5] The division commander urged on his men relentlessly. In one instance, he rode across an open field, deliberately exposing himself to enemy fire. When his officers protested, he brushed aside their concerns. "I did it for a purpose," he said. "I saw that our men were wavering, and I wanted to give them confidence."[6] Johnston's plan had called for Huger to flank the Federals on the right and Longstreet to do the same on the left. Now Hill was doing all the fighting and he needed help. "Had my boys been supported," he would write his wife, the enemy "would have been driven like chaff before the wind."[7]

Longstreet continued to mismanage the battle. He sent one of his brigadiers, Pickett, off on detached duty. Then he assigned three more, Wilcox, Colston and Pryor, to wait on the Charles City Road with Huger's three-brigade command, where due to his indecision they wasted the afternoon marching and countermarching instead of going to Hill's aid. Later Longstreet pretended he had never given these orders. "You have taken a good deal of time to reach this [Williamsburg] road," he told Wilcox. "For that reason," Wilcox replied, "I reported the . . . marches and countermarches he had given, and that I had made in obedience to his orders."[8] Of the nine brigades other than Hill's under Longstreet's command, only two, Richard Anderson's and James Kemper's, came to Hill's support and only the former saw action. Only 12,500 of his 30,000 men were committed.

When Anderson's brigade of South Carolinians did come up, Harvey Hill used it well. Two regiments under the reliable Anderson fell on the enemy's center, bolstering the Confederate front. Two others under Colonel Micah Jenkins, together with the 27th Georgia, rushed on a flanking movement to the left. Finding a seam in the Federal lines, the 26-year-old Jenkins quickly went on the attack. From 3 P.M. to dusk he encountered and routed the enemy in five separate actions, passed through three lines of breastworks, and took 250 prisoners. "Having to pass across an open field on this advance, I lost heavily," Jenkins said, "but succeeded in routing and dispersing the enemy in my front, driving them at least a quarter of a mile; then, gathering up my men promptly . . . I moved by the flank . . . and took up line of battle oblique to the [Williamsburg] road and to the left, so as to present front at once to the enemy's advance by the road and to any rallied party that might recover from my last attack. . . ."[9]

Just before the last engagement, Captain William D. Smith of the Palmetto Sharpshooters described Jenkins's reaction to a Yankee charge: "Someone called to Jenkins, 'Colonel, just look at them coming on the double-quick.' He replied, 'We will meet them at the double-quick!' He gave the command to change fronts . . . and I never saw on ordinary parade a prettier maneuver. Jenkins was magic. He could come nearer making men work like machinery than any other man I ever saw."[10] With night falling the Federals fell back to a third position, perhaps a mile and a half behind Seven Pines. "Thus we closed our busy day," said Jenkins, "the last seen of the enemy being his broken and disorganized squads of from five to twenty men, visible for one-half mile over an extensive wheat field."[11] Out of a command of 1,900 men he had lost 700, but he had turned the tide.

While Harvey Hill was fighting and Longstreet dithering at Seven Pines, the Confederates on their left near Fair Oaks Railroad Station were left wondering what was going on. Not until sometime after 4 P.M. did Johnston learn from a courier that Hill was engaged in fierce fighting. Now at this late hour Longstreet, saying he was "disappointed" he was not being supported, was blithely asking for an advance down the Nine Mile Road, *where his division should have been all along*. What Johnston at this point was thinking we do not know, but he ordered forward the division of G.W. Smith. Because Smith was in ill health, the unit was led by Chase Whiting, the officer whose resistance months before to unifying regiments of the same state had so angered the president.

In the van was the brigade of Evander McIvor Law of South Carolina. Suddenly Law's men came under strong artillery fire from hidden Union positions a thousand yards to their left, threatening their rear if they moved farther and causing consternation in the ranks. "I joined Generals Whiting and Johnston, who were riding toward the [railroad] crossing," explained B.W. Frobel, then a major on Whiting's staff. "General Whiting was expostulating with General Johnston about taking the division across the railroad— insisting that the enemy were in force on our left flank and rear. General Johnston replied: 'Oh! General Whiting, you are too cautious.' Nearly at the same moment . . . the enemy opened up an artillery fire from the direction pointed out by General Whiting. [Law's brigade] had been ordered forward to charge the batteries. . . . The brigade was repulsed, and in a few minutes came steaming back. . . ."[12] In the rueful words of Porter Alexander: "We all stood & watched Whiting's charge, which was met by a musketry fire so heavy that a very large force of the enemy was indicated & [he] was driven back with severe loss."[13]

What had happened was that the long-delayed Confederate attack at Seven Pines had given elements of Union General John Sedgwick's division time to cross the Chickahominy at Grapevine Bridge and come to the aid of their comrades at Fair Oaks. Now the Confederates were in danger of being flanked. Whiting desperately threw in three more brigades: those of Wade Hampton, who had been promoted to brigadier and whose Hampton Legion had been folded into his new command; Robert Hatton, a former U.S. Congressman from Tennessee; and James J. Pettigrew, a lawyer who had graduated first in his class at the University of North Carolina. But the Federal guns, firing canister, and the Federal riflemen were not to be denied. Thomas Herndon of the 14th Tennessee remembered his regiment "fought and scratched our way to within twenty to thirty yards of the enemy's line, when they gave us the deadliest volley we received all during the war."[14] Major Joseph Brent, a staff officer at the scene, wrote that "the victorious enemy did not show himself, but a constant stream of rifle and artillery fire made the retreat a rapid one."[15]

Darkness brought the engagement at Fair Oaks to a close. The Confederates lost some 1,270 men, the Federals some 470. Hampton had been wounded, taking a bullet in the foot, Hatton killed, Pettigrew wounded and captured. What little ground Harvey Hill had won at Seven Pines, Johnston and Whiting had lost at Fair Oaks. Johnston himself, watching the action from a nearby hill, was wounded twice, once by a bullet in the right shoulder, next by a shell fragment in the chest.

The next day—Sunday, June 1—with G.W. Smith nominally in command but still ailing, the fighting around the Nine Mile and Williamsburg Roads resumed. Now Longstreet committed the brigades he had held back, but with inconclusive results. The sole action of brilliance was that of George Pickett who, realizing he would be attacked on his front near the railroad and not be supported by Smith, sent to Harvey Hill for reinforcements. Hill sent him a brigade, and Pickett repulsed the attack. "Pickett held his ground against the odds of ten to one for several hours longer," said Hill, "and only retired when the Yankees ceased to annoy him."[16] Over the two-day period Confederate losses were some 6,100; Union losses, some 5,000. The serious bloodletting was beginning.

That afternoon, Robert E. Lee by presidential order took command of the Army of Northern Virginia. "General Lee had up to this time accomplished nothing to warrant the belief in his future greatness as a commander," Evander Law would say. "There was naturally a great deal of speculation among the soldiers as to how he would 'pan out.' The general tone, however, was one of confidence, which was invariably strengthened by a sight of the man himself. Calm, dignified and commanding in his bearing, a countenance strikingly benevolent and self-possessed, a clear, honest eye that could look friend or enemy in the face . . . simply and neatly dressed in the uniform of his rank, felt hat, and top boots reaching to the knee, sitting his horse as if his home was in the saddle; such was Robert E. Lee as he appeared when he assumed command. . . ."[17]

With the battle over, let us look more closely at some of the participants. Fifty-six-year-old Benjamin Huger, a South Carolinian of French Huguenot stock, was a product of the Old Army. Self-important, putting on weight with middle age, he seldom showed initiative. He could be relied on to obey orders, however, and if Longstreet had not confused him, he doubtless would have been capable of positioning his division in the right place at the right time. Not particularly articulate, he became Longstreet's scapegoat for went wrong at Seven Pines. Scholarly Samuel Garland, a descendent of James Madison, was a V.M.I. graduate and distinguished lawyer. Because his wife and infant son had died tragically the year before, some thought his grief made him overly reckless in combat. He was the last of his family line. Thirty-four-year-old Robert Rodes, he of the V.M.I. background and the handlebar mustache, had added to his reputation as a hard-hitting brigadier. Within the month, before his wound was properly healed, he would insist on returning to duty. No better fighter dwelt in the army.

John Brown Gordon, Rodes's senior colonel during the battle and a man with no military training, emerged as a natural leader. His gaze was intense, his body straight and slim as a ramrod. Gordon had attended the University of Georgia, for a time practiced law in Atlanta, later gone into the coal-mining business. In 1854, when he was 22, he married Fanny Haralson, then 17, of La Grange, Georgia. She would give him two sons and, when war came, refuse to be separated from him. "Yielding to the promptings of her own heart and to her unerring sense of duty," said Gordon, "she . . . [announced] that she intended to accompany me to the war, leaving her children with my mother."[18] During the fighting at Seven Pines, she climbed with her uncle to a vantage point outside Richmond. "The cannonade was rolling around the horizon like some vast earthquake," he wrote. "It was evident that her anxiety became more and more intense with each passing moment. . . . Pale and quiet, with clasped hands, she sat statue-like, with her face toward the field of battle."[19]

Cadmus Marcellus Wilcox, whom Ulysses S. Grant had asked to be best man at his wedding, was well liked throughout the army. He was also one of the few people who had seen Thomas Jackson in high alcoholic spirits. This happened shortly after the graduation of the West Point class of 1846, when Jackson, Wilcox and others visited Washington and took a hotel room for the evening. Wilcox went out for dinner and did not return until late. "The sounds of boisterous revelry were roaring within," recalled a classmate. "For some time [Wilcox] demanded entrance in vain, and when at last admitted, found . . . Dominie [another classmate] and 'Old Jack' . . . singing with stunning effect [the West Point drinking song] 'Benny Haven's, O!' and executing a bare-footed back-step in time to the music. . . . This was 'Old Jack's' first and last frolic."[20] On duty Wilcox was a stickler for detail; off duty, he was relaxed and convivial. In battle he sometimes affected a broad-brimmed straw hat, and waved a hickory switch instead of a sword. Days after the action, he continued to be vexed over the orders Longstreet had given him on the Charles River Road.

Gifted and strong-willed Micah Jenkins, one of six children of a wealthy plantation owner, was born into a life of luxury on Edisto Island, South Carolina. He attended The Citadel, the state military college, where in 1854 he graduated first in his class in both scholarship and soldiership. Thereafter he embarked on an educational career, establishing a military preparatory school. In 1856 Jenkins, then 20, married Caroline Jamison, 19, herself the daughter of a wealthy planter. She would give him five sons. At Manassas, leading the

5th South Carolina in D.R. Jones's brigade, he had skirmished on the right, away from the main action. At Williamsburg his newly raised Palmetto Sharp- shooters had laid down a withering fire on the foe. Now at Seven Pines he had come into his own, leading the penetration of the Union lines.

G.W. Smith's limited but puzzling role in the battle would be endlessly debated. Few questioned his courage. "I was much struck by [Smith's] cool- ness, while shot and shell were falling about him," said Major Brent, the staff officer. "I only recollect among the many I heard two voices of high officers in battle, which preserved their ordinary and usual tones. One was Gen. Gus- tavus Smith, and the other was Gen. Dick Taylor."[21] Porter Alexander was equally supportive. "I had always been a great friend of Gen. G.W. & believed him a great soldier. In the Mexican War he had been a lieut . . . & had had an unusual amount of hard & close fighting, & he came out of that war with several brevets, & a reputation for personal gallantry second to none in the army. But somehow, in our war, the fates were against him. He started with high rank but had never had a chance in battle until this fight. . . . Smith was a martyr to physical ailments which greatly reduced his energy, &, especially made riding almost impossible. . . ."[22] His adjutant offered his own thoughts: "General Smith finds himself utterly unable to endure the mental excitement incident to his actual presence with the army. Nothing but duty under fire could possibly keep him up, and there is danger of his entire prostration."[23] Whether Smith's neurological problems were physical or mental, they were real. His collapse removed him from further field command.

Colonel Evander McIvor Law and Generals Wade Hampton and James Pettigrew, who had been in the midst of the carnage at Fair Oaks, would continue to serve with distinction. Evander Law, like Micah Jenkins a 26- year-old graduate of The Citadel, flourished as a brigade commander. Trouble ensued, however, when each man vied to command the same division. Quar- rels were commonplace in an army whose officers valued their honor above their lives, but the future dispute between Law and Jenkins would be partic- ularly bitter. Wade Hampton was still fighting as an infantryman, but by Second Manassas he would be commanding a cavalry brigade, and by early September he would be second-in-command to Stuart. James Pettigrew would be released by the North two months later under the liberal exchange of prisoners both sides then favored, and later be assigned to coastal duty. He would not rejoin the army until Gettysburg.

John Bell Hood and his Texas Brigade, serving under Chase Whiting on the Nine Mile Road, saw no action. The first day he was dispatched cross- country toward the Williamsburg Road, instructed to support the Confederate left at Seven Pines. But he and his men soon found themselves mired in a swamp, wading through waist-high water and making little progress. Ordered back to Fair Oaks to support the action there, he did not return until the fighting was over. The next day the brigade was idle.

Raised in the Bluegrass Region of Kentucky, Hood was the son of a prosperous physician and a socially prominent mother. Following his graduation
from West Point in 1853, he served under Lee with the 2nd U.S. Cavalry in
Texas, the state he came to regard as his home. Tall and rawboned, he projected a rustic image. One staff officer would describe him as a "country-
looking man, with little of the soldierly appearance that West Point often gives
its graduates. He looked like a backwoodsman, dressed up in an ill-fitting
uniform."[24] Hood's brigade then consisted of the 1st, 4th and 5th Texas, the
only Texas regiments in the Army of Northern Virginia, plus the 18th Georgia. In times to come, it would be in the thick of the fighting.

Longstreet completely ignored the fact he had advanced along the wrong road,
thereby ruining Johnston's plan, instead claiming that Huger's lateness was
responsible for the fiasco. "I have reason to believe," he said, managing to
imply that Whiting had been remiss as well, "that the affair would have been
a complete success had the troops upon the right [Huger's] been put in position within eight hours of the proper time. The want of promptness on that
part of the field and the consequent severe struggle in my front so greatly
reduced my supply of ammunition that at the late hour of the move on the
left [Whiting's advance] I was unable to make the rush necessary to relieve
the attack."[25] Johnston, amazingly, backed up this canard. "Had General
Huger's division been in position and ready for action when those of Smith,
Longstreet and Hill moved," he said, "I am satisfied that Keyes's corps would
have been destroyed instead of being merely defeated. Had it gone into action
even at 4 o'clock the victory would have been much more complete."[26]

Huger, of course, attempted to defend himself. He hotly contended that
early in the morning his division, still on the Williamsburg Road before veer-
ing off on the Charles City Road, had been blocked for hours at Gillies Creek
by Longstreet, who insisted on crossing his troops first and in the slowest
possible way. Admitted Raleigh Colston, one of Longstreet's own brigadiers:
"A little brook [Gillies Creek] near Richmond was greatly swollen, and a long
time was wasted crossing it on an improvised bridge made of planks, a wagon
mid-stream serving as a trestle. Over this the division passed in single file, you
may imagine with what delay. If the division commander [Longstreet] had
given orders for the men to sling their cartridge boxes on their muskets and
wade without breaking formation, they could have crossed by fours at least,
with water up to their waists . . . and hours would have been saved. . . . When
we got across we received orders to halt on the roadside until Huger's division
passed us. . . . There we waited for five or six hours."[27]

Later that afternoon on the Charles City Road, Huger stressed, more hours
were wasted while Longstreet marched and countermarched his division, together with the brigades of Wilcox, Colston and Pryor, up and down the
Charles River Road. "When General Longstreet's troops moved to support

General Hill's attack," he said, "[my] division moved down the Charles City Road at the same time with three brigades of Longstreet's division. . . . I have only to say that if [my division] did not go into action by 4 o'clock, it was because General Longstreet did not require it, as [the division] was in position and awaiting his orders."[28]

That Longstreet was on the wrong road, creating complications for himself and others, is apparent from G.W. Smith's original report on the engagement. "On arriving at the headquarters of General Johnston about sunrise (May 31), I learned from him that . . . Longstreet's division should move by the Nine Mile Road. . . . General Johnston's intentions, as then explained to me, were, that whilst General D.H. Hill's division was attacking the enemy's advanced position on the Williamsburg Road in front . . . Longstreet's division would engage the enemy on Hill's left." About 9 A.M., Smith continued, "I learned by note from Captain Beckham [his aide] that neither General Longstreet nor any part of his command was on Nine Mile Road. This note was immediately shown to General Johnston. . . ." While it was soon learned that Longstreet was on the Williamsburg Road, little else was apparent about his aims. Hours passed with Johnston completely in the dark. Then, said Smith, "about 4 or 5 o'clock a note was received from General Longstreet, stating that he had attacked and beaten the enemy after several hours severe fighting; that he had been disappointed in not receiving assistance upon his left; and although it was now nearly too late, that an attack, by the Nine Mile Road, upon the right flank and rear of the enemy would probably enable him to drive them into the Chickahominy before night."[29]

This report was for many years suppressed, however, because of Johnston's intervention. "I enclose herewith the first three sheets of your report," he wrote Smith, "to ask for a modification—or omission, rather . . . I refer to the mention of the misunderstanding between Longstreet and myself in regard to the direction of his division, and that of his note to me, received about 4 o'clock, complaining of my slowness. . . . As it seems to me that both of these matters concern Longstreet and myself alone, I have no hesitation in asking you to strike them out of your report. . . ."[30] Why Johnston made this request is a matter of conjecture. Perhaps he simply wanted to be fair to Longstreet, feeling that his verbal orders had not been clear. What is most unfortunate, however, is that he accepted Longstreet's charges against Huger at face value, even denying him a proper court of inquiry. Huger became the dupe and Longstreet, far from finding his reputation tarnished, found it enhanced.

# FOUR

\* \* \* \*

# JACKSON'S VALLEY CAMPAIGN

From March through early June Stonewall Jackson's series of rapid movements in the Shenandoah, supported by Lee the military advisor from his desk in Richmond, would befuddle, divide and ultimately rout his opponents. With never more than 16,000 men, he would tie up 70,000 Federal troops, keeping 40,000 or more of them from joining McClellan on the Peninsula. His tactics came down to two precepts. "Always mystify, mislead, and surprise the enemy, if possible," he said, "and when you strike and overcome him, never let up in the pursuit. . . . The other rule is, never fight against heavy odds, if by any possible maneuvering you can hurl your own force on only a part, and that the weakest part, of your enemy. . . ."[1]

Just a few months before these triumphs, however, an indignant Jackson had to be talked out of resigning. The contretemps resulted from a dispute with one of his subordinates, General William Loring, the selfsame Loring who had given Lee so much trouble the previous year. Jackson had led his men in early January into northwestern Virginia to occupy the town of Romney, which he regarded as a communications center. The decision was probably a bad one. During the two-week expedition the army endured snow and ice storms, freezing temperatures and widespread illness. Loring became particularly irate when Jackson ordered him to stay with three brigades in Romney, while the rest of the army returned to the comparative comfort of Winchester in the Valley. Soon thereafter Jackson received a curt note from Secretary of War Judah Benjamin: "Our news indicates that a movement is making to cut off General Loring's command; order him back immediately."[2]

Observed a commentator: "This order had been issued without reference to General Johnston, Jackson's immediate superior. . . . It had been brought about by most discreditable means. . . . Loring's officers had sat in judgement on [Jackson]. Those who had been granted leave . . . had repaired to Richmond, and had filled the ears of the Government and the columns of the newspapers with complaints. Those who remained at Romney formulated their grievance in an official remonstrance, which Loring was indiscreet enough to approve and forward. . . ."[3]

The danger that Loring would be cut off, of course, was nonexistent. Jackson recalled him to Winchester, but then on January 31 submitted his resignation to Johnston for forwarding to the War Department. "With such interference in my command," he wrote, "I cannot expect to be of much service in the field, and, accordingly, I respectfully request to be ordered to report for duty to the superintendent of the Virginia Military Institute at Lexington. . . ."[4] Meanwhile he wrote his old friend from Lexington, Governor John Letcher. "As a single order like the Secretary's may destroy the entire fruits of a campaign," he said, "I cannot reasonably expect, if my operations are thus to be interfered with, to be of much service. . . . If I have ever acquired through the blessing of Providence any influence over troops, this undoing of my work . . . may greatly diminish that influence. . . . I desire to say nothing against the Secretary of War. I take it for granted he has done what he believed to be best, but I regard such a policy as ruinous."[5]

This last letter, luckily, saved for the Confederacy the services of one of its greatest soldiers. The ordinarily mild-mannered Letcher could barely contain his anger over what Benjamin had done. He rushed to the secretary's office and demanded he hold up Jackson's resignation, which the startled Benjamin, now realizing the seriousness of the matter, was more than willing to do.

In days to come, repeated entreaties from Governor Lechter and others finally convinced Jackson to change his mind. "If my retiring from the Army," he wrote Lechter, "would produce the effect upon our country that you have named . . . I of course would not wish to leave the service."[6] Explained Robert L. Dabney, soon to be Jackson's chief of staff: "Had the system of encouragement to the insubordination of inferiors, and of interference with the responsibilities of commanders in the field . . . become established, military success could only have been won by accident. By [Jackson's] firmness, the evil usage was arrested, and a lesson impressed both upon the government and the public opinion of the country. . . ."[7] Loring was transferred, and Jackson's authority upheld.

When Johnston began withdrawing on March 8 and 9 from the Manassas line to the Rappahannock, Jackson to protect his own flanks shortly thereafter retreated up the Valley from Winchester to Strasburg. To appreciate his tactics, let us look at the Shenadoah's topography. Lying between the Alleghenies to the west and the Blue Ridge to the east, the Valley extends from Harpers Ferry on the Potomac in the north to Lexington in the south, including such townships as Winchester, Strasburg and Harrisonburg. About 165 miles long and 25 miles wide, it is split for some 50 miles by the Massanutten Mountains, which extend from Strasburg to Harrisonburg. At their northern end Strasburg connects with Front Royal to the east, and at their southern end Harrisonburg connects with Conrad's Store. But the Massanuttens themselves are passable only at their mid-point, from New Market to Luray to the east. They essentially divide the Shenandoah into two 50-mile corridors, the wider Great Valley with its vastly better turnpike to the west, and the smaller Luray Valley to the east.

To Jackson the tactical implications of the two corridors were obvious. An army in the Great Valley that did not control the New Market to Luray passage across the Massanuttens could only move north or south. But an army in the Luray Valley could still move east, through the gaps in the Blue Ridge. Last, an army moving up the Great Valley on the turnpike was vulnerable to an enemy moving down the Luray Valley and falling on its rear. Using these two all but impenetrable corridors to screen his movements he would offset the enemy's superior numbers, playing a deadly game of hide-and-seek.

If Robert E. Lee personified Virginia's aristocracy, then Thomas Jackson surely represented its proletariat. Born on January 20, 1824, in the mountains of western Virginia, the son of an impecunious lawyer and an intelligent but sickly mother, he knew nothing but hard times. His father died when he two, his mother when he was seven, and he was raised thereafter by relatives. Only his iron determination to make something of himself, and a bit of luck, secured his appointment to West Point. The man originally named, appalled by the discipline, had resigned before classes even started. Two weeks later, mud-splattered and disheveled after a 250-mile journey to Washington, Jackson convinced his Congressman he should be the new appointee. Barely earning passing grades at first, he showed continual improvement, eventually graduating seventeenth in a class of fifty-nine. Even in his senior year, however, cadet officer rank eluded him. It was felt he had no gift for command.

Gallantry in Mexico followed, then his tragic first marriage and his happy second marriage to Mary Anna Morrison. Now he was Jackson the general. "In face and figure Jackson was not striking," his aide Henry Kyd Douglas would say. "Above the average height, with a frame angular, muscular and fleshless, he was, in all his movements from riding a horse to handling a pen, the most awkward man in the army. His expression was thoughtful, and, as a result I fancy of his long ill health (he was dyspeptic), generally clouded with an air of fatigue. His eye was small, blue and in repose as gentle as a young girl's. With high, broad forehead, small sharp nose, thin pallid lips generally tightly shut, dark rusty beard, he was certainly not a handsome man. . . . He rode boldly and well, but not with grace and ease; and 'Little Sorrel' [his mount] was as little like a Pegasus as he was like an Apollo."[8]

Jackson was quiet, Douglas explained, but far from morose. "He often smiled, rarely laughed. He never told a joke but rather liked to hear one, now and then. He did not live apart from his personal staff, although they were nearly all young; he liked to have them about, especially at table. He encouraged the liveliness of their conversation at meals, although he took little part in it." Some wondered if Jackson ever slept; whether in camp or in battle, he seemed a constant presence. "In fact, he slept a great deal. Give him five minutes to rest, he could sleep three of them. Whenever he had nothing else to do he went to sleep, especially in church. He could sleep in any position, in a chair, under fire, or on horseback." He was insistent on secrecy, even with his generals, and on quick marching. "As he never told his plans, he never discussed them. He didn't offer advice to his superiors, nor ask it of his subordinates. Reticent and self-reliant he believed 'he walks with speed who walks alone' . . . Such reticence at times was neither judicious nor defensible. . . . Swiftness of execution was his most popular virtue. . . . He was the most rapid mover in the South, and his old brigade got the name of 'Jackson's Foot Cavalry' from the outset of the war."[9]

Douglas summed up Jackson thusly: "He was a soldier of great ability, activity and daring, and not an irresponsible, erratic genius. In manner he was deferential, modest and retiring, in the presence of women diffident to excess. He never blustered and even on the field of battle was rarely severe except to incompetency and neglect. He judged himself more harshly than anyone else did. . . . In religion he was a quiet Christian gentleman, absolutely liberal and nonsectarian: he was a Presbyterian but might just as easily have been a Methodist or an Episcopalian or, perchance, a Catholic. . . ."[10]

Key to Jackson's success in the Valley was the bold riding of the swarthy, hardy Turner Ashby, his chief of cavalry. For Ashby's 500 troopers, there were outposts to be harassed, prisoners to be taken, bridges to be burnt. Jackson demanded more than this, however: He wanted his cavalry to inform him of the enemy's movements. Where they were camped, in what strength, where they might be heading—this was the information he needed to outguess the foe. "To penetrate the enemy's lines, to approach his camps, and observe his columns—these were the tasks of Ashby's riders, and in these they were unrivaled," a commentator wrote. "Many of them were no more than boys; but their qualifications for such a life were undeniable. . . . They were acquainted with every country lane. . . . They had friends in every village. . . . More admirable material for the service of intelligence could not possibly have been found."[11]

Born in 1828 in Fauquier County, Virginia, the grandson of Captain "Jack" Ashby of Revolutionary War fame, young Ashby spent far more time in the saddle than the schoolroom. Participating in hunts and riding competitions, he had "a dash and a fire few young men ever possessed . . . for it was seldom that he failed to carry off the first honors. . . . His superb management of his horse, his daring feats, and his grace were the marvel of his day."[12] He grew up to be a well-to-do businessman, a part-time politician and the captain of a cavalry militia company. With the outbreak of war, he offered his services to the Confederacy.

Now the full-bearded Ashby, mounted alternately on a pure white or coal black stallion, was in Winchester serving under Jackson. There he organized the first horse artillery, mounted gunners who could ride with the cavalry. Leading that first battery was Captain R. Preston Chew, 19, who by war's end would command all the horse artillery in Lee's army. Ashby was "without consciousness of danger," Chew would say, "cool and self-possessed and ever alert and quick as lightning to take advantage of any mistake of the enemy." His credo was boldness: "A officer should always go to the front . . . in order to keep his men up to the mark."[13] Describing Ashby's conduct in one engagement, William Poague of the Rockbridge Artillery would write: "The enemy seemed to be searching the whole region with his fire. . . . Did I dodge? Yes: just as low as my saddle pommel would allow. But who was that man out there walking slowly back and forth . . . with arms folded apparently enjoying a quiet promenade, totally indifferent to the hellish fire. . . . That was Turner Ashby—a man of the coolest courage and finest nerve I ever knew."[14]

On March 15 Jackson withdrew from Strasburg, reluctantly resuming his retreat up the Valley. His total force was perhaps 6,000 men. Opposing him under General Nathaniel P. Banks were Federal troops totaling some 38,000. A former governor of Massachusetts, Banks was no soldier, but that seemed irrelevant; his numerical superiority was overwhelming. Days later, however, hearing from Ashby that Banks was sending many of his troops to join McClellan and was himself withdrawing toward Winchester, Jackson resolved to fall on his rear guard. On Sunday, March 23, he made a forced march to engage the enemy at Kernstown, just outside Winchester. Supported by the horse artillery and the 3rd Brigade, Ashby was to hold the Valley Turnpike, while the Stonewall Brigade under Richard Garnett and the 2nd Brigade were to move to the left and turn the Federal right. In this particular action Ashby's reconnaissance was only partly correct. Banks was sending troops to McClellan, but Union forces were still at Kernstown and Winchester in great numbers. Instead of just a few regiments, the surprised Jackson with 3,500 men found himself facing the 7,000-man division of General James Shields.

For the next two hours the battle raged. The action on the Confederate left was particularly fierce, with wave after wave of Federals assailing the lines. The 2nd Brigade of Colonel Samuel Fulkerson on the extreme left took shelter behind a stone wall but the Stonewall Brigade, between Fulkerson and Ashby, found little protection. John Echols of the 27th Virginia suffered a nasty leg wound; the regiments grew thin and tired. Still the enemy came on. Now Garnett, aware that his men had run out of ammunition, felt he had no recourse but to retreat. The 2nd Brigade also withdrew. "All our ammunition being gone, we gradually retired," said John Worsham of the 21st Virginia. "One of our company in going to the rear was encountered by General Jackson who inquired where he was going. He answered that he had shot all his ammunition away, and did not know where to get more." Jackson was livid. "Then go back and give them the bayonet!" he shouted.[15] Seeing his men give way infuriated him; seeing the Stonewall Brigade fall back was almost more than he could bear. Nonetheless he could not stem the tide. The withdrawal was orderly, but Kernstown was a Confederate defeat. For the rest of his life, James Shields, an Irish immigrant and Democratic politician, would boast he was the only Union officer who had bested Jackson. Confederate losses were some 700, about 20 percent of the men engaged; Federal losses, some 600.

Despite the fact the Stonewall Brigade had suffered the heaviest casualties, about 25 percent, Jackson could not forgive Garnett for retreating without orders. Two regiments were still in reserve; the battle could still have been won—that was his thinking. Soon Jackson relieved him of command. A member of one of Virginia's finest families and a former West Pointer and Indian fighter, the distinguished-looking Garnett would serve with distinction in future engagements, but never under Jackson, until he fell at Gettysburg. Wrote a staff officer: "The chief error of the battle, [Jackson] believed, was the unexpected retreat of the Stonewall Brigade. . . . His disapprobation was strongly expressed against its brave General, Garnett, nor was he willing to accept the justification, that their ammunition was expended. . . . This instance may serve to show Jackson's rigid ideas of official duty, which were always more exacting, as men rose in rank."[16] His old brigade, Jackson believed, should set the standard. "We had to pay dearly for our reputation," Private John O. Casler would say, "for whenever there was any extra hard duty to be performed, General Jackson always sent [us] to that post of duty for fear the other brigades . . . would think and say that he favored his old command."[17]

On the way back toward Mount Jackson that night, with the enemy making no effort to pursue, the army bivouacked along the Valley Pike. Ordinary soldiers were not shy about voicing their opinions on the conduct of the war, so it was not altogether surprising when one young trooper sought out Jackson as he was standing before a campfire lost in thought. "The Yankees don't seem willing to quit Winchester, General!" he said. "Winchester is a very pleasant place to stay in, sir," Jackson replied. Nothing daunted, the trooper went on: "It was reported they were retreating, but I guess they're retreating after us." Jackson kept his eyes on the blazing logs. "I think I may say I am satisfied, sir!" was his answer.[18] Jackson could not know, of course, the full impact of Kernstown, but he could hope, as he stood before the campfire in reverie, that the attack would panic Washington. This is precisely what happened. Even as McClellan was leaving for the Peninsula, Lincoln kept most of McDowell's 40,000 men to defend the capital. Some 28,000 Federals stayed under Banks's command in the Valley, and 9,000 more were dispatched to General John Charles Frémont in western Virginia. In effect Kernstown created in Virginia four uncoordinated Union armies.

Jackson in the aftermath of the battle, while certain he was right about dismissing Garnett, was somewhat defensive about fighting on Sunday. This was in response to a letter he received from Anna, chiding him for launching an attack on the Lord's day. "I hope and pray to our Heavenly Father that I may never be circumstanced as on that day," he said. "I believed that, so far as our troops were concerned, necessity and mercy both called for the battle. . . . Had I fought [it] on Monday instead on Sunday, I fear our cause would have suffered, whereas, as things turned out, I consider our cause gained much from the engagement."[19]

Jackson's assault had given Banks pause. Uncertain of his foe's strength, the Union commander for the next three weeks made little effort to engage, staying in the Strasburg area. Ashby's cavalry easily handled those skirmishers he did throw forward, while Jackson used the time to reorganize. Charles Sidney Winder of Maryland, a West Pointer in the class of 1850 with an impressive record of Indian fighting, replaced Garnett. He had only been a brigadier for a month, but already he had the reputation of a disciplinarian. Tall and slim, well dressed and well mounted, he maintained an austere appearance. Excerpts from his diary, however, revealed the real man. "Oh that I was with my own precious darling wife & children as happy as one year ago," he wrote on one occasion. "Up early, thinking of my own darling pets, longing so sadly to be with them," he wrote on another. "God grant this war may soon end and we be restored to each other. In God is my trust."[20]

For chief of staff Jackson chose the Rev. Robert L. Dabney, a Presbyterian minister and a professor at Union Theological Seminary in Hampden Sydney, Virginia. "Your rank will be major," Jackson told him, adding that "your duties will require early rising and industry." Dabney leaped at the offer, understandably so since Harvey Hill had rejected his earlier overture to serve as a mere chaplain. "Our Regimental Chaplains, as a general thing," the sarcastic though religious Hill told him, "are as trifling as the Regimental Surgeons, which is the strongest denunciation I can make."[21] Early on in his service with Jackson, Dabney eschewed uniform and sword, instead preferring a beaver hat, a Prince Albert coat and an umbrella. Naturally his appearance on the march brought jeers from the men. "Come out from under that umbrella!" . . . "Come out! I know you're under there, I see your feet a-shaking" . . . " 'Fraid you're going to get your beegum spoiled?"[22] To get Dabney away from the catcalls

Jackson ordered his mounted aides to trot with him through some dense woods. By the time the party emerged Dabney's beaver hat was gone, his umbrella wrecked. He soon bought a uniform.

Jackson, who relished theological discussions, clearly had a weakness for clerics—and their progeny. One young aide, Lieutenant Alexander ("Sandie") Pendleton, was the son of Episcopal minister William Pendleton, who began the war as captain of the Rockbridge Artillery (the guns were christened Matthew, Mark, Luke and John) and then became Lee's chief of artillery. Twenty-two-year-old Henry Kyd Douglas, a lawyer and the youngest member of the staff, was the son of the Rev. Robert Douglas of Shepherdstown, Virginia. Kyd Douglas was a worldly sort, however, and he kept out of Jackson's sight when he drained the occasional glass and smoked the occasional cigar. No cleric's son but nonetheless a staunch Presbyterian was Jedediah Hotchkiss, a onetime New Yorker turned Virginia schoolteacher who was Jackson's topographical engineer. "I want you to make me a map of the Valley," Jackson told him, "from Harpers Ferry to Lexington, showing all the points of offense and defense."[23] In the weeks to come, Hotchkiss's mapmaking skills and knowledge of terrain would prove invaluable.

In mid-April, with Banks now advancing up the Great Valley on Mount Jackson and Harrisonburg, Jackson fell back to Conrad's Store at Swift Run Gap. There he was in ideal tactical position, threatening Banks's flank and lines of supply if he advanced farther, and simultaneously controlling the Luray Valley. Complained one Union officer: "Jackson was ready to run, and began to do so as soon as we begun to move. But perhaps we hastened him a little. Here we are, eighty miles from our supplies, all our wagons on the road, our tents and baggage behind, our rations precarious, and following a mirage into the desert."[24] Position Jackson might have, but the odds against him seemed enormous. To the west Union General Frémont with 20,000 men was marching on Edward ("Allegheny") Johnson's 3,000. Banks with his 20,000 troops faced Jackson's own 6,000-man army at the south end of the Massanuttens. To the east across the Blue Ridge Jackson could look for help only to the 8,000-man division of Richard Ewell.

Within his immediate command, moreover, he had the problem of Turner Ashby. That splendid officer was a warrior, not an administrator. He could not or would not see that the cavalry, now up to 1,200 troopers, badly needed drill and discipline. When Jackson ordered it be organized into two regiments and supervised by more officers, Ashby submitted his own letter of resignation. "For the last two months I have saved the Army of the Valley from being utterly destroyed," he said. "This I have done without the aid of [Jackson] and embarrassed by the want of such information from him which I consider myself entitled to, as not knowing his movements has made my duties much more arduous."[25] Help came from an unexpected source, in the person of Charles Winder. That officer, disciplinarian though he was, had by now won the respect of the Stonewall Brigade and the easygoing Ashby. Citing the good of the service, Winder brought the two men together to resolve their differences. Soon after, Jackson rescinded his order and Ashby withdrew his resignation. "Such was Col. Ashby's influence over his command," Jackson said, "that I became well satisfied that if I persisted in my attempt to increase the efficiency of the cavalry it would produce the contrary effect, as Col. Ashby's influence, who is very popular with his men, would be thrown against me."[26]

While Jackson was at Conrad's Store his correspondence with Lee intensified, culminating with the decision to move some 30 miles west of Staunton into the Bull Pasture Mountains to join with Johnson in repulsing Frémont. Ewell would cross the Blue Ridge at Swift Run Gap to take his place at Conrad's Store and keep Banks in check. If Jackson's attack were successful he then would double back to combine with Ewell in taking on Banks.

Through the first week in May Jackson marched and countermarched his men this way and that in the Staunton area, at one point even leaving the Valley and then returning on railway cars, confusing both friend and foe about his intentions. "We had most wretched weather, rain or snow most of the time," said a member of the Rockbridge Artillery about one such countermarch. "The dirt roads were, of course, almost bottomless. . . . The depth of [mud] was nearly up to my knees. . . . An infantryman was cursing Stonewall most eloquently, when the old Christian rode by, and, hearing him, said, in his short way, 'It's for your own good, sir!' "[27] The deceptions were effective. Banks, thinking Jackson was leaving the Shenandoah to join with Ewell in falling on his rear, began to withdraw down the Valley from Harrisonburg to New Market. Then, early on the morning of May 8, the Confederate commander suddenly appeared in the Bull Pasture Mountains, joining with Johnson on Sitlington's Hill near the village of McDowell. Together they numbered some 9,000. Facing them in the pasture below was the van of Frémont's army, some 6,000 men under General Robert H. Milroy, an Indiana politician.

General Johnson, born in Virginia and raised in Kentucky, was a loud, burly man with a perpetual glower who led his men into battle with a cane so thick it could be called a club. A graduate of the West Point class of 1838, he had fought both in the Mexican War and against the Seminoles in Florida. He was far from handsome, and some found his social behavior crude. "His head is so strangely shaped—like a cone, an old-fashioned beehive," Richmond hostess Mary Chestnut remarked. "He had an odd habit of falling into a state of incessant winking as soon as he was the least startled or agitated. He seemed persistently winking one eye at you, but he meant nothing by it."[28]

Deciding against a frontal attack Jackson spent most of the day reconnoitering, which resulted in Jedediah Hotchkiss finding a path through the mountains to turn Milroy's flank the next day. Then Jackson went to the rear, leaving Johnson in command. About 4:30 P.M., however, the aggressive Milroy decided to take the battle to the enemy. "Milroy . . . was determined to carry the Hill if possible by direct attack," Jackson would report. "Protected in his advance by the character of the ground, and the wood interposed in our front, and driving our skirmishers before him, he emerged from the wood & poured a galling fire into our right, which was returned, and a brisk and animated contest was kept up for some time." The battle would last four hours. "The engagement had now not only become [widespread] along the whole line, but so intense that I ordered Gen. [William] Taliaferro to the support of Gen. Johnson," Jackson continued. "Every attempt, by front or flank movement, to attain the crest of the Hill, where our line was formed, was signally . . . repulsed."[29] By nightfall, wrote Hotchkiss, "our troops were all mingled together, in the greatest disorder imaginable, like a swarm of bees, calling out for comrades, commands, etc., no one being able to distinguish another in the darkness."[30]

During the night Milroy withdrew precipitously toward Franklin, where days later he would join with Frémont's main force. Confederate losses totaled 400; Federal, some 260. Johnson, struck down by a bullet that cracked his ankle, would not return to the army for an entire year. Jackson's communiqué to Richmond was brief: "Providence blessed our arms with victory at Mc-Dowell yesterday," he said.[31] This overstated the case, of course, although Jackson had kept Milroy and Frémont from joining with Banks and, just as important, given the latter the impression his numbers were stronger than they actually were. John Charles Frémont, famed as the "Great Pathfinder" for his explorations in the Rockies, was like McClellan all too willing to see himself beset by imaginary foes. At this point, however, even Jackson's fellow Southerners did not know what he was up to. Wrote the Richmond hostess: "The croakers roll their gloomy eyes and say, 'Ah, General Jackson is so rash,' and a lady even assured me he was known to be crazy when under excitement."[32]

The Confederate pursuit of Milroy on the tortuous road to Franklin was sluggish, and lasted but a few days. The Federals set fire to the woods, literally creating smoke screens and slowing the chase. Jackson basically used the time to block off the three mountain passes into the Valley, further isolating Frémont from Banks. On May 12 he began returning to McDowell, preparatory to reentering the Shenandoah.

Back at Conrad's Store, meanwhile, Richard Ewell was seething. Jackson had told him next to nothing about his intentions, and the excitable and profane Ewell was hopping mad. "Did it ever occur to you that General Jackson is crazy?" he brusquely asked Colonel James A. Walker of the 13th Virginia.

Walker had no reason to defend Jackson, who ten years earlier after a classroom argument had expelled him from V.M.I., but he replied diplomatically. "I don't know, General. We used to call him 'Tom Fool' Jackson at the Virginia Military Institute, but I don't suppose he is really crazy."

"I tell you, sir," rejoined Ewell, "he is as crazy as a March hare. He has gone away, I don't know where, and left me here with instructions to stay until he returns. But Banks's whole army [may be] advancing on me and I haven't the most remote idea where to communicate with General Jackson! I tell you, sir, he is crazy and I will just march my division away from here! I do not mean to have it cut to pieces at the behest of a crazy man!"

Walker later encountered his brigade commander, Arnold Elzey, who likewise was incensed, the cause of *his* anger being an order he had just gotten from Ewell. "I tell you, sir, General Ewell is crazy, and I have a serious notion of marching my brigade back to Gordonsville."

Walker listened for a while, and then replied: "Well, I don't know what to do myself. I was up to see General Ewell just now, and he said that General Jackson was crazy; I come down to see you, and you say that General Ewell is crazy. . . . So it seems I have fallen into evil hands, and I reckon the best thing for me to do is . . . march the rest of my regiment back to Richmond."[33] The two men, seeing the humor of the situation, then laughed over it.

Just about the time Jackson, still some 100 miles away, was turning back to the Valley, Ewell was awakened to some startling news. Banks was dividing his command, sending Shields's division out of the Valley to reinforce General McDowell on the Rappahannock. "He sprung out of bed, with only a night shirt on," said Colonel Thomas A. Munford, his chief of cavalry, "and spreading the map open on the floor, down on his knees he went; his bones fairly rattled; his bald head and long beard made him look more like a witch than a Major General. He became much excited, pointed out Jackson's position, General Shields's, and General McDowell's. . . . Then, with an ugly oath, he said, 'This great wagon hunter [Jackson] is after a Dutchman, an old fool! [German-born Major General Louis Blenker of Frémont's command.] General Lee at Richmond will have little need for [supply] wagons if all of these people close in around him; we are left out here in the cold. Why, I could crush Shields before night if I could move from here. This man Jackson is certainly a crazy fool, an idiot!' "[34]

Richard Stoddert Ewell was born on February 8, 1817, the third son of Elizabeth Stoddert and Thomas Ewell, in the Georgetown area of the District of Columbia. His mother, whose grandfather had been the first secretary of the navy, came from an esteemed family; his father, a physician with a drinking problem, had a lineage almost as distinguished. Thomas Ewell died when Richard was nine, leaving behind a widow and eight children in near poverty, barely able to eke out a living on the family farm near Centreville, Virginia. Wrote a biographer about young Ewell: "Richard possessed Thomas Ewell's violent temper, high intellect, nervous energy, and love of alcohol. Fortunately he escaped most of his father's excesses, but he did not escape his father's eccentricity. . . . Generations of inbreeding among the Ewells had given the

whole family a certain inbalance of mind; just how much may be judged by
the fact Dick was regarded as the only normal member of the clan."[35]

With much pulling of family strings, Ewell secured an appointment to West
Point. He graduated in 1840, thirteenth in a class of forty-two, and for the
next two decades, with time out for the Mexican War, built up his military
credentials fighting Indians on the frontier. There, General Richard Taylor of
Louisiana would say, "as he often asserted, [Ewell] had learned all about
commanding fifty United States dragoons, and forgotten everything else. In
this he did himself injustice . . . but he was of a singular modesty. Bright prominent eyes, a bomb-shaped, bald head, and a nose like that of Francis of
Valois, gave him a striking resemblance to a woodcock; and this was increased
by his bird-like habit of putting his head on one side to utter his quaint
speeches."

Taylor, one of Ewell's brigadiers, knew him well. "He fancied he had some
mysterious internal malady, and would eat nothing but frumenty, a preparation of wheat. . . . His nervousness prevented him from taking regular sleep,
and he passed nights curled around a camp-stool, in positions to dislocate an
ordinary person's joints. . . . After long silence he would suddenly direct his
eyes and nose toward me with 'General Taylor! What do you suppose President Davis made me a major-general for?'—beginning with a sharp accent
and ending with a gentle lisp. Superbly mounted, he was the boldest of
horsemen. . . . He always spoke of Jackson, several years his junior, as 'old,'
and told me in confidence he admired his genius, but was certain of his
lunacy. . . ."[36]

Ewell was a bachelor, but he seems to have been in love all his life with
Lizinka Campbell Brown, a first cousin and "a belle of the first water."
Daughter of a former U.S. senator from Tennessee and minister to Russia (she
was named in honor of the Czarina), Lizinka was both beautiful and accomplished. She "plays finely on the piano," said a family member, "very well on
the harp, speaks French, is learning Italian. . . ."[37] Married to a man who
mistreated her, she was widowed in 1844 at the age of 24 and later, after the
death of her father and brother, became through inheritances one of the
richest women in Tennessee. Through the years she and Ewell stayed in close
touch, so much so that in the 1850s she made him a generous offer to manage
some of her properties. He declined, possibly because his love for her precluded any such business arrangement. Finally in December 1861, the then
44-year-old Ewell proposed and, miracle of miracles, the 41-year-old Lizinka
accepted. They would not marry, however, until May of 1863.

Ewell could hardly believe his good fortune. "My prayer is that I may prove
worthy of the great happiness you have conferred on me & which to my
wildest fancies seemed hopeless," he wrote to her in one letter. "Your expression 'in life or death we shall be united' is to me fraught with promise,"
he said in another. "It has seemed that were our union limited to this world

that it would be comparatively valueless. . . . You may think I am in my dotage but I cannot weight my words."[38] Seeing Ewell and Lizinka together on
one of her visits to Virginia, Jeb Stuart remarked: "Poor Gen Ewell is desperately but hopelessly smitten."[39]

By May 17 Jackson was back in the Valley at Mt. Solon, where he briefly
conferred with Ewell, who had ridden across the 25 miles from Conrad's
Store. That day came word that Shields's division had cleared the Blue Ridge
on its way toward joining with General McDowell. Meanwhile Banks with
the rest of his army had withdrawn northward from New Market to Strasburg. Jackson and Ewell now outnumbered Banks two-to-one, some 16,000
to 8,000, and the two men planned to fall on him with overwhelming force.
"Whatever movement you make against Banks do it speedily," Lee had instructed Jackson, "and if successful drive him back toward the Potomac, and
create the impression, as far as practicable, that you design threatening that
line."[40] Late that night, however, Ewell received a contradictory dispatch from
Johnston, ordering him to leave the Valley and pursue Shields. "Mounting his
horse, without escort, General Ewell rode express, night and day, and met
Jackson on the Sabbath, May 18th, at Mossy Creek to inform him of this
necessity of inflicting so cruel a disappointment upon him. . . ." said Chief of
Staff Dabney. "[Jackson] meekly replied: 'Then Providence denies me the privilege of striking a decisive blow for my country.' . . . [Ewell] then proposed
that if Jackson, under whose immediate orders he was, as ranking Major-
General, would assume the responsibility of detaining him . . . he would remain."[41]

Ewell's support of Jackson, particularly since it involved backing an officer
he had so recently thought "crazy," was most courageous. Jackson that same
day wrote him the following note, to use as justification for his decision:
"General: . . . You state that you have received letters from Generals Lee,
Johnston and myself requiring somewhat different movements. . . . In reply I
would state that as you are in the Valley District you constitute part of my
command. . . . You will please . . . encamp between New Market and Mount
Jackson . . . unless you receive orders from a superior officer. . . ."[42] From this
time onward the mutual respect between the two generals began to grow. On
May 19, the army was on the move, pushing through Harrisonburg and down
the Valley. "On to Harrisonburg," said Private John Casler of the Stonewall
Brigade, "where we were ordered to pile away our knapsacks in the courthouse. We knew there was some game on hand then, for when General Jackson ordered knapsacks to be left behind he meant business."[43]

Then on May 20 came a second, more insistent dispatch from Johnston to
Ewell, ordering him to leave the Shenandoah at once. Jackson's only hope
now was Lee in Richmond. "I am of the opinion that an attack should be
made to defeat Banks," he wired him, "but under instructions just received
from General Johnston I do not feel at liberty to make an attack. Please an-

swer by telegraph."[44] Lee's reply came within hours, authorizing Jackson to advance on Banks. Even Johnston, who did not use the telegraph but preferred couriers, now supported the attack. From him came a third, delayed message in effect rescinding his previous order. The next day Jackson's division accompanied by Taylor's brigade advanced down the Great Valley and crossed over the Massanuttons at New Market, where they joined with the rest of Ewell's command coming down the Luray Valley. Jackson intended, not to fall on Banks directly at Strasburg, but to flank him by taking Front Royal.

Richard Taylor possessed impressive credentials, as we might expect of the only son of a former president. Born in 1826 in Kentucky, he was educated at the University of Edinburgh, Harvard and Yale, and later established a highly profitable 1,700-acre sugar plantation in Louisiana. Scholarly, poised, well connected—those are the terms that apply to him. Despite his lack of military training, he was a confident, competent officer. "I early adopted two customs," he said. "The first was to examine at every halt the adjacent roads and paths, their directions and condition . . . the country, its capacity to furnish supplies, as well as general topography. . . . The second was to imagine while on the march an enemy before me to be attacked, or to be received in my position, and to make the necessary dispositions. . . ."[45]

His Louisiana brigade was comprised of the 6th, 7th, 8th and 9th Infantry Regiments, plus Major Roberdeau Wheat's battalion, and it could not have been more diverse. "The 6th, Colonel [Isaac] Seymour, recruited in New Orleans, was composed of Irishmen," Taylor explained, "stout, hardy fellows, turbulent in camp and requiring a strong hand. . . . The 9th, Colonel [Leroy] Stafford, was from North Louisiana. Planters or sons of planters, many of them men of fortune. . . . The 8th, Colonel [Henry] Kelly, was from the Attakapas—'Acadians,' the race of which Longfellow sings in 'Evangeline.' A home-loving, simple people, few spoke English."[46] The 7th Louisiana, sometimes called the Pelican Regiment, Colonel Harry T. Hayes, was like the 6th Louisiana also from New Orleans, but of a more privileged class, many of its members even belonging to that city's prestigious Pickwick Club. Wheat's battalion of "Louisiana Tigers" in combat we have already observed at First Manassas. Suffice it to say in camp this thieving, riotous outfit was an officer's nightmare, "so villainous . . . that every commander desired to be rid of it."[47] The Tigers were Zouaves, a term originally applied to French auxiliaries in Algeria. Their showy uniforms consisted of baggy red breeches, a blue tunic and a red tasseled fez.

Taylor's first meeting with Jackson was a memorable if condescending one. He would claim that he had just marched his brigade into camp, "over 3,000 strong, neat in fresh clothing of gray with white gaiters, bands playing at the head of their regiments, not a straggler, but every man in his place, stepping jauntily as on parade, though it had marched twenty miles and more. . . .

Jackson's men, by thousands, had gathered on either side of the road to see us pass." Reporting to Old Jack, Taylor said, "I saluted and declared my name and rank, and waited for a response. Before this came I had time to see a pair of cavalry boots covering feet of gigantic size, a mangy cap with visor drawn low, a heavy, dark beard, and weary eyes—eyes I afterward saw filled with intense but never brilliant light. A low, gentle voice inquired the road and distance marched that day.

" 'Keazletown Road, six and twenty miles.'

" 'You seem to have no stragglers.'

" 'Never allow straggling.'

" 'You must teach my people; they straggle badly.'

"A bow in reply. Just then my Creoles started their band and a waltz. After a contemplative suck on a lemon, 'Thoughtless fellows for serious work' came forth. I expressed the hope that the work would not be less well done because of the gaiety. A return to the lemon gave me the opportunity to retire. Quite late that night General Jackson came to my campfire, where he stayed some hours. He said we would move at dawn, asked a few questions about the marching of my men, which seemed to have impressed him, and then remained silent. . . . He sucked lemons, ate hardtack and drank water, and praying and fighting appeared to be his idea of the 'whole duty of man.' "[48]

Ewell's other principal brigadiers were Arnold Elzey and Isaac Ridgeway Trimble, both adopted sons of Maryland. The puffy-faced and protuberant-eyed Elzey, originally Arnold Elzey Jones, had decided to drop his last name when he tired of being one of the Joneses of the world. He had behaved gallantly at First Manassas, as senior colonel of the brigade replacing Kirby Smith when that officer was wounded. Beauregard, referring to the Prussian field marshall, called him the "Blucher of the Day" for coming up to support Jackson, and Davis had promoted him to brigadier on the spot. Bushy-browed and mustachioed, Isaac Trimble at age 60 was one of the oldest generals in the army. He graduated from West Point in 1822, then resigned after ten years of service to build a second career as chief engineer and general superintendent of several East Coast railroads. One more officer should be mentioned: George Hume Steuart, who graduated next to last in his 1848 class at West Point, now was leading a minibrigade called the Maryland Line, a mixed force of infantry, artillery and cavalry. Within days he temporarily would be placed in charge of Ewell's cavalry, led at the regimental level by the senior Colonel Thomas Munford, a V.M.I. graduate and planter, and 51-year-old Colonel Thomas Flournoy, a former U.S. congressman and friend of Lincoln's.

Charles Sidney Winder, John A. Campbell and William Booth Taliaferro commanded Jackson's three infantry brigades, composed entirely of Virginians. Winder's control of the Stonewall Brigade now was absolute, and he was viewed as a rising star. Leading the 2nd Brigade was Campbell, a V.M.I.

graduate and attorney from southwestern Virginia who had served under
Johnson at McDowell.

In charge of the 3rd Brigade was Taliaferro, whose background and relationship with Jackson are worth going into further. Born into the Tidewater
aristocracy, Taliaferro graduated from William and Mary, attended Harvard
Law School and fought in the Mexican War. He had sided with Loring in the
Romney controversy, and had been instrumental in causing the secretary of
war's interference. He could be just as obstinate as Jackson. Over that officer's
heated objections Taliaferro now not only had been promoted to brigadier,
but assigned to Jackson's division. The situation was not pleasant for either
man. In military matters, Taliaferro just could not help second-guessing Jackson. Wrote one of his men in the aftermath of the Valley Campaign: "Genl.
Taliaferro thinks Jackson's army will not be able to fight for a month—thinks
the same of the Enemy—but I reckon Genl. Jack thinks contrary. This army
is much worn out but six days will rest them."[49]

Turner Ashby continued in command of the Valley cavalry, with R. Preston
Chew leading the horse artillery. The combined Confederate artillery force
now boasted eleven batteries, comprising 48 guns, under Colonel Stapleton
Crutchfield. Batteries of note included William Poague's 1st Rockbridge, John
Carpenter's Allegheny, W.E. Cutshaw's Winchester and John Brockenbor-
ough's 2nd Baltimore.

Jackson's army marched down the Luray and closed in on the village of Front
Royal about 2 P.M. on May 23. His plan was to crush the 1,000-man Federal
garrison there before it could get help from Banks at Strasburg, or even alert
him that the Confederates were on his flank. Toward that end both Ashby's
and Flournoy's cavalry was dispatched to the west, to gain control of the
Manassas Gap Railroad and cut the telegraph lines. The 1st Maryland Regiment, commanded by Princeton graduate and lawyer Bradley T. Johnson, led
the attack, along with Rob Wheat's Louisiana Tigers and the rest of Taylor's
brigade. "General Jackson's order that our regiment should take the front . . .
was due to the discovery that it was occupied by the First Maryland Federal
Regiment," said one of Johnson's men. "He thus put us on our mettle to show
which were . . . the truest representatives of Maryland. It must be acknowledged that the 'loyal' Marylanders were made of good stuff. They put up a
gallant fight and when, on their defeat, they were pursued by our cavalry,
they would form in small squares and fight to the death. My record says 'only
a score or so escaped.' "[50]

Driven from the town the Federals massed on the heights beyond, where
their artillery temporarily held up the Confederate assault. "As [Jackson] beheld this picture," said Chief of Staff Dabney, "he was seized with uncon-
trollable eagerness and impatience, and exclaimed: 'Oh, what an opportunity
for artillery! Oh, that my guns were here!' . . . Some guns were, after a little,
brought up; but the enemy had meantime passed the crest of the ridge, and

the pursuit was resumed; the General riding among the skirmishers and urging them on."[51]

Now Colonel Flournoy and his 6th Virginia Cavalry, back from cutting the telegraph lines, appeared on the scene. "General Jackson no sooner saw them," said Dabney, "than he gave the order to charge with a voice and air whose peremptory determination was communicated to the whole party. Colonel Flournoy instantly hurled his forces in column against the enemy, and broke their centre. They, however, speedily reformed in an orchard on the right of the turnpike, when a second gallant and decisive charge being made against them, their cavalry broke and fled, the cannoneers abandoned their guns, and the infantry threw down their arms, and scattered in utter rout. . . . Thus two hundred and fifty men were taught, by the dash and genius of Jackson, to destroy a force four times their number."[52] Federal casualties, including prisoners, totaled some 900; Confederate, about 30. Two ten-pound rifled guns were among the spoils.

"Late in the night Jackson came out of the darkness and seated himself by my campfire," Taylor said. "He mentioned that I would move with him in the morning. . . . For hours he sat silent and motionless, with eyes fixed on the fire. I took up the idea that he was inwardly praying."[53]

By noon the next day it was apparent Banks was evacuating Strasburg for Winchester. Ordering Ewell to continue the advance on Winchester from the south, Jackson with Ashby and Taylor in the van headed west to Middletown, hoping to intercept Banks on the turnpike. When he arrived two hours later he found the Federal columns strung out for miles, raising immense clouds of dust and presenting an inviting artillery target. "On the 24th Gen. Ashby was ordered, with his cavalry, supported by a part of Taylor's Brigade, to take Chew's Battery and two guns from [Poague's] Rockbridge Artillery, and assail the enemy at Middletown," Chew stated. "His advance was stubbornly opposed by the Federal Infantry, but he succeeded in driving them back. . . . Telling me to move with the cavalry, he charged the enemy's cavalry, some 2,000 to 2,500 strong. . . . Our guns charged with [him], and when within a short distance, probably 100 yards from the turnpike, we unlimbered and opened on the Federals. There was a stone fence on either side of the road, and we caught them at a great disadvantage. . . . The enemy fled in every direction."[54] Wrote Jackson in his report: "In a few minutes the turnpike, which just before had teemed with life, presented a most appalling spectacle of carnage and destruction. The road was literally obstructed with the mingled and confused mass of struggling and dying horses and riders. Amongst the survivors, the wildest confusion ensued, and they scattered in disorder."[55] In rushed the Tigers to mop up, followed by Taylor's other units.

"Press on! Press on!" Jackson must have urged his cavalry, intent on inflicting maximum damage on the Federals. For a brief time they did just that, but then at Newtown, four miles north of Middletown and ten miles from

Winchester, the pursuit abruptly halted. Jackson, coming up with the rest of his force, did not learn of this until late in the afternoon. "Upon approaching Newtown, the General [found] his artillery arrested, and wholly unsupported by the cavalry; while the enemy, taking heart from the respite, had placed two batteries in position . . . and again showed a determined front," said Dabney. "Nearly the whole of Colonel Ashby's cavalry present with him, with a part of the infantry under his command, had disgracefully turned aside to pillage. . . . Indeed, the firing had not ceased . . . before some of Ashby's men might have been seen, with a quickness more suitable to horse-thieves than to soldiers, breaking from their ranks, seizing each two or three of the captured horses, and making off across the fields."[56] In fairness, it should be noted that Confederate troopers received no recompense if their mounts were lost through disease or capture; this explains to some degree why the taking of the Yankee horses was so tempting.

The enemy guns were not silenced until sunset, when Jackson resumed the chase. "From dark till daylight we did not advance more than four miles," said Ned Moore of the Rockbridge Artillery. "Step by step we moved along, halting for five minutes, then a few steps and halt again. . . . Occasionally we were startled by the sharp report of a rifle, followed in quick succession by others; then all as quiet as the grave. Sometimes, when a longer halt was made, we would endeavor to steal a few moments' sleep, for want of which it was hard to stand up. By the time a blanket was unrolled, the column was astir again, and so it continued through the long, dreary night."[57]

Jackson seemed oblivious of the minie balls whizzing out of the darkness. "I remember thinking at the time that Jackson was invulnerable," said Taylor, "and that persons near him shared that quality." Up rode his quartermaster with bad news. The supply wagons were far behind, mired in the bad roads of the Luray Valley.

"The ammunition wagons?" Jackson broke in.

"All right, sir. They were in advance, and I doubled teams on them and brought them through."

"Ah!" in a tone of relief.

"Never mind the [supply] wagons," Taylor jokingly told the quartermaster. "There are quantities of stores in Winchester, and the General has invited me to breakfast there tomorrow."[58]

Daybreak on Sunday, May 25, brought on despite Jackson's religious misgivings the battle of First Winchester. His plan called for turning the Federal right. The Stonewall Brigade under Winder moved up to a ridge southwest of the town, the 2nd Brigade under Campbell then moving to Winder's left. Soon they would be joined by the 3rd Brigade under Taliaferro, extending the line still farther to the left. Trimble's brigade of Ewell's command meanwhile positioned itself southeast of the town. Now Jackson's line on the left found itself at right angles to Federal infantry and artillery behind a stone wall on a second ridge, and suffering grievously from enfilading fire. "As we were getting into position," said Cannoneer Poague, seventeen of whose men were killed and wounded, "we were set upon by both infantry and artillery at 300 or 400 yards, an ugly predicament truly. But we managed to change positions under this hot fire and got a less exposed location, to which we held on until the enemy was flanked out."[59] Carpenter's and Cutshaw's batteries soon came to his support, but the Confederates were getting more than they could handle.

Jackson galloped up to Taylor, pointing to the ridge on the left occupied by the enemy. "You must carry it," he said calmly. The Louisiana officer was more than willing to try. He had already noted that there was a break in the ridge, near the extreme right of the Federal line. That was where he would lead the charge.

"Riding on the flank of my column . . . I saw Jackson beside me," Taylor said. "This was not the place for the commander of the army, and I ventured to tell him so; but he paid no attention to the remark." The closer the Confederates got to the ridge, the heavier the fire. Many men fell, and many more began ducking their heads. "What the hell are you dodging for?" Taylor roared. "If there is any more of it, you will be halted under this fire for an hour!"

Taylor never forgot the look of "reproachful surprise" on Jackson's face. "He placed his hand on my shoulder, said in a gentle voice, 'I am afraid you are a wicked fellow,' turned, and rode back to the pike."[60]

Private John Worsham of Campbell's brigade could see nearly all of Taylor's advance. "His march was in an open field, then up the steep foothill or high bank, then on a gentle rise to the top. . . . The enemy poured grape and musketry into [his] line as soon as it came in sight. General Taylor rode in front of his brigade, drawn sword in hand. . . . They marched up the hill in perfect order, not firing a shot! About half way up to the Yankees he gave in a loud and commanding voice . . . the order to charge! And to and over the stone wall they went!" Simultaneously, Jackson ordered up the other brigades. "Our whole line moved forward on the run, the enemy broke and ran. . . . This charge of Taylor's was the grandest I saw during the war."[61] By 10 A.M. Jackson's whole army was pouring through the streets of Winchester, and Banks's troops, in total disarray, were fleeing toward Harpers Ferry.

Now the situation called for aggressive cavalry pursuit. Ashby's regiment was not up to the task; it had not yet regrouped since the looting of the day before. Jackson sent his aide Sandie Pendleton to George Steuart, now commanding Ewell's cavalry, urgently calling for his assistance. That officer showed himself a stickler for regulations; orders must come through Ewell, he insisted. Two hours were lost through Steuart's nonsense. "Never have I seen an opportunity when it was in the power of the cavalry to reap a richer harvest," Jackson would say. "There is good reason for believing that, had the cavalry played its part in this pursuit, as well as the four companies under

Colonel Flournoy, two days before . . . but a small portion of Banks' army would have made its escape to the Potomac."[62] Confederate losses at Winchester totaled some 400; Federal losses, more than 3,500, half of the command. Left behind by the enemy were 9,000 small arms, 500,000 rounds of ammunition, two rifled cannon and immense supplies of food and medicine.

For the next few days Jackson following Lee's instructions contented himself with demonstrating near Harpers Ferry, feinting an invasion of Maryland. On May 29 he began his withdrawal up the turnpike to Winchester, leaving Winder and the Stonewall Brigade, together with Ashby's cavalry, as a rear guard. Worried about the safety of Washington, Lincoln was flooding troops into the Shenandoah. Frémont, with 15,000 men, was pressing down from Franklin in the west. Shields, with 10,000, was approaching Manassas Gap in the east; two of McDowell's divisions, another 20,000, were close behind him. Banks, reinforced to 15,000, was moving up from the Potomac. Some 60,000 Federals now were on the chase.

Jackson continued to withdraw at a rapid pace up the Valley. By the afternoon of May 31 all his men except for Winder's brigade had cleared Winchester on the way to Strasburg. Wagons filled with spoils in the lead, the Confederate column stretched for at least seven miles. Jackson's immediate concern was to reach and pass through Strasburg before Frémont and Shields, assailing the turnpike from the west and the east, could squeeze him between them. This he did, largely because of the enemy's excessive caution. By nightfall, even as his rear guard was leaving Winchester, Jackson occupied Strasburg. At that point in time Frémont was still several miles to the west. Shields, who had retaken Front Royal, was twelve miles to the east. Both Union generals, instead of hurling themselves on Jackson, had become timid. Frémont, moving listlessly, somehow had gotten the idea he might be facing two to three times his numbers. Shields, likewise thinking himself outgunned, was calling for reinforcements. "It cannot be said that Lincoln and Stanton were responsible for the indecision of the generals," pointed out a commentator. "They had urged Frémont forward to Strasburg, and Shields to Front Royal. They had informed them, by the telegraph, of each other's situation . . . and yet, though the information was sufficiently exact, both Shields and Frémont, just as Jackson had anticipated, held back at the decisive moment."[63]

That night Jackson again visited "Dick" Taylor's campfire. "Jackson was more communicative than I remember him before or after," Taylor remarked. "He said Frémont, with a large force, was three miles west of our present camp, and must be defeated in the morning. Shields was moving up the Luray Valley, and might cross Massanutton to New Market, or continue south until he turned the mountain to fall on our trains near Harrisonburg. The importance of preserving the immense trains, filled with captured stores, was great, and would engage much of his personal attention; while he relied on the army, under Ewell's direction, to deal promptly with Frémont. This he told in a low, gentle voice, and with many interruptions, as I thought and believe, for inward prayer."

The next morning, Sunday, June 1, Ewell found Frémont and his army reluctant to fight. "I can't make out what these people are about, for my skirmish line has stopped them," he complained to Taylor. "They won't advance, but stay out there in the wood, making a great fuss with their guns; and I do not wish to commit myself . . . while Jackson is absent." Further reconnoitering left Ewell even more puzzled about Frémont's intentions. "I have just driven [the skirmishers] back to the main body, which is large. Dense wood everywhere. Jackson told me not to commit myself too far." Taylor asked for permission to take his brigade and turn the enemy.

"Do so; that may stir them up, and I am sick of this fiddling about," Ewell replied.

Taylor's advance easily rolled up the Federal flank. "Sheep would have made as much resistance as we met," he scoffed. "Men decamped without firing, or threw down their arms and surrendered. . . . Our whole skirmish line was advancing briskly. . . . I sought Ewell and reported. We had a fine game before us and the temptation to play it was great; but Jackson's orders were imperative and wise. He had his stores to save, Shields to guard against, Lee's grand strategy to promote. . . . He could not waste time chasing Frémont."[64] John Frémont, the first presidential candidate of the new Republican Party in 1856, was proving a disaster as a military commander. Only the year before in strife-torn Missouri he had unilaterally declared martial law and freed the slaves there, forcing an embarrassed Lincoln, still hoping to contain the rebellion, to revoke the premature proclamation.

By midday the engagement ceased, with the Federals retreating farther into the woods and Ewell staying close to the turnpike. Hours later Winder's rear guard safely reached Strasburg and rejoined the army. Only Ashby's cavalry remained behind as a buffer. Wrote Jackson to his wife: "[The enemy] endeavored to get in my rear by moving on both flanks of my gallant army, but our God has been my guide and saved me from their grasp. . . . You must not expect long letters from me in such busy times as these, but always believe your husband never forgets his little darling."[65]

Jackson continued his withdrawal for the next few days up the Great Valley, followed in fits and starts by Frémont. The more aggressive Shields meanwhile had no choice but to move up the parallel Luray Valley, intent on clearing the Massanuttons and uniting with Frémont at Harrisonburg. He could not cross the Massanuttons at New Market because Ashby's cavalry had burned the bridges there over the North Fork of the Shenandoah. Heavy rains on the poor roads in the Luray delayed Shields's progress more than Jackson's on the macadamized turnpike. Old Jack was heading for Port Republic, a village just south of Conrad's Store. By holding the bridge there across the North River—a tributary of the South Fork—while successively destroying the other bridges he could indefinitely delay Shields from joining with Frémont. Jackson's position at Port Republic, moreover, put him on Frémont's flank, all but forcing the Union general to turn and make a frontal attack.

During the retreat up the Valley, Turner Ashby seemingly was every-where—assisting Winder's rear guard, burning bridges, providing constant reconnaissance. Still smarting over his cavalry's misbehavior on the advance to Winchester, he was determined to make amends. Even his promotion to brigadier did not slake his thirst for battle. Sensing his mood, Jackson put all the cavalry under his command, giving Steuart the infantry brigade hitherto led by Colonel William C. Scott. Then came tragedy. On June 6 near Harri-sonburg Ashby set up an ambush of the pursuing Federals, who included the 1st Pennsylvania Cavalry and the 1st Pennsylvania ("Bucktail") Rifles. "They have had their way long enough," he said to Tom Munford of the 2nd Vir-ginia. "I am tired [of] *being crowded* and will make them stop it after to-day."[66] Leaving two guns with a small detachment of Munford's men as a lure on the Port Republic Road, with the rest of the cavalry hidden nearby, Ashby moved with some 500 rifles of Steuart's infantry through the woods to the Union left. His plan was to take the Federals in flank when they rushed the guns, then have Munford complete the job with a spirited charge.

Bradley Johnson of the 1st Maryland recalled that "Ashby's dark face [was] afire with enthusiasm. His hair and head were as black as a crow and his beard grew close up his black eyes, until he looked like a Bedouin chief. He was pointing out the positions and topography, swinging his arm right and left." Johnson remarked to an aide: "Look at Ashby enjoying himself!"[67] Once the assault began, however, the well-disciplined Bucktails took cover from behind a protective fence, laying down a heavy fire and making the attackers reel. "Ashby, seeing at a glance [his men's] disadvantage, galloped to the front, and ordered them to charge, and drive the Federals from their vantage ground," wrote Dabney. "At this moment his horse fell; but extricating him-self from the dying animal, and leaping to his feet, he saw his men wavering. He shouted, 'Charge men; for God's Sake, charge!' and waved his sword; when a bullet pierced him full in the breast, and he fell dead."[68] Minutes thereafter the Confederates took the fence, pouring volley after volley into the enemy and forcing them to flee.

Jackson took the news of Ashby's death hard. He went to his room, shut the door and paced the floor. Despite their differences, he recognized the cav-alryman's worth. "As a partisan officer, I never knew his superior," Jackson would say. "His daring was proverbial; his powers of endurance almost in-credible; his tone of character heroic, and his sagacity almost intuitive in di-vining the purposes and movements of the enemy."[69]

———

Port Republic was sited on what in effect was a peninsula, created by the North and South Rivers flowing on either side of the town and then joining to form the South Fork of the Shenandoah. The North River could be crossed only by the sole remaining bridge, which was in Jackson's possession, while the South River was fordable. On June 8 the Confederate force was split into two segments. Jackson's own division was on the ridge just north of Port Republic and the bridge awaiting Shields, whose van was still one day away coming up the Luray Valley. Ewell's division was four miles to the north of Jackson at Cross Keys, facing Frémont advancing from Harrisonburg. About 9 A.M. that Sunday morning—the third occasion during the Shenandoah Campaign Jackson would give battle on Sunday—a surprise raiding party of Shields's cavalry supported by two guns forded the South River and burst into Fort Republic, threatening the wagon train and the bridge. Only a handful of pickets and scraped-together soldiers and Captain James Carrington's inexperienced gun crew could be mustered to block the raiders, but they succeeded in temporarily bringing the enemy up short.

Jackson, who had spent the night in the town, narrowly escaped to his lines overlooking the bridge. There he directed artillery fire on the foe. "I never saw Jackson as much stirred up at any other time," said Captain William Poague. "He had just made a narrow escape from capture personally and he did not know what force Shields was pushing to his rear. His first and only words, as he reached our battery, which was the nearest force to the bridge, were: 'Have the guns hitched up, have the guns hitched up!' He was addressing no one in particular. Galloping on to the infantry he almost shouted: 'Have the long roll beat, have the long roll beat!' "[70] Colonel Samuel Fulkerson's 37th Virginia, part of Taliaferro's brigade, would be the first infantry unit double-quicking into Port Republic. "We saw a single piece of artillery pass by the lower end of the village," one of Poague's men said, "and, turning to the right, drive quietly along the road toward the bridge. The men were dressed in blue . . . still we were confident they were our own men, as three-fourths of us wore captured overcoats. General Jackson ordered, 'Fire on that gun!' We said, 'General, those are our men.' "

"Fire on that gun!" Jackson insisted. Still the Rockbridge gunners hesitated.

"General, I know those are our men," Poague interrupted.

Jackson decided to take matters in his own hands. Riding to the front of the ridge, he gestured and cried out in a loud voice to the gunners below, "Bring that gun up here!" Finding his order ignored, he called out again, "Bring that gun up here, I say!" The Federal response, for indeed they were Federals, was a cannon blast. "Let 'em have it," Jackson told Poague.[71] Soon the Rockbridge guns were bombarding the raiders, driving them back. Jackson himself joined Fulkerson's men in retaking the bridge. "So rapid and skillful was the attack," said Dabney, "the enemy were able to make but one hurried discharge, before their position and their artillery were wrested from them.

To clear the town was now the work of a moment, for the batteries frowning from the opposite bank rendered it untenable to them."[72] The raiders fell back more than two miles, until they were out of range.

Now about 10 A.M. Frémont assailed Ewell's position at Cross Keys, beginning with a cannonade on its center. There on a ridge atop an open field the Confederate artillery was concentrated, backed up by the brigade of Arnold Elzey. In the woods to the left and right of the guns, respectively, were the brigades of Steuart and Isaac Trimble. Jackson, who rode over from Port Republic briefly to confer with Ewell, was pleased with his defensive lines. "Let the Federals get very close before your infantry fires," he told him. They won't stand long."[73] One Maryland soldier who saw the two drab-looking generals conferring was unimpressed, thinking they looked "like two countrymen higgling over the price of a horse, or a cow or a bunch of hogs."[74]

The Federal artillery barrage lasted for hours, and achieved the only real damage on the Confederates. Randoph McKim, who had just been appointed an officer on Steuart's staff and was riding without spurs on a borrowed horse, found the shelling vexing for personal reasons. "As the battle progressed, I was sent by General Steuart with a dispatch to Major-General Ewell," he said. "I found him surrounded by his staff of young officers. . . . He gave me an order to take back . . . but when I turned to go [the] horse positively refused to face the very heavy artillery fire directly in front. In vain I dug my heels into his side. Whereupon General Ewell laughed aloud and said, 'Ha! Ha! A courier without any spurs!' . . . I was very angry and felt the blood suffuse my face."

"Young man," said Ewell patiently, "you will have to go back another way."[75]

Union General Julius Stahel, a Hungarian-born revolutionary who had fought against the Habsburgs, led off the infantry attack with his New York brigade of German-Americans, assaulting the Confederate right. Here the cantankerous 60-year-old Trimble's brigade lay concealed. "Trimble ordered the three regiments with him to 'rest quietly in the edge of the open wood' until the enemy, after having crossed 'the field and hollow, should come within fifty steps' of his line," wrote an analyst. "Then deadly volleys are poured in the faces of the Germans; their advance is at once checked, and in a few moments they waver and break." When Stahel did not renew the attack, Trimble went on the offense himself. "[He] moves out to his right, and, under cover of a ravine and the woods, approaches [the enemy's] flank. He is joined en route by Col. [James] Walker, of Elzey's brigade, with two regiments. . . . Walker moves on Trimble's right and tries to turn the Federal flank. . . . In a few minutes the Federals retreat. . . . Walker presses forward, and Trimble throws his regiments once more on the Federal lines. . . . In a few minutes the whole Federal left wing is retreating."[76]

About midday Union General Robert Milroy, whom last we saw at the battle of McDowell, tested the Confederate center with his brigade, and Robert Schenck of Ohio, a former U.S. congressman, later did the same on the left. Their advances were tentative and uncoordinated, and though Ewell took the precaution of rushing up reinforcements they accomplished little. "General Ewell awaited for a long time the expected onset upon his [left] flank," said Dabney. "It resulted in nothing more than a feeble demonstration, which was easily repulsed."[77] With darkness coming on, Frémont, disheartened over the reverses Trimble had inflicted on him earlier, broke off the engagement to lick his wounds. He unknowingly outnumbered Ewell's 5,500-man force by more than two-to-one, but lacked the confidence to advance. Trimble pushed for a night attack, ignoring the difficulties such an action would entail, but Ewell overruled him. "You have done well enough for one day," he said, "and even a partial reverse would interfere with General Jackson's plans for [dealing with Shields]."[78] Later Ewell, ever generous with his praise, would tell Thomas Munford, the new chief of cavalry replacing Ashby, that Trimble was "the hero of yesterday's fight. . . . They will call it mine, but Trimble won the fight; and I believe now if I had followed his views, we would have destroyed Frémont's army."[79] Confederate losses were less than 300; Frémont's losses were some 700, two-thirds of them in Stahel's brigade. The most notable Confederate casualty was George Steuart, who was struck in the chest by a canister ball. He would not return to duty for one year.

Jackson's original plan the next morning, June 9, was to cross the South River and smash the lead elements of Shields's army, then to return and finish off Frémont. Leaving two brigades under Trimble in Cross Keys and Taliaferro's brigade in Port Republic, he moved the rest of his force at daybreak. To effect the crossing, wagons were rolled into the water to serve as pontoons, and then connected with planks. This proved an unsatisfactory arrangement. "About the middle of the stream," said one infantryman, "where the planks running from one wagon to the next should have overlapped, only one of the planks did so. . . . When the men in the front reached this place those planks tilted, and the men were thrown into the river. Those who followed . . . refused to cross on those planks, and waited for each other as they crossed on the one. This caused a great delay."[80]

The Stonewall Brigade under Winder led the way across the water, followed because of the faulty footbridge at a considerable interval by Taylor, and a still greater interval by the rest of Ewell's command. Facing them about 7:30 A.M. in a strong, elevated position were the two brigades and 3,500 men of Erastus B. Tyler, his left anchored by a mountain, his right by the South Fork. Tyler's six guns were located on his left, where the dense woodland made them all but unapproachable by infantry. Impatient to get the battle underway Jackson committed Winder's 1,200 men prematurely, with the result that the Stonewall Brigade was soon pinned down on the plain between the mountain and the river by artillery fire. "The musketry was tremendous," Winder wrote.

"Loss great. My horse was shot three times. Obliged to dismount. Thanks to our Heavenly Father I escaped unhurt."[81] Poague's battery, with only his two Parrott pieces having sufficient range to take on the enemy's half-dozen, was simply outgunned. Winder's losses meanwhile were becoming alarming, and his attempt to flank the guns was proving futile. "The thunder of that battery was terrible," said one Confederate. "The thunder of the artillery shook the ground . . . and the air was full of screaming fragments of exploding shells."[82] By the time Taylor arrived on the scene, the situation looked bleak.

"Delightful excitement," Jackson purportedly remarked.

"I replied that it was pleasant to learn he was enjoying himself," Taylor said, "but thought he might have an indigestion of such fun if the six-gun battery was not silenced."[83]

Jackson called over Jedediah Hotchkiss. "Take General Taylor around and take those batteries," he said, pointing up the mountain.[84]

"The head of my approaching column was turned short up the slope," Taylor reported, "and speedily came to a path running parallel with the river. We took this path, [Hotchkiss] leading the way. From him I learned that the plateau occupied by the battery had been used for a charcoal kiln, and the path we were following, made by the burners in hauling wood, came upon the gorge opposite the battery."

The 8th Louisiana whose Creole music and dancing had so bemused Jackson was in the van, led by Colonel Henry Kelly, a New Orleans lawyer. Closely following were the Tigers under Roberdeau Wheat; the 9th Louisiana under Leroy Stafford, a wealthy planter with a growing reputation for gallantry; and the 6th ("Irish") Louisiana under the silver-haired Isaac Seymour, a 58-year-old newspaper editor. "Our approach, masked by timber, was unobserved," Taylor said. "A loud Federal cheer was heard, proving Jackson to be hard-pressed. It was rather an anxious moment, demanding instant action. . . . With a rush and shout the gorge was passed and we were in the battery. Surprise had aided us, but the enemy's infantry rallied in a moment and drove us out. We returned, to be driven a second time." Before leaving, Rob Wheat and some other Tigers drew their knives and cut the throats of the horses to keep the enemy from withdrawing the guns. "It was a sickening sight," wrote one of Taylor's men, "men in gray and blue piled up in front of and around the guns and with the horses dying and the blood of men and beasts flowing almost in a stream. Major Wheat was as bloody as a butcher."[85]

By now it was 9:30 A.M. Tyler's stubborn resistance, so unlike Frémont's half-hearted efforts the day before at Cross Keys, forced Jackson to give up his plan to recross the river. He sent word for Trimble and Taliaferro to join him as quickly as possible, and to burn the bridge behind them. Meanwhile Taylor's fight on the mountainside continued. "The riflemen on the slope worried us no little," he said, "and two companies of the 9th Regiment were sent up the gorge to gain ground above and dislodge them, which was accomplished. The fighting in and about the battery was hand to hand. . . . With a desperate rally, in which I believe the drummer boys shared, we carried the battery for the third time, and held it." Then a fierce fire came on Taylor from the west. Seeing his success against their guns, the enemy had ceased belaboring Winder and the supporting units Jackson sent to aid him and turned on Taylor's flank. "Wheeling to the right, with colors advanced, like a solid wall he marched straight upon us. There seemed nothing left but to set our backs upon the mountain and die hard."

Just in time Dick Ewell came crashing up the mountain, bringing the 44th and 58th Virginia with him. With these reinforcements Taylor turned the Federals' own guns on them, the ardent Ewell himself serving one of the pieces. Winder and the other Confederate units on the plain below attacked in concert, driving in what was now the enemy's exposed flank. By 11 A.M. the battle was over and the pursuit beginning, with Trimble and Taliaferro in the lead. The prizes would include one more field gun, 800 muskets and 450 prisoners.

"Jackson came up," said Taylor, "with intense light in his eyes, grasped my hand, and said the brigade should have the captured battery. I thought the men would go mad with cheering, especially the Irishmen."[86]

Back on the ridge above Port Republic, unable to cross the North River and come to Tyler's aid because of the burnt-out bridge, Frémont could only watch impotently. Confederate casualties during the battle totaled some 800; Federal losses, some 1,000. Colonel Harry T. Hays of the 9th Louisiana, who had been sent to help Winder, received a wound that would keep him out of action until Antietam. By advancing the Stonewall Brigade without proper support, Jackson had mismanaged the battle, but he gloried in the result. Riding up to Ewell he laid his hand on his arm and said: "General, he who does not see the hand of God in this is blind, Sir, blind!"[87] The Federals had been bested. Shields, when Tyler's defeated brigades rejoined him, withdrew to Luray and Front Royal and thence to Manassas. Frémont moved back to Strasburg, close by Banks at Middletown. Over three months, with never more than 16,000 men, Jackson had defeated three separate armies with more than three times that number, capturing thousands of guns and small arms, and tons of supplies. Most important, he had immobilized most of McDowell's 40,000 men at Fredericksburg, keeping them from the Peninsula.

Taking supper one night with Thomas Munford following the victory at Port Republic, Ewell made a resolution. "Look here, Munford," he said, "do you remember a conversation we had at Conrad's Store?"

"To what do you allude?" Munford said smilingly, knowing full well.

"I take it all back," said Ewell, "and will never prejudge another man. Old Jackson is no fool; he knows how to keep his own counsel, and does curious things, but he has method in his madness."[88]

# FIVE

\* \* \* \*

# LEE ASSUMES COMMAND

In the days after Seven Pines, Lee began drawing up an ambitious new plan to rout the besiegers of Richmond. Recognizing that the Union army was still divided, now with only one corps under Fitz-John Porter north of the Chickahominy and the other four south of the river, he resolved to fall on Porter with great force. Toward that end he dispatched Alexander Lawton's Georgia brigade to Jackson in the Valley, together with Chase Whiting's small division consisting of Hood's and Law's brigades. Such reinforcements, about 8,000 men, were calculated to give the impression Jackson was marching on Washington. Instead Lee would bring him to Richmond, where he would hit Porter's right flank. Meanwhile Lee would augment his own strength, bringing up to the capital Roswell Ripley's brigade from South Carolina as well as Theophilus Holmes's three-brigade division of North Carolinians and Robert Ransom's North Carolina brigade. Working in concert with Jackson, he then would assail Porter's left flank with part of his army while keeping McClellan occupied in front of Richmond with the rest. In all, the Confederates had some 90,000 men; the enemy, some 110,000.

Before putting his plan in operation, however, Lee needed to know how far to the right Porter's lines extended. On June 10, accordingly, he summoned Jeb Stuart to his presence and ordered him to find out. In this manner the first celebrated "Ride Around McClellan" was launched. Knowing Stuart's exuberant nature, a trait that would lead to grief in the days before Gettysburg, Lee urged his cavalry chief to be prudent. "You are directed to make a secret movement to the rear of the enemy posted on the Chickahominy," he wrote. ". . . You must bear constantly in mind while endeavoring to execute the general purpose of your mission not to hazard, unnecessarily, your command or to attempt what your judgement may not approve; but be content to accomplish all the good you can, without feeling it necessary to obtain all that might be desired."[1]

For the raid Stuart chose the 1st Virginia Cavalry under Colonel Fitzhugh Lee and the 9th Virginia under Colonel William Henry Fitzhugh ("Rooney") Lee, each bolstered by elements of the 4th Virginia, and 250 troopers from the Jeff Davis Legion and the South Carolina Rangers under Lieutenant Colonel William Martin. The expedition, which included two guns from the horse artillery under Lieutenant James Breathed, totaled 1,200 men. Jovial Fitzhugh Lee, who had so narrowly escaped expulsion from West Point for carousing, was Lee's nephew. The burly and handsome Rooney Lee was Lee's second son. William Martin was a former Mississippi public prosecutor, James Breathed a young Virginia doctor. From his personal staff Stuart chose three redoubtable scouts: gaunt John Singleton Mosby; the highborn, handsome South Carolinian William Farley; and the indefatigable Redmond Burke. Two more aides were chosen: John Esten Cooke, a writer and a cousin of Stuart's wife; and Heros von Borcke, a Prussian officer on leave as an observer.

Leaving on June 12 the column first headed to the northwest, ostensibly to join Jackson in the Valley, then swerved to the northeast and camped at Ashland. Not until 3 P.M. the next day, some fourteen miles past Hanover Courthouse at a place called Linney's Corner, did the Confederates encounter any real resistance. There some 100 Federal troopers blocked the road. Stuart unhesitatingly gave the order: "Form fours! Draw sabers! Charge!" Leading the onslaught was 29-year-old Captain William Latane of the Essex Light Dragoons, a Virginia doctor and plantation owner, who headed straight for his opposite number, Union Captain William Royall. Latane was killed, pierced by several bullets; Royall went down, severely wounded by Latane's saber. The wild melee lasted only a few minutes; then the Federals fled. Fitzhugh Lee pushed on one mile to the village of Old Church, where he captured some members of his old command, the former old U.S. 2nd Cavalry. The prisoners called him "Lieutenant," and inquired about old comrades serving with the Confederacy.

By now Stuart knew what he had been sent to find out: Porter's right flank was unanchored and vulnerable. But he had no intention of returning the way he had come. Instead he would keep on riding, cutting telegraph lines and burning bridges behind him, circling the entire Federal army! *That* would be glorious sport! "Tell Fitz Lee to come along," he informed Cooke. "I'm going to move on."

"I think the quicker we move now, the better," replied the aide.

"Right! Tell the column to move on with a trot."

Toward evening Stuart reached Tunstall's Station, scattering the small garrison there. Now he must have been tempted: a detour of a few miles to the east would bring him to West Point on the Pamunkey River, McClellan's main supply base. If he could destroy it the Union army would have to fall back from Richmond; 1,200 troopers would frustrate 100,000 men! No, the attempt would be too dangerous; the West Point garrison would be heavily armed, and pursuit was close behind him! Stuart turned south toward Talleysville in the growing darkness, concerned about the safety of his command. "Where is Rooney Lee?" he asked Cooke at one point.

"I think he moved on, General."

"Do you *know* it?"

"No, but I believe it."

"Will you *swear* to it? He may take the wrong road, and the column will get separated."

Cooke galloped on ahead to find Lee, and then returned. "Is he in front?" asked Stuart.

"About a mile, sir."

"Good!"[2]

Late that night the entire column camped for a few hours in Talleysville, where they supped contentedly off sutlers' stores. "Never in my life have I enjoyed a bottle of wine so much," said the 250-pound von Borcke, a gourmand with a girth to match.[3] Early on June 14, Stuart headed due south to the Chickahominy, hoping to make a crossing at Christian's Ford. There recent rains has swollen the waters to record depths and power. Rooney Lee stripped and swam into the waters to test them, and barely fought his way back to shore. "What do you think?" Cooke asked him.

"Well, Captain," Rooney replied, "I think we are caught."

Luckily Stuart soon learned of a possible alternate crossing, the remains of an old bridge a mile downstream. "A large, abandoned warehouse stood near at hand," wrote a commentator, "and a party was at once set to work under the direction of Captain Redmond Burke . . . to tear down this house and convey the timbers to the river. Never did men work with more alacrity. In a wonderfully short time a foot-way was constructed, over which the cavalrymen commenced to pass, holding the bridles of their horses as they swam at their side. About one-half of the command was sent over in this manner, while the work of enlarging and strengthening the bridge was prosecuted. Within three hours it was ready for cavalry and artillery, and by one P.M. the whole command had crossed. Fitz Lee was the last man to step upon the bridge."[4] The Confederates quickly set the jerry-built structure afire. Ten minutes later, while it was still burning, the first of the Federal pursuers loomed up on the north bank.

"That was a tight place at the river, General," Cooke would tell Stuart. "If the enemy had come down on us, you would have been compelled to have surrendered."

"No," Stuart replied, "one other course was left."

"What was that?"

"To die game."[5]

Stuart now led his weary men to Charles City Courthouse and thence the 35 miles to Richmond, sweeping around McClellan's left flank. On the morning of June 15 he reported his findings to Lee, and then was reunited with his darling Flora. The next day his exploit would be hailed in the Southern newspapers, to his unabashed delight, with such headlines as "Brilliant Reconnaissance" and "Unparalleled Maneuver." In truth Stuart owed much of his success to the bumbling of Flora's father, Union cavalryman Philip St. George Cooke, who was responsible for guarding the area through which he rode. Cooke accepted wild reports that Stuart was accompanied by a half-dozen brigades of infantry, then procrastinated before mobilizing the pursuit. A cautious soldier, he would die a peaceful death at age 83. In stark contrast was the violent end of young William Latane, the expedition's sole Confederate casualty, who inspired the *Burial of Latane*, a painting depicting grieving women praying over his body in a peaceful glen. Engravings made from the picture, assuring wives and parents their loved ones had been buried with dignity, would be found after the war in countless Southern homes.

Jackson meanwhile with his customary secrecy began leaving the Valley for Richmond, first marching to Charlottesville, then using the Virginia Central Railroad to shuttle his troops east to Gordonsville and Frederick's Hall. Because the railroad did not have enough cars he used a leapfrog technique, picking up the men at the end of the column and moving them to the front, subsequently backing up the cars and repeating the process. Though rumors were rife as to the destination, Jackson chose not to confide in his generals. "The General has gone off on the railroad without entrusting to me, his senior Major General, any order, or any hint whither we are going," Ewell complained to Dabney, "but [John] Harman, his Quartermaster, enjoys his full confidence, I suppose, for I hear he is telling the troops that we are going to Richmond."

"You may be certain, General Ewell, that you stand higher in General Jackson's confidence than anyone else, as your rank and services entitle you to," replied Dabney in his most conciliatory manner.[6]

On Sunday June 22, Jackson was at Frederick's Hall, staying at a private home, his army nearby. He spent the morning meditating and the afternoon at a religious service in Hood's brigade, where Dabney gave the sermon. That evening his hostess asked him when he wanted breakfast. Whenever you usually serve, Jackson replied. But the usual time found him already many hours in the saddle, making the arduous 50-mile, 14-hour ride to Lee's headquarters on the Nine Mile Road. Early Monday afternoon Harvey Hill approached Lee's house, responding to a summons. "I saw an officer leaning over the yard paling, dusty, travel-worn, and apparently very tired," he said. "He raised himself up as I dismounted, and I recognized General Jackson, who till that moment I had supposed was confronting Banks and Frémont. . . . We went together into General Lee's office. . . . Soon after Generals Longstreet and A.P. Hill came in, and General Lee, closing the door, told us he had determined to attack the Federal right wing, and had selected our four commands to execute the movement."

These four major generals were Lee's most dependable fighters. Magruder and Huger were not invited to the meeting; they would be left south of the Chickahominy to defend Richmond. The commanding general's rough plan called for Jackson with his three divisions—his own under Charles Winder, Ewell's and Whiting's—to sweep down north of the river on Porter's right flank near the village of Mechanicsville, then for Powell Hill to cross the river and engage his left flank. Crossing behind Powell Hill would be Longstreet and Harvey Hill, the former in support of Powell Hill, the latter in support of Jackson. Lee then excused himself to handle some paperwork, leaving his subordinates to work out the details. While he was gone, Harvey Hill said, Longstreet raised the crucial issue of when the unified attack could begin. "Longstreet said to Jackson: 'As you have the longest march to make, and are likely to meet opposition, you had better fix the time for the attack to begin.' Jackson replied: 'Daylight of the 26th.' Longstreet then said: 'You will encounter Federal cavalry and roads blocked by felled timber, if nothing more formidable; ought you not to give yourself more time?' "

Other accounts have Jackson impulsively saying that he could arrive by daylight of the 25th, only to be persuaded to take another day. No matter. The 26th was the agreed upon date.

"When General Lee returned," Harvey Hill continued, "he ordered A.P. Hill to cross at Meadow Bridge, Longstreet at the Mechanicsville Bridge, and me to follow Longstreet. The conference broke up about nightfall."[7] Jackson then began a second grueling 50-mile, all-night ride back to Frederick's Hall.

Lee's official order, issued on the 24th, read in part (italics added): "*At three o'clock Thursday morning*, the 26th instant, General Jackson will advance on the road leading to Pole Green Church, *communicating his march to General [Lawrence O'Bryan] Branch* [seven miles above Meadow Bridge], who will immediately cross the Chickahominy and take the road leading to Mechanicsville.

"*As soon as these movements are discovered*, General A.P. Hill will cross . . . near Meadow Bridge and move direct upon Mechanicsville. . . . The enemy being driven from Mechanicsville, and the passage across the bridge opened, Genl Longstreet with his division and that of Genl D.H. Hill will cross at or near that point. . . . *The four divisions keeping in communication with each other and moving en echelon*, on separate roads, if practicable, the left division in advance. . . .

*"Genl Jackson [will bear] well to his left, turning Beaver Dam Creek and taking the direction toward Cold Harbor.* [The divisions] will then press forward toward the York River Railroad, closing upon the enemy's rear. . . ."[8]

On June 25 McClellan on the Richmond front decided to relieve the tedium of the siege by ordering General Joseph Hooker to advance his picket lines toward the capital. The engagement took place at Oak Grove, one mile west of Seven Pines. Facing the Federals there were the Virginia brigades of William Mahone and Lewis Armistead, the mixed brigade of Ambrose Ransom Wright and the North Carolinians of Robert Ransom, all under the command of Benjamin Huger. Lee at first thought McClellan might be launching his own offensive, trying to beat him to the punch. He soon realized, however, the attack was nothing more than a probe. Hold your line, he duly instructed Huger. "I have determined to make no change in the plan," he informed President Davis.[9] Huger gave up no more than one-third of a mile, incurring some 450 casualties. Federal losses were more than 600. So began the series of battles that came to be known as the Seven Days.

The evening of June 25, however, found Jackson's timetable beginning to slip. The countryside north of the Chickahominy, unlike the Shenandoah, was all but unknown to him, and his maps were almost useless. Hotchkiss's instinctive feel for finding the best routes would have been invaluable, but he had been left behind in the Valley. Late that night Ewell and Whiting went to Jackson's tent to suggest the pace could be quickened by moving their columns on two parallel roads. Jackson replied he would give them his decision in the morning.

"Do you know why General Jackson would not decide upon our suggestion at once?" Ewell asked as he and Whiting were walking away. "It was because he has to pray over it, before he makes up his mind." Minutes later, remembering he had forgotten his sword, Ewell returned to the tent. There he found Jackson upon his knees.[10]

It was not until 9 A.M. the next day that Jackson, six hours behind schedule, reached the parallel roads leading to Pole Green Church. There he dispatched a message to Branch, who crossed his North Carolina brigade over the Chickahominy and, staying close to the river, headed south toward Mechanicsville. Branch, a Princeton graduate and astute politician but an inexperienced soldier, was intended to be the link between Jackson and the rest of the army. But for the rest of the day neither Branch nor Jackson informed Lee of their progress. Shortly after 1 P.M. Jackson was still three miles from Pole Green Church, while Ewell on his right was even farther away. Branch on Ewell's right was still five miles from Mechanicsville.

By 3 P.M. Powell Hill, the youngest and most impetuous of the division commanders, decided to hurl his troops across the Meadow Bridge, "rather than hazard the failure of the whole plan by longer deferring it."[11] He did so without telling Lee, who did not know at this point that Hill was moving despite having no idea where Jackson or Branch was. "It had not been General Lee's design to attack the Federal Army in its strong position along Beaver Dam," wrote a commentator. "Jackson's column to the north was intended to turn this position and force the enemy to fall back."[12] In short order Hill's advance of his "Light Division," so named by its commander for its quick marching, uncovered the Mechanicsville Bridge, and Longstreet and Harvey Hill followed him across the river. The Confederate units crowded in one on the other, making coordination difficult.

Now it was 5 P.M. Powell Hill, wearing his battle shirt of red calico, had overrun Mechanicsville but was hesitating to assault head-on Fitz-John Porter's Fifth Corps in its entrenched position along Beaver Dam Creek, hoping that Jackson would miraculously appear and turn the Federal flank. Jackson, a half-day late but now in reasonable position to attack, nonetheless followed orders as closely as Hill did not. Lee's directive called for the divisions to communicate with one another and the assault to be delivered en echelon. Where *was* Powell Hill, Jackson must have wondered. Should he now advance toward the sound of the guns, knowing little of the terrain or what was happening? No, he would wait for further orders. Fatigue undoubtedly played a part in his startling lack of aggressiveness. Dabney recalled him as being "anxious and perplexed. . . . My surmise was and is that he was every moment hoping and waiting for some definite signal from Genl. Lee; and that having reached Hundley's Corner (just south of Green Pole Church) . . . and still no definite instructions, he concluded the risk was too much to go further."[13] With several hours of daylight remaining, Jackson encamped for the night.

Lee meanwhile had little choice but to order the attack on Beaver Dam. Now that Powell Hill had begun the fight, it had to be followed up. Magruder and Huger could be entrusted with the protection of Richmond only so long.

On the high ground behind the waist-deep swampy creek, well protected by abatis and earthworks, waited Porter's men. Charles Field's brigade of Virginians led off the assault against Union General John F. Reynolds on the Federal right, where Hill still hoped Jackson would materialize. Supporting the stocky and normally congenial Field were the Georgians of Joseph R. Anderson—soon to leave the army to run the Tredegar Iron Works, the South's leading maker of guns and munitions—and the Tennesseans and Alabamians of the energetic James J. Archer. Facing some thirty cannon, the Confederates never had a chance. His lines, Field would report, "were momentarily thinned by the most destructive cannonading I have yet known. Our only safety from this fire lay in pushing forward as rapidly as possible and getting so close to the enemy's infantry as to draw the fire upon his own troops should it be continued."[14] Up rushed bespectacled 21-year-old Willie Pegram and his six-gun battery to take on the Federals, with harrowing results. Four of his pieces soon were silenced, while fifty of his ninety men were killed or wounded. Still Pegram kept his last two guns blazing. "Exposed . . .

to the convergent fire of five six-gun batteries, long after night came down the thunder of his guns told that he was tenaciously holding his ground," said a comrade.[15]

Hill was in the forefront of the action, trying to *will* his men across the creek. To no avail. "We fought under many disadvantages," Color-bearer Martin Ledbetter of the 5th Alabama Battalion reported. "It was with great difficulty that we made our way through [the] entanglement of tree tops, saplings, vines, and every other conceivable obstruction, and under a heavy fire. . . . I had to wrap my flag around the staff while crawling through the abattis."[16] The 35th Georgia of Anderson's brigade effected a minor crossing, but could not be reinforced. The Federal right, Hill began to see, was impregnable. "Their position . . . was too strong to be carried by a direct attack without heavy loss," he said.[17] As it was, his three brigades suffered some 550 casualties; the enemy, less than a third that number.

Toward dusk Hill decided to assail the Federal left, defended by Union General Truman Seymour. There William Dorsey Pender's North Carolinians stormed the foe, but with even worse results. "Fragments of shells literally hailed around me," said Pender aide John Hinsdale. "I thought that my life was worth very little."[18] One of Pender's regiments, the 38th North Carolina, lost one-third of its complement—152 of 420 men. Roswell Ripley's brigade of Harvey Hill's division, the nearest unit, rushed in to reinforce Pender. For the hot-tempered Ripley and his men, this was their first battle. Wrote 17-year-old Edgar Jackson of the 1st North Carolina: "Col. [Montford] Stokes (who was mortally wounded) soon orders us to rise up and charge and at it we go with a yell; we proceed half way down the hill, halt and exchange shot for shot with the Yankees, who had the very best of covering."[19] Stopped short of the creek, the 1st North Carolina found what cover it could, pinned down by enemy fire. It took 142 casualties. The 44th Georgia of Ripley's brigade was decimated, losing 335 men. Altogether Pender and Ripley incurred some 850 casualties. "I have passed though a fiery order of grape, canister shells, round-shot and musket balls," Private Jackson reflected, "and was permitted by the All Wise Being to pass through unscathed."

In Richmond Mrs. Roger Pryor, the wife of one of Longstreet's brigadiers, could not bring herself to look toward the battlefield. "I shut myself in my darkened room," she said. "At twilight I had a note from Governor [John] Letcher . . . inviting me to come to the Governor's mansion. From the roof one might see the flash or musket and artillery. No! I did not wish to see the infernal fires. I preferred to wait alone in my room. . . . God only knew what news I might hear before morning."[20] General Pryor was unhurt, but by nightfall the battle cost the Confederates some 1,500 men. Federal losses were only some 360. "It was unfortunate for the Confederates that the crossing was begun before Jackson got in rear of Mechanicsville," Harvey Hill conceded. "The loss of that position would have necessitated the abandonment of the line of Beaver Dam Creek, as in fact it did the next day. We were lavish of blood in those days. . . ."[21]

Despite the Federal success at Beaver Dam Creek, McClellan in the early hours of June 27 ordered Porter to withdraw during the night some five miles east to Boatswain's Swamp, near Gaines's Mill and New Cold Harbor. The fact that Jackson was lurking somewhere on Porter's right, menacing his flank and the supply base at White House, was only part of the reason for the decision. McClellan was convinced that Lee had 100,000 men north of the Chickahominy and another 100,000 south of the river, far more than twice his actual strength. Nothing could dissuade him from this conviction. In his mind he was not retreating, but only changing his base from White House on the Pamunkey to Harrison's Landing on the James.

Lee and Jackson met that morning about 10 A.M. Lee expressed no criticism of Jackson's tardiness the previous day, instead putting both Harvey Hill's division and Stuart's cavalry under his command—fourteen of the twenty-six brigades north of the river. The two men talked for a while, and then were joined by Powell Hill. Now Lee's tactics called for Hill supported by Longstreet to assail Porter's left, which was anchored on the Chickahominy, while Jackson aided by Harvey Hill attacked his right. Stuart's efforts for the next few days would largely be confined to reconnaissance, the terrain and the massed Federal artillery making cavalry charges impractical.

Some hours later Maxcy Gregg's brigade of Powell Hill's division made first contact with the enemy at New Cold Harbor. Bringing up the rest of his brigades Hill then formed them to Gregg's right thusly: Gregg, Branch, J.R. Anderson, Field and Archer, with Pender in reserve. The division pushed forward at 2:30 P.M., moving on the dug-in Federals behind Boatswain's Swamp. Maxcy Gregg, a cultured South Carolinian whose love of the classics was matched only by his knowledge of the sciences, went into battle waving his father's Revolutionary War sword. His brigade, however, could not dislodge the foe. "Men were killed and wounded amongst us everywhere in rapid succession," said Sergeant Barry Benson of the 1st South Carolina. "As I lay, a man on my right . . . suddenly vomited up blood, turned over and died. The wounded were steadily rising and running to the rear."[22] Gregg's brigade incurred 815 casualties, the largest number in the army. Branch's brigade fared almost as badly, suffering losses of some 400. Four of the 7th North Carolina's color-bearers were wounded or killed; the banner itself bore thirty-two bullet holes.

For Hill, the fight was Mechanicsville all over again. "Gregg, then Branch, then Anderson became successively engaged," he said. "The incessant roar of musketry and the deep thunder of the artillery told us the whole force of the enemy was in my front. . . . Pender's Brigade was suffering heavily, but stubbornly held its own. Field and Archer met a withering storm of bullets, but

pressed on to within a short distance of the enemy's works. . . . These brave
men had done all that any brave soldiers could do. . . . From having been the
attacking I now became the attacked; but stubbornly and gallantly was the
ground held. My division was thus engaged full two hours before assistance
was received. We failed to carry the enemy's lines, but we paved the way for
the successful attacks afterward."[23] Powell Hill that day lost some 2,150 men;
two days of fighting at Mechanicsville and Gaines's Mill cost him 25 percent
of his division.

Seeing Hill's predicament but still waiting for Jackson's advance Lee ordered Longstreet to make a diversion on Hill's right, the initial assault beginning about 4:30 P.M. "In front of me the enemy occupied the wooded slope
of Turkey Hill," said Longstreet, "the crest of which is fifty or sixty feet higher
than the plain over which my troops must pass. . . . The plain is about a quarter of a mile wide; the farther side of it was occupied by sharpshooters. Above
these . . . was a line of infantry behind trees felled so as to form a good breastwork. The crest of the hill, some forty feet above the last line, was . . . occupied by infantry and artillery. . . . I was, in fact, in the position from which
the enemy wished us to attack him." Cadmus Wilcox and George Pickett led
the way, with Dick Anderson in support. So strong was the enemy position,
Longstreet soon realized, that a feint would be useless. "I found that I must
drive him by direct assault," he said.[24] Longstreet paused in his attack, then
eventually found his left bolstered by the arrival of Whiting's division, comprised of John Bell Hood's and Evander Law's brigades. These troops were
part of Jackson's command. But where was Jackson?

In truth Stonewall was making another confused march, in part because of
his habitual reticence. Earlier he selected Private John Henry Timberlake of
the 4th Virginia Cavalry, whose family farm was located near Gaines's Mill,
to guide his columns—those of Ewell, Winder and Whiting—around the
Union right. Timberlake had been a member of Stuart's Ride Around Mc-
Clellan, and knew the countryside. Take me to Cold Harbor, Jackson probably told him, that and nothing more. Naturally the guide took the most direct
route, which led past Gaines's Mill to New Cold Harbor.

Approaching Gaines's Mill, where Powell Hill now was heavily engaged,
Jackson heard the sound of cannon.

"Where is that firing?" he demanded sharply of Private Timberlake. From
Gaines's Mill, the guide replied.

"Does this road lead there?" He was told that the road led past Gaines's
Mill to Cold Harbor.

"But I do not wish to go to Gaines's Mill," Jackson broke in. "I wish to
go to Cold Harbor, leaving that place on the right."

"Then," said Timberlake, realizing Jackson wanted to go to Old Cold
Harbor, two miles to the east, "the left-hand road was the one which should
have been taken, and had you let me know what you desired, I could have

directcd you aright at first." This meant reversing the columns, adding four miles to the march and delaying Jackson's offensive for hours.[25] Harvey Hill, arriving at Old Cold Harbor sooner, could only wait for Jackson's arrival.

It was about 3:30 P.M. when Walter Taylor, Lee's aide, finally intercepted Ewell's column and directed him to support Powell Hill's left. One hour later Dabney took it upon himself to correct some orders from Jackson that had been garbled in transmission, and ensured that Whiting's and Charles Winder's brigades also moved toward the fighting. The belated assault was continuing, but in piecemeal fashion.

Ewell quickly pushed in Dick Taylor's, Isaac Trimble's and Arnold Elzey's brigades against the Federal center. Taylor, crippled by a chronic arthritic condition, had turned his command over to Isaac Seymour. Trimble's men, reinforcing Hill's, ignored their plaints: "You need not go in!" "We are whipped!" "You can't do anything!" Shouted the veterans of Winchester and Cross Keys: "Get out of the way!" "We will show you how to do it!"[26]

Earlier that morning Major Rob Wheat of the Louisiana Tigers had a premonition of his death. He called his officers together and passed a brandy flask around, then read a petition for a "Joyful Resurrection" from a prayer book given him by his mother. "Lord, I commend myself to thee," he concluded. "Bury me on the field, boys," he told his officers. During the ensuing fighting Wheat was killed instantly by a bullet that tore through one eye. Seymour also went down, killed in a fusillade. Without their leadership, the brigade faltered. "They have killed the old Major, and I am going home," yelled one Tiger. "I wouldn't fight for Jesus Christ now!"[27]

The slack was picked up by Trimble's 15th Alabama, particularly by a young lieutenant colonel named John F. Trentlen, who held his unit together by conspicuous bravery and heroic language. Backing him up was a dashing horseman who rode up and down the ranks, shaming the timid and lauding the bold. He was no officer, only Private Frank Champion, who in the heat of battle had commandeered a runaway horse.[28]

By 5 P.M. Ewell, aided by Charles Winder's Stonewall Brigade and Alexander Lawton's Georgians, had stiffened Hill's lines and stabilized that part of the front. At this point in time the concave arc of the Confederate line extended from Harvey Hill on the extreme Federal right; to Ewell, Winder and Lawton; to Powell Hill; and thence to Hood, Law and Longstreet. While Jackson knew of the placement of his men, much of their positioning had been taken out of his hands, largely because of his delay on the Cold Harbor Road.

Now Jackson with three hours of daylight remaining rode to the center of the lines, to meet for the second time that day with Lee. Most of the army still had no idea what he looked like, though his reputation from his exploits in the Valley had reached mythic proportions. "He rode in his peculiar forward-leaning fashion," wrote John Esten Cooke, "his old rawboned sorrel, gaunt and grim—but like his master, careless of balls and tranquil in the loudest battle. Moving about slowly and sucking a lemon (Yankee spoil, no doubt) the celebrated General Stonewall looked as little like a general as possible. . . . He had the air rather of a spectator."[29]

"Ah, General," said Lee, "I am very glad to see you. I had hoped to be with you before." Jackson nodded and mumbled a reply, giving no sign of noticing the mild rebuke.

"That fire is very heavy," Lee continued. "Do you think your men can stand it?"

Jackson raised his head, the light of battle glinting in his blue eyes. "They can stand almost anything," he replied. "They can stand that!"[30]

Though the fighting had been raging for some time in Powell Hill's and Ewell's front, it was not until 7 P.M. that the entire Confederate line launched the general assault. Harvey Hill advanced on the extreme left. "I do not know how much of our infantry straggled in the swamp," he said. "[Roswell] Ripley got lost, and his fine brigade was not in action at all. Of [Alfred] Colquitt's brigade, the 6th and 27th Georgia Regiments were engaged; the other three regiments in coming out of the swamp found themselves behind Jackson's corps. . . . [Robert] Rodes, [Samuel] Garland, and [George] Anderson kept their brigades well in hand and did brilliant service."[31]

In the center Lawton's Georgians, 3,600 men strong and largely armed not with muskets but with Enfield rifles, moved forward relentlessly. Gregg's South Carolinians, who had been repulsed earlier, were happy to see them. "Come on, boys, walk right over us!" they called. Just before the attack Colonel Clement A. Evans of the 31st Georgia asked Sergeant James Wright of the 38th Georgia for the battle flag, saying he would bear it. "Wright refused," said a comrade, "told Col. Evans . . . all he wanted him to do was tell him where to carry it and he would go to the cannon's mouth." This Wright did, and the battery was taken. "Col. Evans complimented [him] on his bravery; told him that he wanted to carry him home and show him to his wife."[32]

On the extreme right Longstreet likewise pushed forward. Corporal Edmund Peterson of the 9th Alabama, Wilcox's brigade, remembered: "We met such a perfect storm of lead in our faces that the whole brigade literally *staggered* backward several paces. . . . Just for one moment we faltered, then the cry of Major [Moxley] Sorrel, 'Forward, Alabamians—forward!' and . . . we swept forward with wild cheers."[33]

Who first broke the Federal line that day has been endlessly debated. Certainly Harvey Hill's men have a claim, as do the brigades of Lawton and Wilcox. But the feat of piercing the enemy right center, and then sweeping all before them, probably lies with Hood and Law. "This must be done," Lee earlier had said to Hood. "Can you break his line?" Hood said he could try. "I therefore marched the 4th Texas by the right flank into this open field," he wrote, "halted and dressed the line whilst under fire of the long range guns, and gave positive instructions no man should fire until I gave the order; for I knew full well that if men were allowed to fire, they would halt to load, break the alignment, and very likely never reach the breastworks." Though he was a brigadier, Hood had promised the 4th Texas, his old regiment, that he would lead them into their first major battle. His other regiments advanced in tandem. "Soon we attained the crest of the bald ridge within about 150 yards of the breastworks. Here was concentrated upon us, from batteries in front and flank, a fire of shell and canister. . . . With a ringing shout we dashed up the steep hill through the abatis, and over the breastworks, upon the very heads of the enemy." Now Hood was in the Federal rear. "Meantime, the long line of blue and steel wavered and, finally, gave way as the 18th Georgia, the 1st and 5th Texas and Hampton's Legion moved forward from right to left, thus completing a grand left wheel of the brigade into the very heart of the enemy."[34]

Evander Law was on Hood's right. "Men fell like leaves in an autumn wind, the Federal artillery tore gaps in the ranks," he recalled. "Not a step faltered as the two gray lines swept silently and swiftly on; the pace became more rapid every moment; when the men were within thirty yards of the ravine . . . they rushed for the works. The Confederates were within ten paces of them when the Federals in the front line broke cover . . . carrying their second line with them in their rout."[35] Now the attackers had their turn, pouring fire into the fleeing men. Continuing to advance they leaped into a ravine, clambered up the other side and captured fourteen enemy guns.

"General Hill was in our front until we were within about one hundred yards of the creek," said William R. Hamby of the 4th Texas, "when he wheeled his horse to the right and ordered us to fix bayonets and charge at the double-quick. . . . More than half of our regiment had fallen upon the field, although we had not fired a gun. Raising the Rebel yell we dashed across." After routing the enemy and capturing the guns, Hamby and his comrades endured one last counterattack. "We felt the ground began to tremble like an earthquake and heard a noise like the rumbling of distant thunder," Hamby said, describing the unwise charge of the 250-man U.S. 5th Cavalry. "To see their sabers glistening in the sunlight of the dying day . . . imparted a feeling of awe in the bravest of hearts." The Confederates waited until the horsemen were within forty yards, then delivered a deadly volley. "Horses and riders fell in heaps upon the ground, and the groans of the wounded and the shrieks of the dying could be heard above the roar of battle."[36]

Between them Hood and Law suffered some 1,000 casualties, one-quarter of their strength. Overall Gaines's Mill cost Lee some 8,000 men; Porter, almost 7,000. Colonel Samuel Fulkerson, acting brigadier of Jackson's 3rd Brigade, was killed; Brigadier Arnold Elzey of Ewell's command went down with a crippling facial wound; Brigadier George Pickett of Longstreet's division was seriously wounded. Losses were heavy on the regimental level; seven colonels were killed or mortally wounded at Gaines's Mill; three had been killed at Mechanicsville. But Lee on this Day Three had gained his first victory, Richmond was saved, and McClellan clearly was in retreat.

McClellan had no legitimate excuse, other than his own irresolution, for his predicament. He had permitted one-third of his army under Porter to be assailed north of the Chickahominy by two-thirds of the Confederate army. Simultaneously he kept two-thirds of his army south of the river, idly watching the relatively small force under Magruder and Huger in front of the capital. Magruder's talents for misleading the enemy with demonstrations were impressive, as he had demonstrated at Yorktown, but he should have been overrun. Yet McClellan refused to admit his failings. "I have seen too many dead and wounded comrades to feel otherwise than that the Govt has not sustained this Army," he wired Secretary of War Stanton, ignoring the fact he had not been within miles of Porter's lines or used his 65,000 troops south of the river. ". . . I tell you plainly that I owe no thanks to you or any other person in Washington—you have done your best to sacrifice this Army."[37] Neither Stanton nor Lincoln saw this last bitter charge. It so dismayed the head of the War Department's telegraph unit that he deleted it before passing on the communiqué.

Now under cover of night McClellan moved Porter back across the Chickahominy, later burning the bridges behind him. Hundreds of stragglers were picked up the next morning, including Union General John Reynolds, who worn out from fatigue had fallen asleep in the woods and not been awakened during the pullout. Reynolds, a friend of Harvey Hill in the Old Army, was mortified by his capture. Said Hill: "He sat down and covered his face with his hands, and at length said, 'Hill, we ought not to be enemies.' I told him that there was no bad feeling on my part, and that he ought not to fret at the fortunes of war. . . . He was placed in my ambulance and sent to Richmond."[38]

June 28 provided a lull in the fighting, one that was used in part to help the wounded and bury the dead. "Wrapped in a blanket, the soldier's shroud, the bodies of such comrades as died on the field were laid side by side in shallow trenches, each regiment's dead to itself," wrote an infantryman in the 4th Texas. "At the head of each body was placed a rough, rudely lettered board to tell whose it was, and then the earth was heaped in a high mound over the common grave. A few, whose bodies, it was thought, their friends would likely desire to remove, were buried in separate graves."[39] In the wake of the retreat supplies littered the ground, and the Confederates salvaged what they could. "The whole country was full of deserted plunder," said Dabney. "Army wagons and pontoon trains, partially burned or crippled; mounds of grain and rice, and hillocks of mess-beef smouldering; tens of thousands of axes, picks and shovels . . . blankets lately new, and overcoats torn in twain from the waist up. . . . Great stores of fixed ammunition were saved, while more was destroyed."[40]

Soon it was clear that McClellan was withdrawing his main command eastward toward White Oak Swamp, joining with Fitz-John Porter and thence turning south toward the James and the protection of Federal gunboats. Fitz-John Porter's Fifth Corps and Erasmus Keyes's Fourth Corps would be in the van, together with the immense train of 4,000 supply wagons; William Franklin's, Edwin Sumner's and Samuel Heintzelman's Sixth, Second and Third Corps would bring up the rear, all the while keeping an eye on their flank and the Confederates advancing toward them from Richmond. White Oak Swamp formed a rough half-circle, its arc to the south and stretching perhaps ten miles, its western end near Savage's Station and its eastern near Fisher's Bridge. Roads south through the morass led to White Oak Swamp Bridge, five miles southeast of Savage's Station. Then Long Bridge Road led south to Glendale and the Quaker Road to Malvern Hill. Once McClellan was across the swamp he could use it to protect his rear, and then concentrate on repelling any attacks from the west.

In the early hours of Sunday June 29, Day Five, Lee issued orders to intercept this withdrawal. His intent was not just to defeat McClellan but to destroy him. The roads going east and west were much better than the ones running north and south, affording the Confederates a clear advantage in this regard. The swamp, on the other hand, would make pursuit from the rear difficult. Magruder was told to move his six brigades some five miles eastward on the Williamsburg Road to Savage's Station and engage the enemy in flank later that day. Huger was to advance some eight miles eastward on the Charles City Road to Magruder's right and support him by attacking south of the swamp. To Jackson fell the most difficult assignment, rebuilding the bridges on the Chickahominy, crossing the swamp with his own, Ewell's, Whiting's and Harvey Hill's divisions and falling on McClellan's rear while Magruder was engaged at Savage's Station.

Longstreet and Powell Hill, who had the longest march, were to recross the Chickahominy near Richmond, move on the Darbytown Road to Huger's right and assail the enemy in flank the next day at Glendale. Theophilus Holmes's division was to advance on the New Market Road to Malvern Hill.

Just as at Mechanicsville and Gaines's Mill, Lee's plans for June 29 did not go smoothly. First the fatigued Jackson did not get his entire command over the Chickahominy until the early hours of June 30, in large part because he entrusted the construction of the principal bridge to the Rev. Dabney, who clearly was no engineer. He gave little or no thought to sending across a partial force earlier to help Magruder. This in turn put added pressure on the excitable Prince John, who began to believe as the hours slipped by that his and Huger's commands, perhaps 25,000 men, were being asked to engage most of McClellan's army. Morphine-laced medicine he took for his nervous stomach only heightened his apprehension and slowed his progress. Meanwhile Huger, all too conscious he had been made the scapegoat for Seven Pines, likewise moved no faster than he had to. Two of his brigades at one point were sent to reinforce Magruder and then called back. Thereafter he advanced strictly according to orders down the Charles City Road, and soon bivouacked.

Not until 5 P.M. did Magruder, finally resigned to Jackson's absence and Huger's lack of enthusiasm, launch his attack at Savage's Station. But he did so hesitatingly, using less than half his command of 14,000 troops. Joseph Kershaw's brigade of South Carolinians, Paul Semmes's mixed brigade and two regiments of Richard Griffith's Mississippians under William Barksdale moved up on either side of the Richmond & York River Railroad. Lawyer Kershaw, clean shaven except for a drooping blond mustache, in this contest and others to come would prove a man of conspicuous courage, as would the patrician-looking Semmes, a Georgia banker and politician. The hard-drinking Barksdale, a former U.S. congressman famous for a notable fistfight on the floor of the House, would also emerge as a first-rate combat officer. Contesting their commands were elements of Sumner's and Franklin's corps, twice the number of men.

One piece of armament the Confederates had going for them, however, was a huge 32-pound naval gun mounted on a railroad flatcar. It was Lee's answer to McClellan's highly immobile siege guns, and it out-ranged anything the enemy had on the field that day. "General Kershaw, in person, was immediately in our rear on foot," said D. Augustus Dickert of the 3rd South Carolina. "He called out in a loud, clear tone the single word 'charge.' The troops bounded to the front with a yell . . . the heavy railroad siege gun made the welkin ring with its deafening reports. . . . The enemy fought with great energy and vigor. . . . Much was at stake, and night was near. [Union General] Sumner was fighting for the safety of the long trains of artillery and wagons seeking cover in his rear, as well as for the very life of the army itself." The smoke of the guns and the dense shrubbery made the woods dark as night. "I had not gone far into the thicket before I was struck by a minie ball in the chest, which sent me reeling to the ground momentarily unconscious. Our men lost all semblance of a line . . . and those in front were in as much danger from friend as from foe. While I lay in my semi-unconscious state, I received another bullet in my thigh, which I had every reason to believe came from someone in the rear."[41]

Private John Wood of the 53rd Georgia, one of Semmes's regiments, commented on the confusion in equally sanguine terms. This was his unit's initial engagement and the men showed it, first sending a volley into the friendly troops on their left, then into their comrades on their right. "The only damage we done, I believe, was that of killing our Major's horse," Wood wrote home. The 53rd Georgia recovered its composure and soon, Wood said, "I fired as coolly as if I had been shooting a squirrel."[42] The battle, which resulted in a stalemate, did not end until almost 9 P.M. Much of the fighting was hand-to-hand, and here the antiquated Confederate smoothbore muskets proved lethal. Loaded with "buck-and-ball," a cartridge consisting of three buckshot and a ball, they were ideal short-range weapons. Federal casualties were some 900; Confederate, some 450. Through Sumner's and Franklin's efforts, however, all the Federals and their wagons soon would be across White Oak Swamp, making Jackson's efforts to roll up their rear all the more difficult.

On June 30 the Confederate attack at Glendale and Frayser's Farm suffered similarly from lack of communication and coordination. The lead attack on the center of the Federal column was to be made by the divisions of Longstreet and Powell Hill, now because of losses no more than 20,000 strong, marching down the Darbytown Road some six miles. Supporting them would be Magruder, coming south from Savage's Station and then following in their footsteps. Holmes with 6,000 men would be on their right, Huger with 9,000 on their left. Jackson and Harvey Hill, now with perhaps 20,000 men, were charged with pushing through White Oak Swamp. Lee's intent was to sever the Federal column and overwhelm its rearmost components.

From the beginning the Confederates moved in fits and starts. On the far right the 57-year-old Holmes, quite deaf and out of his depth, during the afternoon advanced on and shelled Malvern Hill, where Porter with the van of the Federal army then had no more than 1,500 men. What Porter did have, however, were thirty-six field pieces and the support of the gunboats in the James. The responding artillery barrage panicked the attackers. "The irregular cavalry stampeded and made a brilliant charge to the rear," wrote Harvey Hill. "The artillerists were also panic-struck . . . and cutting their horses loose mounted them, and with dangling traces tried to catch up with the fleet-footed cavaliers. The infantry troops . . . crouched behind little saplings to get protection from the shrieking, blustering shells." It was at this point that Holmes emerged from a house where he had been conducting some business. "General Holmes," continued Hill wryly, "who from his deafness was entirely unaware of the rumpus came out of the hut, put his hand behind his right ear, and said: 'I thought I heard firing.' Some of the pale-faced infantry thought they also had heard firing."[43] Holmes's subsequent calls for help eventually brought him Magruder, thus depriving Longstreet of Prince John's immediate support. Holmes soon disengaged, taking no further part in the action. Meanwhile Magruder's troops, ordered back to the main front and worn out by twenty miles of marching and countermarching under their high-strung leader, did not get back to Longstreet and Powell Hill until long after the fight was over.

On Longstreet's left, Benjamin Huger's support proved equally lacking. Finding his way on the Charles City Road blocked by felled trees, he put his men to work with axes so his artillery could advance. "As the Confederates

cut away, the enemy continued to deepen the obstruction," wrote one commentator. "The strange spectacle was presented of a battle of rival axemen.
Apparently Huger never considered the possibility of leaving his guns in the
rear, of keeping up an active skirmish and of offering to move his troops
through the woods in support of Longstreet and Hill. He played it safe, and
played a lone hand. As he chopped, the Divisions to his right withheld their
advance."[44]

Jackson's conduct that day would be the most controversial of all. Finding
the White Oak Swamp Bridge completely destroyed and Franklin's massed artillery and 20,000 men—about the same size as his own force—commanding
the high ground on the south side of the stream, he did little more than reconnoiter. Both Tom Munford of the cavalry and Wade Hampton, temporarily leading a brigade in Winder's division, found possible alternate crossings
and Hampton actually built a footbridge, but Jackson seemed uninterested.
At one point he even took a nap. "It looked to me as if on our side we were
waiting for Jackson to wake up," said one of Winder's aides.[45] Critics of
Stonewall in this battle, which was his nadir as a commander, admit that a
head-on assault at the burnt-out bridge would have been suicidal. They say,
however, he should have pursued one of two courses: either swinging several
miles to the west and then moving down the Charles City Road to reinforce
Longstreet, or at least making a forceful demonstration that would tie up
Franklin's troops. The latter point seems more powerful. During the late afternoon the Union general, seeing that Jackson was not attacking, sent four
brigades under his command back to Glendale.

What were the reasons for Jackson's failure? Once again his tendency to
follow orders to the letter, plus mind-numbing fatigue. Lee had ordered him
to push his way across White Oak Swamp and guard the army's left flank,
not to make a turning movement of his own. Nor did Old Jack know the
overall situation. "None of us knew that the veterans of Longstreet and A.P.
Hill were unsupported," Harvey Hill would explain, referring to the absence
of Magruder and Huger in the attack on the Union center.[46] "If General Lee
had wanted me, he could have sent for me," Medical Officer Hunter McGuire
quoted Jackson as saying several days afterward. Declared Dr. McGuire, "If
Lee had wanted Jackson to give direct support to Longstreet he could have
had him there in less than three hours. The staff officer was not sent . . ."[47]

Jackson's malaise, wrote Dabney, "was probably to be explained by physical causes. The labor of previous days, the sleeplessness, the wear of gigantic
cares . . . had sunk the elasticity of his will and the quickness of his invention."
That evening, supping with his staff, Stonewall dozed off at the table. Stated
Dabney: "After dropping asleep from excessive fatigue, with his supper between his teeth, he said, 'Now, gentlemen, let us at once to bed, and rise with
the dawn, and see if tomorrow we cannot *do something*!"[48] Writing Anna
subsequently, Jackson admitted: "During the past week I have not been well,

have suffered from fever and debility, but through the blessing of an ever-kind Providence I am much better. . . ."[49]

Thus it was that at 5:30 P.M. Longstreet and Powell Hill finally assailed the enemy on their own at Glendale, while some 50,000 of their comrades remained unengaged. Opposing them there and at nearby Frayser's Farm were approximately 40,000 Union troops under Philip Kearny, George McCall, Joseph Hooker and John Sedgwick, double their number. In the Confederate van was the Virginia brigade of doughty James Kemper, a former Speaker of the House of Delegates given to high-flown oratory before and after battle. His men double-quicked across 600 yards of open field toward two Union batteries, capturing six of the eight guns. Rejoiced Private David E. Johnson of the 7th Virginia: "The brigade met with a shower of shot, shell, and canister, and a storm of leaden bullets; it never faltered."[50] With them were Cadmus Wilcox's Alabamians and Micah Jenkins's South Carolinians. Edmund Patterson of the 9th Alabama, charging a second battery, reported: "Those of us left standing poured a volley at a distance of not more than ten paces into the faces of the gunners. They fell across their guns and under the wheels, whole teams of horses plunging about in their mad agony, trampling under foot the wounded."[51]

Taking the worse casualties of all were Jenkins's troops; they would lose some 530 soldiers, the highest of any brigade that day. "As I watched the fight of Jenkins' Brigade," said Major Edward Porter Alexander, "a fine, tall, handsome young fellow dropped out of ranks & came back toward me. As he seemed weak I went to meet him & found he had been shot through the lungs, the bullet passing clear through. He had been the color bearer." Alexander gave the soldier some brandy, and assured him he knew of men who had survived such wounds. "He was evidently cheered & said, 'Of course, I'm willing to die for my country, if I must; but I'd a heap rather get well & see my mother & my folks again.' Poor fellow, I hope he did, but I never knew."[52] Soon Roger Pryor's mixed brigade and Winfield Featherston's Mississippians also were engaged.

The battle ebbed back and forth. Now Powell Hill's men came up—the brigades of Field, Pender and Gregg in the lead. The fighting was hand-to-hand. Robert Christian and his brother Eli of Charles Field's 60th Virginia took on four of the enemy. Bayoneted several times, Robert killed three of them; his brother killed the fourth. "My Dear Wife," the slightly built, spirited Dorsey Pender later would write his Fanny, "God has spared me through another day's fight. We drove them again from their position [at Frayser's Farm], taking one General, [George] McCall, and two batteries of fine rifled guns." One of Pender's regiments, the 22nd North Carolina, had just gotten a new battle flag, the old one having been shredded at Gaines's Mill. It promptly squared off against the 20th Massachusetts, whose officers came from Boston's bluest blood. In the ensuing donnybrook, the 22nd North Carolina's colonel noted, "our flag staff was shot in two twice, the Color Bearer killed & 6 out of 8 of the color-guard either killed or wounded." Just beforehand Captain Oliver Wendell Holmes of the 20th Massachusetts lined up his men next to his friend Captain James Lowell. "We caught each other's eye and saluted," said Holmes sadly. "When next I looked, he was gone."[53]

While Longstreet deployed large numbers of men with admirable skill during the battle, displaying his usual calm under pressure, Powell Hill once again showed his bent for personal leadership. Seeing some North Carolinians breaking and heading for the rear, he rode forward and seized their battle flag, crying, "Damn you, if you will not follow me, I'll die alone!" The men stopped in their tracks. Shouted one of them: "Lead on, Hill! Head the North Carolina boys!" The Carolinians soon rallied.

By 8:30 P.M. darkness brought the combat to an end, with the Confederates unable to cut the Federal column. "Longstreet and A.P. Hill made a desperate fight," said Harvey Hill, "but they failed to gain possession of the Quaker Road, upon which McClellan was retreating. That night Franklin glided silently by them. He had to pass within easy range of the artillery of Longstreet and Hill, but they did not know he was there."[54] Many prisoners were taken including Union General McCall, as well as several batteries and thousands of small arms. The cries of the wounded were piteous, but some of the survivors did not notice. Wrote one officer to his wife: "Strange as it may seem to you I never slept sounder in my life. We was so worn out that as soon as we stopped fighting we could hardly keep awake."[55] Confederate casualties totaled some 3,700; Union, some 3,800.

More changes came on the brigade level. Jubal Early, still so bothered by his wound he had to be helped onto his horse, took over Arnold Elzey's command. The slain Richard Griffith of Mississippi was replaced by his senior colonel, William Barksdale. General John R. Jones, one of few officers in the Army of Northern Virginia whose career would be marred by charges of cowardice, now led the Virginians of the 2nd Brigade of Winder's division, formerly under John Campbell. With Richard Taylor still ailing, his Louisiana command devolved on Leroy Stafford. Wounds to Pickett, Featherston and Joseph R. Anderson resulted in new officers for those Virginia, Mississippi and Georgia units. Robert Rodes, his own wound reopened, entrusted his Alabama brigade to the dashing John Brown Gordon.

Early on the morning of July 1, with the entire Federal army and its massed artillery reunited on Malvern Hill, Lee met with his generals to consider still another assault. Jackson had by this time crossed White Oak Swamp in the wake of the retreating Franklin, and Lee's intent was for Harvey Hill, Huger and Magruder, none of whom had seen action the previous day, to bear the brunt of the fighting. Malvern Hill was actually an elevated plateau, some 150 feet high and a mile and one-half in breadth and three-quarters of a mile in width, just one mile north of the James. Assailing it would give the bravest man pause. One informant previously had warned Harvey Hill "of its commanding height, the difficulties of approach, its amphitheatrical form and ample area, which would enable McClellan to arrange his 350 field-guns tier above tier and sweep the plain in every direction." Now he gave Lee the gist of this report, adding, "If General McClellan is there in force, we had better let him alone."

Longstreet, who was standing nearby, scoffed at Hill's suggestion. "Don't get scared, now that we have got him whipped," he said.

The words must have stung, but Hill made no reply. "It was this belief in the demoralization of the Federal army," he would write subsequently of Lee's fateful decision, "that made our leader risk the attack."[56]

Harvey Hill's division was to form on the left of the line, with the rest of Jackson's command in reserve; Huger's division was to be in the center, Magruder's on the right. Hill's men took their position, then waited for further orders. "My five brigade commanders and myself now made an examination of the enemy position," he said. "He was found to be strongly posted on a commanding hill, all the approaches to which could be swept by his artillery." Coming up on Hill's right by midday was the Virginia brigade of Lewis Armistead, soon to be followed by the mixed brigade of Ambrose Ransom ("Rans") Wright. The balding, hard-charging Armistead, a professional soldier, had earned plaudits throughout the Old Army (and expulsion from West Point) for breaking a mess plate over Jubal Early's head. Rans Wright, a Georgia lawyer and politician, had risen from private to brigadier. About 2 P.M. Hill received a badly worded message from Robert Chilton, Lee's chief of staff: "Batteries have been established to act upon the enemy's line. If it is broken, as probable, Armistead, who can witness the effect of the fire, has been ordered to advance with a yell. Do the same."[57]

There were two flaws in this scenario. One was that the Confederate guns at the front were relatively few and widely scattered, no match at all for the Federal artillery, and Lee's chief of artillery, General William Pendleton, was simply not up to the job of bringing the reserve guns forward and positioning them. Pendleton's defenders have pointed out that Lee should have sent aides to spur him on, saying if anyone can be found on the battlefield it is the officer standing beside scores of field pieces, but this does not explain Pendleton's lack of initiative. The second flaw was that the decision to set off the assault was entrusted to a brigadier in his first battle, relying on a rebel yell that might or might not be heard amid the roar of the guns.

More hours passed, and soon it was late afternoon. Lee now realized he was outgunned, and had no intention of making an attack unless it could be heavy and swift. The Federal cannonade was unrelenting and breathtaking, so much so that the men of the Stonewall Brigade joked with gallows humor that it had even silenced the passionately profane Colonel Andrew Grigsby of the 27th Virginia. Hill knew that Armistead was on his right, but where were the rest of Huger's brigades and the whole of Magruder's command? The fact was that Huger had lost control of his troops. Armistead and "Rans" Wright had been sent forward, but thereafter received no direction. Huger, in a bit of a snit, now was holding back William Mahone and Robert Ransom because "I had no one to show us what road to take."[58] When Major Joseph Brent, Magruder's aide, sought him out to ask him where his flank was, Huger hotly replied, "I do not know where my Brigades are, and I hear that at least some of them have been moved without my knowledge . . . and I have no information enabling me to answer your inquiries."[59]

Magruder meanwhile had problems of his own. His three minidivisions— his own (comprising the brigades of Howell Cobb and William Barksdale), David R. Jones's (the brigades of Robert Toombs and George T. Anderson) and Lafayette McLaws's (the brigades of Joseph Kershaw and Paul Semmes)— were once again fruitlessly marching and countermarching. His orders were to come up the Quaker Road. Unfortunately there were two Quaker Roads, and his guides initially chose the one leading away from the action.

Magruder's division heads were David ("Neighbor") Jones, the courtly South Carolinian who had commanded a brigade under Beauregard at First Manassas, and Lafayette McLaws, a sound if punctilious Georgian who had been in Longstreet's class at West Point. Brigadiers Howell Cobb and Robert Toombs were wealthy Georgia politicians, the former brooding and introspective, the other violent and egotistic. George Thomas ("Tige") Anderson, also a Georgian, would become one of Lee's stalwarts. Barksdale, Kershaw and Semmes we have already met.

By the time Magruder did reach the front, hours late, he was in a near panic. More instructions from Lee, ambiguous and delivered verbally, further alarmed him. Mistakenly thinking he was being accused of foot-dragging he abandoned the original plan of hurling his and the absent Huger's 15,000 men simultaneously on the enemy's left and instead, about 5:30 P.M., committed the brigades piecemeal. Some of Armistead's regiments had already advanced and been pinned down; now the rest were ordered forward, as were Rans Wright's troops. Wrote David Winn of the 4th Georgia to his wife: "It is astonishing that every man did not fall; bullet after bullet too rapid in succession to be counted. . . ." Every man was a hero, he maintained, who just summoned up the nerve to charge.[60]

Harvey Hill, like Lee, had come to believe there would be no action that day, that the Federal position was too strong and the hour too late. Now he heard the sounds of battle. "While conversing with my brigade commanders," he said, "shouting was heard on our right, followed by the roar of musketry. We all agreed that this was the signal agreed upon. . . ." Garland's North Carolina Brigade formed up next to Armistead, with Hill's other brigades extending to the left: Rodes's Alabamians under Gordon, then the wounded

George Burgwyn Anderson's North Carolinians under Colonel Charles Tew, then Ripley's and Colquitt's Georgians, North Carolinians and Alabamians. "The brigade moved forward with alacrity about half way to the battery," said Garland, "when the terrible fire of the artillery and the opening fire of the infantry induced them to halt, lie down, and commence firing, without my orders and contrary to them." Remembered Gordon: "The whole ground was swept by the fire of the artillery, which had in rapid succession silenced two Confederate batteries in out front. . . . Never was the courage of troops more severely tried. . . . They moved on under this terrible fire . . . until a little over 200 yards of the batteries. . . . Here the canister and musketry mowed down my already thinned ranks so rapidly that it became impossible to advance without support." Stated Ripley: "Officers and men fell fast, but they maintained their ground, opening and keeping up a severe fire upon the enemy in return, before which his advance battery fell back and his troops wavered."[61] Hill's division together with Armistead's and Wright's brigades totaled no more than 10,500 men; yet, they were attacking McClellan head-on.

Incurring terrible losses but close to cracking the Federal lines, Hill needed immediate and concerted support. He did not get it. Wrote Lee: "A simultaneous advance of other troops not taking place, [Hill] found himself unable to maintain the ground he had gained against the overwhelming numbers . . . of the enemy." Now Magruder compounded the slaughter. Belatedly, almost in slow motion, he continued to commit the rest of his and Huger's troops. Onward they came: scrawny, piping-voiced Billy Mahone's Virginians, jowly Howell Cobb's mixed brigade, white-haired Barksdale's Mississippians and balding Robert Ransom's North Carolinians, one by one and far too late. They met the same devastating fire, achieving nothing. Magruder's subsequent ill-timed assaults, those of Robert Toombs, George T. Anderson, Kershaw and Semmes suffered the same consequences. "As each brigade emerged from the woods," Harvey Hill would say, describing the bloodshed, "from fifty to one hundred guns opened upon it, tearing great gaps in its ranks. . . . It was not war—it was murder."[62] By 9:30 P.M. the last of the fighting mercifully ended. Confederate casualties were almost 5,700; Federal, some 3,000.

"Why did you attack?" Lee asked Magruder late that night.

"In obedience to your orders, twice repeated," was the reply. Ever the gentleman, Lee kept his feelings to himself, but there is no doubt he must have bemoaned Magruder's lack of judgment.[63]

No real attempt was made to pursue McClellan, who withdrew to Harrison's Landing and the protection of Federal gunboats in the James, leaving behind some 50 field pieces and 35,000 rifles. There before beginning his return to Washington he huddled in military limbo for the next five weeks with the Army of the Potomac—some 90,000 men, 290 guns, 3,000 wagons and 27,000 horses and mules. "I think I begin to see some wise purpose in this," McClellan would write Miss Nelly, seeing God's wisdom in the defeat.

"If I had succeeded in taking Richmond now the fanatics of the North might have been too powerful & reunion impossible."[64]

In the days before and after Malvern Hill the disappointed Lincoln made two key appointments. Henry ("Old Brains") Halleck, renowned in the Old Army as a planner and strategist, was named general-in-chief. Halleck, as flabby in physique and colorless in personality as McClellan was muscular and charismatic, would serve Lincoln well. The second appointment would prove less fortunate. John Pope, who had achieved some success in the West, was recalled to lead the newly formed Army of Virginia—combining Frémont's Mountain Department, Banks's Department of the Shenandoah, McDowell's Department of the Rappahannock and the Washington garrison. While the unification decision was wise, Pope's selection was not. First he alienated his new command by implying Federal troops in the West were fighters and they were not: "Let us understand each other. I have come to you from the West, where we have always seen the backs of our enemies. . . ." Then his bombast exposed him to ridicule. Where would he make his headquarters? "In the saddle," Pope replied, giving rise to the comment his hindquarters were where his headquarters should be.[65]

The exhausted Army of Northern Virginia meanwhile licked its wounds. "So far as I can now see," Lee wrote Davis on July 4, explaining why he was not assaulting Harrison's Landing, "there is no way to attack [the enemy] to advantage, nor do I wish to expose the men to the destructive missiles of his gunboats." Confederate killed and wounded during the Seven Days totaled approximately 19,200, with 950 missing or captured. Federal killed and wounded totaled some 9,800, with 6,100 missing or captured. Thirteen brigades, one-third of the army and most of them in Longstreet's and Powell Hill's divisions, suffered more than half of the casualties. In Longstreet's command Cadmus Wilcox's brigade had 1,055; Roger Pryor, 862; Richard Heron Anderson, 787; Winfield Featherston, 666; and George Pickett, 654. In Powell Hill's division, Maxcy Gregg suffered 939; Lawrence O'Bryan Branch, 839; and Dorsey Pender, 800. In Harvey Hill's command Roswell Ripley had 908; George Burgwyn Anderson, 863; and Samuel Garland, 844. Rans Wright incurred 666 casualties and John Bell Hood 623.

In his official report Lee later voiced deep regret that McClellan had gotten away. "Under ordinary circumstances," he wrote, "the Federal Army should have been destroyed."[66] The Seven Days, however, did not take place under ordinary circumstances. Lee the master strategist had been in command less than a month, with little time to assess his personnel. The fatigued Jackson's performance had been dismal, but such would never again be the case. Longstreet, Powell Hill and Harvey Hill were still learning to direct large bodies of men. Poor communications and poor staff work would have to be improved. But Lee's aggressiveness had reinvigorated the army, saving Richmond and humiliating McClellan. For his next major battle he would reorganize his command, putting the methodical Longstreet in charge of its "right wing" with fifteen brigades, and the offensive-minded Jackson of its "left wing" with fourteen.

The shortcomings of Prince John Magruder, Benjamin Huger and Theophilus Holmes, senior officers all, soon resulted in their transfer to other commands. Magruder ended up in charge of the District of Texas, New Mexico and Arizona; Huger was named inspector of artillery and ordnance; Holmes went to the Department of the Trans-Mississippi. Chase Whiting, still the opinionated officer who had offended Davis, would be exiled to coastal duty in Wilmington, North Carolina. Daniel Harvey Hill also would be briefly transferred, not at this point for his outspokenness but because he was needed in his native North Carolina. He would return for the battles at South Mountain and Antietam.

# SIX

\* \* \* \*

# CEDAR MOUNTAIN
# AND SECOND MANASSAS

For Lee the weeks following the Seven Days were spent in refitting the army, in great part with the spoils the Federals had left on the field, and swelling its ranks with the recovered wounded and new conscripts. Then in mid-July, even while retaining the bulk of his command to keep McClellan's Army of the Potomac checkmated at Harrison's Landing, Lee dispatched Jackson with 12,000 men west to the Gordonsville rail junction to confront and deal with Pope's 50,000-strong Army of Virginia. Soon afterward he reinforced him with 11,000 more troops under Powell Hill. That proud warrior had been engaged in a brouhaha with Longstreet, not entirely of his making, as to whose division had borne the brunt of the fighting at Glendale. It took all of Lee's tact to resolve their differences, but it was clear Hill could no longer serve under Longstreet. Putting him together with the aggressive Jackson must have seemed a good match. "A.P. Hill you will find I think a good officer with whom you can consult and by advising with your division commanders as to your movements much trouble will be saved," Lee wrote Jackson, nudging him to be less secretive.[1] The hint would prove useless.

On August 3 Jackson attended Sunday services at an Episcopal church in the Gordonsville area. His aide Charles Minor Blackford, despite being disappointed by what he called a "trashy sermon," was impressed by the sight of the generals—Jackson, Hill, Winder, Pender—sitting side by side in the pews and later taking communion. "The clanking swords sounded strangely," he said, "as each man arranged his so as to enable him to kneel at the chancel rail."[2] Devout though he was, Jackson nodded off through most sermons. "What is the use of General Jackson going to church?" said Ewell. "He sleeps all the time."[3] Writing Anna, who was six months pregnant, Jackson permitted himself a mild lament. "My darling wife, I am just overburdened with work, and I hope you will not think hard at receiving only very short letters from your loving husband . . . though let me say no more. A Christian should never complain. The apostle Paul said, 'I glory in tribulations!' What a bright example for others."[4]

On the eve of still another campaign Ewell was less stoic. "It may be all very well to wish young heroes to be in a fight," he told his Lizinka, "but for my part I would be satisfied never to see another field. What pleasure can there be in seeing thousands of dead & dying in every horrible agony, torn to pieces by artillery. . . . Since March I have been almost constantly within hearing of skirmishing, cannon &c &c. and I would give almost anything to get away for a time."[5] Ewell also regretted the loss of the hard-fighting Richard Taylor, who had been sent to the District of Western Louisiana, though he thought him in some ways peculiar. In truth the stresses of the war were deepening the fault lines among many Confederate officers, making them ever more prone to take offense over real or imagined deficiencies or slights. "Most of us are in the estimation of our best friends more or less eccentric," commented Ewell's brother Ben. "So Taylor and Ewell thought Jackson, and so Taylor thought Ewell, and so Ewell thought Taylor, and I have no doubt that if Jackson's mind hadn't been full of more important matters he would have thought so of Ewell and Taylor."[6]

On August 7 within hours after learning that the van of Pope's army, exposed and vulnerable, had advanced to Culpeper some thirty miles north of Gordonsville, Jackson moved on the attack with overwhelming force. Noted Edward Porter Alexander, now Lee's chief of ordnance: "To Pope came orders from [Henry] Halleck to make some demonstrations toward our railroad at Gordonsville so as to attract part of Gen. Lee's troops from Richmond, in order that McClellan might safely weaken his army by beginning to ship it to the Potomac. Nothing could have suited Gen. Lee better. No sooner did Pope send some of his troops across the Rappahannock, than Lee sent Jackson with his own division, Ewell's & A.P. Hill's to look after him."[7] The first day of the march to Culpeper was uneventful, but the second day was a disaster, and it widened the personality gulf that had existed between Hill and Jackson since their days at West Point. Marching orders called for Ewell to be in the lead, then Hill, then Jackson's own division under Winder. Instead Jackson without informing Hill sent Ewell forward on a different road. Patiently waiting in the early morning for Ewell's troops to pass so he could fall in behind with the Light Division, Hill found out too late they were Winder's. Confusion followed confusion, compounded by the stifling heat of the day. Ewell made only eight miles, Powell Hill no more than two. Jackson did not blame himself; he blamed Hill. Nightfall found the army stretched out for miles, with Hill far in the rear.

Jackson rushed into battle August 9 at Cedar Mountain, therefore, with his largest division not yet on the field. His plan called for Ewell on the Confederate right to cross the mountain with two of his brigades in the early afternoon and turn the Federal left. Jubal Early, back from the wound he had incurred at Williamsburg, would advance in the center. Winder, who had been sick but was insistent on taking the field, would move up the Culpeper Road, extend the line to the left and simultaneously envelop the Federal right. Opposing Jackson across the intervening wheat and cornfields was Nathaniel Banks, his old adversary from the Shenandoah, smarting over his defeat in the Valley and eager for revenge.

From 3 to 5:30 P.M. the combatants bombarded each other with heavy artillery fire. Here Charles Sydney Winder, a highly capable division head, suffered a mortal wound that deprived the left flank of his leadership. "Between my gun and limber, where General Winder stood," said Edward Moore of the Rockbridge Artillery, "was a constant stream of shells tearing through the trees and bursting close by. While the enemy's guns were changing their position he gave some directions, which we could not hear for the surrounding noise. I, being nearest, turned and walking toward him asked what he had said. As he put his hand to his mouth to repeat the remark, a shell passed through his side and arm, tearing them fearfully. He fell straight back at full length and lay quivering on the ground."[8] The Maryland officer in recent weeks had alienated some of his men by ordering corporal punishment for straggling and absenteeism. It was hard for them to forgive the harsh discipline. "His death was not much lamented," said one member of the Stonewall Brigade dispassionately, "for it probably saved some of them the trouble of carrying out their threats to kill him. I would not have done it had I the chance; but I firmly believe it would have been done by some one in that battle."[9]

McHenry Howard, a staff officer, reached Winder's side when he was brought to the rear on a stretcher.

"General, do you know me?" Howard asked.

"Oh yes," Winder replied. For a while he spoke in snatches about his beloved wife and children before relapsing into shock.

"General, lift up your head to God," a chaplain urged.

"I do, I do lift it up to him," Winder said, shortly before he died.[10]

In late afternoon the Federal infantry on the Confederate center and left stepped up their pressure. Rather than turning the Federal right, Winder's brigades now commanded by Taliaferro were themselves being flanked. Some 1,500 Federals were making the assault. The 2nd Brigade under Thomas Garnett, a Virginia physician, began to fall back, as did the 3rd Brigade now under Colonel Alexander Taliaferro, the 54-year-old uncle of the brigadier. The Stonewall Brigade, temporarily led by attorney Charles Ronald, rushed up but lost its momentum and became separated in the thick woods. Regiment by regiment, the entire Confederate left was panicking. This in turn put Early's left flank at risk, at one point forcing the removal of the artillery. "For a few moments," wrote a commentator, "the blue and the grey were mingled in close conflict amid the smoke . . . the troops were mingled in a tumultuous mass. . . . But fortunately for the Virginians the Federal right wing was unsupported."[11]

Into the fray rode Jackson, hatless and waving a battle flag, crying: "Rally brave men, and press forward! Your general will lead you. Jackson will lead you. Follow me!"[12] Remembered Charles Blackford: "Jackson usually is an indifferent and slouchy looking man but then, with the 'Light of Battle' shedding its radiance over him his whole person had changed. . . . The men would have followed him into the jaws of death itself. . . . Even the old sorrel horse seemed endowed with the style and form of an Arabian."[13] Inspired by Jackson's words, the Virginians began to rally. Garnett's and Taliaferro's brigades stopped their flight, and Ronald's efforts to restore the gaps in the Stonewall Brigade's line began to take effect.

In the center meanwhile, Early was more than holding his own, bolstered by the arrival of Edward Thomas's Georgians, the first of Powell Hill's brigades to arrive on the field. Old Jube placed them next to one of his own regiments, the 12th Georgia, by attrition led by its senior field officer, Captain William F. Brown.

"General," said Brown, a veteran of the Valley, "my ammunition is nearly out; don't you think we had better charge them?"

Though he thought the suggestion imprudent, the sharp-eyed Early admired its gallantry. "This brave old man was then 65 years old," he would write, "and had a son, an officer in his company. The position was held . . . and the day was thus prevented from being lost." Only Early, Thomas and the three brigades of Jackson's division had been engaged up to this time, but now the rest of Hill's men were coming up. "The temporary advantage gained by the enemy was soon wrestled from him," Early said, "and he was forced back into the wheat field, and then across it over the ridge beyond."[14]

Jackson himself urged on the next of Hill's brigades, Lawrence Branch's North Carolinians. "Branch, when in Congress, was an orator of great force," said a staff officer, "and while waiting orders, he took occasion to give his troops the benefit of it, by making them a speech. . . . But no harm was done on this occasion, for General Jackson hearing of this delay and the cause of it started with an unfathomable smile and galloped to the spot."

"Push forward, General, push forward!" he ordered.[15]

Branch quickly moved to the front, followed by James Archer and Dorsey Pender. "Branch and Archer advanced rapidly," said one of Archer's Tennesseans, "pushing back the Federals until they reached a wheat field occupied by their reserve lines. Here an obstinate stand was made . . . but opportunely Pender threw his brigade upon their right flank. . . . They hesitated a moment, then broke and fled in confusion from the field."[16] Jackson had won the battle of Cedar Mountain, but Hill had tipped the balance and the knowledge must have been sweet for Little Powell. In sweat-soaked shirtsleeves and with sword in hand he exhorted his men on, with no tolerance for shirkers. "Who are you, sir, and where are you going?" he called to a lieutenant moving toward the rear.

"I am going back with my wounded friend," came the answer.

Hill angrily leaned from his horse and ripped the man's bars from his collar. "You are a pretty fellow to hold a commission," he said, "going to the rear with a man who is scarcely badly enough wounded to go himself. . . . If you do not go to the front and do your duty, I'll have you shot as soon as I can find a file of men for the purpose."[17]

The Confederates, with 20,000 men available for action, suffered less than 1,300 killed and wounded. Six hundred of these were in Garnett's and Alexander Taliaferro's brigades. Banks, with only 9,000 men, incurred some 2,400 casualties, including 400 prisoners. By going into combat before all his troops were up, Jackson had committed a serious blunder. Nonetheless his subsequent conduct, and that of his men, could not be faulted. James Binford of the 21st Virginia, Thomas Garnett's brigade, went into battle with eighteen comrades, twelve of whom were killed or wounded. "Thanks to a merciful Providence," he told his kin, "I breathe & have all my limbs. I have had enough of the glory of war. I am sick of seeing dead men, & men's limbs torn from their bodies."[18]

Both sides under truce spent the next few days burying the dead. The Confederates, the victors, also fell heir to six full wagonloads of captured rifles.

"It is hard to see our nice rifles going that way," said one Union soldier to another.

"Yes, but they are theirs," was the reply, "they won them fairly."[19]

The energetic Jeb Stuart during August continued his effective raiding and reconnaissance, always with a quip on his lips or a smile on his face. Just as conscientious a Christian as Jackson and likewise a teetotaler, he nonetheless enjoyed parties, music and dancing, even to the extent of providing his own musicians. The two officers were genuinely fond of each other, and Stuart was the only man who could josh Jackson for his stodginess. He and his cavalry staff, in their cocked felt hats, long black plumes, yellow sashes and top boots, cut dashing figures—the impression Stuart sought to make. "He liked his staff to present a handsome, soldierly appearance," said William Blackford, his engineering officer, "and he liked a handsome man as much almost as he did a handsome woman." Superficial observers made the mistake of considering

Jeb frivolous, but this was not so. "I have often seen him arranging for some of his most brilliant cavalry movements," Blackford continued, "and after all was prepared, come out of his tent, call for [Joe] Sweeney and the banjo, and perhaps for some of the men to dance for him and then, to our amazement, order everybody to mount and be off. . . . The gayer he was the more likely we were to move. . . . But it was in action Stuart showed to the greatest advantage. I have never seen his like on a battlefield."[20]

On August 13 Lee, with most of his troops either around or on the way to Gordonsville, ordered Stuart to cross over into Pope's rear and destroy the railroad bridge at Rappahannock Station, preparatory to launching an all-out attack on the Federals. Since Pope's force was tucked into the angle formed by the confluence of the Rapidan and the Rappahannock, this would deny him his primary means of retreat. On the evening of August 17, Stuart and his staff arrived at Verdiersville to rendezvous with the brigade of Fitz Lee and carry out the plan. Near dawn a cavalry column shrouded by mist clattered into the hamlet. They were not Fitz's troopers, however, but Federal soldiers. Stuart and most of his men barely had time to make their escape, Jeb leaping onto his already-saddled mount Skylark and vaulting a fence, the huge von Borcke galloping through an open gate. Meeting up with Stuart an hour later William Blackford found him without his new plumed hat and his cloak and, more important, his haversack with maps and papers revealing Robert E. Lee's intentions. "Expecting Fitz Lee's command by that road, the approach of the enemy's troops . . . had attracted no special attention," explained Blackford, "until they fired and charged."[21] For the rest of the day, with the sun rising hotly, Stuart used his handkerchief to shield his head, while hearing the same biting question: "Where's your hat?" Pope, alerted to Lee's intent, drew back across the Rappahannock.

Stuart vowed revenge and it was not long in coming. Lee soon approved his plan for a new cavalry attack on Pope's rear, crossing over the Rappahannock and riding to Warrenton, then moving east to destroy the supply base and bridge at Catlett's Station and disrupt the Federal rail line from Washington. The night of August 22 Stuart with 1,500 men from Fitzhugh Lee's and Beverly Robertson's brigades stormed with guns blazing into the enemy camp. Some of the Union officers had just made some drinks and were sipping them when someone remarked, "Now this is something like comfort. I hope Jeb Stuart won't disturb us tonight." Just then rebel yells and gunfire burst the silence of the evening.

"There he is, by God!" yelled the speaker, never finishing his glass.[22]

Presently all resistance was over, and tents and supplies were put to the torch. "I now got a detail of men and had the telegraph wires cut in several places, taking out lengths so as to delay repairs as much as possible," said Blackford, "and then exerted myself in keeping the men at work burning, and collecting the mules and prisoners. . . . The way they went through the trunks in the tents was amusing; the blow of an ax answered the place of a key and a kick from the foot spread the contents out for inspection."

Earlier Stuart had learned that Pope's headquarters train with his dispatch book was at the camp. Seizing this book proved invaluable. From it, said Blackford, "we learned as much about his force as he knew himself. . . . We also secured his army treasure chest which I afterwards heard contained $500,000 in greenbacks and $20,000 in gold. From Pope's private baggage a full dress uniform coat and hat was taken to General Stuart as a trophy."[23] Jeb knew just how to capitalize on his acquisition. "General," he wrote Pope, "you have my hat and plume. I have your best coat. I have the honor to propose a cartel for a fair exchange of the prisoners."[24] The Federal commander made no reply. In only one respect was the raid a failure. Before the bridge could be burnt, a pelting rain foiled all attempts to fire the timbers.

Poring over the dispatch book subsequently, Lee confirmed what he already suspected. Pope was delaying his offensive until McClellan's troops could join him. Within days his 50,000 men would grow first to 70,000, then to 130,000. Lee could not let this happen. He resolved that Jackson should go on the attack forthwith.

Because McClellan's men in late August were slowly disembarking at Aquia Creek and then moving up the Rappahannock, Pope was forced to keep his left flank at Fredericksburg. This pinned him down and left his right flank vulnerable to a turning movement. Lee's strategy again called for dividing his army, initially sending Jackson's divisions up the Rappahannock and around the Federal right behind the Bull Run Mountains, then having him drive east through Thoroughfare Gap to the huge supply depot at Manassas Junction. Pope would have no choice but to fall back and protect his rear. This would lengthen the distance McClellan would have to march to reinforce him and give Lee the maximum time to make an assault. Longstreet's columns would demonstrate on the river until Pope realized his danger and withdrew; then Lee and Longstreet would follow Jackson behind the mountains and through the gap.

Lee had by now completed the army's first reorganization and much of its deadwood was gone. For the Second Manassas campaign Jackson's 25,000-man Left Wing consisted of the same three divisions as at Cedar Mountain—his own under William Taliaferro, Powell Hill's and Dick Ewell's—but their complement had been somewhat changed. In Taliaferro's division the Stonewall Brigade was now led by William S. Baylor, the commonwealth attorney for the city of Staunton. While he lacked formal military training, he was an impassioned fighter and a favorite of Jackson. Replacing Thomas Garnett in charge of the 2nd Brigade was Bradley T. Johnson of Maryland, a Princeton graduate and lawyer. Alexander Taliaferro retained the 3rd Brigade. Taylor's 2nd Louisiana Brigade, now in Taliaferro's division, was headed by General

William E. Starke, a Virginian who had served under Charles Field during the Seven Days.

Hill's Light Division remained the same, its brigades comprised of Lawrence Branch's and Dorsey Pender's North Carolinians, Edward Thomas's Georgians, Maxcy Gregg's South Carolinians, James Archer's Tennesseans and Field's Virginians. Ewell's division was comprised of Alexander Lawton's Georgians, Isaac Trimble's mixed brigade, Jubal Early's Virginians and the 1st Louisiana Brigade under Colonel Henry Forno, a former New Orleans chief of police.

Longstreet's 30,000-man right wing consisted of the divisions of Major General Dick Anderson, David "Neighbor" Jones, Cadmus Wilcox, John Bell Hood and James Kemper. Anderson commanded Lewis Armistead's and William Mahone's Virginians, and Ambrose "Rans" Wright's Georgians. One of David Jones's brigadiers was the Georgia politician Robert Toombs, currently under arrest for pigheadedly recalling pickets from the Verdiersville fords, thus almost causing Stuart's capture. Replacing Toombs was the part Cherokee Colonel Henry ("Rock") Benning. Jones's other commanders were Thomas Drayton, a 54-year-old West Pointer of uncertain competence, and the stalwart Georgian, Colonel George ("Tige") Anderson. Wilcox's division consisted of his own Alabamians; Winfield Scott Featherston, recovered from his wound, and his Mississippians; and Roger Pryor's mixed brigade. Hood commanded a minidivision—his own Texans and Georgians and Evander Law's mixed brigade. Kemper's men included the Virginia brigades of Banker Montgomery Corse and the wounded George Pickett, the latter now led by Lawyer Eppa Hunton, and the South Carolinians of Micah Jenkins. Back with the army from coastal duty in South Carolina was the colorful Nathan "Shanks" Evans of First Manassas fame, marching to his own drummer and commanding a so-called independent brigade.

In charge of the cavalry was Major General Jeb Stuart, whose two brigades at Second Manassas were headed by Beverly Robertson and Fitzhugh Lee. Robertson led the Laurel Brigade, the Virginia troopers who had been Ashby's, but he was no favorite of Jackson or Stuart. The former complained ceaselessly about his lack of initiative; the latter could not forget that he had been an old beau of Flora's and the protégé in the Old Army of his father-in-law. Robertson's regiments included the 2nd Virginia of Thomas Munford and the 6th Virginia of Thomas Flournoy, whom we have met, and the 7th Virginia of William E. ("Grumble") Jones. With a disposition as sour as Stuart's was sunny, Jones would continually clash with his superior. It was a pity, for he was an able and hard-fighting cavalryman. Fitz Lee's troopers included the 9th Virginia of Colonel W.H.F. ("Rooney") Lee, the 5th Virginia of Thomas Rosser and the 4th Virginia of Williams Carter Wickham. The broad-shouldered Rosser, a classmate and friend of Union cavalryman George Armstrong Custer at West Point, had resigned from the academy to join the

Confederacy. Wickham, severely wounded at Williamsburg and captured at his home during McClellan's advance, had just returned to duty after being exchanged for a kinsman of his wife.

Jackson was elated by his marching orders. Just as Lee in May had set him on Banks in the Valley, now he was unleashing him against Pope. He moved forward within hours: Ewell's division in the lead, followed by Hill, then by Taliaferro. Over the next two days, August 25–26, his columns would tramp a remarkable 54 miles, moving circuitously over Waterloo Bridge to Salem, then through unguarded Thoroughfare Gap to Bristoe Station and Manassas. "Now Hill's 'Light Division' was to earn its name and qualify itself for membership in Jackson's corps," said one member of the 55th Virginia, Field's brigade. "The hot August sun rose, clouds of choking dust enveloped the hurrying column, but on and on the march was pushed without relenting . . . haversacks were empty by noon, for the unsalted beef spoiled and was thrown away, and the column subsisted upon green corn and apples from the fields devoured while marching; for there were no stated meal times, no systematic halts for rest." A few hours for sleep, then on again. "There was no mood for speech, nor breath to spare if there had been—only the shuffling tramp of the marching feet, the steady rumbling of wheels . . . with an occasional order, uttered under the breath and always the same: 'Close up! Close up, men!' "[25]

The weary column at one point passed by Jackson, who had dismounted to observe their progress. "His men burst forth into their accustomed cheers, forgetting all their fatigue," said Dabney, "but, deprecating the tribute by a gesture, he sent an officer to request that there be no cheering as it might betray their presence to the enemy. . . . They at once passed the word down the column to their comrades."

Jackson could not conceal his pleasure over the army's spirit. "Who could not conquer, with such men as these?" he told his staff.[26]

Late on August 26 the Confederates fell on Bristoe Station, where the destruction of the rails would cut Pope's supply line from Washington. Munford's cavalry regiment and Henry Forno's Louisiana Brigade, brushing aside the pickets, took the station and accomplished the task in short order. One supply train was derailed; then a second crashed into the rear of the first in the gloom and compounded the damage. That night old Isaac Trimble, leading the 800 muskets of the 21st North Carolina and the 21st Georgia and accompanied by Stuart's cavalry, pressed on five miles to capture the rich Federal supply base at Manassas. Will two regiments be enough, Jackson had asked the Marylander. "I beg your pardon, General, but just give me my two Twenty-ones and I'll charge and capture hell itself!" was the reply.[27] Trimble was as good as his word. Advancing in the darkness his men crushed the Union pickets, took the guns and put the infantry to rout. The whole affair was over in minutes, at a cost of four Confederate casualties.

"Halloo, Georgia, where are you?" one North Carolina officer called out in the blackness.

"Here, all right! We have taken a battery!"

"So have we!" the Carolinian hollered.

Reported Trimble proudly: "Each of the two batteries contained four field pieces, horses, equipments, and ammunition complete."[28]

Next morning, August 27, Powell Hill's and Taliaferro's divisions moved to Manassas Junction, Ewell's temporarily remaining at Bristoe Station. Still the Federal high command in Washington had little inkling that Pope had been flanked, instead thinking the action a cavalry raid. "Our troops had barely been placed in position," said Taliaferro, "when a gallant effort was made by General [George] Taylor, with a New Jersey brigade, to drive off the supposed raiding party and recapture the stores; but, rushing upon overwhelming numbers, he lost his own life, two hundred prisoners, and the train that had transported them from Alexandria."[29] Later that day Ewell fought a delaying action at Bristoe against the van of Pope's army advancing from the Rappahannock, then fell back to Manassas.

Between battles, Jackson's troops feasted on the food and drink at the Federal supply base as only near-starving men could, later destroying what they could not carry or consume. "I soon found a room filled with officer's rations and several soldiers supplying themselves with coffee, sugar, molasses, etc.," said a member of the Stonewall Brigade. "We found a barrel of whiskey, which we soon tapped; but as we had our canteens full of molasses, and our tin cups full of sugar, we had nothing to drink out of. We found an old funnel, however, and while one would hold his hand over the bottom of it another would draw it full. In this way it was passed around." Explained one of Bradley Johnson's men: "It was hard to decide what to take, some filled their haversacks with cakes, some with candy, others oranges, lemons, canned goods, etc. I know one who took nothing but French mustard . . . and it turned out to be the best thing taken, because he traded it in for meat and bread." Marveled one of Maxcy Gregg's South Carolinians: "Fine whiskey and segars circulated freely, elegant lawn and linen handkerchiefs were applied to noses hitherto blown by the thumb and forefinger. Hard-tack and bacon, coffee and sugar, soap even was distributed to us, and we were invited to help ourselves to anything in the storehouses, from a dose of calomel to a McClellan saddle." Leaving Manassas to take up new positions, Jackson's tough troops looked almost comic. "Here was one fellow bending beneath the weight of a score of boxes of cigars," said Kyd Douglas, "another with as many boxes of canned fruits, another with coffee enough for a winter encampment, or perhaps with a long string of shoes hung around his neck."[30]

The lethal business of war, however, was never far from mind. Edward Moore of the Rockbridge Artillery reflected on the guns and munitions taken from the Federals, including two pieces "made of a bronze-colored metal, and of a different style from any we had yet seen. In our last battle, that of [Cedar] Mountain, we had noticed a singular noise made by some of the guns pointed at us, quite like the shrill note of a tree frog on a big scale. . . . Here it was, and known as the three-inch rifled gun, a most accurate shooter. . . . In view of the fact that almost all the field artillery used by the Confederates was manufactured in the North, a supply for both armies seems to have been wisely provided."[31]

Learning that Pope had awakened to his flanking movement and was advancing on Manassas to destroy him before Longstreet could come to his support, Jackson on August 28 moved along various routes to Groveton, a hamlet at the intersection of the Warrenton-Washington Turnpike and the Sudley Springs Road no more than ten miles from Thoroughfare Gap. There he concealed his divisions—Hill's men to the far left near Sudley, Ewell's in the center, Taliaferro's on the right—behind a ridge just north of and parallel to the pike. Jackson did not know of course just when the lead elements of McClellan's army would reinforce Pope but, outnumbered more than two-to-one, he was intent on engaging him before they came up.

In late afternoon a courier arrived, bringing the news that Lee was at Thoroughfare Gap and would cross the next morning. "Where is the man who brought this dispatch?" asked Jackson. "I must shake hands with him." Old Jack celebrated with cold buttermilk provided by William Blackford. Soon a mile-long Federal column, the 10,000-man division of General Rufus King, appeared on the pike. "Jackson rode out to examine the approaching foe," Blackford said, "trotting backwards and forwards among the line of the handsome parade marching by, and in easy musket range of their skirmish line, but they did not seem to think that a single horseman was worthy of their attention." Every officer in his command, still concealed behind the ridge, now was watching his every movement. "All felt sure Jackson never could resist the temptation, and the order to attack would come . . . even if Longstreet was beyond the mountain." Near sunset he wheeled and galloped back to his generals and staff.

"Here he comes, by God," said several.

"Bring out your men, gentlemen," Jackson said in a soft voice, touching his hat in military salute.

"The men," said Blackford, "had been watching their officers with as much interest as they had been watching Jackson, and when they dashed toward them they knew what it meant, and from the woods arose a hoarse roar like that from cages of wild beasts at the scent of blood."[32]

In truth the Confederate attack, while violent, was piecemeal. Hill's troops, too far away, never did engage. Taliaferro initially committed only Colonel William Baylor and the Stonewall Brigade, Ewell only the Georgians of Alexander Lawton and the Georgians, Alabamians and North Carolinians of Isaac Trimble. Facing them were the rugged Wisconsin and Indiana men of

General John Gibbon, soon to become famous as the "Iron Brigade." Though outnumbered, they refused to budge. "There was no disposition on the part of the Federals to avoid the onset, but on the contrary they met us half-way," reported Taliaferro. "A farm-house, an orchard, a few stacks of hay, and a rotten 'worm' fence were the only cover afforded to the opposing lines of infantry; it was stand-up combat, dogged and unflinching, in a field almost bare." The lines were no more than one hundred yards apart. "They stood as immovable as the painted heroes in a battle-piece. . . . In this fight there was no maneuvering, and very little tactics—it was a question of endurance, and both endured."[33] John Casler's company in the Stonewall Brigade went into battle with seventeen men and suffered eleven casualties. "We had a terrible fight, which lasted until 9 o'clock at night, neither party giving back . . . and being guided in our firing by the flash of each other's guns. . . . My brigade was behind an old fence, and would lie down, load and fire, and it seemed that everyone who would raise up was shot."[34]

This encounter at Groveton, while only a prelude to Second Manassas, produced severe casualties for those engaged. Confederate losses were 1,200 out of 4,500, the enemy 1,100 out of 2,800. The Stonewall Brigade was reduced to some 430 men, less than regimental strength. Gibbon's Iron Brigade suffered more than one-third casualties. Jackson moreover lost two more division chiefs. William Taliaferro went down with wounds to the foot, neck and arm, though he would return in time for Fredericksburg. Far worse was the able Dick Ewell's plight. Personally leading a regiment against the 6th Wisconsin, he took a bullet in the left knee and tibia that necessitated the amputation of the leg. He would return just before Gettysburg, nursed back to health by Lizinka, but he would not be the same soldier. General William E. Starke, a prosperous New Orleans cotton broker who had been commanding Taylor's old 2nd Louisiana Brigade, replaced Taliaferro and was succeeded in turn on the brigade level by Leroy Stafford. Alexander Lawton, a West Pointer and graduate of Harvard Law School, replaced Ewell.

Walking through the battlefield that night while men were doing what they could for the wounded, William Blackford came across a sobbing boy, no more than fifteen or sixteen years old. Before he could go to his aid the young soldier's father, the captain of his company, came up in the darkness.

"Charley, is that you?"

"Oh yes!" was the reply. "Father, my leg is broken but I don't want you to think that is what I am crying for; I fell in a yellow-jackets' nest and they have been stinging me. . . . That is what makes me cry." His father could only hold him until he died.

By light of day the lines of battle, marked by corpses, were still distinct. Noted Blackford: "The bodies lay in so straight a line that they looked like troops lying down to rest. On each front the edge was sharply defined, while toward the rear it was less so . . . showing how men had staggered backward after receiving their death blow."[35] Despite the cost, Groveton for Jackson was a resounding tactical success. His intent had been to draw Pope's army into battle, and he had achieved his goal. Soon 50,000 or more Federals, luckily for Jackson in an uncoordinated way, would be converging on his 18,000. But if Longstreet joined him in time, the two Confederate wings would have Pope in a deadly trap.

August 29 found Jackson falling back one mile from the ridge, forming most of his mile-and-a-half defensive line along the protection afforded by an unfinished railway bed. Powell Hill was on the left near Bull Run Creek; Ewell's men under Lawton held the center, Taliaferro's under Starke the right near Groveton. Pope meanwhile was having difficulty concentrating his forces. His assaults this day while bloody were sequential, and chiefly aimed at Hill on the left. There Maxcy Gregg's South Carolinians stood, their front in an obtuse angle, facing elements of Samuel Heintzelman's Third Corps. Seeing the Federals coming up that morning, Gregg the lover of Greek and Latin poetry ordered a charge. "The battle raged furiously," said one of his officers. "On the right the 13th and the 1st [South Carolina] pressed back the stubborn enemy through the thick undergrowth, killing large numbers, and losing heavily themselves." Colonel Oliver Edwards, a pious Baptist, was in command. "High above the roar of battle rang his clear voice, as he moved up and down his line, cheering on his men, directing their fire, and even supplying them with cartridges." On the left Colonel Dixon Barnes, a wealthy planter with a long white beard, "charged the enemy with his characteristic impetuosity, and cleared the woods, for two or three hundred yards, of all the troops they could throw against him." Colonel Jehu Marshall, a lawyer, then advanced with his Orr's Rifles, "and the two regiments charged and routed a fresh line moving against our position."

Recalled at noon to their original placement on the railroad, Gregg's men soon found themselves in greater peril when the Federals exploited a 150-yard gap between their line and that of Edward Thomas's Georgians to their right. "The railroad cut was quite deep opposite this opening . . . the enemy were enabled to crawl into the cut and creep up unseen," the officer continued. "Then they suddenly made a dash forward and almost drove through the belt of woods in which we were, thereby cutting the brigade completely off." Colonel Samuel McGowan, the son of Scotch-Irish immigrants, rushed into the breach with the 14th South Carolina and fell "promptly and vigorously on the intruders and, after a brief and desperate struggle, sent them flying in disorder." Still the Federals came on. In mid-afternoon, "they closed in upon us from front and right and left, pressing up with an energy never before witnessed by us. . . . The firing was incessant. They seemed determined not to abandon the undertaking; we were resolved never to yield. There was a perfect death storm all around."[36]

Fragmented as the Federal attacks were, sheer weight of numbers was telling. "Late in the afternoon I had occasion to visit A.P. Hill," remembered Kyd Douglas, Jackson's staff officer. "The last two attacks had been directed particularly against him, and the last of the two barely repulsed. One of his brigades was out of ammunition, and details were out on the field collecting cartridges from the boxes of the dead and wounded." Hill told the aide to ride to Jackson and inform him he could not hold out. "Such a message from a fighter like Hill," said Douglas, "was weighty with apprehension."

When he heard the news, Jackson's expression darkened.

"Tell him if they attack him again he must beat them," he said sharply.

Douglas galloped off, only to find Jackson following. Soon the two of them met Hill.

"General, your men have done nobly," Jackson pointedly told Little Powell. "If you are attacked again, you will beat the enemy back."

Gunfire interrupted the meeting.

"Here it comes!" Hill shouted, turning his horse toward the front.

"I'll expect you to beat them!" Old Jack called after him.[37]

Now Maxcy Gregg came into his own. "Tell General Hill that my ammunition is exhausted, but that I will hold my position with the bayonet!" he informed an aide.

"This was absolutely true," recalled Lieutenant Colonel Edward McCrady of the 1st South Carolina Volunteers. "The ammunition we had carried into action had been expended for some time. . . . General Gregg drew up the remnants of his five regiments, now reduced to a mere handful, in two lines. . . . We were upon the top of the hill, the point to which we had been driven back, some two or three hundred yards from the railroad excavation." Here after enduring five attacks they awaited the final assault.

"I can see him now," McCrady continued, "as with his drawn sword, that old Revolutionary scimitar we all knew so well, he walked up and down the line, and hear him as he appealed to us to stand by him and die there. 'Let us die here, my men, let us die here.' And I do not think that I exaggerate when I say that our little band responded to his appeal."

In the midst of this last attack the South Carolinians, shoulder to shoulder with Edward Thomas's Georgians, heard alarming shouts behind them. "Was all the glorious fight we had made the livelong day to end in our capture by an unseen movement to our rear? Terror stricken we turned, when lo! there were our friends coming to our assistance. . . . Field with his Virginians and Pender with his North Carolinians, relieved by Early and Forno, came rushing up. . . . The Federals halted, turned and fled."[38]

Longstreet's column had been up on Jackson's right for hours, and while it took no part in the fighting that day, its arrival had released Jubal Early's Virginians and Henry Forno's Louisianans from the task of protecting Jackson's flank. Now they had double-quicked to where they were most needed.

A courier brought Jackson the news. "General Hill presents his compliments and says the attack of the enemy was repulsed."

"Tell him I knew he would do it," answered Jackson, while rebel yells of triumph resounded through the air.[39]

When darkness ended the battle, the Confederates listed their casualties. Gregg's brigade understandably had suffered the most, losing some 600 men. Forty-one of his forty-three officers had been either killed or wounded. Of the brigade commanders Generals Trimble and Field were severely wounded, as was Colonel Forno.

The big question of course was whether Longstreet, whose divisions had been up since late morning, should have assailed Pope that day instead of waiting for the next. Old Pete was already showing he was a defensive commander who preferred that the enemy come to him, and when they did not he could drag his feet. "Longstreet, with a complacency it is difficult to understand, has related how he opposed [Lee's] wishes," said a critical commentator. "Three times Lee urged him forward. The first time he rode to the front to reconnoitre and found that the position, in his own words, 'was not inviting.' Again Lee insisted that the enemy's left might be turned. While the question was under discussion, a heavy force (Fitz-John Porter, leading some of the first troops returning from the Peninsula, and Irwin McDowell, the defeated commander at First Manassas) was reported advancing from Manassas Junction. No attack followed, however, and Lee repeated his instructions. Longstreet was still unwilling. A large portion of the Federal force on the Manassas road now marched north to join Pope, and Lee, for the last time, bade Longstreet attack toward Groveton. 'I suggested,' says the latter, 'that the day being far spent it might be as well to advance just before night upon a forced reconnaissance, get our troops in the most favorable positions, and all things ready for battle the next morning. To this [General Lee] reluctantly gave consent.' "[40] This frustrating exchange would be a harbinger of future events at Gettysburg.

Longstreet, a solid and capable officer, viewed his conduct not as procrastination but prudence. "At half-past four on the afternoon of the 29th," he wrote, "[Pope] issued an order for Porter to attack Jackson's right, supposing I was at Thoroughfare Gap, when in fact I had been in position since noon, and was anxiously awaiting attack. . . . If I had advanced upon Pope I would have been under enfilade fire from Porter's batteries, and if I had advanced upon Porter I would have been under fire from the batteries on Pope's front. . . . Had Porter attacked me. . . . The result would have been Porter's retreat in confusion, and I might possibly have reached Pope's left and rear in time to cut him off."[41] Porter in part because of muddled orders did not attack, however, and Jackson's troops that day did all the fighting.

Colonel Evander Law, who was marching with Hood at the head of Longstreet's column, felt Old Pete should have attacked on the 29th. "Before 10 o'clock [we] reached Jackson's battle-field, where heavy artillery fire then was going on," he said. "I am absolutely certain that Hood's division reached there not later than [that] time. . . . Our division was thrown quickly into line . . . until Jackson's flank was cleared. . . . The other troops of Longstreet's command were now rapidly coming up. [James] Kemper with three brigades took position to the right of Hood, and D.R. Jones' Division still farther to the right. [Shanks] Evans' Brigade came up in rear of Hood, and [Cadmus] Wilcox' three brigades were posted in rear of the interval between Longstreet's left and Jackson's right."[42] Soon they would be joined by Dick Anderson's division and Stephen D. Lee's artillery battalion.

Not until dusk, however, did Law's and the Texas brigades move forward for the reconnaissance in force Longstreet belatedly suggested, and then with little effect. "Longstreet seemed disposed to let Jackson maintain the contest unaided save by the artillery under his command," commented one Texan. "General Lee, at sunset, ordered [us] forward. . . . Much to its surprise the Texas Brigade was not fired upon by even Federal skirmishers . . . and by the time the main line reached the open ground . . . it was too dark to distinguish friends from foes at ordinary musket range." Unable to keep a straight line in the darkness, Law's and the Texas brigades began to converge.

"Halt!" a voice cried out, followed by several shots.

"The brigade came to a sudden stop, the men standing motionless. A minute later the caution came whispered from man to man: 'Silence! We are surrounded by the enemy.'

"We asked each other in whispers how in the mischief we had got ourselves into such a trap. It had been easy to do so; moving forward on converging lines, the two brigades had simply driven themselves, wedge-like, into the unoccupied space between two Federal brigades."[43]

Waiting some time to restore the silence of the night, and then moving as noiselessly as possible, Hood's men made their escape.

Hour after hour passed on August 30 with the two armies poised motionless. Jackson did not ask for troop reinforcements but Lee nonetheless placed the artillery of Colonel Stephen D. Lee (no relation) on his right flank. Sited on a 60-foot ridge and at right angles to Jackson's lines, the guns could sweep the open meadow in his front for a mile or more. Together with other artillery they would provide a deadly crossfire. "Since the experience of the Seven Days," Porter Alexander said, "Gen. Lee had begun to throw his isolated batteries together into battalions of artillery. Usually four batteries (three of 4 guns each & one of 6, making 18 guns in all) constituted a battalion, which was commanded by two field officers. But one of Longstreet's battns. was an unusually large one, comprising 5 batteries—22 guns—under Col. Stephen D. Lee and Maj. Del Kemper. . . . It had a beautiful position in easy range & the weight of its fire was very effective in breaking up the enemy's lines."[44]

At 3 P.M. the boom of a single cannon signaled the Federal attack. Either ignorant or uncaring of Longstreet's whereabouts in his determination to crush Jackson once and for all, the befuddled Pope this day sent Fitz Porter's columns rapidly toward the Confederate right, where the Stonewall Brigade and the rest of Jackson's old division under William Starke awaited them. "It was one continuous roar," said a man in the 33rd Virginia of the assault. "My brigade was in a small cut, with a field in front sloping down about 400 yards to a piece of wood. The enemy would form in the woods and come up the slope in three lines as regular as if on drill, and we would pour volley after volley into them as they came; but they would still advance until within a few yards of us, when they would break and fall back to the woods, where they would rally and come again."[45] But on the part of the line manned by Lieutenant Ezra Stickney of the 5th Virginia, the enemy seemed to come out of nowhere. "The Federals came up in front of us as suddenly as man rising up out of the ground," he said, "showing themselves at the old railroad line . . . in double battle phalanx and coming forward in slow time, pouring shot into our ranks in unmerciful volume."[46]

When the color-bearer of the 33rd Virginia fell mortally wounded Colonel Baylor snatched the banner.

"Boys, follow me!" he yelled.

"We did follow him, shouting and firing, out into the field," said one of his men, "only to see the brave man shot down, wrapped in the flag he carried, pierced by many bullets and dead." Next taking up the colors was Captain Hugh White, a minister-in-training who had worshipped with Baylor at a prayer service the night before. He too went down with mortal wounds. Command now devolved on the hard-swearing Colonel Andrew Jackson Grigsby, who sent an aide to Jackson to tell him that Baylor was dead and the brigade was crumbling.

"What brigade, sir?" said Jackson, not hearing Baylor's name amid the gunfire.

"The Stonewall Brigade, sir," repeated the aide.

"Go back," said Jackson, "give my compliments to them, and tell the Stonewall Brigade to maintain her reputation."[47]

On the Stonewall Brigade's left Bradley Johnson's Virginians and Leroy Stafford's Louisianans likewise found themselves under intense pressure, as did Trimble's old Brigade, now commanded by Captain William Brown, the sexagenarian whose spirit had impressed Jubal Early at Cedar Mountain. The Federals, remembered one man in the 15th Alabama, "were so thick it was impossible to miss them. . . . What a slaughter! What a slaughter of men that was." Here the lines came within yards of each other. Stated Bradley Johnson: "I saw a Federal flag hold its position for half an hour within ten yards of a flag of one of the regiments in the [railroad] cut and go down six or eight times, and after the fight 100 dead were lying twenty yards from the cut, some of them within two feet of it." But the killing was using up the ammunition. In Johnson's and Stafford's brigades the fire began to lessen, simply because the men had no more bullets.

"Boys, give them the rocks," one of Stafford's men cried.[48]

That the Louisianans did, picking up the ample supply of stones lying in the cut and hurling them at the enemy. Fist-sized rocks were thrown like baseballs; larger ones were tossed up in the air to fall on the foe crouched below. Before the battle ended, Stafford's brigade would incur some 385 casualties.

On the far Confederate left Powell Hill's men, facing elements of Irwin McDowell and Samuel Heintzelman's commands, suffered less grievously than the previous day. "In perfect array," said an officer of the 47th Virginia in Field's brigade, "[the Yankees] kept step as if on dress parade, and bore their banners proudly. I looked for a terrific shock, but before they came to close quarters with us, the Confederate artillery . . . opened up on their closed ranks and wrought such fearful destruction as, I believe, was not dealt in any other battle of the entire war." One of Pender's men was more direct: "We slaughtered them like hogs. I never saw the like of dead men in all my life."[49]

Jackson was holding his own, but barely. With both his reserves and his ammunition running out, he reluctantly asked for help. Lee ordered Longstreet, who still had not yet launched his attack on Porter's flank, to send a division to Jackson's support. Here Old Pete made a sensible decision. Realizing it would take infantry an hour or more to reach Jackson, he instead rushed additional batteries to Stephen Lee and instructed him to open fire immediately. That Pope's assault was blunted, so soon after it began, was due to large part to the enfilading fire of these massed guns on Jackson's right. The Federals who had reached the railway cut were pinned down by the awesome shellfire in the open ground behind them. Meanwhile reinforcements venturing through the storm of iron were devastated. "As shell after shell burst into the wavering ranks," said one of the gunners, "and round shot ploughed broad gaps among them, you could distinctly see, through the rifts of smoke, the Federal soldiers falling and flying on every side. With the dispersion of the enemy's reserve, the whole mass broke and ran like a flock of wild sheep."[50]

Now about 4 P.M. Longstreet moved his divisions forward, intent on destroying Porter's shattered lines and turning the Federal left. His object was Henry Hill on the old Manassas battlefield, where he would control the Warrenton Pike and cut the line of retreat to Washington.

John Bell Hood's command backed by Shanks Evans spearheaded the assault, pushing straight up the pike. Emerging from some woods the 5th Texas soon found itself face to face with the 5th New York Zouaves, clad in their distinctive red trousers, blue jackets and white leggings. "The Zouaves were first to fire," said a regimental officer, "but most of their shots went far astray from the mark. . . . Following almost on the instant, but with far better aim, was the volley of the Fifth Texas and seemingly one-half of the Zouaves fell, cut down in their tracks." Within the next ten minutes 120 of them would be killed and 180 wounded out of 500. Beyond the Zouaves the 4th Texas overwhelmed a Federal battery commanded by Captain Mark Kerns, a native Virginian. "Although nearly all his men had fallen," said one admiring Texan, "he loaded and fired his guns until he himself was struck down when we were only a few steps from him."

"I promised to drive you back, or die under my guns, and I have kept my word," Kerns said, almost with his last breath.[51]

By 5 P.M., however, Hood's swift advance against Porter came to a standstill. Longstreet's other divisions, all experiencing problems with terrain and distance, needed more time before closing to his support. Kemper, D.R. Jones and Dick Anderson eventually assembled on his right, Wilcox on his left. The respite gave McDowell, now in charge on the Federal left, the opportunity to rally his troops in strong defensive lines—first on Chinn Ridge, then on Henry Hill itself. When darkness fell, they then withdrew across the Stone Bridge and Bull Run Creek, leaving the ground littered with dead comrades and abandoned guns. Second Manassas cost the Federals more than 16,000 casualties; the Confederates, some 9,200. Pope had been routed, but he had escaped Lee's trap.

Still there was ample cause for rejoicing. The Army of Northern Virginia, just two months before huddled on the banks of the Chickahominy, now loomed on the banks of the Potomac. Lee proudly wired Jefferson Davis: "This army achieved today on the plains of Manassas a signal victory over combined forces of Genls McClellan and Pope. On the 28th and 29th each wing under Genls Longstreet and Jackson repulsed with valour attacks made on them separately. . . . Our gratitude to Almighty God for His mercies rises higher and higher each day, to Him and the valour of our troops a nation's gratitude is due."[52]

That night Jackson saw a soldier crawling with difficulty out of the railroad cut, and inquired if he was wounded.

"Yes, General, but have we whipped 'em?"

Jackson told him the Confederates had swept the field, and asked the man his unit.

"I belong to the 4th Virginia, your old brigade, General. I have been wounded four times but never as bad as this. I hope I will soon be able to follow you again."

"You are worthy of the old brigade," said Jackson in a grave voice, "and I hope with God's blessing you will soon be well enough to return to it."[53]

On the brigadier level Charles Field, Billy Mahone and Micah Jenkins had been wounded as well, as had Colonel Jerome Robertson of the 4th Texas. Of Shanks Evans's four regimental commanders, two were killed and two wounded.

Just before the battle General Field's wife, Nimmie, had dreamed presciently about her husband's injury. "He was carried to a house, & the building being already full of wounded, was laid under a tree in the yard," said Porter Alexander, to whom she recounted the story. "Soon the surgeons examined the wound, &, believing it mortal, did nothing more . . . passing on to other sufferers where prompt attention might save life. He lay under the tree all night. A surgeon's operating table stood near & amputations were going on upon it, the sights & sounds distressing Mrs. Field in her dream very much. In the morning she saw the surgeons re-examine the wound & heard them say that if he lived ten days he would recover."

The next morning she began her journey to her husband's bedside, arriving before the ten days had elapsed. Continued Porter Alexander: "She and Gen. Field always asserted that on comparison they found an accurate agreement of all the details of her dream. Gen. F. also mentioned in talking to her how he was himself distressed by the proximity of the operating table. But she would not tell him about the ten-day opinion until after that day had passed, though he had asked her specially, 'Nimmie is that *all* you dreamed?' She would evade a direct reply, but after the tenth day she told him what she had dreamed."

"Yes, the surgeons did say that very thing," he answered, "& I overheard them, & I was trying to find out if you had dreamed that also when I questioned you, but I did not want to tell you until the time was over."[54]

# SEVEN

\* \* \* \*

# STANDOFF IN MARYLAND

In the aftermath of Second Manassas emotions in Washington ranged from panic to plain indignation. How could a Federal force so superior in numbers and guns, radical Republicans wanted to know, so easily be put to rout? Charges of treason against McClellan, for moving too slowly to reinforce Pope, filled the air. In the midst of the brouhaha Lincoln and General-in-Chief Henry Halleck made some hard decisions. The Army of Virginia was merged with the Army of the Potomac, the defeated Pope transferred to the Northwest to fight the Sioux and, amazingly, the less than combative McClellan restored to overall command. "We must use the tools we have," Lincoln told his aide John Hay, viewing the appointment as a necessary evil. "There is no man in the Army who can . . . lick these troops of ours into shape half as well as he. If he can't fight himself, he excels in making others ready to fight." McClellan, of course, was as confident as ever. "[Lincoln] asked me if I would, under the circumstances, as a favor to him, resume command and do the best that could be done," he said. "Without one moment's hesitation and without making any conditions whatsoever, I at once said that . . . I would stake my life I could save the city."[1] Little Mac's reappointment, as Lincoln knew it would, invigorated the army.

"General McClellan is here!" the cry went out the first night he visited his troops.

"The enlisted men caught the sound!" said one witness. "Whoever was awake aroused his neighbor. Eyes were rubbed and those tired fellows . . . sent up such a hurrah as the Army of the Potomac had never heard before.

Shout upon shout went out. . . . The effect of the man's presence was electrical, and too wonderful to make it worthwhile attempting to give a reason for it."[2]

In early September Lee crossed the Potomac into Maryland, in large part not to seek out battle but to feed his army. He could not live off the land in the devastation of northern Virginia, and falling back to the fertile Shenandoah would encourage the enemy to follow or even march again on Richmond. Moving into the bountiful farmland of Maryland, where men hopefully could find provisions and animals forage, seemed far the better course. Meanwhile the Federals would have no choice but to pursue him. "The army is not properly equipped for an invasion," he acknowledged in a letter to President Davis. "It lacks much of the material of war, is feeble in transportation, the animals being much reduced, and the men are poorly provided with clothes, and in thousands of instances are destitute of shoes." Lee would not shy from battle, however. "Though weaker than our opponents in men and military equipment," he would "endeavor to harass [them] if we cannot destroy them. . . . I do not consider success impossible."[3]

However tattered, hungry and footsore they might be, Lee's men after their successes in the Valley, the Seven Days and Second Manassas now possessed an esprit de corps of inestimable value. "His army had acquired that magnificent morale which made them equal to twice their numbers, & which they never lost," said Ordnance Officer Porter Alexander. "And his confidence in them, & theirs in him, were so equal that no man can yet say which was greatest. . . . By going into Maryland Gen. Lee could at least subsist his army for a while upon the enemy, & he doubtless hoped, too, for the chance to force the Federal army to come out & fight him under favorable conditions." By September 7, his entire force was in Frederick, Maryland. "We laid there and took a much needed rest for man & beast for four days," said Alexander. "And even that was scarcely enough, for stragglers were lining the roads, &, what with these & the killed and wounded at Second Manassas, divisions had sunk to little more than brigades, & brigades nearly to regiments."[4]

Lee nonetheless was ever the aggressor. If fortune smiled, his grand strategy in heading north even called for penetrating into Pennsylvania. Examining a map with General John G. Walker of Missouri, newly come to the army, he placed his finger on Harrisburg.

"That is the objective point of the campaign," he said, referring to the major bridge that carried the Pennsylvania Railroad across the Susquehanna River near Harrisburg. "I wish effectually to destroy that bridge, which will disable the Pennsylvania railroad for a long time. With the Baltimore and Ohio in our possession [that line would be captured earlier on the march through Maryland] and the Pennsylvania railroad broken up, there will remain to the enemy but one route of communication with the West, and that very circuitous, by way of the Lakes. After that I can turn my attention to Philadelphia, Baltimore or Washington, as may seem best to our interests."

"I was very much astonished at this announcement," said Walker, "and I suppose [Lee] observed it."

"You doubtless regard it hazardous to leave McClellan practically on my line of communication, and to march into the heart of the enemy's country?" the commander asked.

Walker admitted as much.

"Are you acquainted with General McClellan?" Lee said. "He is an able general but a very cautious one. His enemies among his own people think him too much so. His army is in a very demoralized and chaotic condition, and will not be prepared for offensive operations—or he will not think it so—for three or four weeks. Before that time I hope to be on the Susquehanna."[5] Fortune, alas, would not smile on this ambitious plan.

The Confederate force marching into Maryland, what with the problem of stragglers and the casualties of Second Manassas, totaled no more than 55,000 men. Longstreet's wing had been reinforced with the divisions of Lafayette McLaws and John G. Walker. McLaws's command consisted of Joseph Kershaw's South Carolinians, Howell Cobb's Georgians, Paul Semmes's mixed brigade and William Barksdale's Mississippians. Walker's minidivision was comprised of Robert Ransom's North Carolinians and his own mixed brigade, led by Colonel Van H. Manning, an Arkansas lawyer.

Longstreet's other full divisions were headed by Richard Heron Anderson and David "Neighbor" Jones. Dick Anderson's people consisted of Cadmus Wilcox's Alabamians under West Pointer Alfred Cumming, the wounded Billy Mahone's Virginians under Planter William Parham, Winfield Featherston's Mississippians under Carnot Posey (who had served with Jefferson Davis's Mississippi Rifles in Mexico), Lewis Armistead's Virginians, Roger Pryor's mixed brigade and Ambrose "Rans" Wright's Georgians. Jones's division was comprised of Robert Toombs's Georgians, Thomas Drayton's mixed brigade, the wounded Pickett's Virginians under Richard Garnett (he who had retreated without orders at Kernstown and was still anathema to Stonewall Jackson), James Kemper's Virginians, the wounded Micah Jenkins's South Carolinians under Colonel Joseph Walker, and George "Tige" Anderson's Georgians. Hood's minidivision, consisting of his own Texans under William Wofford and Evander Law's mixed brigade, completed Longstreet's command, along with Shanks Evans's independent brigade.

Jackson's wing had been reinforced by his brother-in-law Harvey Hill's division, comprised of Roswell Ripley's mixed brigade, Robert Rodes's Alabamians, Samuel Garland's and George Burgwyn Anderson's North Carolinians, and Alfred Colquitt's Georgians.

Jackson's three other divisions were Powell Hill's, Ewell's command under

Alexander Lawton and his own under John R. Jones. Hill's division was comprised of Lawrence Branch's North Carolinians, Maxcy Gregg's South Carolinians, the wounded Charles Field's Virginians under Lawyer John ("Beau") Brockenbrough, James Archer's Tennesseans, William Pender's North Carolinians and Edward Thomas's Georgians. Lawton's division included his own brigade under Marcellus Douglas, Jubal Early's Virginians, the wounded Trimble's mixed brigade under Colonel James A. Walker (whose quarrel with Jackson while a cadet at V.M.I. had brought on his dismissal) and Harry Hays's Louisianans. Jones's division was composed of the slain Winder's Virginians under Andrew Jackson Grigsby, the wounded Taliaferro's mixed brigade under Colonel Edward T. Warren, Jones's own Virginians under Bradley Johnson and William Starke's Louisianans.

William Pendleton's reserve artillery was added to the army's guns. Stuart's cavalry division also saw some changes: Fitz Lee retained his brigade but Beverly Robertson did not, being replaced by Thomas Munford, while Wade Hampton added a third brigade to the unit. Three batteries of horse artillery continued to be led by Major John Pelham.

The Confederate high command, meanwhile, was in battered condition during this period. Lee's stallion Traveler had become frightened and thrown him to the ground, severely injuring both hands and forcing him to wear splints. Jackson was suffering from a badly bruised back, the result of an unbroken mount rearing up and falling on him. Longstreet was in carpet slippers because of an ulcerated heel.

Upset one morning that his column's 4 A.M. start with Powell Hill in the lead was not yet underway, Jackson rode into camp to find out why. Coming across Gregg's men just then filling their canteens, he realized the division head had not checked on his brigades to see the marching order was obeyed and issued a mild rebuke. "Hill took this reprimand rather sullenly, his face flushing up, but said nothing," reported Jedediah Hotchkiss. To reinforce his point Jackson then raised his voice, telling Little Powell and the partially deaf Gregg: "There are but few commanders who properly appreciate the value of celerity!" By the time the column did break camp both Jackson and Hill were steaming. The latter officer set a fast pace in the van, determined he not again be accused of dawdling, but he made no periodic checks to make sure the Light Division kept closed up. Soon his column was badly strung out, with heavy straggling. When Hill did not even stop for the usual midday break to tighten ranks, the angry Jackson took matters in his own hands. Riding up to Edward Thomas, whose Georgians marched just behind Hill and his staff, he ordered a halt. Some minutes later, when Hill looked over his shoulder and saw no one following him, he galloped back to his troops.

"Why did you halt your command without orders?" he asked Thomas.

"I halted because General Jackson told me to do so," the brigadier said.

For Hill this was the ultimate insult: Jackson had given an order to one of his subordinates and ignored the chain of command. He hurled himself from his horse, whipped his sword from its scabbard and presented it to Jackson.

"If you take command of my troops in my presence, take my sword also," he said.

Jackson ignored the proffered blade. "Put up your sword and consider yourself under arrest," he replied.[6]

Lawrence Branch would temporarily take command of the Light Division. Hill would march forlornly on foot at the rear of his brigades, seething over the injustice he felt Jackson had done him.

Porter Alexander talked about Jackson's ways with his brother-in-law Alexander Lawton. "He told me that he was the only division commander in Jackson's corps not at that moment in arrest," Alexander wrote. "It seems that Gen. Jackson, at times, was something of a martinet—& this was one of his times. All, I believe, were arrested because Gen. J. had seen some of their men straggling on the march; & Lawton was in hourly fear lest Jackson might perhaps catch one of his men somewhere in the rear up an apple tree & send an aide ahead & tell Lawton to consider himself in arrest." Alexander conceded the army was straggling badly. "Provisions were scarce, but green-corn and apples were abundant. That diet, however, weakened the men, causing sickness, and had much to do with the straggling. But Gen. J. very soon released his unfortunate generals, and nothing came of it, though I can recall that A.P. Hill's arrest caused a great deal of talk. Possibly . . . Gen. Jackson saw the point of Gen. [Jubal] Early's reply; who, when he received a note with Gen. Jackson's compliments, & desiring to know why he saw so many stragglers in rear of Early's division that day, answered with his own compliments that it was probably because Gen. Jackson rode in rear of the division."[7]

Longstreet, of course, could be just as autocratic as Jackson. After Second Manassas John Bell Hood had commandeered several Federal ambulances left on the field. Sometime later Shanks Evans, recently named a major general with nominal authority over Hood, ordered that they be turned over to his South Carolina brigade. Hood refused, saying: "I would cheerfully have obeyed directions to deliver them to General Lee's Quartermaster for the use of the army [but] I did not consider it just that I should be required to yield them to another Brigade of this Division, which was in no manner entitled to them."[8] Longstreet sided with Evans, placing Hood under arrest and nearly causing the Texans to mutiny.

Lee, Jackson and Longstreet pitched their tents close together during their stay in Frederick, and all received a stream of Southern sympathizers and well wishers, but Jackson unwillingly received the lion's share of attention. On one occasion, said Kyd Douglas, "he met an open carriage containing two bright Baltimore girls, who at sight of him sprang from the carriage, rushed up to him, one took his hand, the other threw her arms around him, and talked with the wildest enthusiasm, both at the same time, until he seemed simply miserable. In a minute or two their fireworks were expended, and they were driven away happy and delighted; he stood for a moment cap in hand, bowing, speechless, paralyzed. . . ." Jackson attended a church service on Sunday, September 7, falling asleep as usual during the sermon and awakening only when the choir began to sing. The preacher, said Douglas, "was afterward credited with much loyalty and courage because he prayed for the President of the United States in the presence of Stonewall Jackson. Well the General didn't hear [the prayer]; but if he had I've no doubt he would have joined in it heartily."[9]

Just a few miles to the southeast in Urbanna, Jeb Stuart gave a ball one night to show his appreciation for Maryland hospitality. Regimental flags bedecked the walls of a former school building, the band of the 18th Mississippi furnished the music, and moonlight and candles provided the lighting. Von Borcke led off the dancing with the queen of the ball, a visitor from the North called the "New York Rebel," and suggested a polka. He quickly switched to "a very lively quadrille" when the young lady informed him she could not join in a round dance with a man not of her own family.

"The dancing began, the strange accompaniments of war added zest to the occasion, and our lovely partners declared that it was perfectly charming," said William Blackford. "But they were destined to have more of the war accompaniment than was intended by the managers." Soon there came the boom of artillery, followed by the rattle of musketry. McClellan's advance guard was making a reconnaissance. "Being assured that it was probably only a night attack to feel our position, and that we might all return to finish the evening, [the ladies] agreed to await our return." After a sharp skirmish Stuart and his men returned and resumed the dance. "We hastened back 'covered with glory,' at least in the ladies' eyes," said Blackford. "Dancing was at its height again when it was doomed to a final interruption." Heavy tramping of feet attracted the attention of Blackford's partner, who looked through a doorway, saw the wounded being carried to the rooms upstairs and uttered a piercing scream. "It was no use talking of any more dancing that night," he continued ruefully. "There, like a flock of angels in their white dresses assembled around the stretchers, they bent over the wounded men, dressing their wounds and ministering to their wants, with their pretty fingers all stained with blood. . . . All that was left for us now was to escort the 'lovely angels' home by the light of the moon. . . ."[10]

Lee's expectation when he entered Maryland had been that the Federals at Harpers Ferry would evacuate the position and return to Washington. They had not done so, and now that he was moving farther north to Hagerstown he could not afford to leave them along his lines of communication. Earlier Longstreet had persuaded him to defer action on Harpers Ferry. Now Lee, knowing that swift action was needed, called Jackson to his tent and outlined his plan. Old Jack was to take his three divisions on a circuitous march and approach the town from Bolivar Heights to the south. McLaws with his own and Dick Anderson's divisions would have the most difficult task, scaling Maryland Heights from north of the Potomac, while John G. Walker's mini-division would approach from Loudoun Heights to the east. With guns on the heights on three sides the Confederates should quickly force the garrison's surrender. Jackson would be leading twenty-six of the army's forty brigades. Longstreet meanwhile would proceed to Boonsboro (en route to Hagerstown) with Hood's and Neighbor Jones's divisions, and Harvey Hill's brigades would be left near South Mountain as a rear guard. These instructions were listed in Lee's Special Order 191, dated September 9, and delivered to the division heads.

Jackson was again elated at the chance of semi-independent command. General Walker would remember that "he seemed in high spirits, and even indulged in a little mild pleasantry about his long neglect of his friends in 'the Valley,' General Lee replying that Jackson had 'some friends' in that region who would not, he feared, be delighted to see him."[11]

Within days Jackson, McLaws and Walker were menacing Harpers Ferry with their three-pronged assault and Lee and Longstreet were encamped in Hagerstown. On September 13, however, a private of the 27th Indiana in a vacated Confederate campsite near Frederick found three cigars wrapped in a copy of Special Order 191 addressed to Harvey Hill. This blatant bit of care-lessness was not Hill's fault, but that of some staff officer. Rushed to Federal headquarters and authenticated, the order informed McClellan not only that Lee had split his army but also exactly what he was doing with it, giving Young Napoleon a priceless opportunity to smash the foe. Late that night Lee learned through an informant that the Federals knew of his plans. Disaster now threatened. Harpers Ferry had not yet fallen, and only Harvey Hill's division was at South Mountain. Once the enemy streamed through its passes the divided Confederates would be at McClellan's mercy. Lee reacted force-fully. He ordered Jackson to speed up his bombardment, warned McLaws on Maryland Heights his rear might be threatened by Federals at South Mountain and dispatched Longstreet to Hill's support.

Just before Jackson's columns closed in upon Harpers Ferry, a conciliatory Powell Hill was restored to command. "[He] sent for me," said Kyd Douglas, "and requested me to say to General Jackson that it was evident a battle was at hand and he did not wish anyone else to command his division . . . he asked to be restored to it until the battle or battles were over, when he would (again) report himself under arrest." Douglas was more than happy to oblige. "I gave the message as forcibly as I could and ventured to add that no one could command Hill's division as well as he could. The General could not refuse a request to be permitted to fight. . . . Hill was soon in the saddle."[12]

Essential to reuniting the army was the quick capture of Harpers Ferry. The Confederate divisions were on their respective heights above the town by September 14, but moving forward the necessary artillery to crumble its resistance required the entire day. Walker's batteries opened up about 1 P.M., then Powell Hill's and Lawton's an hour later, then McLaws's an hour after that. "But the range from Maryland Heights being too great," said General Walker, "the fire of McLaws' guns was ineffective, the shells bursting in midair without reaching the enemy. From my position on Loudoun Heights my guns had a plunging fire on the Federal batteries a thousand feet below and did great execution. By 5 P.M. our combined fire had silenced all the opposing batteries. . . ." During the night the Confederates tightened the noose. Powell Hill advanced his cannon, "placing them on the slope of Loudoun Mountain, far below me, as to command the enemy's works. McLaws got his batteries into position nearer the enemy, and at daylight of the 15th the batteries of our five divisions were pouring their fire on the doomed garrison."[13]

One hour of heavy bombardment silenced all the Federal guns, and the garrison soon surrendered. "Owing to the heavy fog I was ignorant of what had taken place," Walker continued, "but surmising it, I ordered my batteries to cease firing. Those of Lawton, however, continued some minutes later. This happened unfortunately, as Colonel Dixon S. Miles, the Federal commander, was at that time mortally wounded by a fragment of shell while waving a white flag." In truth the late firing may have come not from Lawton's but from the Stonewall Brigade, which joined the bombardment that morning. "While engaged [on Bolivar Heights] early on the 15th," said Gunner William Poague, "I noticed on the enemy's works what I took to be a white flag and reported the fact to Colonel [Andrew] Grigsby commanding the brigade. . . . He either could not or would not see the flag, which now looked like a small tent fly, and ordered 'damn their eyes, give it to them.' " Even after the cease-fire, Grigsby remained bellicose. When Poague sent a messenger to ask in what direction he should discharge his still-loaded guns, Grigsby replied: "Tell him to fire them off the way they are pointed. He won't kill more of the damn Yankees than he ought to."[14]

Subsequently Powell Hill, with Jackson observing, was given the honor of accepting the surrender. The ranking Federal officer, Douglas noted, "was mounted on a handsome black horse, was handsomely uniformed, with an untarnished sabre, immaculate gloves and boots, and had a staff fittingly equipped. He must have been somewhat astonished to find in General Jackson the worst-dressed, worst mounted, most faded and dingy-looking general he had ever seen anyone surrender to, with a staff not much for looks or equipment." Old Jack nonetheless drew appreciative stares from Yankee soldiers, many of whom saluted him. "Boys, he's not much for looks," one of them yelled, "but if we had him we wouldn't have been caught in this trap!"[15] Verbal exchanges between the men in the ranks were still more irreverent.

"Hello, Johnny," one of the impressively uniformed prisoners challenged a captor, "why don't you wear better clothes?"

"These are good enough to kill hogs in," came back the reply.[16]

At 8 A.M. on September 15 Jackson informed Lee: "General: Through God's blessing, Harpers Ferry and its garrison are to be surrendered. . . . [Hill] will be left in command until the prisoners and public property shall be disposed of. . . . The other forces can move off this evening so soon as they get their rations."[17] The almost unscathed Confederates had taken 11,500 prisoners, 13,000 small arms, 73 guns, 200 wagons and a vast store of supplies. Wrote Jackson to Anna: "Our Heavenly Father blesses us exceedingly."[18] Hungry men spent much of the day feasting. "We fared sumptuously," reported one of Maxcy Gregg's men. "In addition to meat, crackers, sugar, coffee, shoes, blankets, underclothing, etc., many of us captured horses roaming at large, on whom to transport our plunder. The writer of this sketch confesses to the appropriation of two, of which, however, the quartermaster's department soon deprived him."[19]

Early on September 14, even as Lee was hurrying back to Boonsboro and South Mountain with Longstreet's divisions, Harvey Hill at Turner's Gap with no more than 5,000 men was watching the bulk of McClellan's 90,000-man force deploy against him in the valley to the east of his position. Luckily for the Confederates the Union general was moving with his usual lack of vigor. "The Federal were under the self-imposed illusion that there was a very large force opposed to them," said Harvey Hill, "whereas there was only one weak division until late in the afternoon. They might have brushed it aside almost without halting." (McClellan had interpreted the lost order as saying that Longstreet's troops would billet just behind the mountain at Boonsboro.) "It was a battle of delusions also," Hill went on, "for by moving about from point to point and meeting the foe wherever he presented himself, the Confederates deluded the Federals into the belief that the whole mountain was swarming with rebels."[20]

Thus far only two of Hill's five brigades were yet on hand. He quickly posted Alfred Colquitt's Georgians on both sides of the turnpike at Turner's Gap and sent Samuel Garland's North Carolinians to Fox's Gap, a smaller pass a half-mile to the south. There about 9 A.M. the first of the day's engagements took place, with some 1,000 North Carolinians defending against 3,000 troops comprising the van of the Federal Ninth Corps under Jesse Reno. Garland, the descendent of James Madison who had so tragically lost wife and daughter, was on the verge of future happiness. Richmond society was abuzz with the news that one of the city's most accomplished young women would soon be announcing their engagement. Such prospects did not cool Garland's fighting ardor. Lieutenant Colonel Thomas Ruffin Jr. of the 13th

North Carolina was in the midst of the assault when he noticed him at his elbow.

"General, why do you stay here? You are in great danger," Ruffin told him.

"I may as well be here as yourself," Garland answered.

"No, it is my duty to be here with my regiment, but you could better superintend your brigade from a safer position."

Just then Ruffin was struck down with a hip wound. Since he was the sole field officer left in his regiment he asked Garland to send someone to lead it. Instantly the brigadier also was hit. "He turned and gave some order," said Ruffin. "In a moment I heard a groan and looked and found him mortally wounded and writhing in pain."[21]

One of the regiments assailing the North Carolinians was the 23rd Ohio whose colonel, Rutherford B. Hayes, went down with an arm wound shouting, "Give 'em hell! Give the sons of bitches hell!" Likwise serving with the 23rd Ohio was Sergeant William McKinley, perhaps setting a regimental record for future presidents.[22]

It was now about noon. "Garland's Brigade, demoralized by his death and by the furious assault on its center," said Hill, "now broke in confusion and retreated behind the mountain. . . . The brigade was too roughly handled to be of any further use that day." Instead of moving directly on Turner's Gap, however, Union General Jacob Cox stopped to wait for support. "There was nothing to oppose him," Hill continued. "My three other brigades had not come up; Colquitt's could not be taken from the pike except in the last extremity." In desperation Hill ordered two guns forward to bluff the foe, forming a line of dismounted staff-officers, couriers, teamsters and cooks behind them to give the appearance of battery supports. "I do not remember ever to have experienced a feeling of greater *loneliness*. It seemed as though we were deserted by 'all the world and the rest of mankind.' " The ensuing lull would last for hours. By the time the three other divisions of the Union Ninth Corps came up, Hill had his remaining brigades in place. George Burgwyn Anderson's North Carolinians and Roswell Ripley's mixed brigade moved to the south near Fox Gap, Robert Rodes's Alabamians to the far north.

Still the lull continued, McClellan imparting no sense of urgency to his troops. "About 3:30 P.M. the advance of Longstreet's command arrived and reported to me—one brigade under Colonel [George "Tige"] Anderson and one under General [Thomas] Drayton. They were attached to Ripley's left, and a forward movement was ordered." The excitable Ripley, just as he had at Gaines's Mill, at this point lost his sense of direction. "In half an hour or more," Hill said mordantly, "I received a note from Ripley saying that he was progressing finely; so he was, to the rear of the mountain on the west side. Before he returned the fighting was over, and his brigade did not fire a shot that day."[23]

By now John Bell Hood also had been restored to command. Hundreds of his men, marching by Lee near Boonsboro on their way to reinforce Harvey Hill, one after the other shouted, "Give us Hood!"

"You shall have him, gentlemen," the impressed Lee responded, raising his hat in assent.

Resolute man that he was, Hood refused to apologize to either Longstreet or Evans for refusing to give up the ambulances.

"Well," Lee wisely said, "I will suspend your arrest till the impending battle is decided."[24] Hood rejoined his men amid wild cheering, and nothing further ever came of the charge.

Ripley's misdirection created a breach to the south or right of the pike between Tige Anderson and Drayton that the Federals swiftly penetrated. Desperate fighting closed the opening, but the lines swayed back and forth. Then Hood came up with his minidivision, his own Texas Brigade under Lawyer William Wofford and Evander Law's brigade. "McClellan's long lines could be seen moving up the slope in their front," said one Texan, "intending to dislodge the Confederate forces posted on the sharp ridges overlooking the valley." Hood took in the situation at a glance, moving "the command to the right of the turnpike, our troops on that side having been driven back. In the new position taken, the men were ordered to fix bayonets, and when the enemy came within a hundred yards, to fire and charge. The charge was made to the accompaniment of a rebel yell, and sent the Federals flying pell-mell."[25] Toward dusk in this engagement Union Major General Reno fell mortally wounded.

Like so many of Lee's men, Hood was inspirational in battle. Remembered his Richmond hostess: "When he came, with his sad Quixote face, the face of an old crusader who believed in his cause, his cross, his crown—we were not prepared for that type exactly as a beau ideal of wild Texans. Tall—thin— shy. Someone said that great reserve of manner he carried only into ladies' society. [Charles] Venable [an aide to Lee] added he had often heard of the 'light of battle' shining in a man's eyes. He had seen it once. He carried [Hood] orders from General Lee and found [him] in the hottest of the fight. 'The man was transfigured. The fierce light of his eyes. I can never forget.' "[26]

To the north of Turner's Gap and the pike the 17,000-man Union First Corps under Joseph ("Fighting Joe") Hooker meanwhile was assailing the Confederate left. It had taken them seven hours, but the Federals at 4 P.M. finally were advancing on two flanks, pincer-fashion, against Hill's defenders. There Hooker's men encountered the mustachioed and hard-fighting Robert Rodes and his 1,200-man Alabama Brigade, whose personnel included John Brown Gordon, the ramrodlike colonel of the 6th Alabama. Rodes fought tenaciously, falling back but buying time. He would suffer some 400 casualties, a third of his complement. Soon more of Longstreet's brigades came up in support—Evans, Richard Garnett and James Kemper. Here on the north the Federals gained more ground than on the south, but not control of the gap. Just before darkness came they made one more effort to break through, marching straight up toward Colquitt's Georgians and Alabamians, who had been posed in the Confederate center since early morning and seen little action. Chosen for the effort was John Gibbon's "Black Hat" Brigade, the tough Wisconsin and Indiana men who had gone head-to-head with Jackson at Groveton. One of the many ironies of the war was that Gibbon, a native North Carolinian, had been Harvey Hill's best man at his wedding.

"Oh you damned black hats, we gave you hell at Bull Run!" one Georgian yelled as the lines closed together.

"You thieving scoundrels, no McDowell after you now!" shouted a Yankee.[27] This last a not-so-veiled acknowledgement of Irvin McDowell's failures at First and Second Manassas.

The Midwesterners strove mightily but could not dislodge Colquitt's men from their position behind stone fences on the high ground. With darkness the tired men of both sides lay down to rest within a hundred yards of each other. The Federals suffered 1,800 casualties overall at Turner's Gap, the Confederates some 2,300.

McClellan could not believe that Hill's two brigades had for hours been the only troops blocking his way. In his official report, he insisted: "The force opposed to us at Turner's Gap consisted of D.H. Hill's corps (fifteen thousand), and a part if not the whole of Longstreet's, and perhaps a portion of Jackson's—probably thirty thousand in all." Rejoined Hill: "Thus it was that a thin line of men extending for miles along the crest of the mountain could afford protection for so many hours to Lee's trains and artillery and could delay the Federal advance until Longstreet's command did come up and, joining with mine, saved the two wings of the army from being cut in two."[28]

Six miles to the south at Crampton's Gap a more successful Federal assault on the mountain, one that threatened McLaws's rear, took place that same September 14 shortly after 2 P.M. Even as the Georgian was pushing his guns forward through the heavy underbrush on Maryland Heights, he learned that two divisions of William Franklin's Sixth Corps, some 12,000 men, were assailing 1,000 Confederates at Crampton's. "To observe the caution with which the Yankees, with their vastly superior numbers, approached the mountain," said one rebel, "put one very much in mind of a lion, king of the forest, making exceedingly careful preparations to spring on a plucky little mouse."[29] By 4 P.M. Crampton's defenders, Mahone's brigade under Colonel William Parham and Thomas Munford's dismounted Laurel Brigade, were in danger of being overwhelmed. "When they charged us I loaded my gun and took aim at an officer who was as large as Pa," one Virginian remembered, "and who was behaving very bravely bringing his men up cheering and talking to them all the while. I waited until they were 75 or 100 yards from where I was. I let fly at him and he threw his arms up in the air and fell."[30]

Howell Cobb's brigade, rushed back by McLaws from Maryland Heights to help, soon found itself caught up in a rout. Cobb, a former Speaker of the

U.S. House of Representatives, tried bravely to rally the men but to no avail. Paul Semmes's Georgians, likewise sent back by McLaws, fared no better. The best the two men could do was position some artillery to slow down the onrushing Federals.

By now both McLaws and Jeb Stuart, drawn by the accelerating gunfire, were on the scene. "Dismount, gentlemen, dismount, if your lives are dear to you!" Cobb feverishly greeted them. "The enemy is within fifty yards of us; I am expecting their attack every minute. Oh, my dear Stuart, that I should live to experience such a disaster! What can be done? What can save us?"[31] The normally self-possessed Howell Cobb was a statesman but not a soldier. Expletives flowing from the tongue of McLaws quickly extinguished his panic. Soon Stuart's troopers established that Franklin had halted at Crampton's and, for reasons unclear, was not pressing his advantage. The respite gave McLaws his opportunity. "I at once ordered up [Cadmus] Wilcox' Brigade . . . and rode toward the gap," he said. "Fortunately, night came on and allowed a new arrangement of the troops to meet the changed aspect of affairs. The brigades of Generals [Joseph] Kershaw and [William] Barksdale, excepting one regiment of the latter, and two pieces of artillery were withdrawn from the heights . . . and formed line of battle across the valley and about one and one-half miles from Crampton's Gap, with the remnants of the Brigades of Generals Cobb, Semmes and Mahone, and those of Wilcox, Kershaw and Barksdale . . . under command of General [Dick] Anderson."[32] Federal losses would be some 530; Confederate, 930.

From now through Gettysburg, Lafayette McLaws would command a division that was among the army's best. Kershaw's South Carolinians, Barksdale's Misisssippians and two brigades of Georgians under Howell Cobb (and later his younger brother Thomas Cobb) and Paul Semmes would establish themselves as pugnacious foes. McLaws, said one aide, "was an officer of much experience and most careful. Fond of detail, his command [always] was in excellent condition, and his ground and position well examined and reconnoitered."[33]

Late that night, just as the Confederate reverses at Turner's and Crampton's Gaps were forcing Lee to consider retreating across the Potomac, he received a message from Jackson advising him that the advance on Harpers Ferry, "which commenced this evening, has been successful thus far, and I look to Him for complete success tomorrow."[34] Confident that Jackson soon would be victorious and his army reunited, Lee instead resolved to fall back westward to a crossroads village called Sharpsburg, bordered by a creek named Antietam. Even if McClellan failed to follow him, and turned on McLaws, Lee would be on the Union general's flank and rear. So far as he was concerned, only the lost order had thus far spoiled his plans; the Army of Northern Virginia was a superb fighting machine, McClellan was his ineffectual self, and the Federals were demoralized. Two of those beliefs were true.

But the third, that the Federals were less than eager to take the field, was not, and the battle of Sharpsburg would be the bloody result.

Porter Alexander, Lee's ordnance officer, would be critical of his decision to fight. "Longstreet and D.H. Hill's divisions retreated from the South Mountain or Boonsboro battlefield on the night of the 14th, Sunday," he said. "About noon on [the] 15th they halted after crossing Antietam Creek & took position between the creek & Sharpsburg, which are nearly a mile apart." Soon Lee learned Harpers Ferry had surrendered. "That was the time for him to have taken those two divisions & recrossed into Va. & saved the bloodshed," Alexander continued. "Next morning 2 of Jackson's 3 divisions, J.R. Jones's and Ewell's under Lawton . . . were brought across & later [John G.] Walker's division also came over. By noon an immense Federal force was apparent on the other side of Antietam Creek." On the morning of September 17 some 75,000 Federal troops and 275 guns were massed in front of the Confederates. Lee thus far had perhaps 27,000 troops and 135 guns. "A.P. Hill's Division was still at Harpers Ferry 12 miles away," the ordnance officer explained. "McLaws's Division (with Dick Anderson's on its heels) had been marching all night & had halted near the river for breakfast. McLaws was forever afterwards called slow, because he did not come into the battle until about ten o'clock . . . but when he did come his men were in good condition & did beautiful & successful fighting." Even when the absent divisions arrived, Lee with the Potomac at his back would have no more than 40,000 troops and 195 guns.

Three of McClellan's corps would be on the Confederate left where Jackson commanded—the First under Joseph Hooker, the Twelfth under Joseph Mansfield and much later the Sixth under William Franklin. Opposite the Confederate center and right, where Longstreet stood poised with Harvey Hill's, Neighbor Jones's and John G. Walker's divisions, were Edwin Sumner's Second Corps and Ambrose Burnside's Ninth Corps. Fitz Porter's Fifth Corps was likewise at the center, but would see little action. "Had McClellan attacked along our whole line at dawn we had not the force to have withstood him long," Alexander concluded. "He let us get through the day only by making partial attacks & giving us the chance to concentrate nearly all we had to meet each one in succession."[35] Lee's line was about three miles long. Its right rested on the 60-foot-wide creek at what came to be called Burnside's Bridge, a mile in front of Sharpsburg, and its left bent back toward the Potomac, ending several miles north of the village and straddling the Hagerstown Turnpike near the infamous Cornfield.

At first light Hooker with some 10,000 men stormed Jackson's position, intent on turning his flank. The 4,000 defenders were at right angles to meet him—Jackson's old division under John R. Jones and Ewell's old division under Alexander Lawton. Jubal Early's Virginia Brigade, Lawton's command, was on the extreme left, anchoring the flank and protecting Jackson's artillery, most of which had been placed on Nicodemus Hill under Stuart and Captain John Pelham, his chief of horse artillery. (Stapleton Crutchfield, Jackson's chief of artillery, was still at Harpers Ferry.) Next came Jones's troops: the Stonewall Brigade under Andrew Grigsby and Bradley Johnson's Virginians, backed up by Taliaferro's Virginians and Alabamians under Lawyer Edward Warren and William Starke's Louisianans. On Jones's right were the other brigades of Lawton's command: Marcellus Douglas's Georgians, James A. Walker's Georgians and Alabamians and Richard Taylor's old brigade of Louisianans under Harry Hays. A few hundred yards in the rear, at the Dunkard Church near Lee's left center, Hood waited with his men, ready to lend support where needed. Near Hood, with four batteries, was Colonel Stephen D. Lee of Longstreet's command.

Behind the Dunkard Church was the West Woods, where many rocky ridges provided the Confederates with excellent cover from gunfire. Five hundred yards to the right, across the Cornfield, was the dense East Woods, and a like distance to the left the equally dense North Woods. Both the West Woods and the Dunkard Church were vulnerable to the enemy using these screened approaches. The Federals moreover had the artillery advantage, not just in numbers but in range and quality of ammunition. From the ridge east of Antietam their 20-pounders could inflict great harm, while most of the Confederate guns west of the stream lacked the range to retaliate.

The brigades of Douglas and Walker had the misfortune to be posted in the Cornfield during Hooker's initial advance. There about 6:30 A.M. they were caught in an enfilading fire from the Federals in their front and his artillery on their flank that decimated their ranks. "Every stalk of corn in the northern and greater part of the field," Hooker would say, "was cut as closely as could have been done with a knife, and the soldiers lay in rows precisely as they had stood in their ranks moments before. It was never my fortune to witness a more bloody, dismal battlefield."[36] Supported by Hays's brigade, the Confederates nonetheless rallied. Wrote one of Hays's officers to his wife: "I thought, Darling, that I heard at Malvern Hill heavy cannonading, but I was mistaken."[37] The nouveau Louisiana Tigers, composed of troops ranging from Irish immigrants to French Creoles, found themselves going toe-to-toe with old-line Yankees of the 12th Massachusetts, staunch abolitionists all. The Tigers lost 60 percent of their complement, the 12th Massachusetts some 67 percent. Lawton was severely wounded, Marcellus Douglas killed and James A. Walker disabled.

To the left of the Cornfield, Jones's men similarly fought with fierce resolution. "But the opposing infantry, constantly reinforced, pressed irresistibly forward," said one commentator, "and the heavy guns beyond the Antietam, finding an opening between the woods, swept the thin gray line from end to end." Soon the Confederates found themselves forced back to the West

Woods. Jones himself was stunned by a shell burst and left the field. Starke, taking over the division, then led the Virginia regiments once more into the open field. "The battle swayed backwards and forwards under the clouds of smoke; the crash of musketry, reverberating in the woods, drowned the roar of the artillery; and though hundreds were shot down at the shortest range neither Federal nor Confederate flinched from the dreadful fray."[38] Starke was killed soon thereafter. Grigsby, entrusting the Stonewall Brigade to Charles Ronald, next took command—a colonel commanding a division.

Jubal Early's brigade now came on the scene. Jackson had ordered him from Nicodemus Hill to replace the fallen Lawton. On the way he found Grigsby and Leroy Stafford rallying a few hundred Virginians and Louisianans and came to their support. "I halted my brigade and formed line in rear of Grigsby and Stafford, and they at once advanced against the enemy's skir- mishers, who had penetrated some distance into the [West] Woods, driving them back," he said. Subsequently the crusty Early formed line of battle with Grisgby and Stafford on a ridge at the end of the woods. "Heavy bodies of the enemy were now discovered in the field beyond the woods. . . . I left my brigade under the command of Colonel William Smith of the 49th Virginia, with directions to resist the enemy at all hazards, and rode across the Hag- erstown Pike toward the right to find the brigades which had been engaged early in the morning, but I found that they had been very badly cut up and had gone to the rear, Hood having taken their place."[39]

Hood's men under William Wofford and Evander Law had entered the battle promptly, interrupting their breakfasts to come to Lawton's relief in the Cornfield. The Texan, who knew only one way to fight, immediately or- dered his men to advance on the double-quick. "Tell General Jackson," he informed an aide, "that unless I get reinforcements I must be forced back, but I am going on while I can!" Then he pushed forward, riding over rows of dead men who had perished in Hooker's first onslaught. "Never before," he said, "was I so continuously troubled by fear that my horse would further injure some wounded fellow soldier, lying helpless on the ground."[40]

Wofford's and Law's regiments moved with dispatch, but none so swiftly as the 1st Texas. Just as the 4th Texas had its day at Gaines's Mill and the 5th Texas at Second Manassas when it devastated the New York Zouaves, it was the turn of the 1st Texas at Sharpsburg. Lieutenant Colonel Philip Work described his regiment's charge: "As soon as [it] became engaged with the enemy in the cornfield, it became impossible to restrain the men, and they rushed forward, pressing the enemy close until we had advanced a consider- able distance ahead of both the left and right wings of the brigade. . . . It was not until we reached the farther side of the cornfield that I could check the regiment." By this time the 1st Texas had broken the first line of the enemy and advanced within 30 yards of the second line, crouched behind fence rails and backed by a battery of guns. "My men continued firing, a portion of them at the enemy's men and a portion at the artillerists, the result of which was that the second line broke and fled, and the artillery was limbered up and started to the rear, when the whole fire of my regiment was concentrated on the artillerists and horses with such effect that the artillery was abandoned." Colonel Work wisely chose not to carry the guns. "I was aware that a heavy force of the enemy was massed upon my left, and [if] I moved farther to the front I would be attacked upon my left and rear and annihilated."[41] As it was, the 1st Texas lost 75 percent of its men.

Jeb Stuart throughout the early morning had done much to arrest Hooker's initial success. Sharpsburg offered no terrain suitable for troopers on horseback but the irrepressible cavalryman, who had forged a strong if incongruous friendship with Jackson, had been entrusted with the tactical disposition of the left wing's guns on Nicodemus Hill, one of the few points relatively safe from McClellan's artillery. Stuart in turn relied heavily on John Pelham, the handsome 23-year-old son of Dr. and Mrs. Atkinson Pelham of Benton County, Alabama. Young Pelham had grown up with five brothers on a 1,000-acre estate, and then gone on to West Point, where he excelled in cavalry tactics before resigning two weeks before graduation to throw his lot with his native state.

From Nicodemus Hill Pelham's nineteen guns, including 12-pound Napoleons and 10-pound Parrotts, inflicted terrible damage on Hooker's flank, pouring double canister into the Federals as they marched through the North and East Woods and the Cornfield. The smoothbore Napoleons, with an effective range of one mile, were particularly effective at this close-up work against infantry. The rifled Parrotts, though with twice the range more suited to long-distance dueling, added to the cannonade. Helped by Stephen Lee's massed guns at the Dunkard Church, they exerted a murderous crossfire.

Now Hooker's corps was spent. On its heels about 7:30 A.M., however, came Mansfield's 8,000-man Twelfth Corps, thrashing through the East Woods and the Cornfield. Hood's men under Wofford and Law slowly fell back toward the West Wood and the Dunkard Church under the counterattack, even while fresh Confederate units were coming up to support them. Harvey Hill sent in Roswell Ripley's brigade on their right flank, personally leading the charge, then committed Colquitt's brigade and Garland's under Duncan McRae. Why do you take such risks? Hill's chief of staff asked him. Would you not rather live than die?

"Oh yes," Hill casually replied, "when I think of my wife and babies I would, but God will take care of them, if he allows anything to happen to me."[42]

Ripley's men, many of whom were still armed with old smoothbores, poured a vicious enfilading fire on the Federals. Firing "buck-and-ball"— buckshot and a standard ball—their muskets at close range had the effect of shotguns. "Very soon our Reg was under fire the balls whisin over us," said Private Calvin Leach of the 1st North Carolina. "I commenced loading and shooting with all my might but my gun got chooked the first round, and I picked up a gun of one of my comrades who fell by my side and continued to fire."[43] Ripley was wounded but stayed on the field.

Mansfield gained ground, but at terrible cost. Two of his brigades suffered 1,000 casualties before advancing a foot. Soldiers stood like duelists, firing muskets at fifty paces. Hood's bullet-ridden ranks grudgingly continued their withdrawal and Harvey Hill's troops, their own flank exposed, soon joined them. "There was no rout, no frantic running to the rear," said an officer in Hood's division. "The men fell back in squads—often stopping to replenish their empty cartridge boxes from those of the dead and wounded. . . . When they reached the woods from which they had debouched about two hours before [1,800] strong, only 700 could be mustered."[44]

Now Stuart and Pelham, conscious that the Confederate line in their front was becoming more and more concave, shifted their guns farther to the right to Hauser's Ridge behind the Dunkard Church. The closer the Federals came, the more exposed they were to Pelham's field of fire. Stephen Lee's guns, almost at right angles, supported him admirably. "Pelham, joined by [William] Poague, meanwhile had moved 13 pieces to a position just in rear and to the immediate left of Jones' old line," wrote one military historian, "from which he was able to sweep the open ground from the Nicodemus house to the Dunkard church. . . . No one movement on either side bore a greater influence upon the final issue of the battle than did the advancement of Pelham's group during the interval between Hooker's and Mansfield's attacks."[45]

By 9 A.M. this second Federal assault on the Confederate left was almost at a standstill. Not only had Hooker's First Corps been cut to pieces, losing 2,500 men, but Mansfield's Twelfth corps, losing more than 1,500, was riddled. Hooker had been wounded by a sharpshooter, and the white-haired Mansfield, a 40-year army veteran, had incurred a fatal wound. The Federals controlled the ground north of the church and east of the Hagerstown Pike, but Jackson's left was still intact. So far some 9,000 Confederates with 35 guns had stymied both Hooker's and Mansfield's corps, comprised of 18,000 men and 60 guns. Confederate casualties had been severe as well, none more so than in Hood's command.

"Where is your division?" a general officer, possibly Shanks Evans, asked the Texan.

"Dead on the field," was the laconic answer.[46]

Within the week Lee would be writing an earnest plea to Senator Louis Wigfall of Texas: "I have not heard from you in regard to the new Texas regiments which you promised to raise for the army. I need them very much. I rely upon those we have in all our tight places, and fear that I have to call upon them too often. . . . You must help us in this matter. With a few more regiments such as Hood now has . . . I could feel more confident of the campaign."[47]

Despite the carnage, George Greene of Mansfield's Corps nonetheless pushed his division forward, trying to envelop the Dunkard Church. Jubal Early, who with Grigsby's and Stafford's survivors was concealed with his brigade in the West Woods, moved parallel with Greene and fell upon his right flank. "I saw the column on my right and rear suddenly move into the woods in the direction of the rear of the church," Early said. "The limestone ridges enabled my troops to keep out of view of the enemy . . . and they moved rapidly so as to get up with them." He ordered Colonel William Smith of the 49th Virginia, whose regiment was in the lead, to open fire. "They ran in on the main body, which was taken by surprise by the fire from the unexpected quarter from which it came." Early then signaled a general advance that hurled Greene's troops back several hundred yards across the Hagerstown Pike. "My brigade was faced to the front as soon as the whole of it had passed from behind the ledge, and opened fire on the enemy, who commenced retiring toward the pike in great confusion."[48]

The third attack on Jackson's left wing came about 10 A.M. Edwin ("Bull Head") Sumner of the Union Second Corps led John Sedgwick's 5,400-man division out of the East Woods straight toward the West Woods, thinking he would meet little resistance. In so doing he bared Sedgwick's entire left flank to Confederate reinforcements coming up from the south behind the Dunkard Church. Greene's withdrawal added to the peril. The reinforcements were McLaws's men—Kershaw's South Carolinians and Barksdale's Mississsipians. George "Tige" Anderson's Georgians and John G. Walker's two brigades of North Carolinians, who had been shifted from the right wing of the army, likewise threw themselves into the action.

For the first time, Stonewall had superior numbers and he took full advantage of it. In a wild melee, McLaws, Anderson, Early and Walker struck Sedgwick from flank and front with stunning impact. "Back, back, boys, for God's sake, move back!" Sumner shouted, waving his hat and riding through the Union ranks. "You are in a bad fix!" Sedgwick himself, a beloved officer who had already lost an arm on the Peninsula, went down with several wounds. Within minutes almost half his division was killed or wounded and the other half was fleeing to the rear. The scene was horrendous. "You could hear laughing, cursing, yelling and the groans of the wounded and dying, while the awful roar of musketry was appalling," one of Tige Anderson's Georgians said. "Where the line stood the ground was covered in blue, and I believe I could have walked on them without putting my feet on the ground." Riding with McLaws in the midst of the shellfire, Jackson gloried in the Confederate advance. "God," he said, "has been very kind to us this day." The Federals soon rallied and Jackson withdrew back to the West Woods, but by 10:30 A.M. all assaults on the left wing ceased. Franklin's Sixth Corps when it later reached the field would for the most part be held back in support, attacking neither Jackson nor Harvey Hill. Both Sumner and McClellan concurred in this decision. "If I were defeated," Sumner would be quoted as saying, "the [Union] right would have been entirely routed, mine being the only troops left on the right that had any life in them."[49]

Following the cease-fire on the left General Lee rode up to Captain William Poague, whose 1st Rockbridge Artillery had been in the midst of the fighting around the Dunkard Church, to inquire about the battery's condition and its supply of ammunition.

"I replied," said Poague, "that we could make out to use all three guns from our present position, but for any rapid movement only one piece was equipped, as our teams had suffered severely." When a soldier approached, his face smudged with gunpowder, it took Lee a moment to recognize his youngest son, Rob, serving as a private in the battery.

"You are not going to put us in the fight again in our crippled condition, are you?" the 19-year-old asked.

"Yes, my son," was the reply. "I may need you to help drive these people away."

Poague later marveled at the elder Lee's equanimity, saying he exchanged "a few pleasant words with his son," then "rode away as quietly and composedly as if nothing special was going on."[50]

Sumner's two other divisions, six brigades in all, meanwhile had sharply diverged from Sedgwick, compounding his vulnerability, and were assailing Harvey Hill's position in the Confederate center. There Hill had placed two of his strongest brigades, the Alabamians of Robert Rodes and the North Carolinians of George Burgwyn Anderson, in a sunken roadbed to the east of and perpendicular to the Hagerstown Pike, 500 yards south of the Dunkard Church. Soon this road would be called the Bloody Lane. The Federals totaled some 11,000 men; Rodes and G.B. Anderson, perhaps 2,200. To stiffen his regiment's resolve Colonel John Brown Gordon of the 6th Alabama shouted out to Lee, who had come up to observe, "The men are going to stay here, General, till the sun goes down or victory is won!"[51]

Hill, Lee and Longstreet then rode up a nearby ridge, but Hill unlike his companions did not dismount.

"If you insist on riding up there and drawing the fire," Longstreet told him, "give us a little interval so we may not be in the line of fire when they open up on you."

Within minutes a cannon shot came through the air that took off the front legs of Hill's mount, bringing the animal down on his stumps. "The horse's head was so low and his croup so high that Hill was in a most ludicrous position," said Longstreet, not without satisfaction. "With one foot in the stirrup he made several efforts to get the other leg over the croup, but failed. Finally we prevailed upon him to try the other end of the horse, and he got down."[52] Hill would have three horses shot from under him that day.

In the moments before the attack Gordon, squarely in the middle of a line that formed an inverted V, ordered his men to hold their fire until the enemy was all but upon them. "Now the front rank was within a few rods of where I stood," he said. "It would not do to wait another second, and with all my lung power I shouted 'Fire!' My rifles flamed and roared in the Federals' faces like a blinding blaze of lightning. . . . The entire front line, with few exceptions, went down in the consuming blast." Still the enemy persisted. "The result, however, of this first effort did not satisfy the intrepid Union commander. Beyond the range of my rifles he reformed his men into three lines and on foot led them to the second charge. . . . This advance also was repulsed; but again and again did he advance in four successive charges."[53] Similarly, to Rodes's and Gordon's right, George Burgwyn Anderson's brigade repelled attack after attack. Anderson eventually went down with a shattered ankle; his senior colonel was killed, his next-senior colonel wounded.

This stalemate continued until noon. The Federals would advance over the crest above the Bloody Lane, endure withering volleys, then fall back. The Confederates for their part would make periodic sallies to flank the foe, but with little success. Incessant musket fire at such close range produced shocking numbers of casualties. Gordon himself was wounded five times, the last one nearly killing him. "The first volley from the Union lines sent a . . . ball through the calf of my right leg," he said. "Higher up in the same leg I was again shot; but still no bone was broken. I was able to walk along the line and give encouragement." Later a third ball pierced his left arm, tearing tendons and mangling flesh. A fourth bullet ripped through his shoulder, leaving its base and a wad of clothing in the wound. "I could still stand and walk, although the shocks and loss of blood had left but little of my normal strength . . . I looked at the sun . . . it seemed to stand still."

The last bullet struck Gordon square in the face and passed through his neck, barely missing the jugular. "I fell forward and lay unconscious with my face in my cap; and it would seem that I might have been smothered by the blood running into my cap . . . but for the act of some Yankee who, as if to save my life, had at a previous hour during battle, shot a hole through the cap, which let the blood out."[54]

Hill placed four brigades of Richard Heron Anderson's division, which had come up with McLaws from Harpers Ferry, in support of Rodes and George Burgwyn Anderson in the Bloody Lane. Early on, however, Dick Anderson suffered a severe thigh wound and command devolved on Roger Pryor, his senior brigadier. Newspaper publisher Pryor proved no more a soldier at Sharpsburg than politician Howell Cobb had at Crampton's Gap. With the able Anderson gone from the field, Pryor could not give the division proper direction. "Rans" Wright's Georgians made it to the Bloody Lane, but Wilcox's Alabamians under Colonel Alfred Cumming, Featherston's Mississippians under Carnot Posey, and Pryor himself saw little action. (William

Parham's brigade, down to some 80 men after its encounter at Crampton's Gap, had been merged with Pryor's; Armistead's Virginians had been sent elsewhere.) Wright and Cumming went down with wounds, compounding the command problem. Harvey Hill and Rodes did what they could to offer guidance but to little avail.

With Gordon borne unconscious to the rear his lieutenant colonel, James N. Lightfoot, went to Rodes for orders. Knowing that the 6th Alabama's casualties had been severe, in part because the position it held in the Bloody Lane exposed it to enfilading fire, Rodes instructed him to pull back and straighten his line. Then the brigadier helped a wounded aide to the rear. When he turned around he could not believe his eyes. His battle-hardened Alabamians were withdrawing from the Bloody Lane, exposing the entire Confederate center. Lightfoot had drawn his regiment back, ordering, "About face!" and the entire brigade, mistakenly thinking the order was meant for them, had precipitously withdrawn.[55] On Rodes's right, George Burgwyn Anderson's men had no choice but to fall back themselves. The two Confederate brigades lost some 700 of 2,200 men; the two divisions attacking them lost some 3,000 of 11,000.

Hill and Longstreet reacted with desperate courage. "As I rode along the line with my staff I saw two pieces [of Captain M. B. Miller's Battery] of the Washington Artillery," Longstreet said, "but there were not enough men to man them. The gunners had been either killed or wounded. . . . I put my staff officers to the guns while I held their horses. It was easy to see that if the Federals broke through our line there, the Confederate army would be cut in two and probably destroyed, for we were already badly whipped and only holding our ground through sheer force of desperation." Longstreet, still wearing carpet slippers for his injured heel, quickly became a cannoneer. "We loaded up our little guns with cannister and sent a rattle of hail into the Federals as they came over the crest of the hill. . . . So warm was the reception we gave them that they dodged back behind the crest. We sought to make them believe they had many batteries before them. . . . We made it lively while it lasted."[56]

Harvey Hill serendipitously found Captain R. Boyce's South Carolina battery, Evans's brigade, nearby and added their cannister fire to Longstreet's. Then he rallied a few hundred men, grabbed a rifle and led a charge. The effort was fruitless, of course, but it gave the enemy pause. "The Yankees were so demoralized," Hill insisted, "a single regiment of fresh men could drive the whole of them in our front across the Antietam."[57] Colonel John R. Cooke had not one but two regiments: the 27th North Carolina and 3rd Arkansas of Walker's division, and at this point his fierce musket fire made the Federals hesitate anew. The North Carolinian, whose disdain for the decision of his father, Philip St. George Cooke, to fight for the Yankees matched that of Jeb Stuart, his brother-in-law, took a page from Harvey Hill's book and emulated his recklessness. Standing behind a bullet-shredded hickory tree 15 yards in front of his men, he directed their fire through shouts and gestures. Then Cooke even led a charge of his own, joined by Cobb's brigade under William Macrae.

Longstreet, who was still scraping together scattered defenders, noted the assault approvingly. Old Pete, whose great strength was in seeing the battle-field as a whole and moving troops accordingly, sought to encourage Cooke.

"Major Sorrel," he told an aide, "go down to that regiment with my compliments to the colonel. Say he had fought splendidly and must keep it up. We are hard pressed and if he loses that position there is nothing behind him."

Cooke had no thought of retreating. "Major, thank General Longstreet for his good words," he replied, "but say, by God almighty, he needn't doubt me! We will stay here, by J.C., if we must go to hell together!"[58]

Just after 1 P.M., with victory in his grasp, McClellan halted the assault on the razor-thin Confederate center. Once again, expecting a counterattack from imaginary hordes of rebels, he was playing not to lose. With Franklin's and Porter's Corps still fresh, he chose not to commit them. More than 20,000 Federals would not see action. Lee meanwhile had committed his entire command.

John Brown Gordon and George Burgwyn Anderson, who had fought so bravely in the Bloody Lane before succumbing to their wounds, suffered different fates. Gordon, whose wounds appeared far more serious, would live. "Mrs. Gordon was soon with me," he would write of his Fanny. "When it was known that the battle was on, she had at once started toward the front." The doctors were doubtful about letting her visit his room, but Mrs. Gordon prevailed. "My face was black and shapeless—so swollen that one eye was entirely hidden and the other nearly so. My right leg and left arm and shoulder were bandaged and propped with pillows." Fanny was shocked.

"I saw at once that I must reassure her. Summoning up all my strength, I said: 'Here's your handsome husband; been to an Irish wedding.' Her answer was a suppressed scream."

For weeks thereafter, while Gordon's life hung in the balance, "she sat at my bedside, trying to supply concentrated nourishment to sustain me against the constant drainage. With my jaw immovably set, this was exceedingly difficult and discouraging." Fanny nonetheless persevered. Then infection set into his limbs. "The doctors told Mrs. Gordon to paint my arm above the wound three or four times a day with iodine. She obeyed the doctors by painting it, I think, three or four hundred times a day. Under God's providence, I owe my life to her incessant watchfulness."[59]

George Burgwyn Anderson's ankle wound, while extremely painful, at first did not appear life-threatening. Surgeons thought a shell fragment had simply glanced off his foot. A 31-year-old West Pointer with a taste for literature, Anderson possessed, in the words of a friend, "a smile as gentle and winning as ever beamed from a human face." For ten days he endured the agony of wagon transport back to Raleigh, intent on seeing his wife, Mildred, and their baby. Only when he reached home, his ankle badly swollen with infection, did his own physician find a minie ball imbedded in the wound. Amputation followed, but too late. The man who told his aides he "would prefer being shot through the head" to being captured died in his wife's embrace.[60]

In early morning the Federals had tested Jackson on the Confederate left and at noonday Hill and Longstreet in the center. Now the right, also under Longstreet's command, was in danger. So many troops had been shifted from this position to stymic attacks elsewhere that only five small brigades—some 2,800 men—under David "Neighbor" Jones remained there. Toombs's Georgians on the far right guarded the Rohrbach Bridge and the downstream fords, Thomas Drayton's brigade and James Kemper's Virginians were on their left, and Jenkins's South Carolinians under Joseph Walker and Pickett's Virginians under Richard Garnett were still farther to the left in front of Sharpsburg. Neighbor Jones, like McLaws, was a dependable if not exciting division commander. Only 37 years old, the congenial South Carolinian suffered from a heart condition. Though he would survive the battle he would succumb to cardiac failure four months later.

The Rohrbach Bridge, some 125 feet long but only 12 feet wide, would henceforth be called Burnside's Bridge. Union General Ambrose Burnside, instantly recognizable with his muttonchop whiskers, had been trying to cross the Antietam with his 12,000 men since midmorning. His problems were manifold. The bridge's narrow width created an instant bottleneck, the roads leading up to it exposed his troops for lengthy distances to devastating shot and shell, and the four-to-five-foot-deep creek bed made fording under fire hazardous. Burnside's advantage, of course, was the almost absurd thinness of the Confederate line. Robert Toombs's men, the bridge's principal defenders, numbered not more than 400. Though backed up by artillery, at some point they had to crack.

Toombs, the overbearing Georgian politician whose disdain for following orders had led to Longstreet's temporarily relieving him of command before Second Manassas, was convinced his enemies wanted him out of the army. He would not leave, he told his wife, until he had fought one great battle. "The day after such an event," he said, "I will retire if I live through it."[61] Defending the Burnside Bridge he would make his mark. In this action he was handsomely aided by his fellow Georgian and senior colonel, Henry "Rock" Benning, a former state Supreme Court judge. Solidly built and deep-voiced, Benning was a natural leader. For three precious hours, waiting for Powell Hill to come up from Harpers Ferry where he had been paroling thousands of prisoners and allocating captured guns and supplies, Toombs and Benning kept Burnside from crossing the creek. "From the nature of the ground on the other side," Toombs said, "the enemy was compelled to approach mainly by the road which led up the [creek] for near three hundred paces parallel with my line of battle and distant therefrom from fifty to a hundred and fifty feet, thus exposing his flank to a destructive fire."[62]

Time and again the Federals fruitlessly strove to cross the bridge. General Jacob Cox, Burnside's second-in-command, found the Confederate position virtually impregnable. "The column approaching it was not only exposed at pistol-range to the perfectly covered infantry of the enemy and to two batteries which were assigned to the special duty of supporting Toombs, and which had the exact range of the little valley with their shrapnel," he said, "but if it should succeed in reaching the bridge its charge across it must be made under a fire plowing through its length, the head of the column melting away as it advanced, so that, as every soldier knows, it could show no front strong enough to make an impression upon the enemy's breastworks, even if it should reach the other side."[63]

By 1 P.M., however, the situation changed. Toombs and Benning, seeing that the Federals finally had found fords over the creek, left their positions opposite the bridge and withdrew up the steep ground toward Sharpsburg. The enemy had lost some 500 men, Toombs some 200. Luckily the fighting at the Confederate center now had almost ceased, and Burnside would need two more hours to complete the crossing and then reorganize. If Jones could hold on the right until Powell Hill came up, the battle still might be won. Meanwhile Longstreet, his aide Moxley Sorrel wrote, "seemed everywhere along his extended lines, and his tenacity and deep-set resolution, his inmost courage, which appeared to swell with the growing peril to the army, un-doubtedly stimulated the troops to greater action."[64]

When the Federal line did move forward, its force seemed unstoppable. Garnett and Joseph Walker on one side of the road leading up to the town, and Kemper and Drayton on the other side, were pushed back relentlessly. Defeat seemed inevitable, but the stigma of a wound from behind was intol-erable. "I was afraid of being struck in the *back*," said Private John Dooley, one of Kemper's men, "and I frequently turned half around in running, so as to avoid if possible so disgraceful a wound." The captain beside Dooley did him one better, running backward while keeping his face to the foe.

From a hill behind the town, Lee could see that Jones's division was dis-integrating. Only Toombs's brigade held its ground. Then at 4 P.M. he noticed a column of men advancing from the south. With his hands still in splints from his fall two weeks before, he called a passing officer to use a spyglass for him.

"What troops are those?" Lee asked.

A long pause ensued. "They are flying the Virginia and Confederate flags," he eventually was told.

"It is A.P. Hill from Harpers Ferry," Lee said calmly.[65]

So it was. Wearing his red battle shirt Powell Hill had driven his Light Division on a punishing 17-mile, 8-hour march—rivaling anything Jackson's foot cavalry had ever done and justifying Lee's gamble. Some 3,000 of his men soon would be assailing the Federal left flank, even as Confederate artillery bombarded its front. Hill conferred briefly with Jones, then ordered his lead brigades—Archer, Gregg and Branch—into action. James Archer was so ill with fever he had to be brought to the field by ambulance. Now he drove his Tennesseans, many of whom were partially clad in the blue uniforms captured at Harpers Ferry, straight toward the 8th Connecticut, whose men hesitated to shoot. Point-blank fire from Archer, together with enfilading volleys from the beleaguered Toombs, wasted the enemy's ranks. Maxcy Gregg's South Carolinians and Lawrence Branch's North Carolinians followed close behind, extending Archer's left. As usual Gregg was in the midst of the fray. When a bullet in his hip knocked him from his horse, he first thought he was wounded.

Finding no hole, an aide told him, "General, you aren't *wounded*; you are only *bruised*." With that Gregg limped back into the battle. The next morning, sitting down to eat his breakfast of an ear of corn, he pulled his silk handkerchief out of the tail pocket of his frock coat and out dropped a rifle ball, flat as a half dollar. It was the ball that had knocked him from his horse.[66]

Lawrence O'Bryan Branch was not so fortunate. "He had just swept the enemy before him and driven them in such confusion and dismay, that all firing had ceased in his immediate front," one of his men said, "when Generals Gregg and Archer directed his attention to a V-shaped column of the enemy that was advancing on his left. He stepped forward and formed with these generals a little group, which evidently attracted the attention of some sharpshooter. For, just as he was raising his glasses to his eyes, a single shot was fired."[67] The bullet tore through Branch's skull, killing him instantly. The former U.S. congressman had matured into a professional soldier since the Seven Days, and his presence would be missed. "He was my senior brigadier," mourned Hill, "and one to whom I could have entrusted the command of the division with all confidence."[68]

Within the hour the Confederates, temporarily at least, were in control. Burnside's divisions were thrown back in confusion from Sharpsburg to the ridges along the banks of the Antietam, where they dug in as darkness fell. Powell Hill had instinctively taken the battle to the enemy, assailing troops vastly outnumbering him and putting them to flight. Reported Lee: "[Hill] drove the enemy immediately from the position they had taken, and continued the contest until dark, restoring our right, and maintaining our ground."[69] Casualties for the daylong battle were incredible. Federal losses totaled some 12,400; Confederate, some 10,300.

In the deep quiet of the night Lee, still mounted, took the reports of his generals as they wearily rode back from the front. One by one he asked them the same question, "How is it on your part of the line?" Each reply was the same: the men are exhausted; the enemy's numbers are overwhelming; we must retreat across the Potomac immediately. Even Jackson offered no other counsel, saying he had never before fought against such odds. After all the generals had spoken, a lengthy silence ensued.

"Gentlemen," Lee finally said, rising in his stirrups, "we will not cross the Potomac tonight. You will go to your respective commands, strengthen your lines; send two oficers from each brigade towards the ford to collect your stragglers and get them up. . . . If McClellan wants to fight in the morning I will give him battle again. Go!"[70]

Lee held his ground in front of Sharpsburg all the next day. Not until late on September 18 did he begin to cross the Potomac and withdraw into Virginia. Not a shot from McClellan was fired after him.

Far less resolute was the conduct of the Rev. William Nelson Pendleton, chief of artillery, whom Lee entrusted the next night with guarding the army's rear at Boteler's Ford on the Potomac. The 53-year-old Pendleton, a West Point graduate who had been rector of Grace Episcopal Church in Lexington, Virginia, clearly was not the man for such responsibility. He had been found wanting at Malvern Hill, had missed Second Manassas because of illness and had seen no action earlier at Sharpsburg. Moreover there were continual questions, not only about his competence, but his courage. Gunner Ham Chamberlayne, in one of his milder comments about the preacher-soldier, observed, "Pendleton is Lee's weakness. He is like the elephant, we have him and we don't know what on earth to do with him, and it costs a devil of a sight to feed him."[71]

Lee had already been reducing Pendleton's authority, quietly shifting more and more of the reserve artillery's guns to batteries directly attached to the various divisions of the army. The decision to place him at Boteler's Ford, therefore, is puzzling. With some 40 guns but with only limited and inferior ammunition and a skeleton infantry force of 300, the man the troops called "Old Mother" Pendleton was being asked the night of September 19 to don the warrior's mantle. This was not to be. Lee's orders had been to hold the ford unless Federal pressure risked the loss of the guns. In that case he was to fall back in orderly fashion: first the guns and only then the infantry, with cavalry also providing cover. Toward dusk, when enemy sharpshooters stepped up their musket fire, Pendleton soon persuaded himself he would be flanked and a withdrawal was necessary. It was far from orderly, however, and he was neither informed enough nor forceful enough to restore discipline. Infantrymen simply melted away in the darkness and unprotected artillerymen soon followed, leaving their guns behind. "Worn as were these men, their state of disorder, akin to panic, was not, justly, to be met with harshness," he would say. While this was true—most of the troops had barely slept and not eaten for forty-eight hours—it was no justification for abandoning the guns. "Somebody blundered again or was grossly negligent," Kyd Douglas commented. "It would have been no difficult matter to defend that ford from passage."[72]

Sometime after midnight Pendleton caught up with the rear of the army and found Lee with his staff, sleeping under an apple tree. Rousing him from slumber, he matter-of-factly stated he had lost all the reserve artillery.

"All?" said the dazed Lee.

"Yes, General, I fear all," said Pendleton before going off to sleep himself.

One staff officer, hearing the news, said that it "lifted me right off my blanket, and I moved away, fearful that I might betray my feelings." So far as he could tell Lee "exhibited no temper, made no reproach that I could hear, either then, or ever afterwards."[73]

In reality Lee was so flustered that, for perhaps the only time in the war, he could not think straight. "I hear from one messenger that the enemy have crossed the river and captured a few pieces of artillery, by another that they have crossed in force and have possession of all the reserve artillery," he said. "I can hear nothing reliable." Happily for Lee, however, Stonewall Jackson when he learned of the debacle reacted without waiting for orders. "The affair disgusted General Jackson beyond words," said Kyd Douglas. "He took the matter in his own hands and his staff were little out of the saddle that night." Powell Hill's men, who were closest to the ford, were dispatched by Jackson to reclaim the guns. Early the next morning, September 20, they did just that. With Dorsey Pender, Maxcy Gregg and Edward Thomas in the lead they slammed into the Federal van, enduring heavy artillery fire from the north bank before driving the enemy back across the Potomac and recapturing all but four of the guns. "It was as if each man felt the fate of the army was centered in himself," Hill declared. Pender was more matter-of-fact about the engagement. "Some of our miserable people allowed the Yankees to cross the Potomac before they ought and ours ran away, making it necessary for us to go and drive them back," he wrote his wife, Fanny. "It was as hot a place as I wish to get in."[74]

Pendleton treated the matter with his usual blandness. "I had the privilege of accompanying a force, under General Jackson, sent to punish the enemy . . ." he said, "and of witnessing the destructive chastisement inflicted upon the several thousands that had crossed and remained on the south side of the river." Lee's two-sentence report was interesting for what it left out: "General Pendleton was left to guard the ford with the reserve artillery and about [300] infantry. That night the enemy crossed the river above General Pendleton's position, and his infantry support giving way, four of his guns were taken." Young Ham Chamberlayne did not mince words: "Brig. Gen. Pendleton is an absurd humbug; a fool and a coward. Well known to be so among those who see & know, & do not hear."[75]

# EIGHT

\* \* \* \*

# FREDERICKSBURG

In the weeks after Sharpsburg the army rested south of the Potomac while replenishing its ranks and reorganizing its command. In the latter regard Lee saw to it that Longstreet and Jackson officially were named lieutenant generals, each in command of a corps, with major generals and divisions apportioned between them. Old Pete had been at his best in Maryland, ever defensive-minded and showing his mastery at reacting to crises and moving large numbers of troops to meet them. His tendency to procrastinate or even dissemble if orders did not suit him was still not that apparent. Lee did not have the rapport with him that he had with Jackson, or even Stuart, but he relied on him. "Here comes my war horse just from the field he has done so much to save!" he greeted Longstreet in the aftermath of the battle.[1] Jackson's offensive gifts were obvious. Though he had faltered during the Seven Days, he had been brilliant earlier in the Shenandoah and then again at Second Manassas and Sharpsburg. Only his continuing quarrel with Powell Hill must have been a cause of concern.

Still bridling over what he felt was his unfair arrest Hill asked for a court of inquiry, sending the application as protocol required through Jackson to Lee. With his usual tact the commanding general sought to end the controversy. "Respectfully returned to Gen. A.P. Hill," he wrote, "who will see from the remarks of General Jackson the cause of his arrest. His attention being now called to what appeared to be neglect of duty by his commander, but which from an officer of his character could not be intentional and I feel assured will never be repeated, I see no advantage to the service in further investigating this matter nor could it be done without detriment at this time." The hotheaded Hill then renewed the application, forcing Jackson, who at this point would have been content to drop the charges, to restate and elaborate on them. Observed Jedediah Hotchkiss, Jackson's mapmaker: "I hope all may blow by. Gen. Hill is a brave officer but perhaps too quick to resent seeming over-stepping of authority. [Now] Gen. Jackson intends to do his whole duty. May good and not evil come out of this trouble."[2]

Lee effectively tabled the whole issue, saying he did not have the time to give the papers proper study and putting them in the deepest recesses of the files. "My opinion of the merits of General Jackson has been greatly enhanced during this expedition," he wrote Davis. "He is true, honest, and brave; has a single eye to the good of the service and spares no exertion to accomplish his object." Meanwhile, in recommending Longstreet and Jackson to the president for promotion, he gave Hill singular praise. "Next to these two officers, I consider A.P. Hill the best commander with me. He fights his troops well and takes good care of them."[3]

Longstreet now commanded five divisions: those of Major Generals Lafayette McLaws and Dick Anderson, newly promoted Major Generals John Bell Hood and George Pickett, and Brigadier General Robert Ransom Jr. The brigades of David R. Jones, whose heart condition forced his retirement, went to Hood and Pickett. John G. Walker's two brigades went to Ransom; Walker himself, whose service in Lee's army was confined to Harpers Ferry and Sharpsburg, was promoted to major general and sent to the Trans-Mississippi.

McLaws's division still consisted of Joseph Kershaw's South Carolinians and William Barksdale's Mississippians, but Paul Semmes now led an all-Georgia brigade, and Thomas Cobb led the Georgians formerly commanded by his older brother Howell. The brigades of Dick Anderson, recovered from his wound, included Cadmus Wilcox's Alabamians, Billy Mahone's Virginians and Ambrose "Rans" Wright's Georgians, while Winfield Featherston returned to lead his Mississippians. A newcomer to Anderson's division was Brigadier Edward A. Perry, a Yale-trained lawyer, who led the Florida regiments and in effect replaced the hapless Robert Pryor. (Incensed by his demotion Pryor in one of the war's oddities would resign his commission and enlist in the 3rd Virginia Cavalry as a private.) Hood now commanded four brigades: the Texas Brigade under Jerome Bonaparte Robertson, Evander Law's Alabamians and North Carolinians, "Tige" Anderson's Georgians and Robert Toombs's old Georgia unit now under "Rock" Benning. The untested Pickett, a favorite of Longstreet, led most of the latter's former division: the Virginia brigades of Richard Garnett, Lewis Armistead, James Kemper and Monty Corse, and the South Carolina brigade of Micah Jenkins. Brigadier Robert Ransom, a gallant soldier but a stiff disciplinarian, took over John G. Walker's old two-brigade command, his own North Carolinians and those of John R. Cooke.

Gone from the army to the Carolinas with his independent brigade, now for good, was the colorful if erratic Nathan "Shanks" Evans, he who had responded so promptly to the Federal threat at First Manassas. "Evans was difficult to manage," a Longstreet aide admitted. "He had a Prussian orderly, with a wooden vessel holding a gallon of whiskey always strapped on his back, and there was the trouble."[4] Gone too was Thomas Drayton, a close friend of Jefferson Davis, whom Lee personally liked but felt lacked the capacity to command.

Jackson's corps was comprised of four divisions: those of Major Generals Powell Hill and Harvey Hill, Dick Ewell's old command under the proven Brigadier Jubal Early, and Jackson's former division under Brigadier William Taliaferro.

Powell Hill's Light Division included six brigades: the Georgians of Brigadier Edward Thomas, the South Carolinians of Brigadier Maxcy Gregg and the North Carolinians of Brigadiers James Lane, who replaced Lawrence Branch, and the esteemed Dorsey Pender, as well as the Tennsseans of Brigadier James Archer and the Virginians of Colonel John Brockenborough. Harvey Hill's division consisted of Brigadier Robert Rodes's Alabamians, Brigadier Alfred Colquitt's Georgians, the wounded Roswell Ripley's mixed brigade under Brigadier George Doles, the slain Samuel Garland's North Carolinians under Brigadier Alfred Iverson and George Burgwyn Anderson's North Carolinians under Colonel Bryan Grimes. (John Brown Gordon was appointed a brigadier but not formally confirmed, possibly because of concern over his wounds.) Jubal Early's division was comprised of Lawton's Georgians under Colonel Edmund Atkinson, Trimble's mixed brigade under Colonel Robert Hoke, Early's own Virginia brigade under Colonel James A. Walker, and Brigadier Harry Hays's Louisianans. Taliaferro's division included the Stonewall Brigade under the newly named Brigadier Elisha Franklin Paxton, Brigadier John R. Jones's Virginians, Colonel Edward Warren's mixed brigade and Colonel Edmund Pendleton's Louisianans.

Needing to know more about McClellan's intentions Lee now sent Stuart on a second "Ride around McClellan" into Pennsylvania, instructing him to record troop dispositions, disrupt communications and commandeer Yankee horses. The cavalry commander selected for the expedition 1,800 of his best men under Wade Hampton, Rooney Lee and William ("Grumble") Jones, together with four guns under John Pelham. Irrepressible as ever, Stuart even held a dance and musicale the night before leaving, delivering several solos himself. On October 9 the force crossed the Potomac far west of Harpers Ferry and headed north, avoiding heavily garrisoned Hagerstown and riding a circuitous 40 miles to Chambersburg. En route William Blackford learned of a local resident who owned a detailed map of the countryside and "called at the house for it, as these maps have every road laid down and would be of the greatest service to us." Only the women of the household were home, and they "flatly refused to let me have the map." Blackford dismounted, pushed past them into the sitting room and took it by force. "Angry women do not show to advantage," he reflected, "and the language and looks of these were fearful, as I cooly cut the map out of its rollers and put it in my haversack."[5]

Once in Chambersburg Stuart torched the Cumberland Valley Railroad's machine shops, destroyed 5,000 muskets and rounded up some 1,200 horses. Then he embarked on a dangerous cross-country return. "Of course I left nothing undone," he said, "to prevent the inhabitants from detecting my real route and object . . . I started directly toward Gettysburg but . . . started back toward Hagerstown for six or eight miles, and then crossed to Maryland by Emmitsburg." In three days he would cover 180 miles, 80 of these nonstop in the last 24 hours of the raid. "Not a man should be permitted to return to Virginia!" barked Union General-in-Chief Halleck, as he and McClellan organized a feverish pursuit.[6] On October 12 Stuart's weary five-mile-long column nonetheless outraced the Federals, and reached the Potomac at White's Ford. "The last files of the last division were entering the water," recounted Blackford, "when General Stuart rode down the bank to where I was."

"Blackford, we are going to lose our rear guard," he said, in a voice heavy with concern.

"How is that, General?"

"I have sent four couriers to [Mathew Calbraith] Butler [of the 2nd South Carolina Cavalry] to call him in, and he is not here, and you see the enemy is closing in upon us."

Blackford immediately volunteered to ride back and find Butler. "As I rose the bank I passed Pelham who with one gun, kept back for the purpose, was rapidly firing alternately up and down the river at masses of the enemy not a quarter of a mile away. We waved our hats at each other as I passed." Three miles in the rear he found Butler, who quickly had his command with drawn sabers galloping toward the ford, prepared to cut their way through. But there was no need. "There stood Pelham with his piece and there the enemy, just as I had left them, with an open gap for us to pass through," said Blackford. "In a moment we were at the ford and Pelham's gun rumbling along with us into the water."[7]

McClellan sought to explain Stuart's success by saying his own cavalry was badly in need of fresh horses. To this the fuming Lincoln made on October 24 the following reply: "I have just read your dispatch about sore tongued and [fatigued] horses. Will you pardon me for asking what the horses of your army have done since the battle of Antietam that fatigue anything?"[8]

Thus prodded, McClellan finally crossed the Potomac and reentered Virginia. But whither would he march, through the Shenandoah or to the east of the Blue Ridge Mountains? To guard against either contingency Lee on October 28 again split his command, placing Jackson near Winchester in the

Valley and sending Longstreet across the Blue Ridge to the Culpeper area. Quite soon, however, divining McClellan's plans would be academic. On November 11 Lincoln again relieved his reluctant warrior of command. Named to succeed him was the personable Ambrose Burnside, a former West Pointer and close friend of McClellan who had been in the railroad business with him until the outbreak of hostilities.

During these weeks Jackson received joyful personal news, learning from Anna that she had given birth to a healthy baby girl. The man who had suffered the loss of his first two daughters fell to his knees and gave God thanks. "My Own Dear Father—" the charming missive read, "As my mother's letter has been cut short by my arrival, I think it but justice that I should continue it. I know that you are rejoiced to hear of my coming, and I hope that God has sent me to radiate your pathway through life. I am a very tiny little thing. I weigh only eight and a half pounds, and Aunt Harriet says I am the express image of my darling papa, and so does our kind friend, Mrs. Osborne, and this greatly delights my mother. My aunts both say I am a little beauty. . . . My mother is very comfortable this morning. She is anxious to have my name decided upon, and hopes you will write and give me a name. . . . I was born on Sunday (November 23) just after the morning services at church. . . ."

Jackson was ecstatic. "Oh, how thankful I am to our kind Heavenly Father for having spared my precious wife and given us a little daughter!" he wrote. "I cannot tell you how gratified I am, nor how much I wish I could be with you and see my two darlings." Ever the disciplinarian, he cautioned: "Do not spoil it, and don't let anybody tease it. Don't permit it to have a bad temper." The baby, he decided, would be named Julia in honor of his mother. "How I would dearly love to see the darling little thing! Give her many kisses from her father." He tried to curb his emotions, lest he tempt fate. "Do not set your affections upon her," he told Anna, "except as a gift from God. If she absorbs too much of our hearts, God may remove her from us."[9]

Lee meanwhile was suffering a grievous loss, the sudden death of his 23-year-old daughter, Annie. "Tidings reached General Lee, soon after his return to Virginia," wrote his aide Walter Taylor, "of the serious illness of one of his daughters—the darling of his flock." One morning several hours after mail was received Lee and Taylor conducted business as usual, dealing with assorted military matters. "I then left him, but for some cause returned in a few moments . . . when I was startled and shocked to see him overcome with grief, an open letter in his hands. That letter contained the sad intelligence of his daughter's death."

To Taylor this stoicism was typical of the man. "He was the father of a tenderly loved daughter, one who appealed with peculiar force to his paternal affection . . . but he was also charged with the command of an important and active army. . . . His army demanded his first thought and care; to his men, to their needs, he must first attend, and then he could surrender himself to his private, personal affairs." Duty was the first rule of Lee's life, and his every thought, word and action was made with an eye to its needs.

Just as impressive, Taylor continued, was the commanding general's self-discipline. "General Lee was naturally of a positive temperament, and of strong passions; and it is a mistake to suppose him otherwise; but he held them in complete subjection to his will and conscience." In view of his burdens, "the occasional cropping-out of temper which we, who were constantly near him, witnessed, only showed how great was his habitual self-control."[10]

Before the year was out Lee would bear one more personal blow, the result of the high infant mortality of the times: the death of the daughter of Rooney Lee and his wife, Charlotte, the second child they had lost. "I heard yesterday, my dear daughter, with the deepest sorrow, of the death of your infant," he wrote Charlotte just before Fredericksburg. "I was so grateful at her birth. I felt she would be such a comfort to you, such a pleasure to my dear Fitzhugh, and would fill so full the void still aching in your hearts. But you have now two sweet angels in heaven. What joy there is in the thought!"[11]

Not all soldiers in the army were so rocklike in their faith as Jackson and Lee. The pragmatic William Porter Alexander, for instance, newly promoted to colonel and heading an artillery battalion in Longstreet's corps, thought it was a weakness that "many of our generals really & actually believed that there *was* this mysterious Providence always hovering over the field & ready to interfere on one side or the other, & that prayers & piety might win its favor from day to day." Acid-tongued Jubal Early, still only a brigadier though commanding Ewell's division, once would scandalize a congregation hearing a sermon on the Resurrection.

"What would be your feelings on that day?" the preacher fervently asked. "What would be your feelings at seeing those gallant ones who have given up their lives for their beloved country, rising in their thousands and marching in solemn procession?"

Early could not contain himself. "I would conscript every damned one of them," he growled semi-audibly from his pew.

Even the spirited Dorsey Pender, now Powell Hill's senior brigadier and a man Lee held in high regard, alluded to his lack of commitment. "Oh how I do wish I could be a Christian," he told his wife. "I feel now how far I am from what I would believe myself and what we should be, particularly one who has taken such solemn vows as I have. Oh that I could be filled with the living Faith necessary to salvation. We are taught that the prayers of the just avail much—honey, pray for me continually for my conversion and that I may not go astray."[12]

Let us look for a moment at these men in modest detail. Porter Alexander, a son of Leopold and Sarah Alexander, was born in 1835 on Fairfield plantation in Washington, Georgia, and raised in privileged circumstances. His father, one of whose neighbors was the politician Robert Toombs, placed such store in education that a series of private tutors were imported from the North to instruct the boy and his nine siblings. "I was passionately fond of shooting & fishing," he wrote, "& my friendship with two old gentlemen, growing from this fondness, was a source of great amusement to my older sisters." When he was fifteen his then antisecessionist views provoked an argument with two older boys. "Every barkeeper and every rowdy in the town was a hot secessionist," he said. The upshot was that Alexander and one of his adversaries drew pistols on each other, his piece misfired, and the fight was broken up. "Gratitude to a Providence which saved me so narrowly from a calamity which would have ruined my whole life" made him resolve "to avoid & eschew politics, as too prolific of quarrels for one who, like myself, is liable to become reckless of consequences when in a passion."[13]

Alexander entered West Point with Toombs's help in 1853, and a photograph taken during this period already reveals his innate self-confidence. He proved a more than able student, graduating third in the class of 1857, and for much of the next three years he remained at the academy as an instructor in the engineering department. During this time he met his future wife, 24-year-old Bettie Mason of King George County, Virginia, the daughter of a physician who was spending the summer in the Hudson Valley. He also helped develop the signal flag method, the so-called "wig-wag" system he used so effectively at First Manassas. In 1860 he and Bettie, whom he had taken to calling Miss Teen, were married. By the time of Lincoln's election Alexander had turned full circle in his political beliefs, becoming a fervent secessionist. "As soon as the *right to secede* was denied by the North," he said, "I strongly approved of its assertion & maintenance by force if necessary."[14]

When Georgia seceded Alexander found himself with Bettie on the West Coast, with fresh orders to report for engineering duty in San Francisco Harbor. He thereupon informed his commanding officer, James B. McPherson, he would be resigning and requested a leave of absence to return home.

"Aleck, if you must go I will do all I can to facilitate your going," McPherson told him. "But don't go. These orders, sent by pony express to stop you here, are meant to say to you that if you wish to keep out of the war that is coming you can do so. You will not be required to go into the field against your own people, but will be kept out on this coast on fortification duty."

"Mac, my people are going to war, & war for their *liberty*," Alexander replied. "If I don't come and bear my part they will believe me a coward—and I will feel that I am occupying the position of one. I must go & stand my chances."

"I suppose in your situation I should feel as you do," said McPherson.

Soon Alexander was serving with the Confederacy, advancing from captain of signals at First Manassas to chief of ordnance in ensuing battles. "His was the happiest and most hopeful nature," said Moxley Sorrel, commenting on his abilities. "He was sure of winning in everything he took up, and never did he open his guns on the enemy but that he knew he should maul him into smithereens. . . . He was often called on both by Lee and Longstreet for technical work. . . . Longstreet thought so well of his engineering and reconnoitering abilities that he kept him very near headquarters."[15]

Alexander's new command had been the crack artillery battalion of Stephen D. Lee, who was promoted to brigadier and sent to the West. From Vicksburg Lee wired his congratulations: "Well, Aleck, I am glad you took my battalion—manage them right & they will make you a brig."[16]

Jubal Anderson Early was born in 1816 in remote western Virginia, one of ten children of Joab and Ruth Early, prominent and wealthy Franklin County landowners. His youthful years were uneventful, marred only when he was sixteen by the death of his mother. "She was a most estimable lady," he said, "and her death was not only the source of the deepest grief for her immediate family, but caused universal regret." Even as a young man, however, he evinced a tendency to be disputatious and, sometimes, disagreeable. He entered West Point in 1833 and, before the year was out, had his storied quarrel with Lewis Armistead. Early made some scathing remark on the drill field, tempers boiled over in the mess hall, and Armistead broke a serving plate over Early's head. For this he was dismissed from the academy, while Early continued in his curmudgeonly ways. In his senior year he received 189 demerits, placing him 195th in a corps of 211. He did better academically, finishing eighteenth in a class of 50.[17]

Following graduation in 1837 Early fought Indians for a year in the Florida swamps, then resigned from the army and spent the next two decades in Rocky Mount, Virginia, practicing law and serving in the state legislature.

His only break in this regimen came in 1847 when he served as a major in the Virginia Volunteers during the Mexican War. He arrived after the fighting was over but his soldierly abilities impressed both Jefferson Davis, colonel of the 1st Mississippi Rifles, and General Zachary Taylor. The former man became a lifetime friend; the latter appointed him military governor of Monterrey. "Being rather a strict disciplinarian," Early said, "and naturally regarded by inexperienced troops as harsh in my treatment of them, I was by no means popular with the mass of the regiment . . . but I can safely say that, on the day they were mustered out . . . I had the satisfaction of receiving from a great many of the men the assurance that they had misjudged me in the beginning and were now convinced that I had been their best friend all the time."[18] In Mexico he contracted the fever that developed into the painful and chronic arthritic condition that bent his body and, already in 1848, made him appear far older than his thirty-two years.

Back in Rocky Mount, Early resumed his law practice and took rooms at the local inn and tavern, where he would regularly voice his opinions in the evening over a convivial drink. The lifetime bachelor also began a relationship with 17-year-old Julia McNealey, whom he kept in a small house near the inn. She would serve him supper, come into his bed and bear him four children. While he did not flaunt the relationship he made no effort to conceal it, acknowledging and supporting the children and naming the last one, a boy born in 1864, Jubal L. Early. "I was never blessed with . . . captivating manners," he would acknowledge, "and the consequence was that I was often misjudged and thought to be haughty and distainful in my temperament. When earnestly engaged about my business . . . I would frequently pass an acquaintance without noticing him, because of the preoccupation of my mind, and this often gave offense."

Now he was serving the Confederacy with distinction. At First Manassas he had rushed up to tip the balance; at Williamsburg he had been wounded in his brave but reckless charge; at Cedar Mountain, Second Manassas and Sharpsburg he had shown his coolness under fire. Often confused with Dick Ewell—with whom he shared a piping voice, an irascible nature and a bent for profanity—Early spared neither his friends nor his foes. "I was never what is called a popular man," he said unabashedly.[19]

William Dorsey Pender, born in 1834 in Edgecombe County, North Carolina, was the son of James and Sarah Pender, who by all accounts were doting parents. Growing up on the family farm he soon elected for the soldier's life, and in 1850 entered West Point, where his classmates included Jeb Stuart, Stephen D. Lee and John Pegram. Following graduation the handsome, dark-haired Pender visited the North Carolina home of another classmate, Samuel Shepperd, son of a longtime U.S. congressman. Shepperd's petite 14-year-old sister, Fanny, captivated him from their first meeting and for the next five years, while stationed on the frontier, he conducted a long-distance courtship. They were married in 1859 at her parents' home and then journeyed to his posting in Washington Territory, where Fanny gave birth to Samuel, their first son.

Back in North Carolina on furlough with his family in 1861 as the possibility of secession became a reality, Pender offered his services to the Confederacy. He did not see action, however, until the following year at Seven Pines as colonel of the 6th North Carolina in Evander Law's brigade. There in the action at Fair Oaks, when his well-drilled regiment was in danger of being flanked on its left by Yankees streaming across the Chickahominy, he sized up the situation immediately. "By the left flank, file left, double-quick!" he shouted in a ringing voice. This quick reaction, said one of his officers, "was the only possible combination of commands that could have saved us from capture, and they were molded into a single order without hesitating for an instant." President Davis, witnessing the maneuver and Pender's ensuing assault on the enemy, rode up and said, "General Pender, I salute you," giving him a battlefield promotion on the spot.[20] Thereafter his brigade served in the Light Division.

Throughout the war Pender kept up a remarkable correspondence with Fanny while they were apart, writing letters that revealed an intense and loving relationship. On one occasion, however, she became incensed. First she quoted his offending letter: "I was at a little gathering two nights ago, and had a very nice time dancing and flirting with a very nice girl. I am trying to get her to knit you a sack [a sort of hairnet] but she says she is not going to work for my wife, *but will do anything for me.*"

Then Fanny unleashed her anger. "Now, I ask you candidly, in your sober senses, why you wrote me such a thing as that? Was it to gratify your vanity by making me jealous, or to make me appreciate your love still more? You are very much mistaken. . . . I feel indignant that any woman should have dared to make such loose speeches to my husband and that he should have encouraged it by his attentions."

Within days a remorseful Pender was abjectly apologizing. "Oh! Fanny, Fanny, how could you suppose a dishonorable act. . . . [Your] letter was in my mind awake and sleeping, and again and again would my grief have to be relieved by tears. If you had simply said I do not love you I could have stood it, for I should have known that you did not mean it, but to accuse me of dishonorable acts! But honey let it pass . . . if you knew how much I suffered you would believe me sincere [in] what I've said."[21]

More typical were his letters to Fanny in the aftermath of the army's battles. Following Gaines's Mill: "I did not tell you yesterday that I was slightly wounded in the right arm. Merely a flesh wound which has not caused me to leave the field. . . . We will try to see each other if God should spare my life through this, for if I do not go to see you, possibly you may come on to see me." Following Second Manassas: "We have been fighting for several days. I am safe and sound with the exception of a small cut by shell on the top of the head. . . . May God have mercy upon me and protect me as he had thus far. . . . I am very anxious to know how Dorsey is [Dorsey, their second son, had been sick]." Following Sharpsburg: "Gen. Hill gave me command of half his division when we attacked Harpers Ferry and two [brigades] this morning on the retreat. . . . My dear the prayers of the righteous availeth much, pray for my deliverance from the enemies [*sic*] balls, but darling if my fate should be that of too many, you must rest in the hope of our meeting in a better world."[22]

Union General Burnside, who had been so slow getting his troops into action at Sharpsburg, moved with far more dispatch upon replacing McClellan, heading his troops in mid-November straight toward Fredericksburg. Pressure from Lincoln and General-in-Chief Halleck undoubtedly spurred him on his way.

Burnside's reorganized 115,000-man Army of the Potomac now consisted of three so-called grand divisions under Edwin Vose Sumner, Joseph Hooker and William Franklin.[23] But on November 21, when the Federals drew up north of the Rappahannock opposite the town, they found that the pontoons needed to bridge the river had not arrived. This mishap gave Lee almost three weeks to fortify his lines, bring Jackson from the Valley and unite his 78,000-man command.

There was little question but that Burnside would make his main attack at Fredericksburg. The Rappahannock there was some 400 feet wide; upstream it was narrower but choked with impediments to mass crossings; farther downstream it widened to some 1,000 feet. Stafford Heights on the north bank, 150 feet high, dominated the town, which was at waterside on the opposite bank. There Burnside concentrated some 200 cannon, along with Sumner's and Hooker's divisions. Behind the town for some 500 yards the ground sloped upward, culminating in Marye's Heights. Here Lee placed Longstreet's First Corps: McLaws and Ransom in the center, Dick Anderson to the left, Pickett and Hood to the right. Burnside stationed Franklin's division a mile downstream. Opposite on elevated ground between the mouth of Deep Run and Hamilton's Crossing was Jackson's Second Corps in three lines: Powell Hill's division in the first, Early's and Taliaferro's in the second, Harvey Hill's in reserve. All in all, the Confederate front extended for some seven miles.

The decision to engage the Federals at Fredericksburg had not been unanimous. Obviously the guns on Stafford Heights made the town itself indefensible and a crossing inevitable; only the high ground behind it could be held. More important, the cannon would protect the enemy should they be forced to withdraw, making pursuit impossible.

"I am opposed to fighting on the Rappahannock," Jackson told Harvey Hill. "We will whip the enemy but gain no fruits of victory. I have advised the line of the North Anna, but have been overruled."[24] Here Jackson was not considering the larger picture. Falling back 35 miles to the North Anna would have exposed even more of northern Virginia to destruction, and would have devastated Southern morale. Lee had to stand and fight.

Early on the morning of December 11 Federal engineers and workmen finally began laying their pontoons across the river. Waiting for them in well-concealed rifle pits were Barksdale's Mississippians, the only Confederates left in the town, who were under orders to delay the bridge building. "About 4 o'clock a battery posted on the ridge back of the town fired a few shots at the bridge," said Captain James Dinkins of the 18th Mississippi, "then the . . . pickets immediately along the river . . . maintained such a destructive fire that the enemy was compelled to abandon the work. Very soon, however, they returned . . . but the fire of the Mississippi boys was too deadly, and the enemy was forced to withdraw." By 10 A.M. Burnside decided to level the town.

"The bombardment was kept up for over an hour. . . . The deafening roar of cannon and bursting shells, falling walls and chimneys, brick and timbers flying through the air, houses set on fire, the smoke adding to the already heavy fog, the bursting of flames though the housetops, made [an appalling] scene."[25] Then the bridge building resumed, only to be interrupted time and again by the sharpshooting of the Mississippians. The portly, white-haired Barksdale was exultant. "Tell General Lee," he instructed a messenger, "that if he wants a bridge of dead Yankees, I can furnish him with one!"[26]

By mid-afternoon the stymied enemy began to cross the river above and below the town in rowboats, determined to root out the defenders in hand-to-hand fighting. "Barksdale's Brigade watched them from their hiding places and awaited their near approach," continued Dinkins. "Suddenly, when within about 75 yards of our line, as if by common impulse, a volley rang out from the rifle pits on the cold air . . . and hundreds fell dead in their tracks." Other Mississippians previously concealed in cellars now emerged, firing in the enemy's rear and flanks and inflicting heavy damage. Then Barksdale's men slowly began to retire, fighting as they withdrew. "When the Mississippians, who had thus far stood the brunt of the attack, marched over the ridge to rest . . . cheer after cheer rang out from along the [Confederate] line. When they held their ground after the bombardment had ceased . . . the other troops . . . felt a pride in their comrades which they could not conceal."[27]

For the rest of the night and the next day the Federals constructed bridges and moved their troops across the river. By morning of Saturday, December 13, Burnside had two of his grand divisions on the south side of the Rappahannock—Sumner's 30,000 men in the town and Franklin's 45,000 downstream at Deep Run. Later Sumner would be reinforced by elements of Hooker's 40,000-man force. Longstreet had some 40,000 men; Jackson, 38,000. "Lee stood upon his chosen hill of observation . . . with his two great Lieutenants beside him," wrote Major Dabney, "and reviewed every quarter of the field with his glass." Longstreet, for whom Fredericksburg would be the perfect defensive battle, was in a jovial mood.

"General, do not all these multitudes of Federals frighten you?" he asked Jackson.

"We shall see very soon," came the grim answer, "whether I shall not frighten them."[28]

As Jackson rode back to his lines the enthusiasm of his troops seemed boundless, their cheers rolling up and down the ranks. "He was wearing a new and handsome coat, the present of General J.E.B. Stuart," one of his aides explained, "and a new cap sent him by his wife, with a wide braid of gilt about it, which he disliked exceedingly but which he feared it might offend Mrs. Jackson to remove." His men could scarcely believe their eyes. "The unwonted splendor of their great general was greeted as a good omen on the morn of battle."[29]

Back with his corps Jackson coldly, almost disinterestedly, watched Franklin's troops march toward his position on the Fredericksburg Railroad embankment. When Heros von Borcke of Stuart's staff evinced some concern over the coming attack, he brought the Prussian up short. "Major, my men have sometimes failed to take a position," he said, "but to defend one, never!"[30] About 9 A.M. Major John Pelham of the horse artillery rolled forward two guns on the extreme right, well in front of the Confederate lines, and boldly opened an enfilade fire on the advancing Federals, creating panic in their ranks. Four batteries, 16 cannon in all, opened up on him in return but Pelham was in no way intimidated. When one of his guns was silenced he moved the remaining piece, a 12-pound Napoleon, all the more frequently to keep the enemy from again finding the range and fired it all the faster. For two hours he kept up the cannonade. Three orders from Stuart were required to make him retire, and then only when his caissons were nearly empty. "It is glorious to see such courage in one so young," Lee commented.[31] His efforts, combined with Confederate fire on the enemy's front from such stalwart artillerymen as Willie Pegram and David McIntosh, forced a withdrawal. The gallant Pelham, so boyishly handsome his West Point classmates called him "Sallie," thrived on battle. "He saw guns shattered and dismounted, or men tore to pieces, without any signs of emotion," wrote a comrade. "His nature seemed strung and every muscle braced to a pitch which made him rock; and the ghastliest spectacle of blood and death left his soul unmoved—his stern will unbent."[32]

About 1 P.M. the Federals again assailed Jackson, this time with more tangible results. Five hundred yards of swamp on Powell Hill's line, thought to be impassable, had been left undefended. But the ground had frozen over, enabling the enemy to smash through the gap between the right of James Lane's North Carolinians and the left of James Archer's Tennesseans. Escalating the impending disaster was the fact that Maxcy Gregg, who should have plugged the breach, in his deafness did not react quickly enough. "The attack was sudden and unexpected," said Colonel Alfred Scales of the 13th North Carolina, "and mistaking the enemy for our own troops, Orr's Rifles of [Gregg's] Brigade were thrown into momentary confusion, and Gen. Gregg, while attempting to rally them, fell mortally wounded."[33]

Here Jubal Early met the Federal attack head-on. Without waiting for orders he rushed his veterans into the gap—Edmund Atkinson's Georgians, Robert Hoke's mixed brigade, James A. Walker's Virginians. "Here comes old Jubal!" his men shouted as they passed through Hill's ranks. "Let old Jubal straighten that fence! Jubal's boys are always getting Hill out o' trouble!" Desperate was the struggle that followed. "The Federals fought manfully," said a combatant, "but the artillery on our right, together with the small arms, literally mowed them down."[34] Pushing through the grove where the South Carolinians had been surprised and routed some of Early's men saw Gregg, his hands on a tree, painfully pulling himself to his feet. "The old hero, unable to speak, unable to stand alone," said Scales, "raised himself to his full height by a small tree and, with cap in hand, waved them forward."[35]

William Poague now moved elements of the Rockbridge Artillery closer to the enemy, turning some 20-pound Parrotts on them with deadly effect but paying the price. "I do not recall the number of casualties, but our lossses were heavy," wrote gunner Edward Moore. "One of the drivers . . . was lying on the ground, his head toward the enemy. A shell entered the crown of his head and exploded in his body! Not long after this I heard someone calling me, and, looking back, I saw 'Doc' Montgomery prostate. I ran to him . . . and began to examine his wound. 'There is nothing you can do for me,' he said. 'I am mortally wounded and can live but a little while. Take a message for my mother. . . . Tell her how I died—at my post—like a man.' It was about this time, I think, that Pelham came up and said, 'Well, you men stand killing better than any I ever saw.' A little while later . . . I received two severe wounds myself, one of them disabling my right arm for life."[36]

Soon the Federals were thrown back to the railroad embankment and the low ground whence they had come. There Edmund Atkinson was severely wounded and captured. During the battle Dorsey Pender, in the thick of the action, was shot in the left arm.

"General, I see you are wounded!" exclaimed Scales, one of his colonels.

Pender waved off the injury. "No bone is broken," he said. "I want you to send at least two companies down to the railroad and drive those scoundrels out!"[37] He left the field briefly to have the wound dressed, then rejoined his men. By mid-afternoon it was apparent the attack on Jackson's front had been blunted. Franklin had suffered some 4,800 casualties; Jackson, some 3,400.

The Federal assault on Longstreet and the Confederate left, meanwhile, began about noon. Here Lafayette McLaws's division, backed up by the North Carolina brigades of Robert Ransom and John Rogers Cooke, was entrenched on Marye's Heights behind and above Fredericksburg. Their position was all but impregnable. Not only were the enemy guns across the river largely unable to damage the Confederate lines, but Union General Sumner's men faced the challenge of advancing toward them across some 800 yards of open plain. "My line of defense was a broken one, running from the left along the sunken road near the foot of Marye's Hill, where General [Thomas] Cobb's Brigade was stationed," said McLaws. "Then the line was retired a hundred or more yards to the foot of the hills in the rear, along which was extended Kershaw's Brigade of South Carolina troops, and General Barksdale's Mississippians, from left to right, the brigade of General Semmes being held in reserve." The Washington Artillery under Colonel James B. Walton was on the crest of Marye's Hill over the heads of Cobb's men, as initially were the brigades of Ransom and Cooke. "The enemy, from their position, could not see the sunken road," McLaws continued, "nor do I think they were aware, until it was made known to them by our fire, that there was an infantry force anywhere except on top of the hill."[38]

Years later Longstreet still marveled at the strength of his position. "An idea of how well Marye's Hill was protected," he wrote, "may be obtained from the following incident: E.P. Alexander, my engineer and superintendent of artillery, had been placing the guns, and in going over the field with him before the battle, I noticed an idle cannon. I suggested that he place it so as to aid in covering the plain in front of Marye's Hill. He answered: 'General, we cover that ground now so well that . . . a chicken could not live on that field when we open up on it.'"[39]

Crouching in the sunken road, Tom Cobb and his Georgians were spoiling for a fight. Though Longstreet had alerted him he might at some point have to withdraw to a second defensive line, Cobb was having none of it. "Well, if they wait for me to fall back," he had snorted, "they will wait a long time!"[40] Just recently, in letters to his wife, he had thought it unlikely the enemy would attack at all. On December 6: "I returned from picket last night in a beating snow storm, and reached my camp half frozen. My men, God bless the brave fellows, came in with a cheer, and not a murmur was heard from them. The snow this morning was four inches deep, and tonight it is bitter cold." On December 8: "The snow lies on the ground unmelted, and what is worse, the commissary department has failed to furnish any rations for two days, except some flour." On December 10: "I do not now anticipate a battle at this place, at least for some time. Do not be uneasy about my being 'rash.' God helping me, I will do my duty when called upon, trusting the consequences to Him."[41]

Sumner's advance, spearheaded by the divisions of Winfield Scott Hancock, Oliver Otis Howard and William French, was spirited but doomed. "They came on at the double-quick, with loud cries of 'Hi! Hi! H!' " one Confederate said. "Their bright bayonets glistening in the sunlight made the line look like a huge serpent of blue and steel. . . . We could see our shells bursting in their ranks, making great gaps; but on they came, as though they would go straight through and over us." As the Federals closed in, the rebel batteries switched from shell to canister, staggering them anew. "A few more paces onward, and the Georgians in the road below us rose up and, glancing an instant along their rifle barrels, let loose a storm of lead into the faces of the advance brigade. This was too much; the column hesitated and then, turning, took refuge."[42]

But on and on the enemy came. The futile Federal charges, one historian wrote, could be "likened to successive waves of surf dashing a against a shore, breaking up, receding, leaving a thin line on the sand to mark the farthest reach."[43] Already crippled by artillery fire, each brigade as it neared the sunken road and the stone wall simply disintegrated, torn to pieces by the fire of Cobb's men. Longstreet was in his element. "By the time the third attack was repulsed, the ground was so thickly strewn with the dead that the bodies seriously impeded the approach of the Federals," he said. "General Lee . . . became uneasy when he saw the attacks so promptly renewed and pushed forward with such persistence. . . . He said to me: 'General, they are massing very heavily and will break your line, I am afraid.' 'General,' I replied, 'if you put every man now on the other side of the Potomac on that field to approach me, and give me plenty of ammunition, I will kill them all.' "[44] Though the Federals outnumbered their foes almost two-to-one, they were advancing in a narrow corridor, allowing the Confederates to focus their fire on the assaults.

To William Pettit, a young gunner observing them, Lee and Longstreet seemed indifferent to the shells and rifle fire coming up from the town. "I did not once see them stoop," he said, "tho' others say they sometimes did." Longstreet's appearance particularly intrigued him. "Lt. Gen. Longstreet wore a gray military coat and pants, the coat with remarkably short skirts or tail. . . . He wore a gray or lead colored shawl wrapped closely about his neck and shoulders, and kept in place by holding it together with his hands and arms, which were generally wrapped up in it. No marks of insignia of rank were visible. . . . He is about six feet 2 inches high, of strong round frame, portly and fleshy but not corpulent or too fat. . . . Next to Lee I should prefer entrusting the chief command of our armies to him."[45]

In the midst of the carnage Tom Cobb, fighting his first engagement as a brigadier, fell victim to a sniper's bullet. The minie ball pierced his thigh, severing the femoral artery, and he soon died from loss of blood. On Marye's Heights John Rogers Cooke likewise went down, hit above the eye by a bullet that fractured his skull. He would not return to the army until Gettysburg.

To bolster Cobb's men, who had already been joined by elements of Cooke's and Kershaw's commands, McLaws dispatched Joseph Kershaw and the rest of his South Carolinians to the sunken road. Down the crest along the Telegraph Road the blond-mustachioed Kershaw promptly galloped, his booming voice urging his brigade to follow. Thousands of soldiers watched his conspicuous ride, wondering if still another sniper's bullet would blow him from the saddle. Luck was with him, however, and he arrived unscathed. "I found on my arrival that Cobb's Brigade . . . occupied our entire front," Kershaw said, "and my troops could only get in position by doubling up on them. This was accordingly done, and the formation along most of the line during the engagement was consequently four deep. . . . Notwithstanding that their fire was the most rapid and continuous that I have ever witnessed, not a man was injured by the fire of his comrades."[46]

By 1 P.M. all three leading Union divisions were largely immobilized, flat in the dirt in front of the stone wall among the bodies of their dead comrades. They could move neither forward nor rearward without drawing a withering fire. Still convinced he could crush the Confederates by sheer weight of numbers, Burnside now ordered Sumner and Hooker to push forward more of their men.

Through the afternoon the assaults continued. "I think the fourth time the Federals charged," recalled Longstreet, "a gallant fellow came within one hundred feet of Cobb's position before he fell. Close behind him came some few scattering ones, but they were either killed or they fled from certain death. This charge was the only effort that looked like certain danger to Cobb, and after it was repulsed I felt no apprehension, assuring myself that there were enough of the dead Federals on the field to give me half the battle."[47] By 3:30 P.M., with his caissons running out of ammunition, Colonel Walton of the Washington Artillery called on Porter Alexander's battalion to relieve him. "All the [gun] pits were in open ground & some were a little troublesome to get to," said Alexander. "But it was my first fight in command of troops & I was only too glad of the chance." Spurring forward he encountered a Parrott shell spinning end over end directly toward him. "I had no time to dodge & wondered where it would hit. It passed under the horse's belly somehow— without touching & struck about fifteen feet beyond her. . . . The sharpshooters & the enemy's guns all went for us, but we were emulating greased lightning just then & we got off very lightly, some 6 men & 12 horses, I think it was, only who were struck."[48]

Alexander barely had set up his cannon when the Federals made their sixth and final charge. "The enemy had just brought up a fresh division under command of Gen. [Andrew] Humpreys, of my old corps—the engineers, a splendid old soldier," he said. "Word was sent back to them that our artillery on the hill had been withdrawn. This raised their hopes & Humpreys, to diminish the temptation to stop & fire, which is the bane & danger in all charges, ordered that his whole division should go with empty muskets & rely on the bayonet alone." With a great hurrah the enemy rose up and swarmed forward in three long lines of battle. Alexander raked them with canister and shrapnel as fast as his guns would fire. "It was plainly a disagreeable surprise to them, but they faced it very well & and came along fairly until our infantry at the foot of the hill opened up. . . . Then Humphreys broke all up. . . . His line got no further than the others had come & his men scattered about & laid down & fired from behind houses, but the charge was over." [49]

Humpreys's immediate superior, Joseph Hooker, summed up the devastation in bitter terms: "Finding that I had lost as many men as my orders required me to lose, I suspended the attack."[50] Sumner and Hooker had incurred some 8,800 casualties; Longstreet, only 1,900. Federal losses at Fredericksburg altogether totaled some 13,600; Confederate, 5,300.

All that night and through Sunday, December 14, with Burnside's troops still in the town and Lee's on the heights, the dreadful sounds of the wounded and the dying filled the air on the corpse-strewn slope. Nobody moved to help them, lest sharpshooters from either side add more bodies to the toll. Finally 19-year-old Sergeant Richard Kirkland of the 2nd South Carolina asked Brigadier Kershaw if he could go to their aid.

"I can stand it no longer," he said. "I come to ask permission to go and give them water."

"Kirkland, don't you know that you would get a bullet through your head the moment you stepped over the wall?" Kershaw replied.

"Yes, sir, I know that. But if you will let me, I am willing to try it."

The officer hesitated. "I ought not to allow you to run a risk," he finally said, "but the sentiment [that] actuates you is so noble that I will not refuse your request, trusting that God may protect you. You may go."

The sergeant saluted and took his leave, only to return in a few moments. Kershaw thought he had lost his courage.

"General, can I show a white handkerchief?"

"No, Kirkland, you can't do that." Kershaw knew that neither side had agreed to a truce.

"All right," said the sergeant, "I'll take my chances."

The brigadier watched with deep concern as Kirkland hurdled the wall and reached the nearest of the wounded, raising his head and giving him water. That done, he went on to another man, and then a third. By this time his purpose was well understood, and all danger was over. From everywhere on the slope came fresh cries of "Water! Water! For God's sake, water!" For the next hour and a half he tended to all the wounded he could, then returned to his post unhurt.

The selfless Sergeant Kirkland would be killed the next year at Chickamauga in far-off Tennessee. "He was but a youth when called away," Kershaw would remember, "and had never formed those ties from which might have resulted a posterity to enjoy his fame and bless his country; but he has bequeathed . . . an example that dignifies our common humanity."[51]

Dawn on December 16 revealed that Burnside, covered by darkness and stormy weather, had withdrawn his men back across the river. The Union army had sustained its most ignoble defeat since First Manassas. "I had my suspicions that they would retire during the night," Lee wrote his wife, "but could not believe that they would relinquish their purpose after all their boasting & preparations, & when I say the latter is equal to the former, you will have some idea of its magnitude. This morning they were all safe on the north side of the Rappahannock. They went as they came, in the night. They suffered heavily as far as the battle went, but it did not go far enough to satisfy me."[52]

# 1 8 6 3

O N E

\* \* \* \*

## T H E   A R M Y   R E S T S

The winter of 1863 was both boon and bane for the Army of Northern Virginia. Boon because the army had been fighting almost without letup in the seven months since Lee had taken command and badly needed the rest. Bane because the snow and cold and temporary halt to the bloodletting made the men's lack of proper clothing and rations all the more desperate and noticeable. Some 400 of the 1,500 men in one of the Louisiana Brigades, for instance, had no shoes. Thousands more had no shirts, socks or undergarments, while undercoats were so rare as to draw stares. Indeed many regiments were so threadbare they could not drill or go on picket duty. Daily rations were thought fulsome if they contained eighteen ounces of flour and four ounces of bad bacon, supplemented by infrequent and meager amounts of rice, sugar or molasses. Symptoms of scurvy were appearing, and to find vegetables regiments combed the woods for sassafras buds, wild onions and garlic.[1]

The seasoned soldiers in Lee's army, both officers and enlisted men, were if anything now more resolute than ever. "They were still, for the most part, volunteers," wrote one military historian, "but they were volunteers of a very different type from those that had fought at Kernstown or Gaines's Mill. Despite their protracted absence from their homes, the wealthy and well-born privates still shouldered the musket. Though many had been promoted to commissions, the majority were content to set an example of self-sacrifice . . . and the regiments were thus still leavened with a large admixture of educated and intelligent men." Nine out of ten had been farmers, craftsmen and laborers, but the remainder were lawyers, businessmen, teachers and other professionals. During these months in winter quarters Latin, Greek, mathematical and even Hebrew classes were instituted by the soldiers, while most traces of social distinction vanished. "Between the rich planter and the small farmer or mechanic there was no difference either in aspect or habiliments. Tanned by the hot Virginia sun, thin-visaged and bright-eyed, gaunt of frame and spare of flesh, they were neither more nor less than the rank and file of the Confederate army; the product of discipline and hard service, moulded after the same pattern, with the same hopes and fears, the same needs, the same sympathies."[2]

The average soldier stood just five feet, eight inches and weighed some 140 pounds. He had long since discarded his heavy and bulky knapsack, knowing he had to travel light during the army's frequent forced marches. Over his left shoulder he slung a horseshoe roll, a blanket and incidental clothing rolled lengthwise inside an oilcloth or rubber sheet—if he was fortunate enough to have one. On his left hip he carried a foot-square haversack filled with rations and personal effects; over the sack dangled his canteen and under it hung his bayonet. His cartridge box with its forty rounds was worn on his belt, close to his right hand, and near the belt buckle was a small pouch for percussion caps. Over his right shoulder, of course, he carried his rifle. His two prized possessions were a large tin cup, invaluable for making coffee, and a bowie knife, used more as a tool than a weapon. "I had a very good oilcloth haversack to carry my rations in, a tin cup, a splendid rubber cloth, a blanket, a pair of drawers, and a pair of woolen socks," said one soldier in the 2nd Virginia proudly. "Every article captured from the enemy!"[3]

Uniforms originally called for gray forage caps, short gray jackets and blue trousers, with blue collar and cuff trim signifying the infantry. But the men often wore wide-brimmed slouch hats, and their clothing soon evolved into all shades of gray from charcoal to butternut. Shoes were always in short supply, and dead and captured Yankees were relied upon as a prime source of footwear. Few men had comfortable or well-fitting shoes, and fewer had socks and, as a consequence, the pain from raw and bleeding feet was extreme. "It was a common practice, on long marches," said a private in the Richmond Howitzers, "for the men to take off their shoes and carry them in their hands or swung over the shoulder. Bloody footprints in the snow were not unknown!" Troops were generally so good-humored that outsiders did not realize how much they were suffering. "In summer time . . . the nostrils of the men, filled with dust, became dry and feverish, and even the throat did not escape. The 'grit' was felt between the teeth, and the eyes were rendered almost useless." Other times the men endured mud, cold, rain and snow. "Rain was the greatest discomfort a soldier could have. . . . Wet clothes, shoes and blankets; wet meat and bread; wet feet and wet ground; wet arms and ammunition. . . ."

Young staff officers galloping along the line in well-cut uniforms elicited merciless catcalls from the ranks. "The expressions of good-natured fun, or contempt, which one regiment of infantry was capable of uttering . . . would fill a volume. . . . They would shout, 'Come out of that hat—you can't hide in thar!' 'Come out of that coat, come out—there's a man in it!' 'Come out of them boots!' The infantry seemed to know exactly what to say to torment . . . and generally said it."[4]

Cooking rations was a haphazard affair. Sometimes company-level kitchens were set up and some of the men designated as cooks. More often it was every man for himself. A soldier would grind some coffee beans in a bucket with the butt of a rifle, pour the particles into a cup and add boiling water, then sip the brew while considering his culinary options. If he had some scraps of bacon or salt pork he might fry them in a borrowed skillet until it was full of boiling grease. Then he'd pour some flour mixed with water or some crumbled cornbread into the pan to create a sort of stew called "slosh." A variation of this recipe called for using less grease and less water, producing a pancake browned in one piece on each side called "slapjack." Observed one Texan of these barely edible dishes: "It would kill a horse to digest them."[5] Hardtack, a stale three-inch-square cracker often filled with worms, was another staple. "When on the march . . . a piece of solid fat pork and a dry cracker was passable or luscious, as the time was long or short since the last meal," remarked one man. "When there was leisure to do it, hardtack was soaked well and then fried in bacon grease. Prepared thus, it was a dish which no Confederate had the weakness or strength to refuse."[6]

"Foraging," a euphemism for supplementing rations that could range from stealing to begging, became an art form. "The soldiers began to appropriate anything in the way of grub, such as hogs, chickens, apples, corn, etc., to their own use," said the irrepressible John Casler of the 33rd Virginia. "We would not allow any man's chickens to run out into the road and bite us as we marched along. We would not steal them! No! Who ever heard of a soldier stealing? But simply take them." Other Confederates were more subtle. One Georgia soldier, before knocking on a farmhouse door, would put on his most mournful face. "Please, m'am, give me a drink of water," he would say. "I hain't had a single bite for the last three days, and hain't slept on a bed for a week." Stonewall Jackson was a fierce foe of foraging, but one of his men nonetheless endorsed the practice by parodying a passage from the Bible. "Man that is born of a woman," he intoned, "and enlisteth in Jackson's army, is of few days and short rations. He cometh forth at reveille, is present also at retreat, and retireth apparently at taps. When lo! he striketh a bee-line for the nearest hen-roost, from which he taketh sundry chickens, and stealthily returneth to his camp. He then maketh a savory dish, wherewith he feasted himself and a chosen friend. But the Captain sleepeth, and knoweth not that his men are feasting."[7]

Inadequate and badly cooked rations, as well as poor hygiene, often brought on crippling intestinal problems. Diarrhea and dysentery were the scourge of the army and, because of the fatigue of the soldiers and their exposure to the elements, difficult to cure. Men from the primarily rural South, moreover, usually had developed no immunity to childhood diseases. Crowded together in campsites early in the war, they endured virtual epidemics of measles and upper respiratory infections. Later the lack of proper immunizations brought on waves of smallpox, further riddling the ranks. Typhoid fever borne by ticks became a problem, killing a quarter of its victims, as did the debilitating effects of malaria. Confederate deaths from disease during the conflict would total some 166,000, compared to deaths on the battlefield of 94,000, some 260,000 in all. (Confederate casualties—both dead and wounded—would total 486,000 out of a white male population—age 10 to 49—of only 2.8 million.) "It is surprising how the Confederacy got along with such a small variety of medicines, which consisted, in the field, almost entirely of blue powders, one kind of pills, and quinine," commented one Virginia infantryman.

Sick call was perfunctory.

"What is the matter with you?"

"I don't know, doctor, but I have a terrible misery here," the man replies, placing his hands on his stomach.

"Give him a blue powder," the doctor tells an orderly.

The next man is examined the same way, and given some quinine. Then the doctor might mix the medicines. The third patient gets a pill and quinine, the fourth a blue powder and quinine, and so on.

"Occasionally some favored [patient] was given a gill of whiskey," the soldier concluded. "Nearly every man thereafter developed the same symptoms!"[8]

Battlefield wounds were almost all caused by bullets, constituting some 93 percent of all injuries. Cannon fire, while frightening, accounted for just 6 percent, and bayonets less than 1 percent. On entering the body the so-called minie ball—the bullet universally in use—dragged fragments of clothing and skin with it, compounding the damage. The ball would shatter any bone it struck and, if it passed through the body, leave a gaping exit hole. Some 71 percent of bullet wounds were in the arms and legs, 18 percent in the torso, only 11 percent in the head and neck. Stomach injuries were almost invariably fatal, those men with major hemorrhaging dying on the field, and the amputation of limbs—while commonplace—usually depended on how badly the bones were shattered. Splintering and compound fractures resulted in immediate amputation; lesser breaks sometimes were treated more conservatively. But sterile techniques were all but non-existent, the dangers of bacteria were unknown, and infections following surgery resulted in many deaths.

By now the standard weapon of Lee's infantry was the rifled musket—a long-barreled, muzzle-loading single-shot piece that fired the minie ball. The minie (the invention of a French man named Minié but commonly pronounced "mini") was not a ball but a bullet. It was hollow-based and conical, and it expanded on firing to fit snugly into the riflings of the barrel, affording improvements in range and accuracy. During the first year of the war the standard weapon had been the smoothbore musket, with a range of perhaps 75 yards. The musket would be loaded with a single round, or with "buck-and-ball," three buckshot behind a single bullet. Attackers could charge on the dead run from 100 yards away, take a volley, and be on the enemy before they could reload. If they had the advantage in numbers the rout would be on. The rifled musket, however, had a range of at least 300 yards, and a skilled marksman using the piece could kill from 700 to 800 yards away. The minie ball, moreover, made the reloading process simpler and quicker, so that well-trained defenders with clean weapons could get off two to three rounds a minute. This created a revolution in tactics, forcing attackers in most instances to abandon frontal assaults in favor of turning the enemy's flanks. Their artillery pieces could no longer unlimber within 300 yards of the defenders and blast them to pieces; their cavalry were largely useless in head-on charges. Dug-in infantrymen dominated the field.

If a commander did order a frontal attack he more often than not paid a bloody and costly price. We have just seen how Burnside fared at Fredericksburg. Soon Lee, desperate to end the war in one smashing victory, would come to grief at Gettysburg. Later Ulysses S. Grant, through sheer arrogance, would litter the field with Union bodies at Cold Harbor. If men were on the attack and lacked cover, moreover, putting new rounds in the long-barreled muzzle loaders was hazardous. The soldier tore open a cartridge, which consisted of a minie ball and a charge of powder wrapped in paper, poured the powder down the barrel and inserted the bullet, then used a ramrod to tamp them down. Last he half-cocked the hammer to insert the firing cap, then full-cocked it before aiming and firing. During this time he was an inviting target, the length of the barrel requiring him to stay on his feet, or at the least on one knee, perhaps in plain view of the defenders. Some men reloaded while flat on their backs, with their heads toward the enemy, but this slowed the procedure and required even greater courage. Soldiers under fire want to see their foes.

In line of march the columns of the army usually plodded four-men abreast, meaning that brigades and divisions stretched for miles along country roads, and any halt or delay extended the column even farther. Straggling was a continual problem, as men searched for food or water, or just could not keep up the pace. To ensure better control, divisions took parallel roads if they were available.

Forming line of battle the eight or ten companies of each regiment turned left or right off the road, throwing a handful of men forward as skirmishers and creating a two-deep front with the regimental colors in the center. Each of perhaps four regiments then extended the line farther until the brigade was in place. Typically an infantry division went on the attack with four brigades. The leading unit would be in line of battle; the second brigade would be some 200 yards behind, partially extending the left or right flank as the case might be; the third brigade would back up the second in the same manner. The fourth brigade would be kept in reserve. Officers had to exercise constant vigilance, both to keep the ranks in alignment and to keep the men moving forward.

While directing one assault at Fredericksburg, Colonel William Stiles of the 60th Georgia saw a soldier drop out of line and crouch behind a tree. Coming up behind the man Stiles gave him a resounding whack across the back with the flat of his sword.

"Up there, you coward!" he shouted, pointing toward the front.

The skulker, thinking a Yankee bullet had struck him, instantly raised his hands to the Heavens and keeled over backwards, yelling, "Lord, receive my spirit!"

Nothing nonplussed, Stiles promptly delivered a kick to the man's ribs.

"Get up, sir!" he exclaimed. "The Lord wouldn't receive the spirit of such an infernal coward!"

The soldier blinked. "Ain't I killed?" he asked. "The Lord be praised!" he yelled with sudden comprehension, picking up his rifle and running to rejoin his comrades.[9] Thereafter, we are told, he was a model soldier.

On January 1 Abraham Lincoln formally issued the Emancipation Proclamation, which despite its title neither immediately freed the slaves nor satisfied the abolitionists, since it applied only to slaves in areas in rebellion against the United States. It abolished slavery in the Confederate states, where Lincoln could not enforce the decree, but not in the non-Confederate slave-holding states—Delaware, Maryland, Kentucky and Missouri. Nonetheless it was a watershed event, a first step toward total emancipation that provided for former slaves to serve in the Union armed forces. Before the war was over, some 180,000 blacks would flock to the colors.

On the north side of the Rappahannock meanwhile, the Army of the Potomac regrouped, wondering what had gone wrong. "I say now that I do not blame 'Sides' for the Fredericksburg disaster," wrote an officer of the 96th Pennsylvania, "but I do blame . . . Abolitionists at home for crying out 'on to Richmond' until at last he succumbed." The *New York Times*, likewise blaming the politicians for the fiasco, thundered "that the direct assault upon Fredericksburg Heights should never have been ordered by the Government against the settled judgment of General Burnside." In the midst of the brouhaha Burnside manfully set the record straight. "For the failure in the attack I am responsible," he told General-in-Chief Henry Halleck. "The fact that I decided

to move from Warrenton onto this line . . . and that you left the whole movement in my hands, without giving me orders, makes me responsible."[10] Mc-
Clellan remained as popular as ever in the ranks and many soldiers, feeling
he had been unjustly removed from command after the impasse at Sharpsburg,
called for his reinstatement. The man who had painstakingly reduced the defenses at Yorktown by siege guns alone, they insisted, would never hurl his
infantry against the massed guns on Marye's Heights. "Give us back Mc-
Clellan is the cry of the army," insisted a member of the 7th Pennsylvania.[11]

Compounding Burnside's problems was the disloyalty of many of his generals. William Franklin and William ("Baldy") Smith both wanted McClellan
reinstated as commander of the army, and took the lead in lobbying Washington for Burnside's dismissal. Joseph Hooker likewise pulled strings to oust
his chief, but only so he could be named in his place. Though a longtime
Democrat, he took pains to court favor with radical Republicans. Matters
came to a head when Burnside, determined to redeem himself, took a desperate gamble. On January 20 he ordered his troops four miles upriver from the
town to Banks's Ford, where he hoped to cross the river and turn Lee's left.
Unwillingly leading the way were Franklin and Hooker.

That night the Army of the Potomac suddenly found itself in the middle
of a full-blown winter nor'easter, complete with howling winds, sheets of rain
and near-freezing temperatures. For 48 hours the storm raged, turning the
roads into cauldrons of mud. Infantry could make some headway by getting
off the roads and into the woods, but the army's wagons, guns and pontoons
could not be moved. "The ground was so soft that the wagons settled to the
hub," said one quartermaster, "and the mules over the fetlock." In some spots
the mud seemed bottomless. "It is solemnly true," Union General Alpheus
Williams wrote, "that we lost mules in the middle of the road, sinking out of
sight in the mud-holes. A few bubbles of air, a stirring of the watery mud,
indicated the last expiring efforts of many a poor long-ears." One engineering
officer resorted to sarcasm, requisitioning "50 men, 25 feet high, to work in
mud 18 feet deep." Summed up General Williams: "I don't know . . . how the
world's surface looked after the flood in Noah's time, but I am certain it could
not have appeared more saturated than does the present surface of the Old
Dominion." Confederate soldiers viewed the debacle with bemusement, taunt-
ing their adveraries. "Say! Yanks! We'll be over in the morning and haul your
guns and pontoons out of the mud for you," shouted a reb.[12] The luckless
Burnside had no choice but to call off the expedition.

Back in camp from the so-called "Mud March" the Federal commander
learned the full extent of his officers' intrigues from the editor of the *New
York Times*, who was outraged by their deceit. Burnside promptly drew up
General Order No. 8, which would have cashiered a number of his critics.
Prominent among them were Franklin and Smith, who would be relieved of

their commands, and Hooker, who would be dismissed from the service. On January 24 Burnside met with Lincoln, giving the president a choice: approve General Order No. 8 or accept his resignation.

Lincoln took no more than 24 hours to assert himself. Believing that "Fighting Joe" Hooker now was the best of his generals, he named him commander of the Army of the Potomac. The straightforward Burnside was prevailed upon to withdraw his resignation and assigned to the West. Franklin and Smith were transferred from the army. Then Lincoln wrote Hooker an extraordinary letter. "I have placed you at the head of the Army of the Potomac," he said. "Of course I have done this upon what appear to me to be sufficient reasons. And yet I think it best for you to know that there are some things in regard to which, I am not quite satisfied with you. I believe you to be a brave and skillful soldier, which, of course, I like. . . . You are ambitious, which, within reasonable bounds, does good rather than harm. But I think that during General Burnside's command of the army, you have taken counsel of your ambition, and thwarted him as much as you could, in which you did a great wrong to the country, and to a meritorious and honorable brother officer. . . . Of course it was not *for* this, but in spite of it, that I have given you the command."[13] Hooker would be Lee's fifth foe since taking command—McClellan, Pope, McClellan again, and now Burnside proving unequal to the task.

Generals would likewise be restive this winter in the Army of Northern Virginia—albeit to a lesser degree. Harvey Hill, with the onset of cold damp weather plagued by habitual spinal troubles, sought to resign his commission. In truth he was also feeling unappreciated. Lee valued him as a fighting man but deplored what he perceived as Hill's lack of administrative ability and unquestionable tendency to fault-find. After much negotiation he agreed to stay in the service, and in early February was again sent to his native state, where he was placed in charge of the Department of North Carolina.[14]

Longstreet soon afterward also left the lines along the Rappahannock, dispatched by President Davis and James Seddon, the new secretary of war, to head temporarily what Old Pete chose to call the Department of Virginia and North Carolina. Eager to be his own man he left out the phrase "Southern Virginia." There is no doubt, however, that the command was only semi-independent and that he still reported to Lee. (The reader will note that in the battles thus far the offensive-minded Lee has remained close to Longstreet, but has given Jackson considerable leeway. Could this have chafed?) Going with Old Pete were the divisions of John Bell Hood and George Pickett. His mission, not all that clearly defined, was to collect food and fodder and simultaneously harass Federal garrisons along the coast. It was assumed he would readily return to the main army should Hooker move across the river.

February and March saw Lee once more reorganizing his command. Three new major generals were named: hawkish Jubal Early, who during Dick Ewell's lengthy convalescence had led Ewell's division so brilliantly; ornery Isaac Trimble, the 61-year-old Marylander whose severe wound at Second Manassas would delay his return until Gettysburg; and Edward "Allegheny" Johnson, likewise incapacitated with the wound he had suffered in the Valley. Ewell, who had slipped on the ice over Christmas in Richmond and further damaged the stump of his leg, could not have been happier for Early's promotion. "The injustice you and Colonel James A. Walker have suffered has been a source of constant anxiety to me," he wrote Early. "And I should already have made efforts to have it repaired, but the absence of the President and the injury I have suffered have prevented me." Trimble had no doubts his own recognition was overdue. "If I am to have promotion I want it *at once*," he wrote Adjutant General Cooper, "and I particularly request that my [promotion] date may be from 26 August, the date of the capture of Manassas—which General Jackson was pleased to say he considered 'the most brilliant exploit of the war.' "[15] Johnson's promotion was largely due to Jackson's efforts. Stonewall had become quite impressed with the burly officer during their brief engagement with Frémont.

The two strong Longstreet divisions still with Lee, those of Lafayette McLaws and Dick Anderson, experienced minor changes. In McLaws's command the Georgian brigade of the slain Tom Cobb now was led by William Wofford, while the rest of the units remained the same: Paul Semmes's Georgians, Joseph Kershaw's South Carolinians and William Barksdale's Mississippians. In Anderson's division Carnot Posey took over the Mississippi brigade of Winfield Featherston, who was transferred to the Gulf States, joining Cadmus Wilcox's Alabamians, Ambrose Wright's Georgians, Billy Mahone's Virginians and Edward Perry's Floridians.

In Jackson's corps the division heads were Powell Hill, the mustachioed Brigadier Robert Rodes filling in for Johnson (who would have been replacing Harvey Hill), Early, and Raleigh Colston filling in for Trimble. The last appointment was something of a surprise. Though Colston had led a brigade under Longstreet at Seven Pines, he had been on sick leave ever since. Now Jackson, who had known him since their teaching days at V.M.I., was giving great responsibility to a largely untried officer. The opening for Colston only came about because Brigadier William Taliaferro requested a transfer. The Tidewater aristocrat had commanded Jackson's old division since Cedar Mountain. His relations with Jackson had long been strained, and he was upset about not being promoted.

Powell Hill, whose own feud with Jackson continued to simmer, now had two new brigadiers. Henry Heth, a close friend of Lee and reportedly the only man in the army to call him by his first name, took over the Virginia brigade of Charles Field, who had come so close to death at Second Manassas and was still bedridden. Samuel McGowan, former colonel of the 14th South Carolina who had been fighting since the Peninsula, replaced Maxcy Gregg, his old chief. Hill's other brigades remained in familiar hands: Edward Thomas's Georgians, James Lane's and William Pender's North Carolinians and James Archer's Alabamians.

In Rodes's division Edward O'Neal took over Rodes's old brigade of Alabamians. Alfred Colquitt and George Doles continued to lead their respective Georgia brigades, and Stephen Dodson Ramseur and Alfred Iverson their North Carolina units.

Jubal Early welcomed back the Georgia Brigadier John Brown Gordon, recovered from his five wounds at Sharpsburg through his wife's nursing, and eager for further combat. Robert Hoke, who had enlisted as a private in the 1st North Carolina at the onset of war and commanded Trimble's brigade at Fredericksburg, officially took over the unit. William ("Extra Billy") Smith, who had led a regiment at Sharpsburg, now settled into Early's old Virginia brigade. A former governor of Virginia, Smith had earned his nickname because of the many extra fees he charged the government for the mail-coach service he founded. Harry Hays's Louisianans completed Early's command.

Colston, the least experienced officer, ironically headed the most unsettled division. Elisha Franklin Paxton had swelled the once-depleted ranks of the Stonewall Brigade and ably led his men at Fredericksburg, it was true, and Colonel Edward Warren had performed well in the battle. But Francis Nicholls, who had served with Richard Taylor's Louisianans in the Valley under Jackson and at Winchester had lost an arm and been captured, had not fought since then. Most troubling was the case of John R. Jones, who commanded the 2nd Brigade of Virginians in Jackson's old division. Jones, who had left the field at Sharpsburg after being stunned by an artillery blast, had been accused of cowardice by a fellow officer at Fredericksburg and later brought before a court-martial board. Though he was acquitted, rumors persisted about his courage.

The reorganization also affected the artillery, whose branch of service color called for red collar and cuff trim. In the beginning of the war batteries had been assigned to individual brigades and divisions, and had formed close attachments to them. Orders to serve even temporarily in other units, where they might be more needed, were strongly resisted and resulted in glaring deficiences. Then during 1862 consolidation began to take place. The batteries, which averaged 100 officers and men and 60 horses to haul the guns and wagons for hay and grain, came under the control of divisional artillery chiefs. But if a battle required the massing of cannon, they still were expected to come from the reserve, even though those of another division might be closer to hand and not in use. Now Lee and Chief of Artillery William Pendleton grouped the army's guns into battalions of four or more batteries each, 16 or more guns in all, each battalion usually headed by a colonel reporting directly to a corps commander. The First and Second Corps each would have four divisional and two reserve battalions—26 batteries and 112 guns in the First Corps and 27 batteries and 116 guns in the Second Corps. Brigadier Pendleton, whose duties were becoming more and more administrative, would retain only two battalions in the general reserve.

In the First Corps Colonel James B. Walton was named chief, and he continued to command the Washington Artillery, one of the two reserve battalions. Colonel Porter Alexander led the other. In the battles to come, however, Lee and Longstreet would place more and more reliance on Alexander, who was 20 years younger. The other battalions were commanded by Colonel Henry Cabell, a Virginia lawyer who at 43 was old man of the group; Lieutenant Colonel John Garnett, 24; Major James Dearing, 23; and Major Mathis Henry, 35, who previously had served in Stuart's horse artillery. In Jackson's Second Corps, command devolved on Colonel Stapleton Crutchfield, 28, who had taken first honors at V.M.I. The four divisional batteries were led by Colonel Reuben Lindsay Walker, 36, who would fight in sixty-three engagements without suffering a wound (Willie Pegram, 26, was serving as a major in his command); Lieutenant Colonel Thomas Carter, 32, a V.M.I. graduate; Lieutenant Colonel R. Snowden Andrews, 32, a Washington, D.C., architect; and Lieutenant Colonel Hilary Jones, 30. The reserve batteries were commanded by Colonel John Thompson Brown, 28, and David McIntosh, 27, a South Carolina lawyer (Major William Poague, 27, formerly of the Rockbridge Artillery, was serving under him).

Most artillery batteries were elite units, whose officers and men were well educated and enjoyed considerable social station. Rob Lee, the commander's youngest son, fought as we have seen at Sharpsburg as a private in the Rocksbridge Artillery. By now the artillery's principal weapons were the smoothbored, bronze 12-pound Napoleon, designed by Napoleon III; the rifled, wrought-iron 10-pound Parrott gun, with its distinctive iron tube encircling and reinforcing the breech (the 20-pound and 30-pound Parrotts had a disturbing tendency to explode); and the rifled, iron, 3-inch Ordnance gun. All were muzzle loaders.

The Napoleon had a range of almost a mile, and a similar-looking piece was used as a howitzer to throw shells in a high arc rather than the usual trajectory. Most battles were not fought in open spaces, and Napoleons could be used effectively in the rolling, heavily wooded countryside. They had a high rate of fire, and when using case or canister at close range were devastating. Case was a shell filled with musket balls and fitted with a time fuse; employed at a range of 400 or more yards it exploded while still in the air, raining metal down on the enemy. Canister, a can filled with balls and metal scraps, was used at under 400 yards and exploded directly in the enemy's line of advance. The rifled Parrotts and Ordnance guns had a range of some two miles, and were used for dueling with enemy batteries, or throwing solid shot against massed troops and incendiary shells against fortifications. Throughout the war the artillery would be plagued by defective ammunition, the fuses in particular being unreliable.

The cavalry command under Major General Jeb Stuart continued to grow. From the single regiment he had led at First Manassas he now had four brigades, headed by Brigadiers Wade Hampton, Fitzhugh Lee, Rooney Lee and William ("Grumble") Jones. By late spring, when Lee ordered Beverly Robertson's brigade up from North Carolina to join him, Stuart would supposedly be commanding almost 20,000 horsemen. These numbers, however, are misleading. Because the Conferate cavalry was forced to provide its own mounts, no more than half would be present at any one time. Each man was paid perhaps fifty cents a day for the use of his horse but was reimbursed only if the animal was killed in battle. It was the owner's loss if the horse broke down or fell sick, as by far the greater number did. Besides the monetary burden there was the additional problem, even for well-to-do cavalrymen, of replacing their steeds. Virginians had the best chance of going home, refitting and returning to the ranks within a reasonable time, but men from the Deep South had much longer treks. Even midway through the war, moreover, finding mounts was becoming difficult.

Calvalrymen, whose branch of service color was yellow, may have been the best-armed soldiers in the army. Weapons included the three-foot-long saber, Colt revolvers and single-shot, muzzle-loading rifled muskets with cut-down barrels. The cavalry's principal responsibilities involved guarding the flanks, harassing the enemy's rear when victorious and its van when in retreat and screening the army's own movements even while ascertaining those of the foe. Stuart's men would charge enemy cavalry, but full-scale assaults against infantry were a tactic of the past, a tribute to the deadliness of the minie ball.

At this point Stuart's men still generally outclassed their opposite numbers, but the Federals were fast improving. In an encounter on March 17 near Kelly's Ford, upriver from Fredericksburg, Fitz Lee with 800 sabers found himself facing Union General William Averill with 2,100 horsemen advancing up Culpeper Road. The initial clash was close-up and bloody, with the 3rd Virginia charging the enemy's van, which had dismounted and taken cover behind a stone fence. With them rode Major John Pelham of the horse artillery, who would not have been involved in the action but for the fact he was in the neighborhood calling on a young belle and had impulsively decided to join in. "Forward!" he shouted, waving his sword and racing to the front of the charge. Then a shell burst sent a sliver of metal into the back of his head. He was still alive when he fell from his saddle, mortally wounded. When the regiment briefly was forced to give way, two officers slung his body across a horse and took him to the rear.[16]

The engagement would last all day, with men on both sides fighting with great intensity. Surely no soldier was more heroic than Sergeant W.J. Kimbrough of the 4th Virginia. "Wounded early in the day, he refused to leave the field," said Fitz Lee in his official report. "In the last charge he was the first to spring to the ground to open the fence; then dashing in at the head of the column, he was twice sabered over the head, his arm shattered by a bullet, captured and carried across the river, when he escaped, and walked back twelve miles to his camp."[17]

By the time the encounter ended, with the Federals ultimately stymied and forced to withdraw, Pelham was dead. "During the winter Pelham and I had become more intimate than we had ever been before," said William Blackford. "Our tents were next [to] each other and we had built our stables together . . . [he] and I had been reading aloud to each other [Sir Charles] Napier's 'Peninsular War,' and the day he left us . . . I marked the place we stopped and I have never had the heart to read more in it since." Wrote Robert E. Lee to the president: "I mourn the loss of Major Pelham. I had hoped that a long career of usefulness and honor was still before him." By slow trains the body was taken home to Alabama, escorted by Heros von Borcke, who had a small window placed in the coffin lid so friends and admirers could take a last look at the smooth, handsome face. "The noble, the chivalric, the gallant Pelham is no more," Stuart told the cavalry, not bothering to restrain his tears. Just months before, Stuart had lost his 5-year-old daughter, Flora, to illness. Soon he would name his next child Virginia Pelham Stuart.[18]

Unswerving Christian faith made most soldiers willing to accept death, whether in battle or in their personal lives. They would lift their voices in prayer, and then embrace God's will. Never was this more evident than in the series of religious revivals, largely evangelical and nondenominational, that began during the spring. The meetings started, fittingly enough, in Jackson's corps. "We are having a glorious time about now," said one private. "We commenced a protracted meeting in this Brigade about four days ago. Gen. Jackson (God Bless him) has given us the privilege to be exempt from Morning's Drill in order that we may attend preaching . . . we have two sermons each day & . . . we all sit around on the ground and listen to the sweet sound of the Gospel." Jackson would quietly take a seat on a campstool, and listen raptly to the singing and sermons. Young men, carried away during the services by their emotions, could become boisterous. But order would quickly be restored with the admonition, "Keep quiet! Old Stonewall is praying for you."[19]

Religion was deeply personal, not in the sense that it was private—indeed it was very public—but because it involved direct communication with God, and it offered both solace and inspiration. "We were cut off from home & had not much hope of ever meeting again the loved ones at home," said one Tennnessean. "I thought of earthly home sweet home & cried." Writing his brother, another Confederate expressed his faith this way: "The greatest pleasure that I have is when I am reading my Bible and praying to my Creator my Heavenly Father for in his care alone do I feel safe." God was in their everyday lives, and men were comfortable talking to him. "Oh Lord, we have a mighty big fight down here, and a sight of trouble," said one North Carolinian, "and we hope, Lord, that you will take the proper view of the matter, and give us the victory."[20]

Randolph McKim, who fought with the army from the Valley through Gettysburg before joining the ministry, recalled his first days as a chaplain with a cavalry unit. "I mounted my horse, and took my place as a matter of course in the column as it marched. This was a surprise to many of the men."

"Hello, Parson, are you going with us into battle?" one asked.

"Oh yes," McKim replied with a laugh, "I'm an old infantry soldier—I don't mind these little cavalry skirmishers."

"That's right, Parson," a rough-looking trooper yelled, rising in his stirrups. "You stick to us, and we'll stick to you!"

"I recall his appearance to this day," McKim wrote. "He had long yellow hair almost to his shoulders . . . and his eyes were so light that they almost looked white. From that moment on he was my fast friend."[21]

Many general officers likewise made professions of faith. Jackson, Lee and Stuart, of course, were lifetime Christians. But now such men as Dick Anderson, Robert Rodes, Dorsey Pender and the Stonewall Brigade's Franklin Paxton embraced the faith. Even Dick Ewell became a communicant, vowing he would give up swearing.

Chaplains, it must be admitted, seldom shared the deprivations of the men, although at least fifty died in combat and another fifty were wounded or died of disease. Even while praising one of the clerics attached to his own unit, Paxton allowed that "we have few such in the army. Chaplains are frequently away, whilst others stay at houses in the neighborhoods of the camps." During battle, moreover, chaplains often went to the rear. Jubal Early met one such cleric during Fredericksburg.

"Chaplain," yelled Early, "where are you going?"

"General, I am going to a place of safety," was the reply.

"Chaplain, I have known you for the past thirty years," jibed Early, "and all that time you have been trying to get to Heaven, and now that the opportunity is offered, you are fleeing from it. I am surprised."[22]

Under Longstreet's command in the south, meanwhile, were the heads of three sub-Departments: Arnold Elzey, never fully recovered from the facial wounds he had suffered at Gaines's Mill, in Richmond; punctilious Samuel G. French in southern Virginia; and Hill in North Carolina. Though his own divisions numbered only 16,000 men, his total force exceeded 40,000. It was an opportunistic situation, and he would strive to make the most of it. Exiles from

Lee's army like imperious Chase Whiting and bibulous Shanks Evans were, respectively, on duty at Wilmington and Kinston, North Carolina. (Even our old friend Pierre Beauregard with his Napoleonic delusions, though not reporting to Longstreet, was nearby at Charleston, South Carolina.) More valued officers included Robert Ransom, who had been sent to North Carolina after Fredericksburg with his brigade and that of the wounded John R. Cooke, and James Johnston Pettigrew, who had been exchanged following his capture at Seven Pines.

Longstreet soon found, however, that getting these strong-willed individuals to work together was no easy matter, no matter what his ambitions. In mid-March he ordered an attack on New Berne by Harvey Hill, but when Whiting failed to provide proper support the expedition failed. "The spirit manifested by Whiting has spoiled everything," Hill railed. "If I am to be cut down to two brigades I will not submit to the swindle." On March 30 Longstreet next moved against Washington, North Carolina, an operation that similarly came to naught because of bickering. Here Whiting did cooperate with Hill, sending him Ransom's brigade, though he fretted that he had stripped himself of reliable infantry. "I place but little reliance on Evans' Brigade," he said, referring to his remaining force, "which is certainly in worse condition than any I have ever seen." For his part Ransom protested that the combative Hill, of all officers, was dragging his feet. "I am not partial to service where there has been so little done," he said.[23]

There was some justification, of course, for Longstreet's assaults on New Berne and Washington. His quartermaster had insisted he could not collect supplies if his wagons were subject to Federal raiding parties, so bottling up the enemy in the garrison towns made sense. But Old Pete, whose success in gathering provisions was no more than adequate, seemed to be forgetting he might be needed on the Rappahannock, despite Lee's reminders that he stay mobile. There was little reason, for instance, for his siege of Suffolk, 120 miles away from Fredericksburg, which began on April 11.

Even if the town could be taken it could not be held, because Union gunboats could level it. Besides, the area had long since been stripped of foodstuffs. Longstreet initiated the action without consulting with Sam French, in part because he wanted to supplant him with Micah Jenkins, a personal favorite. "The next thing I knew," said French, "[Longstreet] . . . took from me a division and a number of batteries, and was on his way to Suffolk." There over the next few weeks this expedition likewise ground to a halt. "The Yankees have a very strong position," Hood beseechingly wrote Lee. "I presume we will leave here so soon as we gather all the bacon in the country. When we leave it is my desire to return to you." Longstreet nonetheless hung on in front of Suffolk, oblivious to the threat the Federals posed to Lee in the north. "I am of the opinion," he blandly said on April 29, ". . . that I can hold my position against any attack from the front." That same day Hooker made his move, throwing the bulk of his infantry across the river above Fredericksburg. "The enemy crossed the Rappahannock today in large numbers," Lee wired Davis. ". . . Besides the force which was reported by Genl Stuart to have crossed on the pontoon bridges laid below Kelly's Ford, I have learned this evening by couriers from Germanna & Ely's Fords that the enemy's cavalry crossed the Rapidan at those points about 2 P.M. today. . . . I hope if any reinforcements can be sent they may be forwarded immediately."[24]

Longstreet with the divisions of Hood and Pickett would not rejoin Lee in time for the battle of Chancellorsville. His excuse was that he could not leave his wagons, which were widely scattered and vulnerable to the enemy. "In view of Lee's repeated warnings," said one critic, "the excuse is not valid. Longstreet did not move because he did not wish to move."[25]

In the midst of the army's latest reorganization, the question of who would be advanced was raised anew. Tactical skill and bold deeds earned most promotions, but political considerations also counted, as did personal relationships. Dorsey Pender, for instance, complained that the rift between Powell Hill, his division chief, and Jackson would block his own promotion. "I understand Gen. Jackson has been making inquires about me," he wrote Fanny, "and said he was sorry he did not know more of me personally—the old humbug—this was when Gen. Hill sent up his last recommendation. He [Jackson] asked an officer of his staff in whom he has great confidence who was the best Brigadier in the Corps, and I think he told him that I was." Regardless of Jackson's real or imagined prejudices, Hill's recommendation of Pender touched off an amusing protest. The wife of fellow North Carolinian Robert Ransom entered the fray, writing Lee's adjutant that if anyone from the state deserved advancement it was her husband. Such rivalries made for good gossip during the long winter. Writing John Cooke, his convalescing brother-in-law, Jeb Stuart took the high road: "Now if Mrs. Jeb ever takes it upon herself to write to any official a letter of that kind in my behalf, she will have an account to settle with the aforesaid Jeb. It is *far better* to be neglected than to seek promotion by such means."[26]

That the quarrel between Hill and Jackson would ever be settled, even by so conciliatory a man as Lee, seemed more and more remote. Continuing to demand a trial Hill wrote Lee: "The General must acknowledge that if the charges preferred against me by General Jackson were true, then I do not deserve to command a division in this army; if they were untrue, then General Jackson deserves a rebuke as notorious as the arrest." Then in April he initiated a further contretemps when he directed that all orders from Jackson and his staff, even those dealing with mundane matters in the commissaries, ordnance units and signal departments, must first pass through him. Otherwise they would not be obeyed in the Light Division. This was too much for Stonewall. "When an officer orders in his command such disregard for the orders of his superiors, I am of the opinion that he should be relieved from duty," he told Lee on April 24. "It is very important to have harmony in my command."[27] Just days before Chancellorsville, then, with the army already weakened by Longstreet's absence, Jackson was calling for the removal of his best and most experienced division head.

# TWO

\* \* \* \*

# CHANCELLORSVILLE

Joseph Hooker likewise had reorganized his 115,000-man army, which now primarily consisted of seven corps, most comprised of three divisions. John Reynolds led the First Corps, Darius Couch the Second, Daniel Sickles the Third, George Meade the Fifth, John Sedgwick the Sixth (replacing Baldy Smith), Oliver Otis Howard the Eleventh and Henry Slocum the Twelfth. With the exception of Sickles, a New York politician, all were professional soldiers. The outspoken Couch had perhaps the best division chiefs: Winfield Scott Hancock, John Gibbon and William H. French. Howard, an old-line Yankee from Maine, led a command filled with German immigrants, as the names of many of his officers—von Steinwehr, Schurz and Schimmelfennig—attested.

On April 28 Hooker began his march upriver from Fredericksburg. The next day he turned Lee's left, sending Meade, Howard and Slocum across the Rappahannock at Kelly's Ford. The columns then turned south, crossed the Rapidan at Germanna and Ely's Fords unopposed and late on April 30 were at a crossroads called Chancellorsville, soon to be joined by Couch and Sickles. The upcoming battlefield was simply a clearing in an almost-impenetrable, densely wooded forest of pitch pine and scrub oak called the Wilderness, which stretched north and west of the crossroads for many miles. Its main feature was a large, brick two-story house, occupied by the George Chancellor family, and several outbuildings. Fording the river back at the town, meanwhile, were Reynolds and Sedgwick. The Federals now had some 80,000 men on or near Lee's flank, with 35,000 more facing his front. In three days

Meade, Howard and Slocum had marched 46 miles over rough roads, had forded and bridged two chest-high rivers with artillery and wagons and were threatening the enemy's rear. Hooker was already savoring victory. "I think this plan was decidedly the best strategy conceived in any of the campaigns ever set foot against us," conceded Porter Alexander.[1]

The Confederate lines on April 29 were largely where they had been since December: Jackson's corps with Colston, Powell Hill, Rodes and Early below Fredericksburg, McLaws's division behind the town and Dick Anderson's division upriver. In spite of the Federal demonstrations in his front Lee had sensed the major assault would be on his left. "I will notify Generals McLaw and Anderson to be on the alert," he told Jackson the week before, "for I think that if a real attempt is made to cross the river it will be above Fredericksburg." Once Stuart brought him news of the crossing and Hooker's progress he acted decisively, sending Anderson west up the Orange Plank Road that very night. "Cover the road leading from Chancellorsville . . . taking the strongest line you can," he told him. The next morning the industrious Anderson was digging in at Tabernacle Church, some four miles from the crossroads. "The work of intrenching was commenced immediately after the line had been selected, and was continued with great diligence and activity," that unassuming officer reported.[2]

Now Lee made a key decision. While it was true Hooker was in his rear, it was equally true that the two wings of the Federal army were 14 miles apart. "Beware of rashness, General Hooker," Fitz Lee would comment. "Some 50,000 'rebellious Rebels' have, by your own act, been placed between your two wings, and what is worse for you, they are commanded by Lee and Jackson. . . . General Lee perfectly understood the military problem thus presented to him. Drive the wedge in and keep the two parts asunder. If possible, hold one part still by a feint, or, if necessary, retard its march by a fight. Concentrate upon and overwhelm the other. Sedgwick, in command of the troops in the Confederate front, lay quiet while Hooker was massing at Chancellorsville."[3] Lee promptly ordered McLaws's division up the Orange Turnpike toward the enemy, with Jackson's division on its heels. With less than 50,000 men he would meet Hooker head-on. Only Barksdale's brigade of McLaws's command, Jubal Early's division and the reserve artillery under Pendleton—some 10,000 soldiers—were left on the river to fend with Sedgwick.

In the early hours of May 1 Jackson reached the lines at Tabernacle Church and at once ordered an advance. "My spirits rose with a sense of the wicked power of which I was in control & which I was soon going to turn loose," said Alexander, referring to his artillery battalion. "Immediately we knew that all our care and preparation to that point was work thrown away. We were not going to wait for the enemy to come & attack us in those lines, we were going out on the warpath after him." Anderson was to march up the plank road toward Chancellorsville, McLaws up the pike. Hours later, when the van of Hooker's column emerged from the Wilderness down these same roads, it encountered what it took to be the whole of Lee's army. Skirmishing was brisk, and Paul Semmes's Georgia brigade was in the thick of it. The Yankees were firing too high to bother his regiment, one man in the 53rd Georgia said, "but the left of our brigade suffered a sight, especially the 51st. . . ." The latter regiment lost perhaps 100 men, its colonel, William Slaughter, was mortally wounded, and the executive officer, Lieutenant Colonel Edward Ball, also was wounded. "The enemy, after a sharp contest," said Semmes, "retired a short distance and took shelter under a crest . . . advancing once more only to be again repulsed."4

By 2 P.M. Hooker, unnerved by Lee's challenge, decided to fall back to Chancellorsville. There in the Wilderness, he believed, his lines would be much stronger and his flanks unassailable, and Sedgwick would have more time to join him. Despite his superior numbers he was going on the defensive. "It was all wrong to stop—at least for the man who had to fight Lee & Jackson," Alexander argued. "But that is just what Hooker did. And what made him do it seems to me largely to have been the moral oppression of knowing who were his antagonists, & feeling himself outclassed. . . . Jackson had the reputation of making mysterious moves, & [Hooker] became demoralized and hesitated." Union General Couch, writing years afterward, was irate about the withdrawal. "Turning to the officers around me, Hancock, [George] Sykes, [Governeur] Warren and others," he said, "I told them what the order was, upon which they all agreed with me that the ground should not be abandoned. . . . The position was high ground, more or less open in front, over which an army might move and artillery be used advantageously; moreover, were it left in the hands of an enemy, his batteries, established on its crest and slopes, would command the position at Chancellorsville." Presently Couch was back at headquarters, making his report.

"It is all right, Couch, I have got Lee just where I want him," Hooker said. "He must fight me on my own ground."

The man who had schemed so endlessly to gain control of the army had, his own officers felt, lost the capacity for command.

"To hear from his own lips that the advantages gained by the successful marches of his lieutenants were to culminate in fighting a defensive battle in that nest of thickets was too much," said Couch, "and I retired from his presence with the belief that my commanding general was a whipped man."5

Soon Hooker's lines would form a V with Chancellorsville at the apex. His left extended to the Rappahannock, his right along the Orange Turnpike and into the Wilderness. Lee's right straddled the pike and extended toward the river, and his left was anchored at the old Catharine Furnace.

Through the night Lee and Jackson pondered the situation. Hooker had to be attacked forthwith, but it was self-evident that the Federal center, heavily fortified with abatis, could not be stormed successfully. Lee himself had scouted Hooker's left, but found no openings. "Returning . . . he found Jackson," explained Fitz Lee, who had been reconnoitering with his cavalry, "and asked if he knew any place to attack.

"Jackson said 'No.'

"Lee said, 'Then we must get around on the Federal right.'

"Jackson said he had been inquiring about roads by [Catharine] Furnace. Stuart came up then, and said he would go down to the furnace, and see what he could learn about roads. He soon returned with the Rev. [Beverly] Lacy [Jackson's chaplain, and a man familiar with the countryside], who said, 'A circuit could be made around by Wilderness Tavern,' and a young man living in the county, and then in the cavalry, was sent for to act as guide."

Within hours the plan firmed up. "Lee then took up the map and pointed out to Jackson the general direction of his route by the Furnace and Brock roads," Fitz Lee said. "Some conversation took place as to the importance of . . . [concealing] the movement from the enemy, and as to the existence of roads further to the enemy's right." Lee had made his decision. The details were being left to Jackson. "I . . . stated to General Jackson," Lee would write, "we must attack on our left as soon as practicable. . . . In consequence of a report received about that time from General Fitz Lee, describing the position of the Federal army, General Jackson, after some inquiry concerning the roads . . . undertook to throw his entire command entirely in Hooker's rear."[6]

Just before daybreak Lee and Jackson, seated on two cracker boxes—the debris of an issue of Federal rations the day before—conferred for the last time. "Well, General Jackson, what do you propose to do?" Lee asked rhetorically.

"Go around here," Jackson said, indicating some changes in the route that Chaplain Lacy and Jed Hotchkiss, his mapmaker, had recommended.

"What do you propose to make the movement with?"

"With my whole corps."

"What will you leave me?"

"The divisions of Anderson and McLaws."

Lee smiled, knowing that his lieutenant's daring matched his own.

"Well, go ahead," he ordered.[7]

Jackson would make his flanking march the morning of May 2 with 15 brigades—almost 30,000 men. Thomas Munford's 2nd Virginia Cavalry fanned out in front, and Stuart's and Fitz Lee's sabers guarded the right, intent on blocking the byways and shielding the column from the enemy. Soon the infantry was on the road. Rodes's division, with Colquitt's brigade in the van, led the way, followed by Colston's Division and Powell Hill's. Jackson, whose last days in camp before the battle had been cheered by a visit from Anna and five-month-old Julia—the first time he had seen the child—was reflective.

"Nothing earthly can mar my happiness," he told a friend. "I know that heaven is in store for me; and I should rejoice in the prospect of going there tomorrow." One aide remarked that many of the officers on the march had ties to the Virginia Military Institute. Jackson had taught there, of course, as had Rodes and Colston. Tom Munford was a V.M.I. graduate, and so was Stapleton Crutchfield, the Second Corps chief of artillery. "The Institute will be heard from today," said Jackson.[8]

There were two main obstacles to a surprise attack. The first was that the Federal cavalry might discover their route, and here Hooker, unbeknowst to Lee, had done the Confederates a great service. Earlier he had sent off the bulk of his horsemen, some 10,000 men under George Stoneman, on what turned out to be an ineffectual raid on Richmond. The enemy cavalry would not be a factor.

The second obstacle was time, and how many hours of daylight might remain when the attack was launched. "It would seem that with only ten miles to go, & the roads being in average fair country cross-road condition, we should have reached our goal in five hours," said Porter Alexander. "But no one who has ever marched with a long column can form any conception how every little inequality of ground, & every mud hole, especially if the road be narrow, causes a column to string out and lose distance. So that, though the head may advance steadily, the rear has to alternately halt & start, & halt & start . . . wearing out the men and consuming precious daylight." Hunter McGuire, the Second Corps medical director, stated that he would never forget "the intensity of Jackson on that march. His face was pale, his eyes flashing. . . . In his eagerness, as he rode, he leaned over the neck of his horse as if in that way the march might be hurried. 'See that the column is kept closed and that there is no straggling,' he more than once ordered, and 'Press on! Press on!' was repeated again and again." The enemy meanwhile did not divine his intentions. By 1:30 P.M. Union General Sickles, clashing with Jackson's rear guard at Catherine Furnace after the main column had passed, leaped to the conclusion the Confederates were retreating. Hooker, receiving this report from Sickles, heard what he wanted to hear.[9] During the whole time Jackson was making his march Hooker stayed in his lines, making no assaults on his front, where Lee with only Anderson's and McLaws's 12,000 men was so vulnerable.

The Confederate flanking column, its progress both concealed and impeded by the denseness of the Wilderness, trudged on. "For hours our silent columns swept along the roads at the quick step, now turning to the right, and now to the left," said a captain in the 14th South Carolina. "We lost the points of the compass and became about as much bewildered in regard to courses or directions, as we already were in regard to the object of the expedition." Now Fitz Lee reached the Orange Plank Road, five miles west of Chancellorsville. Crossing it he rode through the woods in the direction of the Orange Turnpike, then cautiously ascended a hill. "What a sight presented itself before me!" he said. "Below, and but a few hundred yards distant, ran the Federal line of battle. I was in rear of [Oliver] Howard's right. There were the lines of defence, with abatis in front, and long lines of stacked arms. Two cannon were visible. . . . The soldiers were in groups in the rear, laughing, chatting, smoking."[10]

Rejoining his cavalry he galloped back to Jackson and made his report. "General," he said excitedly, "if you will ride with me, halting your column here out of sight, I will show you the enemy's right." Soon Jackson was viewing Howard's unsuspecting Eleventh Corps for himself. "I only knew Jackson slightly," Fitz Lee went on. "I watched him closely as he gazed upon Howard's troops. His eyes burned with a brilliant glow. . . . To the remarks made to him while the unconscious line of blue was pointed out, he did not reply once during the five minutes he was on the hill, and yet his lips were moving . . . I know now what he was doing then. . . . While talking to the Great God of Battles, how could he hear what a poor cavalryman was saying?" Wheeling his horse, Jackson abruptly addressed a courier. "Tell General Rodes," he said, "to move across the plank road; halt when he gets to the old turnpike, and I will join him there." By 3 P.M. he was advising Lee: "The enemy has made a stand at Chancellor's [Melzi Chancellor's house, also known as Dow Dall's Tavern], which is about two miles from Chancellorsville. . . . I trust that an everkind Providence will bless us with great success."[11]

Two hours later Rodes's command was drawn up perpendicular to the pike—the line from left to right comprised of Alfred Iverson's North Carolinians, Edward O'Neal's Alabamians and George Doles's and Aldred Colquitt's Georgians, with Dodson Ramseur's North Carolinians behind Colquitt. On the second line were three brigades of Colston's division: from left to right Francis Nicholls's Louisianans, John R. Jones's Virginians and Edward Warren's mixed unit. On the third line, still coming up, was Hill's division. "Each brigade commander received positive instructions, which were well understood," said Rodes. "The whole line was to push ahead from the beginning, keeping the road for its guide. The position at [James] Talley's house was to be taken at all hazards as . . . it commanded a second position of the enemy at Melzi Chancellor's house. . . . Under no circumstances was there to be any pause in the advance. As there was possibility of pressure on my right flank, Ramseur was directed to watch that flank carefully, thus leaving Colquitt free to push ahead."[12]

Captain James Power Smith, a Jackson aide, recalled the order to attack. "Upon his stout-built, long-paced little sorrel General Jackson sat, with visor low over his eyes and lips compressed, and with his watch in his hand. Upon his right sat General Robert E. Rodes, the very picture of a soldier, and every inch all that he appeared.

" 'Are you ready, General Rodes?'

" 'Yes, sir,' said Rodes, impatient for the advance.

" 'You can go forward then.'

"Suddenly the woods rang with the bugle call, and back came the responses from bugles on the right and left, and the long line of skirmishers, through the wild thicket of undergrowth, sprang eagerly to their work."[13]

The surprise was complete. Porter Alexander picks up the story: "There was no longer any embargo on noises & the mingled roar of our musketry, & the famous Confederate yell, shook the woods. . . . Howard was an excellent soldier. His corps was composed almost entirely of Germans. A few stood their ground, & fought well for a while; but within twenty minutes the whole corps was thrown into such a wild panic as was never seen in either army before or after. . . . It was now after six, and the sun set at 6:50. Our lines of battle had been, practically, broken up by the advance through the thick woods, & they did not halt to reform but pressed forward, the men singly & in groups, firing stopping to load, & then pressing forward again." Doles was in the forefront, on his left O'Neal and Iverson. "Doles at this moment debouched from the woods and encountered a force of the enemy and two guns entrenched," said Rodes. "Detaching two regiments to flank the position, he charged without halting, sweeping everything before him, and, pressing on to Talley's, gallantly captured the works there, and captured five guns by a similar flank movement." Thus far, however, only three of Rodes's five brigades had been engaged. Colquitt on the right had become indecisive. At this critical moment the Princeton graduate, despite his orders, had held up his men. "General Colquitt, soon after starting, was misled by the appearance of a small body of the enemy's cavalry," said Rodes coldly, "and, notwithstanding the instructions . . . halted his brigade. . . . Ramseur, being ordered to follow Colquitt and watch his flank, was deprived of any active participation."[14]

Twilight was falling on the woods. Melzi Chancellor's house had been taken, but still the Confederates pressed on. Rodes's and Colston's divisions had become so mingled that officers could not find their men nor men their officers, but Jackson, galloping into the ranks, urged them to press the pursuit. Some 10,000 Federals had been utterly routed and his men were in rear and within a mile-and-a half of the enemy's center, but until Chancellorsville was reached and the road to United States Ford was cut, Hooker could still make his escape. The field was strewn with bodies. Porter Alexander passed one wounded Yankee, lying by the roadside and calling out, loudly and repeatedly, " 'Water! Water! Water!' I noticed that he was shot through the forehead & the brain was protruding. I asked, 'What State are you from?' He changed his cry & began to shout, 'New York! New York! New York!' just as he had been shouting 'Water!' and kept it up as long as I could hear."[15]

In the growing darkness Powell Hill's troops with their full cartridge boxes passed through and relieved the first two lines of Rodes and Colston, struggling to maintain both their own ranks and the pressure on the enemy. The brigade of James Lane, the former mathematics professor at V.M.I., was in the van. "Push right ahead, Lane!" Jackson had told him, and Jim Lane did just that, dividing his four regiments in line of battle across the plank road.

Then in the midst of carnage occurred a bizarre interlude. Lieutenant Colonel Levi Smith of the 128th Pennsylvania came forward under a white flag, asking whether Lane's men were Confederates or Federals. "Considering this an illegitimate use of a white flag, as he expressly stated it was not his object to surrender, and not wishing to let him return," said Lane, "I sent [a courier] to General Hill to know what I should do." In the meantime the matter became moot when his skirmishers returned with Smith's regiment, which had thrown down its arms, causing its commander "to remonstrate with me for allowing it to be captured while he was in my lines with a white flag." Lane sent both Smith and his men to the rear and resumed his advance. Behind him as night fell were Samuel McGowan's South Carolinians, the former command of Maxcy Gregg. "The scene was terrible," said a second lieutenant in the 1st South Carolina. "Volley after volley of musketry was poured by the Confederate line in front of us upon the enemy; cheers wild and fierce rang over the whole woods; officers shouted at the top of their voices, to make themselves heard; cannon roared and shells burst continually. We knew nothing, could see nothing. . . . Night engagements are always dreadful. . . . To see your danger is bad enough; but to hear shell whizzing and . . . not know from whence death comes to you, is trying beyond all things."[16]

While Lane and McGowan and the rest of Hill's brigades were advancing in the moonlit darkness to less than a mile from Chancellorsville, Jackson about 9 P.M. became impatient. Riding on or near the Orange Plank Road during a lull to see how far the Federals had fallen back, he and some aides moved beyond the main Confederate lines. "General," said Sandie Pendleton, "don't you think this is the wrong place for you?" Jackson dismissed the warning. "The danger is over. The enemy is routed. Go back and tell A.P. Hill to press on." Powell Hill, feeling it was his duty to go where his commanding officer led, rode with his own aides some 50 yards behind Jackson.

Minutes later a single shot rang out hundreds of yards to the southwest, probably from a rebel picket and entirely unrelated to Jackson's reconnaissance. It set off a chain reaction along the Confederate lines—first scattered firing and then some volleys—that spread to the 18th North Carolina of Lane's brigade. These shots from behind—from their own men—unhorsed Hill and killed and wounded several of his aides but initially left Jackson and his party unhurt. Instinctively galloping back to their lines, Jackson's group rode into a second fusillade from the 18th North Carolina. This battle-hardened regiment had served bravely in Lee's army since the Seven Day but, stated one of its officers, the noise of Jackson's horses in the darkness "seemed to the average infantryman like a brigade of cavalry."[17]

The second burst of fire wounded Jackson in three places. One minie ball passed through his right palm, another through his left forearm, the last through his upper left arm, splintering bone and ripping tendons. By this time ten of the nineteen horsemen in the two parties had been killed or wounded.

Hill soon rushed to his stunned commander's side. "I have been trying to make the men stop firing," he said. He asked Jackson with genuine anguish if his wounds were painful.

"Very painful," came the dazed reply. "I think my arm is broken."

The man who had been bitterly quarreling with Jackson since Second Manassas cradled his head while helping to rip away his clothing and treat the wounds. Hill's concern was obvious. Soon a surgeon came on the scene.

"I will try to keep your accident from the knowledge of the troops," Hill said before Jackson was taken to the rear. "Thank you," Jackson answered. Hill, who assumed command of the corps, would not see him again.[18]

The shots from Lane's brigade had roused the Federal gunners, who thought an attack was underway and answered with a full-scale artillery barrage. "When the shells and grapeshot come tearing through the ranks the scene is indescribable," said a soldier in the 2nd Louisiana. "The men seem almost panic stricken, the groans & shrieks of the wounded were heart rending, artillery horses riderless came thundering back with pieces & caissons . . . all combined a most horrible spectacle." In the midst of the frenzy a shell ripped through the belly of the mount ridden by Francis Nicholls, commanding one of the two Louisiana brigades (his was in Colston's division; Harry Hays's Louisiana brigade was in Early's), and tore off his left foot. Nicholls, who had lost his left arm in the Valley Campaign, lay semiconscious in the darkness. Soon an ambulance crew found him, but seeing his empty sleeve and missing foot left him for dead. Later Nicholls, trying to tend his mutilated leg, "found to my upper surprise the wound did not bleed at all." Subsequently some of his Tigers carried him to the rear, and somehow he survived.[19]

Hill likewise was wounded during the barrage when a shell fragment cut off his boot tops and badly lacerated his lower legs, incapacitating him. Though command should have devolved on Brigadier Rodes, the senior division chief, Hill sent for Major General Stuart and at midnight gave him the leadership of the corps. The thought of infantry being led by the head of the cavalry was a novel one, but Rodes understood the decision. "I feared that the information that the command had devolved on me, unknown except to my own immediate troops, would in their shaken condition be likely to increase the demoralization of the corps," he said. "General Stuart's name was well and very favorably known to the army, and would tend I hoped to re-establish confidence."[20] Command of Hill's division, in turn, went to Henry Heth. When the firing finally ceased, the Confederates settled down in the darkness, straightening their ranks and awaiting the morning.

———

Sunday May 3 brought on fierce fighting both in the Wilderness and back at Fredericksburg on Marye's Heights. Let us look first at the Wilderness, where at daybreak Stuart launched an all-out attack to push Hooker back from Chancellorsville and reunite his right flank with Lee's left. Powell Hill's division, now under Heth, made up the first line of battle. Dorsey Pender's North Carolinians and Edward Thomas's Georgians advanced up the north side of the plank road, while James Lane's North Carolinians, Samuel McGowan's South Carolinians, James Archer's mixed brigade and Heth's brigade of Virginians under Colonel John Brockenbrough moved up on the south side. Colston's division was in the second line, Rodes's in the third.

Stapleton Crutchfield had lost a leg the night before and Porter Alexander was commanding the artillery. "The action was commenced by advancing our infantry until it developed the enemy's line," Alexander wrote. "This was found close at hand everywhere, & was generally strengthened by trenches, breastworks of logs, & with trees felled in front. Tremendous musketry fire was at once opened by both parties. . . . I remember thinking at the time that the roar of the battle would be easily heard at Mr. Wortham's [the house nearby where his wife and child were staying] & would tell them all what was going on. I was interested afterward to hear that our little 18 months old daughter was greatly excited over it, & made the longest sentence she had yet produced, 'Hear my papa shoot Yankee. Boo!' "[21]

By 7:30 A.M. Heth's men were still stymied or repulsed, with their only success being James Archer's seizing of Hazel Grove, one of the few positions in the forest where artillery could be used effectively. Taking this clearing, however, would tip the balance of the battle. "As the sun lifted the mist that shrouded the field," Jeb Stuart said, "it was discovered that the ridge on the extreme right (Hazel Grove) was a fine position for concentrating artillery. I immediately ordered 30 pieces to that point and, under the happy effects of the batallion system, it was done quickly. The effect of this fire upon the enemy's batteries was superb."[22] Both Alexander and the gentle-looking Willie Pegram, now leading a battalion, had earlier realized the importance of Hazel Grove and had rushed additional guns up the plank road, a move that would catch the Yankee artillery in a north-south converging fire. Up and down the mile-long field the fighting continued to rage, with Heth's command in the forefront of a desperate melee.

South of the road near Hazel Grove the experience of McGowan's brigade was typical as it surged forward, was driven back, then advanced again. "Now we were at a standstill," said J.F.J. Caldwell of the 1st South Carolina. "The enemy became emboldened, and advanced upon the unprotected right flank of the brigade. . . . The Rifles gave way, the 1st Regiment followed it slowly . . . seventy or eighty yards from the late position. Gen. McGowan arranged us as well as possible here, and . . . was wounded standing upon the works. The ball entered below the knee, inflicting such injury that he did not recover until the next winter. . . . Brig. Gen. Colston brought in a fresh line, himself and his staff riding up the works, conspicuous marks to the enemy. The Stonewall Brigade passed over us, some of them saying, with not very pleasant levity, that they would show us how to clear away a Federal line. . . . They were forced back into the woods with us. The firing continued, unintermitted, deadly."[23]

The human cost of the struggle would be high. Prior to the war Brigadier Franklin ("Bull") Paxton of the Stonewall Brigade had been a profane and godless man, but Jackson's example and the bloodletting had made him a believer, and now he was never without a small Bible, kept in a breast pocket. Just the night before, he had told Henry Kyd Douglas he would not survive the next day's fighting. "He did not seem morbid or superstitious but he spoke with earnest conviction," Douglas said. "He then told me exactly where certain private and personal papers were to be found in his desk. . . . He requested me to see to it that they were not lost but were sent [home] to Lexington. He had the picture of his wife and his Bible with him. He concluded by asking me to write to his wife as soon as he was killed, and to see that his body was sent to Lexington. . . . Paxton was not an emotional man. . . . I had no doubt of his sincerity and his awful prescience."[24] Later, while leading the Stonewall Brigade through McGowan's lines, Paxton wore a new uniform his wife had sent him, the insignia of his rank proudly sewn on its collar. Urging his men forward by example, he was shot in the chest and died within minutes.

Colston would lose all four of his brigade commanders at Chancellorsville. Besides Paxton, the night before he had lost Nicholls and within the hour Edward Warren would also be wounded. Meanwhile John R. Jones, that rarest of creatures in Lee's army—an officer of suspect courage—had left the field with what he claimed was an ulcerated leg. He would not serve in the army again. Their subordinates nonetheless soldiered on. In the 10th Virginia, Warren's brigade, Captain James Melhorn remembered: "I was shot in the foot, and fifteen minutes after I was shot in the hip, which near disabled me." Though the enemy called on him to surrender, "I crawled over the breastworks & layed down." Then reinforcements arrived, and as he was escaping he received a third wound. "I made my exit from the field by the assistance of a friend." Included in the 10th Virginia's 150-odd casualties were 17 officers.[25]

By 9:30 A.M., however, Stuart's unrelenting pressure was beginning to crumble the Federal defenses south of the plank road. Jeb galloped up and down the lines, shouting words of encouragement, and at one point led two charges by the 28th North Carolina. Reported one officer: "When the 28th rejoined me . . . its colonel, [Samuel D.] Lowe, was perfectly carried away with Stuart. He not only spoke of his dash, but he told me he heard him singing,

'Old Joe Hooker, won't you get out of the Wilderness!' and he wound up by saying, 'Who would have thought it? Jeb Stuart in command of the 2nd army corps!' "[26]

Now all three of Stuart's divisions were heavily engaged, and the guns at Hazel Grove were rolling out their cannonades in earnest, dominating the enemy artillery position at Fairview. "A glorious day, Colonel, a glorious day!" the bespectacled, gunpowder-blackened Pegram enthused to Porter Alexander. Grudgingly the Federals began to fall back. North of the plank road Dorsey Pender's North Carolinians from the beginning had been a pounding force. "We had the most terrible battle of the war," he later wrote Fanny, "not because [the enemy] fought better but because they had such terrible odds and such a strong position. . . . Hooker thought he had us but . . . after five terrible hours we drove him from his position. I was in the front line to start at them and went through to the last. Fought my brigade until the final repulse. . . . If not before, I won promotion last Sunday, and if it can be done I think I shall get it. Our N.C. troops behaved most nobly."[27]

It was not Pender, however, but his fellow North Carolinian, the 25-year-old Brigadier Dodson Ramseur, who to the south headed directly toward the enemy artillery and first opened a breach in the Federal lines. Chancellorsville was his first battle at the head of the slain George Burgwyn Anderson's old brigade, and Ramseur made the most of the opportunity. Pushing his unit forward into some breastworks he encountered John R. Jones's huddled and demoralized brigade. When he ordered them forward, "not a man moved." Ramseur promptly asked Stuart if he might "run over the troops" in his front, and permission was just as promptly given. "Forward!" he yelled, and his men advanced, literally treading on the backs of the Virginians. "I, myself, put my foot on the back and head of an officer on high rank, in mounting the work," said Colonel Bryan Grimes of the 4th North Carolina, "and, through very spite, ground his face in the earth." In short order but with appalling casualties Ramseur's men closed with the enemy, neutralizing the Federal cannon who could not shoot without killing their own men. Later the Stonewall Brigade came up to his support. Ramseur would lose almost 800 of his 1,500 troops. "On beholding the shattered remnants of the . . . brigade," an officer of the 2nd North Carolina would say, "[Ramseur] wept like a child."[28]

Events now moved swiftly. Elements of Dick Anderson's division, which were on the left of Lee's lines facing Hooker, had marched during the morning through Catharine Furnace and reached Hazel Grove, reuniting the Confederates in a concave front against the Federals. By 10 A.M. Lee was ordering James Archer, who was still in support of Pegram's batteries, to assault the enemy's guns at Fairview. Soon Anderson's fresh brigades—Carnot Posey's Mississippians, Rans Wright's Georgians and Edward Perry's Floridians—joined with Stuart's corps in the attack. Within the hour Hooker's entire force was pushed north of the plank road and Chancellorsville taken, but the enemy still held the escape route to U.S. Ford. The morning-long battle in the Wilderness incurred frightful casualties: almost 9,000 for the South, some 8,600 for the North. During this period the Federal defense was further weakened when a shell struck the George Chancellor farmhouse, where Hooker had his headquarters, and knocked him unconscious. Even when he came to, he remained for a time in a confused condition.

Back at Fredericksburg on Saturday morning, May 2, even as Jackson was making his flank march, Jubal Early was watching Sedgwick, wondering when and where he would strike. Expecting any Federal attack to be downriver from the town, he had strung out in that area his whole division—comprised of John Brown Gordon's Georgians, Robert Hoke's North Carolinians, William "Extra Billy" Smith's Virginians and Harry Hays's Louisianans—leaving Barksdale's Mississippians on Marye's Heights. Then about 11 A.M. Colonel Robert Chilton, Lee's chief of staff, arrived with urgent verbal orders: Early was to march to Chancellorsville immediately, leaving behind only William Pendleton with the reserve artillery and one brigade of infantry. Early could not believe what he was being told. "I remarked to Colonel Chilton," he said, "that I could not retire my troops without their being seen by the enemy, whose position on Stafford Heights not only overlooked ours, but who had one or two balloons which he was constantly sending up from the heights to make observations, and stated that he would inevitably move over and take possession of Fredericksburg and [Marye's] Heights."

Chilton was insistent. "The Colonel said he presumed General Lee understood all this, but that it was much more important for him to have troops where he was than at Fredericksburg," Early continued. "This was astounding to us, as we were satisfied that we were keeping away from the army opposed to General Lee a much larger body of troops than my force could neutralize if united to [his] army near Chancellorsville." Orders were orders, however, and Early soon had his command heading toward the Orange Plank Road, leaving behind Hays's brigade, Pendleton and one of Barksdale's regiments. Chilton had misunderstood Lee's wishes, however, a not uncommon occurrence when verbal orders were relayed during times of stress. "Upon getting near the plank road, a little before dark, I received a note from General Lee which informed me that he did not expect me to join him unless, in my judgment, the withdrawal of my troops could be done with safety, and I think he [said] that if I could . . . check a large force of the enemy, I could do as much or perhaps more service than by joining him."[29] A fuming Early turned his column around, getting back to Fredericksburg about 11 P.M.

Left behind to picket the Rappahannock during this futile march was Colonel Benjamin Humphreys and the 21st Mississippi. "The only instruction I received from [General] Barksdale was, 'Watch your flanks, hold the picket line as long as you can, then fall back . . . and hunt for your brigade.' I cannot well describe my feelings when I found my regiment thus left alone, stretched out three miles long, with only a small river between us and thirty thousand well-armed and hostile men, purposely displayed to magnify their numbers." Shortly after dark a courier brought Humphreys, a 58-year-old planter, welcome news: Barksdale and the Washington Artillery were returning to Fredericksburg, and the rest of Early's division was in their wake. Toward midnight Humphreys went back to Barksdale on the heights for further orders. He found him wrapped in a heavy blanket, lying at the foot of a tree.

"Are you asleep, General?" he whispered.

"No, sir," came the gruff reply. "Who could sleep with a million armed Yankees all around him?"

The next morning, Sunday, while Stuart was throwing Jackson's Second Corps against Hooker, Early was still trying to anticipate where Sedgwick would make his main assault. The Federals made feint after feint to conceal their intentions. Early continued to think the attack would be downriver from the town and concentrated his main force there, but to placate Barksdale, who insisted it would be on Marye's Heights, he sent him Hays's brigade in support. Barksdale turned out to be right. Following one demonstration against Marye's Hill, the enemy requested a truce to remove their wounded. "This truce was granted," Humphreys said, "and the enemy, with one eye on their wounded, and the other on our trenches, discovered that our redoubts were nearly stripped of guns, and our infantry of the 18th Regiment stretched out to less than a single rank." Subsequently forty pieces of artillery were directing their fire on his position, and "three columns of infantry seemed to rise out of the earth and rushed forward with demonic shouts—one from a valley in front of Marye's Hill, one from the [town] on the plank road, and one up the valley of Hazel Run." Soon the stone wall and the sunken road, where Tom Cobb and John Rogers Cooke had made their stand the previous December, were overrun. "The first intimation I had of disaster at the stone wall," continued Humphreys, "was from a sharpshooter's minie ball striking the visor of my cap, and driving it back against and blinding for the time my left eye. I saw enough to satisfy myself that I was cut off from the brigade, with the enemy on my right flank. I attempted to change front and form on the plank road . . . but found that road enfiladed . . . which forced us to retreat."[30]

The capture of Marye's Heights could have resulted in the Federals cutting off Hays's brigade on the left of the town from the rest of the command, but Early quickly organized a skillful withdrawal. He fell back in stages to a strong position two miles south of the heights and proceeded to regroup his left and right wings. In this he was helped by Sedgwick's lack of aggressiveness. The Federal commander had received orders from Hooker at midnight to advance and join him at Chancellorsville, but could not get started until dawn. Now his attack had consumed almost the entire morning, and Sedgwick thought it prudent to regroup before marching on. This would be a mistake, for there was plenty of fight left in Early and his men. "Where are your guns?" someone asked a retreating member of the Washington Artillery. "Guns!" replied the cannoneer angrily. "I reckon now the people of the Southern Confederacy are satisfied that Barksdale's Brigade and the Washington Artillery can't whip the whole Yankee army." Barksdale put the setback in more optimistic terms. "Our center has been pierced, that's all," he said; "we will be all right in a little while."[31]

Here Providence entered the picture in the person of Cadmus Marcellus Wilcox, whose Alabama brigade had been detached to guard the river at Banks's Ford, some five miles upstream from Fredericksburg. Disturbed like so many officers by lack of promotion, the capable Wilcox had asked to be reassigned from the army, only to be talked out of the request by Lee. May 3 proved to be his great day. "Having visited my line of pickets on the morning," he said, "I found that the . . . sentinels on post had their haversacks on, a thing unusual. This induced me to believe that most of the force from Banks's Ford had been sent to Chancellorsville." Leaving a token force to guard the ford, Wilcox was preparing to go there himself when he learned that the enemy was massing in force at Fredericksburg. "I determined not to move my command . . . until I knew definitely the intention of the enemy, and ordered them in the ravine opposite Dr. Taylor's, where they would be near and yet out of sight."

About 2 P.M. he learned that Barksdale was hard pressed and Marye's Heights had been lost. He made contact with Harry Hays, who was on Early's extreme left, and suggested the two of them make a stand on the plank road. "This [Hays] declined doing, having been ordered [by Early] to fall back to the Telegraph Road, and was soon out of sight. . . . Finding myself alone on the left of the plank road, with the enemy in full view on the crests of the first range of hills in the rear of Fredericksburg . . . I felt it a duty to delay the enemy as much as possible in his advance, and to endeavor to check him. . . . With this view I formed my brigade promptly in line near Stansbury's house, at right angles to the road." Wilcox positioned his four guns on his flanks, sent out skirmishers and opened fire on Sedgwick's lines some 800 yards distant, holding the enemy in check for some time. "At length they deployed skirmishers . . . and began to advance. This was slow, and, delayed by frequent halts. . . . From this slight affair . . . I felt confident, if forced to retire along the plank road, that I could do so without precipitancy, and that ample time could be given for reinforcements to reach us from Chancellorsville; and, moreover, I believed that, should the enemy pursue, he could be attacked in rear by General Early, reinforced by Generals Hayes and Barksdale."[32]

Subsequently Wilcox, employing classic delaying tactics, fell back to Salem Church. Sedgwick pursued again in halting fashion, giving Lee time to rush reinforcements the twelve miles from Chancellorsville to his aid. About 5 P.M., when Sedgwick did make his assault, McLaws's three brigades—Semmes's and Wofford's Georgians, and Kershaw's South Carolinians—were in support of Wilcox, as were Mahone's Virginians. Deploying below a ridge and out of sight, their presence was not immediately noted. Cautious as Sedgwick was, he nonetheless marched straight into great peril. Expecting one brigade, he encountered five.

Wilcox's and Semmes's brigades, straddling the plank road, did by far the bulk of the fighting. For Private John Wood of the 53rd Georgia, the artillery fire was second only to what he had experienced at Malvern Hill. "It sounded like a large cane brake on fire and a thunder storm with repeated large thunder claps," he said. His regiment's position behind an embankment was greatly to his liking because "we could load and fire without exposing anything except our heads and arms. In shooting our company fired [an average of] 15 to 20 rounds apiece at the vandals." An officer in the 53rd Georgia, referring to the smoothbores his men were firing as the enemy closed in, wrote his wife: "You may believe that we gave them buck and ball in a hurry. . . . Mollie you ought to have been there to see the dead and wounded Yankees and to see what they had, and seen our boys robbing their knapsacks."[33]

The force of the Federal assault temporarily unnerved the 10th Alabama, which wavered and fell back, endangering the line. Standing beside the 9th Alabama, his only reserve regiment, Wilcox remained calm. Recalled one of his officers: "Wilcox twice sang out . . . look at that dammed 10th . . . steady 9th Alabama. . . ." Only at the last moment did he give the order to fire. "One solid sheet of flame arose from this noble Reg., the enemy waver and return the fire. . . ." Led by its commanding officer, Major Jeremiah Williams, the 9th Alabama countercharged into a point-blank volley. "This fire did most of the damage of the day," said another officer. "Nine men of Co. K fell dead in their tracks without firing a gun, as almost twice as many suffered severely." The 9th Alabama did not flinch, rolling into Sedgwick's lines with the force of a pile driver. Inspired, the rest of Wilcox's regiments followed, pushing the enemy back. With darkness coming on, Sedgwick broke off the action and withdrew toward Fredericksburg and the river.

"That is the best regiment I ever saw," McLaws said in admiration of the 9th Alabama's reckless onslaught.

"General," Wilcox proudly answered, "that is the best regiment on the American continent."

Later the courtly Wilcox, he who had seen the young Thomas Jackson doing the buck-and-wing during their post–West Point graduation visit to Washington, wrote his sister: "My brigade acted nobly in this fight of the 3rd. . . . You can see how our men fight and how much better they fight than the Yankees."[34] Lee's reinforcement of the lines against Sedgwick, of course, meant that the

Confederates could take little action against Hooker at Chancellorsville late Sunday afternoon or the following day. On May 4 the battle would be at Fredericksburg.

Six days of marching, fighting and countermarching had ensued, and the positions of both armies were truly extraordinary. "A heavy force of Federals— about fifteen thousand—occupied Fredericksburg and Stafford Heights," Colonel Humphreys recalled. "Barksdale and Early, with their backs to each on the plank road, with five thousand men, between Fredericksburg and Sedgwick; Sedgwick between Early and Lee, with twenty thousand men; Lee with Anderson, McLaws and Wilcox, between Sedgwick and Hooker's main army, with twenty thousand men; Hooker's main army—ninety thousand strong— between Lee and Stuart; Stuart, now commanding Stonewall Jackson's Corps, with twenty-five thousand men; all stretched out along a straight road within a space of twelve miles." With Jackson wounded and Longstreet absent, moreover, Lee was without his two best men. "With the genius that never deserted him," Humphreys said, "[Lee] boldly issued his orders. Barksdale was to hold back any Federal force left in Fredericksburg, Stuart and Anderson were to threaten Chancellorsville, while in person Lee advanced with McLaws and Wilcox and a portion of Anderson's Division, composed of [Carnot] Posey's and [Edward] Perry's Brigades, to attack Sedgwick in front, while Early attacked him in the rear."[35]

On Monday morning at Fredericksburg the Confederates were gambling that Hooker would stay within his lines and not go on the offensive, and in this expectation the Federal commander did not disappoint. The day began auspiciously when Jubal Early, who had massed his troops during the night, moved up the Telegraph Road, intent on retaking Marye's Heights and cutting Sedgwick off from the town. "[John Brown] Gordon's Brigade was placed in line at light," said Early, "while ["Extra Billy"] Smith and Barksdale were ordered to take their positions and be in readiness to follow. . . . I then went with Generals [Harry] Hays and [Robert] Hoke . . . across Hazel Run to point out to them the positions they were to take. After doing this I rode back and found to my surprise that Gordon had moved off under a misapprehension of my order, as he was to have waited."

Gordon, new to brigade command and hearing only that his Georgians were to spearhead the assault, had reacted with characteristic fervor. In this case, his impetuosity was rewarded. Resistance was minimal, and the heights were soon recaptured. "When we were under full headway and under fire from the heights," said Gordon, "I received an order to halt, with the explanation that the other troops were to unite in the assault. . . . My men were already under heavy fire. . . . I replied to the order that it was too late to halt them and that a few minutes more would decide the result of the charge. General Early playfully but earnestly remarked after the fort was taken that success had saved me from being court-martialed." The Confederate plan now called for McLaws to assail the enemy right while Early applied pressure on the left. With the Federal salient bulging out from the river in the shape of a six-mile-long horseshoe, however, communication was difficult and the strategy failed, with McLaws in particular being hesitant to commit his command.[36]

This development did not put Lee in the best of humors. "About ten o'clock Gen. Lee in person with his staff came up to where I was on the line," said Porter Alexander, "& for the first time . . . I saw him in a temper." The cause of the commander's ire was manifold: "1st. That a great deal of valuable time had already been uselessly lost by somebody, somehow, no particulars being given. 2nd. Nobody knew exactly how or where the enemy's line of battle ran & it was somebody's duty to know. 3rd. That it now devolved on him personally to find out." The best way to find out all about the enemy, Alexander felt, would be to move on them at once, "but the old man seemed to be feeling so real wicked, I concluded to retain my ideas exclusively in my own possession." Lee then spent the balance of the day reconnoitering, giving Sedgwick hope he would not attack. "He knew that their right flank (which was in front of *us*) rested on the river; but where was their left?"[37] Lee was missing Longstreet. Old Pete might be stubborn, even at times self-serving, but he understood the importance of knowing the terrain when directing large bodies of men in the field.

Finally establishing that the enemy's left flank also rested on the river, Lee and Early drew up new plans. McLaws and Wilcox would stay where they were, blocking the plank road, only later in the battle advancing Wofford's Georgians and Kershaw's South Carolinians; Early would open the attack on the enemy left with Gordon's Georgians, Hays's Louisianans and Hoke's North Carolinians; Dick Anderson would extend the lines with Rans Wright's Georgians, Posey's Missisippians and Perry's Floridians and assail the center. Hopefully Sedgwick's lines would be broken before darkness gave him the opportunity to escape across the river.

In part because of difficulties getting the troops into position, the attack did not begin until 6 P.M., when Alexander sounded the signal with three cannon shots. Early enjoyed initial success, routing the 20th New York, which was comprised of Germans from New York City. So fast did the 20th run, in fact, that its men thereafter—along with those of Oliver Howard's unfortunate Eleventh Corps—were called the Flying Dutchmen. Other Federal units, particularly the Vermont brigade known as the Green Mountain Boys, were made of sterner stuff, and soon the defensive lines stiffened. Then Robert Hoke went down with an arm wound and his North Carolinians, lacking leadership, floundered about. On their right Hays's brigade likewise lost cohesion. "Owing to the rapidity of our charge," said one officer in the 9th Louisiana, "the brigade became inextricably confused. One half the men were so broken down by previous hard marching as to be unable to keep up with rest. Officers lost their companies, and companies their officers."

John Brown Gordon on the far right made the best showing, taking Taylor's Hill and then coming close to the enemy position at Banks's Ford. "The boys raised a yell enough to frighten any living thing on earth," said a man in the 13th Georgia, ". . . and it was all the skirmishers could do to keep in shooting distance." Even Gordon eventually was repulsed, however. On Early's left Dick Anderson's people accomplished less, succeeding in driving in the Federal skirmishers but never closing with the main lines. McLaws, ordinarily a solid commander, continued to show a reluctance to engage. "Alexander opened his batteries," he would say of his part in the fighting, "and Generals Kershaw and Wofford advanced to the front through a dense woods. Night now came on, and nothing could be observed of our operations." McLaws heard the clatter of Sedgwick's troops crossing the river on pontoons at Banks's Ford, but seemed curiously detached. While he did order Alexander to shell the crossing in the darkness, he showed little else by way of initiative.[38]

By dawn on May 5, learning that Sedgwick was safely on the north side of the Rappahannock, an increasingly frustrated Lee turned his attention back to the Federals at Chancellorsville. But heavy rains had turned the roads into seas of mud, delaying the launching of the attack, and Hooker that night used the darkness to effect a similar withdrawal at U.S. Ford, despite the protests of George Meade and Oliver Howard. When Dorsey Pender the morning of the 6th reported the Yankees gone, Lee again lost his temper. "This is the way that you young men are always doing," he said. "You have again let these people get away. I can only tell you what to do, and if you do not do it, it will not be done. . . ." In his report to President Davis, Lee was more restrained: "I returned on the 5th to Chancellorsville with the divisions of Genls McLaws and & Anderson. Their march was delayed by a storm which continued all night & the following day. In placing the troops in position on the morning of the 6th to attack Genl Hooker, it was ascertained he had abandoned his fortified position."[39]

If truth be told, the men in the ranks on both sides welcomed the respite. Horrific is the word to describe the results of the battle, particularly at the Chancellorsville crossroads. Wrote one member of the 33rd Virginia on burial detail there: "The dead and badly wounded . . . were lying where they fell. The woods, taking fire that night from the shells, burnt rapidly and roasted the wounded men alive. . . . We could see where they had tried to keep the fire from them by scratching the leaves away as far as they could reach. But it availed not; they were burnt to a crisp. The only way we could tell to which army they belonged was by turning them over and examining their clothing where they lay close to the ground . . . so we could see whether they wore the blue or the gray. We buried them all alike by covering them up with dirt where they lay."[40]

The Federals suffered some 16,800 casualties overall, the Confederates a little more than 13,000. Of the latter number, some 6,000 were in Rodes's and Powell Hill's divisions and were equally divided. Jackson's wounds would be mortal and, as we have seen, the Stonewall Brigade's Paxton was shot and killed. Indeed that unit had been so bloodied that it would never again return to anything resembling full strength. Nicholls, McGowan, Crutchfield and Hoke had been badly wounded, and Hill, Heth, Pender, Ramseur and Edward Warren less severely so. Rodes had lost 237 officers, and Hill's division had been commanded by four different men—Hill, Heth, Pender and last James Archer. Once again Lee had thrown every brigade he had into the struggle. Hooker, like the Federal commanders before him, had not. John Reynolds's First Corps and George Meade's Fifth Corps had seen little action.

No one can say with certainty that the presence of Longstreet, with Hood's and Pickett's divisions, would have enabled Lee to crush Hooker rather than merely defeat him. Nonetheless the assertion is a tempting one to make, though Lee seems to have given it little thought. Just after the battle, in fact, he sent Longstreet in southern Virginia a communiqué that was notable for its blandness: "The emergency that made your presence so desirable has passed for the moment so far as I can see, and I desire that you will not distress your troops by a forced movement to join me, or sacrifice for that purpose any public interest that your sudden departure might make it necessary to abandon."[41]

The greatest casualty of the battle was, of course, Stonewall Jackson. Even getting him to the rear the night of May 2 presented a problem because of the shell bursts and the darkness, and on at least two occasions he was hurled from his litter, landing heavily on his wounded shoulder and arm. The pain must have been excruciating. Later he was transferred to an ambulance, which he shared with Stapleton Crutchfield, and then attended to by surgeon Hunter McGuire, who gave him morphine. "Could I have directed events," Lee would write him, "I should have chosen, for the good of the country, to have been disabled in your stead."[42] Once Jackson reached the Second Corps field hospital the 27-year-old McGuire, a graduate of the University of Pennsylvania Medical School, saw that the arm bones were so badly shattered that the limb could not be saved. Immediate amputation was necessary before gangrene set in. In the early hours of May 3 chloroform was administered, the arm sawed away and the arteries ligated. Soon Jackson was conscious again, taking a cup of coffee and giving every indication of being on the road to recovery.

With the military situation still so fluid Lee the next day ordered him farther to the rear, telling McGuire and others to accompany him. For his temporary place of recuperation Jackson chose the home of an old friend, Thomas Chandler, which was some 25 miles away at Guiney Station. During the long journey in the ambulance Jackson talked freely.

"Have you heard of anyone that is killed?" he asked his aide, James Power Smith, while they were discussing the Stonewall Brigade.

"Yes, sir," Smith replied. "I am sorry to say, they have lost their commander."

"Paxton? Paxton?" Jackson exclaimed.

"Yes, sir, he has fallen."

Jackson turned his face, closed his eyes and labored to control his emotions. Reminded that Paxton had died a committed Christian, he instantly brightened.

"That's good! That's good!" he exclaimed.

Someone asked Jackson what he thought of Hooker's campaign plan.

"It was, in the main, a good conception, sir," he answered. "But he should not have sent away his cavalry; that was his great blunder. It was that which enabled me to turn him. . . . Had he kept his cavalry with him, his plan would have been a very good one."[43]

During the next two days in the Chandler house, Jackson continued to show improvement. Chaplain Lacy brought him a second message from Lee: "Give him my affectionate regards, and tell him to make haste and get well, and come back to me as soon as he can. He has lost his left arm, but I have lost my right arm." Then in the early morning of Thursday, May 7, Jackson began to experience nausea and paroxysms—pain that grew worse with each intake of breath. He was developing pneumonia and falling in and out of delirium. By that afternoon Anna had arrived from Richmond and was at his bedside. "I know that you would give your own life for me," he told her, "but I am perfectly resigned. Do not be sad. I hope I may yet recover. Pray for me, but always remember in your prayers to use the petition, 'Thy will be done.' " Over the next 48 hours his labored breathing further exhausted him. "I see from the number of physicians that you think my condition dangerous," he said to Dr. McGuire, "but I thank God, if it is His will, that I am ready to go." He asked to see Julia and caressed the baby girl with his splinted hand, saying, "Little comforter . . . little comforter." Mostly he dreamed of battle: "Order A.P. Hill to prepare for action. . . . Pass the infantry to the front."

On Sunday, May 10, Jackson knew the end was near. "It is the Lord's Day. . . . My wish is fulfilled. I have always desired to die on Sunday." He sank into coma, then revived to utter these last words: "Let us cross over the river, and rest under the shade of the trees."[44]

News of Jackson's death brought cries and tears of rage throughout the South, and President Davis decreed a state funeral in Richmond. When the Stonewall Brigade asked that it be permitted to escort the body to the capital, Lee reluctantly denied the request. "Those people across the river are again showing signs of movement and I cannot leave my Headquarters long enough to ride to the depot and pay my dear friend the poor tribute of seeing his body placed upon the cars," he explained. "His friends of the Stonewall Brigade may be assured their General will receive all the honor practicable. He never neglected a duty while living and he would not rest the easier in his grave if his old brigade had left the presence of the enemy to see him buried." On May 12 in Richmond tens of thousands watched as Jackson's coffin was borne through the streets. Leading the procession were Jefferson Davis and four of the generals Old Jack had led into battle: Arnold Elzey, now commanding the defenses in the capital; Dick Ewell, the stump of his leg nearly healed; George "Maryland" Steuart, wounded at Cross Keys; and Richard Garnett, the onetime commander of the Stonewall Brigade whom Jackson had relieved for retreating without orders at Kernstown. "You know of the unfortunate breach between General Jackson and myself," Garnett had said to Jackson's aides Kyd Douglas and Sandie Pendleton the night before, his voice trembling with emotion. "I can never forget it, nor cease to regret it. But I wish to assure you that no one can lament his death more sincerely than I do. I believe he did me great injustice, but I believe he acted from the purest motives. He is dead. Who can fill his place!"[45]

Three days later Stonewall Jackson was buried in Lexington. "Such an executive officer," Lee said in final tribute, "the sun never shone on." Now the question of who would succeed him was the talk of the army, with three front-runners emerging: Ewell, Jackson's staunch lieutenant who had not been with the army since Groveton; Powell Hill, whose Light Division was perhaps the army's finest; and the cavalryman Jeb Stuart, who had commanded the infantry of the Second Corps so well at Chancellorsville.[46]

# LEE HEADS NORTH

Lee moved swiftly to fill the vacancies created by Chancellorsville, and in late May created three corps when hitherto there had been two, naming Richard Ewell and Powell Hill lieutenant generals. Jeb Stuart, it seems, would not be joining the infantry after all. Ewell was, to an extent, an unknown factor. He had fought bravely and well under Jackson's guidance but now would have to make the hard decisions himself. Nonetheless he seemed eager to take the field. Doubts remained about his fitness, however, since he had to be lifted onto his horse and strapped to the saddle. Within days of his promotion the bald, piping-voiced Ewell married his great love, the widow Lizinka Campbell Brown, who had been "watching over [her fiancé] with sleepless vigilance." Pushing the 45-year-old bachelor into the nuptials was his brother Benjamin, who warned that only marriage would keep him from falling back "on some of his old habits—hard swearing, and drinking." So awed was Ewell with his bride that he sometimes did not seem to realize marriage had changed her name, introducing her to his fellow officers with the phrase, "My wife, Mrs. Brown."[1]

Powell Hill's promotion seemed well merited. "I think upon the whole," Lee told Jefferson Davis, he "is the best soldier of his grade with me." The question, of course, was whether Hill could channel the combative spirit that made him a sterling field commander into the requirements of his new position. The day after his promotion, learning that the 58th Virginia had lost its colors while suffering heavy losses, he brusquely rejected its request for a new flag. "I am constrained to recommend to the general commanding," he said, "that the regiment not be allowed to carry a color until it has redeemed its own by capturing one in battle."[2] Such insistence on gallantry was commendable, but it did not show that Hill could handle detailed planning—let alone restraint. There the jury was still out.

Following these promotions the structure of the Army of Northern Virginia evolved thusly: Longstreet continued to command the 1st Corps. Lafayette McLaws, George Pickett and John Bell Hood led his divisions. Pickett with his perfumed and flowing ringlets will soon be taking a more prominent place in our story. This 38-year-old widower and protégé of Longstreet had seen little action since his wounding at Gaines's Mill, and now was courting LaSalle ("Sally") Corbell, a girl half his age.

McLaws's brigades consisted of Joseph Kershaw's South Carolinians, Paul Semmes's and William Wofford's Georgians and William Barksdale's Mississippians. Pickett's division was comprised of Richard Garnett's, Lewis Armistead's and James Kemper's Virginians. Hood's division included the Texas Brigade under Jerome Robertson, Evander McIvor Law's Alabamians and George ("Tige") Anderson's and Henry ("Rock") Benning's Georgians. The First Corps's artillery continued under the titular leadership of 60-year-old Colonel James Walton, but age was tiring him, and Longstreet was relying increasingly on Porter Alexander.

Dick Ewell took over the Second Corps, with Jubal Early, Edward ("Allegheny") Johnson (replacing 53-year-old Isaac Trimble, whose osteoporosis was complicated by other illnesses) and newly promoted Major General Robert Rodes heading his divisions. The sometimes coarse Johnson had been recuperating in Richmond since suffering his wound in the Valley, and his behavior had provided the social set with titillating gossip. "Old Edward, our pet general, sat diagonally across the room," said Mary Chestnut, "with the leg straight out, like a poker wrapped in red carpet leggings. . . . There he was, with a loud voice and a thousand winks, making love to Mary P. I make no excuse for listening. . . . Mary P. cannot altogether control her own voice, and her shrill screams of negation—'No, no, never'—utterly fail to suppress her wounded lover's asseverations of his undying affection for her."[3]

Early's brigades were composed of Harry Hays's Louisianans, Robert Hoke's North Carolinians under Colonel Isaac Avery, "Extra Billy" Smith's Virginians and John Brown Gordon's Georgians. The 66-year-old Smith, newly elected to a second term as governor of Virginia, was a brave man but an inept soldier. Nonetheless, he would insist on fighting at Gettysburg before taking office. Johnson's units included Francis Nicholls's Louisianans under Colonel Jesse Williams, the Stonewall Brigade now under James A. Walker, and the Virginians of the ignoble John R. Jones under—most confusingly—John M. Jones. Walker was the V.M.I. student whose quarrel with Jackson in the long ago had resulted in his expulsion and then his challenging Jackson to a duel. Now he was the sixth commander of the dwindling Stonewall Brigade. John M. Jones, whose West Point nickname was "Rum" because of his drinking habits, had promised Lee his bouts with alcohol were over for the duration of the war—a commitment he kept. Rodes's division was comprised of newcomer Junius Daniel's, Alfred Iverson's and Dotson Ramseur's North Carolinians, George Doles's Georgians and Edward O'Neal's Alabamians. With Stapleton Crutchfield out of action indefinitely because of the loss of his leg, the Second Corps's guns were under the command of J. Thompson Brown.

Powell Hill's Third Corps included the divisions of Dick Anderson ("that most silent and discreet of men"), and the new Major Generals Henry Heth and Dorsey Pender. Heth, the close friend of Lee, would have the distinction of precipitating the battle at Gettysburg. Anderson's brigades were composed of Cadmus Wilcox's Alabamians, Billy Mahone's Virginians, "Rans" Wright's Georgians, Edward Perry's Floridians under Colonel David Lang, and Carnot Posey's Mississippians. Heth's brigades were comprised of newcomer Johnston Pettigrew's North Carolinians, Colonel John Brockenbrough's Virginians, James Archer's Tennesseans and Alabamians and newcomer Joseph Davis's Mississippians. Davis, nephew of the president, led a brigade as courageous but unseasoned as himself. Pender's command consisted of the wounded McGowan's South Carolinians under Colonel Abner Perrin, James Lane's and Colonel Alfred Scales's North Carolinians and Edward Thomas's Georgians. Heading the Third Corps artillery was R. Lindsay Walker, and serving under him were D.G. McIntosh and Willie Pegram.

Back with his beloved cavalry was Jeb Stuart, leading the Virginia brigades of Fitz Lee, Rooney Lee, William "Grumble" Jones and Albert Jenkins, and the Carolina brigades of Wade Hampton and Beverly Robertson. Of these men Fitz Lee and Hampton were the clear standouts. Grumble Jones and Stuart had no more use for each other than ever. "Do not let your judgment be warped," Lee was forced to chide his cavalry chief about Jones. Robertson, expert at training and drill, was not thought combative enough in the field. Replacing John Pelham of the horse artillery was the reliable Robert Beckham, who had been his chief lieutenant.[4]

Leaving the army at this time was Raleigh Colston, who Lee felt had not been sufficiently energetic in following up Hooker's retreat from the Chancellorsville crossroads on May 3. The fact that his division was reeling—having lost all four of its brigade commanders—did not, in Lee's eyes, excuse his foot-dragging. Ordered up the road toward U.S. Ford in the late afternoon, Colston had told Stuart that his division "was not able to attack with any prospect of success." Giving no reason, Lee wrote Davis: "I think it best to relieve Colston from duty."[5] Likewise found wanting and dispatched to North Carolina, at least temporarily, was Alfred Colquitt, who had halted his brigade during the flank attack the night of May 2 despite orders to push ahead.

Offsetting the good news of Chancellorsville was unsettling news from the West. There a Confederate army had been forced back into Vicksburg, a key stronghold on the Mississippi, where it was under siege from the Federal navy on the river and Ulysses S. Grant on the ground. Hoping to relieve the pressure on Vicksburg by bringing the war to the enemy while simultaneously foraging for food and fodder, Lee drew up plans to invade Pennsylvania. In early June he began sending Longstreet's and Ewell's corps west to Culpepper Courthouse, preparatory to moving down the Blue Ridge and the Shenandoah and north across the Potomac. Hill's corps would remain on the Rappahannock until Hooker abandoned his position on the river and moved west in pursuit. "We should not conceal from ourselves," Lee wrote President Davis, "that our resources in men are constantly diminishing, and the disproportion in this respect between us and our enemies . . . is steadily augmenting. . . . Under these circumstances we should neglect no honorable means of dividing and weakening our enemies that they may feel some of the difficulties experienced by ourselves."[6]

In the midst of these preparations Stuart on June 5 staged a grand review of his command on the level plains near Brandy Station, with some 10,000 cavalrymen taking part. Invitations had been issued far and wide, and throngs of visitors were there to cheer the spectacle. Stuart and his aides galloped down the front of the lines and came back by the rear, the general officers and their staffs joining them as they passed until nearly a hundred horsemen reined up at the reviewing stand. Then the cavalry broke into a column of squadrons and marched by at a walk, making the entire circuit. Next it came around at a trot, at the last moment breaking into a gallop near the reviewing stand and sweeping past at full speed with rebel yells and brandished sabers. "The effect was thrilling, even to us," said William Blackford, "while the ladies clasped their hands and sank into the arms, sometimes, of their escorts in a swoon if the escorts were handy, but if not they did not. While the charging was going on, Beckham with the Horse Artillery was firing rapidly and this heightened the effect. It would make your hair stand on end to see them."[7] That night there was a ball, with moonlight and huge bonfires illuminating the fete, while hundreds of couples danced on the grass.

On June 8 Stuart held a second review for Lee's benefit. This one was more restrained. The commanding general, ever mindful of taxing his men unnecessarily, did not allow the cavalry to break into a gallop, nor did he permit the cannoneers to work their guns. Later the brigades went their separate ways: Fitz Lee's troop, under Colonel Tom Munford, guarded the upper Rappahannock; Rooney Lee moved toward Welford's Ford; Grumble Jones blocked Beverly Ford; Beverly Robertson moved toward Kelly's Ford, four miles down the river; and Wade Hampton, who had missed Chancellorsville because he and his men were in southern Virginia finding badly needed mounts, bivouacked between Brandy Station and Stevensburg. Stuart himself bedded down on Fleetwood Hill, a half-mile from Brandy Station and four miles from Beverly Ford.

Just before dawn two strong columns of Alfred Pleasanton's Federal cavalry, some 11,000 men, advanced across the Rappahannock under a thick fog, making a reconnaissance in force to investigate rumors Lee was moving his army westward. One column under John Buford thundered over at Beverly Ford, the other under David Gregg at Kelly's Ford. With the largest cavalry battle of the war about to begin, Stuart's men clearly were unprepared, some of them forced to leap onto horses without putting on coats or saddling up. Buford overwhelmed the pickets at Beverly Ford and drove them back toward Grumble Jones's encampment, where he came close to capturing the guns of the horse artillery. There 23-year-old Major Cabell Flournoy of the 6th Virginia scraped together some troopers, charged Buford head-on and succeeded in delaying him. Grumble Jones now brought up the 7th Virginia. "A charge was instantly made to support Flournoy, but it was repulsed by the enemy," said one of Stuart's aides, "and in the recoil the 7th was carried back past the guns stationed on the road. These gallant cannoneers . . . proved that they were able to take care of themselves. Although now exposed to the enemy, they covered their own retreat with cannister, and safely retired to the line at St. James Church (in front on Fleetwood Hill), where they found efficient support."[8]

Jones extended his regiments to the left of the church, in the direction of Rooney Lee's command, and Hampton came up on the right, for the moment stabilizing the situation. The Federals fell back to the protection of some woods, then regrouped and charged again. This onslaught, over a plateau some 800 yards wide and aimed at the artillery at the church, proved futile. Buford's troopers, said Captain James F. Hart of the horse artillery, "dashed up to the very muzzles, then through and beyond our guns, passing between Hampton's left and Jones' right. Here they were simultaneously attacked from both flanks, and the survivors driven back."[9]

Undoubtedly Stuart was congratulating himself on his cavalry's spirited reaction to the surprise attack when, about 11 A.M., a courier from Grumble Jones brought an unwelcome message. Jones reported that a second Federal column, later found to be Gregg's, was coming up from the south and threatening his right flank.

Stuart could not believe the news. Hadn't he placed Robertson's brigade to block an attack from Kelly's Ford? Grumble, besides being an irritant, must be an alarmist. "Tell General Jones," he said, "to attend to the Yankees in his front, and I'll watch the flanks."

Mused Jones aloud when he heard Jeb's reply: "So he thinks they ain't coming, does he? Well, let him alone; he'll damn soon see for himself."[10]

Soon Stuart did see his peril, as other couriers confirmed the report: Gregg's column was galloping toward Brandy Station, endangering the Confederate right and rear. Coming up from Kelly's Ford the Federals had made no effort to engage Robertson, but simply swept around him. That officer, perhaps reluctant to divide his small command, had made no effort to follow them and simply held his position. Stuart now ordered a general pullback from the St. James Church line to Fleetwood Hill, which dominated the whole battlefield. But who would get there first, Stuart or Gregg?

Here occurred a fortuitous circumstance. Left on the hill with a handful of men and one six-pound howitzer when Stuart had rushed forward to direct operations against Buford was Henry B. McClellan, his adjutant. McClellan ordered the gun pushed forward to the crest, found a few shells and some round shot in the limber chest and began a slow fire on the oncoming foe. "The enemy was deceived by appearances," he said. "That the head of his column should have been greeted by the fire of artillery . . . must have indicated to General Gregg the presence of a considerable force upon the hill; and the fact that his advance had been entirely unopposed, together with his ignorance of what had transpired with Buford, must have strengthened the thought that his enemy, in force, here waited an attack." Though McClellan's ammunition was soon exhausted, he succeeded in slowing Gregg's progress. Nonetheless the Federals were only 50 yards from the hill when the first of Jones's troopers stormed up, touching off a furious contest that lasted all afternoon.

While the fighting ebbed to and fro, with Jones bearing the brunt, Hampton was gathering his brigade of Carolinians for a massive assault on Fleetwood. The 45-year-old patrician planter hated war as much as Stuart, fifteen years his junior loved it, but both men were merciless in battle. Captain Hart's battery was abreast of Hampton when he began his gallop toward the hill. "This charge was as gallantly made and gallantly met as any [I] ever witnessed during four years of active service," he remembered. "Taking into estimation the number of men that crossed sabers (nearly a brigade on each side) it was by far the most important hand-to-hand combat between the cavalry." The blue and the gray riders hacked and thrust with their sabers in the smoke and the dust, with the battle in the balance. "At last the intermixed and disorganized mass began to recede, and we saw that the field was won to the Confederates." Buford meanwhile was kept from aiding Gregg by the presence of Rooney Lee on his right, who would have taken him in flank if he had done so.[11] Thus ended Gregg's threat to Fleetwood Hill, with Major Beckham placing his guns on the ridge and Hampton and Jones deploying their troopers behind the cannon.

Giving up on taking Fleetwood directly, the Federals under Buford now turned their attention to Lee's brigade on Stuart's left. "An engagement of dismounted men—in which portions of the 2nd Massachusetts and 3rd Wisconsin infantry participated—was the prelude to a charge of the 6th Pennsylvania and the 2nd U.S. Cavalry," said McClellan. This charge was met by the 9th Virginia, which broke the assault and drove it back, only to be attacked in flank. "Here the 9th was reinforced by the 10th and 13th Virginia and the . . . Federal cavalry was driven back across the crest of the hill." During this action 26-year-old Rooney Lee was wounded in the leg and carried from the field. (Later he would be captured while recuperating at his home near Richmond, and not exchanged until March 1864.) Now Tom Munford galloped up from the north with elements of Fitz Lee's brigade, further strengthening Stuart's lines. Soon Buford and Gregg, who had effected a junction, began to withdraw across Beverly Ford.[12]

One more Federal force remained to be dealt with. Earlier, when Gregg was advancing toward Brandy Station, some 1,900 troopers under Union General Alfred Duffie had split from the column and ridden west toward Stevensburg. Duffie met no real opposition until he passed through the town and headed north to Brandy Station. There he was met by the 4th Virginia under Colonel Williams Wickham, whom he initially put to rout, and the 2nd South Carolina under Colonel Matthew Calbraith Butler. The Confederates rallied, however, and soon made a stand. "Colonel Butler ordered me to hold my position," said Major Thomas Lipscomb of the 2nd South Carolina, "and if they pressed me on the right to move in that direction. The firing on my right gradually got to my rear, and I was in the act of moving when Captain [Will] Farley [Stuart's chief scout] brought to me a squadron of the 4th Virginia, with orders to hold. . . ." [13]

Butler and Farley later were side by side on horseback when an enemy shell suddenly struck the ground near them and ricocheted, cutting off Butler's right foot, then passing through both mounts and severing the other man's leg. A staff officer and a civilian observer rushed to the aid of Butler, who would recover from his wound and calmly urge that they help Farley. "I wish that you two gentlemen," said the well-bred Butler, who usually led his troopers carrying no weapon but a silver-mounted riding whip, "as you have placed me in the hands of my own men, would go and take charge of Captain Farley." The observer, James T. Rhett, takes up the story. "We went to Captain Farley . . . and placed him in a old flat trough. He was very cool, in fact pleasant and smiling, though evidently in great pain. Just as we were about to send him away, he called me to him, and pointing to the leg that had been cut off by the ball . . . he asked me to bring it to him. He took it, pressed it to his bosom as one would a child. . . ."

"It is an old friend, gentlemen, and I do not wish to part from it," he said.

"[We] shook hands with him . . . expressing the hope that we should soon again see him."

"Goodbye, gentlemen, and forever," he replied. "I know my condition, and we will not meet again. . . . It is a pleasure to me that I have fallen into the hands of good Carolinians at my last moment." He died within a few hours.

"I have never seen a man," Mr. Rhett marveled, "whose demeanor in the face of certain, painful and quick death, was so superb."[14]

Eventually Duffie, knowing he was far removed from the rest of the Federal cavalry, broke off the action and withdrew across the Rappahannock.

Confederate losses on June 9 totaled some 525 men; Federal losses, some 485. For Stuart, fifteen regiments did all the fighting—five of Hampton's, five of Jones's, four of Rooney Lee's, one of Fitz Lee's. Robertson's brigade was not engaged.

The Federal reconnaissance in force at Brandy Station learned nothing about Lee's intentions. But it did have one profound effect. "It *made* the Federal cavalry," said McClellan, Stuart's aide and, incidentally, a cousin of Union General George McClellan. "Up to that time confessedly inferior to the Southern horsemen, they gained on this day that confidence in themselves and in their commanders that enabled them to contest so fiercely the subsequent battlefields."[15]

Though Stuart refused to admit he might have been lax in anticipating the attack, newspaper commentaries and the opinions of his fellow officers were almost all negative. "Vigilance, vigilance, more vigilance, is the lesson taught us by the Brandy surprise," editorialized the *Richmond Sentinel* in one of the milder rebukes, "and which must not be forgotten by the victory that was wrested from defeat. Let all learn from it, from the Major General down to the picket." Wrote Dorsey Pender to Fanny: "I suppose it is all right that Stuart should get all the blame, for when anything handsome is done he gets all the credit. A bad rule either way. He however retrieved the surprise by whipping them in the end." Used to basking in praise, Stuart must have chafed under these sentiments. In the campaign to come, seeking to burnish his reputation, he would take liberties with his orders—with fateful results.[16]

Some ten days later in a minor cavalry skirmish north of the Rappahannock, Heros von Borcke, the Prussian officer serving on Stuart's staff, was badly wounded. "The bullets patterned around us on the hardened, hoof-trodden grounds like drops of rain," said William Blackford. "Just then I heard a thump like someone had struck a barrel a violent blow with a stick. I knew well enough what it meant." Turning, he saw that von Borcke was shot in the neck and slipping from the saddle. Blackford and others tried to get the 250-pound Prussian back on his horse before the enemy closed in, but the rearing, panicked mount made the task all but impossible. "I was at my wit's end. I then recollected a thing von Borcke had once told me . . . and I made a courier twist the horse's ear severely and keep it twisted . . . the horse becoming perfectly quiet immediately." Blackford got von Borcke back in the saddle and they made their escape. "The bullet passed through the collar of his jacket an inch or two from the spine and entered his throat, and for months he coughed up pieces of his clothing. . . . He was never able to enter active service again with us."[17]

Lee's plans to invade Pennsylvania continued apace. To safeguard the invasion route, the first step in the drive north called for Ewell's Second Corps to cross the Blue Ridge Mountains and oust the Federals from Winchester in the Shenandoah. There Union General Robert Milroy with some 8,000 men held a fortified position, with 2,000 more of the enemy nearby. On June 14 Ewell sent Early's division on a concealed and circuitous march west of the town, leaving Gordon's brigade and Allegheny Johnson's division to hold Milroy's attention with demonstrations to the south and east. Early's objective was Little North Mountain. From this height his artillery would dominate West Fort, the principal bastion protecting Winchester, and force its evacuation. The march took most of the day but at 6 P.M. Early's twenty guns laid down a withering barrage, soon silencing the enemy cannon. Harry Hays's spirited Louisiana Tigers led the charge on the double-quick that followed, their shrill rebel yells piercing the air. "Hoist those colors in the 9th!" shouted Hays when a minie ball brought down the 9th Louisiana's color-bearer. With no pause in the advance, eager hands swiftly raised the battle flag once more.

Within minutes the Tigers were over the walls and into the fort, routing the defenders and turning their own guns on them as they fled. "Bully! Bully! By God! Bully!" cried out William Peck, the portly colonel of the 9th, gasping for breath from his exertions. Watching from his command post, Ewell was just as excited. "Hurrah for the Louisiana boys!" he yelled. Just then a spent ball struck him in the chest, giving him a painful bruise. Hunter McGuire, insisting that Ewell lie down, for a time had to take away his crutches. But soon he was upright again, cheering the Tigers on. Father James Sheeran, chaplain of the 14th Louisiana, would write that Ewell for days afterward was profuse in his praise of Hays's bold assault: "He said, next to God, he was indebted to [the Tigers] for the almost bloodless victory."[18]

Expecting Milroy's withdrawal from Winchester under cover of darkness, Ewell during the night sent Johnson to Stephenson's Depot, four miles east of the town, to cut off the enemy. It was a wise decision. By 4 A.M. Johnson was fully engaged and the Federals, strung out on the Martinsburg Road, found their column severed. Confused and disoriented, ever-growing numbers of them began to surrender. With the break of dawn, Ewell and Early marched triumphantly through the town. Only as the day wore on, however, did the Confederates realize the full extent of their victory. Some 4,000 prisoners would be taken, as well as 23 pieces of Milroy's artillery and hundreds of wagonloads of ammunition and supplies. Soon Rodes would defeat a smaller Federal force at Martinsburg, capturing five more cannon and additional ordnance. Confederate losses overall were less than 300. "[Ewell] did well," allowed John Casler of the Stonewall Brigade, "but Jackson in my opinion would have marched all night . . . and by daylight would have had his line of battle around Winchester, and captured the whole command."

Later the women of the town presented Ewell with a Confederate flag they had made from two captured Union banners. Then they called on him to say a few words.

"I can't make a speech to ladies," the newly married Ewell replied. "I never made a speech but to one lady in my life. My friend General Early"—here he pointed out Jube—"can speak. He will address you."

Early the bachelor answered in kind. "I never have been able to make a speech to one lady," he said, "much less to so many."[19] The two generals then took tea with the women.

With Winchester secure, Ewell swiftly crossed the Potomac. Not until June 22, however, did Lee order him to move farther north into Pennsylvania. His mission was to move rapidly through the fertile countryside, collecting horses, cattle and supplies for the entire army and pulling Hooker away from the Rappahannock. Screened by the Blue Ridge, Longstreet's and Powell Hill's corps would follow in his wake when prudent. Still, wrote the ever-combative Lee, "If Harrisburg [the state capital] comes within your means, capture it." Over the next few days Ewell split his corps, leading Rodes's and Johnson's divisions through Greencastle and Chambersburg to Carlisle, while Early's division veered eastward at Chambersburg, passing through Greenwood and Gettysburg to York. Meanwhile the foraging was bountiful. By the time Ewell reached Carlisle he had collected hundreds of horses, 3,000 head of cattle, 5,000 barrels of flour and great quantities of ammunition and medicine. "The people are fearful of retribution from us," said Jed Hotchkiss, "but some were disposed to joke and spoke of our being in the Union now. . . . We occupied the houses of some Union people for the night, but no damage was done to anything. The land is full of everything and we have an abundance."[20]

His successes put Ewell in a good mood. When a group of Carlisle ministers visited him on Saturday, June 27, to inquire if he would object to their offering prayers for President Lincoln on the Sabbath as was their custom, he could not have been more gracious.

"Certainly pray for him; pray as much as ever you can," he said. "I don't know anybody that stands more in need of prayer!"[21]

Jubal Early, as might be expected, was more bellicose. Passing through Greenwood, he took pains to put the ironworks owned by Thaddeus Stevens, a radical Republican, to the torch. "The enemy had destroyed a number of similar works . . . in those parts of the Southern states he had been able to penetrate," he explained, "upon the plea they furnished us the means of carrying on the war. . . . Finding in my way these works of Mr. Stevens who . . . had been advocating the most vindictive measures of confiscation and devastation, I determined to destroy them. This I did on my own responsibility. . . ."

Early found nothing amusing, therefore, in the shenanigans of "Extra Billy" Smith, the governor-elect of Virginia, who with his brigade led the Confederate column into York. With his band playing "Yankee Doodle," the bare-headed and smiling Smith waved and saluted everyone in his path, courting the townspeople as if he were running for office. In short order, he had them applauding him. "It was a rare scene," said one onlooker, "the vanguard of an invading army and the invaded and hostile population hobnobbing on the public green in an enthusiastic gathering. The general did not dismount, but from the saddle he made a rattling humorous speech, which both the Pennsylvanians and his own brigade applauded to the echo." The gist of Smith's remarks went like this:

"My friends, how do you like this way of coming back into the Union? I hope you like it; I have been in favor of it for a good while. But don't misunderstand us. We are not here with any hostile intent. . . . We are not burning your houses or butchering your children. On the contrary, we are behaving ourselves like Christian gentlemen, as we are. You see, it was getting a little warm down our way. We needed a summer outing. . . . We are sorry, and apologize that we are not in better guise for a visit of courtesy, but we regret to say our trunks haven't gotten up yet; yet we were in such a hurry to see you that we could not wait for them. . . ."

Now Early impatiently pushed his way through the crowd, demanding to know what was going on. "General Smith, what the devil are you about! Stopping the head of this column in this cursed town!"

Ever the unruffled politician, "Extra Billy" had a ready retort. "Having a little fun, General, which is good for all of us, and at the same time teaching these people something that will be good for them and won't do us any harm."[22] Whatever his chagrin, Early could console himself with the supplies that York eventually provided—several tons of meat, 3,500 pounds of sugar, 3,000 gallons of molasses and 1,500 pairs of shoes.

On June 28, even as Ewell was making plans to advance on Harrisburg, Lee with Longstreet's and Hill's corps was encamped at Chambersburg. The Southern commander had heard nothing from Jeb Stuart, who had been ordered to screen the army's right on its march north, and was desperate for information. "Every officer who conversed with General Lee for several days previous to the battle of Gettysburg," said Major General Henry Heth, "well remembers having heard such expressions as these: 'Can you tell me where General Stuart is?' 'Where on earth is my cavalry?' 'Have you any news of the enemy's movements?'" Then Lee learned from a spy, a Mississippian named James Harrison, that the Army of the Potomac was marching against him, with two of its corps already at Frederick, Maryland. Hooker, who had lost Lincoln's confidence with his conduct at Chancellorsville, had been relieved and the new army head was George Meade, a courageous if aloof officer. "It was on this, the report of a single scout, in the absence of cavalry, that the army moved," said Moxey Sorrel, Longstreet's adjutant. "[Lee] sent orders to bring Ewell immediately back from the north about Harrisburg, and join his left. He started A.P. Hill off at sunrise for Gettysburg, followed by Longstreet. The enemy was there, and there our General would strike him."[23]

Ewell's orders from Lee were to advance on either Cashtown or Gettysburg as circumstances might dictate, a decision that literal-minded officer did not welcome. "The General was quite testy and hard to please," said Jed Hotchkiss, "and had everyone flying around. I got up in the night to answer questions and make him a map." Nearing both towns on the morning of July 1, however, and learning that Hill was making a reconnaissance in force on Gettysburg from the west, Ewell resolved to do the same from the north. Rodes's and Early's divisions marched in parallel, the former on the Carlisle Road, the latter on the Harrisburg Road. Johnson's division was temporarily absent, detached to shield Ewell's immense wagon train.[24]

Both armies were blundering into battle—each with only its advance elements on the field, each not quite aware of the other's strength. Lee's instructions had been to avoid a general engagement until the 75,000-man Army of Northern Virginia could be reunited, but events were taking on their own momentum. Ewell's and Hill's corps, converging on Gettysburg thinking they were reconnoitering, would find themselves drawn into a desperate fight. Opposing them would be John Buford's cavalry division, newly confident after Brandy Station; the First Corps of John F. Reynolds, who many thought should have been in command instead of Meade; and the Eleventh Corps of Oliver Howard, smarting after its rout at Chancellorsville.

In the days before Gettysburg, what was Jeb Stuart doing? Lee had ordered him on June 22 and 23 to leave two brigades in the Blue Ridge to screen the passes from the enemy while Hill and Longstreet were moving down the Shenandoah and across the Potomac. Stuart himself was to proceed with his remaining three brigades "into Maryland and take position on General Ewell's right, place yourself in communication with him, guard his flank, keep him informed of the enemy's movements, and collect all the supplies you can for the use of the army." Stuart, whom Lee regarded as a surrogate son, was given discretion, or he so interpreted his orders, as to whether he should ford the Potomac west or east of the Blue Ridge. This point is crucial. If he crossed west of the mountains he would be tying himself to the main army; if he crossed east of them he would have more freedom. For Stuart the choice was obvious. He would ride east to ford the river between the Federals and Washington, do some raiding while making still another triumphant ride around the Army of the Potomac and then take up his duties on Ewell's right.

Leaving Grumble Jones and Beverly Robertson to guard the passes, Stuart left Salem on June 25 with the brigades of Wade Hampton, Fitz Lee and the wounded Rooney Lee under John R. Chambliss. Frequent halts were necessary to rest the mounts and find forage. Though his orders were to cross the Potomac as soon as practicable, he could not do so until June 28. In Rockville,

Maryland, he intercepted a 125-wagon supply train and, making a second bad decision, commandeered it rather than burned it. This further delayed his progress. "The wagons were brand new, the mules fat and sleek, and the harness in use for the first time," said Colonel Richard Beale of the 9th Virginia defensively. "Such a train we had never seen before and did not see again."

Not until June 30 did Jeb and his troopers ride into Pennsylvania. No longer was there any possibility of his screening the army's right. So rapid in fact had been the northward advance of the 90,000 Federals under Meade, their new commander, and so halting had been Stuart's own movements that he was nowhere near the head of the Federal column, which he would have had to turn if he were to rejoin Lee. In fact he was in the rear and middle of the enemy, with half of them ahead of him and half behind. For six long days, with events largely out of his control once he committed himself to his ride, he had deprived Lee of the cavalry's eyes. He did not even know with any certitude where the Army of Northern Virginia was. Stuart, normally not given to introspection, must have realized he had made an egregious error. Still another arduous ride would be necessary, through Dover and Carlisle, before he led his exhausted troopers with the cumbersome wagons into Gettysburg the afternoon of July 2. "Well, General Stuart, you are here at last," Lee is reputed to have remarked.[25] The rebuke was all the stronger for what was left unsaid.

# GETTYSBURG

Gettysburg in 1863 was a town of some 2,400 people, a bustling county seat where a number of roads converged—including turnpikes to Chambersburg, Baltimore and York. Surrounded by lush open meadows and pastures—even the woods were largely clear of underbrush—it was framed by a series of long, relatively flat ridges. To the southwest the closest of these was Seminary Ridge, three-quarters of a mile from the town; then McPherson's Ridge a half-mile farther west; then Herr Ridge another mile distant. Directly south of the town, along three-mile-long Cemetery Ridge, the ground was much higher. There it rose and curled like an inverted fishhook, its barbs at Culp's Hill and Cemetery Hill close to the town, its eyelets at the Big and Little Round Tops. On these crests, defenders could dominate the terrain. Both armies at this point were still strung out—Hill's Third Corps with Henry Heth and Dorsey Pender nearing the town from the west, Ewell's Second Corps with Robert Rodes and Jubal Early doing the same from the north. Longstreet's First Corps was well behind Hill. Coming up from the south were the lead elements of the Federal army.

James Archer's Tennesseans and Joseph Davis's Mississippians of Heth's division touched off the fighting at Gettysburg the morning of July 1, marching down the Chambersburg Pike. By Heth's account he was hoping to find stores of badly needed shoes, even though Early had just passed through the town and found little worth requisitioning. Only the day before, moreover, Johnston Pettigrew had warned him the enemy might be in Gettysburg in considerable numbers. He mentioned this to Powell Hill while asking permission to make the raid. "The only force at Gettysburg is cavalry," Hill told him, "probably a detachment of observation. I am just from General Lee, and the information he has from his scouts corroborates that I have received from mine—the enemy are still at Middleburg [some 30 miles south], and have not yet struck their tents."

"If there is no objection," said Heth, "I will take my division . . . and get those shoes."

"None in the world," was the reply.[1]

Little Powell was not well—fellow officers described him as looking quite pale and much fatigued. Whether he was being bedeviled by a flare-up of his prostate troubles or some other illness we do not know, but his condition kept him from noticing that Heth was putting his weakest brigades in the forefront. Archer's command had been reduced to 1,000 men. Davis was seeing action for the first time. Putting Pettigrew's fresh North Carolinians and John Brockenbrough's tested Virginians in the van, rather than keeping them in reserve, would have been more prudent.

When about 8 A.M. Archer and Davis began driving in the Federal pickets, it soon became apparent the opposition was no mere detachment. The defenders were comprised of John Buford's 2,900-man 1st Cavalry Division, armed with breech-loading carbines that gave them a rapid and effective rate of fire. Three-quarters of the troopers fought dismounted, taking cover on McPherson's Ridge wherever they could find it, while the rest tended the horses in the rear. Their grim resistance held the two infantry brigades at bay for two hours, giving Union General Reynolds time to move the First Corps into the fight. Now the Confederates came to grief. On the right of the pike Archer, whose taking of Hazel Grove had been key to the victory at Chancellorsville, was overwhelmed by the Iron Brigade, those Midwesterners who had distinguished themselves at Groveton. The Iron Brigade's regiments moved en echelon, charging in waves. "Forward, men, forward for God's sake and drive those fellows out of the woods!" shouted Colonel Lucius Fairchild of the 2nd Wisconsin. Archer and scores of his men were captured, and his brigade pushed back to Herr Ridge. During this time Reynolds fell dead, instantly killed by a sniper's bullet that struck him in the head.

Soon the fuming and frustrated Archer encountered General Abner Doubleday, whom he had known in the Old Army and who had replaced Reynolds.

"Good morning, Archer," said Doubleday. "How are you? I am glad to see you."

"Well, I am not glad to see you by a damned sight," was the answer.

"Take him to the rear," said Doubleday. "Take him to the rear."

On the left of the pike the inexpert Davis, who initially had enjoyed success while fighting from a railroad cut, found himself turned. With several hundred of his men trapped and captured in the cut, he too was routed. "The enemy had now been felt, and found to be in considerable force," Heth would say with vast understatement.[2]

Oliver Howard with the Union Eleventh Corps arrived on the field around noon during a temporary lull in the fighting. Placing a reserve brigade on Cemetery Hill, he led the rest of his command into and beyond Gettysburg, forming on Doubleday's right and facing Rodes and Early coming in from the north. By 2 P.M. the battle resumed in piecemeal fashion. Robert Rodes, seeing the enemy coming out of the town toward him, had little choice but to engage. Leaving George Doles's Georgians to anchor his left he went on the attack himself, pushing forward Alfred Iverson's and Junius Daniel's North Carolinians and Edward O'Neal's Alabamians even as elements of Doubleday's corps joined Howard's men in assaulting him. "Finding that the enemy was rash enough to come out of the woods to attack me," said Rodes, "I determined to meet him when he got to the foot of the hill I occupied. I caused Iverson's Brigade to advance, and . . . gave in person to O'Neal the order to attack, indicating to him precisely the point to which he was to direct the left of the four regiments then under his orders. . . . Daniel was at the same moment instructed to advance to support Iverson if necessary, if not, to attack on his right as soon as possible." But Rodes's brigadiers could not keep their lines, Iverson came under withering fire, confusion spread, and soon the whole of the command was in peril. From their posts near the Chambersburg Road, both Lee and Heth watched the fighting with concern.[3]

"Rodes is very heavily engaged," Heth asked, "had I not better attack?"

"No," Lee replied, "I am not prepared to bring on a general engagement today. Longstreet is not up."[4]

Fortunately the first of Early's brigades, the fiery John Brown Gordon's Georgians, now arrived on Rodes's left on the double-quick, hurling themselves on Howard's men and turning the tide. "With a ringing yell, my command rushed upon the line posted to protect the Union right," Gordon said. "Here occurred a hand-to-hand struggle. That protecting Union line once broken left my command not only on the right flank, but obliquely in rear of it. . . . There was no alternative for Howard's men except to break and fly, or throw down their arms and surrender. Under the concentrated fire from front and flank, the marvel is that any escaped." Riding a coal black stallion, standing in the stirrups, waving his hat, using his voice like a trumpet, Gordon was everywhere. "Our loss, at least in Gordon's Brigade, was slight," said one staff officer. "I distinctly remember . . . calling out to [him], 'General, where are your dead men?' and his reply, 'I haven't got any, sir; the Almighty has covered my men with His shield and buckler!' "[5]

With the battle thus joined Lee rescinded his orders and committed the rest of his force, ordering Heth forward with Pettigrew's and Brockenbrough's brigades toward McPherson's Ridge. "Never was a grander sight beheld," said a private in the 26th North Carolina. "The lines extended more than a mile, all distinctly visible to us. . . . The roar of artillery, the crack of musketry and the shouts of the combatants, added grandeur and solemnity to the scene." This martial panorama was the last the 23-year colonel of the 26th, Henry Burgwyn, would see before suffering a mortal wound. Casualties here were brutal, with some men firing at each other from 20-yard distances. Heth took a ball in the head and, stunned, toppled unconscious from the saddle. All that saved him from death was the thick wad of paper he had stuffed in his head-band, almost unconsciously, to keep his oversize hat in place.[6]

Next Dorsey Pender pushed his division into the fray. "Here we found and marched over Pettigrew's Brigade," said Lieutenant James Caldwell of McGowan's 1st South Carolina. "The field was thick with wounded . . . and the ground gray with dead and disabled. There was a general cheer for South Carolina as we moved past them. [Pettigrew's men] had fought well but, like most new soldiers, had been content to stand and fire, instead of charging." Colonel Abner Perrin, who had replaced McGowan, led the assault. Contin-ued Caldwell: "Filled with admiration for such courage as defied the whole fire of the enemy—naturally drawn to his horse, uniform and flashing sword—the brigade followed, with a shout that was itself half a victory." Pender's men rushed into the mouths of the enemy cannon. "It was done with the fierce might that always made Pender's charges terrifying," a commentator would write. When a shell all but tore off the right arm of the color-bearer of the 13th North Carolina, he shifted the staff to his left hand, his pace never slackening. "Still they came on," said a Union gunner, "the gaps being closed by regiments from the second line, and . . . by a second column which was coming over the hill. Never have I seen such a charge. Not a man seemed to falter. Lee may well be proud of his infantry." Pender succeeded, but at great cost. "Only a squad here and there marked the place where regiments had rested," said Alfred Scales, who suffered a severe wound, of his riddled North Carolinians.[7]

Under pressure from both the west and the north the Federal lines began to crumble, with Doubleday's First Corps evacuating first McPherson's Ridge and then Seminary Ridge, and Howard's Eleventh Corps streaming back through the streets of Gettysburg. By 4 P.M. Lee's men were victorious, and the enemy was digging in on Cemetery Ridge. Of 18,000 Federals who had gone into battle, almost half were casualties—many of them prisoners. Of 25,000 Confederates engaged, 6,000 were casualties. Rodes had lost some 2,900 men, Heth 2,000, Pender 1,100. With four hours of daylight remaining, Lee's instinct was to follow up the attack while he still had the advantage. How soon would the rest of Meade's corps be up? he must have wondered. "I cannot think what has become of Stuart; I ought to have heard from him long before now," he earlier had told Dick Anderson, the third of Hill's di-vision heads. "I am in ignorance as to what we have in front of us here."[8]

While Lee was deliberating, John Brown Gordon was having a curious encounter. In the midst of putting Howard's men to rout north of the town he had come upon a Union officer sprawled on the ground among the dead. "Quickly dismounting and lifting his head," Gordon said, "I asked his name and the character of his wounds." The officer was Brigadier General Francis Barlow of New York, one of Howard's division heads, and a minie ball had struck him near the spinal cord, numbing his limbs. "Neither of us had the remotest idea that he could possibly survive many hours. . . . Before parting he asked me to take from his pocket a package of letters and destroy them. They were from his wife. . . . He [also] asked me to assure her that he had died doing his duty." That evening Brown learned Barlow's wife was with the Union army and near the battlefield. "When it is remembered how closely Mrs. Gordon followed me, it will not be difficult to imagine that my sympathies were especially stirred. . . . I dispatched under flag of truce the promised message to Mrs. Barlow." Barlow recovered, however, and much later heard that a kinsman's of Gordon with the same initials, General James B. Gordon of North Carolina, had been killed near Richmond. "To me, therefore, Barlow was dead," said the Georgian, "to Barlow, I was dead."

Some fifteen years passed, and the war was a distant if distinct memory when the two former officers met at a Washington dinner party.

"General, are you related to the Barlow killed at Gettysburg?" Gordon idly asked.

"Why, I am the man, sir," was the reply. "Are you related to the Gordon who killed me?"

"I am the man, sir," was the response.

Both men were dumbstruck. "Nothing short of an actual resurrection from the dead could have amazed either of us more," Gordon would say.[9]

On the Confederate left opposite Cemetery and Culp's Hills, a hesitant Dick Ewell at this 4 P.M. moment of triumph was finding corps command difficult. When Kyd Douglas, now serving on Allegheny Johnson's staff, galloped up to report that Johnson was less than three miles away, with his division well rested and ready to go into action, Ewell seemed uninterested. "I gave General Ewell my message and tried to express General Johnson's earnestness as well as I could. When I finished General Gordon seemed to second it, saying that he could join in the attack and they could carry that hill—pointing to Cemetery Hill—before dark." Gordon indeed advocated attack. "Had [Jackson] been there," he said, "his quick eye would have caught at a glance the entire situation, and instead of halting me he would have urged me forward . . . notifying General Lee that the battle was on and he had decided to occupy the heights. . . . General Meade's army at that hour was stretched out along the line of his march for thirty miles. General Lee's was much more concentrated."[10]

Ewell's reply was cautious: "General Lee told me to come to Gettysburg and gave me no orders to go further. I do not feel like advancing and making an attack without orders from him." Sandie Pendleton, Ewell's chief of staff, could not conceal his chagrin. "Oh, for the presence and inspiration of Old Jack for just one hour," he said quietly. "It was a moment of most critical importance," remarked James Power Smith, another Ewell aide. ". . . Some of us who had served on Jackson's staff sat in a group in our saddles, and one said sadly, 'Jackson is not here.' Our corps commander, General Ewell, as true a Confederate soldier as ever went into battle, was waiting for orders, when every moment of the time could not be balanced with gold."[11]

Major General Isaac Trimble likewise urged a prompt attack. The 61-year-old Trimble's illnesses had deprived him of command—Allegheny Johnson was heading the division that would have been his—but he was serving as an officer-at-large and was just as aggressive as he had been at Cross Keys and Second Manassas.

"Well, General," he said to Ewell, "we have had a grand success. Are you not going to follow it up and push our advantage?"

Ewell replied, in so many words: "General Lee has instructed me not to bring on a general engagement without orders, and I will wait for them."

"I said," Trimble continued, "that hardly applies to the present state of things, as we . . . should secure the advantage gained. He made no rejoinder."

Disturbed by the silent dismissal Trimble decided to reconnoiter for himself, and soon discovered that Culp's Hill, which dominated the terrain, was unoccupied. Returning to Ewell, he pointed this out.

"General," he said stridently, gesturing toward Culp's Hill, "*there* is an eminence of commanding position, and not now occupied, as it ought to be by us or the enemy soon. I advise you to send a brigade and hold it if we are to remain here."

"Are you sure it commands the town?" Ewell asked.

"Certainly it does, as you can see, and it ought to be held by us at once."

Obviously not wanting to hear anything more about an advance, Ewell made some impatient reply.

"Give me a brigade and I will engage to take that hill!" Trimble reputedly demanded. Ewell shook his head. "Give me a good regiment and I will do it!" Again Ewell shook him off.

Trimble then stalked away, believing that Ewell, his old friend from the Valley Campaign, was wasting a precious opportunity.[12]

Ewell next received a dispatch from Jubal Early that echoed Trimble's counsel, recommending that Johnson's division immediately on arrival move on Culp's Hill, the more vulnerable of the two promontories from the direction of the town. Early himself was in a foul mood. "Extra Billy" Smith, guarding the left flank, had sounded a warning that the enemy was advancing down the York Pike on the Confederate rear. Investigating this rumor, which turned out to be false, consumed more valuable time.

Now a series of messages, notable for their fuzziness, ensued between Lee and Ewell. From his position on Seminary Ridge the commanding general stated he could see the enemy retreating into the hills "without organization and in great confusion," and he urged Ewell that they should be pressed "if possible." Ewell conferred with Rodes and Early and then laid down a condition, dispatching James Power Smith to Lee to request that Hill's corps support his attack. But Heth and Pender's commands were licking their wounds, and Dick Anderson's division was not yet up. Back came the reply that Lee "regretted that [Hill's] people were not up to support [Ewell] on the right, but he wished him to take Cemetery Hill if it were possible; and he would ride over and see him very soon."[13] These ambiguous exchanges did nothing to expedite matters.

The upshot was that Ewell as the hours passed simply waited. He halted Johnson in line of battle, moved against neither Cemetery Hill nor Culp's Hill, put off decisions until he could meet with Lee. To be fair, his orders were to advance "if practicable," and he was concerned about the strength of his own corps.[14] Rodes's division had been badly bloodied and only part of Early's division was available, as Gordon had been sent to look into Smith's panicky rumor.

No one knows if audacity would have been rewarded. The Federals until perhaps 6 P.M. were disorganized, and largely comprised of the survivors of the First and Eleventh Corps and Buford's cavalry—no more than 9,500 men. But by sunset two hours later, when the Twelfth Corps under Henry Slocum and the Third Corps under Daniel Sickles were positioning themselves on Cemetery Ridge, their number had risen to some 27,000. Meade himself would arrive about midnight. The Second Corps under Winfield Scott Hancock and the Fifth Corps under George Sykes would arrive in the morning, swelling the ranks further. Hancock, who had been sent ahead to the ridge by Meade and took temporary command there about 4 P.M., would state that the Confederates might have been successful if they had struck quickly to take the heights: "If [they] had continued their pursuit of General Howard . . . they would have driven him over and beyond Cemetery Hill. After I [came] upon the field . . . and made my disposition for defending that point, I do not think the Confederate force then present could have carried it."[15] If we assume that Hancock's "disposition" took no more than two hours, Ewell's window of opportunity extended no longer than 6 P.M.

Lee rode around dusk to Ewell's headquarters, where Early and Rodes joined them. He did not ask why the Second Corps commander had not advanced on the heights, and he received no explanations. "It was evident from the first," said Early, "that it was [Lee's] purpose to attack the enemy as early as possible the next day. . . . It was a point taken for granted." There was some discussion about the position and strength of the enemy, and then Lee asked Ewell: "Can't you, with your corps, attack on this flank at daylight tomorrow?" When his chief was slow to answer, Early broke the silence. "The purport of what I said was, that the ground over which we would have to advance on our flank was very rugged and steep; the enemy was evidently concentrating and fortifying in our immediate front, and by morning would probably have the greater part of his force concentrated on that flank . . . that we could not move through the town in line of battle, and would therefore have to go to the left of the town right up against Cemetery Hill . . . and that the result of an attack there might be doubtful, but if successful it would inevitably be at very great loss."

Early then called Lee's attention to the Round Tops, saying that an attack from the right would have more chance of success. The Round Tops dominated the lower ridge, but were thought to be less fortified. Ewell and Rodes concurred.

"Then perhaps I had better draw you around to my right," Lee asked, "as the line will be very long and thin if you remain here, and the enemy may come down and break through it?"

Moving to the right was not what Early wanted to do. "I did not like the idea of giving up anything we had gained," he would acknowledge. To Lee he said, in effect, "that you need have no fear that the enemy would break through our line . . . that on that part of the line it was more difficult for the enemy to come down from the heights to attack us than for us to ascend them to attack him, as difficult as the latter would have been." Again Ewell and Rodes supported him.[16]

Though Lee agreed to leave Ewell's command on the left, the decision was not well considered. Reconnaissance by Johnson's men later that night showed that the Federals, unimpeded by the Confederates, had occupied Culp's Hill in force. During the next two days, whenever elements of Ewell's command did assail the heights, they essentially butted their heads against impenetrable positions. "Gen. Ewell had seen some ground he thought he could take & asked permission to stay & take it," said Porter Alexander. "Gen. Lee consented, but it turned out early the next morning the position could not be taken. Yet the orders to come out from the awkward place [Ewell] was in— where there was no reasonable probability of his accomplishing any good on the enemy's line in his front & where his artillery was of no service—were never renewed and he stayed there till the last." This was Ewell's true failure. Not that he had failed on July 1 to take the heights, but that he and his officers convinced Lee they should remain on the left, stringing out the lines and making the assaults of the Third Corps on the Federal center and the First Corps on the right all the harder the next day.[17]

Why Lee permitted this is unclear. Perhaps, as many commentators have suggested, he was disappointed that his Second Corps commanders were content to remain on the defensive. Ewell, Early, Rodes—these officers were among his top men. But he was finding them singularly passive.

"Well, if I attack from my right," Lee finally said, "Longstreet will have to make the attack." He paused for a moment, held his head down in deep thought and then added: "Longstreet is a very good fighter when he gets in position and gets everything ready, but he is *so slow.*" These last words came out reluctantly.

Jubal Early maintained he was surprised by Lee's comment. "Ewell, Rodes and myself all knew that Longstreet did not move or maneuver with the celerity that characterized Jackson, and had been transmitted in great to the officers and troops who had served under him;" he said, ". . . but I was a little startled to hear it from General Lee, with the emphasis he gave the assertion . . . as well as the time of making it. We knew, however, that Longstreet had a corps of very fine fighting men . . . and we had no doubt he would be up in time to make the attack." Here Early was wrong. Just as he had resisted assaulting Cemetery and Culp's Hills, Longstreet would foot-drag in attacking the Round Tops and the ridge.[18]

The root of the problem was that the First Corps commander had come to see himself as Lee's equal, or even superior, as a strategist. This notion may have been engendered by the success Longstreet enjoyed at Sharpsburg and Fredericksburg, which for the Confederates essentially were defensive battles. He had not wanted to invade Pennsylvania, thinking it would only inflame the North, and he certainly did not want to attack a strong defensive position. He believed in entrenching, and letting the enemy attack him. "The question is not whether the maneuvers suggested by Longstreet would have been more successful than those executed by General Lee," said one military historian, "but whether [he] did everything which lay within his power to carry out, loyally and unhesitatingly, [Lee's] wishes and instructions." Here the answer is a resounding no. If the opening battles of the Seven Days marked the weary Jackson's nadir as a commander, the same can be said of the stubborn Longstreet's behavior July 2 and 3 at Gettysburg.[19]

Consider Lee's circumstances the night of July 1. He had moved with such rapidity through Pennsylvania, notwithstanding Stuart's unwise ride, that he was far to the northwest of Washington before his columns were threatened by the enemy's advance. On that day he found a Federal force on his right flank. His troops became engaged and scored a signal victory, mauling two Federal corps and throwing them back on Cemetery Ridge. There the enemy occupied a strong position it is true, but they would be badly outnumbered—perhaps two-to-one—provided the Confederates attacked at daybreak. Every passing hour, as each of Meade's corps came up, reduced Lee's advantage. Yet Longstreet's attack on the right would not be made until 4 P.M. How could this delay happen?

Quite late on the night of July 1, while surveying the terrain with Longstreet after leaving Ewell, Lee's thinking could not have been more at odds with his chief lieutenant.

"We could not call the enemy to position better suited to our plans," Longstreet would recall saying to Lee. "All that we have to do is file round his left, and secure good ground between him and his capital."

"If he is there tomorrow I will attack him," Lee replied.

From the outset, therefore, there was a profound difference of opinion between the two men. Lee, finding that his advance guard had been successful and that the enemy was not yet concentrated, was determined to attack. Longstreet thought the sounder move would be to turn the Federal left and take up a defensive position.

The First Corps commander would always maintain that Lee never specifically ordered him to attack at daybreak or soon thereafter. This is literally true, but if words mean anything Lee's intent was clear. The fact that his instructions included such courteous phrases as "if possible," "if practicable" and the like was a reflection of Lee's character, as well as his confidence in his subordinates. "There can be no question that General Lee intended to attack very early in the morning of the second day, July 2nd," said James Power Smith. "He said so to Ewell and his generals the night before on the Carlisle road. He said so to Longstreet a little while later, near Cemetery Hill. General Pendleton, his Chief of Artillery . . . says that General Lee told him that night that he 'had ordered General Longstreet to attack on the flank at sunrise the next morning.' [Armistead] Long, of General Lee's staff, writes that in his opinion 'orders were issued for the movement to begin on the enemy's left as soon as practicable.' "[20]

By sunrise on July 2 Lee was already on Seminary Ridge, still deprived of the reconnaissance Stuart's cavalry would have provided, but determined to put the final touches on his plans. Powell Hill and Longstreet were there, as were two of Longstreet's division heads, McLaws and Hood, and many aides. Lee's tactics called for McLaws and Hood to approach the battlefield by a series of subsidiary roads, then advance up the Emmitsburg Road, which ran at an angle between Seminary and Cemetery Ridges. When he was just south of the Peach Orchard and the adjacent Wheat Field, McLaws was to march off the road and extend his brigades in order of battle. Hood when abreast of the Round Tops was to do the same, taking up a position on his right. Dick Anderson's division of Hill's corps was to come up on McLaws's left and assail the midpoint of Cemetery Ridge. Once the main attack on the center and right was underway, Ewell was to attack on the left to keep the enemy from shifting troops from one part of their lines to the other. These orders were clear.

Lee was happy to see the hard-fighting Hood, whose troops had marched through the night to get into position. "The enemy is here," he told him, "and if we do not whip him, he will whip us." Then Lee turned his attention to McLaws, pointing out on a map how he was to lead the advance and stressing the importance of doing so without being seen.

"Can you do it?" he asked.

"I know of nothing to prevent me," McLaws replied, "but I will take a party of skirmishers and reconnoiter."

Captain S.R. Johnston of Lee's staff, who had just returned from going over the ground, had found that there were no defenders on Little Round Top. McLaws told Lee he would like to go with Johnston and survey the terrain again.

Longstreet interrupted. "No, sir, I do not wish you to leave your division," he said to McLaws. Then he placed a finger on the map. "I wish your division placed so."

"No, General," Lee said, calmly but firmly, "I wish it placed just the opposite."

Longstreet was visibly angry. "General Longstreet," said McLaws, "appeared as if he was irritated and annoyed, but the cause I did not ask."[21]

There matters rested. McLaws and Hood, under Old Pete's direction, were at earliest opportunity to make an oblique attack on Cemetery Ridge and the Round Tops. "I think you had better move on," Lee urged Longstreet before riding over to coordinate the advance with Ewell. During his absence Longstreet nonetheless remained at headquarters most of the morning, doing little or nothing. "The General is a little nervous this morning," he told Hood. "He wishes me to attack; I do not wish to do so without Pickett. I never like to go into battle with one boot off." Pickett's was the third of his divisions, and it was still far from the field.

Lee returned about 11 A.M., irritated that Longstreet had not touched off the assault. "It would not do to have Ewell open the attack," he said by way of remonstrance. Then he broke with long-standing habit and issued a direct order: Longstreet was to push forward immediately.[22]

Concentrating the command took more time, however, and it was not until 1 P.M. that the First Corps column got underway, with Captain Johnston as its guide and Kershaw's brigade at its head. Even then its advance to the Emmitsburg Road was slow. McLaws at some point halted his division, worried that his line of march would be seen by the enemy. Johnston pointed out a shortcut that entailed leaving the feeder road they were on and crossing a field, but Longstreet demurred. Nothing would do but that the column countermarch to find a second feeder road, though this entailed jumbling McLaws's division with Hood's and further delaying matters. "After considerable difficulty, owing to the rough character of the country in places . . . the countermarch was effected," said McLaws, "and my troops were moving easily forward . . . when General Longstreet rode up to me, and said: 'How are you going [to attack]?'"

"That will be determined when I can see what is in my front," answered McLaws.

"There is nothing in your front," Longstreet assured him, "you will be entirely on the flank of the enemy."

"Then I will continue my march in column of companies, and after arriving on the flank . . . will face to the left and march on the enemy."

"That suits me," said Longstreet, riding away.

Not until 4 P.M. did McLaws begin to close with the foe on the Emmitsburg Road at the Peach Orchard and the Wheat Field. There he received a wicked surprise. "One rapid glance showed them to be in force much greater than I had," he said, "and extending considerably beyond my right. My command, therefore, instead of marching on as directed, deployed at once. Kershaw, a very cool, judicious gentleman, immediately turned the head of his column and . . . put his men under cover of a stone wall. Barksdale, the impetuous Mississippian, came into line on the left of Kershaw, his men sheltered by trees. . . ."

With the Peach Orchard teeming with Yankees, McLaws saw he needed substantial artillery support. "An order came from General Longstreet, borne by Major [Osmund] Latrobe, asking why I did not charge," he recalled, "as [supposedly] there was no one in my front but a regiment of infantry and a battery of artillery." Longstreet plainly did not want to hear that the Federals were in the Peach Orchard and on lower Cemetery Ridge in force. The man who all day had interpreted Lee's orders so loosely now was following them to the letter. Continued McLaws: "In a very short time after this the order was repeated, and I informed [Major Latrobe] again that the enemy was so strong . . . that it required careful preparation for the assault . . . that the opposite artillery was numerous, and it was necessary to break its force by the fire of our artillery." When the order to charge was repeated a third time, McLaws despite his reservations prepared to move his men forward. "But while collecting my staff to send the orders for a simultaneous move of the whole line, a courier dashed up with orders for me to wait until Hood got into position."[23]

John Bell Hood was having his own difficulties with Longstreet. The Texan had likewise discovered that the Federal lines extended down toward Big Round Top, but that the southern slope of the hill was undefended. Marching up the Emmitsburg Road behind McLaws made no sense to Hood—it would expose his flank and rear to enemy fire. Far better to turn Big Round Top, and then assail Little Round Top from the south. "I found that in making the attack . . . up the Emmitsburg Road," he said, "I should have, first, to encounter and drive off [the enemy's] line of battle; secondly, at the base and along the slope of the mountain, to confront immense boulders of stone, so massed together as to form narrow openings which would break our ranks. . . ." He dispatched a messenger to Longstreet, asking permission to make a flanking move.

Back came the reply: "General Lee's orders are to attack up the Emmitsburg Road."

"I sent another officer to say that I feared nothing could be accomplished by such an attack, and renewed my request," said Hood.

Again came Longstreet's reply: "General Lee's orders are to attack up the Emmitsburg Road." At the urging of Evander Law, one of his brigadiers, Hood sent Longstreet still a third request to turn Round Top rather than assail it head-on. Still a third reply: "General Lee's orders are to attack up the Emmitsburg Road." Just as he was moving his men into position, Longstreet himself rode up and the Texan made a fourth request. "We must obey the orders of General Lee," Longstreet said. Hood and Law, among the bravest of Lee's officers, would make the assault under formal protest. "I do not know whether the protest ever reached General Lee," said Law. "From the brief interval that elapsed between the time it was sent to General Longstreet and the receipt of the order to begin the attack, I am inclined to think it did not."[24]

Longstreet's delay in putting the First Corps into action on July 2 was a blot on his record. His strict obedience to orders thereafter, worse still. "The question then arises," said McLaws, "was it General Longstreet's duty . . . when he became aware that General Lee's orders could not be obeyed, that the reconnaissance on which they were based had been faulty, and that therefore he had given those orders under mistaken or false information, to have halted his command, and going back to General Lee, informed him of the true status of the enemy?"[25]

The ensuing Confederate attack along its seven-mile front would be conspicuously uncoordinated, with long intervals between the assaults on the right, center and left, permitting the enemy with its much shorter lines to reinforce danger points almost at will. Hood's division was on the far right, with Jerome Robertson's Texas Brigade and Law's Alabamians in the first line, backed by George "Tige" Anderson's and Henry "Rock" Benning's Georgians. These were the men who would go up against the Round Tops and Devil's Den, the boulder-strewn, heavily forested area between the two hills. To Hood's left was McLaws, with Barksdale's Mississippians and Kershaw's South Carolinians in the forefront, and William Wofford's and Paul Semmes's Georgians behind them. These were the troops, for the most part, who would be engaged at the Peach Orchard and the Wheat Field, the low ground a half-mile to the west of Little Round Top. Once Hood launched his attack he would be on his own. Longstreet would be with McLaws, and the nature of the battlefield did not permit easy communication.

To McLaws's left in the center, posted since noon, was Richard Heron Anderson's division of Hill's Third Corps. Until the army's latest reorganization Dick Anderson had always served under Longstreet. Doubtless helped by Hill's impaired state of health this would lead to confusion, with Little Powell to some degree thinking Longstreet would be supervising Anderson and vice versa. The result was that Anderson would be acting semi-independently, and on this occasion none too forcefully. His brigades lined up, from left to right, thusly: Carnot Posey's Mississippians, Rans Wright's Georgians, David Lang's Floridians and Cadmus Wilcox's Alabamians. On the far left the Second Corps under Ewell, still strung out disadvantageously in the shadow of Cemetery and Culp's Hills, had been ready since dawn. There Allegheny Johnson was on the left, Early in the center, then Rodes.

Hood launched his assault about 5 P.M., initially sending Robertson and Law straight toward Devil's Den and the Round Tops. "For half a mile we were exposed to a heavy and destructive fire of canister, grape and shell from six pieces of their artillery . . . and the same number on a commanding hill but a short distance to the left of the mountain," said Jerome Robertson, "and from the enemy's sharpshooters from behind the numerous rocks, fences and houses in the field." His brigade consisted of the 1st, 4th and 5th Texas Regiments, together with the 3rd Arkansas Regiment.

Soon Robertson's and Law's brigades divided and became entwined. The 1st Texas and the 3rd Arkansas with two Alabama regiments veered leftward toward Devil's Den, while the other Texas regiments with the rest of the Alabamians marched toward the Round Tops. "The enemy stood their ground bravely, until we were close on them, but did not await the bayonet," said Private James Bradfield of the 1st Texas, speaking of the assault on Devil's Den. "They broke away from the rock fence as we closed with a rush and a wild rebel yell, and fell back to the top of the ridge, where they formed on their second line." There they poured fire on the Confederates. "We saw that this would never do," said Bradfield, "and so, without awaiting orders every man became his own commander and sprang forward toward the top of the hill at full speed." Now Rock Benning's brigade, coming up from the reserve, put added pressure on the enemy. "The opposing lines stood with only the sheltering rocks between them—breast to breast, and so close that the clothing of many of the enemy was set on fire by the blaze from the Confederate rifles. This continued for some time, but finally . . . the Federals could no longer endure it, but gave way and fled. . . . The Lone Star flag crowned the hill."[26]

In short order the Federals regrouped and, preceded by a deafening artillery barrage, sought to retake the crest of Devil's Den. Here Sergeant Will Barbee of the 1st Texas, not yet 20 years old, inspired his comrades with an act of reckless courage. Springing atop a boulder, standing fearlessly erect, he fired again and again at the oncoming foe, the wounded men below passing up loaded muskets as fast as he emptied them. In a few minutes he was knocked off the rock by a ball that struck him in the right leg. Climbing back he resumed shooting, only to go down with a wound in the other leg. Still a third time he mounted the boulder, until another ball struck him in the chest. "Too seriously wounded this time to extricate himself," said Private Bradfield, "he called for help . . . crying and cursing because the boys would not . . . help him back on the rock." The counterattack failed.[27]

Meanwhile the assault on the Round Tops was if anything even fiercer. "Every tree, rock and stump that gave any protection from the rain of minie balls that was poured down upon us, from the crest above us, were soon appropriated," said Private Val. C. Giles of the 4th Texas. "John Griffin and myself pre-empted behind a moss-covered old boulder about the size of a 500-pound cotton bale. . . . To add to this confusion, our artillery on the hill in our rear was cutting its fuses too short. The shells were bursting . . . over our heads, and all around us. Nothing demoralizes troops quicker than to be fired on by their friends. . . . This mistake was soon corrected." The lines in front of Big Round Top were in places no more than 50 yards apart. "Everything was on the shoot; no favors asked, and none offered," added Giles. "My gun was so dirty that the ramrod hung in the barrel, and I could neither get it down nor out. I slammed the rod against a rock a few times, and drove home ramrod, cartridge and all, laid the gun on a boulder, elevated the muzzle, ducked my head, halloed 'Look out!' and pulled the trigger. She roared like a young cannon and flew over my shoulder. . . . It was no trouble to get another gun. The mountain side was covered with them."[28]

By this time Hood had been taken to the rear, brought down by a ball that all but pulverized his left arm. Robertson likewise would be wounded, and command of the division would devolve on Law. "Confusion reigned supreme everywhere," said Private Giles. "Nearly all our field officers were gone. . . . Major [Jefferson] Rogers, then in command of the 5th Texas, mounted an old log near my boulder and began a Fourth of July speech. He was a little ahead of time, for that was about 6:30 o'clock on the evening of the 2nd. Of course, nobody was paying attention to the oration as he appealed to the men to 'stand fast.' He and Captain [John] Cussons of the 4th Alabama were the only two men I saw standing. The balance of us had settled down behind rocks, logs and trees."

Just then a courier galloped up from Evander Law, shouting: "General Law presents his compliments and says hold the place at all hazards!"

Major Rogers glared down at the messenger from his perch.

"Compliments, hell!" he yelled. "Who wants compliments in such a damned place as this! Go back and ask General Law if he expects me to hold the world in check with the 5th Texas Regiment!"[29]

Somehow the 4th and 5th Texas, together with Law's Alabamians, not only maintained their lines but slowly pushed them forward—the Texans and some Alabamians skirting the base of Big Round Top and advancing on Little

Round Top from the west, the 47th and 15th Alabama approaching it from the south. The latter hill, some 600 feet high, was the key to the whole Federal position. If the Confederates took it, the enemy would have little choice but to evacuate Cemetery Ridge. Reported Law, who had learned his soldiering at The Citadel: "My brigade, on the right, had swept over the northern slope of Round Top, cleared it of the enemy, and then, making a partial change of front to the left, advanced upon Little Round Top."[30] Here in bitter action the Texans and most of the Alabamians were thrice stopped cold by torrents of fire from the crest. The barrages came from the fresh, 1,100-man brigade of Union Colonel Strong Vincent, a Harvard graduate with little military training who, seeing that Little Round Top was undefended, had without orders rushed his troops onto the heights. Like Law, Vincent was only 26 years old—the youngest brigade commander in Meade's army—and a fearless fighter. Within the hour he would be killed.

Confederate hopes to turn Little Round Top now rested solely on the 15th Alabama under Colonel William Oates, which was on the extreme right of Law's line. Oates's men had taken Round Top, driving Federal sharpshooters before them, and at this point were clambering up its smaller sibling, trying to turn Vincent's left and unhinge the Union position. Opposing them, in one of the war's classic regimental matchups, was the 20th Maine under Colonel Joshua Chamberlain. The two commanders were studies in contrast. The 29-year-old Oates grew up a brawler and a wanderer, and then returned to Alabama, where he settled down and began practicing law. Dark, handsome and vigorous, he would be described by a fellow soldier as being "regarded by many as too aggressive and ambitious but he usually was well to the front and did not require his men to charge where he was unwilling to share the common danger."[31] Chamberlain, 35, was a farm boy who had graduated from Bowdoin College and the Theological Seminary at Bangor, Maine, and at the outbreak of the war was teaching at Bowdoin. His mien was professorial, his gaze idealistic. By all accounts he took his position on Little Round Top less than fifteen minutes before the 15th Alabama attacked.

Slowly moving up the craggy hillside, Oates met a fire so intense his lines "wavered like a man trying to walk into a strong wind." But he persisted, spotting a position that would afford at least some protection, and crying, "Forward, men, to the ledge!" Once it was taken the two sides then settled into a hot and desperate fight, seesawing up and down the slope. The 15th Alabama was a veteran outfit, so tough one of its officers forced a shirker into the front lines, making sure he was an easy target. A sergeant held the man there until a bullet took his life. "Now I guess you will not run away," said the noncom, letting the body fall to the ground. The 20th Maine, by contrast, had seen little action. Both regiments this day went at each other with a vengeance. The firing was so loud that Oates's officers could not hear his commands, the gunpowder smoke so heavy his men could not see where to shoot.

"Colonel, I can't see them," Private William Holloway complained. Oates told him to crouch below the smoke and fire from there. Holloway did so, and a moment later received a bullet in the head. Captain Henry Brainard, standing near Oates, also went down with a mortal wound, crying at the last, "Oh, God, that I could see my mother!" Lieutenant John Oates succeeded to his command, and then fell with several wounds himself. Sick that day with fever, he had reached the field only because Colonel Oates, his brother, had found him a horse. The suggestion he remain in the rear appalled him. "Brother, I will not do it," he had said. "If I remain here people will say that I did [so] through cowardice."

With the action in places hand-to-hand and the lines continually shifting, the wounded literally found themselves being fought over, as those on their feet pushed back and forth over the fallen. Oates used his pistol again and again on Federals who came within paces of his command post. On one occasion a Maine man got so close to the 15th Alabama's flag he almost grabbed it. The color-bearer pulled the staff back just as a comrade put a bayonet through the assailant's head.[32]

Oates and Chamberlain now made fateful decisions. Both colonels were on their own, with no hope of support and little knowledge of the strength of the men they were fighting. Both realized their own men were on the verge of exhaustion, and both with darkness coming on needed to end the engagement. Oates, fearful of being overrun, ordered an expeditious retreat. "Run in the direction from whence [you] came and halt on the top of Round Top."

Chamberlain, fearful of being surrounded, ordered his men to fix bayonets and charge. "The word was enough," he said. "It ran like fire along the line." Here audacity triumphed. The retreat quickly became a rout, with the pursuers scampering downhill and their foes running "like a herd of wild cattle." One of the men fleeing with Oates had a bullet in his windpipe, and he sprayed blood on the colonel with every step he took. Oates lost 172 of 380 men; Chamberlain, 136 of 358.[33]

Night brought an end to the fighting on Hood's front. Though the Confederates controlled Devil's Den, they had been repulsed at Little Round Top. Here their lines stretched along the foot of its western slope, extending to the northwestern face of Big Round Top. The cries of the wounded men left on the field were continual and plaintive. Wrote John Mosely, in a note sent between the lines, to his mother in Alabama: "I am a prisoner of war and mortally wounded. I can live but a few hours at best. . . . Do not mourn my loss. I had hoped to have been spared, but a righteous God had ordered it otherwise. . . . Farewell to you all. Pray that God may receive my soul."[34]

---

On the lines where McLaws waited, opposite the Peach Orchard and the Wheat Field, the battle did not begin until 5:30 P.M. Here Union General Daniel Sickles, thinking the area would provide better terrain for his guns, had advanced his Third Corps from Cemetery Ridge without orders, creating a bulge and a weakness in the Federal front. Sickles was used to acting impulsively. In 1859, while a U.S. senator from New York, he shot and killed a man who was having an affair with his wife. Pleading temporary insanity for the first time in legal history, he was acquitted.

Fresh from his confrontation with Hood about the wisdom of assailing the Round Tops frontally, Longstreet galloped up to McLaws in a foul mood.

"Why is not a battery placed there?" he demanded, pointing to a gap in the lines.

Nothing intimidated by his West Point classmate, McLaws made a quick retort: "General, if a battery is placed there it will draw the enemy's artillery right among my lines formed for the charge . . . and tend to demoralize my men."

Longstreet peremptorily ordered that some guns be brought up immediately. Predictably their fire brought a crushing response from the enemy. "The bursting shells . . . wounded or killed a number [of my men] whilst in line . . . producing a natural feeling of uneasiness among them," said McLaws. "I got on my horse and rode among them, directing them to lie down so as to escape as much as possible from the shot and shell." Chafing under the cannonade, Barksdale sought orders to charge the enemy guns. "General, let me go; General, let me charge!" he repeated several times. McLaws, who was himself awaiting orders, advised him to be patient.[35]

When Longstreet did signal an advance, McLaws quickly unleashed his men. Barksdale's Mississippians, William Wofford's Georgians, Kershaw's South Carolinians and Paul Semmes's Georgians—from left to right—rushed across the Emmitsburg Road toward the Peach Orchard and the Wheat Field. Helped by George "Tige" Anderson's Georgians coming up from Devil's Den, they pushed the enemy back on both flanks, threatening to envelop Sickles's vulnerable salient. In the wake of the charge Porter Alexander called up additional artillery under Major James Dearing from the reserve. When rows of fences slowed the advance of his guns, Dearing put several hundred prisoners to work. "God damn you," he shouted, waving his sword in their faces, "pull down those fences!" With the barriers gone, "the batteries charged within cannister distance of the enemy and poured a deadly fire into their retreating ranks."[36]

Kershaw bypassed the Peach Orchard and advanced through the Wheat Field to Sickles's left. Semmes, who soon received a fatal wound when a ball cut an artery in his thigh, closely followed him. "Kershaw was on foot," said one of his officers, "prepared to follow the line of battle immediately in rear, looking cool, composed and grand, his steel-gray eyes flashing the fire he felt in his soul. . . . The battery in the orchard began grapeing [our] left as soon as it came in range, the right being protected by a depression in the ground. . . . Men fell here and there from the deadly minie-balls, while great gaps or swaths were swept away by batteries from the hills. . . . On marched the determined men across this open expanse, closing together as their comrades fell out." Halfway through the Wheat Field, the enemy fire intensified. "It was thought by some that it was our flag that was drawing the fire, four color guards having gone down, [and] someone called out, 'Lower the colors, down with the flag.' " The newest color-bearer would not have it so. "Moving to the front where all could see, [he] called out in loud tones, 'This flag never goes down until I am down.' "37

To Sickles's right the pugnacious Barksdale—backed by Wofford—assailed the Peach Orchard, completing the envelopment and forcing the Federals back toward Cemetery Ridge. "I had witnessed many charges marked in every way by unflinching gallantry," said one of McLaws's aides, "but I never saw anything to equal the dash and heroism of the Mississippians. . . . When I carried [Barksdale] the order to advance his face was radiant with joy. He was in front of his brigade, hat off, and his long white hair reminded me of the 'white plume of Navarre.' I saw him as far as the eye would follow, still ahead of his men, leading them on." Porter Alexander backed up the Mississippians with his guns. "Every battery was limbered to the front," he said, "and all six charged in line across the plain and went into action at the position the enemy had deserted. . . . An artillerist's heaven is to follow the routed enemy, after a tough resistance, and throw shells into his fleeing masses. . . . Now we saw our heaven. . . . Now we would have our revenge."38 Such was not to be. The retreat of Sickles's Third Corps to the ridge, together with the elements of the Fifth and Second Corps sent to support it, would be relatively orderly, but casualties were heavy. By twilight Tige Anderson would be severely wounded, Barksdale would suffer a mortal chest wound, and Sickles would lose his right leg.

Farther to the north quiet Dick Anderson next advanced his own division from Seminary Ridge on McLaws's left, putting added pressure on the foe. Wilcox's Alabamians were closest to McLaws, then David Lang's Floridians, Rans Wright's Georgians and Carnot Posey's Mississippians. Of the four brigades, the Georgians pushed forward to the ridge, but this would be their undoing. "Thus we worked our way across that terrible field for more than a mile, under the most furious fire of artillery I had ever seen," Wright wrote his wife. "We were now within a few hundred yards of the enemy's guns, and had up to this time suffered little loss. . . . But we were in a hot place. . . . The side of the mountain was so precipitous here my men could with difficulty *climb* it, but we strove on, and reaching the stone fence, *drove the Yankee infantry from behind it*, and then taking cover *shot all the gunners of the enemy's artillery*, and rushing over the fence seized the guns." At this point

Wright noticed a heavy column of Federal infantry on his right flank. "They had taken advantage of the gap left in our line by the falling back of [Lang's] Brigade and were rapidly getting in our rear. *Posey had not advanced on our left. . . .*"

Anderson in the center was encountering the same problems that had plagued Hood and McLaws on the right. The Confederate attacks in some places drove back the enemy, but overall lacked the sledgehammer force and coordination to break his lines and take Cemetery Ridge. Here Longstreet's willfulness and, to a lesser degree, Powell Hill's illness—the failures of the corps commanders to implement Lee's plans—must be acknowledged. Meade meanwhile was using his shorter interior lines to move troops up and down the heights, reinforcing his positions where needed. "The enemy had now gotten completely in our rear," Wright continued, "*and were advancing upon us over the very ground we had passed in attacking them. . . .* With cheers and good order we turned our faces to the enemy in our rear, and abandoning our captured guns we rushed upon the flanking column and *literally cut our way out*, and fell back about one-half the distance we had gone over."[39]

During these three hours of fighting the three Confederate divisions on the right and center suffered some 6,000 casualties. Hood and McLaws had 2,200 each, a rate of 30 percent; Anderson had 1,600 in Wright's, Wilcox's and Lang's brigades, a rate of 40 percent. Sickles's corps lost some 4,200 men, a rate of 30 percent, and Federal casualties overall totaled 9,000.

Though not engaged on July 2, the formidable Dorsey Pender of Hill's corps just before sunset suffered a mortal wound. He and some fellow officers were waiting for orders when the cannonading reached a crescendo and he could bear the inactivity no longer. "Major," he said to Joseph Englehard, his aide, "this indicates an assault, and we will ride down our line." Near the front a small shell fragment struck Pender in the leg. Unable to mount a horse, he had to be taken to the rear. In his last letter to his wife he had praised his men and asked God's blessing. "I never saw troops march as ours do; they will go 15 or 20 miles a day without leaving a straggler and hoop and yell on all occasions" he told Fanny. "Confidence and good spirits seem to possess everyone. . . . Now darling, may our Good Father protect us and preserve us to each other to a good old age. Tell Turner [one of their sons] I have a pretty pair of low patent leather shoes with heels for him."

Days later the main artery in Pender's leg began hemorrhaging and the bleeding could not be stopped. "Tell my wife I do not fear to die," he informed a chaplain. "I can confidently resign my soul to God. . . . My only regret is to leave her and our two children." Powell Hill mourned the "irreparable loss" of his favorite lieutenant. "We learned to admire and love him while living," said one of Pender's officers, "and to regret him with all our hearts when dead." On hearing the news, 23-year-old Fanny closeted herself in her bedroom for three days. Months later she gave birth to their third son.

She never remarried, died at age 82 and was buried next to her husband in Tarboro, North Carolina.[40]

Last to go on the attack that afternoon were Ewell's divisions and they did so, despite Lee's admonitions, with the same lack of cohesion that marked the overall Confederate effort. "We did not or we could not pursue the advantage of yesterday, and now the enemy are in a good position," he had pointedly told Old Bald Head that morning, referring to the Federal lines on Cemetery and Culp's Hill. Yet Ewell remained indecisive, giving no specific instructions to Johnson, Early and Rodes as to how to coordinate their assaults. The upshot was that Johnson ordered his artillery under Major Joseph Latimer to move to Benner Hill, some 1,000 yards to the east of Culp's Hill, and open up an ill-advised barrage about 4 P.M., long before the infantry was ready to move forward. There these sixteen guns, joined by four guns of the Rockbridge Artillery, would be in an exposed position, facing twice the number of enemy pieces. To a Marylander in George Steuart's brigade, their advance nonetheless was "a splendid sight. Sixteen guns, sixteen caissons, with their attending cavalcade of company and field officers, steaming over the field in bustle and bust speed and enveloped in clouds of dust."[41]

Latimer, not yet 20 years old, was an artillery prodigy in the mold of William Poague, John Pelham and Willie Pegram. Nicknamed "The Boy Major," he had joined the army straight out of V.M.I. Campbell Brown, Ewell's stepson and aide, described him as being "small & slight of his age . . . but one of those born soldiers whose promotion is recognized by all to be a consequence of their own merit."

With Ewell's infantry still immobile, the Federals concentrated all their fire on Latimer's men, over the next few hours decimating the battalion. "As soon as his guns were unmasked, the enemy replied with a superior number of guns from Cemetery Hill and Culp's Hill, causing many casualties," wrote one historian. "Soon the Federals planted some guns well out to Latimer's left front, enfilading [Joseph] Carpenter's Battery and practically silencing it. By this time one section of [William] Dement's Battery had entirely exhausted its ammunition and one of [William] Brown's pieces had been disabled. Brown himself was wounded and his men so cut up but that two pieces could be maintained in action."[42]

Describing the scene in Brown's battery, a second historian was more graphic: "When no ammunition was brought to his gun, Pvt. Jacob F. Cook . . . ran to the limber to see what had gone wrong. He found Sgt. Robert A. Crowley, the chief of piece, there, and when he asked where the other crewmen were, Crowley showed him. Cpl. Daniel Dougherty was cut in half, Pvt. Frederick Cusick's head was torn off, Doctor Jack Brian had lost his head, and there were other wounded lying nearby." Yale-educated Robert Stiles, once a gunner at Malvern Hill and now an aide to Jubal Early, was no stranger to artillery battles. He would say of the carnage on Benner Hill, "Never, before or since, did I see . . . such a condition of wreck and destruction as this battalion was. It had been hurled backward, as it were, by the very weight and impact of metal from the position it had occupied on the crest . . . into a saucer-shaped depression behind it . . . guns dismounted and disabled, carriages splintered and crushed, ammunition chests exploded, limbers upset, wounded horses plunging and kicking. . . ."

Leaving four guns on the hill, Latimer with heroic effort managed to remove the others, fitting them with salvaged wheels from the caissons. Then he returned to his post, just as Johnson's division moved on Culp's Hill. There, though he suffered a leg wound that eventually cost him his life, he continued to support the attack. In his final hours, the attending physician asked him if he feared death. "No," he replied, "for my trust is in God."[43]

By the time Johnson crossed Rock Creek and neared the hill's eastern slope, it was about 7:30 P.M. Steuart's Marylanders, North Carolinians and Virginians were on the left of his line, then Nicholls's Louisianans under Jesse Williams, then John "Rum" Jones's Virginians. The Stonewall Brigade under James A. Walker, lacking sufficient cover, stayed behind until darkness fell. Nicholls's and Jones's brigades reached the base of the heights, but were unable to advance farther. Jones took a bullet in the leg, and the two units eventually dug in, preparing for an early morning assault. Steuart had better luck, taking some Federal lines on the lower slope and about 9:30 P.M. coming within 500 yards of the Baltimore Pike, Meade's supply line. In the blackness men could not tell friend from foe, and were guided by musket flashes. Randolph McKim, Steuart's aide, was guiding some North Carolina troops forward when he saw such flashes on his right. "Fire on them, boys! Fire on them!" he shouted, only to learn they were his own men. "Owing to the din the command to fire had not been heard except by those nearest to me," he said, "and I believe no injury resulted from my mistake." Now Steuart likewise paused and waited for morning.[44]

Just as Johnson became engaged, a determined Jubal Early pushed Hoke's North Carolinians under Isaac Avery and Hays's Louisianans up the east slope of Cemetery Hill. The plan called for Rodes simultaneously to hurl his division up the west slope, catching the enemy in a pincers. Hearing the bugle call for the advance, admitted Joseph Jackson, one of Hays's officers, "I felt as if my doom was sealed, and it was with great reluctance that I started my skirmishers forward." During the attack Avery, the scion of a notable North Carolina family, was shot from his horse and mortally wounded. "Tell my father I died with my face to the enemy," were his scribbled last words. Early's men enjoyed initial success, overrunning the first line of Yankee artillery and putting Oliver Howard's infantry to flight. "With bayonets and clubbed guns we drove them back," said Jackson.[45] Sprinting ahead of his men to be the first into the Federal cannon was Colonel Leroy Stafford of the 9th Louisiana, serving Old Jube as gallantly as he had Stonewall Jackson at Port Republic. But the enemy was already rushing up reinforcements. Early and Hays needed support. Where was Rodes?

Handsome, mustachioed Robert Rodes was not often tardy, but this was one of the rare occasions. To be fair he had his reasons. Not only were his brigades posted in the narrow streets of Gettysburg, slowing their movements, but they were twice as far away from Cemetery Hill as Early's—some 1,200 yards. Moreover, Rodes needed assurances that Pender's division would be guarding his right flank, and in the confusion following that officer's wounding this guarantee was lacking. Early was in no mood for such excuses. "When my brigades started," he said, "I sent word to Rodes that I was moving, and while they were making their way up the rugged slopes I sent again to urge him to go forward. . . . I have nothing to say in regard to the causes of his delay, except that I imagine he and the division commander on his right were discussing the question as to whether the latter should also move. . . . There was no attack here by 'piecemeal' in any sense. Johnson and I attacked together, but Rodes did not attack at all." Early's men, unsupported, were forced to fall back in the darkness. Rodes never did come up and all fighting ceased.

Like Harvey Hill, the arthritic Early seldom could restrain his caustic tongue. He was, said aide Robert Stiles: "a bundle of inconsistencies and contradictions; of religion and irreligion, of reverence and profanity. I have heard my father (a Presbyterian minister) speak of the General's deep interest in religious work. . . . I do not think I ever knew one human soul to look up to another with a feeling nearer akin to worship than that with which Early regarded Lee and Jackson . . . yet he was the only man known to swear in General Lee's presence. The General used to reprove him gently, yet at the same time express his special affection . . . calling him 'My bad old man.' "[46]

Thus the second day of battle ended. Near the inverted fishhook that was Cemetery Ridge the Confederate positions were hard-won but tenuous: on the right, the western foot of the Round Tops and boulder-strewn Devil's Den; on the left, the eastern slope of Culp's Hill; in the center, the Peach Orchard.

Still confident he could crack the Federal lines, Lee during the night issued orders to Longstreet, Ewell and Hill for an all-out assault at dawn on July 3. "The general plan was unchanged," he would say. "Longstreet, reinforced by [George] Pickett's three brigades . . . was ordered to attack the next morning, and General Ewell was directed to assail the enemy's right at the same time." Porter Alexander, who was at Longstreet's bivouac, would remember the instructions: "I was told that we would renew the attack early the next morning. That Pickett's Division would arrive and would assault the enemy's line. My impression is the exact point for it was not designated, but . . . would be to our left of the Peach Orchard." These directions well suited Ewell, who was

eager to exploit Johnson's toehold on Culp's Hill. During the night he reinforced him with two of Rodes's brigades—Junius Daniel's North Carolinians and Edward O'Neal's Alabamians. Hill likewise was enthusiastic, and
had his divisions poised to give support where needed. "What Lee wanted
above all," one military historian would say, "was to strike both extremities
of the enemy line at exactly the same time, Ewell the left and Longstreet the
right. . . . The formidable character of the Union position never awed him
as it did Longstreet, and he felt sure his incomparable infantry if properly
handled could take any height."[47]

What ruined this plan was Longstreet's continued recalcitrance. Just as
Johnson at 4:30 A.M. was launching his attack on William Slocum's Twelfth
Corps, Old Pete was once more resisting a frontal assault and giving orders
to move around Meade's left and take a defensive position between the Federals and Washington. Lee only learned of this at dawn, when he rode up to
Longstreet's bivouac and found his troops unprepared to attack. While he put
an instant halt to the flanking movement, he could not stop Ewell's attack.
"General Longstreet's dispositions were not completed as early as was expected," Lee reported, "but before notice could be sent to General Ewell,
General Johnson had already become engaged, and it was too late to recall
him." Longstreet later would say he was "depressed" by Lee's reaction to his
tactics. Lee was far more than "depressed" by Longstreet. Here with Jackson's
death was his chief lieutenant, the only officer he had who had proven he
could exercise corps command, and he was opposing his instructions to a
point just short of insubordination.[48]

Longstreet tried to justify his actions. "Fearing [Lee] was still in his disposition to attack," he would say, "I tried to anticipate him, by saying: 'General, I have had my scouts out all night, and I find that you still have an
excellent opportunity to move around to the right of Meade's army and maneuver him into attacking us.'

"He replied, pointing with his fist at Cemetery Hill: 'The enemy is there,
and I am going to strike him.' "

How many men would be making the assault? Longstreet asked. Perhaps
some 15,000, Lee answered.

"General," Longstreet said, "I have been a soldier all my life. I have been
with soldiers engaged in fights by couples, by squads, companies, regiments,
divisions and armies, and should know, as well as anyone, what soldiers can
do. It is my opinion that no 15,000 men ever arrayed for battle can take that
position." He protested no more, but turned away. "I felt that my record was
such," he would say, "that General Lee would or could not misconstrue my
motives."[49]

Whether Longstreet was right or wrong is not the point. At dawn on this
third day at Gettysburg he had thwarted Lee's original intent. Even as Johnson's troops at 5:30 A.M. were hopelessly assailing Culp's Hill without sup-

port, the Confederate commander was being forced to scrap his plans and rethink his tactics.

On Culp's Hill meanwhile Steuart's brigade desperately held the left of the line, with Nicholls's Louisianans and "Rum" Jones's Virginians on its right. "Maryland" Steuart was the pedantic cavalry officer in the Valley Campaign, we will remember, who refused an urgent order from one of Jackson's aides because it did not come through the chain of command. Now with the infantry, he had become a dogged fighter. For the next several hours, the two sides traded blows to little effect. When Steuart's men ran short on ammunition Randolph McKim took three men and went back on foot to the wagons, about a mile and a half away, to bring up two boxes of cartridges. "We emptied each box into a blanket," said McKim, "and swung the blanket on a rail, and so carried it to the front."

About 9 A.M. Johnson moved Daniel's North Carolinians to Steuart's right and ordered a general advance. Junius Daniel was a solidly built West Pointer who was building an equally solid reputation as a brigadier. Neither he nor Steuart thought the attack wise, but they plunged ahead. "Well might they despair of success," Lieutenant McKim explained. "The works to be stormed ran almost at right angles to those we occupied. Moreover, there was a double line of entrenchments, one above the other, and each filled with troops. In moving to the attack we were exposed to enfilading fire from the woods on our left, besides the double line of fire we had to face in front, and a battery of artillery posted on a hill on our left rear opened upon us at short range." Steuart had his brigade leap over their breastworks and formed them in line of battle at right angles to their previous position. "Then drawing his sword, he gave the command, 'Charge bayonets!' and moved forward on foot with his men. . . . Soon, however, the left and center were checked and then repulsed. . . . We were beaten back to the line from which we had advanced with terrible loss." Steuart's total casualties at Gettysburg were almost 700; Daniel's were 916, the highest in Ewell's corps. "My poor boys! My poor boys!" Steuart cried out, clenching his fists while tears ran down his cheeks. By 10:30 A.M. the battle for Culp's Hill was over and Johnson had evacuated his position.[50] Overall casualties in Johnson's division would be some 1,800, with losses in Daniel's, O'Neal's and "Extra Billy" Smith's brigades almost doubling the total. Federal losses in the Twelfth Corps, the most heavily engaged, would be 1,080 men.

By now Lee had devised new tactics. Rans Wright the day before had reached Cemetery Ridge but been forced to withdraw because of lack of support on his flanks. "The trouble is not in going in there," he had said. "The trouble is to stay there after you get there." Lee's plan called for pushing forward under artillery cover enough infantry to crush the defenders beyond hope of recovery. Explained a commentator: "His troops would converge on one point [on the ridge], say that small clump of trees he could see with his naked eye; they would form something like a flying wedge of sufficient depth to sustain their momentum and sufficient breath to protect their flanks." That clump of trees offered another advantage. "Once gained and firmly held, his men could curl around to the left and threaten Cemetery Hill from the flank and rear. Federal troops south of the captured position would be able to do little to help their comrades for fear their counterfire would be as destructive to friend as foe."[51]

Standing in the open fields in front of the ridge with Longstreet and his other generals, Lee's first thought was that the entire First Corps would make the assault. When Longstreet argued the decision, saying that Hood and McLaws had been too bloodied the previous day, Lee conceded the point and named Heth's division and part of Pender's to replace them. The eight brigades of Hood and McLaws, as well as Hill's remaining five brigades, would become involved as circumstances warranted. Ewell's thirteen brigades remained semi-isolated to the north of Cemetery and Culp's Hills. Stuart's cavalry had been sent east of Gettysburg, its mission to get in Meade's rear and disrupt his communications.

The final order of battle would consist of eleven brigades. Pickett's all-Virginia division would be on the right, with Richard Garnett and James Kemper in the first line and Lewis Armistead in the second. Guarding the Virginians' right flank would be Marcellus Wilcox's Alabamians and David Lang's Floridians of Dick Anderson's division. The wounded Heth's division under Johnston Pettigrew would be on the left, with Robert Mayo's Virginians, Joseph Davis's Mississippians, James Marshall's North Carolinians and Birkett Fry's Tennesseans and Alabamians from left to right in the first line; behind Pettigrew in the second line would be two of Pender's brigades under Trimble—James Lane's and W. Lee Lowrance's North Carolinians. In all, the force totaled some 13,500.

These would be the men, then, who would be involved in what came to be known as Pickett's Charge. Major General George Pickett, he of the perfumed ringlets and beard, was a contradiction in terms. Martial in spirit, coming from a family that was one of Virginia's ruling elite, he was nonetheless a dandy and a drinker, someone who flaunted the pieties of the day, and he could be rowdy and arrogant. His indolence, at least in his youth, resulted in his graduating last in his class at West Point. After his first wife died in childbirth, he fathered a child by an Indian woman while on army duty in Washington State, and when she died soon after giving birth he rarely saw the boy again. His rise to divisional command in the Army of Northern Virginia is something of a mystery, although his strong friendship with Longstreet did him no harm. When three of Longstreet's children died suddenly of fever in 1862, in fact, Pickett was said to have handled the burial arrangements for the distraught parents. Wounded at Gaines's Mill, he had seen little action since.

Now he was courting LaSalle "Sallie" Corbett, a cultivated young woman half his age. So close was the relationship that, during Longstreet's siege of Suffolk, Pickett had galloped off to see her almost every night. "Here when all was quiet along the lines," Sallie said, "my Soldier would ride in from his headquarters . . . between the hours of sunset and sunrise to see me—a ride of about thirty miles." Some saw his ardor as neglect of duty. One officer of the 56th Virginia complained to his wife that Pickett was "continually riding off to pay court to his young love, leaving the division details to his staff." Moxley Sorrel, Longstreet's adjutant, once denied him permission to leave camp. "Pickett went all the same," he said, "nothing could hold him back from that pursuit. . . . I don't think his division benefited from such carpet-knight doings."[52]

Pickett's three brigadiers were Garnett, Kemper and Armistead. Though we have met them before, they are worth looking at again. The able Richard Garnett, a Tidewater aristocrat, had spent the months after Kernstown redeeming himself in Longstreet's corps. Jackson's decision to relieve him for retreating without orders was wrong, he felt, and he had shown his courage since at Sharpsburg and Fredericksburg. Sick with fever he insisted on taking the field, wearing a heavy overcoat to control the chills racking his body despite the July heat.

Full-bearded James Kemper, a boyhood friend of Powell Hill, was a country lawyer from Madison County, Virginia. With the army since First Manassas, his leadership was without blemish. Fine bearing, fearlessness and dash—these are the words used to describe him. Forty years old in 1863, he had been married for ten years to the former Cremora ("Belle") Cave. He was given to full-blown oratory both before and after battles, and beloved by his brigade. "You have made yourself dear to all your men," his mother-in-law wrote him. "I do feel so glad where from every tongue, I learn something of your kindness and bravery."[53]

Lewis Armistead, whose forebears had been in Virginia since 1636, came from a family of soldiers. One of them, Colonel George Armistead, had defended Fort McHenry during the War of 1812; the flag that waved over it during the bombardment, immortalized by Francis Scott Key, was a treasured heirloom. His own father, when he died in 1848, was second-in-command of the U.S. Army. Expelled from West Point because of his storied quarrel with Jubal Early, Armistead later received a commission and served for more than twenty years with the Old Army. He had been with his brigade since the Peninsula, and had made it a disciplined, battle-hardened unit. "He was a strict disciplinarian, but never a martinet," one of his officers said. "Obedience to duty he regarded as the first qualification of a soldier. For straggling on the march . . . he held the officer in immediate command strictly responsible. The private must answer to the officer, but the officer to him."[54]

On Pickett's right and rear were Wilcox and Lang. Marcellus Wilcox, who years before, like Powell Hill, had been an honored guest at the wedding of West Point classmate George McClellan and Ellen Marcy, was a much-admired officer. Everyone seemed to know the role he had assumed without orders at Salem Church during the battle of Chancellorsville, stopping the Federals cold and contributing to their withdrawal across the Rappahannock. He could be fussy with the details of soldiering, however, and his men called him "Old Billy Fixing." For Longstreet he still had little regard, remembering how that officer had muddled the line of march at Seven Pines, and then shifted the blame to others. Colonel David Lang, 25, had enlisted in the 1st Florida as a private. Now he commanded Edward Perry's small brigade, that officer being ill with typhoid fever.

Brigadier Johnston Pettigrew, who had been wounded and captured at Seven Pines and had only recently rejoined the army, was on Pickett's left. He was tough and resolute, but with Heth's wounding was completely new to division command and, additionally, impaired by understrength and inexperienced brigades. His division, cut to pieces the first day of the battle, totaled no more than 4,300 men. Colonel Robert Mayo, 27, a V.M.I. graduate and lawyer, replaced John Brockenbrough, who had been disabled at Fredericksburg. Brigadier Joe Davis, the unpretentious nephew of Jefferson Davis and son of his beloved older brother Joseph, was still green in battle. Colonel James Marshall, 24, a V.M.I. graduate and teacher, took over Pettigrew's brigade. Colonel Birkett Fry, who had been dismissed from West Point for failing mathematics, had been wounded three times in previous battles. Now the bald, solemn officer replaced the captured James Archer.

Walrus-mustached, cantankerous Major General Isaac Trimble commanded the second line behind Pettigrew. Old Man Trimble was back in action for the first time since Second Manassas, and he hoped to make the occasion a memorable one. Brigadier James Lane and Colonel W. Lee Lowrance led his North Carolina brigades. The diminutive and sad-eyed Lane, a V.M.I. graduate highly regarded for his intelligence and diligence, had been with the army since the Peninsula. One of his regiments, the 18th North Carolina, had ironically enough been the unit that mortally wounded Stonewall Jackson at Chancellorsville. Colonel Lowrance, a 26-year-old merchant, replaced the wounded Alfred Scales.

No keener observer of the Confederate assault existed than Edward Porter Alexander, Longstreet's chief of artillery, poised with his eighty-four guns to provide the main support for the Confederate advance on the clump of trees. To his left were Hill's cannon on Seminary Ridge and curling still farther left, out of his sight, were Ewell's guns in front of Cemetery Hill. Subsequently he would have two regrets about the performance of his artillery counterparts that day. "Between eleven & twelve o'clock there was a severe artillery duel, between Hill's guns & the enemy, which seemed to me to begin in a fight between the skirmishers over a barn. The artillery got into a duel . . . that lasted a half-hour & then finally died out. . . . I think it was a mistake to use that much ammunition prematurely." He was more critical of Ewell, who he believed could have opened up with enfilading fire on Cemetery Ridge. "Only one of Ewell's five fine battalions . . . participated in our bombardment at all. It only fired a few dozen shots, for, apparently, it could not see what it was doing. But every shot was smashing up something, &, had it been increased and kept up, it is hard to say what may have resulted."

Pickett's men were behind Alexander's cannon in the woods. Again Lee's orders were clear. Longstreet at 1 P.M. was to give the signal for the bombardment on the Federal lines to begin and, when Alexander judged its effectiveness was at its height, he would be responsible for ordering Pickett forward. It was not a question as to *whether* Pickett would advance, but *when* he would do so. "I had, at first," Alexander said, "taken no very special thought as to how long I would let the fire continue, before telling Pickett to go. Some 20 to 30 minutes I supposed would be about right. Not shorter than 20, for the longer the time the more punishment the enemy would have. But not longer than 30, because [the infantry] had a long charge & I must allow plenty of time for them to cover the distance. . . . I believed that it would come out all right, because General Lee had planned it." Then Alexander received an upsetting message. "Colonel:" Longstreet wrote him, "If the artillery fire does not have the effect to drive off the enemy, or greatly demoralize him . . . I would prefer that you not advise Gen. Pickett to make the charge. I shall rely a great deal on your good judgement to determine the matter. . . ."

Alexander, a poised young officer, was shocked. "It was no longer Gen. Lee's inspiration that this was the way to whip the battle," he said, "but my cold judgement to be founded on what I was going to see." He did not think it appropriate that he should make such a decision and, in measured but respectful words, he told Longstreet so. "General: I will only be able to judge the effect of our fire on the enemy by his return fire, for his infantry is but little exposed to view and the smoke will obscure the whole field. If, as I infer from your note, there is any alternative to this attack, it should be carefully considered before opening our fire, for it will take all the artillery ammunition we have left to test this one thoroughly. . . ." Back from Longstreet came an ingenuous reply: "Colonel: The intention is to advance the infantry, if the artillery has the desired effect of driving the enemy's off, or having other effect such as to warrant us in making the attack. When the moment arrives advise Gen. Pickett. . . ."

Rans Wright was standing nearby when this message was received, and Alexander showed it to him. "He has put the responsibility back upon you," Wright said. Reflected Alexander: "Gen. Lee had originally planned [the attack], & half the day had been spent in its preparation. I determined to cause no loss of time by any indecision on my part." After conferring with Pickett, whom he found "in excellent spirits & sanguine of success," he sent Long-street a simple acknowledgement. "General: When the artillery fire is doing its best I shall advise General Pickett to advance."[55]

At 1 P.M. the boom of two cannon sounded the signal for the Confederate bombardment, and immediately the enemy answered in kind. "His whole line from Cemetery Hill to Round Top seemed . . . to be emulating a volcano in eruption," said Alexander. "Lots of guns developed which I had not before been able to see, & instead of saving ammunition, they were surely trying themselves how much they could consume. . . . I saw at once that I must wait longer . . . & hope meanwhile to silence some at least of their guns. And so I waited, 15, 20, 25 minutes. . . ." At exactly 1:25 P.M., fearful of running out of ammunition himself, he sent Pickett a note: "If you are coming at all you must come at once, or I cannot give you proper support, but the enemy's fire has not slackened at all. At least 18 guns are still firing from the [point of attack]." Soon Alexander noticed these guns had been withdrawn. At 1:35 P.M. he wrote Pickett: "For God's sake, come quick. The 18 guns are gone. Come quick or I can't support you."

On getting the first note Pickett rode up to Longstreet and showed it to him.

"General, shall I advance?" he asked.

Longstreet turned his face aside. Pickett waited a few seconds, then saluted.

"I am going to move forward, sir," he said, wheeling his horse back toward his men.

While Pickett's division was moving forward toward the ridge and the clump of trees some 1,400 yards away, Longstreet rode to see Alexander. "I expressed impatience at Pickett's delay," Alexander remembered, ". . . & said I feared the support I could give might not be all I wished."

"Gen. L. spoke at once, & decidedly, 'Go and halt Pickett right where he is, & replenish your ammunition.'

"I said, 'General, we can't do that. We nearly emptied the [supply] trains last night. Even if we had [the ammunition], it would take an hour or two & meanwhile the enemy would recover from the pressure he is under. Our only chance is to follow it up now. . . .'

"I don't want to make this attack," Longstreet said. "I believe it will fail—I do not know how it can succeed—I would not make it even now, but that Gen. Lee has ordered and expects it."

For long minutes the two men sat on their horses in embarrassed silence.

Now Pickett's troops were streaming through Alexander's lines, headed at a fast pace toward the ridge. "Ahead of his men," said Alexander, "rode good & lovable Gen. Dick Garnett. I had crossed the plains with him, & Gen. Armistead also, in 1858, & grown very fond of them both. Their favorite songs, 'Willie Brewed a Peck of Malt' and 'Wife, Children & Friends,' have been among mine ever since." He returned Garnett's salute, wished him good luck and turned his attention to his guns.[56]

Dressing their lines in order of battle, with Heth's division under Pettigrew on their left and regimental flags flapping in the breeze, the Virginians were high-spirited.

"Sergeant," said Armistead to the color-bearer of the 53rd Virginia, "are you going to put those colors on the enemy's works today?"

"I will try, sir, and if mortal man can do it, it shall be done!" was the reply.

"Armistead, hurry up!" Kemper cried. "I am going to charge those heights and carry them, and I want you to support me."

"I'll do it!" said Armistead. "Look at my line; it never looked better on dress parade."

"Forward! Quick time! March!" came the commands.

"Remember, men, what you are fighting for!" cried Armistead. "Remember your homes and firesides, your mothers and wives and sisters and your sweethearts!"

Closing with the enemy about 3 P.M., moving through cannon blasts in front and flank, the Confederates accelerated the pace. Garnett and Kemper were in the front line, Armistead just behind. The stone fence was the first obstacle, and clearing it was a major problem. There Colonel Joseph Mayo of the 3rd Virginia, Kemper's brigade, noticed "Captain Lewis, of Company C, looking as lazy and as lackadaisical and, if possible, more tired and bored than usual . . . addressing his [men] in that invariable plaintive tone, half command, half entreaty, 'Don't crowd, boys; don't crowd.' "

"Pretty hot, Captain," Mayo said in passing.

"It's redicklous, Colonel; perfectly redicklous," replied Lewis, meaning the situation was as bad as bad could be.

Soon Mayo realized he was being flanked. "I hastily gathered a small band together and faced them to meet the new danger. After that everything was a kaleidoscopic whirl. A man near me seemed to be keeping a tally of the dead for my especial benefit. First it was [W. Tazewell] Patton, then [Alexander] Callcote, then [James] Phillips, and I know not how many more. Colonel [Lewis] Williams was knocked out of the saddle by a ball in the shoulder . . . and in falling was killed by his sword. His little bay mare kept up with the men in the charge. . . . Seeing the men as they fired throw down their guns and pick up others from the ground, I followed suit, shooting into a flock of blue coats that were pouring down from the right."

"Oh, Colonel," one of his beleaguered men asked Mayo, "why don't they support us?"

"It was Walker," said Mayo, "General Kemper's orderly . . . unscathed and undaunted, awkward, ungainly, hard-featured, good-natured, simple-minded, stout-hearted Walker . . . only a private doing his duty. . . ."[57]

With Garnett's and Kemper's ranks becoming increasingly tattered, Armistead moved up. "Double-quick! Double-quick!" he yelled. Here are the words of Captain James Poindexter of the 38th Virginia, describing the scene that followed: "Putting his black hat on the point of his sword, [Armistead] led the advance, all the time in front of his line of battle, marching straight ahead through a hail of bullets. . . . The sword pierced through the hat and more than once we saw the naked steel. As often as the hat slipped down the old hero would hoist it again. . . . It caught the eye, it nerved the hearts of his devoted men."

Recounted another of Armistead's officers: "As we got within 40 yards of the stone wall, came all along the line the order to charge. . . . From behind the fence the Yankee infantry rose and poured into our ranks a murderous fire. Garnett's Brigade and Kemper's had almost entirely disappeared, their brave commanders, gallant officers, with hundreds of rank and file, were stretched on the field, and it remained for [us] to finish the work."[58]

The Confederates took the fence, then halted but only for an instant. To halt meant ruin. Just ahead, bristling with cannon, lay Cemetery Ridge. Beyond it Winfield Scott Hancock was hurrying up his reserves. On the right and on the left the enemy's lines were still intact.

"Colonel," said Armistead to Colonel Rawley Martin of the 53rd Virginia, "we cannot stay here."

"Forward with the colors!" Martin shouted.

Armistead rushed toward the enemy with him, crying, "Follow me, boys. Give them the cold steel!"

Captain Poindexter takes up the story. "They left behind them the stone wall. They passed the earth works. They seized the cannon that, double-shotted . . . had torn our ranks with cannister. Victory seemed within their grasp. But alas! The support they looked for never came." Hancock's reserves were at hand instead, four lines deep, pouring fire on the Virginians and dashing their hopes. Garnett already was dead; Kemper was severely wounded and would soon be a prisoner. Here in the clump of trees and the bend in the enemy lines called the Bloody Angle, Armistead about 3:45 P.M. fell with mortal wounds, trying in vain to turn a captured cannon on the foe. All fifteen of the regimental commanders in the three brigades were killed or wounded. They were lawyers, teachers, businessmen, even a physician and a pharmacist. Almost all were in their early 30s or younger. More than half were V.M.I. graduates.[59]

Pettigrew on Pickett's left was enduring similar damage. He had pushed forward his brigades at the same time as Pickett—aligning Robert Mayo, Joe Davis, James Marshall and Birkett Fry from left to right with the Virginians in line of battle and sighting on the clump of trees. But Robert Mayo's Virginians and Davis's Mississippians, still enfeebled by their losses on July 1, soon withered. Beset by enfilading fire, these two brigades fell into panic and rushed to the rear.

Marshall's North Carolinians and Fry's Alabamians and Tennesseans for a while made more progress. "At a signal from Pettigrew," said Fry, "I called my command to attention. The men sprang up with cheerful alacrity, and the long line advanced. . . . It moved steadily on, and even when grape, canister and musket balls began to rain upon it the gaps were quickly closed." Looking to his right, Fry saw Garnett of Pickett's command bellowing an order. "I am dressing on you," Garnett called out. Minutes later he fell dead, and moments after that Fry went down with a thigh wound. "I was so confident of victory," he said, "that to some of my men who rushed up to carry me off I shouted, 'Go on; it will not last five minutes longer!' " The soldiers left him and rushed forward into the gun smoke, which was so dense he could see little of what was going on. "But a moment later I heard General Pettigrew, behind me, calling to some of his staff to 'rally them on the left.' The roll of musketry was then incessant, and I believe that the Federal troops—probably blinded by the smoke—continued a rapid fire . . . after none but dead and wounded remained in their front."

When the firing did cease, Fry found himself a prisoner. "As evidence of how close was the fighting at that part of the line," he said, "I saw a Federal soldier with an ugly wound in his shoulder, which he told me he received from the spear on the end of one of the regimental colors; and I remembered having that morning observed . . . that the color-bearer of the 13th Alabama had attached to his staff a formidable-looking lance head."

Major John T. Jones, commanding Marshall's brigade when that officer was shot dead, remembered the melee: "When within 250 or 300 yards of the stone wall . . . we were met with a perfect hailstorm of lead. . . . The brigade dashed on and may have reached the wall when we received a deadly volley from the left . . . we were rapidly being flanked. . . . We therefore fell back. . . ."[60]

Even as Isaac Trimble was coming up to Pettigrew's support with James Lane's and Lee Lowrance's North Carolinians, Pettigrew took some grapeshot in the hand. Nonetheless he refused to retire from the field. "Notwithstanding the losses as we advanced, the men marched with the deliberation and accuracy of men on drill," Trimble said. "I observed the same in Pettigrew's line. When the latter was [near] the Emmitsburg Road, they seemed to sink into the earth under the tempest of fire poured into them. We passed over the remnant of their line and immediately after someone . . . sang out, 'Three cheers for the Old North State . . . on which I said to my aide, 'Charley, I believe these fine fellows are going into the enemy's line.' "

Such optimism was ill founded. "They did get to the road," said Trimble, "and drove the opposing line from it. They continued there some minutes, discharging their pieces at the enemy. The loss here was fearful, and I knew that no troops could long endure it." Now both Lane and Lowrance went down with wounds. Looking to the right, in Pickett's direction, Trimble saw that the Federal fire was slackening. "By this I inferred that Pickett's Division had been repulsed. . . . I therefore did not attempt to rally the men who began to give back from the fence."[61] Trimble, who suffered a severe leg wound that required amputation, like Kemper and Fry eventually would end up a prisoner.

Pickett's Charge was over. Longstreet nonetheless had not thought to rescind the orders of Wilcox and Lang, who had been told to support Pickett's flank. These officers soon pulled back on their own, fearful their brigades would be slaughtered. "Not a man of the Division that I was ordered to support could I see," said Wilcox.[62] Meanwhile Powell Hill with the rest of the Third Corps had remained inactive. The gallant but doomed assault on Cemetery Ridge—doomed from the start because of procrastination and lack of commitment—cost some 5,600 Confederate casualties.

What of Stuart, sent with four brigades far east of Gettysburg on July 3 to wreak mischief in the enemy's rear? Once again he met David Gregg's fast improving Federal cavalry and the results were at best a standoff. Just about the time Pickett was assailing the ridge, Wade Hampton and Fitz Lee were attacking Gregg. "They marched with well-aligned fronts and steady reins," said an admiring Captain William Miller of the 3rd Pennsylvania. "Their polished saber blades dazzled in the sun. . . . As they drew nearer, cannister was substituted by our artillerymen for shell, and horse after horse staggered and fell. Still they came on." When Hampton and Lee broke into a gallop, George Armstrong Custer led the Union countercharge. "So sudden and violent was the collision," said Miller, "that many of the horse were turned end over end and crushed their riders beneath them. The clashing of sabers, the firing of pistols, the demands for surrender and cries of the combatants now filled the air." The Federals held in the midst of the maelstrom, however, and the Confederates slowly fell back. The encounter was brief but fierce, costing Stuart some 180 casualties—including a severely wounded Hampton—and Gregg some 250.

Going over the field later, a burial party saw proof of the desperate fighting firsthand. There they found two troopers—one a Virginian, the other a Pennsylvanian—who had "fought on horseback with their sabers until they finally clinched and their horses ran from under them. Their heads and shoulders were severely cut, and when found, their fingers, though stiff in death, were so firmly imbedded in each other's flesh that they could not be removed without the aid of force."[63]

Back on Cemetery Ridge meanwhile, Meade was staying within his lines, making no effort to attack the regrouping Confederates. The damage he had inflicted was not to be squandered, he felt, by going on the offensive and suffering the same fate. Union General Judson Kilpatrick unwisely ordered the one Federal sally, a charge by Elon Farnsworth's 8th Illinois Cavalry against Law's division about 5:30 P.M., and its repulse showed the wisdom of Meade's judgment. Farnsworth, who led the assault under protest, lost his life and almost one-quarter of his men were killed or wounded.

Overall Federal losses at Gettysburg were 23,000, perhaps a quarter of Meade's command; Confederate, somewhere between 21,000 and 25,000, more than one-third of Lee's. In the days that followed the battle the Confederates slowly fell back to Virginia, with Henry Heth, now recovered from his head wound, covering the rear. During one skirmish on the banks of the Potomac during the withdrawal, the luckless Pettigrew was mortally wounded. His death punctuated the end of the expedition.

Subsequently it was inevitable that Pickett would become a subject of controversy. All the divisional and brigade commanders during the charge, it seems, were conspicuous on the field except Pickett himself. This gave rise to rumors that he was less than heroic, or even cowardly, in his leadership. It seems more likely, however, that he became paralyzed in disbelief of what he was seeing. Many officers confirmed that his initial ebullience quickly became despair. Explained one commentator: "Honor and military procedures both demanded that he should gallop forward, join his troops and either inspire them to advance, or give them orders suitable to the emergency." Instead he became useless. "General," he cried to Longstreet following the repulse, "I am ruined, my division is gone—it is destroyed."

Pickett's report on Gettysburg was a litany of complaints, all centering on lack of support. Lee would have none of it. "We have the enemy to fight and must carefully, at this critical moment, guard against dissentions which the reflections in your report would create," Lee told him, refusing to accept the document. On September 15, Pickett and LaSalle Corbell would marry at St. Paul's Church in Petersburg—though Sallie claimed the wedding was in Richmond, with President and Mrs. Davis toasting the happy couple and Lee's wife, Mary, giving them a fruitcake. This hyperbole would be typical of LaSalle, who spent the next six decades celebrating her husband in books and lectures. For her, fact never interfered with fiction. Following the wedding Pickett, accompanied by LaSalle, was posted to garrison duty south of Richmond.[64]

Lee took full responsibility for the failure at Gettysburg, submitting his resignation to Jefferson Davis. "The general remedy for the want of success in a military commander is his removal," he wrote Davis on August 8. "This is natural, and in many instances proper. . . . I have heard and seen of expressions of discontent in the public journals as the result of the expedition. I do not know how far this feeling extends in the army. My brother officers have been too kind to report it, and so far the troops have been too generous to exhibit it. It is fair, however, to suppose that it does exist. . . . I therefore, in all sincerity, request Your Excellency to take measures to supply my place."

The 56-year-old Lee then brought up the state of his health. "I am becoming more and more incapable of exertion, and am thus prevented from making the personal examinations and giving the personal supervision to the operations in the field which I feel to be necessary. I am so dull that in making use of the eyes of others I am frequently misled. . . . I have no complaints to make of anyone but myself. I have received nothing but kindness from those above me, and the most considerate attention from my comrades and companies in arms."

Back came Davis's warm reply, showing how far he and Lee had come since First Manassas: "Suppose, my dear friend, that I were to admit, with all their implications, the points which you present, where am I to find the new commander who is to possess the greater ability which you believe to be required? . . . My sight is not sufficiently penetrating to discover such hidden merit. . . . To ask me to substitute you by someone in my judgement more fit to command . . . is to demand an impossibility. . . ."[65]

It remained for Lafayette McLaws and others to put the reasons for the defeat at Gettysburg in perspective. "The enemy were compact and protected," said McLaws, "and had free intercourse between their signal stations everywhere, in every commanding position. They could see all over our positions and commanded all the approaches . . . yet our army attacked them in detached masses at different points. . . . Why this was, or whose fault it was, I do not pretend to assert; but that it was so, no one will deny."

Reflected Colonel William Allan, a member of Ewell's staff: "The Confederate line was a long one, and the perfect cooperation in the attack needed to prevent General Meade, whose line was a short one, from using the same troops at more than one point, was difficult of attainment. Two of the corps commanders, Hill and Ewell, were new in their places. Longstreet's attack on the Federal left on the 2nd was delayed beyond the expected time, and was not promptly seconded by Hill and Ewell when made." General Lee subsequently informed him, Allan said, "that had the Confederate Corps attacked Meade simultaneously or either the 2nd or 3rd, he would have succeeded. . . . [Lee] said that he had consulted Ewell, and told him if he could not carry his part of the line, he would move his corps to the right of Longstreet and threaten the Federal communications with Baltimore." Concluded Allan: "There was nothing foolish in Pickett's attack had it been executed as designed. Pickett carried the works before him; had Pettigrew and Wilcox moved with him, and Hill and Ewell vigorously seconded this onset, General Lee never doubted that the Federal army would have been ruined."[66]

"General, this has been a hard day on you," General John Imboden said to Lee in the late aftermath of the battle. Imboden, commanding an independent cavalry brigade, had been operating apart from Stuart.

"Yes, it has been a sad, sad day to us," Lee answered. There was a pause, and then he continued, in a voice choked with emotion: "I never saw troops behave more magnificently than Pickett's Virginians did today in that grand charge upon the enemy. And if they had been supported as they were to have been—but, for some reason not yet explained to me, were not—we would have held the position and the day would have been ours." There was a second pause, and then he repeated with growing emphasis: "Too bad! *Too bad!* TOO BAD!"

Where was this support to come from? "The storming column proper, of 9 brigades," explained Porter Alexander, "was distinctly put under Long-street's control, though only three of the brigades were his own. But the five brigades of supports (Dick Anderson's Division) all belonged to A.P. Hill's Corps, and I have never heard that Longstreet was charged with launching them into the battle. . . . Now whose duty was it to start those five brigades to Pickett's support? . . . I will not pretend to say." Alexander would have committed Ewell's divisions as well, swinging two of them around Cemetery Hill and adding them to the assault. "We would have practically forged our storming column into a sort of armor piercing projectile, & could surely have driven its head a long ways into Meade's body."

Undoubtedly the lack of written orders contributed to the confusion. Due to Longstreet's procrastination the morning of the 3rd Lee was forced to im-provise, leaving no time for such niceties. "I believe that *nobody* was directly designated to launch Anderson's Division to Pickett's support," Alexander continued. "For surely no one would have neglected or disobeyed instructions so grossly. . . . Had a written order given the details of that charge there could have been neither omission or misunderstanding on that important matter."[67]

Many were the reasons then that Lee failed at Gettysburg: Stuart's egotism, Longstreet's intransigence and Powell Hill's and Ewell's inadequacies among them. One more explanation should also be cited as to why, ultimately, the Confederates never did succeed in taking Cemetery Ridge. "I think the Union army had something to do with it," George Pickett would say with pungent understatement. Few of the men in that last bloody charge would have con-tradicted him.[68]

# FIVE

\* \* \* \*

# LONGSTREET IN TENNESSEE

The inexorable movements of Union General Ulysses S. Grant down the Mississippi, which began with his capture of Forts Henry and Donelson eighteen months before, culminated on July 4 with the surrender of the besieged Confederate force at Vicksburg. John C. Pemberton's 29,000-man Army of Mississippi laid down its arms, Grant took possession of the city, and the Confederacy was split in half. This defeat, one day after the disaster at Gettysburg, shook the confidence of the South. The cautious Joseph Eggleston Johnston, now commanding the Department of the West, promptly withdrew the rest of his troops into the pinewoods of Mississippi, where Grant did not pursue. "If he has any other plan than that of watching the enemy it has not been communicated," said Jefferson Davis of Johnston.[1]

With the Confederacy thus in crisis, the public outcry to strike back at the enemy reached a crescendo in the ensuing weeks. The South's leaders concurred. The question was where to strike—out West in Mississippi or Tennessee, or in the East in Virginia? Mississippi was never seriously discussed. The troops remaining there were dispirited and the leadership pessimistic. In the East the Army of Northern Virginia, still a dangerous force, needed time to regroup. Armistead, Garnett, Semmes, Barksdale, Pender and Pettigrew had been killed or mortally wounded. Archer, Kemper and Trimble had been captured. Hood and Hampton had been severely wounded. "You cannot fill the places of these men," a visiting British journalist told Powell Hill. "Your men do wonders, but every time at a cost you cannot afford."[2]

Into the breach stepped Longstreet, both because he believed the strongest blow could be delivered in Tennessee and because he wanted independent command. There the indecisive and irritable Braxton Bragg, a Louisiana plantation owner and now commander of the Army of Tennessee, was being outmaneuvered by Union General William Rosecrans, a former West Pointer turned civil engineer and businessman. Longstreet's first suggestion was that he replace the Confederate commander, but Davis did not want to do this. Bragg was a close friend, and the president was loyal to his friends. Instead Davis and Lee in September agreed that Longstreet should be sent to the West with two divisions of the First Corps to reinforce Bragg and stiffen his spine. His instructions were to crush Rosecrans and return quickly to Virginia. "Now, General, you must beat those people out in the West," Lee told him.

Passing through Richmond in September en route to Chattanooga, Longstreet received a hero's welcome. He had shaken off the lethargy of Gettysburg, and both he and his troops were refreshed and eager for action. "It was a very remarkable body," said Moxley Sorrel, "inspired by great sacrifices and victories . . . and with a cohesive strength and belief in itself that spoke nobly for the future." Longstreet's chief regret was that he and his men would have a long and roundabout rail trip, the direct route by way of the Virginia and Tennessee Railroad having been cut by the Yankee capture of Knoxville. They would have to ride south though the Carolinas and Georgia to reach their destination.[3]

Going with him to Tennessee would be McLaws's and Hood's divisions, as well as Alexander's artillery. Though still weak, with his crippled arm in a sling, Hood was on his feet again. When his men appealed to him to lead them, he courageously agreed. The homespun Texan used his brief time in Richmond to see 20-year-old Sally Buchanan ("Buck") Preston, whom he had been courting, or at least doing his best to court. Educated in Paris, stylishly dressed, alternately elusive and attentive in manner, Buck was an accomplished flirt. She was a striking young woman, with a slender yet voluptuous figure, and she drew men to her effortlessly. "Buck, the very sweetest woman I ever knew," said Mary Chestnut, a Richmond society hostess, "had a knack of being 'fallen in love with' at sight and of never being 'fallen out of love' with. But then, there seemed a spell upon her lovers—so many were killed or died of the effects of wounds. . . ."

In this regard Sally Preston had developed a reputation. When Mrs. Chestnut asked one officer if he were succumbing to Buck's fascinations, the man became alarmed.

"No, never," he answered. "I dare not. I would prefer to face a Yankee battery. They say so-and-so is awfully in love with Miss S.P. Then I say, look out! You will see his name next in the list of killed and wounded."

During Buck and Hood's first meeting, outside the Chestnut home in March of 1863 when he was marching his men through Richmond, he was instantly smitten. "Buck stood somewhat apart, rather as a spectator of this scene," said Mrs. Chestnut, who kept what amounted to a salon for officers in her home. "She had refused to appear the night Hood came to tea." They did not speak but before he rode away he looked in her direction and addressed a remark to a nearby officer. Buck later approached the man and asked, "What was that he said to you? About me?"

"He says, 'You stand on your feet like a thoroughbred,' " was the reply.

Now at the Petersburg train station on his way to Tennessee the lovelorn Hood proposed marriage.

"She half-promised me to think of it," he would say. "She would not say yes, but she did not say no, that is not exactly. At any rate, I went off, saying, I am engaged to you, and she said, I am not engaged to you. . . ."[4]

In McLaws's and Hood's divisions, Longstreet had some of the army's toughest soldiers. McLaws's command consisted of Joseph Kershaw's South Carolinians, William Wofford's Georgians, Benjamin Humphreys's Mississippians (Humphreys replacing Barksdale) and Goode Bryan's Georgians (Bryan replacing Semmes). Humphreys had been Barksdale's senior regimental officer; Bryan, a former West Pointer, had been colonel of the 16th Georgia. Only Kershaw and Humphreys would fight at Chickamauga, Wofford and Bryan arriving too late. Hood's brigades included Jerome Robertson's Texans and Arkansans, "Tige" Anderson's and "Rock" Benning's Georgians, Evander McIvor Law's Alabamians and Micah Jenkins's South Carolinians. The last named brigade would not arrive on the field until the battle was over.

Hood's return to duty delayed, at least for a few weeks, the smoldering contest between Law and Jenkins for command. While Law had handled the division with distinction at Gettysburg when Hood went down, he was two months junior to Jenkins in the date of his commission. Law, moreover, was Hood's protégé, while Jenkins was Longstreet's. Photographs reveal two determined 27-year-old brigadiers: Law, with high cheekbones and an intense gaze; Jenkins, clean shaven save for a close-trimmed mustache and square-jawed, with a no-nonsense look. Between the two hard-fighting officers, stated Sorrel, "there was the most intense rivalry. They were both from South Carolina, and it was a continuation, it was said, of what stirred them at school together, at college, at military exercises, and finally in Longstreet's Corps. They had been made colonels about the same time—Law of an Alabama regiment—and had advanced almost contemporaneously to be brigadier generals . . . They were both unquestionably officers of high attainments and the greatest promise."[5]

The rail trip to Tennessee was lengthy but the men enjoyed it. "The cars on all the railroads in which troops were transported were little more than skeleton cars," said one of Kershaw's men. "The weather being warm, the troops cut all but the framework loose with knives and axes. They furthermore wished to see outside and witness the fine country . . . that lay along the route; nor could those inside bear the idea of being shut up in a box car while their comrades on top were cheering and yelling themselves hoarse at the waving of handkerchiefs and flags in the hands of the pretty women . . . as the trains sped through the towns, villages and hamlets of the Carolinas and Georgia."[6]

Outside of Chattanooga meanwhile, the situation was taking a grimmer turn. Though Braxton Bragg had evacuated the city on September 9 and withdrawn southward, the Army of the Cumberland under Rosecrans had become widely scattered, encouraging Bragg to make a stand. In the days that followed he began moving his troops across West Chickamauga Creek, which ran roughly in a north-south direction below Chattanooga, intent on cutting Rosecrans off from the city and his supply line. The battle of Chickamauga, which would be fought September 19 and 20, was the result, with some 60,000 men on either side taking part, and the Confederates for once having a slight advantage in numbers.

Bragg would have been wiser, of course, if he had delayed the start of the engagement. Though Hood completed the rail journey in time to see action the first day of the battle, Longstreet did not arrive until the afternoon of September 19, and would not take the field until the second day. "Bragg had nothing to gain by an immediate attack, & as his reinforcements from Virginia were beginning to arrive," said Porter Alexander, "he should certainly have remained on the defensive until they were all on hand . . . it was wretched play to bring on an offensive battle while [all] of Longstreet's splendid brigades and all of my 26 guns were not yet arrived."[7]

Chickamauga was fought along a five-mile front in heavily wooded terrain, with visibility limited to 150 yards at best. The first day's fighting was heavy, but the results amounted to no more than the two armies exchanging bloody punches. Orders were confusing and the action chaotic, and while the Confederates pushed the enemy back it was only a short distance and at severe cost. "All that day we fought," Hood said, "slowly but steadily gaining ground. Fierce and desperate grew the conflict, as the foe stubbornly yielded before our repeated assaults; we drove him, step by step, a distance of fully one mile."

Longstreet and his aides, finding the rail station deserted upon their arrival on September 19, left the train with ruffled feelings. "A sharp action had taken place during the day," said Sorrel, "and it would appear that if Bragg wanted to see anybody, Longstreet was the man. But we were left to shift for ourselves, and wandered by various roads and across small streams through the growing darkness of the Georgia forest." At one point they blundered into some enemy pickets. "A sharp right-about gallop, unhurt by the pickets' hasty and surprised fire, soon put us in safety, and another road was taken for Bragg, about whom by this time some hard words were passing."[8]

Reaching the Confederate encampment just before midnight, Longstreet roused Bragg from slumber and the two men conferred. The commander of the Army of Tennessee at this time was under immense pressure, as much from his own officers as from the enemy. "[He] was the subject of hatred and contempt, and it was almost openly so expressed," said Sorrel. "His great officers gave him no confidence as a general-in-chief. The army was thus left a helpless machine." This night at least, Bragg seemed determined to make good use of the new arrivals. He had already put Hood in command of Bushrod Johnson's division, together with McLaws's division and the Texan's own. Now on the eve of battle he took the risky step of dividing the army into two wings. Longstreet would have control of the left wing—Hood's three divisions plus three more, 17 brigades in all. The pompous Leonidas Polk, who like Bragg was close to Davis, would lead the right wing. Polk had resigned from the army 35 years before to become an Episcopal minister and, eventually, bishop of Louisiana. "The Lord had made him a splendid bishop," Porter Alexander would say. "So all our pious people with one consent & with secret conviction that the Lord would surely favor a bishop . . . made him a lieut. Gen., which the Lord had not."[9]

Bragg's tactics on Sunday, September 20, were sound enough. They called for Polk's right wing to assail the Federal left at dawn, slamming it back on its heels and cutting Rosecrans off from Chattanooga. Harvey Hill, now nominated for lieutenant general and commanding a corps in the Army of Tennessee, was to have spearheaded the assault. But Polk's courier could not find Hill during the night, and Polk was negligent in following up. "Neither of my division commanders had heard anything of the early attack," said Hill, "and cooked rations were being distributed to our men, many of whom had not eaten anything for 24 hours." Then at 7:30 A.M. came an order from Polk, slightingly directed not to Hill but to his major generals, to begin the attack. "I sent a note to him that I was adjusting my line," said Hill, who had proved his own worth on many a battlefield, "and that my men were getting their rations. [He] soon after came up, and assented to the delay."

Bragg meanwhile was impatiently waiting for the sound of Polk's guns. He sent his aide, Major Pollok Lee, to urge him to advance. Major Lee found the bishop unconcernedly seated at a comfortable breakfast, surrounded by attentive staff officers, and delivered his message. Polk replied that he had ordered Hill to open the action and that he was waiting for him to proceed.

"Do tell Gen. Bragg that my heart is overflowing with anxiety for the attack—overflowing with anxiety, sir," he said.

Hearing these words repeated Bragg turned livid with rage and uttered a string of oaths.

"Major Lee," he roared, "ride along the line and order every captain to take his men instantly into action!"[10]

When the battle was finally joined about 9:30 A.M. the enemy had been given four more hours to entrench, and their defensive lines held up under assault after assault by Polk's wing. "The Confederate attack on the right was mainly unsuccessful because of the [enemy] breastworks," Hill wrote, "but was so gallant and persistent that [George] Thomas [commanding the Union Fourteenth Corps] called loudly for reinforcements, which were promptly sent, weakening the Federal right, until finally a gap was left." Into this opening Longstreet on the Confederate left about 11:30 A.M. hurled his divisions. "Discovering, with the true instinct of a soldier, that he could do more by turning to the right," Hill continued, "he disregarded the order to wheel to the left and wheeled the other way, striking the corps of [Thomas] Crittenden and [Alexander] McCook in flank. . . ."

Rushing into the gap, Hood's 11,000-man command endured some of the harshest fighting. Bushrod Johnson's Tennesseans and Arkansans led the way, then Robertson's Texans and James Sheffield's Alabamians, then Benning's Georgians, then Kershaw's South Carolinians and Humphreys's Mississippians. Both the Federal right and left crumbled under their onslaught, with most of the Twentieth and the Twenty-first Corps and Rosecrans and his commanders fleeing to Chattanooga. "All became confusion," said one Union officer. "No order could be heard above the tempest of battle. With a wild yell the Confederates swept on far to their left. They seemed everywhere victorious. Rosecrans was borne back in the retreat. Fugitives, wounded, caissons, escort, ambulances thronged the narrow pathways. He concluded that our whole line had given way, that the day was lost, that the next stand must be made at Chattanooga."

Only Union General George Thomas in the center made a stand, rallying four of the ten Federal divisions and digging in on Snodgrass Hill and to his left at Kelly Field, some ten miles south of the city. Here throughout the long afternoon he earned his sobriquet "the Rock of Chickamauga," not only blocking the advance but launching a series of devastating counterattacks. Now Hood's men fell victim to their own success. Neglecting to put out flank guards in the dense woods, overeager to follow up their advantage, they soon found their ranks riddled by enfilading fire. "It was now our turn to run, and we ran as fast as the nature of the ground permitted," said one Georgian.[11]

The brigades of Robertson, Sheffield and Benning streamed to the rear under the unexpected barrage. "We wrestled with the resolute foe till about 2:30 P.M.," Hood said, "when, from a skirt of timber to our left, a body of Federals rushed down upon the immediate flank and rear of the Texas Brigade. . . ." Riding forward to straighten the lines, Hood himself went down, a minie ball crushing his right leg below the hip and necessitating a battlefield amputation. During these hours Longstreet again showed his coolness. "A sudden counterstroke of the enemy had smashed [Benning's] Brigade and they were badly scattered," said Moxley Sorrel. "Benning thought that they were 'all gone.' Seizing an artillery horse that was galloping by, harness flying, he threw himself on the terrified animal and found Longstreet."

"General," he said, "I am ruined; my brigade was suddenly attacked and every man killed; not one is to be found. Please give orders where I can do some fighting."

"Nonsense, General, you are not so badly hurt," replied Longstreet. "Look about you. I know you will find at least one man, and with him on his feet report your brigade to me, and you two shall have a place in the firing line."

Concluded Sorrel: "Benning . . . took the hint, hunted up his men, who were not so badly mauled after all, and with a respectable body was soon ready for work."[12]

Longstreet thus stabilized the situation, realigning Hood's command and restoring discipline. Bushrod Johnson's two brigades weighed in with their support, as did those of Kershaw and Humphreys. "I could see but little of the enemy's line," Longstreet said, "and only knew of it by the occasional exchange of fire between the lines of skirmishers." If he could not see the whole field he could envision it. When he fought from instinct and forsook dreams of grand strategy, Lee's "War Horse" was a fierce and formidable antagonist.[13]

Following an unhurried lunch of sweet potatoes Longstreet conferred with Bragg in the rear. "[He] told him of the steady and satisfactory progress of the battle," said Harvey Hill, "that sixty pieces of artillery had been reported captured [probably the number was overestimated], that many prisoners and stores had been taken." He then asked for additional troops to hold the ground gained, while he pursued the enemy and turned Thomas's flank on Snodgrass Hill. "Bragg replied that there was no more fight left in the troops of Polk's wing," Hill continued, "that he could give Longstreet no reinforcements. . . . He seems not to have known that [Benjamin] Cheatham's Division and part of [St. John] Liddell's had not been in action that day."

Late in the afternoon Polk put Hill in charge of the attacking forces on the right wing and told him to renew the assault. This Hill did not do with his usual competence. Perhaps he was resentful that Bragg had given Polk, a less experienced combat officer, command of the right wing. He bickered over the routes to be taken, and in general dragged his feet. But when at last his troops did go forward they did so with elan. "The men sprang to their arms," Hill said, "though they had not heard of Longstreet's success, and they showed by their cheerfulness there was plenty of 'fight in them.' " His brigades pushed onward to Kelly Field, rolling up the enemy left and step by bitter step driving the Federals back. "As we passed into the woods west of the [Chattanooga] road, it was reported to me a line was advancing at right angles to ours. I rode to the left to ascertain whether they were foes or friends, and soon recognized General [Simon] Buckner [of Longstreet's wing]. The cheers that went up when the two wings met were such as I have never heard before. . . ."[14]

Chickamauga would be a hollow triumph. With nightfall coming on, Thomas and his remaining troops withdrew from their final position on Snodgrass

Hill, slowly retiring into the Federal lines at Chattanooga. Both sides had suffered dreadful losses. The Confederates had almost 18,500 casualties; the Federals, some 16,200.

Next morning, September 21, a faltering Bragg asked Longstreet whether he should renew the battle. "Move instantly against Rosecrans's rear to destroy him," was the forthright reply. Polk and Hill gave similar advice, but Bragg did not move, believing his troops were exhausted, and the Confederate advantage was lost. "Whatever blunders each of us in authority committed before the battles of the 19th and 20th, and during their progress," admitted Hill, "the great blunder of all was that of not pursuing the enemy on the 21st." Cavalryman Nathan Bedford Forrest was early in the saddle and recognized the enemy's vulnerability. Disorganized masses of men had still not yet reached the safety of the city; batteries of artillery were inextricably mixed with trains of wagons; confusion pervaded the broken ranks. "Every hour [is] worth a thousand men," Forrest informed Bragg. The Confederate commander remained passive. "Rosecrans spent the day and the night of the 21st in hurrying his trains out of town," mourned Hill. "A breathing-space was allowed him; the panic among his troops subsided, and Chattanooga—the objective point of the campaign—was held."[15]

In the days after Chickamauga the resentment of Bragg's officers over his leadership deepened, with Longstreet taking a leading role in the protests. "To express my convictions in a few words," he wrote Secretary of War James Seddon on September 25, "our chief has done but one thing he ought to have done since I joined this army. That was to order the attack upon the 20th. . . . I am convinced that nothing but the hand of God can save us or help us as long as we have our present commander. . . . Can't you send us General Lee?" Knowing it was highly unlikely Lee could or would leave Virginia, Longstreet might well have again been angling for command. It is more likely, however, that he wanted to get out of what he saw as an impossible situation. The unpleasantness promptly escalated. When Polk wrote Lee, entreating him to come to Tennessee, Bragg relieved him of command. In response on October 4 Longstreet and Hill, joined by ten other officers, sent a petition to Jefferson Davis citing Bragg for incompetence and asking for his removal.[16]

On October 9 the president arrived at Bragg's headquarters, intent on resolving the quarrel. There he heard testimony against Bragg from his senior officers, with the commanding general present. "The opinion was given, in substance," said Longstreet, "that our commander could be of greater service elsewhere than at the head of the Army of Tennessee." The next day Davis joined Longstreet for a ride to the top of 1,800-foot Lookout Mountain, which towered above Chattanooga to the southwest of the city. Who if anyone should replace Bragg? the president asked. Here Longstreet made the mistake of suggesting Joseph Johnston, whose slights in the early months of the war

Davis had not forgotten. The very mention of the name, Old Pete recalled, led to his receiving a "severe rebuke." Davis dealt with the near-mutiny in his own inimitable style. His friend Bragg kept his command and was declared "worthy of confidence." His friend Polk was restored to duty and transferred to Mississippi. The chief casualty of the affair was not Longstreet but Harvey Hill, who was incorrectly suspected of drafting the petition. Davis removed him from the Army of Tennessee, withdrew his nomination for lieutenant general and let him languish in North Carolina.[17]

Tensions nonetheless continued to build between Longstreet and Bragg, who in effect were commanding two separate armies in front of Chattanooga. The former remained with the left wing on Lookout Mountain, the latter with the right on the rugged heights of Missionary Ridge, and they communicated as little as possible. Now Longstreet was beginning to experience divisiveness within his own ranks. The festering relationship between Micah Jenkins and Evander Law again came to the fore on October 28, when he sent Hood's division, now under Jenkins's command despite Law's protests, on a night attack to disrupt newly opened Federal supply lines west of the city.

Jenkins was to take two brigades and assail one Union strong point, while Law was to take his own and Jerome Robertson's brigades and block another Federal force from joining the fight. The operation soon miscarried, with Jenkins finding Yankees in his rear. He suffered some 350 casualties, while Law's losses were negligible. Longstreet charged the road had been improperly blocked and attributed the debacle to a "want of conduct" on Law's part. Jenkins went further and later said, referring to the failure of the assault, "I should perhaps have taken official notice of the disobedience of General Law, had it not been for my knowledge of his feelings in reference to my having command of this division as his senior. . . ." These comments infuriated Law, who saw his honor being impugned. Jenkins, it turned out, was attacking a Federal force of 4,000 men with some 2,400, in itself unwise; but Law was being asked to block a relief column of 7,000 men with just 1,700. He angrily demanded a court of inquiry.[18]

Before any action could be taken in the matter, Bragg called Longstreet into conference and suggested he go some 100 miles to the northeast to assault Knoxville, where Ambrose Burnside was sitting on the direct rail line to Virginia. Weakening his army in this manner was indefensible, particularly since Ulysses S. Grant had been named commander of all Federal forces in the Chattanooga area, and reinforcements under William Sherman and Joseph Hooker were near at hand. "Longstreet, always ready with suggestions, declared that the move was feasible," wrote one of his critics. "He urged a concentration of the main army behind Chickamauga Creek while he himself should make a hasty campaign against Burnside and return before Sherman reached Chattanooga. Longstreet evidently was moved by a desire to leave Bragg, for more fatuous reasoning never was. How could he, with the poorest transportation facilities, expect to move into East Tennessee and fight a battle and return, all while Sherman, hastening from Memphis, was still on the way?"

On November 4 Longstreet began pulling out of the lines. "Bragg realized, almost as soon as Longstreet was detached," the critic continued, "that he had made a false move and that he was in a position of great peril. He wished Longstreet to do what he could do and return. But he had made an irreparable blunder in ever sanctioning so hare-brained a maneuver and he had to pay the penalty." In the days that followed, Longstreet's slow progress drove Bragg to distraction. "He tore his hair as he watched the growing Union strength in Chattanooga and realized that Longstreet could not be driven, that that mule-like personage would do only what he pleased to do and as it pleased him."[19]

It was not until November 17 that the Confederate van reached the vicinity of Knoxville, only to find that any assault on Burnside would require much more time than originally thought. "He had as many [men] as we in a strong position fortified," Longstreet said, seemingly uncaring of Bragg's peril. "We went to work, therefore, to make our way forward by gradual and less hazardous measures, at the same time making examinations of the enemy's entire positions." What was to have been a swift attack on Burnside had become a campaign in itself.[20]

Back at Chattanooga, Grant had amassed some 70,000 men against Bragg's 50,000. On November 24 he went on the attack, sending Sherman against the Confederate right and Hooker the left. Sherman's attempt to seize the northern end of Missionary Ridge proved futile, but Hooker, advancing up Lookout Mountain in clouds of mist produced by a cold, drizzling rain, was more successful. "After fighting for nearly two hours, step by step up the steep mountain-side, over and through deep gullies and ravines, over great rocks and fallen trees," said one Union brigadier, "the earth works on the plateau were assaulted and carried, and the enemy was driven out." It was now 2 P.M. "A halt all along the line was ordered by General Hooker, as the clouds had grown so thick that further advance was impracticable, and as his ammunition was almost exhausted and more could not well be brought up the mountain."

The next day was the crucial one, with Sherman continuing to assail the Confederate right on Missionary Ridge and Hooker coming down the mountain to attack the left, all to little effect. Then about 4 P.M. a desperate Grant ordered George Thomas, who had replaced Rosecrans in command of the Army of the Cumberland, to make a frontal assault against the Confederate center. The Federals promptly took the first line of enemy riflemen at the base of the ridge, where Grant thought they would pause. "There was a halt of but a few minutes," continued the brigadier, "to take breath and re-form lines; then, with a sudden impulse, and without orders, all started up the ridge.

Officers, catching their spirit, first followed, then led. There was no thought of supports or protecting flanks, though the enemy's line could be seen, stretching on either side."

Watching the charge up the 600-foot slope, Grant angrily turned to Thomas and said: "Thomas, who ordered those men up the ridge?"

"I don't know," Thomas replied in his quiet, deliberate manner, "I did not."

Grant turned to Union General Gordon Granger. "Did you order them up, Granger?"

"No," said Granger, "they started up without orders. When those fellows get started, all hell can't stop them."

Grant muttered that "somebody would suffer" if the attack did not turn out well, and then, turning, watched the assault.[21]

He had no cause for worry. Not only had the Confederates in the center been improperly positioned—placed on top of the ridge where they were silhouetted, rather than just below where they would have been protected—but the artillerymen on the crest found they could not depress their cannon sufficiently to fire on the men coming up the slope. Most important, the fight had gone out of the Confederates. The dissatisfaction of the senior officers with Bragg had seeped down to the ranks. Is it not possible that Hood's and McLaws's stalwarts, if they were there, would have shored up the defense? We think so. However, they were not, and in short order Thomas's spirited troops tore a half-dozen gaps in the Confederate line, panic set in, and Bragg's army fled the field. No one felt the shame of the defeat more than he. "The disaster admits of no palliation," he later wrote Davis, submitting his resignation. "I fear we both erred in the conclusion for me to retain command here after the clamor raised against me. The warfare has been carried on successfully, and the fruits are bitter. You must make other changes here, or our success is hopeless."[22]

Federal losses at Chattanooga were some 5,800; Confederate, some 6,700. But the strategic loss was even greater. The whole Chattanooga area now was firmly in Federal hands, and in 1864 it would be the staging point for Sherman's vengeful march through Georgia. In the meantime, Davis swallowed another bitter pill. Feeling there was no better choice to command the Army of Tennessee, he recalled Joseph Johnston from Mississippi, where he had been in virtual exile.

Even as rumors of the rout at Chattanooga were reaching him, Longstreet on the morning of November 29 was launching an attack on the Federal defenses at Knoxville. His target was Fort Loudon, an outlying bastion on a hill just northwest of the town that was surrounded by a ditch of undetermined depth and protected by a parapet. If Fort Loudon could be taken, Confederate guns would look down on Knoxville and force its surrender. On the eve of the attack, however, both Jenkins and McLaws expressed their reservations about going ahead with the operation. Jenkins's concern was that the distance from the bottom of the ditch to the top of the parapet might be as much as ten or twelve feet, a problem that was being ignored. "Alexander," he said at one point to Porter Alexander, "I want you to go back with me to Longstreet's. McLaws's troops are to form the storming column tomorrow, & I don't think McLaws has provided any ladders. I am going to urge Longstreet to order him to do so, for we don't know what we are going to find. . . . I want you to go back with me & add your influence to mine."

"Jenkins," Alexander replied, "your influence will be enough. The matter is very simple & obvious. . . . You can tell the general that you met me . . . & that I asked you to say I heartily concur in your opinion."

Longstreet valued Jenkins highly, but in this instance he pooh-poohed his concern. "Keep your men well at their work, and do not listen to the idea of failing and we shall not fail," he told him. "If we go in with the idea that we shall fail, we will be sure to do so. But no men who are determined to succeed can fail."[23]

McLaws's point involved the events at Chattanooga. "If the enemy has been beaten at Chattanooga," he wrote Longstreet, "do we not gain by delay at this point? If we have been defeated at Chattanooga, do we not risk our entire force by an assault here? . . . If we should be defeated or unsuccessful here, and at the same time General Bragg should have been forced to retire, would we be in condition to force our way to the army in Virginia?"

Longstreet disagreed. "It is a great mistake," he said, "to suppose that there is any safety for us in going to Virginia if General Bragg has been defeated, for we leave him at the mercy of his victors. . . . There is neither safety nor honor in any other course than the one I have chosen and ordered."[24]

Now Longstreet at the last moment changed his attack plans. Instead of the assault beginning at sunrise and being preceded by an artillery barrage, it was to take place before dawn and with infantry alone. "This was a bitter disappointment to the artillery," said Alexander. "We believe that in daylight, with our aid, the result would have been different." Late that night skirmishers went forward to capture the enemy's pickets. "Our sharpshooters established themselves in the enemy's line of rifle-pits within 150 yards of the fort," he continued. "But it put the enemy on the alert." Those assigned to the storming column were Benjamin Humphreys's Mississippians, Goode Bryan's and William Wofford's Georgians (the latter under Colonel Solon Z. Ruff), all of McLaws's division. George "Tige" Anderson's Georgians were to support their left flank. Each brigade numbered perhaps 1,000 men.

Three signal guns fired in rapid succession touched off the engagement. The assaulting column swarmed through the rifle pits in the dim predawn light and rushed toward the fort, only to find themselves entangled in telegraph wires stretched a foot or so above the ground and fastened to stakes and tree

stumps. Pressing on, McLaws's men jumped into the ditch under severe musket fire. Here they milled about, unable to scale the parapet. "On the western
face, indeed, [the ditch] proved to be only about four-and-a-half feet deep,"
said Alexander, "and ordinarily a ditch of that depth would not a be a serious
obstacle. But that morning the ground was frozen and very slippery." Moreover, the Federal engineers had cut away the so-called "berm," the foot-wide
space between the top of the ditch and the foot of the parapet, creating one
continuous wall. "It will be readily seen that to a man attempting to scale the
parapet the berme is a great assistance, giving a foothold whence it is easy to
rush up the exterior slope, which cannot be made steeper than forty-five degrees."[25]

Few Confederates reached the top of the parapet, and the enemy easily
dispatched those who did. Meanwhile the Federals added to the confusion in
the ditch, tossing bombs with short fuses into the mass of men below. For
twenty minutes the carnage went on, until Longstreet finally sounded the recall. Even then the casualties mounted, with the troops finding it as difficult
to retreat as it had been to attack. The action was a humiliating setback for
Old Pete and the doughty men of the First Corps. They suffered some 800
casualties, almost all inflicted by a Union garrison numbering no more than
250 and commanded by an obscure lieutenant of artillery. "Detached from
General Lee, what a horrible failure," sniffed Mary Chestnut, secure in the
comfort of her Richmond home, upon hearing the news. "What a slow old
humbug is Longstreet."[26] She was being unjust, of course, but there is no
denying Longstreet's stay in Tennessee was a mixed bag. Just as he had redeemed himself at Chickamauga for Gettysburg, he ensured defeat at Chattanooga by his quixotic expedition to Knoxville.

With the word of Bragg's debacle confirmed, Longstreet pondered where
he next should take his army. Following a council of war with his senior
officers the night of November 29, he decided to withdraw into east Tennessee, establish a winter camp and live off the countryside. Once there, he found
plenty of provisions. "Pumpkins were on the ground like apples under a tree,"
he said. "Cattle, sheep, and swine, poultry, vegetables, maple sugar, honey
were all abundant for the immediate wants of the troops." His failures in the
aftermath of Chattanooga rankled, however, and, attributing them to disloyalty, Longstreet like Bragg attempted to clean house.

In mid-December his first move was to relieve Major General McLaws of
command, charging him with dereliction of duty in the assault on Fort Loudon. McLaws hit back. In a letter circulated to influential friends, he wrote:
"[General Longstreet] attempted to make me a blind to run public inquiry off
his complete failure in the whole Tennessee campaign—then forwarded his
charges but did not ask that a court be ordered to investigate them. . . . The
difficulty with Gen. L. and myself commenced at Chickamauga when I, not

believing that he was a greater man than Genl. Bragg, kept aloof from the coalition which was forming against him, headed by Gen. L." Demanding a trial, McLaws asserted that Longstreet's long delay before Knoxville "was the cause of much of Bragg's disaster at Chattanooga," adding for good measure that his former superior "has nothing to recommend him as a commander but the possession of a certain bullheadedness."[27]

Simultaneously Longstreet filed charges against Jerome Robertson of the Texas Brigade, whom he blamed, along with Evander Law, for not properly supporting Jenkins earlier at Brown's Ferry. He cited him for making discouraging remarks intended "to prevent that hearty and hopeful cooperation necessary to success." While there had been some mutterings concerning Robertson's tactical skills, his courage and dedication heretofore had been unquestioned. A physician in private life, he was devoted to his men, who warmly called him "Aunt Polly."[28]

When McLaws did go before a court-martial, he was found guilty on only one of the specifications against him, namely that he had neglected at Fort Loudon to provide his men with proper scaling equipment. The War Department was unwilling even to have that charge stand, later dismissing it for lack of evidence. McLaws, while he kept his rank, never again did serve in the Army of Northern Virginia—Longstreet's feelings taking precedent in this regard. Eventually he would be assigned to the defense of Savannah. Robertson's case did not go to trial. He too would keep his rank and be forced from Lee's army, taking command of the reserve forces in Texas.

Evander Law, the third object of Longstreet's ire, would be far more of an irritant. He averted possible charges of misconduct by submitting his resignation on December 19 and, before it was formally accepted, going to Richmond to seek another command. Longstreet even let him carry the paper to the War Office in person, happy that it might open up the way for Micah Jenkins to take over Hood's old division. Once Law arrived at the capital, however, he had a change of heart. Longstreet began suspecting that he was petitioning the War Office to transfer his crack Alabama brigade elsewhere. Law had led Hood's division at both Gettysburg and Chickamauga when that officer went down with wounds, and he would not accept Jenkins as his superior. Furious, Old Pete now preferred charges against Law, accusing him among things of "conduct highly prejudicial to good order and military discipline."[29]

What seems to have happened is that Law's old mentor John Bell Hood, who was recuperating from his wounds in Richmond, prevailed upon him not to resign but to endure the situation. When Law did return to Longstreet's winter camp, he stepped into a hornet's nest. His officers, independent of him, were indeed asking that the brigade be sent back to Lee or to Mobile, and when Law sent the petition to Longstreet for approval he found himself under arrest for obtaining leave under false pretenses and destroying his own letter of resignation. Before this tangled situation was resolved, it would drag on for months.

So ended Longstreet's second attempt at independent command, in regret over what might have been and in rancor over who should take the blame. It had been no accident that Lee, when Jackson was alive and the army was divided into only two corps, almost invariably stayed close to Longstreet while dispatching his other lieutenant on tactical maneuvers both desperate and distant. The commander of the First Corps, technically adept though he was in handling large numbers of troops, needed spurring to be at his best. Left to his own devices at Suffolk and at Knoxville, as we have seen, he had lost sight of the larger picture. Spring would find him back with the Army of Northern Virginia.

# SIX

\* \* \* \*

# BRISTOE STATION TO MINE RUN

Lee in Virginia meanwhile, commanding Dick Ewell's and Powell Hill's corps and Jeb Stuart's cavalry, was solidly entrenched behind the Rapidan River, with the Army of the Potomac under George Meade making no move to advance against him. The Confederate commander had used the weeks since Gettysburg to good advantage, building up morale and finding replacements for the fallen. In Ewell's corps, the division heads remained the same: Jubal Early, Edward Johnson and Robert Rodes. New to Early's command was John Pegram, older brother of artilleryman Willie Pegram. Exchanged after John Pemberton's surrender at Vicksburg, he had asked to serve in the East. Now he led the Virginia brigade of "Extra Billy" Smith, who took office as governor. Early's three other brigades were Harry Hays's Louisianans, John Brown Gordon's Georgians and Robert Hoke's North Carolinians. Replacing the crippled Francis Nicholls in Johnson's division was Leroy Stafford, the wealthy Louisiana planter who had served since the Valley Campaign. Johnson's other brigadiers were James Walker of the Stonewall Brigade, George Steuart's Virginians and North Carolinians and John "Rum" Jones's Virginians. Rodes's division saw two changes. Robert Johnston, who had been with the army since the Peninsula, took over the North Carolina brigade of Alfred Iverson, whose health had broken. Cullen Battle, a lawyer and self-taught soldier, now led the Alabama brigade of Edward O'Neal, who had been found wanting. Junius Daniel's and Stephen Ramseur's North Carolinians, and George Doles's Georgians, completed Rodes's command.

In Powell Hill's corps, Dick Anderson and Henry Heth remained as division heads. Replacing the slain Dorsey Pender and promoted to major general was Cadmus Marcellus Wilcox. Anderson's division saw one change: South Carolinian Abner Perrin soon would lead Wilcox's Alabama brigade. Billy Mahone's Virginians, Carnot Posey's Mississippians, "Rans" Wright's Georgians and Edward Perry's Floridians remained in place. In Heth's division William Kirkland now led Pettigrew's North Carolinians, and John Cooke had recovered from his wound at Fredericksburg to rejoin his North Carolina brigade. H. Harrison Walker, who had been on leave since his wound at Gaines's Mill, took over the Virginia brigade Robert Mayo had led at Gettysburg. Joseph Davis's Mississippians and James Archer's Tennesseans completed the division, though Archer was still a prisoner of war. Wilcox's division consisted of James Lane's and Alfred Scales's North Carolinians, the wounded Samuel McGowan's South Carolinians and Edward Thomas's Georgians.

Stuart's cavalry was composed of two divisions, one under Wade Hampton and the other under Fitz Lee. Grumble Jones, James B. Gordon and Pierce Young led Hampton's brigades, though Jones's bitter disputes with Stuart would soon lead to his transfer from the army. This was a pity, for he was a gifted officer. In Fitz Lee's division, John Chambliss continued to lead the brigade of the captured Rooney Lee, while Lunsford Lomax and Williams Wickham headed the other commands.

During these days Lee's ranks swelled with recruits and the recovered wounded, food and clothing arrived in ample quantities, and spirits soared. Morale was especially good in Hill's corps. "Our elastic spirits revived from the depression of July," said one of his officers, "and satisfaction with the present and confidence of the future were almost unanimously expressed." Hill himself recovered some of his old elan. Not only did he drill his men relentlessly, but he staged colorful and regular reviews. On September 12, Lee arrived with his daughters for one such pageant. Stated an onlooker: "The scene was graced by the presence of ladies from surrounding country and many officers' wives, who generally flocked like gentle doves to the army when war's wild alarms had for a time subsided." Lee observed the troops on horseback with Hill mounted behind him. "As [Lee's] veterans passed in review . . . the great soldier's face seemed to light up with admiration for the men whose confidence and affection he knew he possessed."[1]

Simultaneously the religious revival continued. "The most ordinary preachers drew large congregations," said James Caldwell of McGowan's brigade. "Scarcely a day passed without a sermon; there was not a night, but the sound of prayer and hymn-singing was heard. Often, two or three sermons were preached at once in the brigade, and if there was none among us, we went to the other brigades to hear." Hill's troops participated fully in the revival, with some regiments reporting up to sixty converts in a single week. Wrote one man in the 8th Alabama: "Probably when we fear and love God, we will be blessed with peace. He can close this war whenever he chooses to do so." Hill himself remained a sedate Episcopalian, attending church on Sunday but other services only if his wife, Dolly, wished to. He was welcoming to many of the visiting chaplains though, and particularly to the Rev. John Broadus, a boyhood friend. "His duties have not puffed him up," Broadus noted, "but have only sobered him."[2]

On October 10 Lee decided to take the battle to the foe. Noting that Meade had weakened the Army of the Potomac by sending reinforcements to the West following Chickamauga, he ordered an advance across the Rapidan, hoping to turn the enemy's right. Over the next few days he was eminently successful, pushing the Federals back across the Rappahannock toward Manassas and Centreville, capturing tons of supplies and inflicting 2,300 casualties. Then on the afternoon of October 14, Powell Hill in the Confederate van rode to a crest above Bristoe Station and saw what he thought was a golden opportunity. Thousands of troops belonging to William French's Third Corps were huddled on the banks of Broad Run, totally vulnerable as they waited to ford the swift-moving stream. "The whole face of the earth in that vast plain seemed covered with Yankees," said a North Carolinian. "I never saw so many of them at one time during the war." Without making a careful reconnaissance of the terrain or waiting for his other two divisions to come up, the overly eager Hill ordered Henry Heth to make an immediate attack on the fugitives.[3]

The luckless Heth, whose division soon would be as battered at Bristoe as it had been that first day at Gettysburg, swung into action. From left to right the brigades of William Kirkland's and John Cooke's North Carolinians quickly formed line of battle and began the advance. Now Heth and Cooke noticed something troubling: Federal skirmishers were poised behind a railroad embankment on their right flank. Evidently not all the enemy were withdrawing across Broad Run. They relayed this information to Hill, who assumed the skirmishers were few in number. Push on, he told them. Don't let the enemy escape. Dick Anderson's division will soon be up to cover your right. Cooke's courage was unquestioned—the boyish-looking brother-in-law of Jeb Stuart had already been wounded seven times during the war—but he was not happy about his orders. "Well, I will advance," he said, "and if they flank me, I will face my men about and cut my way out."[4]

Cooke was prescient. Concealed behind the railroad cut were not just an enemy detachment but the 3,000 men of General Gouverneur Warren's Second Corps. Two Confederate brigades, double-quicking toward the stream, were about to be mowed down in a crossfire by three Federal divisions. In short order, said one North Carolinian, "we were suffering from the terrific fire of the enemy's artillery posted in the thickets on the elevation beyond the railroad, and from the murderous fire of their infantry in safe position behind the embankment." The rebel ranks, said another Tarheel, "were mowed down like grain before a reaper." Cooke was felled with a leg wound; Kirkland was hit in the arm but stayed on the field. The battle lasted no more than forty minutes, with the two decimated North Carolina brigades falling back in disorder. Then the Federals re-formed and continued their retreat. Cooke suffered 700 casualties; his superb 27th North Carolina lost 290 out of 420 men and 33 out of 36 officers. Kirkland suffered 600 casualties. Total losses in Hill's division were some 1,360. Casualties in Anderson's division, when it did arrive, were light; but Carnot Posey, who had led his Mississippi brigade with distinction under Anderson since Chancellorsville, suffered a mortal wound.[5]

Hill took responsibility for the debacle. "I am convinced that I made the attack too hastily," he said, "and at the same time that a delay of half an hour and there would have been no enemy to attack. In that event I believe I should equally have blamed myself for not attacking at once."

Reported Lee: "General Hill explains how, in his haste to attack the Third Army Corps of the enemy, he overlooked the presence of the Second, which was the cause of the disaster that ensued."

Jefferson Davis was more blunt. "There was a want of vigilance," he wrote.[6]

Riding with Lee over the battlefield the next morning, even as a steady rain fell on the Confederate dead, Hill repeatedly tried to explain what had happened. Lee listened silently, his disappointment showing in his face. Then he spoke quietly, in words that must have hit the sensitive Hill all the harder for their forbearance. "Well, well, General," he said, "bury these poor men, and let us say no more about it."[7]

Bristoe Station shook Hill's confidence in himself. The hard-hitting commander of the Light Division, used to being in the thick of the action, was not thriving as the head of a corps. Jackson had been zealous and Longstreet certainly was unflappable, but neither man could be called impetuous. Now in a post where he had to make considered judgments before he acted, Hill found himself fettered. The burden of command was taking its toll.

Lee pursued Meade north to Bull Run Creek but then declined to attack the stout Federal defenses at Centreville. On October 18, tearing up the tracks of the Orange & Alexandria Railroad behind him, he began moving his army back to the Rappahannock. In the midst of this backing and filling, Jeb Stuart was having his own adventures. Sent by Lee on October 13 to reconnoiter at Catlett's Station, commanding the division of the wounded Hampton, he found that he was cut off late in the afternoon by the retreating Federal columns. "A large body of the enemy . . . were marching on the road we had crossed at Auburn," said his aide William Blackford. "Their advance had driven Lomax (with the rear guard) away and there they were steadily marching across our rear . . . but entirely ignorant of the fact. The ground to the north of us was steep, broken and wooded, and to the south as ill luck would have it there was a wide and deep canal. . . . It was thus impossible for us to escape on either side."

Providentially, Stuart located a hiding place. "He found almost in sight of Auburn the mouth of a little valley opening on the wood and covered with woods," said Blackford, "and finding this valley large enough to hide his command in, he marched it in there, just about dark." There his brigades, augmented with seven guns and five ordnance wagons, fitfully passed the night, while their pickets crouched in the bushes alongside the road and Federal columns unconcernedly trudged by. "General Stuart threw himself down by my side and laid his head on me and in an instant was fast asleep. Hour after hour passed and the General's head on my middle became rather heavy for comfort. . . . It got so bad at last that I was compelled to move it gently . . . but this awoke him and I then snatched a few hours' sleep." The biggest problem was keeping the mules from braying and betraying the position, and designated troopers were assigned to the task. "The poor beasts needed food and water, and often we would hear an incipient bray brought to a premature close by a whack over the head from a sabre scabbard."[8]

Stuart did not fight at Bristoe Station the next day, but he did play a major role in the reconnoitering and skirmishing that went on as Lee pursued Meade to Centreville. His biggest coup came on the subsequent retreat to the Rappahannock while guarding the army's rear. "Fitz Lee suggested that Stuart should withdraw past [the village of] Buckland and that he would attack [Union General Hugh] Kilpatrick in flank," said Blackford, "and at the first gun [Stuart] should wheel and attack him in front." Still leading Hampton's division, Stuart fell back through the village of Buckland on October 19 and formed in two columns behind a range of hills. Fitz Lee meanwhile came up on the enemy's right from the direction of Auburn. "It was a broad, straight turnpike road," Blackford remembered, "and as far as the eye could reach [Kilpatrick's] splendidly equipped cavalry came marching on with flags fluttering and arms glittering in the bright autumn sunshine."

The minutes ticked by while Stuart waited. "Not seeing us, the enemy was just ascending the little rise behind which we were, not two hundred yards distant, when rapid fire of cannon in Lee's direction announced his attack, and at the same moment our two columns were let loose, and at them we went." Hit in front and flank, the Federals turned tail. "Then it was a race like a fox chase for five miles," Blackford said, ruing the fact that the enemy's superior horses and the open countryside enabled most of them to escape. Some 250 prisoners and a dozen wagons were taken, however, in a chase that came to be known as the "Buckland Races." One of the wagons contained the correspondence of Union General George Armstrong Custer. "Some of the letters to a fair, but frail, friend of Custer's were published in the Richmond papers and afforded spicy reading, though the most spicy parts did not appear."[9]

For Stuart the triumph at Buckland was a return to the glory days. His nature was such that he could not admit that the Federal cavalry, with more and better-fed horses, had come of age. Explained his adjutant Henry McClellan: "He could never see or acknowledge that he was worsted in an engagement. It was the enemy who *ought* to be whipped, and *must be* whipped." But the fact that his command was breaking down was self-evident. On any given day more than ten percent of Stuart's 9,500 troopers were dismounted, searching far and wide for replacements. Those who did have mounts faced the constant problem of feeding them, especially during the winters. Federal horses were taking in ten pounds of grain daily, while their counterparts often existed on as little as a pound of corn and the bark of trees.

Stuart had two maxims for war: "If you are in doubt of what to do, attack," and "Believe that you can whip the enemy, and you have won half the battle." Good mottoes, these, for a soldier. How closely Stuart would cleave to them in the months to come, even in view of the dearth of horses and fodder, would never be in doubt. Summed up McClellan: "Devotion to duty . . . was the ruling principle of his life."[10]

Opposing Lee on the Rappahannock on November 7, Meade launched two near-simultaneous attacks. The first was about noon at Kelly's Ford, where he soon succeeded in establishing a bridgehead against Dick Ewell on the south bank. Here Rodes's and Johnson's divisions fell back, the terrain favoring the Federal artillery. The second assault was upriver toward dusk at Rappahannock Station, where Lee stood guard with Early's division. Here Harry Hays's Mississippians and Archibald Godwin's North Carolinians, perhaps 2,000 men, were entrenched on the north bank. (Godwin was substituting for Robert Hoke, off on detached service.) Hays's and Godwin's lines were in a semicircle, with both flanks anchored on the river. Behind them a narrow pontoon bridge afforded their only means of retreat. The Rappahannock Station position was key. So long as the Confederates held it, the incursion at Kelly's Ford might be contained.

In the growing darkness, Lee and Early could see little of what was happening on the far bank. "They watched as [Hays's] trench line suddenly erupted in jagged flashes of musket fire," said a Louisiana Tiger historian. "A strong wind drowned out all noise of the firing, and when the flashes abruptly ceased, Lee dismissed it as a skirmish." The Federals heretofore had never made a night attack against the Army of Northern Virginia. Lee went back to his headquarters, convinced the action was a feint. "Early had no reason to believe otherwise, until an aide sent to check on [Hayes's] rations came galloping back saying that Tigers were streaming across the bridge in an apparent retreat." What had happened was that the enemy, moving up in the dark behind a concealing ridge, had made a massive assault on the Confederate lines. Lead elements of the Union Fifth and Sixth Corps under John

Sedgwick, some 2,000 of 20,000 men in his overall command, had overwhelmed Hays's three regiments on the right, gained control of the bridge and cut them off from retreat. "Scores of Yankees were cut down . . . but the mass of Federals behind them never slowed and soon swarmed over [Hays's] position."[11]

So briskly was the attack delivered that Early could only pace in frustration. "Godwin's regiments had not yet been captured, and I had the mortification of seeing the flashes of their rifles, and hearing their capture without being able to render them the slightest assistance, as it would have been folly to attempt to cross the bridge, and I could not open with the guns on the south side . . . we would have been as apt to fire into our own men as the enemy."[12]

Hundreds of Tigers and Tarheels were captured but some escaped, either slipping across the bridge in the darkness or swimming the river. Harry Hays made one of the more dramatic bolts for freedom. "General Hays had effected his escape," said Early, "after he was entirely surrounded by the enemy and was in their power, by his horse's taking fright at a musket fired near him and dashing off, when a number of shots were fired at him, and finding he had to run the gauntlet anyhow, he made for the bridge and escaped unhurt." Of the 2,000 Confederates on the far shore, perhaps 400 got away. Almost all the rest were prisoners, including Godwin and a half-dozen other colonels and lieutenant colonels. Some of the Louisiana regiments, acknowledged to be among the army's elite, all but ceased to exist. Editorialized the *Richmond Whig* about Hays's dwindling command: "The nine hundred remaining Louisianans were worth their weight in gold. . . . If they are now lost to Lee's army, we know not where the material will be found to replace them."[13]

Early was bitter about the debacle, calling it "the first serious disaster that had befallen any of my immediate commands . . . since the commencement of the war." He did not consider himself the culprit, though, saying he had not wanted to occupy the north bank in the first place. "When the enemy reached the works he had no trouble in walking over them, as there were no ditches or obstructions in front. . . . In constructing these works . . . there was but one mode of approach to or retreat . . . so that when the works were carried in front of the only bridge, the fate of the rest of the command was sealed."[14]

Having dinner a few days later with Robert Chilton, the Lee aide who had brought him the garbled message at Chancellorsville, Early showed considerable self-restraint when Chilton blamed the design of the bridgehead on him.

"You, General Early, thought it a strong one; those works were yours," Chilton said with characteristic certainty.

"No, sir," Jubal replied, "I objected to the engineering and pointed out where I thought it was bad."[15] While no mess plates were broken on this occasion, neither were enduring friendships made.

Who then should be blamed for the rout? One could name Lee, who had clearly underestimated the enemy's resolve. Or even Early, whose lines of communications with Hays and Godwin were tenuous at best. Certainly it is plausible the reverse is true: the battle was won because Sedgwick and his men had executed a night attack with great precision and daring, and badly beaten their unwary foes in the process.

Within hours of the defeat at Rappahannock Station, a crestfallen Lee had his men falling back to the Rapidan. Sandie Pendleton, who felt that Ewell had not been aggressive enough in resisting Meade at Kelly's Ford, continued the criticism of his chief he had first voiced at Gettysburg. "Oh, how each day is proving the inestimable value of General Jackson to us," he wrote his mother. In a letter to his sister he complained about his "superannuated chieftain," saying that Ewell was not physically up to the job, and he castigated him for "doting so foolishly upon his unattractive spouse." In truth a badly fitting wooden leg had ulcerated Ewell's stump, putting him temporarily on sick leave. Lizinka, who had joined her husband within days of the Kelly's Ford setback and must have been a distraction, went to the rear with him.[16]

It was not until November 26 that Meade moved some 60,000 men in bitter cold against Lee's line, attempting to turn the Confederate right. The two forces made initial contact the next day in the vicinity of Locust Grove, some two miles northeast of rain-swollen Mine Run, one of the Rapidan's tributaries. There Ewell's corps under Early—with Early's division under Hays, and Rodes's division—began forming line of battle. Hays and Rodes were held back, however, until Allegheny Johnson's division arrived. "I found the enemy occupied commanding ground in and around Locust Grove," said Early, "while the position Hays had been compelled to assume was low and very unfavorable. . . . Causing Hayes to connect his left with Rodes's right and so post his troops as to make them as secure as possible, I rode to Rodes's position, which I found equally disadvantageous." When Johnson did come up about 3 P.M. on Rodes's left, taking the road by Bartlett's Mill, the situation suddenly changed. Seeing he was in danger of being flanked by French's Third Corps, which had blundered across the Rapidan at Jacob's Ford, he wheeled to face the threat.[17]

Confused and seesaw fighting now occurred on Johnson's front. There the 2nd Brigade of John "Rum" Jones slogged through a swamp before engaging the enemy. "How the men crossed it I don't know," said John Worsham of the 21st Virginia. "Many left one or both shoes in the mud, the horses could not cross, the officers were compelled to dismount and take the mud too." Gaining some hilly ground, the troops took what cover they could and hunkered down. Middle-aged Captain John Johnson of the 50th Virginia, a large, stout man, then took the initiative. "Thinking that some of the men were not doing as well as they ought," said Worsham, "[he] walked out to the brow of the hill, lay down on its top, broadside to the enemy, and then called to some of his men to come up; and if they were afraid, they could use him as a breastwork. Several of them promptly accepted his challenge, lying down behind him, resting their guns on him, firing steadily from this position." Johnson was not even wounded.

Leroy Stafford likewise sought to inspire his Louisianans, galloping along the front lines in full view of the foe. Though he would dismiss all credit for his gallantry, insisting the only way he could keep his panic-stricken horse under control was to let it run, not all his men were impressed. When he rode back to a gun emplacement to direct its fire, one artilleryman asked, "General, who was that crazy fellow on horseback trying to get himself killed . . . prancing his horse up and down the line of fire?"

Stafford had to laugh. "Oh, that was one of the officers in my brigade," he said before riding off.[18]

Waving his clublike cane and booming orders to his officers, Johnson by nightfall succeeded in blunting the Third Corps assault and securing Early's lines. "Johnson effectually checked the enemy's advance," said Early, "driving his troops back, and maintaining full occupation of the [Bartlett's Mill] road . . . and by the check thus given . . . saved the whole corps from a very serious disaster, for if the enemy had got in possession of this road, he would have been able to come up in rear. . . ." Confederate casualties were some 545; Federal, 950. Under cover of darkness, Lee withdrew Early's command to more advantageous ground behind Mine Run, forming him on Powell Hill's left. "Our position was a very good one," continued Early, "and it was rapidly strengthened with the ordinary rifle trenches and some epaulments for artillery. The enemy's position on the opposite banks . . . was also a strong one. . . . A direct attack from either side would have been attended with great difficulties. . . ."[19]

For the next three days the two entrenched armies stared at each other in the frigid weather. Riding along the lines on Sunday, November 29, Lee and some aides came upon a group of soldiers having a prayer service. He at once drew rein, and listened to the singing of the men. "He heard the entire hymn," said his adjutant Walter Taylor, "and as the benediction was pronounced, reverently raised his hat from his head, received the blessing, and then continued his ride around the fortifications. It was a striking scene. . . . The parapet was crowded with men; here and there at proper intervals waved battle flags; and from many dozen embrasures frowned the now silent artillery . . . it was a cheering thing to see that, while ready for action, our men did not forget that, to secure victory, divine help should be implored." Edward Moore of the Rockbridge Artillery, noting the ground was strewn with playing cards, expressed the religious impulse more simply: "I never saw or heard of a Bible or prayer-book being cast aside at such a time, but cards were always thrown away by soldiers going into battle."[20]

But further battle there was not to be. On the night of the 30th, even while Lee was making plans to launch an attack, Meade withdrew across the Rapidan, heading back to the Rappahannock. He had no taste for going on the attack himself, and he saw no advantage in spending the winter in front of Mine Run. Lee berated himself for not going on the offensive sooner. "I am too old to command this army," he said the next morning. "We never should have permitted those people to get away." Others saw the retreat in a more positive light. "A mountain in labor, and behold at parturition a mouse is brought forth," rejoiced one Richmond paper. "Meade has marched up the hill and then marched down again."[21]

From Bristoe to Mine Run, the Confederates had suffered some 4,300 casualties, troops they could ill afford to lose. Now both sides would pause to bind their wounds, waiting for another winter to pass and another spring campaign to begin. Between North and South in the months to come there would be no compromise, and many more brave men would die.

# 1 8 6 4

ONE

* * * *

## THE ARMY IN LIMBO

In January of 1864 the wartime table talk at the home of Richmond hostess Mary Chestnut tended to be as despondent as it was spirited, reflecting the growing concerns of her guests:

"After the battles around Richmond, hope was strong in me. All that has insensibly drifted away."

"I am like David after the child was dead. Get up, wash my face, have my hair cut, &c&c."

"I think we are more like the sailors who break into the spirits closet when they find out the ship must sink. There seems to be for the first time a resolute feeling to enjoy the brief hour. . . ."

"I now long, pine, pray and grieve—and—well, I have no hope. . . ."

"One more year of Stonewall would have saved us."

"Chickamauga is the only battle we have gained since Stonewall went up."

"And no results—as usual."

"General Lee can do no more than keep back Meade."

"One of Meade's armies, you mean. They have only to double on [Lee] when he whips one of theirs."

"General Edward Johnson says he got Grant a place. Esprit de corps, you know, would not bear to see an old army man driving a wagon. That was when [Johnson] found him out west. Put out of the army for habitual drunkenness."

"[Grant] don't care a snap if they fall like the leaves fall. He fights to win, that chap. He is not distracted by a thousand side issues."

"Yes, like Lincoln, they have ceased to carp at him because he is a rough clown, no gentleman, &c&c. You never hear now of his nasty fun, only of his wisdom. . . . They talked of Lincoln's drunkenness, too. Now, since Vicksburg, they have not a word to say about Grant's habits."

"He has the disagreeable habit of not retreating before irresistible veterans. . . ."

"Listen, if General Lee had Grant's resources, he would have bagged the last Yankee or had them all safe back, packed up in Massachusetts. . . ."

"Damn splay-footed Yankees, every man jack of them."

"As they steadily tramp this way, I must say. . . ."[1]

Mrs. Chestnut's companions were a privileged sort, and other than the field officers she cultivated largely immune from the horrors of the war, but they recognized that in Ulysses S. Grant they had a relentless adversary. On March 12 Lincoln would name him general-in-chief of all the Federal armies, and he would devise a sweeping three-pronged plan to crush Confederate resistance.[2] In the East as soon as weather permitted Grant would send George Meade's 120,000-man Army of the Potomac south against Lee's 65,000-man Army of Northern Virginia, even while the 40,000-man Army of the James under Benjamin Butler would advance up the James River in Lee's rear. To meet this latter threat Beauregard with some 24,000 men, including George Pickett's division, would face Butler at Petersburg, 20 miles below Richmond. Simultaneously Union General Franz Sigel would march on the Shenandoah Valley, intent on denying that fertile breadbasket to the Confederacy. Opposing him would be General John C. Breckinridge of Kentucky, the Southern Democrat who lost to Lincoln in the four-candidate election of 1860.

The nondescript Grant was the prototype rural Midwesterner, declaimed one historian, "bearing somehow the air of the little farm on the empty dusty road and the small-town harness shop, [now] plunked down in an army predominantly officered by polished Easterners. He was slouchy, round-shouldered, a red bristly beard cropped short of his weathered face, with a look about the eyes of a man who had come way up from very far down; his one visible talent seemingly the ability to ride any horse anywhere under any conditions." Somewhere deep inside the Union general-in-chief was "the proud, shy little West Point graduate who had put on the best uniform a brevet second lieutenant of infantry could wear when he went home to Ohio after graduation, and got laughed at for a dude by livery-stable toughs, and who forever after preferred to wear the plain uniform of a private soldier, with officer's insignia stitched on the shoulders."[3]

He breakfasted on coffee and sliced cucumber soaked in vinegar, ate meat only if it was cooked to a near crisp and smoked as many as two dozen cigars daily. He loved his wife, Julia, as a young man loves his first sweetheart—this woman who still referred to him as "Mister Grant"—writing her long letters during the times they were apart, and he doted on his children. Isolated in

California at a small army post, far from his family and wracked by loneliness, he had turned for solace to drink. In 1854 he resigned from the service to avoid court-martial for drunkenness, and his fortunes subsequently went downhill. Before the war rescued him from a hand-to-mouth existence, he was reduced to working as a store clerk. Then his dogged leadership during 1862 and 1863 in the battles out West at Forts Henry and Donelson, Shiloh and Vicksburg transformed him into a national figure.

"Who's this Grant that's made a lieutenant general?" one Ohio soldier on picket duty along the Rappahannock asked some of his friends.

"He's the hero of Vicksburg."

"Well, Vicksburg wasn't much of a fight. The Rebels were out of rations and they had to surrender or starve. They had nothing but dead mules and dogs to eat, as I understand."

The men nodded wisely, and another soldier opined that Grant never could have penned up Lee's generals that way. Longstreet or Stuart "would have broken out some way and foraged around for supplies."[4]

Though Longstreet had seen Grant but once since West Point and Jefferson Barracks, he retained great respect for him. "That man will fight us every day and every hour till the end of the war," he warned his rebel comrades.

For the average Federal soldier, however, the jury on Grant was still out.

"Well, what do you think?" one private in the 5th Wisconsin asked another when they first caught a glimpse of their new commander.

The second soldier took in Grant's watchful eyes and hard straight mouth. "He looks as if he [means] it," he said.

"Well, we'll see for ourselves before long," was the reply.[5]

Through the winter months the recuperating John Bell Hood continued his courting of Sally Buchanan Preston, who often stayed in Mrs. Chestnut's home. He too had been named a lieutenant general and would soon be transferred to the Army of Tennessee, but for the moment he was in Richmond on crutches, ignoring the twin handicaps of a mangled arm and an amputated leg. Here was the man who had fought ferociously at some of the army's greatest triumphs—Gaines's Mill, Second Manassas, Sharpsburg and Chickamauga—and he was acting like a lovesick adolescent.

"When I am gone, it is all over. I will not come back," he said to Mrs. Chestnut and Buck one day, lamenting the on-again, off-again affair.

"Are you not threatening the wrong end of the sofa?" Mrs. Chestnut asked.

Hood laughed heartily, turned his back on Buck, who was also sitting on the sofa, and inquired, "Will she care?"

"How do I know?" said Mrs. Chestnut as she rose and walked away.

Buck could be needlessly cruel. In early February Hood escorted Varina Davis to a dinner party. There the two of them heard the young woman's ringing voice coming from another room, telling some friends, "Absurd! Engaged to that man! Never! For what do you take me?" To cover the awkward moment, the first lady told Hood that people were marveling at his courage, saying that if they had suffered such wounds they would wince at every shot they heard. "Why wince—when you would thank God for a ball to go through your heart and be done with all?" he responded.

"This is high drama and not farce," Mrs. Davis later said of the incident, "for there was the bitterness of death in his tone *for a moment*—and the silvery voice from the other room [again] came, calm and clear, 'Absurd—oh, you foolish creatures—to fancy I would.' "

One week afterward Buck and Hood were out riding when he took her hand in his.

"Ah, don't do that," she said. "Let it all rest as it is. You know I like you. You want to spoil it all."

"Say yes or no," Hood said. "I will not be satisfied with less. Yes—or no, is it?"

"Well, he would keep holding out his hand," she subsequently told Mrs. Chestnut. "What could I do? So I put mine in his. Heavens, what a change came over his face. I pulled my hand away by main strength."

"Now I will speak to your father," said Hood. "I want his consent to marry you at once."

"Did you ever know so foolish a fellow?" Buck asked Mrs. Chestnut.

Much of Richmond society was by now amused over Hood's "rough Texan wooing." One evening his passion overcame his judgment. "I think it began with those beautiful, beautiful silk stockings that fit so nicely," Buck told Mrs. Chestnut. "You ought to hear him rave about my foot and ankle. Before that he was so respectful. . . . But as I stood by the [fireplace] fender, warming my feet, he seized me round the waist and kissed my throat—to my horror—and when he saw how shocked I was, he was frightened . . . and so humble and full of apologies."

Before going to the West, Hood saw Buck once more at a Sunday church service. She was seated near him but did not raise her head or acknowledge his presence. "I was a little nervous when I saw who it was," he said. "[She] took my breath away."[6]

Let us look now briefly at a random sampling of officers who have been playing roles in our story. One such man was 26-year-old Stephen Dodson Ramseur, who had led his North Carolina brigade with elan at Chancellorsville, charging the enemy cannon when John R. Jones's unnerved brigade refused. This first son of Jacob and Lucy Ramseur, the second of their nine children, was born in Lincoln County, North Carolina, and raised in affluent circumstances. His parents were fervent Presbyterians and while both shaped his character, it was his mother, with her "judgment clear and firm," as well as her "tenderness and sympathy," who had the greater influence. In later years Dodson's on-the-field daring and off-the-field gentleness would mirror these qualities. Going off to Davidson College in 1853, he welcomed the school's religious teachings but had only disdain for its low academics and unruly students. He found a mentor, however, in the person of Harvey Hill, newly hired by the trustees to raise standards. This Hill did, and when he learned that the young man was interested in a military career, he facilitated his transfer from Davidson and appointment to West Point as well. "Who knows," Dodson wrote a friend, "but that 'I may write my history with my sword'?"[7]

Ramseur's leadership abilities were soon recognized at the academy, where he would hold every rank from cadet corporal to captain. During this time his merchant father fell victim to a dishonest partner, losing most of his money. The fact that the partner was a Northerner added fuel to Dodson's indignation. His family had been "robbed of all earthly goods" by "a miserable Yankee, a villain, a liar, a fiend of Hell. . . ." Northern efforts to ban slavery in the territories likewise infuriated him. "I am a *Secessionist* out and out," he said, "in favor of drawing the dividing line from the Atlantic to the Pacific." Meanwhile he saw no incongruity in mingling with Northerners at West Point for twice-a-week services conducted by then Lieutenant Oliver Otis Howard of Maine, nor in celebrating his graduation at Benny Haven's Tavern, just before he left the academy in 1860, with Union stalwart George Custer of Michigan.[8]

With the coming of secession, Ramseur resigned from the Old Army and offered his services to the Confederacy. By 1862 he was colonel of the 49th North Carolina in Robert Ransom's brigade, preoccupied with making his regiment ready for combat. "I will leave nothing undone that I can do to make them effective troops," he said. A photograph shows him looking older than his years, his closely cropped hair at odd variance with his newly grown beard. "God grant that we may overthrow entirely our base and merciless invaders," he wrote on the eve of the Seven Days. At Malvern Hill, where he first distinguished himself, the 49th North Carolina lost 100 of its 500 men, and Ramseur went down with a severe wound, his right arm shattered. His convalescence was long and painful, complicated by the fact the minie ball that struck him had impaired the nerves. Ramseur used the respite to become engaged. His fiancée was his cousin Ellen ("Nellie") Richmond, two years younger and his "long cherished ideal of womanly perfection."

Realizing Ramseur's potential, Lee in November 1862 saw to it he was promoted to brigadier, taking over the North Carolina command of George Burgwyn Anderson, who had been mortally wounded in the Bloody Lane at Sharpsburg. Throughout the winter and spring Dodson trained his men rigorously, honing their fighting edge. One day the brigade "marched 7 miles through blinding snow, waded two deep creeks, reached camp at 9 P.M.," he wrote Nellie. Following his success at Chancellorsville, he endured the disappointment of Gettysburg, where his men on July 1 were among the first to oust the enemy from the town. There his chief characteristic, one of his officers would say, was the effortless way he directed troops under fire, as he drew "his line . . . at a right angle to the wall . . . wheeled the line to the left, and then sent us forward at the double-quick. . . ." In the battle's aftermath, Ramseur had no illusions about the grim days that lay ahead. "Our great campaign . . . has failed," he said. "I look the thing square in the face, and am prepared to undergo dangers and trials to the end."[9]

In October 1863 Dodson took leave to marry Nellie, and while he was gone two of his regiments were pounded at Kelly's Ford, "which affair," he lamented, "was rather badly managed by the [officers] in command." But when he returned for Mine Run his presence, said one of his men, "seemed to reanimate the brigade. . . ." The winter of 1863–64 found him daily drilling his troops, permitting no slackness in their regimen. He was elated when Nellie joined him over the holidays in camp, where she would stay until the spring. "Can you imagine *how* much I enjoy her society?" he wrote a friend. ". . . Nellie and I have all the evening to ourselves. You *know* we have a cozy, comfortable, *spooney* time."[10]

Modest, quiet, undersized, pious—these are the words often used to describe 22-year-old Major William Johnson Pegram, who had been a law student at the University of Virginia when war broke out. Peering through thick, gold-rimmed spectacles, he now led one of the army's premier artillery battalions. "There was a certain magnetism about Willie Pegram that impressed all who came into his presence," said a private who served under him. "Never excited, possessing at all times that perfect equipoise so much prized in a commander, he embodied all the qualities of a soldier." In battle after battle, he had performed superbly. "He was, in some respects, of the type of Stonewall Jackson," said Robert Stiles, one of Lee's aides, "and like him combined the strongest Christian faith . . . with the most intense spirit of fight." Pegram's favorite tactic, Stiles went on admiringly, was "to rush to close quarters with the enemy and open at the shortest possible range. He admitted that it seemed deadly, but insisted that it saved life in the end."[11]

His gallantry first had been noted as a battery commander at Mechanicsville where, though his six guns were outnumbered five-to-one, he had kept them blazing away far into the night. Every one of his officers was killed or wounded; some 60 of his 80 men were casualties.

"I think we can take it for granted that Pegram's Battery was so nearly annihilated as not to be counted in forces available," remarked one of Powell Hill's brigadiers the next day.

At this moment a slim young officer, his face still begrimed with gunpowder, joined the conference. "I am Pegram of Pegram's Battery," he said. "I bring you a message from my men. It is this: 'In recognition of service done yesterday, what is left of Pegram's Battery claims as its right the most exposed position on the firing line this morning.' " His request was granted.[12]

Pegram flourished in combat. "At first our infantry behaved badly," he wrote his sister Jennie after Cedar Mountain. "My support ran, and the battery was charged by the enemy. I kept a sharp lookout, and played upon them with canister to the last, and then got out in time, with the loss of one man wounded, three horses killed, and a caisson. After we drove them back, I [retrieved] my caisson." On the part he played during the two days Pope pounded Jackson's line at Second Manassas, Pegram wrote: "God assisted us and we drove them back with great slaughter." When a shell burst in the midst of one of his crews, he was coolly analytical: "It was the worst shot I ever saw . . . killing two of my best men, wounding two, stunning the remainder, killing three horses, disabling a wheel and cutting through a tree." Later, pushing up from Harpers Ferry under Hill to relieve Lee at Sharpsburg, he arrived in time to deliver a brutal enfilading fire on the enemy left.

Pegram may have made his greatest battlefield contribution at Chancellorsville where, temporarily leading a battalion, he joined with Porter Alexander to dominate the Federals at Hazel Grove and Fairview. "A murderous fire was kept upon them," he said, "killing and wounding a very large number until our infantry came up on their flanks, and we drove them entirely off. . . ." Wrote Lieutenant John Munford to a cousin: "This was the first battle Major Pegram commanded us in . . . he is the bravest and noblest fellow I ever saw, has won the confidence & esteem of the whole command. . . . Present my compliments to [his mother] when you see her & tell her Willie is the adoration of this Batt: & of all who know him. . . ."[13]

In the aftermath of Gettysburg Pegram's battalion saw minor action along the Rappahannock and the Rapidan. From winter quarters in February 1864 he shared his frustrations and cares with his sister Mary: "I wish that when active operations once commence, they could continue until the war is brought to an end. Camp is getting to be insufferable. The music of a shell would be delightful." He worried that "Richmond must be getting fearfully corrupt," complaining of the "bad taste and hard-hearted conduct" of those people who gave dances and dinner parties while others mourned for their dead. "I fear that God will not favor us as long as such is the case." His biggest problem was finding and feeding horses. "Mine, unfortunately, are at this time in low order, & I have lost many, owing to . . . an epidemic among them."[14]

Within a few months Pegram, by then a lieutenant colonel, would be hearing the sound of continual cannonades. Grant would be driving south through the Wilderness, where Joe Hooker had been humbled, and this time Lee would be in peril.

William "Little Billy" Mahone, who led a brigade of Virginians in Richard Heron Anderson's division, Powell Hill's corps, stood perhaps five feet tall and weighed no more than 125 pounds. He had huge, hollow-rimmed blue eyes, long brown hair and a flowing beard—all wildly out of proportion to his slender frame—and his unconventional uniform included straw hats, hunting shirts, pleated trousers that tapered at the ankles and boots as elegant as a woman's. Quick-tempered and energetic, he suffered from a nervous stomach, often surviving for days on milk provided by the cow he brought along on the march. Growing up the son of a tavern keeper in Southampton County, Virginia, young Billy early became wise in the ways of the world. He filled in one night for his sleepy father in the midst of a card game with a wealthy patron, and by the time the elder Mahone returned the son had won the pot. When the father asked for the winnings, he refused to give them up. "I am going to keep [them] and educate myself," he announced.[15]

Mahone graduated from V.M.I. in 1847, went on to teach mathematics and study engineering and soon became a railroad surveyor. Blessed with good judgment, an entrepreneurial nature and alliances with politicians who wanted to expand the rail lines, he rose quickly in his chosen field. By 1855 he was chief engineer for a newly chartered railroad, the Norfolk and Petersburg, and shortly after its completion three years later he was named its president. Meanwhile he married Otelia Butler, who would give him thirteen offspring, ten of whom would die in childhood.

Commissioned the colonel of the 6th Virginia, he participated at the outbreak of hostilities in the capture of the Norfolk navy yard and was soon named a brigadier. On May 15, 1862, Mahone commanded the troops on Drewry's Bluff when Confederate shore batteries, in a four-hour duel, succeeded in repulsing the Federal ironclad *Monitor* as she steamed up the James to threaten Richmond. At Seven Pines two weeks afterward, however, he incurred the wrath of Harvey Hill while serving under him. There during the height of the fighting Hill repeatedly ordered some of Mahone's men out of a ditch, where they had taken cover, to fill a gap in the lines. When the men would not move, Hill became enraged.

"Colonel Scales!" he shouted, rising in his stirrups. "Colonel Scales, come and occupy the position that these cowardly Virginians have fled from!"

Alfred Scales, then the colonel of the 13th North Carolina, double-quicked his men forward over the backs of the huddled Virginians. Now Mahone came on the scene.

"You should not abuse my men," he said, "for I ordered them out of the fight."

"Why did you do so?" Hill answered. "Do you not see that you have left a gap open for the enemy to pass through and break our line?" Then he added bitingly, "But if you ordered them out, then I beg the soldiers' pardon for what I have said and transpose it all to you."[16]

Mahone was livid, but the battlefield was no place to pursue the argument.

Instead he rallied his men and pushed them forward, where they fought bravely until nightfall. Later he considered challenging Hill to a duel, but then thought better of it. Everyone in the army knew Hill's religious beliefs precluded dueling, his courage was unquestioned and such a challenge would be an empty gesture.

Soon afterward Mahone's brigade was transferred to Dick Anderson's division. At Malvern Hill he and his men fought with distinction, suffering some 26 percent casualties, and they were equally conspicuous at Second Manassas. There a minie ball struck Mahone full in the chest, badly wounding him. When a messenger brought Mrs. Mahone the news, he sought to reassure her by saying the injury was only a flesh wound.

"Now I know it is serious," she reportedly replied, "for William has no flesh whatever."[17]

Mahone did not return to service until Fredericksburg, where his brigade played a minor role. Nor was he given much opportunity at Chancellorsville where he came up on May 4 to support Marcellus Wilcox at Salem Church, or at Gettysburg where he was ordered to protect Pegram's batteries. But in the fourth year of the war, in the Wilderness and the defense of Petersburg, his star would rise. "As a brigadier he is not lacking in diligence but he is without special distinction . . ." one historian would write. "Promotion transforms him. Dispute and caution give place to fierce action. His men become the most renowned shock troops of the army. . . ."[18]

In April the army found a new hero. Robert Hoke, who was on detached duty in North Carolina, would be entrusted with the task of retaking the coastal town of Plymouth from the Federals. It would be a land-sea expedition, with three Confederate brigades, a regiment of cavalry and the ironclad ram *Albemarle* participating. Since Hoke was in charge of the operation, his own brigade—consisting of one Georgia and three North Carolina regiments—was commanded by Colonel John T. Mercer of the 21st Georgia. Matt Ransom's North Carolinians and James Kemper's Virginians under Colonel William Terry completed the infantry detachment, while Colonel James Dearing led the cavalry.

The scion of a wealthy North Carolina family and a close friend of Dodson Ramseur since childhood, Hoke had been with the army since the early days of the war, enlisting as a private and fighting as a second lieutenant under Harvey Hill at Big Bethel Church. He served as a major and lieutenant colonel in the 33rd North Carolina under Lawrence O'Bryan Branch during the Seven Days, Second Manassas and Sharpsburg, then became colonel of the 21st North Carolina in Isaac Trimble's brigade. When Trimble's wounds kept him from Fredericksburg, Hoke as the senior officer assumed command.

Just before the battle he turned to one of his staff and asked what kind of men he would be leading. "I am a stranger to your brigade," he said. "They have the reputation of being good fighters but I wish to know whether they are impetuous or stolid in action."

"We dash right into them; we either promote our commanders or get them shot," the officer replied. "I hear Burnside is crossing the river. If you are the right kind of stuff and will lead, we will make you Brigadier General Hoke tomorrow or get you killed."

Hoke brightened visibly. "That's the kind of talk I like to hear," he said.[19]

Standing in reserve on the Confederate left, he showed himself just such a leader. When the Federals poured through a gap they had found between James Archer's Tennesseans and James Lane's North Carolinians, he was in the forefront of Jubal Early's assault that restored the lines. "I saw that it would not do to allow [the enemy] to remain in the railroad [cut] as that point commanded a large portion of our entrenchments," he said. "So I immediately ordered a charge, and drove them from this place, killing about 200 and wounding a large number, 100 of whom fell into my hands. . . . I also captured about 300 prisoners."

Two days later he met Harvey Hill, who asked him, "How are you, General Hoke?"

"General Hill, you are poking fun at me," he replied.

"No, I am not," said Hill. "Jackson witnessed that charge!"

Hoke's promotion came through in January of 1863. In 21 months he had advanced from private to brigadier.[20]

At Chancellorsville on May 4, leading an advance the third day of the battle that recaptured Marye's Heights from the enemy, he was seriously wounded in the left shoulder. Taken from the field he refused to let the surgeons amputate the arm, despite the high risk of gangrene. His recovery was long and painful, keeping him from his brigade for the rest of the year. His mother, who initially thought he had been killed, even composed a prayer of requiem: "Almighty God, thou who alone canst see my misery, canst alone cure it. Give me, I implore thee, the faith, the hope, the love, the Christian courage that I need. . . ."[21]

Now the 26-year-old Hoke was leading some 7,000 men in an attack on the 3,000-man garrison at Plymouth, a key supply depot for Federal forces in tidewater North Carolina. His tactics called for approaching the town and its various forts on three sides—Ransom from the east, Kemper and Mercer from the south and west—and bombarding them into submission. Meanwhile the ram *Albemarle* was to destroy the enemy gunboats offshore. The assault began in earnest on April 18. Late that night Mercer's troops, while Ransom was conducting a diversion, stormed the breastworks at Fort Wessels and forced its surrender, making the first breach in the lines. Here Mercer fell with a mortal wound. Then about 3 A.M. on April 19, the *Albemarle* bore down under a full moon on the Federal gunboats, using her 18-foot prow and 8-inch guns to send one to the bottom, disable another and drive off the rest.

The final attack by Hoke's men came at first light the next day. "Fix bayonets! Trail arms! Forward march!" one officer would say of the charge, which was punctuated by screaming men and bursting shells. "At first we start in quicktime. . . . Soon it becomes double-quick, and 'yells' break from the whole line. . . ." One journalist likened the onslaught to "the wildest gust of tornado as it prostrates the forest, or the mad fire as it dashes through the prairies. . . ." By 10 A.M. the enemy had little choice but to raise the white flag.

"General Hoke, this is the saddest day of my life," said the Union commander, offering up his sword.

"General, this is the proudest day of mine!" Hoke responded. Then he handed the officer his weapon, saying, "You are too brave a man to part with your sword; take it back!"

In all the Confederates took some 2,400 prisoners, 40 pieces of artillery, 5,000 small arms, 200 horses and huge stores of food and ammunition. An elated President Davis telegraphed Hoke: "Accept my thanks and congratulations for the brilliant success which had attended your capture of Plymouth. You are promoted to be a major general from that date." Lee likewise was cheered by the triumph. Nonetheless he took pains to let Davis know he hoped for Hoke's men to be restored to his command as soon as possible. "I am glad of General Hoke's promotion," he wrote the president, "though sorry to lose him, unless he can be sent to me with a Division."[22] When the Federals did make their move, Lee knew his outnumbered army could hold the Rapidan only so long. Despite the odds, however, he would carry the fight to the foe.

TWO

\* \* \* \*

# THE WILDERNESS TO
# SPOTSYLVANIA

Before beginning the spring campaign, the army underwent another of its periodic reorganizations. Two of the divisions of the First Corps, whose leadership Longstreet had shredded in the aftermath of Chickamauga, received new commanders. (The third division, Pickett's, remained south of the James, serving under Beauregard to block the Federals advancing toward Petersburg.) One new major general was Joseph Kershaw, promoted to replace the ousted Lafayette McLaws. But the other was not, as Longstreet wished, Micah Jenkins to replace Hood. Much to Old Pete's irritation, Davis and Lee settled the rivalry between Jenkins and McIvor Law by promoting Charles Field and giving him Hood's old command. Field had been absent from the army for almost 18 months, convalescing from the serious wound he received at Second Manassas. His wife, Nimmie, we will recall, had dreamed that if he lived for ten days he would eventually recover—a premonition that proved correct.

Taking over Kershaw's old brigade was Colonel John Henagan, a former sheriff who had led the 8th South Carolina. The other commands stayed in place: Benjamin Humphreys's Mississippians, and William Wofford's and Goode Bryan's Georgians.

In Field's division, supplanting Jerome Robertson, the pugnacious John Gregg commanded the Texas Brigade. Gregg was a former Texas district judge, and his wartime experience thus far had been in the West. As colonel of the 7th Texas he had surrendered to Grant at Fort Donelson in February 1862, then spent several months as a prisoner of war. Following his exchange, he the next year served under Joe Johnston in the unsuccessful attempt to relieve the garrison at Vicksburg. Transferred to the Army of Tennessee, he was seriously wounded at Chickamauga. Now healthy again, he was eager for combat. The South Carolinians Micah Jenkins and Evander McIvor Law, to their credit, swallowed their chagrin over Field's promotion and remained with their respective South Carolina and Alabama brigades. Nonetheless Longstreet kept Law under arrest until mid-May, just before North Anna, when Davis personally ordered that all charges be dropped. In the Wilderness and at Spotsylvania, Colonel William Flake Perry would lead Law's brigade. George "Tige" Anderson and Henry "Rock" Benning continued to head their Georgia commands.

Dick Ewell was back leading the Second Corps, but clearly was impaired by the loss of his leg and in moments of stress, as we have seen at Gettysburg, tended to be indecisive. Just before the battle of the Wilderness, one of Lee's aides would remember him as looking usually thin and pale, and mounting his horse with difficulty. "He was accustomed to ride a flea-bitten gray named Rifle, who was singularly like him. . . . I knew Rifle well and noted that both he and his master looked a little as if they had been up all night and not had breakfast."[1] Lee would have liked him to retire from field service, but Ewell was choosing to ignore his chief's gentle hints.

Old Bald Head's division heads stayed the same: Jubal Early, who despite his increasingly high-handed ways exercised great influence over Ewell; Edward "Allegheny" Johnson; and Robert Rodes. Early's brigades were down to three, Hoke still being south of the James: Harry Hays's Louisianans, John Pegram's Virginians and John Brown Gordon's Georgians. Johnson's division was comprised of the Stonewall Brigade under Jim Walker, George Steuart's North Carolinians and Virginians, John "Rum" Jones's Virginians and Leroy Stafford's Louisianans. Rodes had the largest division: three brigades of North Carolinians under Dodson Ramseur, Junius Daniel and Robert Johnston; George Doles's Georgians; and Cullen Battle's Alabamians.

Doggedly leading the Third Corps was Powell Hill, whose prostatitis was worsening as the war continued. Urination was excruciating for him, and continual infections brought on chills and fevers. Sitting and riding could be equally painful. Moreover his need for frequent urination kept him from getting enough sleep, leading to extreme fatigue. The wonder was that Hill could command at all. Though he would falter at the Wilderness, he would come back strong in the siege of Petersburg.

Hill's division chiefs remained Dick Anderson, Harry Heth and Marcellus Wilcox. Anderson's division consisted of Billy Mahone's Virginians, Abner Perrin's Alabamians, Ambrose "Rans" Wright's Georgians and Edward Perry's Floridians. His fifth brigade was commanded by Nathaniel Harris, replacing Carnot Posey, who had been mortally wounded at Bristoe Station. Harris, a former lawyer who had served since the Peninsula, had led the 19th

Mississippi at Gettysburg. Heth's division was comprised of Joseph Davis's Mississippians, now battle-scarred and on their way to becoming veterans; John Cooke's and William Kirkland's North Carolinians; Harrison Walker's Virginians; and the Tennesseans of James Archer, newly exchanged after his capture the first day of Gettysburg. Wilcox led four brigades: James Lane's and Alfred Scales's North Carolinians; Edward Thomas's Georgians; and the South Carolinians of Samuel McGowan, back from his wounding at Chancellorsville.

Porter Alexander commanded the First Corps Artillery, Armistead Long that of the Second and Lindsay Walker that of the Third Corps. Both William Poague and Willie Pegram headed battalions under Walker.

Though Jeb Stuart was not raised in rank from major general, he now led a cavalry corps. Serving as major generals and division chiefs under him were Wade Hampton, Fitz Lee and Rooney Lee—the last named also exchanged following his capture. Hampton's brigades consisted of Pierce Young's Georgians, Tom Rosser's Virginians and Calbraith Butler's South Carolinians; Fitz Lee's of Lunsford Lomax's and Williams Wickham's Virginians; and Rooney Lee's of John Chambliss's Virginians and James B. Gordon's North Carolinians. Robert Preston Chew headed the horse artillery.

On May 4 Grant sent the 120,000-man Army of the Potomac across the Rapidan at Germanna and Ely's Fords, marching it south on the Germanna Plank Road toward Wilderness Tavern. George Meade remained in charge of the Union force, but General-in-Chief Grant in the campaigns to come would be looking over his shoulder every step of the way. To meet the threat Lee sent Ewell and Hill, respectively, eastward on the nearly parallel Orange Turnpike and the Orange Plank Road, approaching the enemy at a right angle. Though the two columns would never be more than three miles apart, the scrub forests and dense underbrush of the Wilderness precluded virtually all communication. Ewell had all his divisions up, but Hill only two—Dick Anderson being hours behind. Longstreet, who had been ordered to protect the railroad at Gordonsville, was a full day's march away. In all, Lee's force was no more than 65,000 men.

Ewell's corps initially encountered the enemy at 11 A.M. the next day at a clearing in the woods called Saunders Field. Lee would have preferred to wait until his command was unified but circumstances, as they had at Gettysburg, dictated otherwise. Ewell drew up his troops in line of battle—Early, Johnson and Rodes, from left to right—and at first enjoyed considerable success. "We drove the enemy through the jungle to an open field extending on both sides of the [Orange Pike]," said one of Johnson's officers, "and as they were pressed across it a destructive fire was poured into them, so that it appeared to me the ground was more thickly strewn with their dead and wounded than I had ever seen." About 1 P.M., however, additional elements of the Fifth

Corps, now commanded by Gouverneur Warren, fell heavily on "Rum" Jones's Virginians, shattering their ranks. Trying to rally them Jones was killed, as was his aide Robert Early, Jubal's nephew, compounding the confusion. Soon the panic spread to Cullen Battle's and George Doles's brigades. The whole Second Corps line was in danger of collapsing. Ewell galloped back to John Brown Gordon, whose Georgians were with the reserve.

"General Gordon," the commander yelled in his piping voice, "the fate of the day depends upon you, sir!"

"These men will save it," Gordon told him, immediately pushing his troops into position and ordering a countercharge. "With a deafening yell that must have been heard miles away," he remembered, "that glorious brigade rushed upon the hitherto advancing enemy, and by the shock of their furious onset shattered [them] into fragments." Then a problem arose. Gordon's brigade had pierced the Federal line directly in its front, but on both sides Warren's men held fast, pouring fire on the rest of the retreating Confederates. "My command . . . was in the remarkably strange position of being identically on the same general line with the enemy, the Confederates facing in one direction, the Federals in the other." Instead of withdrawing, Gordon wheeled half his men to the left and half to the right, and then, "with another piercing yell, they rushed in opposite directions upon the left and right flanks of the astounded Federals . . . capturing large numbers, and checking any further effort by General Grant on that part of the field."

Gordon by this time was becoming a legend. His troops were devoted to him and would follow him into the fiercest fight. "[He] always had something pleasant to say to his men, and I will bear my testimony that he was the most gallant man I ever saw on a battlefield," said one observer. "He had a way of putting things to the men that was irresistible, and he showed [them] that he shrank from nothing in battle on account of himself."

Ewell hopped up and down in pride over Gordon's charge. "Isn't that magnificent!" he said of the maneuver. "It ought to make Gordon a major general."[2]

For the rest of the afternoon Ewell skillfully set up his defenses and more than held his own with the foe. "Dear, glorious, old, one-legged Ewell," said Porter Alexander, "with his bald head & his big bright eyes & his long nose . . . sat back & not only whipped everything that attacked him but he even sallied out on some rash ones & captured two guns & quite a lot of prisoners. In between the attacks & during the night he intrenched himself nicely. This was the first that Gen. Grant ever saw of the fighting of the Army of Northern Virginia, and, good soldier as he was, I am sure that he must have admired it mightily."[3] The stalemate on the pike on May 5 was a bloody one, with casualties on both sides in the thousands. Besides Brigadier Jones, the Confederates lost Leroy Stafford with a mortal wound and John Pegram with a leg wound.

Over on the Orange Plank Road near its junction with the Brock Road, where Lee rode with Hill, the fighting did not begin until 4 P.M. This delay, which was brought about by the Federals' decision to entrench, was fortuitous. Lee was buying time, waiting for Anderson and Longstreet to come up. Winfield Scott Hancock's Second Corps and elements of John Sedgwick's Sixth Corps—some 38,000 men—now pushed forward against Hill's 14,000, almost equally divided between Heth and Wilcox. Straddling the road on the open ground near the Widow (Eliza) Tapp's House, Heth's division bore the brunt of the attack—Davis, Cooke and Walker, from left to right, forming line of battle, with Kirkland in reserve. Taking what cover they could, the Confederates repelled assault after assault. "The whole Wilderness roared like fire in a canebrake," said one of Cooke's North Carolinians. Watching the action, a *New York Tribune* reporter wrote: "No room in that jungle for maneuvering; no possibility of a bayonet charge; no help from cavalry, nothing but close, square, face-to-face volleys of fatal musketry. The wounded stream out, and fresh troops pour in. Stretchers pass out with ghastly burdens, and so back reeking with blood for more."[4]

Despite his physical pain Hill drove himself relentlessly, personally directing some of the brigades. Even a captain of sharpshooters, coming up with his command, did not escape his notice. "Face the fire and go in where it is hottest," Hill told him.

Now Wilcox's division, which had been on Heth's left trying to form a link with Ewell, was called back in support. "Just as we reached the Plank Road, three or four shells fell among us . . ." said one of McGowan's South Carolinians. "We pressed on, guide left, through the thick undergrowth, until we reached Heth's line, now much thinned and exhausted. . . . We passed over this line cheering. There was no use of this. We should have charged without uttering a word until within a few yards of the Federal line. As it was, we drew upon ourselves a terrific volley of musketry."[5] Lane's and Scales's North Carolinians and Thomas's Georgians likewise moved up. Still the deadly dance continued, each side all but locked in each other's arms. Hill at this point had no more men to commit, except for 125 Alabamians in charge of the prisoners, but somehow he managed to hold.

Darkness brought the engagement to a close. It had been "a butchery pure and simple," said a weary soldier. In the 55th North Carolina, one of the harder-hit regiments, some 200 of 340 men were casualties. In their front rested some 160 enemy dead.[6]

That night Hill's exhausted Confederates lay sprawled on the ground in obvious disarray. Units had lost all cohesion, with a soldier remembering that "none of the brigades seemed to be in line—some regiments isolated entirely from their brigades—in fact, no line at all, but just as they had fought." But when Heth went to Hill and proposed that he and Wilcox be allowed to reform their defenses, he met with a rebuff.

"Longstreet will be up in a few hours," Hill assured him. "He will form in your front. I don't propose that you shall do any fighting tomorrow; the men have been marching and fighting all day and are tired. I don't wish them disturbed."

Still troubled, Heth later returned and made a second plea. Wilcox called on Hill as well with similar concerns. Both were turned away.

When Heth returned a third time Hill, who was wracked with pain in the aftermath of the battle, grew angry. "Damn it, Heth," he said, "I don't want to hear any more about it; the men shall not be disturbed."[7]

Hill had reasons for his decision, of course. Re-forming the lines in the darkness, so close to the enemy, would be no simple matter, and it would necessitate leaving behind his wounded. Moreover he had been assured by an overly optimistic Lee that Longstreet would arrive by 1 A.M. on May 6. Nonetheless he was showing poor judgment.

With Longstreet's corps not yet up, Hancock struck the unprepared Confederates at 5 A.M. Scattered and short of ammunition, Heth's and Wilcox's troops offered little resistance, and within an hour their whole position was in danger of collapsing. Hill reacted with his old-time verve. Galloping to a ridge above the melee, where William Poague's guns were situated, he took the radical step of ordering him to hurl double canister toward the enemy over the heads of the fleeing men. "This cannot be delayed!" he yelled. "The guns must open fire!" The resulting salvos momentarily halted the advancing Bluecoats, even as Hill helped man one of the cannon.

Lee likewise took an active role in the action. Finding himself in the midst of McGowan's fleeing brigade, he uttered uncharacteristically harsh words.

"My God, General McGowan!" he cried. "Is this splendid brigade of yours running like a flock of geese?"

"General," McGowan answered, "these men are not whipped! They only want a place to form, and they will fight as well as they ever did!"[8]

Longstreet chose this moment to arrive on the scene, marching his troops in double column up the plank road toward Hill's beleaguered command. "Like a fine lady at a party," said one artilleryman, "Longstreet was often late in his arrival at the ball, but he always made a sensation . . . with the grand old 1st Corps, sweeping behind him, as his train." Hood's Texas Brigade, now under Gregg, led the way on the left of the road; Barksdale's old Mississippi brigade under Humphreys, and Kershaw's former brigade under Henagan, were in the van on the right. "Now the battle was on in earnest . . ." said Captain Augustus Dickert of Kershaw's command. "The roar of the small arms, mingled with the thunder of the cannon that Longstreet had brought forward, echoed and reechoed up and down the little valley, but never to die away, for new troops were being put rapidly in action to the right and left of us." Regiments were left without colonels, companies without captains. "Still the battle roared on. It seemed as if the whole Federal army was upon us—so thick and fast came the death-dealing missiles. . . . Both armies stood at extreme tension, and the cord must soon snap one way or the other. . . ."[9]

Just as Kershaw's men were moving to stabilize the front on the right of the road, Lee rode up to the Texas Brigade on the left. "Having given General Gregg an order to advance at once and check the on-coming enemy," said a member of the 4th Texas, "[Lee] added: 'The Texas Brigade always has driven the enemy, and I want them to do it now. And tell them, General, that they will fight today under my eye—I will watch their conduct. I want every man of them to know that I am here with them.' "

Barely had Gregg passed on this message and shouted, "Forward!" when "Lee himself came in front of us, as if intending to lead us. The men shouted to him to come back, that they would not budge an inch until he did so, and to emphasize the demand, twenty or more of them sprang forward and made an effort to lead or push his horse to the rear . . . [then] General Longstreet rode up and said something, whereupon General Lee rode silently back through our ranks."[10] Precisely what Gregg's men shouted to dissuade him is in dispute, but "Lee to the rear!" is the most dramatic version.

The Texas Brigade more than justified Lee's confidence, and with "Rock" Benning's Georgians pushed back the Federals and regained much of the lost ground. Both commands paid a terrible price, however, losing half their number to death or wounds. Law's brigade under William Perry now came up to relieve them, streaming through their ranks to put additional pressure on Hancock. By 10 A.M. both sides were back where they had started.

Lee's five-mile-long line at this juncture looked like this: on the far left Early, Johnson and Rodes under Ewell stretched across the turnpike; in the center Wilcox's and Heth's divisions, recovered from their panic, under Hill; on the right Field and Kershaw under Longstreet holding the plank road. Supporting Longstreet on the right was Dick Anderson's division of Hill's command.

Longstreet soon learned from reconnaissance that the Federal left, which could be approached unseen through an unfinished railroad bed, might be turned. A flank attack of this nature, eerily reminiscent of Jackson's assault in the Wilderness the year before, could roll up the entire enemy line. After conferring with Lee, he called Moxley Sorrel to his side and offered him every staff officer's dream. "Colonel," he said, "there is a fine chance of a great attack by our right. If you will quickly get into those woods, some brigades will be found much scattered from the fight. Collect them and take charge. Form a good line and then move. . . . Hit hard when you start. . . . I shall be waiting for your gunfire, and be on hand with fresh troops. . . ."

Riding off to the right Sorrel quickly found three stray brigades. One was Billy Mahone's, whose Virginians the last two days, much to their dismay, had seen little action. The second was the Georgia brigade of William Wofford, who had once served under Hood and absorbed much of his aggressiveness. The reliable "Tige" Anderson and his Georgians completed the command. Eventually some men from Joseph Davis's unit also joined them. Within an hour, Sorrel was ready. "The word was given, and then with heavy firing and ringing yells we were upon Hancock's exposed left," he said. "[The enemy was] rolled back line after line. I was well mounted, and despite the tangled growth could keep with our troops . . . riding most of the charge with Mahone's men. . . . A stand was attempted by a reserve line of Hancock's, but it was swept off its feet in the tumultuous rush, and finally we struck the Plank Road. . . ." There the flanking party fell on Union General James Wadsworth's division. The 57-year-old Wadsworth, who had read law in Daniel Webster's office, tried in vain to rally his command, but "his men would not stay. A volley from our pursuing troops brought down the gallant New Yorker, killing both rider and horse."[11]

For Longstreet the audacious assault must have meant vindication. He had for some time endured the whispers that he was merely a "defensive" general. Now he was emulating Stonewall's greatest triumph, on the brink of bringing the enemy to "utter rout with heavy loss." He and his officers had reason to be proud. Micah Jenkins, riding with Longstreet on the plank road in the wake of the attack, could not contain his emotions. "I have felt despair for the cause for some months," he said, "but am relieved, and feel assured that we will put the enemy back across the Rapidan before night."[12]

It was almost noon. "I hastened back to General Longstreet to press for fresh troops," continued Sorrel. "There was no need with him. He had heard our guns, knew what was up, and was already marching." Longstreet's party numbered perhaps ten men, and it was closely followed by Jenkins's brigade. Besides Jenkins and Sorrel, it included Kershaw, Wofford and several aides. Eager to push the assault Old Pete rushed into dangerous terrain, passing the body of General Wadsworth as he went. Then a burst of shots rang out from the woods. They came from one of Mahone's regiments who, half-blinded by the underbrush and the smoke from the incessant musketry, had mistaken the group for Federal cavalry. Like Jackson on the same plank road earlier, Longstreet was being fired on by his own men. He took a minie ball that entered at the throat, almost choking him in his own blood, and smashed into his right shoulder, even as Jenkins and some others went down with mortal wounds. "He was a heavy man," said Sorrel of his chief, "with a very firm seat in the saddle, but he was actually lifted straight up and came down hard."

Just as Jenkins's and Mahone's men on opposite sides of the road were about to fire on each other, Kershaw galloped between them with drawn sword, repeatedly shouting, "We are friends!" and bringing the confrontation to a close.

Helped down from his horse and propped against a tree, Longstreet had thoughts only for immediately following up the assault. "Tell General Field to take command, and move forward with the whole force and gain the Brock Road," he managed to rasp through his torn throat as a surgeon attended him. This was not to be. Since Field's troops were perpendicular to the road, while the flanking force was parallel, the advance could not continue until all were realigned. Longstreet might have been able to do this speedily. Capable officer though he was, Field was unfamiliar with the situation and needed more time, which the enemy used to create new breastworks. "Could we have pushed forward at once," he said, "I believe Grant's army would have been routed." When about 4 P.M. the final attack on the plank road did get underway, the Federal lines held until the sun went down and the fighting ceased.[13]

Lee aide Robert Stiles meanwhile rode up to the ambulance bearing Longstreet to the rear. "They had taken off [his] hat and coat and boots . . ." he recalled. "While I gazed at his massive frame, lying so still, except when it rocked inertly with the lurch of the vehicle . . . he quietly moved his unwounded arm and . . . carefully lifted the saturated undershirt from his chest, holding it up a moment, and heaved a deep sigh. He is not dead, I said to myself, and he is calm and entirely master of the situation—he is both greater and more attractive than I have heretofore thought him."[14] Longstreet would not return to the army until October, when Petersburg and Richmond were under siege.

Back on the Confederate left on May 6, where Ewell was facing Warren and Sedgwick on the turnpike, John Brown Gordon discovered what he thought was a major weakness in the enemy's lines. Guided by scouts he rode forward in the early morning toward the enemy's extreme right and found that it too might be turned. "Dismounting and creeping slowly and cautiously through the dense woods, we were soon in earshot of an unsuppressed and merry clatter of voices," he said. "A few feet nearer and through a narrow vista, I was shown the end of General Grant's temporary breastworks. There was no line guarding this flank. As far as my eye could reach, the Union soldiers were seated on the margin of the rifle-pits, taking their breakfast. . . ."

Gordon sped back to corps headquarters, where soon after 9 A.M. he urged Ewell and Early that he be permitted to make a flank attack. The front was quiet at the moment, Pegram having handily beaten off an earlier Federal assault. Early peremptorily dismissed the suggestion. "He said that Burnside's (IX) corps was immediately behind Sedgwick's right to protect it . . . that if I should attempt such movement, Burnside would assail my flank and rout or capture all my men," continued Gordon. "He was so firmly fixed in his belief that . . . he was not perceptively affected by the repeated reports of scouts, nor my own statement. . . ." Ewell hesitated, then denied Gordon's request. "In view of General Early's protest, he was unwilling to order the attack . . .

even upon my proposing to assume all responsibility of disaster, should any occur."

Early, it appears, was totally wrong about Burnside's location. Instead of being on the Federal right, he was advancing that morning on the center and left, near the plank road. Wrote Grant: "Burnside, who was coming up with two divisions, was directed to get in between Warren and Wadsworth. . . . Sedgwick and Warren were to make attacks in their front. . . . Burnside was ordered, if he should succeed in breaking the enemy's center, to swing around to the left and envelop the right of Lee's army." Gordon's flanking plan might well have worked.[15]

For hours thereafter, Ewell made no offensive thrust. Despite the frantic fighting on the plank road he stayed in his lines along the turnpike, content to repulse occasional Federal sallies. "Both General Early and I were at Ewell's headquarters," said Gordon, "when, about 5:30 in the afternoon, General Lee rode up and asked: 'Cannot something be done on this flank to relieve the pressure upon our right?' After listening for some time to the conference which followed this pointed inquiry, I felt it my duty to acquaint General Lee with the facts as to Sedgwick's exposed flank. . . ." Early again vigorously opposed any such move, saying Burnside would thwart it. Gordon just as powerfully supported it, saying Burnside was nowhere in evidence. "The details of the whole plan were laid before [Lee]," said Gordon. "There was no doubt with him as to its feasibility. His words were few, but his silence and grim looks, while the reasons for that long delay were given, and his prompt order to me to move at once on the attack, revealed his thoughts almost as plainly as words could have done."[16]

In the brief time before darkness Gordon's Georgia brigade, aided by Robert Johnston's North Carolinians, scored impressive gains. With minimal casualties they rolled up the Federal right, capturing two brigadiers and several hundred men, and killing perhaps 400 more. Insisted Gordon: ". . . had the movement been made at an earlier hour and properly supported . . . it would have resulted in a decided disaster to the whole right wind of General Grant's army." Instead, night brought the engagement to a close, letting the enemy re-form his lines.[17]

The two days of fighting in the Wilderness cost the Federals 18,000 casualties, while the Confederates suffered 12,000. During the night crackling flames ignited by the musketry swept through the tangled brush, consuming the bodies of the dead and wounded just as they had at Chancellorsville. Leroy Stafford, John M. Jones and Micah Jenkins were dead or dying; John Pegram, "Rock" Benning and Longstreet were wounded, with the latter struck down when needed most. Soon Powell Hill would go on sick leave, missing the upcoming battle of Spotsylvania and adding to the leadership crisis.

On May 7 both sides spent the day recovering, staring at each other from behind their entrenchments. Lee used the time, in part, to consider who should replace Longstreet. Summoning Sorrel to his tent, he came directly to the point, saying he had three major generals in mind: Jubal Early, Edward "Allegheny" Johnson and Dick Anderson.

"You have been with the corps since it started as a brigade," he told Sorrel, "and should be able to help me."

"I said that probably Early would be the ablest commander of the three named," the staff officer said, "but would be the most unpopular in our corps. His flings and irritable disposition had left their marks. . . . I feared he would be objectionable to both officers and men."

"And now, Colonel, for my friend Ed Johnson," Lee went on. "He is a splendid fellow."

"All say so, General, but he is unknown to the corps. His reputation is so high that perhaps he would prove all that could be wished, but I think someone personally known to the corps would be preferred." Lee then brought up Anderson, who until Gettysburg had served in Longstreet's corps.

"We *know him* and shall be satisfied with him," Sorrel answered.

Dick Anderson would be named temporary commander of the First Corps. Replacing him as acting division head in Hill's Third Corps would be Billy Mahone. Filling in for Powell Hill would be Jubal Early, while the irresolute Ewell remained as head of the Second Corps. Replacing Early would be Gordon. Drastic changes these, in the critical months ahead.[18]

Late that night Grant withdrew from his lines and sidestepped the Confederate right, marching south on the Brock Road toward Spotsylvania Courthouse in an effort to put himself between Lee and Richmond. "That was his little game, & not a bad one," said Porter Alexander. "Fortunately, Gen. Lee correctly anticipated it, & the night was devoted to a footrace. Grant had a slight advantage in distance, say 12 to our 15 miles, & a more material one in having the initiative." Here credit must be given to quiet, professorial Dick Anderson who, ordered to move with Kershaw's and Field's divisions on parallel roads to Spotsylvania by 3 A.M., took it upon himself to start four hours earlier. Credit likewise must be given to Fitz Lee, whose cavalry stubbornly slowed the Federal advance. "Fitz Lee had cut down trees, & blockaded the roads, & defended the blockades so well," added Alexander, "that the task of opening the road had to wait for daylight, & for Warren's corps of infantry."[19]

In the early morning of May 8, when Anderson's van neared the Brock Road, the ever-rising sound of gunfire indicated that Lee's troopers were hard pressed. "Soon we see an old Virginia gentleman, bareheaded and without his shoes, riding in haste towards us," said one of Kershaw's men. "He reports that our cavalry are holding the enemy . . . but that the Federal infantry are seen to be forming for an attack. . . . General Kershaw orders us forward at the double-quick. . . . Then it was that a gallant cavalryman rushes to us and said, 'Run for our rail piles; the Federal infantry will reach them first, if you don't run.' Our men sprang forward. . . . We occupy the rail piles in time to see a column moving towards us, about sixty yards away. Fire, deadening fire, is poured into that column by our men. . . . The column staggers and then falls back."[20]

The diligent Anderson had won the race to Spotsylvania. In short order he extended his corps in line of battle from the Po River to the Brock Road, stopping the enemy cold. Later Ewell came up, bolstering the defense when he was most needed and eventually moving to Anderson's right. Hill's division under Early, arriving on May 9, formed to the right of Ewell.

By then the Confederates were well entrenched, their breastworks a formidable tangle of logs, dirt and underbrush. Lee's lines extended in a five-to-six-mile arc from the Po in the west to Spotsylvania Courthouse in the east, with a three-quarter-of-a-mile salient in the center, where Ewell's corps was positioned. This bulge, located on a low ridge and originally called the Mule Shoe, would be renamed the Bloody Angle. "This is a wretched line," Lee observed. "I do not see how it can be held!" Ewell agreed the salient was vulnerable but argued for remaining where he was, pointing out that if he withdrew the enemy would move up guns onto the ridge and gain an advantage. When he promised he would place two battalions of artillery in support, Lee consented to his staying.[21] This day the most significant action was on the Confederate left, where the Federals crossed over the Po near Block House Bridge. There they paused in their probing movement, waiting for morning.

This day too marked the death of Union Major General John Sedgwick, who fell victim to a rebel sharpshooter while directing the placement of his artillery. The sniper was probably armed with a Whitworth, an imported English rifle with a telescopic sight that was accurate up to 2,000 yards. When the first balls whistled by, some of the Federals ducked.

"What! What! Men dodging this way for single bullets!" Sedgwick said with a laugh. "What will you do when they open fire along the whole line? I am ashamed of you. They couldn't hit an elephant at this distance."

A moment later another ball passed close by, sending a soldier diving to the ground. The general prodded him gently with his foot. "Why, my man, I am ashamed of you, dodging that way," he joked, again saying, "They couldn't hit an elephant at this distance."

More balls whistled past, followed by a thud. Sedgwick collapsed into the arms of an aide, blood spurting in a steady stream from a wound under his left eye. He died instantly, a smile still on his lips.[22]

On May 10 the fighting intensified. Heth's division accompanied by Early rushed all the way from the far right to the far left of the lines, falling on Hancock's troops on the south side of the Po and in the course of the afternoon forcing them back across the river. Here Early told his artillery chief,

David McIntosh, where to place his guns in a "low whining voice" that Mc-
Intosh could not understand. He asked the general to repeat himself, but again
could not make out the words. When he asked a third time, Jubal exploded:
"Well, God damn it, if you don't understand, go put them where you damn
please!" McIntosh did just that, putting an effective enfilading fire on the
enemy left. Meanwhile Joe Davis's Mississippians, John Cooke's and William
Kirkland's North Carolinians and Harrison Walker's Virginians broke
through the Federal lines. "The Rebs came up yelling as if they'd got a special
license to thrash us," said one Yank. "The surroundings were appalling," said
another. "The men knew that everyone was getting to the rear, that soon the
bridges would be cut away and their only chance of escape gone." Stated a
Pennsylvanian: "Our men were falling like game before hunters."[23] In the
course of the fighting Walker suffered a foot wound that necessitated amputation, while Cooke incurred a minor injury.

No sooner was the threat to their left flank removed than the Confederates
found themselves dealing with Gouverneur Warren's assault on their left center at Laurel Hill. Here Charles Field commanded, with Gregg's Texans,
"Tige" Anderson's Georgians, Law's Alabamians under William Perry, Benning's Georgians under Dudley DuBose, and Jenkins's South Carolinians under John Bratton from left to right forming the line. "Giving no notice of their
attentions," said a Texan of the Federal attack, "five of their brigades, under
cover of the heavy timber, crawled close up to [our] breastworks. Then, with
loud huzzas, they sprang forward in a seemingly reckless charge . . . and for
a few seconds it looked as if the enemy would win (the works). But when his
hope was strongest, a sheet of flame and a yell of defiance burst from the
entrenchments, the bullets mowing down the assailants by the hundreds, and
in front of the 4th and 5th Texas and the 3rd Arkansas the onset was soon
checked."

The 1st Texas had a more harrowing experience, as the Federals exploited
a 40-foot gap in its breastworks, "and into this a double line of Union soldiers
poured, shooting right and left, and to some extent using their bayonets. But
although being taken more by surprise than the other regiments . . . and driven
from their works, the 1st Texas immediately rallied, and joining in a hand-
to-hand contest with their assailants, drove them back . . . and as by this time
the balance of the brigade was idle and turned their fire on the Federals still
in front of the 1st, they were soon compelled to precipitate flight." One Connecticut soldier who lived to tell the tale put the repulse succinctly. "How we
got through it all I don't know," he marveled.[24]

The third of the Union assaults took place at 6:30 P.M., when 24-year-old
Colonel Emory Upton of the slain Sedgwick's Sixth Corps led twelve picked
regiments—some 5,000 men—against the Mule Shoe that was the Confederate center. Upton's men would attack in four waves, and they were under
strict orders not to fire until they reached the breastworks. Firing and reload-

ing during the charge only would consume precious minutes. Directly facing them on the northwest tip of the salient were George Doles's Georgians, flanked on one side by Junius Daniel's and Dodson Ramseur's North Carolinians and on the other by Jim Walker's Stonewall Brigade. Bursting from the woods where they had been concealed, the Federals advanced in wave after wave across 200 yards of open ground toward Doles's breastworks. "Many a poor fellow fell pierced with Rebel bullets before we reached the rifle pits," said a soldier in the 96th Pennsylvania. "When those who were left reached the pits we let them have it." Quickly Doles's lines were broken, his men overrun. Ewell galloped up in front of Daniel's brigade to lend encouragement. "Don't run, boys!" he shouted. "I will have enough men here in five minutes to eat up every damn one of them!"

Daniel's troops took heart and surged forward toward the incursion, refusing their ranks at right angles to bottle up Upton's men and keep them from widening the gap. Ramseur and Cullen Battle rushed up in support, as did Walker and "Maryland" Steuart. Ewell put Robert Johnston's brigade into the breach as well, with the admonition, "Charge 'em, General! Damn 'em, charge 'em!" Now Upton's assault, which had once seemed so threatening, slowly lost its impetus. Perhaps Sedgwick's death had left a void in the chain of command. In any event Federal reinforcements for Upton were not forthcoming. Within the hour he had little choice but to retreat whence he had come, leaving at least 1,000 dead and wounded behind him.[25]

The next day saw only intermittent skirmishing and cannonading. Informed by scouts that Grant might be withdrawing to Fredericksburg, the Confederates pulled back most of their artillery from the salient's front lines at dusk so that the guns would be poised to pursue the enemy in the morning. This would be a crucial mistake. During the night it became apparent that Grant, unruffled by Upton's repulse, might be launching a second assault on the Mule Shoe. Becoming alarmed, Allegheny Johnson sent a message to Ewell urgently requesting the return of the artillery. Such were the delays in transmitting orders, however, that the bulk of the guns were just coming up to the front when the Federals attacked.

At 5 A.M. on May 12 Hancock hurled his eleven brigades against the northeast tip of the salient, the so-called "Bloody Angle," with concentrated force. Emerging at dawn from under a heavy mist, a sea of blue uniforms suddenly topped a ridge and surged toward Ewell's position. "Never have I seen such an exciting spectacle as then met my gaze," said a Louisiana officer. "As far as the eye could reach, the field was covered with the serried ranks of the enemy, marching in close columns to the attack." Wrote Porter Alexander, bemoaning the absence of the Second Corps artillery: "This column was 20 men deep & from front to rear there was probably less than 100 yards. The question at once arises how such a column would [endure] artillery fire, which would be very destructive in such masses. . . . But that can never be known." Bearing the brunt of Hancock's attack were from left to right Harry Hays's Louisianans under Colonel William Monaghan (Hays having been wounded earlier), Jim Walker's Stonewall Brigade, the slain Leroy Stafford's Louisianans under Colonel Jesse Williams, the slain "Rum" Jones's Virginians under Colonel William Witcher, and "Maryland" Steuart's mixed brigade.[26]

The Confederates swiftly found themselves overwhelmed. In the Stonewall Brigade the wetness of the morning made rifles all but useless. His men "with a practiced aim would have created havoc in [the Federal] ranks," said Walker. "But the searching damp had disarmed them, and instead of the leaping line of fire and the sharp crack of muskets came the pop! pop! pop! of exploding caps as the hammer fell upon them. Their powder was damp, and with their muzzle-loading muskets there was no help for them." Walker fell wounded, his left elbow shattered, as did William Terry, his second-in-command. The 4th, 5th, 27th and 33rd Virginia were captured almost to a man, with survivors joining with the remnants of Williams's Louisianans and Witcher's Virginians, and falling back to the limited support that Monaghan's Louisianans could offer. In the midst of the action Williams went down with a mortal wound. "All that escaped had to 'run for it,' " a member of the Stonewall Brigade allowed.

"Old Allegheny" Johnson limped along the breastworks in the hand-to-hand fighting, using his huge cane like a club and trying to rally his division, "swatting at Yankees . . . as if they were a pack of wild dogs," but to little effect. Soon he was taken prisoner. Steuart's brigade suffered fearful losses, with their commander likewise falling into enemy hands. The scene was one of bloody pandemonium. Herman Seay, a member of Steuart's 23rd Virginia, grew so frustrated by the unequal odds that he threw down his weapon and challenged one of the attackers to a no-holds-barred wrestling contest. "Damn your soul," he yelled, "put down that gun and I'll be damned if I can't throw you down!" The two men rolled in the dirt until Seay jammed his thumbs in his opponent's eyes. "I surrender!" the Yank cried. Captives and captors alike found the incident highly amusing. In the immediate wake of the assault, however, one sobering fact remained: Johnson's division had all but ceased to exist. In forty-five minutes the enemy had taken two general officers, some 2,000 men and a score of guns. Only Monaghan's Louisianans on the northwest of the salient held out. Again and again the enemy assailed their position but, one soldier said of the Tigers' grit, "those houseless, landless warriors of Louisiana . . . presented a front as firm as a ledge of rock," keeping the Union breakthrough from widening.[27]

Both Johnson and Steuart later were brought to Hancock in the rear. Johnson accepted his fate philosophically, telling his captor and fellow West Pointer, a close friend from the Old Army, "This is damn bad luck, yet I would rather have this good fortune fall to you than you than to any other man living." Steuart, like James Archer when he was captured the first day at Gettysburg, was far more irate.

"How are you, Steuart?" Hancock asked, extending his hand toward a man he knew only slightly.

"Under the circumstances, I decline to take your hand," Steuart sniffed.

"And under any other circumstances, I should not have offered it," Hancock shot back.[28]

In front of the Mule Shoe, John Brown Gordon, "with that splendid audacity that characterized him," about 6 A.M. took it upon himself to meet the Federals head-on. Now commanding Early's division under Ewell, he threw Robert Johnston's North Carolinians into the teeth of the enemy column. Johnston's brigade took heavy casualties, and he himself suffered a severe wound, but they slowed the onslaught. Rushing up Pegram's Virginians, now under Colonel John Hoffman, and his old Georgia brigade under Colonel Clement Evans, Gordon somehow formed a line of battle. One of the many minie balls whistling through the air pierced his uniform coat from side to side but only grazed his back. "General," cried an aide who was hugging his mount's neck for protection, "didn't that ball hit you?"

"No," answered the iron-willed Gordon. "But suppose my back had been in a bow like yours? Don't you see the bullet would have gone straight through my spine? Sit up or you'll be killed."

Now Lee, with the army in danger of being cut in two, arrived on the scene. "General Lee knew," said Gordon, "that nothing could rescue it except a counter-movement, quick, impetuous and decisive. As he rode majestically in front of my line of battle, with uncovered head and mounted on Old Traveler, [he] looked a very god of war." Gordon saw to his dismay that Lee himself, just as at the Wilderness, intended to lead the charge. Instantly he spurred his horse across Traveler's front, and grasped Lee's bridle in his hand.

"General Lee," he insisted, "you shall not lead my men in a charge. . . . These men behind you are Georgians, Virginians and Carolinians. They have never failed you on any field. They will not fail you here. Will you boys?"

"No! No! No!" came the cries from the ranks.

"You must go to the rear!" Gordon told his chief.

"General Lee to the rear! General Lee to the rear!" chanted the men.

The entire episode lasted no more than a few minutes but, continued Gordon, "it was a powerful factor in the rescue of Lee's army. It had lifted the soldiers to the highest plane of martial enthusiasm. . . ."

"Forward!" he bellowed and his men—less than one-third the Federals in number but with the advantage of fighting on a narrow front—fell on Hancock's column with "the fury of a cyclone."[29]

William Stringfellow of the 13th Virginia, Pegram's brigade, vividly recalled the counterattack: "Immediately in front of our brigade was a growth of old field pines. . . . It was not until we had emerged from the thicket that we saw the enemy. . . . I don't think I exaggerate when I say [they] poured a volley into our faces at not over twenty yards. It was then . . . that the 'rebel yell' rose wild and clear upon the morning air. Never pausing a second, our boys mounted the works. In a moment the blue and the gray were mixed in a dense, struggling mass." Onward Gordon's division surged toward the east of the salient. "Pistols, guns, bayonets, swords, all came into play. A lieutenant of the 52nd Virginia was just to my right, almost touching me. I saw him put a hand upon a Yankee's shoulder, ordering him to surrender. The Yankee jerked away, and making a half turn, drove his bayonet through the lieutenant's body. . . . I had a loaded revolver in my hand, and I emptied it, in many instances close enough to burn their clothing. . . . We were now, I think probably about 150 yards from [the Bloody Angle]. . . ." Here Colonel Hoffman, the brigade commander, temporarily stopped, pawing the ground with his hands.

"Are you hit?" one of his officers asked. He was looking for his spectacles, Hoffman replied. While a soldier helped him search, the rest of his men pushed on.[30]

Clement Evans's Georgians, moving on Hoffman's flank, were just as fierce in their assault. "Our brigade was very close to the place where [the enemy] broke through," he wrote his wife Allie. ". . . In order to check them I changed front of the brigade and charged them immediately with such success that I checked their advance . . . and even recovered part of the works."

Restoring the lines on the west of the salient fell to Robert Rodes's division, and initially to Dodson Ramseur's North Carolinians. A sergeant in Junius Daniel's brigade watched as Ramseur and his regiments, who "always seemed to be in the right place at the right time," double-quicked toward the enemy. "For a moment it seemed to me our brigade ceased firing and held its breath as these men went forward, apparently into the very jaws of death." Ramseur went down with a bullet in his right arm but his troops never faltered, a tribute to his training. Someone began to sing "The Bonnie Blue Flag," and others took it up. Relentlessly the North Carolinians reclaimed the ground earlier lost, pouring "a continuous storm of leaden hail into the enemy's ranks, as he slowly but stubbornly retired until he reached the line of works . . . from which he was driven at the very point of the bayonet." Refusing to leave the field Ramseur hurried in his men's wake, his arm hanging useless at his side.[31] The stalwart Junius Daniel, advancing on Ramseur's flank, about this time went down, taking a ball in the abdomen and suffering a mortal wound.

Lee fed additional brigades piecemeal into the fray. Abner Perrin, who with his Alabamians had been stationed with Billy Mahone's division on the Po River, arrived at Ewell's headquarters about 7 A.M. While waiting for orders, he told his men to lie down to avoid the random fire coming their way. Catching sight of the prone figures, Ewell began to berate the Alabamians:

"Oh boys, for God's sake don't lie down—it don't look well for a soldier to lie down in the presence of the enemy." One soldier leaped to his feet, angry over the slur. "Oh well, if you were ordered to lie down that's all right," Ewell replied. "No, General, I don't want to do anything that looks badly in a soldier," the man insisted. In short order all of Perrin's troops were on their feet and double-quicking toward the front. Close to the Bloody Angle they were caught in a withering crossfire, enduring terrible losses before they could take cover. Galloping ahead of them, Perrin was shot dead from his horse.

Nathaniel Harris and his Mississippians, likewise of Mahone's division, next came on the field. "Whose brigade is this?" Lee demanded.

"Harris's brigade," came the proud response from a dozen men.

"Where is the general?" Lee said. His face was flushed, his eyes anxious. "Never mind, I'll command this brigade myself. . . . Left face, forward, march!" he ordered, turning the column toward the sound of the guns. Harris galloped up at this point, like Gordon before him, insisting that his chief go back. Lee agreed, but only on condition that the Mississippians bridge the gap in the salient between Ramseur and Gordon. "If you will promise me to drive those people from our works, I will go back!" he cried.

"We will! We will!" the soldiers shouted.

"The morning was dark and rain was falling slowly from lowering clouds," remembered one Mississippian. "An almost impenetrable fog hovered near the surface of the ground, which with the smoke of battle, rendered it difficult to see."

Harris's men soon were scaling the high ground toward the Bloody Angle. "The breastworks were slippery with blood and rain," said one soldier, "dead bodies lying underneath half trampled out of sight." Recalled another man: "No Mardi Gras Carnival ever devised such a diabolical looking set of devils as we were. It was no imitation affair of red paint and burnt cork, but genuine human gore and gun powder smoke that came from guns belching death at close range." Harris succeeded in coming up besides Ramseur, but at hellish cost, losing one-third of his command.[32]

About 10 A.M. Lee threw one more brigade into the struggle—Samuel McGowan's South Carolinians of Wilcox's division. The troops moved forward on Harris's right, slogging through knee-deep mud. Here McGowan again was wounded. "The sight we encountered was not calculated to encourage us," one soldier would say of the disputed breastworks. "The trenches, dug on the inner side, were almost filled with water. Dead men lay on the surface of the ground. . . . The wounded bled and groaned, stretched or huddled in every attitude of pain. . . . The enemy still held the works on the right of the [Bloody Angle], and fired across the traverses. Nor were these foes easily seen. They barely raised their heads above the logs at the moment of firing. It was a case of bravery and endurance now." By noon, seven hours after the assault began, the battle was a stalemate. Yet neither side would give way. "No, sir! *We fought for this dirt, and we're going to hold it!*" summed up the sentiments of the antagonists.[33]

Hour after hour through the afternoon and night the carnage continued. The brigades of Daniel, Ramseur, Harris and McGowan under Rodes were dug in on the west; these of Hoffman, Johnston and Evans were under Gordon on the east. "Bullets came in torrents," wrote one historian. "Even the dead did duty: Often the soldiers placed the hand of a fallen comrade in such a position that, when it stiffened, it would hold their cartridges. . . . Where the bluecoats were driven out of a part of the works near the apex of the salient, they took shelter under the trench and threw bayoneted rifles over the parapet." The hand-to-hand combat became one long primal scream. "Firing into one another's faces, beating one another down with clubbed muskets, the front ranks fought across the embankment's crest almost within an arm's reach," Gordon said, "the men behind passing up to them freshly loaded rifles as their own were emptied." Nor did the breastworks offer protection. "Many were shot and stabbed through crevices and holes between the logs," explained a Union officer. "Men mounted the works, and . . . kept up a continuous fire until they were shot down, when others would take their places."

On one occasion the fighting did stop, but only because of a misunderstanding. Colonel Joseph Brown, commanding the wounded McGowan's brigade, "observed the enemy standing in our front, their colors flying and arms pointing upward. I called to them to lay down their arms and come in. An officer answered, that he was awaiting our surrender—that we had raised a white flag, whereupon he had ceased firing. I replied that 'I commanded here . . . and unless he came in, firing would be resumed.' " Stated James Caldwell of the 1st South Carolina: "A Babel of tongues succeeded—officers ordering the resumption of the firing; men calling out to the Federal line, questioning each other, imploring for the fire to be held. . . . So the two lines stood, bawling, gesticulating, arguing. . . . At length a gun was fired. . . . All of both lines joined in, and the roar of battle was renewed."[34]

Midnight came and went, with little slackening in the crash of musketry. In the darkness a massive oak tree, set squarely between the combatants, toppled to the ground. Hundreds of minie balls had cut into its 22-inch trunk as deeply as a woodsman's axe. "The water became a deeper crimson," Caldwell said of the scene. "The corpses grew more numerous. . . . Numbers of the troops sank, overpowered, into the muddy trenches and slept soundly." Though he and his comrades had no way of knowing, Lee and his engineers some three-quarters of a mile to the rear, using the 600-man remnants of Johnson's division, had been building a second line of breastworks along the Mule Shoe's base. Only at 3 A.M., after 22 hours of bloody, bestial confrontation, did the word come to fall back.[35]

———

Jeb Stuart meanwhile with just 5,000 men—Fitzhugh's two Virginia brigades under Williams Wickham and Lunsford Lomax as well as the North Carolinians of James B. Gordon—was in pursuit of Union cavalry chief Philip Sheridan, who had left the vicinity of Spotsylvania with his entire 12,000-man command to lead a raid south toward Richmond. On May 10, when Stuart crossed the North Anna River and rode into Beaver Dam Station, he beheld a sickening sight. Sheridan's 13-mile-long column had put the torch to the Confederate storehouse there hours before, destroying a million and a half rations of meat and bread, as well as the army's reserve medical supplies. Stuart reacted with bitter resolve, sending James Gordon to follow in the enemy's wake and galloping with Lee's brigades down the Telegraph Road to interpose himself between the Federals and the capital. Stopping during the night only for a few hours' sleep, Stuart reached Yellow Tavern, an abandoned roadhouse at a dusty crossroads, at 10 A.M. the next day. Riding with him was his aide Henry McClellan. "He was more quiet than usual, softer, and more communicative," McClellan remembered. "It seems now that the shadow of the near future was already upon him."

Here Stuart planned to assail Sheridan's flank as he approached Richmond, no more than a half-dozen miles away, provided its defenses were strong enough to repel the enemy's frontal attack. Dispatching McClellan to the city to find out, he put Wickham to the left of the road and Lomax on the right, dismounted, in a position that looked like an inverted L.

Before McClellan could return, the van of Sheridan's column arrived about noon at Yellow Tavern. Instead of galloping past, however, the enemy changed direction and headed straight up the Telegraph Road toward the Confederate lines. Sheridan, just as aggressive as Stuart, was more intent on destroying his rebel counterpart than raiding the capital. Initially the heaviest fighting occurred on Lomax's front, where the open fields offered little protection. Temporarily leading the brigade was Colonel Henry Clay Pate of the 5th Virginia, a fierce fighter who, through a series of misunderstandings, was on no better terms with Stuart than "Grumble" Jones had been. During a lull in the skirmishing, Jeb rode over to Pate's position to congratulate him on the skillful way he had handled the defense.

"Colonel Pate, you have done all that any man could do," he reputedly said. "How long can you hold this position?"

"Until I die, General," was the answer.

The two men then shook hands, all differences healed in the heat of battle.[36]

When the attacks resumed, Sheridan's overwhelming numbers all but guaranteed success. The enemy inexorably pushed forward, turning Pate's flanks and throwing his dismounted troopers into disorder. Pate fell with a bullet in his head even as his Virginians were huddling in the roadbed, taking enfilading fire from both sides. "The question was whether to remain in the ditch, where we were safe . . . and surrender," said one survivor, "or take the hazard of crossing that newly plowed field in front of their whole line." Like most of his comrades Leiper Robinson of the 5th Virginia chose to run the gamut. Racing for safety, he saw the man in front of him grazed by a bullet. "He yelled out and seemed to redouble his speed," Alexander said. "He left me away behind."[37]

Wickham came to the support of Lomax's troopers at this point, briefly stabilizing the situation. By 2 P.M. the Confederates were reorganized in a straight line across the Telegraph Road, awaiting Sheridan's next assault. McClellan now returned, with the news that the Richmond defenses were satisfactory and that reinforcements were being recalled from south of the James. Ever optimistic, Stuart sent off a second messenger with the request that these infantry brigades be dispatched from the city to attack Sheridan in flank. If this were done, he said to Reid Venable, another aide, "I cannot see how [the enemy] can escape." Quite soon however, the Federals under George Custer of Michigan again moved forward. "About 4 o'clock," said McClellan, "the enemy suddenly threw a brigade of cavalry, mounted, upon our extreme left, attacking our whole line at the same time. As he always did, the general hastened to where the greatest danger threatened."

Captain Gus Dorsey of the 1st Virginia takes up the story. "The enemy's charge captured our battery . . . and drove back almost the entire left. Where [I] was stationed . . . about eighty men had collected, and among these the general threw himself, and by his personal example held them steady while the enemy charged entirely past their position." Within minutes the Federals came staggering back, put to flight by a countercharge of the 1st Virginia. "Give it to them! Give it to them!" cried Stuart, emptying his pistol into the fleeing Bluecoats. "As they retired," continued Captain Dorsey, "one man who had been dismounted in the charge, and was running out on foot, turned as he passed the general . . . discharging his pistol. . . ." The shot came from point-blank range. Stuart reeled in the saddle, his plumed hat falling to the ground. The bullet had struck him in the stomach, severing blood vessels and puncturing the intestines.

"Are you wounded badly?" someone asked.

"I am afraid I am," Stuart replied, "but don't worry, boys: Fitz will do as well for you as I have done."

Even before he could be taken to the rear, Fitz Lee was at his side.

"Go ahead, Fitz, old fellow," Stuart said, turning over command. "I know you will do what is right!" These were words Lee always would remember, calling them "his most precious legacy."[38] Though the engagement that climaxed at Yellow Tavern would be a Confederate defeat, with Wickham and Lomax losing perhaps one-quarter of their commands, it blunted the impact of the Federal raid. Fitz Lee subsequently withdrew northward while Sheridan, increasingly concerned about the possibility of meeting Confederate infantry, made no serious attacks on the capital.

Even with him prostrate in the ambulance, Stuart's fighting spirit could not be quenched. Seeing some shirkers making for the rear, he shouted at them with all his remaining strength: "Go back! Go back and do your duty, as I have done mine, and our country will be safe! Go back! Go back! I had rather die than be whipped!" Later Reid Venable poured him some whiskey as a stimulant. Stuart at first refused to take it, citing his pledge to his mother years before, but Venable prevailed. "Old fellow, I know you will tell me the truth," Stuart said. "Tell me, is the death pallor on my face?" Venable made a guarded reply: "I hope not; there is some flush on your forehead."

Stuart's wound would be mortal. He spent the next day at a relative's home in Richmond, asking to see Flora and enduring recurring spasms of pain. Before delirium set in, he disposed of some personal effects. "I wish you to take one of my horses and Venable the other," he told McClellan. "Which is the heavier rider?"

The aide answered that Venable was. "Then let Venable have the gray," said the peerless cavalryman, "and you take the bay." Stuart had been carrying a small Confederate flag in his hat, the gift of a woman from Columbia, South Carolina. "The flag should be returned to her," he instructed McClellan. His spurs he had promised to a woman in Shepherdstown, Virginia. His sword should go to his son. As the aide was leaving, Jefferson Davis arrived. "General, how do you feel?" he inquired.

"Easy, but willing to die," Stuart answered, "if God and my country think I have fulfilled my destiny and done my duty."

Just after 7 P.M. everyone in the house gathered at his bedside. Flora and the children would not arrive for hours, too late to see him alive. Episcopal prayers were intoned, and Stuart's favorite hymn, "Rock of Ages," was sung. "God's will be done," were his last words.

In the midst of the horror of the Bloody Angle, Lee learned by telegram of Stuart's fall. "Gentlemen," he said to his officers, barely controlling his emotions. "We have very bad news. General Stuart has been mortally wounded." Then he added, almost to himself: "*He never brought me a piece of false information!*" Later he would say of his surrogate son: "I can scarcely think of him without weeping."[39]

From May 14 to 17, while Ewell solidified his new defensive line at the base of the Mule Shoe, Grant and Meade slowly shifted the bulk of their troops to the Fredericksburg Road and the right of the Confederate perimeter. Then, thinking that Lee had weakened his center to shadow the movement, Grant on May 18 unwisely ordered Hancock's Second Corps and Horatio Wright's Sixth Corps (Wright replacing Sedgwick) back to the Bloody Angle to duplicate their assault of six days earlier.

This time Armistead Long and the 30 guns of the Second Corps were ready for them. "About 8 A.M. attention was attracted to the commotion of the enemy in and near the old deserted works, apparently about to advance," said Major Wilfrid Cutshaw, one of Long's battalion heads. "All were astonished at this and could not believe a serious attempt would be made to assail such a line. . . . So when it was found that an assault was to be made, it was welcomed by the Confederates as a chance to pay off old scores." Solid shot first greeted the Federal infantry as they "stepped out rapidly with their muskets at 'right shoulder shift' in successive lines, apparently several brigades deep, well aligned and steady . . . a most magnificent and thrilling sight." Case shot or shrapnel then rained on them at midrange, "tearing great gaps in their ranks." Canister finally came into use at 300 yards "and under this fire of combined canister and case he could not stand, and broke in confusion, leaving the field in disorder." In less than thirty minutes, some 12,000 infantrymen were driven from the field with heavy losses by artillery alone. Confederate casualties were negligible.

Meade was sickened by the repulse. "We found the enemy so strongly entrenched," he said, "that even Grant thought it useless to knock our heads against a brick wall. . . ." Earlier the Union general-in-chief had written Chief of Staff Henry Halleck: "I propose to fight it out on this line if it takes all summer." Then he added: "I am satisfied that the enemy are very shaky, and are only kept up to the mark by the greatest exertion on the part of their officers." Grant's determination was commendable, but he was underestimating the Army of Northern Virginia. "Fragments of broken iron are welded closest and strongest in the hottest fires," said John Brown Gordon. "So the shattered corps of Lee's army seemed to be welded together by Grant's hammering— by the blood and sweat and fury of the flames that swept over and around them."[40]

The next day brought the last of the clashes at Spotsylvania. Worried that Grant again was sidestepping his right and moving toward Richmond, Lee sent Ewell around the enemy's right to reconnoiter. Before the Wilderness the Second Corps had boasted 12,000 muskets; now it had perhaps half that number. Rodes's division led the way, with Ramseur's North Carolinians in the van, then Cullen Battle's Alabamians and the slain Junius Daniel's North Carolinians under Colonel Bryan Grimes. Next came Gordon's division, with his old Georgia brigade under Clement Evans, the Louisianans consolidated into one brigade, the pitiful remnants of Johnson's division, finally the wounded John Pegram's Virginians under Colonel John Hoffman.

About 3 P.M. Ewell, courting disaster by moving without artillery to speed his progress, blundered into elements of Hancock's corps. Ramseur, seeing that the Federals on his front were so strong that to await attack "would cause disaster," ordered a charge that "drove the enemy rapidly and at great loss." His attack, however, only delayed the inevitable. Union weight of numbers, plus the lack of cannon, left Ewell exposed to a series of flanking maneuvers. With darkness coming on, the timely arrival of Wade Hampton and his battery of horse artillery provided much-needed support, permitting the Confederates to disengage.[41]

Ewell had delayed Grant's departure for the North Anna River by twenty-four hours, but he had paid for it with 900 additional casualties. Overall at Spotsylvania the North suffered some 18,000 casualties; the South, 11,000, of whom 4,600 were prisoners. Allegheny Johnson and Steuart had been captured, and nine brigadiers and a comparable number of regimental commanders killed or wounded. Though Grant could replace these losses, Lee could not. His army was being bled to death.

# THREE

\* \* \* \*

# DREWRY'S BLUFF
# AND NEW MARKET

On May 5, even as Meade's Army of the Potomac was about to assail Heth and Wilcox on the Orange Plank Road in the Wilderness, Major General Benjamin Butler's 40,000-man Army of the James steamed up from Fort Monroe to land at Bermuda Hundred, the peninsula formed by the convergence of the James and Appomattox Rivers. This was the second stage of Grant's master plan: to place a force in Lee's rear that would threaten both Richmond and Petersburg, and disrupt the rail and supply lines between the two cities and the Carolinas. From their new base the Federals were just fifteen miles south of the capital and seven miles north of Petersburg, and just three miles from the railroads. The area, moreover, was virtually defenseless. Richmond was garrisoned by four infantry brigades under Robert Ransom, Petersburg by a single regiment, and Pierre Beauregard—newly named to command south of the James—had been taken sick and was still in Charleston.

Luckily for the Confederates Butler, who had earned the sobriquet "Beast" for his treatment of Southern women during the occupation of New Orleans, was as incompetent a general as he was influential a politician. Though Lincoln had long wanted to ease him out of the military, his connections had saved him.

Serving Jefferson Davis in Richmond as chief military advisor, meanwhile, was Braxton Bragg. This was the same post Lee had held the first year of the war, and Bragg here was in his element, proving himself far better at staff work than in providing field leadership. Despite his best efforts to move up troops from the Carolinas by rail, however, no more than 600 South Carolinians of Johnson Hagood's brigade, Colonel Robert Graham commanding, were available to meet the van of Butler's advance the afternoon of May 6. So fierce was their resistance, however, that they repulsed not just one but two sorties. By the next morning, when Graham was joined by Bushrod Johnson's Tennesseans, who had recently been posted to the Richmond garrison, and more of Hagood's brigade, the defenders totaled some 2,700. With them was the exiled Harvey Hill, who had volunteered his services to Beauregard, and whose combat expertise would prove invaluable.

For the next five days, the tentative Butler contented himself with quick raids inland to tear up railroad track and cut telegraph lines. Instead of marching out in force from Bermuda Hundred, he spent the bulk of his time constructing elaborate breastworks across the base of the Peninsula, fortifications in view of his strength that he did not need. The Confederates used this grace period to build up their own works and further reinforce their troops. Not until May 12, during the desperate hours of fighting for the Bloody Angle at Spotsylvania, did Butler begin moving toward Richmond. Barring his way were the works at Drewry's Bluff, whose guns in 1862 had prevented Union warships from steaming up the James to shell the capital. Here the bulk of the defense, in desultory skirmishing under constant rain, initially was provided by the men of Hoke's division, just arrived from North Carolina via Petersburg. On May 14 Beauregard came on the scene, bringing with him Alfred Colquitt's two brigades.

No sooner had the Louisianan assumed command than he once again, as in the halcyon days after First Manassas, bombarded Jefferson Davis and the War Department with his views on grand strategy, proposing that the beleaguered Lee disengage from Grant, fall back to the defenses of Richmond and send him 15,000 men. Then with some 30,000 muskets in all, he said, "I would attack Butler's right flank, separate him from his base at Bermuda Hundred . . . thus obtaining an easy victory over him." Simultaneously he would move up Chase Whiting's division from Petersburg to fall on Butler's rear and "insure his unconditional surrender." Later, continued Beauregard, he would cross the James to attack Grant on the flank while Lee sallied forth from the city to take him in front. "Bragg, circumstances have thrown the fate of the Confederacy in your hands and mine," he reportedly said. "Let us play our parts boldly and fearlessly! Issue those orders and I'll carry them out to the best of my ability. I'll guarantee success!"[1]

How Lee was safely to disengage from the tenacious Grant was left unexplained. Dryly commented Bragg: "The retreat of General Lee, a distance of 60 miles, from the immediate front of a superior force, with no less than 8,000 of the enemy's cavalry between him and the Chickahominy to retard his movement, at least endangered the safety of his army if it did not involve its destruction." In a face-to-face meeting at Drewry's Bluff, Davis told Beauregard that, while the prospect of getting help from Lee was not practical, he would augment his command with Robert Ransom's division from Richmond. The Louisianan was ordered to march out from Drewry's Bluff and attack Butler in front, while Whiting moved up from Petersburg and took him in rear.[2]

Beauregard for the most part took the rejection of his plan manfully. He took care to point out, however, that his scraped-together troops lacked cohesion ("The moral force . . . which springs from old association was entirely wanting") and that some of his officers, while serving in the Army of Northern Virginia, likewise had been found wanting. Hoke and Ransom were capable men; there were uncertainties about others. Nonetheless Beauregard quickly drew up his order of battle. Heading his three divisions were the North Carolinians Hoke and Ransom and the Georgian Colquitt. Hoke's background and his triumph at Plymouth we have just explored. Ransom, who was subject to illness, had served under Lee until Fredericksburg, later gone to Tennessee and now come back to defend the capital. Colquitt, the Princeton-educated lawyer who had been dilatory during Jackson's flanking attack at Chancellorsville, had been posted in the Carolinas and Florida.

Hoke's division at Drewry's Bluff consisted of Montgomery Corse's Virginians, Thomas Clingman's North Carolinians, Bushrod Johnson's Tennesseans and Johnson Hagood's South Carolinians. He also commanded the 3rd North Carolina Cavalry and the Washington Artillery. Corse, an Alexandria banker who had been severely wounded at Sharpsburg, had been with Longstreet at Chickamauga. Clingman, a former U.S. senator who had graduated first in his class at the University of North Carolina, had been posted to the coastal defenses. Bushrod Johnson, we have seen, had fought with distinction in Tennessee. Hagood, a graduate of The Citadel and a lawyer, had been serving in Charleston.

Ransom's unit was comprised of Archibald Gracie's Alabamians, James Kemper's old Virginia brigade under William Richard Terry (not to be confused with William Terry, the last commander of the Stonewall Brigade), the slain Armistead's Virginia brigade under Colonel Birkett Fry, and Hoke's old North Carolina brigade under Colonel William Lewis. Gracie, who was born in New York City and educated in Germany, had been serving in Tennessee, where his conduct had been bold and zealous. William Richard Terry, a V.M.I. graduate and businessman, had just recovered from a wound incurred in Pickett's Charge. Birkett Fry, a lawyer slight in build but "of gunpowder reputation," he who had been dismissed from West Point for failing mathematics, had been wounded for the fourth time at Gettysburg. Lewis, a railroad engineer, most recently had been with Lee at Gettysburg, Bristoe Station and Mine Run, and then with Hoke at Plymouth.

Colquitt's minidivision had only two brigades: the Georgians of his own command and the North Carolinians of Robert Ransom's older brother Matt, a lawyer, planter and legislator.[3]

---

On May 16, with Lee still tied down at Spotsylvania, Beauregard launched his attack. Ransom shortly before 5 A.M. advanced on the left in a dense fog, intent on turning Butler and cutting him off from his base at Bermuda Hundred. Hoke was to demonstrate on the right, with Colquitt constituting the reserve in the center. Ransom initially was successful, pushing back the enemy while capturing a brigadier and taking some 400 prisoners. Then the fog wreaked its havoc, creating confusion in his ranks and forcing him to stop and re-form his lines. Hoke meanwhile came under heavy pressure, with the Federals driving a wedge between the two divisions, for "on his front the enemy had been allowed to mass his forces by the inaction on the left." Colquitt filled the gap, but the result was stalemate. "Ransom," said Beauregard, "not only reported the enemy in strong force in his front, but expressed the opinion that the safety of his command could be compromised by an advance."[4]

Whiting's assault on Butler's rear now became imperative. "Press on and press over everything in your front," Beauregard wired him at 9 A.M., "and the day will be complete." Whiting's command consisted of Henry Wise's Virginia and James Martin's North Carolina brigades, plus James Dearing's Georgia and North Carolina cavalry. The 58-year-old Wise, the former Virginia governor who had clashed with Lee in western Virginia in 1862, had been on coastal duty in South Carolina. Martin, a West Pointer and lawyer who had lost his right arm in the Mexican War, had been instrumental in raising and training North Carolina troops for the Confederacy. Dearing, only 24, was a cavalryman of conspicuous valor and energy.

The brutal fighting continued for hours, but still Whiting did not appear. By 1:30 P.M., with Davis looking on, Beauregard was becoming edgy. The sound of gunfire from the South cheered him temporarily, but it soon faded away. Then from a courier Beauregard learned that "I need not rely on any advance being made that day by General Whiting." The gunfire had resulted when Dearing, "impatient at his commander's tardiness to obey my orders . . . had encountered the enemy's pickets . . . and had gallantly driven them in. . . ." By 4 P.M. Beauregard felt he had no choice but to break off the engagement. Under cover of night the Federals subsequently retreated behind their works across the neck of Bermuda Hundred. "We had defeated Butler and forced him to take refuge within his fortified lines," Beauregard said. "The communications south and west of Richmond were restored. . . . But though unable for the present to do us any harm—though hemmed in, or 'bottled up,' as was said of him—he was nonetheless there. . . . We could and should have done more. We could and should have captured Butler's entire army."[5] During the Drewry's Bluff campaign the Federals lost 4,160 out of 15,800 troops engaged; the Confederates, 2,500 out of 18,000.

What *had* happened to Whiting, the Mississippian whose arrogance years before had so angered Davis? With Harvey Hill at his side directing the advance, he had on May 16 started Wise's and Martin's brigades toward Dre-wry's Bluff, driving in the enemy pickets and making substantial progress. Then unaccountably, much to Hill's dismay, he ordered a halt and a with-drawal, saying he feared leaving Petersburg unprotected. Later he would have no memory of having given these instructions.

Turning back to Petersburg created a logjam of monumental proportions on the turnpike, leaving Whiting's command vulnerable to cavalry assaults. Seeing this, Hill at midday galloped up with a warning.

"What ought I to do?" Whiting asked him.

"I wrote you two hours ago," Hill answered angrily, "to press the Yan-kees."

"I did not receive your note," Whiting replied.

Hill at this point threw up his hands. "Fearing that General Whiting might be embarrassed by the seeming divided responsibility of my presence," he said, "and feeling that I could accomplish nothing more, I retired. . . ."

Back at Petersburg, Whiting at 3 A.M. the next day received a dispatch from Beauregard ordering him once again to Drewry's Bluff. When his troops moved out, however, they were not under his command, but under Hill's. "I having re-linquished [command] to him," said Whiting, "in consequence of the dissatis-faction expressed by Generals Wise and Martin with my movements . . . deeming that harmony of action was to be preferred at that time to any personal consideration, and feeling—as indeed I had felt for twenty-four hours—phys-ically unfit for action."[6]

Some people ascribed Whiting's erratic behavior on May 16 to his being drunk. This was the view of General Wise, who was with him several times that day. But the outspoken Hill, who likewise observed him firsthand, saw no evidence of intoxication. Nor did Whiting's aide, who had been constantly in his presence. Perhaps the best explanation is the most obvious one: Whiting had been thrust into a combat role after two uneventful years in the coastal defenses at Wilmington, and had been four days largely without sleep. Stress had taken its toll.

To Union Major General Franz Sigel in mid-May fell the task of carrying out the third stage of Grant's strategy: uprooting the Confederates from the Shen-andoah Valley, which provided them both with a route into Maryland and Pennsylvania and an abundant source of produce and livestock. Sigel, a former revolutionary leader in Germany and a hero among German immigrants, led some 9,000 troops up the Valley toward New Market at the southern end of the Massanuttens. Opposing him with 5,600 men was John C. Breckinridge of Kentucky, a spellbinding orator who had been vice president in the James Buchanan administration and had finished second to Lincoln in the 1860 elec-toral college voting. You must meet Sigel and rout him, Lee had told Breck-inridge. Outnumbered two-to-one by Grant in the Wilderness and at

Spotsylvania, he could not risk another enemy attacking his left through New Market Gap in the Blue Ridge Mountains.

Breckinridge had been fighting with distinction in the West, most recently at Chickamauga and Chattanooga. Clean shaven except for a handlebar mustache, he was a charismatic presence. "I knew him as intimately as a boy from 17 to 20 could know a man," said one of his aides, "and I can say . . . he was the truest, greatest man I was ever thrown in contact with." Leading his two Virginia infantry brigades were John Echols and Gabriel Wharton. Echols, a V.M.I. graduate and Harvard-trained lawyer who stood six-foot-four and weighed some 260 pounds, had been severely wounded while serving under Jackson at Kernstown. Plagued with a heart condition, he nonetheless soldiered on. The full-bearded Wharton, likewise a V.M.I. graduate, came from a family with a long military tradition. Posted to the command, though not expected to serve on the front lines, were the 247 untested cadets of the Virginia Military Institute itself, whose average age was just 18. With their clean gray uniforms and their cadenced march, led by a fifer playing "The Girl I Left Behind Me," they were the objects of much ragging from the grizzled veterans.[7]

Skirmishing between the two sides broke out in earnest during May 13 and 14. Informed that the enemy was approaching New Market by John Imboden, now the Valley District's chief of cavalry, Breckinridge soon realized that Sigel had allowed his superior force to become strung out, making it vulnerable. Early in the morning on May 15 he resolved to go on the attack, marching straight up the Valley Pike toward the village. His left would be protected by the North Fork of the Shenandoah, his right by the marshy ground around Smith's Creek. To be doubly sure about his right flank, he sent Imboden there with the 18th Virginia Cavalry and a 6-gun battery of horse artillery. Wharton was on the west of the pike, Echols on the east, with the cadets in reserve. "Young gentlemen," Breckinridge said, "I hope there will be no occasion to use you, but if there is, I trust you will do your duty."

When the infantry reached the outskirts of New Market, Imboden rode forward on the flank through some woodland to reconnoiter. "I was rewarded," he said, "by the discovery of Sigel's entire cavalry force massed in very close order in the fields beyond the woods." He swept his command down Smith's Creek and unlimbered his horse artillery in record time. "The guns were rapidly worked, whilst my cavalry kept on down the creek as if aiming to get in the enemy's rear. The effect was magical. The first discharge of the guns threw [Sigel's] whole body of cavalry into confusion." With Breckinridge and Major William McLaughlin's guns assailing his front and Imboden and J.R. McClanahan's horse artillery on his flank, Sigel had little choice but to fall back. "The town was thus passed by our troops," Imboden continued, "and a little after noon McLaughlin occupied the ground on which the enemy's batteries had been planted the day before."[8]

Breckinridge paused to regroup, then once more pushed Wharton and Echols forward. Sensing the battle would be decided by cannon, he bunched together most of his artillery, personally supervising the firing of the guns. Initially the infantry encountered little opposition. Then about 2:45 P.M. at Bushong's Farm, under violent thunderstorms and blistering enemy cannonades, Wharton's lines on the west of the pike began to crumble. First the 51st and the 30th Virginia were riddled by Federal canister, later the 62nd Virginia under George H. Smith. Five of the 62nd's color-bearers went down in the space of a few minutes, as did some 100 of his 448 men. Puffing his pipe in the midst of the maelstrom Smith fell back, telling his troop to take cover wherever they could. "The fire," wrote a survivor, "was the hottest I was ever under." Private B. Orndorf in Company B was stooping over to reload when a ball passed between his legs, branding the inside of his thighs. He collapsed in pain, kicking his heels and screaming that he had been killed. His comrade F.D. Kildow grabbed him by the ankles, holding him until the pain eased. Orndorf picked himself up and resumed firing, with Kildow chiding him that he made "a hell of a fuss for a dead man."[9]

With the gap in Wharton's lines widening, the situation on the whole front looked grim. To prevent disaster, the hole had to be plugged. One of Breckinridge's aides galloped up, urging him to commit the V.M.I. cadets. At first he demurred, saying, "I cannot expose them to such a fire as our center will receive."

"The Federals are right on us," the aide persisted. "If the cadets are ordered up, we can close the gap."

Breckinridge hesitated a long moment. "Put the boys in," he finally said, "and may God forgive me for the order."

Led by Scott Ship, their 24-year-old commandant, the cadets double-quicked into the breach. Near the Bushong farmhouse the first of many shells fell in their ranks, killing two and leaving a third writhing on the ground, clutching tufts of grass in his agony. Bullets claimed many others. Private Robert Cousins, using the house for cover, remembered that the thud of Federal minie balls made "a sounding board upon its sides." Once the cadets were past the house and into the fields, casualties mounted. Private Thomas G. Jefferson was hit in the stomach. When comrades tried to help him, he waved them away, pointing toward the front. "That is the place for you!" he shouted. "You can do me no good!" Soon the gap was closed. Now the question was: Could the Confederates hold their ground?[10]

Sigel at this point made a classic mistake. Instead of hurling himself on Wharton's weakened lines he sent some 2,000 cavalrymen under Julius Stahel, another German-American immigrant, against Echols on the east of the pike. Here Breckinridge's artillery turned the tables on the enemy. Firing double canister, his cannon decimated the charging horsemen. The 22nd Virginia, led by Colonel George S. Patton, not only held but advanced, restoring momentum to the assault. "Every gun of the enemy was made effective by his use of the smooth ground," said a Union cavalryman, "and by rapid maneuvering an enfilading fire was kept up most of the time." Wrote one of Patton's soldiers with quiet satisfaction: "It was a hard battle, but we routed them." Stahel seemed bewildered by his setback. "Mein Gott, General Sigel," he asked. "Vare ish mein cavalrie?"

Back on Wharton's front at the Bushong farm the Confederates, given precious minutes to regroup, likewise advanced, with Wharton himself leading a company of the 51st Virginia up the sloping ground in the charge. Conspicuous once more in the assault were the cadets. "It made our hearts leap," said one eyewitness, "to see [them] move forward. . . . Their step was as steady as the tread of veteran soldiers. They never faltered. . . ." With bullets flying past, Charles Randolph shouted some advice: "There's no use dodging, boys. If a ball's going to hit you, it'll hit you anyway." Then a bullet tore through his body. Cadet Frank Gibson suffered four wounds within seconds. One shattered his leg, another hit his thigh, a third passed through his cheek, and a fourth severed two fingers from a hand. John Upshur took a bullet in the leg, then tried to keep his place in line using his rifle as a crutch. "Come on, Upshur, close up!" some told him. "No lagging in C Company today!"[11]

General Imboden continues the story. "There was one six-gun battery on elevated ground west of the turnpike that was particularly destructive . . . and Breckinridge decided to dislodge or capture it." Smith's 62nd Regiment and the cadets were given the task. "It so happened that when they got to within 300 yards of the battery, they had to cross a deep rocky gulch. . . . The boys from the Military Institute were more agile and ardent than Smith's veterans, and got out [of it] first." In short order the cadets put the artillerymen to flight, capturing a 12-pound cannon. "A wild yell went up when a Cadet mounted a caisson and waved the Institute flag over it," said Imboden. "The battery was taken, but at fearful cost."

Now Wharton's entire command was on the crest of the slope, turning the high ground to their advantage and pouring down fire on the fleeing enemy. Though the fighting continued the rest of the day, the battle to all intents was over. Federal casualties were some 840; Confederate, 530. The cadets lost 55 men, almost one-quarter of their number. Thereafter Breckinridge was never able to speak of them without tears coming to his eyes. Imboden about 5 P.M. sought him out. "[Breckinridge] was soon found at about 100 yards in rear of McLaughlin's guns, on foot and muddy to the waist," said Imboden. "He had been much of the time off his horse during the day, mingling with and cheering his brave, tired, hungry, drenched and muddy infantry and artillery. . . ."[12]

Seldom would such a small triumph have a more significant effect. Lee was much relieved, wiring Breckinridge his congratulations. Not only did the victory enable him to preserve his lines against Grant, but it ensured that the Valley's crops could be harvested over the next few weeks, providing his army with food. Combined with Beauregard's bottling up of Butler at Bermuda Hundred, this action in the Shenandoah would substantially prolong the war.

# NORTH ANNA TO COLD HARBOR

Seeing that Grant was again sidestepping his right and moving to the south-east, Lee with some 53,000 men fell back from Spotsylvania on May 21 to the North Anna River near Hanover Junction, arriving there the next day. Powell Hill, returning from sick leave, commanded the Third Corps on the left of the line, facing Horatio Wright's Sixth and Gouverneur Warren's Fifth Corps. Dick Anderson's First Corps held the center, opposite Ambrose Burnside's Ninth Corps, while Ewell's Second Corps, its commander in ever-failing health, was on the right against Winfield Scott Hancock's Second Corps. Noting that he was now within cooperating distance of Beauregard, Lee was eager to go on the offense. "General Grant's army will be in the field, strengthened by all available troops . . . and it seems to me our best policy to unite upon it," he wrote Davis. "I should be very glad to have the aid of General Beauregard in such a blow." Worn out though they were, his men remained optimistic. A member of the 45th Georgia, Bryan Grimes's brigade, wrote that he and his comrades "all look very much like a horse after a week's hard driving on the shortest kind of rations," but added, "I believe this campaign to be the decisive one, and know we are going to whip the detestable enemy." Commented a sergeant in the 7th North Carolina, James Lane's brigade: "Grant was badly whipped at the Wilderness and Spotsylvania . . . and if he still desires to fight, he can be accommodated. . . ."[1]

On May 23 the engagement nonetheless began badly for the Confederates, with the enemy pushing across the river on their left at Jericho Mills and their right at Telegraph Bridge. "Why did you not do as Jackson would have done—thrown your whole force upon those people and driven them back?" Lee would ask Hill in a stinging rebuke. Proud officer though he was, Hill chose not to answer. In his eyes the commanding general could do no wrong. That night Lee called his key people together to announce an ingenious defensive strategy. He reshaped his lines into an inverted V whose tip was fixed at Ox Ford, the crossing he still held. One side of the V rested on the Little River, the other on a bend in the North Anna, anchoring his flanks. Grant and Meade had unwittingly split their 68,000-man force into three pieces: one at Jericho Ford on the south bank, the second at Ox Ford on the north bank, the third at Telegraph Bridge on the south bank. Lee planned to hold the enemy at two points with token strength while falling on and crushing the third with most of his command.

Before the conference broke up, he was interrupted by a teamster loudly berating a mule, whacking him for emphasis. "Gen. Lee could stand anything better than having an animal maltreated," said Porter Alexander. "He hesitated a moment in his speech & gave that peculiar little shake of his head which he used when he was worried, & which we used to call snapping at his ear." The teamster's whacking of the mule only intensified. "Gen. Lee stopped his discourse, snapped at his ear a time or two, & then shouted out in a tone which I thought would scare anybody, 'What are you beating that mule for?' "

Not realizing it was Lee who had cried out and thinking he was being taunted, the teamster responded in kind, yelling back in a sneering voice, "Is this any of you-r-r mule?" Concluded Alexander, "Not one of us dared to crack a smile. The general snapped at his ear a time or two, & then apparently determined to finish with us first, before making good his claim to the mule. I have no doubt he did this as soon as we were gone."[2]

Lee's plan to fall on Grant's divided army on May 24 never came to fruition. The afternoon found him racked with severe dysentery, confined to his tent and prostrated by his illness. "In the midst of his operations on the North Anna," his aide Charles Venable said, "he succumbed to sickness, against which he had struggled for some days. As he lay in his tent, he would say, in his impatience, 'We must strike them! We must never let them pass us again! We must strike them!' He had reports brought to him constantly from the field. But Lee ill in his tent was not Lee at the front." With Jackson dead and Longstreet wounded, the commanding general had no subordinate who could assume his mantle. Ewell was failing; Hill could be quixotic; Anderson was too untested. Lee did not even try to name a leader to take his place during his sickness, and none of his corps commanders volunteered. This is not to say, of course, that these men lacked enterprise. They and the next level of officers under them—Joseph Kershaw and Charles Field of Anderson's corps, Jubal Early, Robert Rodes and John Brown Gordon of Ewell's, Billy Mahone and Marcellus Wilcox of Hill's—all these men but Ewell would make their contributions in the months to come.[3]

The stalemate at the North Anna continued for the next two days, with Lee unable to leave his bed and the Federals slowly withdrawing across the river and digging in on the far bank. Then Grant sidestepped around his right for the fourth consecutive time, moving south and crossing the Pamunkey River some dozen miles from Richmond. Ewell had anticipated the tactic. "We are still in juxtaposition with the Yankees," he wrote Lizinka, "mutually watching, they entrenched so strongly as to make it impossible to attack any part of their lines . . . while they are equally afraid to . . . come against us. This will probably continue until they take advantage of darkness to [pass] our flank. . . . We are getting too near Richmond for this to continue much more. . . ." Barely was Lee back on his feet when Ewell came down with equally severe dysentery, enabling Lee to name Early corps commander in his stead. In turn, Dodson Ramseur took over Early's division.[4]

Meeting the van of the Federal advance across the Pamunkey on May 28 were Confederate cavalry under Wade Hampton. No successor to Stuart had yet been named officially, but he was the senior of the three division heads, given that his commission predated both Fitz Lee's and Rooney Lee's. The strapping, 46-year-old Hampton was fifteen years older than Stuart and he had none of his flamboyance, but his thick muscles and superb coordination made him something of a genetic marvel, and his calmness belied a warrior's spirit. "It was said that his coolness amounted to a defect in a cavalry leader, that he wanted the dash, rush and impetus which this branch of the service demands," said John Esten Cooke, who rode with him, "[but] Hampton was sufficiently headlong when I saw him . . . and certainly seemed to have a natural turn for going in front of his column with a drawn sabre." The Federal cavalry under Sheridan was now for the most part armed with breech-loading repeating carbines. To counter this advantage Hampton—while not abandoning in the slightest the pleasures of slash-and-thrust charges, picketing and reconnaissance—trained his own troopers to fight dismounted. On foot their muzzle loaders became an asset, hurling heavier bullets greater distances with lethal accuracy.

Hampton's own division consisted of Calbraith Butler's South Carolinians, Pierce Young's Georgians and Thomas Rosser's Virginians. Each of these men was 28 years old, six feet tall, handsome, battle-scarred, a hard swearer and on occasion a hard drinker. Rosser had been a West Pointer, resigning before graduation to join the Confederacy; Butler and Young, like Hampton, were self-taught in the art of war. Riding with Butler and Rosser this day on the Pamunkey were Williams Wickham's Virginians of Fitz Lee's division. The 44-year-old Wickham, a lawyer and plantation owner, had been fighting since Williamsburg.

The cavalry of the two armies met at Enon's Church, a short distance west of Haw's Shop, where the action raged inconclusively from 10 A.M. to sunset. Hampton's men fought dismounted in the thick woodland, using their heavy Enfield rifles, which had an effective range of 1,000 yards, to devastating effect. So heavy was their fire, in fact, that Sheridan thought they were infantry. While not as large an encounter as the battle at Brandy Station and Fleetwood Hill, it was just as fierce. Killed during the contest was Private John Huff of Michigan, the man who had shot Stuart at Yellow Tavern seventeen days before. "Up to this time the Cavalry Corps had not learned the style of their new commander," said one of Rosser's officers, "but now they discovered a vast difference between the old and the new, for while General Stuart would attempt his work with whatever force he had at hand, and often seemed to try to accomplish a given result with the smallest number of men, Gen. Hampton always endeavored to carry every available man to his point of operation, and the larger his force, the better he liked it."⁵

For the next three days Lee dug in behind Totopotomoy Creek, blocking the enemy from the capital. Ever aggressive, he even went on the attack on May 30, sending Jubal Early and the Second Corps toward Bethesda Church. There Ramseur, in his first engagement as a division head, proved more eager than wise. Despite Early's reservations he insisted on charging what he thought was a single Federal artillery piece, but turned out to be a battery. The wounded John Pegram's brigade, under Colonel Edward Willis, led the way. One of his regimental commanders was Lieutenant Colonel Charles Christian of the 49th Virginia, who since the current campaign began had lost nine color-bearers. Now he had to choose another.

"Will you carry the colors?" he asked a lanky, beardless youngster named John Orndorff.

"Yes, Colonel, I will," Orndorff said. "They killed my brother . . . now damn them let them kill me too."

Willis's advance began about 6 P.M. Exposing themselves with reckless courage, the Confederates walked into a hail of fire. "Our line melted away as if by magic," said Colonel Christian. "Every brigade, staff and field officer was cut down, mostly killed outright, in an incredibly short time." Led by color-bearer Orndorff, the 49th Virginia plunged on. "We crossed that field of carnage and mounted the parapet of the enemy's works and poured a volley in their faces," continued Christian. "They gave way, but two lines of battle, close in their rear, rose and each delivered a volley into our ranks in rapid succession. . . . Our line already decimated was almost annihilated." A cannon blast struck Orndorff at point-blank range. "His [cap] flew up ten feet, one arm went up one way, the other another—fragments of his flesh were dashed in our faces."

The affair at Bethesda Church soon ended. Casualties on the Confederate side totaled some 1,150; on the Federal, some 730. Colonel Christian was wounded and captured. Colonel Willis, a favorite of Lee, was mortally wounded. "I am no more afraid to die than I was to go into battle," he whispered on his deathbed. Early's report was more notable for what it did not say than what it did. "Colonel Edward Willis . . . was sent forward with one of Rodes's brigades on its right to feel the enemy, and ascertain his strength; but meeting with a heavy force behind breastworks, it was compelled to retire, with the loss of some valuable officers and men. . . ."[6]

On June 1 Grant and Meade would make their final sidestep, moving several miles southeast to Old Cold Harbor, the strategically important crossroads where Jackson had marched and countermarched during the Seven Days. Lee would shift with them, setting the stage for the campaign's climatic battle. Meanwhile he had learned that Union General William F. "Baldy" Smith and the Eighteenth Corps, some 16,000 men, had been detached from Butler's bottled-up position at Bermuda Hundred, sailing down the James and up the York and the Pamunkey to bolster Grant's ranks. For weeks Lee, still not the commanding general of the Confederates but their de facto leader, had been imploring Beauregard for help. Now he desperately needed it. He had received some reinforcements, notably Breckinridge's two brigades and George Pickett's four understrength brigades—perhaps some 6,000 men in all—but he was still vastly outnumbered. Yet Beauregard, with consummate bureaucratic skill, was loath to give up any troops. Lee made one more plea. Back came the Louisianan's bland answer: "War Department must determine when and what troops to order from here. I send to General Bragg all information I receive relative to movement of enemy's troops in my front. Have you been attacked today?"

Lee had no choice but to wire the president: "General Beauregard says the Department must determine what troops to send for him. . . . The result of this delay will be disaster. Butler's troops (Smith's Corps) will be with Grant tomorrow. Hoke's Division, at least, should be with me by light tomorrow."[7] This blunt statement, unlike any Lee had ever made to Davis, sent off shock waves in Richmond. The word "disaster," not softened with any qualifications, roiled the War Department, with the result that Beauregard was ordered to send Hoke and his 7,000-man division to Lee immediately. Even before he received the wire, however, Beauregard came to his senses, informing Davis that he was rushing Hoke to Lee's support.

Though there was hard fighting in the interval, resulting in the death and wounding, respectively, of the experienced brigadiers George Doles of Georgia and James Lane of North Carolina, Grant did not lower his head and launch his main assault until June 3 at 4:30 A.M. He had some 108,000 troops, the Confederates some 59,000. Lee's breastworks stretched for six miles, with the Chickahominy at his back and Richmond only ten miles away. "Breastworks," however, might be too misleading a term. They were for the most part only mounds of earth some four feet high and three to five feet thick, without ditches or other obstructions. What made them formidable were the resolute men behind them. "It was a very thin gray line . . . back of a thin red line of clay," recounted one rebel. "But these lines stuck together very hard, and were very hard indeed to separate." Harry Heth's division of the Third Corps was on the extreme left, separate from the rest of Hill's command. Early's Second Corps, with Rodes's, Ramseur's and Gordon's divisions, held the left, facing Burnside and Warren. Anderson's First Corps anchored the center, opposite Baldy Smith. Hoke's division and Breckinridge's brigades were to Anderson's right, across from Horatio Wright. Hill and his remaining divisions, those of Mahone and Wilcox, were on the far right facing Hancock.[8]

Union Generals Baldy Smith, Wright and Hancock delivered the main attack, simultaneously pushing forward at the appointed hour on Anderson, Hoke and Breckinridge, but their lines soon became fragmented and subject to crossfire. "A strange and terrible feature of this battle was that as the three corps moved on, each was enfiladed while receiving the full force of the enemy's direct fire in front," said an aide in Wright's Sixth Corps. "Shell and shot were plunging through Hancock's battalions from his right. From the left a similarly destructive fire was poured in upon Smith, and from both flanks on the VI Corps in the center. . . . No troops could stand against [it], and the order to lie down was given all along the line. At points where no shelter was afforded, the men were withdrawn to such cover as could be found." Within thirty minutes, at frightening cost, the advance was blunted. Fighting continued for hours, with one senseless Federal assault following another, but it was of a sporadic and isolated nature. "Each corps commander reported and complained to General Meade that the [others], right or left as the case may be, failed to protect him from enfilading fire," the aide went on. "The explanation was simple enough. . . . The three corps had moved upon diverging lines, each directly facing the enemy in its front, and the farther each had advanced the more its flank had become exposed."[9]

Watching the Federals assail the center in three lines of battle during the crucial early morning attack was Augustus Dickert of Kershaw's old brigade, Anderson's corps. "The first line came at a rush with charge bayonets, and our officers had great difficulty in restraining the men from opening fire too soon." When the order was given, volley after volley crashed into the oncoming ranks. "The first line reeled and attempted to flee the field, but were met by the next column, which halted the retreating troops with the bayonet, butts of guns and officer's sword, until the greater number were turned to the second assault. All this while our sharpshooters and the men behind our works were pouring a galling fire into the tangled mass." The second enemy line, like the first, came with a loud huzzah but also was riddled. "The result was telling—men falling on top of men, rear rank pushing forward the first rank, only to be swept away like chaff." Lee's cannon meanwhile compounded the damage. "Our batteries on the hills in rear and those mounted on the infantry line were raking the field," said Dickert, "the former with shell and solid shot, the latter with grape and canister." The third line now mingled with the first two, with blue-clad bodies piling up in heaps. "The loud Rebel yell far to our right told us to be of good cheer, they [too] were holding their own and repulsing every assault."[10]

Evander Law, restored to command of his Alabama brigade in Field's division, likewise Anderson's corps, was in the center of the action. Concerned that his men might be running out of ammunition, he went forward to monitor their fire. On his way he met a panic-stricken soldier from the 15th Alabama. "He had left his hat behind, was crying like a big baby, and was the bloodiest man I ever saw," said Law.

"Oh, General," he blurted, showing off his wound. "I am dead! I am killed! Look at this!" Law realized that the Alabamian's wound was not serious, a minie ball having gone through the fleshy part of his neck, and sternly told the soldier to resume his place in the lines.

"He looked at me doubtfully for a second, as if questioning my veracity or my surgical knowledge, I don't know which; then, as if satisfied with my diagnosis, he broke into a broad laugh and, the tears still running down his cheeks, trotted off. . . ."

Reaching the trenches Law, who shortly went down with a head wound himself, found his brigade in a frenzy of bloodletting. Officers were running up and down the line, slapping riflemen with their hats and urging them to step up their fire. "I found the men in high spirits, laughing and talking as they fired," Law said. "[Now] I could see more plainly the terrible havoc made in the ranks of the assaulting column. I had seen the dreadful carnage of Marye's Hill at Fredericksburg, and on the 'old railroad cut' that Jackson's men held at Second Manassas; but I had seen nothing to exceed this." Then he added, echoing the words Harvey Hill had uttered at Malver Hill, "It was not war; it was murder." When the fight ended, more than a thousand men lay in his front, either killed or wounded.[11]

In Hoke's reconstituted command to Dick Anderson's right, the scene was similar. Captain Charles Elliott of James Martin's brigade reported, "The slaughter was terrific. I did not see one man on our side falter. It was a great victory from the start. . . . No men or officers ever made a braver charge than did these Federals on 3 June. But the flame of continuous fire from Martin's Brigade was too much for them or any men to overcome, and our line would not yield an inch. . . . Never will the scene be effaced from my memory." So quickly was the charge repulsed that Brigadier Johnson Hagood, in his memoirs, confessed he could not believe it was an all-out attack. "It may sound incredible but it is nevertheless strictly true," he said, "that the writer . . . awake and vigilant of the progress of events, was not aware at the time of any serious assault. . . ." Only the dead and wounded testified to the tragedy.

Stated Lieutenant Wilson Lamb of Thomas Clingman's brigade: "In [our] front the enemy's dead were so thickly strewn that one could have walked on their bodies the whole extent."[12]

On the far right of the lines, where Breckinridge and Hill were posted, the battle likewise raged. "Up and down our battle line," said one of Hill's gunners, "the fierce musketry [was] crashing and rolling like the sound of heavy hail on a tin roof, magnified a thousand times, with the cannon pealing out in the midst of it like claps of thunder. Our line, far as the eye could reach, was ablaze . . . and into that furious storm of death, the blue columns were urging their way." One half-hour into the attack, Lee dispatched a courier to Hill for information. Little Powell simply pointed toward the dreadful toll of Yankee dead. "Tell General Lee," he said, "it is the same all along my front."[13]

Overall at Cold Harbor, Federal casualties that day totaled some 7,000; Confederate, 1,500. "I have always regretted," Grant said belatedly, "that the last assault at Cold Harbor was ever made. [There] no advantage whatever was gained to compensate for the heavy loss we sustained. Indeed, the advantages, other than those of relative losses, were on the Confederate side." Wrote a contemporary historian of the Army of the Potomac who was critical of Grant's tactics: "Some hours after the failure of the . . . assault, General Meade sent instructions to each corps commander to renew the attack . . . but no man stirred, and the immobile lines pronounced a verdict, silent yet emphatic, against further slaughter."[14]

During the month-long "Overland Campaign"—from the Wilderness to Spotsylvania to the North Anna to Cold Harbor—the North had lost some 50,000 men; the South, 32,000. Lee moreover had lost more than a third of his generals, and even more of his regimental officers, leaving replacements in short supply. Among the dead general officers: in the First Corps, Micah Jenkins; in the Second Corps, Junius Daniel, John M. Jones and Leroy Stafford; in the Third Corps, Abner Perrin. Among the wounded: in the First Corps, James Longstreet, "Rock" Benning and Evander Law; in the Second Corps, Harry Hays, Robert D. Johnston, John Pegram and James A. Walker; in the Third Corps, John R. Cooke, Samuel McGowan, Edward Perry, Harrison Walker and James Lane. Captured were "Allegheny" Johnson and George Steuart.

Despite these losses Lee had one more unpleasant task to perform. On June 4 he in effect relieved Ewell of his duties, giving Early the temporary rank of Lieutenant General and retaining him as Second Corps commander. While Old Bald Head's courage was unquestioned, such was no longer the case with his leadership. "Everybody was uncomfortable for [Ewell]," said William Allen, his chief of ordnance, "& yet we all felt that his removal was inevitable & indeed was proper." Lee's decision brought about a rupture in the close friendship between Ewell and his former subordinate, the one feeling he was being betrayed, the other that he was being misjudged. Initially Ewell appeared to accept the situation. "I only care about [being replaced] on your account . . ." he told Lizinka perceptively, acknowledging that his strongwilled wife dominated the relationship, "knowing how ambitious you are." Then he added, jokingly, that she only had herself to blame for her discomfort. "You should have thought of this before we were married."[15]

Within days, however, Ewell was petitioning Lee for further service. He was not asking for his corps back, he said. He would accept lower rank, if only he could be restored to field command. The tactful Lee had no heart to tell the old soldier that his usefulness had ended. There was no need to take lower rank, he said. As soon as the current campaign ended and Ewell regained his health, he would give him back his corps. What next ensued was a poignant exchange.

"But, General, I am in as good health now as I ever was," Ewell said. "I was up yesterday 3 A.M. to 1 A.M., not fatigued or unwell. I was sick a little at Hanover Junction, but . . . I went on sick report and was cured by two days' rest."

"I have been constantly uneasy about you since last fall," said Lee. "You will go on exerting yourself, and I have been dreading every movement to hear that you have killed yourself by your exertions. . . ."

"My stump does not show the slightest injury," said Ewell of his amputation, "is perfectly well and is far from impairing my health. . . . The injury last fall was as purely accidental as if it had been cut by a knife. I think highly of Early. If I thought you preferred him for other than mere physical reasons, I would not say a word. . . ."

"I do not prefer Early to you except I think him stronger. I am unable to perform the duties of corps commander, which requires great labor."

"Did I not perform them all?"

"Perfectly well," replied Lee, "but remember how tired you were. You would sleep on the ground, liable to take cold."

"But I never did. I was without dyspepsia for the first time for years so long. I am better for riding all day."

"I am glad to hear you give such an account of yourself," said Lee, trying not to offend, "but I cannot but have my fears. I feel friendly to you, but the public interests are paramount to everything else. My own impression and that acquired from others makes me think that it is possible at any moment you may give way. . . ."

"These last few days are the most anxious I have spent," said Ewell.

"It is due Early and the corps that he receive the appointment just as Anderson has," said Lee, referring to Dick Anderson's recent rise to corps command. ". . . Your best plan is to recover your health."

"It is recovered," said Ewell resignedly. "But I will go somewhere to be out of the way."

"You are not in the way, but you had better take care of yourself."[16]

Soon Lee would intervene with the War Department to see that Ewell received another, far less demanding, assignment. Jackson's irascible but faithful lieutenant would be placed in charge of the defenses at Richmond.

In the immediate aftermath of Cold Harbor, Grant could not bring himself to ask Lee for a truce to bury his dead and care for his wounded. Such an overture might be interpreted as an admission of defeat. Not until June 5, with thousands of bodies putrefying and few wounded left alive in front of the Confederate lines, did he send a note to Lee. Even then he did not use the word truce, but instead proposed that burial parties should go out "when no battle is raging." Lee rejected Grant's suggestion ("I fear such an arrangement will lead to misunderstanding and difficulty"), insisting that he follow protocol. This Grant finally did, asking for a truce on June 7. "The stench from the dead between their lines and ours was sickening," said Colonel William Oates of the 15th Alabama, whom last we met in his assault on Little Round Top the second day at Gettysburg. "It was so nauseating that it was almost unendurable; but we had the advantage, as the wind carried it away from us to them. The dead covered more than five acres of ground. . . ."[17]

For five more days the two armies stared implacably at each other from behind their works, with skilled riflemen adding to the deadly toll. "Sharpshooters, with logs & sand bags, made little loop holes over the parapet through which they watched the opposing lines," explained Porter Alexander. "If one caught a glimpse of an enemy anywhere, he would sight carefully at that spot, & watch with his finger on the trigger to see if like causes would not presently cause another glimpse to be given at the same place. If he did he had only to press his trigger." Looking for John Gregg's Texas Brigade headquarters on one occasion, Alexander himself ran the sharpshooter gamut. "By stooping very low a man might approach within fifty yards of the headquarters. To be safe beyond that point he would have to get on his hands & knees, & perhaps even to be flat and crawl for the last part of the distance." The sun was so hot overhead that Alexander decided, when he neared Gregg's trench, to risk a dash for it. "Not being fired at that I was aware of . . . I jumped headlong into the hole. I landed between two dead Texans, each shot through the head, & a third one, alive & well, squatted in one corner."

"By Gosh!" the Texan said sociably. "You has to be mighty careful how you shows a head around here, or they'll get you certain! Thar's two they got already this morning!"

One more experience of Alexander's underscores the sheer volume of the sniper fire during the impasse. Each night he was responsible for seeing to it that the First Corps guns were loaded with double canister, so they would be ready for instant use in case of attack. "One of [Colonel Henry] Cabell's Napoleon's had had its wheels so cut & torn by bullets . . . that it was thought best to put on new ones. This was done, & the breech of the gun was elevated & 37 musket balls fell out"—all of which had gone down its muzzle in a single day.[18]

With his way to Richmond blocked at Cold Harbor, Grant now looked for an alternate route to the capital. On the night of June 12, under cover of darkness, he began the arduous task of withdrawing his troops from north of the Chickahominy to new positions south of the James. This time he would concentrate his entire force, not just Benjamin Butler's troops, on the rail hub at Petersburg, cutting Richmond's lines of supply. In the first stage of the plan Hancock and Wright pulled back from the center to create breathing room between the armies, even as Warren swung wide and advanced on the Federal left to Malvern Hill to screen the approaches to the river. Baldy Smith simultaneously sailed back the way he had come, going down the York and up the James to Bermuda Hundred. Lee, in large part because Hampton's reconnoitering did not equal Stuart's, was oblivious to these moves. In the months to come, both Petersburg and Richmond would fall under siege, a story we will recount subsequently.

Grant meanwhile in his capacity of general-in-chief was orchestrating his second attempt to oust the Confederates from the Shenandoah. He had removed Franz Sigel from command and replaced him with Major General David Hunter, who in early June moved up the valley with 12,000 men. Other than Imboden's cavalry, the only troops available to challenge him were a single infantry brigade under William "Grumble" Jones, whose feud with Jeb Stuart had earned him exile to southwestern Virginia. The Confederates totaled only 5,600. The two commands met on June 5 at Piedmont, a hamlet of a dozen houses just north of Staunton. There Hunter overwhelmed the hard-fighting Jones, who was killed with a bullet to the head. Six days later, all but unopposed, Hunter entered Lexington, where he burned the Virginia Military Institute down to the ground. For the first time, it appeared the upper Valley would fall to the enemy.

# FIVE

\* \* \* \*

# EARLY'S VALLEY CAMPAIGN

To counter the Federal threat in the Shenandoah, Lee on June 12 dispatched Jubal Early with the Second Corps to Lynchburg, where Hunter was demonstrating. Breckinridge with Gabriel Wharton's and John Echol's brigades was likewise sent to the town, whose warehouses, foundries and factories were vital to the Confederacy. Early's whole command, including cavalry, totaled some 14,000 men. The Second Corps, of course, included the remnants of Jackson's old Army of the Valley. Perhaps more important, its three divisions were headed by stalwart warriors: Robert Rodes, John Brown Gordon and Dodson Ramseur. Rodes's command consisted of his old Alabama brigade under Cullen Battle; the Georgians of Philip Cook, a former lawyer who had been named to succeed George Doles; and the North Carolinians of Bryan Grimes and William Ruffin Cox, the latter recovered from the five wounds he had received while leading a regiment at Chancellorsville.

Gordon's division was comprised of three brigades: Clement Evans's Georgians, Zebulon York's Louisianans and William Terry's Virginians. The first of these was Gordon's old unit, but the others were shells of their former selves. The Louisiana Tigers, originally two oversize brigades some 12,000 strong and officered by such men as Richard Taylor and Francis Nicholls, and then by Harry Hays and Leroy Stafford, were down to perhaps 600 men. Overrun at Rappahannock Station in November of 1863 and again at Spotsylvania, the brigade was the size of six companies. York, who had been with the 14th Louisiana for much of this time, had a lion's heart and a love of cursing that impressed the most obstreperous of his charges. William Terry's

Virginians, even more reduced by the debacle at the Mule Shoe, totaled some 500 men. They were all that remained of fourteen Virginia regiments—including the four that had comprised the Stonewall Brigade—that had once been in Allegheny Johnson's division.

The newly promoted Ramseur commanded the wounded John Pegram's Virginians and the wounded Robert Johnson's North Carolinians, under Robert Lilley and Thomas Toon respectively. His third brigade, the North Carolinians of Archibald Godwin, who had been captured at Rappahannock Station, was under W. Gaston Lewis.

Robert Ransom, in an attempt to bring some discipline to the Valley cavalry, was posted from Richmond to lead them. Just as in the days of Turner Ashby, these troopers were fearless in battle but often feckless in camp. Early would never succeed in bringing them under control, and it would cost him dearly in the upcoming campaign. The cavalry, he would say, "was badly mounted and armed, and its efficiency much impaired by the defeat at Piedmont." Ransom's brigades were those of John Imboden, Bradley Johnson (who replaced the slain Grumble Jones), William Lowther Jackson and John McCausland—Valley horsemen all. Imboden and Johnson we have met before. Jackson, the son of Irish immigrants, was a cousin of Stonewall Jackson. The 28-year-old McCausland, who had graduated first in his class at V.M.I., was an infantryman turned cavalryman.[1]

Once Early arrived at Lynchburg, on June 18, he found the Federals unwilling to fight. Hunter doubtless had expected to be joined there by Philip Sheridan's cavalry, doubling his strength, but Wade Hampton had intercepted Sheridan at Trevilian Station and disrupted these plans. In the days that followed Hunter fell back from the town across the Blue Ridge, eventually taking refuge in western Virginia's Kanawha Valley. Soon Early gave up the pursuit. "A great part of my command had had nothing to eat for the last few days, except for a little bacon," he said. "The cooking utensils were in the trains, and the effort to have bread baked at Lynchburg had failed. . . . I knew that the country through which Hunter's route led for forty or fifty miles was, for the most part, a desolate mountain region; and that his troops were taking everything in the way of provisions and forage they could lay their hands on . . . there was a limit to the endurance even of Confederate soldiers." The Federal retreat, however, opened up the entire Shenandoah. Lee had given Early the option, after disposing of Hunter, to return to Richmond or to march down the Valley, cross the Potomac and advance on the Washington defenses. Hopefully this maneuver would force Grant to send reinforcements there, weakening his operations south of the James.

There was little question that the bellicose Early would go on the offensive. Trudging down the turnpike, he and his men had ample opportunity to witness the havoc Hunter had wrought in the countryside. The enemy now was practicing total war in Virginia, against civilians as much as combatants.

"Houses had been burned, and women and children left without shelter," stated Early bitterly. "The country had been stripped of provisions and many families left without a morsel to eat. Furniture and bedding had been cut to pieces, and old men and women and children robbed of all clothing except what they were wearing."[2]

Entering Lexington, Jackson's old division filed past his grave. "Not a man spoke; not a sound was uttered," said Kyd Douglas, now an aide to Ramseur. "Only the tramp, tramp, tramp of passing feet told that his surviving veterans were passing in review, while the drooping and tattered flags saluted his sacred dust."

Down the Valley the grim march continued. The Second Corps passed through Staunton on June 28, then reached Winchester five days later. Nearing the Potomac the Rebels had a stroke of luck at Martinsburg, routing the few enemy soldiers there so quickly they had no chance to remove their stores and provisions. "They were making big preparations to celebrate [July] Fourth," said John Worsham of the 21st Virginia, "and many of the men had received boxes of good things from home. . . . I looked over some of the boxes and choosing one, opened it, and found it filled with cakes, oranges, bananas, lemons, etc., and a bottle of wine. I got a chair . . . and ate, until I could eat no more. Then I went to work again with renewed energy." By July 6 Early had immobilized the Federals on the heights above Harpers Ferry, crossed the Potomac at Shepherdstown and was advancing on Frederick, Maryland, whose town fathers eventually would pay him $200,000 cash in tribute. "The audacity of Early's enterprise was its safety," said Douglas. "No one who might have taken steps to oppose or cut him off would believe his force was so small. . . . The newspapers and scouts represented 'Old Jubal' as moving on Washington with a veteran column of 30,000 to 40,000 troops."[3]

On July 9 about 6:30 A.M. on the banks of the Monocacy River just below Frederick, Early confronted some 5,800 men under Major General Lewis Wallace, an iconoclastic politician who after the war would write the epic novel *Ben Hur*. Rodes was on the left, Ramseur in the center near the Baltimore & Ohio Railroad, Breckinridge and Gordon on the right. Hour after hour, however, passed in stalemate. "The enemy's position was too strong, and the difficulty of crossing the Monocacy under fire too great," said Early, "to attack in front without greater loss than I was prepared to incur." While reconnoitering to his right at 2 P.M. he noticed that "Tiger John" McCausland's cavalry had impulsively forded the river, initially throwing the Federals into confusion but then falling back through weight of numbers. "Orders were sent to Breckinridge," he continued, "to move up rapidly with Gordon's division to McCausland's assistance, and to follow up his attack." Ramseur and Rodes meantime would keep the enemy busy in the center and on the left.

Clement Evans's Georgians were in the van of Gordon's advance. No sooner had they clambered up the slippery banks of the Monocacy than they found themselves moving through an open wheat field under leveling fire. Compounding their difficulties was the fact the wheat had been gathered into grain stacks, studding the field with obstacles that made it impossible to maintain a line of battle. Just as he closed with the enemy, Evans was knocked from his horse, the minie ball lodging in his left side. "I was galloping along the front . . ." he remembered, "& of course was a conspicuous mark for thousands of Federal rifles." Two soldiers took him to the rear.[4]

York's Louisianans and Terry's Virginians came up on Evans's left. "There was Gordon . . . I shall recollect him to my dying day," said Worsham of the 21st Virginia, ". . . sitting on his horse as quietly as if nothing was going on, wearing his old red shirt, the sleeves pulled up a little, the only indication that he was ready for the fight. . . . As we approached [him] he rode forward to meet us and said, 'Hurry up, boys,' turning his horse and taking the lead." Suddenly a line of Yankees came into view across the field. "The men at the head of our column . . . sang out, 'At them, boys!' Now came Gen. Gordon's part: turning quietly in his saddle he said, 'Keep quiet, we'll have our time presently.' " The men stopped briefly to scale a fence, then resumed their advance.[5]

Gordon described the assault. "*En echelon* by brigades from the right the movement began," he said. "As we reached the first line of strong and high fencing, and my men began to climb over it, they were met by a tempest of bullets. . . . Then came the grain-stacks . . . with no possibility of retaining orderly alignment." It was a fight where success depended on the individual. "The men were deprived of that support . . . imparted by a compact line, where the elbow touch of comrade with comrade gives confidence to each and sends the electric thrill of enthusiasm through all." Close to the enemy, Gordon somehow straightened his line and ordered the charge. "The supreme test of their marvelous nerve and self-control now came. . . . I ordered 'Forward!' and forward they went. . . ." Late in the afternoon the Federals began to break. "Up went our old yell all along the line of our division," said Worsham, "and it was answered by our comrades on the other side of the river."[6]

Gordon's turning movement earned his troops a well-deserved respite. "Our division pursued the enemy a short distance," Worsham went on, "when the pursuit was taken up by Ramseur's division, who had crossed the river on the railroad bridge, as soon as we cleared the way." With sunset coming on, his brigade went to camp in the midst of some wounded Yankees. "One of them asked me for some water, and stated that he had had a canteen but one of our men had taken it from him. Poor fellow! I went to the spring, filled a canteen and carried it to him, and as I had two canteens, gave him this one. . . . I offered him something to eat, but he said he had his own haversack."[7]

During the night the surgeons went about their work. The biggest fear of Clement Evans, the highest ranking of the wounded, was that he would miss the raid on Washington. "The surgeons at my request worked fast and hurried me off because Early was moving. . . . My wound was so threatening that [they] sought to dissuade me from my purpose. . . . But I had a horror of *Captivity*—so I refused to take an opiate. . . . I took the risk myself, but as a consequence of that haste I suffered eleven years from the wound." The ball that struck Evans, it seems, tore through a pocket where he had placed a packet of straight pins and buried them in his flesh. The surgeons did not remove them, and for years afterward they would cause him pain as they worked their way to the surface. But Evans did get his wish, going on to Washington via ambulance and witnessing the raid. Thereafter his wound would keep him from the field for three months.[8]

For reasons not clear, perhaps because he did not have confidence in his cavalry, Early did not push the pursuit. Wallace suffered 2,000 casualties in his 5,800-man command; the Confederates, some 800. Though Early would move south and arrive outside Washington on July 11, Wallace's staunch stand had bought the Federals another 24 hours to shift reinforcements—the Sixth and the Nineteenth Corps—to the capital. In point of fact, he had done his job well.

Early approached a panicked Washington on the 7th Street Pike, which ran through Silver Spring past a redoubt called Fort Stevens, one of the block-houses circling the city. Though the Union garrison there had been drastically reduced, its members sent to make up Grant's losses, its fortifications were impressive. "On the right was Rock Creek running through a deep ravine which had been rendered impassable by the felling of timber on each side," Early said, "and beyond were the works on the Georgetown pike. . . . On the left, as far as the eye could reach, the works appeared to be of the same impregnable character." That night, after consulting with his generals in the commandeered Silver Spring home of Francis P. Blair Sr., the confidant of Lincoln who in 1861 had offered Lee command of the Union army, he re-solved to assault the city. Blair's unwitting hospitality may have contributed to the decision. "However considerate of private property these gentlemen and their staffs were," said Kyd Douglas, "I feel compelled to say that the wine cellar of Mr. Blair was much depleted before [we] got away." By morn-ing, however, with reinforcements from the Sixth and Nineteenth Corps filing into the fortifications, Early cancelled his attack. Later, when the Federals made a brief sortie against him, he decided to return to the Valley.

Just after dark, with preparations underway for the march west, Douglas was ordered to report to Early, whom he found with Breckinridge.

"[Early] seemed in a droll humor, perhaps one of relief," said Douglas, "for he said to me in his falsetto drawl:

" 'Major, we haven't taken Washington, but we've scared Abe Lincoln like hell!'

" 'Yes, General,' I replied, 'but this afternoon when that Yankee line moved out against us, I think some other people were scared blue as hell's brimstone!'

" 'How about that, General,' " said Breckinridge with a laugh.

" 'That's true,' piped Early, 'but it won't appear in history!' "[9]

Led by the Sixth Corps of General Horatio Wright, the Union pursuit of Early was vigorous and in force. On July 20 at Stephenson's Depot just north of Winchester, Ramseur came to grief when he allowed Federal cavalry under William Averill to turn his flank and send it reeling. Though he "by every means endeavored to check the flying panic stricken men," his efforts were fruitless, with his division fleeing "in the most perfect rout I ever saw." Casualties totaled some 250, including two of his brigadiers, one of whom was captured. Four guns also were lost. "My men behaved shamefully," he railed to Nellie. Had his command "behaved like my old brigade would have done . . . a disgraceful retreat would have been a brilliant victory." From North Carolina, his pregnant wife subsequently lent him support, writing that neither his friends "nor *anyone* in this part of the country seems inclined to censure *you* in the least, but simply express regret that the affair should have happened." The rout, however, did have one salutary effect. When Early withdrew up the Shenandoah to reorganize, Wright mistakenly assumed he was leaving the Valley to rejoin Lee in the Petersburg-Richmond area. Wright then led most of his troops back to Washington, preparatory to moving on Petersburg himself, leaving behind only George Crook with some 9,500 men.[10]

Once he learned of this development, Early's response was to move down the Valley with his 14,000 men and engage Crook forthwith. The two armies met on Sunday, July 24, at Kernstown, just south of Winchester. It was at Kernstown, of course, that Jackson had attacked James Shields in 1862 and suffered his only defeat. Ramseur and Gordon advanced on the left about noon, with Gabriel Wharton and Rodes on the right. Robert Ransom's cavalry had been sent wide around both flanks with orders to reunite at Winchester and cut off retreat. "After the enemy's skirmishers were driven in," said Early, "it was discovered that his left, extending through Kernstown, was exposed, and General Breckinridge was ordered to move [Wharton's division] under cover of some ravines on our right and attack that flank." This Breckinridge did, falling hard on the Ohio brigade of future president Rutherford B. Hayes, who rallied his men as best he could but ultimately was forced to pull back. Early's other divisions then pushed forward, and the rout was on. The Confederate cavalry was not in position, however, allowing the enemy with all their guns and most of their wagons to escape down the pike. "General Ransom had been in very bad health . . ." said Early, acknowledging the need for an energetic cavalry commander. "I think, if I had one on this occasion, the greater part of the enemy's forces would have been captured or destroyed."[11] Crook incurred 1,200 casualties, while rebel losses were negligible.

With the Shenandoah again clear of opposition Early soon moved north to Martinsburg, where he tore up track and interrupted service on the Baltimore & Ohio. Then on July 29 he dispatched John McCausland with his own and Bradley Johnson's brigade across the Potomac to Chambersburg, Pennsylvania. McCausland's orders were to burn down the town unless the citizens paid an indemnity of $100,000 in gold or $500,000 in greenbacks. Still smarting over the destruction David Hunter had wreaked in the Valley, Early intended to use this money to help the victims rebuild their homes. "Some were willing to pay the money—others were not," said McCausland of the Northerners. "I urged them to comply . . . and told them plainly what they might expect in the event of their failure." When the indemnity was not forthcoming, he torched the town. Early never regretted these instructions. "For this act I, alone, am responsible," he would say, "as the officers engaged in it were simply executing my orders." Burdened with loot, and in some cases reeling with liquor, McCausland's and Johnson's troopers then withdrew toward Virginia.[12]

William Averell's Union cavalry caught up with them on August 7, while they were camped near Moorefield on the south branch of the Potomac. McCausland's men had been nine days in the saddle in their round-trip raid on Chambersburg, and their exhaustion had made them careless. The Federals fell on them before daybreak while they were still sleeping, capturing 420 men, 400 horses and four pieces of artillery. Bradley Johnson himself was briefly captured, but then escaped. McCausland was not taken because he was sleeping elsewhere. The debacle produced a lasting rift between the two officers, with Johnson insisting that it occurred in large part because McCausland had been negligent in disciplining the troop during the raid. "Every crime in the catalog of infamy has been committed, I believe, except murder and rape. . . . Pillage and sack of private dwellings took place hourly." Nothing came of Johnson's charges, but the troopers clearly needed a strong hand. "This affair," said Early with great understatement of the Moorefield rout, "had a very damaging effect upon my cavalry." Ransom was sent back to Richmond and Lunsford Lomax, one of Fitz Lee's able brigadiers, was assigned to replace him.[13]

The Union defeat at Second Kernstown and the torching of Chambersburg impressed on Grant the need for a strong leader in the Valley. From the James, where he was deeply involved in the assault on Petersburg, he ordered 33-year-old Phil Sheridan on August 5 to take command of the Army of the Shenandoah. He eventually would control some 35,000 infantry and 8,000 cavalry.

Black-haired and swarthy, broad-shouldered and stocky, "Little Phil's" appearance was in sharp contrast with that of the 48-year-old Early, grizzled and stooped beyond his years. Lincoln once remarked that he was "one of those long-armed fellows with short legs that can scratch his shins without having to stoop over to do it." Born to poor Irish immigrants and raised in Ohio, the hot-tempered Sheridan—in an episode reminiscent of Early's mess hall argument with Lewis Armistead—narrowly escaped expulsion from West Point for assaulting a cadet with a bayonet. Progressing from command of a cavalry regiment in May of 1862 to head of an infantry division, he had distinguished himself in the West, notably at Chattanooga. One of Grant's first acts on coming East was to make him chief of cavalry. Ever aggressive, he had clashed almost immediately with George Meade, who saw the Union cavalry's main role as picketing and reconnoitering for his Army of the Potomac. Sheridan, who regarded his men as mounted infantry, sought a more substantial role. Now he was being given it.[14]

The rest of August and the beginning of September were taken up with feints and counterfeints between the two armies. Besides Lomax, two brigades of Fitz Lee's division now joined Early's command, lending him added mobility. "Being compelled to occupy the position where I was," he said, "and being aware of its danger . . . my only resource was to use my forces so as to display them at different points with great rapidity, and thereby keep up the impression that they were much larger than they really were." Up to this point he was fulfilling Lee's expectations, pinning down three infantry corps and three cavalry divisions in the stifling heat and keeping them from the assault on Petersburg. "Old Early outgenerals us all," Brigadier Bryan Grimes wrote home, "for no one can guess where he is going to move . . . and the Yankees begin to think him ubiquitous."[15]

Jubal's opinion of Sheridan, however, was making him overconfident. "The events of the last month had satisfied me," he said, "that the commander opposed to me was without enterprise, and possessed an excessive caution which amounted to timidity." Sheridan was just biding his time, however. On September 19 he advanced against Winchester with a three-to-one superiority in numbers, barely giving Early the opportunity to reunite his scattered troops to the east of the town. Ramseur, on the right of the line, about 9 A.M. bore the brunt of the initial attack. A sudden Yankee surge threatened his position, causing some of his men to break and run. Doubtless with memories of Stephenson's Depot in his mind, he waded into their midst, shouting for them to halt and fight and clubbing those who did not with a musket stock. He swung the musket freely "and by this means and the exertions of my staff . . . and some gallant [officers]" restored order to the ranks. Minutes later he withdrew his division several hundred yards to more favorable terrain, where his troops fought with great tenacity. Never, his aide Kyd Douglas would say of their subsequent behavior, "did that division or any other do better work."[16]

Rodes soon formed to Ramseur's left; then Gordon came up to the left of Rodes. Breckinridge and Wharton, comprising the reserve, subsequently took a position behind and at a right angle to Gordon. Fitz Lee's cavalry guarded

the left flank, Imboden and others the right flank. Gordon, who had marched
his men 14 miles through the night to make the battle, had a special reason
to defend Winchester. The charming and devoted Fanny, she who had nursed
him back to health after Sharpsburg and was rarely far from his side during
the war, was staying there. Jubal Early, a crusty bachelor, at first had been
irked by her presence. "I wish the Yankees would capture Mrs. Gordon, and
hold her till the war is over!" he reputedly exclaimed, but eventually he came
to accept her. "What's that?" he had asked his quartermaster when he noticed
her carriage amid the wagons and caissons.

"That is Mrs. Gordon's carriage, sir," the officer replied.

"Well, I'll be damned," said Jubal. "If my men would keep up as she does,
I'd never issue another order against straggling."

Fanny, who learned of Early's comments about her, had used the occasion of
a recent dinner party to tease him about them. He had taken it with good grace,
replying, "Mrs. Gordon, General Gordon is a better soldier when you are close
by him than when you are away, and so hereafter, when I issue orders that officers' wives must go to the rear, you may know that you are excepted." The rejoinder brought forth a round of applause from all at the table.[17]

Through the morning and into the afternoon the battle raged in front of the
town, with the Confederates hurling back charges, making countercharges and
giving and taking severe losses. Their opponents were the Sixth Corps of Horatio Wright and the Nineteenth Corps of William Emory. When the Federals
made head-on attacks, the Confederates responded with double-canister artillery rounds. From no more than 60 yards, the "guns fired as one, when the front
line of the enemy was close enough to feel the flame of the powder," said Colonel Thomas Carter, chief of artillery. "For a moment the smoke hid all from
view. When it cleared away, we had the joy to see . . . a field of flying, disorganized men, scudding for the woods." Rodes and Gordon, close friends as well
as comrades-in-arms, quickly launched a counterattack. "We raised our well-
known 'Rebel Yell,' " said Captain Robert Park of the 12th Alabama, Cullen
Battle's brigade, of the sally, "and continued our onward run . . . after the
disordered host in our front. We could see they had a much larger force than
ours, but we cared not for numbers." Three Confederate divisions were fighting two enemy corps to a stalemate.

In the midst of the action, while conferring with Gordon, the martial-
looking, mustachioed Rodes was struck by a shell fragment in the back of
the head, killing him almost instantly. He had first been wounded at Seven
Pines, had survived the Bloody Lane at Sharpsburg, had led Jackson's flank
attack at Chancellorsville and had been a bulwark of strength from the Wilderness to Spotsylvania. Now he was no more. "As the last words between
us were spoken," said Gordon, "Rodes fell, mortally wounded, near my
horse's feet. . . . To ride away without expressing my deep grief was

sorely trying to my feelings; but I had to go. His fall had left both divisions in my immediate control. . . ."[18]

With the battle subsiding east of Winchester, Sheridan about 4 P.M. sent the 8,000-man Eighth Corps of George Crook plus perhaps 8,000 in cavalry against the rebels north of the town. Here Breckinridge and Wharton had no more than 1,800 infantry, while Fitz Lee's cavalry, including McCausland's and Imboden's, numbered perhaps 4,000. The Confederates on the left were simply overwhelmed. Coming up to Breckinridge's support, Gordon for once could do little to stop the envelopment that was suddenly turning the tide. "General Breckinridge . . . rode to my side," said Gordon. "His Apollo-like face was begrimed with sweat and smoke. He was desperately reckless—the personification of despair. He seemed literally to court death." To Gordon's urgings that he leave the front, the former vice president of the United States only snorted, "Well, General, there is nothing left for me if our cause is to fail."

Bryan Grimes, who would temporarily take over for Rodes, recalled the scene: "Horses dashing over the field, cannon being run to the rear at the top of the horses' speed, men leaving their command and scattering. . . ." Some cannoneers, of course, held their ground, hoping to delay the enemy as long as possible. One such gun crew was preparing to fire one last round when a shell stuck in the barrel. They wrestled with the charge even as men going to the rear warned it would explode. "Stop that, you damned fools!" said Early when he saw what they were doing. "You'll kill yourself and anybody about you!" One gunner, not recognizing him in the rough, disheveled clothes that passed for his uniform, would have none of this advice. "Go to hell, you damned old clodhopper!" he yelled.

With Early making frantic efforts to restore some semblance of discipline, the disorganized force tumbled south through the town and up the turnpike. "To my horror," said Gordon, "as I rode among my troops . . . I found Mrs. Gordon on the street, where shells from Sheridan's batteries were falling." He had thought she had already gone to the rear. "It was the first time, in all her army experience, that she had seen the Confederate lines broken. . . . As the different squads passed, she inquired to what command they belonged." When someone called back, "We are Gordon's men," Fanny lost her temper. She rushed into the street, calling them cowards and demanding they turn to face the enemy. "She was thus engaged when I found her," said Gordon dryly. He promptly bundled her into her carriage with their six-year-old son, Frank, and two wounded officers and made sure she was driven to safety.[19]

By nightfall Early was digging in on Fisher's Hill, a high ridge fronted by a stream near Strasburg that made for a formidable barrier against pursuit. If truth be told, he should have withdrawn from Winchester and taken this defensive position long before. Besides Rodes, Early had lost the six-foot-six

North Carolina brigadier Archibald Godwin, who had been paroled and had held his commission little more than a month. George S. Patton, leading Echols's brigade of Breckinridge's command, also had been killed. Fitz Lee had received a severe wound, further weakening the cavalry, and the Louisianans' Zebulon York had likewise been wounded. Early had overall suffered some 4,000 casualties; Sheridan, 5,000.

Four days later, on September 22, the Federals assailed Early once more. While the Sixth and Nineteenth Corps demonstrated on his front, George Crook's Eighth Corps moved unnoticed through the mountainous woodland on his left. Early seemingly gave little thought to Crook's whereabouts or the possibility his western flank might be turned. To be fair he did not have enough men fully to man his four-mile line, but he compounded his problems by posting one of his weakest units on the left—Lomax's Valley troopers. Early's best men were in the center and on his eastern flank, astride the turnpike. When Crook's battle line surged forward out of the woods in the late afternoon, the setting sun at its back, the Confederates crumbled. What began as an orderly withdrawal slowly turned into a second rout. Early's army would not rally for several days, until it was well up the Valley past Staunton. Mortally wounded in the Fisher's Hill encounter was Sandie Pendleton, Jackson's former aide. Confederate losses would be some 1,200; Federal, only 500.

News of these victories in the Shenandoah, less than two months before the presidential elections, considerably dampened antiwar sentiment in the North. Combined with William Sherman's taking of Atlanta on September 2, they all but ensured that Lincoln would win a second term. In Georgia Sherman had defeated John Bell Hood and the troubled Army of Tennessee. We last saw Hood at Chattanooga and in the drawing rooms of Richmond. Perhaps too offensive-minded for his own good, he had been selected in July by Jefferson Davis to replace the too cautious Joseph Johnston, Davis's bete noir throughout the war, who in turn had replaced Braxton Bragg after the defeat at Chattanooga.

In the weeks that followed the defeat at Fisher's Hill, Sheridan from his headquarters at Harrisonburg systematically pillaged the entire Valley between Staunton and the Potomac, destroying farms, barns and livestock. The breadbasket of the Confederacy lay a smoldering ruin. In consequence, newspapers and politicians alike called for Early's removal. One of his severest critics was one of his former brigadiers, the militarily inept William "Extra Billy" Smith, now out of the army and in the Virginia governor's mansion, who told Lee that Early "was surprised at Winchester . . . and Fisher's Hill was the terrible sequence." Demanding that he be relieved, Smith conceded that Old Jube was brave and dedicated but insisted that he "has no other qualities for independent command, none whatever."

To Smith, Lee made a judicious reply: "I lament [the] disasters as much as yourself, but I am not prepared to say they proceeded from such want of capacity on the part of General Early as to warrant me in recommending his recall." To Early, Lee from Petersburg gave some advice: "As far as I can judge, from this distance, you have operated more with divisions than with your concentrated strength." Then he offered moral support: "I have weakened myself very much to strengthen you. It was done with the expectation of enabling you to gain such success that you could return the troops if not rejoin me yourself. I know you have endeavored to gain that success. . . . You must not be discouraged, but continue to try. I rely upon your judgement and ability. . . ."[20]

By now Early had regrouped, with every intention of taking the fight to the foe. He had lost the services of Breckinridge, who had been recalled to head the Department of Southwest Virginia, but retained Gabriel Wharton's minidivision. His ranks had been bolstered, moreover, by the arrival of Joseph Kershaw's splendid division, as well as Tom Rosser's cavalry brigade. In the first week of October, his order of battle looked like this:

Dodson Ramseur had been transferred to lead the division of the fallen Rodes. His brigades were those of Cullen Battle's Alabamians, Philip Cook's Georgians and Byran Grimes's and William Cox's North Carolinians. John Pegram, recovered from his wound, took over Ramseur's division. Colonel John Hoffman commanded Pegram's old Virginia Brigade, Robert Johnston his North Carolinians and Lieutenant Colonel William Davis the North Carolinians of the slain Archibald Godwin. Gordon's division remained the same: Clement Evans's Georgians, William Terry's Virginians, and the wounded Zebulon York's Louisianans under Colonel Edmund Pendleton. Reporting to Gordon, too, was Wharton and his three small Virginia brigades. Kershaw's division was composed of James Conner's South Carolinians, Benjamin Humphreys's Mississippians and William Wofford's and Goode Bryan's Georgians.

Lunsford Lomax's Valley cavalry brigades continued to be those of John Imboden, Bradley Johnson, John McCausland and William Jackson. The newly arrived Tom Rosser replaced Fitz Lee, his brigades being his own, and those of Tom Munford and William Payne. Considerable uneasiness existed between the assertive Rosser, a onetime Stuart protégé, and the capable, unassuming Munford. The former had only been a junior officer at First Manassas, the latter a lieutenant colonel. Now Colonel Munford, who despite his experience had never been made a brigadier, reported to Rosser. Colonel Tom Carter commanded the army's artillery battalions. Overall, Confederate strength had grown to some 20,000 men; the Federals totaled 32,000.

Believing Early was more of an irritant than a threat, Sheridan during October began to withdraw down the Valley with an eye toward rejoining Grant, burning what little was left in the countryside as he went. His feelings were reinforced on October 9, when Lomax and Rosser, who had been harassing the enemy and were far ahead of infantry support, were soundly defeated at Tom's Brook, just south of Strasburg. There some 4,000 troopers under Wesley Merritt and George Custer stormed into the Confederate cavalry, breaking its ranks and chasing it for miles, seizing eleven guns and some forty supply wagons in the onslaught. Lomax, whose men lacked sabers and pistols and were armed only with cumbersome Enfield rifles, had little chance. "The consequence is," Early would say, "that they cannot fight on horseback and in this open country cannot successfully fight on foot against large bodies of cavalry; besides the command is and has been demoralized. . . ."[21]

With so little expected of Lomax, most of the blame for the fiasco fell on the six-foot-two Rosser, the self-appointed "Savior of the Valley," who was as rash as he was courageous. For several days his troopers had plagued the Federal rear. "Rosser's head," a critical Colonel Munford would say, "seemed to be completely turned by our success, and in . . . ignorance of their numbers, we suffered the greatest disaster that had ever befallen our command." When Munford saw on the morning of the 9th that the enemy was turning on them at Tom's Brook, he immediately sounded a warning. "After repeated couriers had been sent, [Rosser] came up, and in a vaunting manner asked me, 'What [is] the matter?' I replied, 'The enemy are moving up to attack us, and we can't hold this position against such odds.' In the same tone and spirit he replied, 'I'll drive them into Strasburg by 10 o'clock.' I then said, 'They will turn your left.' Said he, 'I'll look out for that.' "

Unfortunately, Rosser was too sanguine. "While I was . . . engaged on the right," continued Munford, "Rosser superintending the left became heavily engaged at the ford. . . . [He] repulsed the first attack . . . which was intended as a feint." Just as the Federals fell back, a second column, unobserved by Rosser, passed behind a hill to his left and pushed rapidly to his rear. When the enemy in front again moved up, Rosser's troopers were caught in a pincers. They had little choice but to flee for their lives, abandoning their artillery and wagons. "We fell back under fire until we reached a body of timbers which afforded shelter for our men," said Munford, "after which the enemy retired." Though casualties were minor, the loss of guns and supplies was galling. Two years before, he added, "we had followed Stonewall Jackson up and down the Valley . . . and when our toils came to an end we could go to our wagons and enjoy a clean shirt and some of the little comforts. . . . Now we had not even a clean shirt—wagons and all were gone."[22]

In the ensuing days, it would be Sheridan's turn to become overconfident. He and the Army of the Shenandoah went into camp at Cedar Creek, south of Middletown, mistakenly thinking that Early could not mount a challenge. Their position, moreover, was a relatively strong one. Cedar Creek was only some 30 yards wide, but its tortuous curves and steep banks all but precluded a frontal assault and dictated a turning movement. Protecting the Federal right, however, was its entire cavalry force, headed by Alfred Torbert. Protecting the left was the northern end of the towering Massanutten Mountains, at whose base ran the North Fork of the Shenandoah. A flanking attack seemed impossible. Short of provisions in the wasted countryside, Early knew he had little time to waste in formulating a plan.

Reconnoitering on October 17 with Clement Evans and mapmaker Jedediah Hotchkiss, John Brown Gordon made the arduous climb to the top of the Massanuttens. From there he could see through field glasses the enemy position in sharp detail—not only the number of cannon and battle flags, but even the blue, red and yellow jacket trimmings that identified the infantry, artillery and cavalry. Noting that Sheridan was protecting only his right and center, Gordon determined to assail his left. "The plan was to abandon serious attack of Sheridan's forces where all things were in readiness, making only a demonstration upon that right flank by Rosser's cavalry dismounted, and upon the center by a movement of infantry and artillery along the pike." But how to deal with the obstacle of the Massanuttens? "A dim and narrow pathway was found [along the mountainside]," Gordon explained, "along which but one man could pass at a time; but by beginning the movement at nightfall the entire corps could be passed before daylight."[23]

Later, after a council of war, Early approved Gordon's route and devised a three-pronged assault. Under the Georgian's command the entire Second Corps would march all night and cross the North Fork at McInturff's and Bowman's Fords. Kershaw would be on Gordon's left. Wharton would push up the pike and join in the attack. Rosser would be on the extreme left. "The men were stripped of canteens and of everything calculated to make noise, and arouse Sheridan's pickets below us," said Gordon, "and our watches were set so that at the same moment the right, center and left . . . would be assaulted." Ramseur was in a particularly good mood, and not just because of the prospect of battle. He had just received a message, "The crisis is over and all is well," meaning that Nellie, whom he had married one year before, had given birth to their first child. He did not yet know whether the infant was a boy or girl. "Tell Sis Mary," he wrote his wife, "for pity's sake, if not for love's sake, write me a long letter about my little wife and baby. . . . Oh me! I want to see you so bad!"[24]

Before dawn on October 19, all was in readiness. "With every man . . . striving to suppress every sound," Gordon's long gray line had padded single file on the precarious path along and down the Massanuttens. Now his troops were waiting for the appointed time, "resting near the bank of the river in the middle of which the Union vedettes sat upon their horses, wholly unconscious of [their] presence. . . ." One mile away near Bowman's Mill on Cedar Creek, Early paced impatiently amid Kershaw's men, hoping the next few hours would bring him a striking victory—one that would rival Jackson's climatic successes at Cross Keyes and Port Republic. "The minute hand of the watch," said Gordon of the 5 A.M. attack, "admonished us that it was time to move. . . ."

William Payne's Virginia cavalry led the assault on the enemy left flank, splashing across the river and driving in the vedettes. Clement Evans, in charge of Gordon's division, rushed into the cold waters and emerged on the opposite bank, advancing on the double-quick. Evans's troops, explained Gordon, "with Ramseur's farther to the right and Pegram's in support, rushed upon the unprepared and unsuspecting Federals, great numbers of whom were still asleep in their tents. Even those who had been aroused by Payne's sudden eruption . . . [then] were thrown into the wildest confusion and terror by Kershaw's simultaneous assault in front. . . . The intrepid Wharton was soon across with his superb division, adding momentum. . . ." The surprise was complete. "Two entire corps, [Crook's] VIII and [Emory's] XIX, broke and fled," Gordon enthused, "leaving the ground covered with arms, accoutrements, knapsacks and the dead bodies of their comrades. Across the open fields [the enemy] swarmed . . . heedless of all things save getting to the rear." By 7:30 A.M. hundreds of Federals had been killed, some 1,300 taken prisoner and eighteen cannon captured.[25]

Ramseur was elated. Riding an eye-catching bay and in full uniform, a flower on his lapel to celebrate the birth of his child, through the early morning he urged his men on. "His presence and manner," said one of his officers, "was electrical." Kyd Douglas, bringing him a message, encountered him on the turnpike. "Let's drive them, Douglas," Ramseur cried. "I want to win this battle, for I must see my wife and baby!" Now Gordon's and Kershaw's forces merged, pushing the broken ranks of the enemy toward and then past Middletown. Only Wright's Sixth Corps, which had been in a rearward position, held relatively firm. "Men seemed more like demons than human beings," said one dazed member of the Nineteenth Corps, "as they struck fiercely at each other with clubbed muskets and bayonets." A captain in a Vermont brigade would never forget the blood: ". . . splashes of blood, and zig-zag trails of blood, and bodies of men and horses. I never on any battlefield saw so much blood as on this of Cedar Creek. The firm limestone soil would not receive it, and there was no pitying summer grass to hide it."[26]

By 9:30 A.M. Gordon, still in command of the Second Corps, was turning his full attention to Wright's Sixth Corps, the pride of Sheridan's army. "It stood like a granite breakwater, built to beat back the oncoming flood," he said, "but it was also doomed. . . . It was at that hour largely outnumbered, and I had directed every Confederate command . . . to assail it in front and upon both flanks." Simultaneously he ordered Colonel Carter to bombard its position with every gun he had. "General, you will need no infantry," Carter confidently told him. "With enfilade fire from my batteries I will destroy that corps in twenty minutes."

Early at this point came on the scene. "Well, Gordon, this is glory enough for one day," he said. "This is the 19th," he added ruminatively, thinking of the flight from Winchester. "Precisely one month ago today we were going in the opposite direction."

"It is very well so far, General, but we have one more blow to strike . . ." Gordon replied, pointing to Horatio Wright's Sixth Corps's position.

"No use in that," said Early, "they will all go directly."

"That is the VI Corps, General. It will not go unless we drive it from the field."

"Yes, it will go too, directly."

If Gordon's account is even half-accurate, it is clear Early was making a terrible blunder. "My heart went in my boots," the Georgian said. "Visions of the fatal halt on the first day at Gettysburg, and of the whole day's hesitation to permit an assault on Grant's exposed flank the 6th of May in the Wilderness, rose before me."[27]

From 10 A.M. to 4 P.M. Early, perhaps thinking the battle had been won, made no concerted move to follow up his advantage. He would move forward, but only incrementally. Later he would claim in his report to Lee that his troops had been too disorganized to advance, largely as a result of looting. "So many of our men had stopped in the camp to plunder," he said, "the country was so open and the enemy's cavalry so strong, that I did not deem it prudent to press farther. . . ." That there was looting is unquestioned. "Hundreds of the men who were in the charge . . . were barefooted," said one of the Stonewall Brigade's survivors, "every one of them was ragged, many had nothing but what they had on, and *none* had eaten a square meal for weeks! In passing through Sheridan's camp they had a great temptation thrown in their way . . . in plain sight were rations, shoes, overcoats and blankets . . . the temptation to stop and eat was too great . . . and they yielded. Others tried on shoes . . . warm pants in place of tattered ones, others got overcoats and blankets, articles so much needed for the coming cold!" Such looting may have accounted for an hour or two's delay, but not for six hours. In his report, while offering his resignation, Early seemed to acknowledge his mistake: "It is mortifying to me, General, to have to make these explanations of my reverses. They are due to no want of effort on my part, though it may be I have not the capacity to prevent them. . . ."[28]

Other officers besides Gordon decried the lengthy halt in the action. Writing his wife just after the battle, an anguished Clement Evans mourned, "Oh what a victory we had yesterday morning—What a defeat yesterday evening! I hardly know how to write about it to you. . . . Gen. Gordon had command of three divisions and as long as his plans were followed . . . we were victorious, but [then] Early took command, the place was changed, and we were defeated." Stated Gabriel Wharton: "I supposed we were arranging for a general movement to the front, and expected every minute orders to advance; but no orders came." Commented cavalryman Tom Rosser: "Had the fight continued . . . as it was so gloriously begun, Sheridan's ride of twenty miles away would never have been sung. . . ."[29]

Rosser's reference to Sheridan's ride brings us to a remarkable feature of the engagement. To this point the Union commander, who had been in Washington for a conference at the War Department, had not been on the field. Now on the morning of the 19th, riding south from Winchester, he began encountering the panic-stricken fugitives from the Eighth and Nineteenth Corps. "I felt," he said, "that I ought to try to restore their broken ranks, or failing in that to share their fate. . . ." Leaving his escort and, later, a cavalry detachment to stem the flow down the pike, Sheridan put his mount into a canter toward Cedar Creek and Middletown, waving his hat and giving his men words of encouragement. "Boys, if you don't want to fight yourselves, come back and look at others fighting!" he shouted. "We will whip them out of their boots by 4 o'clock!" Soon the troops, buoyed by his optimism, began to cheer and then to turn back. Sheridan's eyes, said one of his aides, "had the same dull red glint I had seen . . . when, on other occasions, the battle was going against us."[30]

By 10:30 A.M. he was conferring with his generals—Wright, Emory, Crook, Torbert and others—north of Middletown. "We've done the best we could," said Horatio Wright. "That's all right, that's all right," answered Sheridan. William Emory then reported that his Nineteenth Corps had rallied sufficiently to cover the retreat to Winchester. "Retreat, Hell!" snapped Sheridan, setting the tone. "We'll be back in our camps tonight." By noon the redeployment was well in hand. Urged on by his aides Sheridan rode up and down the lines so his men could see him, tirelessly waving his hat and shouting, "We'll raise them out of their boots!" His infectious enthusiasm, in stark contrast to Early's caution, was creating a sea change in the ranks.[31]

On the Confederate side of the field, the long hours of procrastination produced in Gordon a rising sense of alarm. His division was on the extreme left of the three-mile-long front that Early had chosen to defend. Kershaw and Ramseur were to his right, then Pegram and Wharton to Ramseur's right. Strung out in open ground with both flanks in the air, the entire Confederate position all but invited a heavy blow from a numerically superior foe. Gordon was particularly vulnerable, concerned his left could be turned. "Sheridan's marchers were coming closer and massing in heavy column . . . while his cavalry was gathering on our flank." Trying to protect his left, he saw that a gap had opened on his front. Repeated calls to Early for help went unanswered. "I myself finally rose to headquarters to urge that he reinforce the left and fill the gap, which would prove a veritable death warrant if left open . . . or else that he concentrate his entire force for desperate defense or immediate withdrawal." But Early, hourly becoming more tentative, could not believe Sheridan was attacking in force. He told Gordon to stretch his lines still farther and use cannon to fill the gap. "I rode back at a furious gallop to execute these most unpromising movements," said Gordon scathingly. "It was too late. The last chance had passed of saving the army."[32]

Sheridan moved forward on the double-quick about 4 P.M., assailing the Confederate left. By the time Gordon rejoined his division Clement Evans was all but enveloped. "It required countercharges of the most daring character," said Gordon, "to prevent the utter destruction of the command." Within thirty minutes, two divisions of the Nineteenth Corps, together with George Custer's cavalry, were rolling up the Georgian's lines. First Edmund Pendleton's Louisianans toppled, then William Terry's Virginians.

When the three divisions of the Sixth Corps added their momentum to the attack, the fear of being flanked spread to Kershaw's and Ramseur's divisions. "Regiment after regiment, brigade after brigade, in rapid succession was crushed," Gordon would say, "and, like hard clods of clay under a pelting rain, the superb commands crumbled to pieces." Captain Dickert of Kershaw's old brigade describes the scene on his front: "Seeing no prospects of succor on our right or left, the enemy gradually passing and getting in our rear . . . the men break and fly. . . . The enemy kept close to our heels. . . . There were no thickets, no ravines, no fences to shield or protect us."

Ramseur held fast the longest, perhaps until 5:30 P.M. Gathering some 600 men and six guns, he and his troops repulsed numerous attacks, even as Pegram and Wharton on his right were withdrawing. If he could hold on until dark the Confederates might yet regroup. With one horse shot from under him, the North Carolinian found another mount and galloped along his front, determined to do just that. When the second horse was killed he looked for another. Suddenly a minie ball crashed through his side and pierced his lungs, inflicting a mortal wound. Deprived of Ramseur's example, his men late on October 19 joined in the flight of their comrades. "They would not listen to entreaties, threats or appeals of any kind," Early would say of the retreat to New Market. "A terror of the enemy's cavalry had seized them, and there was no holding them."[33]

For the Rebels it was the most disheartening of defeats, one that most felt need not have been. Cedar Creek cost the Federals some 5,800 casualties; the Confederates, some 3,000. Equally discouraging was the loss of twenty-four guns and hundreds of supply wagons, plus all the Federal guns and wagons that had been captured in the morning. Only the lethal fire of Colonel Carter's cannon slowed the chase. "The Yankees got whipped; we got scared," was the way Old Jube summed up the debacle. Here the blunt-talking Early may have been using "we" to mean himself as well as his men. Four years of war were taking their toll.

Captured during the retreat, the wounded Ramseur was taken to Sheridan's headquarters and given prompt medical attention, but there was no hope for recovery. Old friends from West Point visited his bedside during the night, doing their best to give him words of comfort. Artillery officer Henry DuPont, who had roomed across the hall from the secession firebrand at the academy, at one point jostled the bedstead, sending "a thrill of pain" through Ramseur, who groaned, "DuPont, you don't know how I suffer." Cavalryman George Custer likewise sat with him, perhaps thinking of the farewell party at Benny Haven's Tavern they had enjoyed not that long ago. Helped by doses of laudanum, Ramseur passed in and out of consciousness. When he was awake he often mentioned Nellie and their newborn child, and how he wished he could see them, just once, before he died. To an aide who had also been taken prisoner, he gave instructions to write his wife and send her a lock of his hair. Twenty-seven-year-old Dodson Ramseur died the next morning. "He told me to tell you," the aide wrote Nellie, "that he had a firm hope in Christ and trusted to meet you hereafter. He died as became a Confederate soldier and a firm believer."[34]

Gallant battler though he was, Early's usefulness was at an end. The storm of criticism over his setbacks continued unabated, ignoring the fact that he had inflicted 14,500 casualties and for months tied down tens of thousands of Federal troops, just when they were most needed for the assault on Petersburg. Though Lee badly needed competent officers, political considerations tied his hands. Early would stay in the Shenandoah with Wharton's division that winter, far up the Valley at Staunton, but the bulk of his command would return to the Petersburg-Richmond area. Kershaw's division left in mid-November. Gordon, leading the Second Corps, left several weeks thereafter.

# SIX

# PETERSBURG AND
# RICHMOND BESIEGED

Back on the Petersburg-Richmond front on June 15, three days after he had so hopefully dispatched Early and the Second Corps to the Shenandoah, Lee found himself on the horns of a dilemma. He knew that the Federals had withdrawn from the lines at Cold Harbor and that elements of the enemy were south of the James, but he could not be sure whether Grant was moving in force against Petersburg or the capital. He needed intelligence and he was not getting it. Grant's rapid movements and convincing feints were serving to conceal his aims, so much so that Lee for the nonce felt compelled to keep his army north of the river. In reality, however, most of the Federals had crossed the James and were advancing on Petersburg. Baldy Smith's Eighteenth Corps had sailed back to Bermuda Hundred, rejoining the still bottled-up Benjamin Butler. Meanwhile the rest of the enemy marched 50 miles to Wilcox's Landing. There Hancock's Second Corps crossed by boat, while Warren's Fifth Corps, Wright's Sixth Corps and Burnside's Ninth Corps took advantage of a superbly engineered 2,100-foot pontoon bridge.

Leading the attack from the east on Petersburg, a city of some 22,000 through which various railroads funneled essential supplies into Richmond, was Smith's 16,000-man corps. He was advancing on the so-called Dimmock Line, a ten-mile-long, artillery-studded breastwork in the shape of a squat horseshoe whose ends rested on the south bank of the Appomattox River. Opposing him was the 58-year-old former Virginia governor Henry Wise with his brigade and some scraped-together militia—perhaps 2,200 men. This would be the first engagement in a siege that would last nine and one-half months, with both sides shuttling troops back and forth between the two cities for some half-dozen battles and scores of lesser actions.

The fighting on June 15 began about 7 A.M. when James Dearing's cavalry brigade and Edward Graham's guns blocked the Federals on the City Point Road. "The stand taken by our handful of cavalry, near their breastworks, was most creditable," said the vainglorious Pierre Beauregard, still in command between Drewry's Bluff and Petersburg. "But the weight of numbers soon produced its almost inevitable result . . . and the breastworks were flanked and finally abandoned." Dearing's encounter, however, alerted Wise to the enemy's intentions and enabled him to concentrate his meager numbers. By 10 A.M., to the Confederates at least, the skirmishing had become alarming. Beauregard thereupon stripped some of his troops from Bermuda Hundred. "To the urgent demands of General Wise for reinforcements, I was enabled at last to answer that part of [Robert] Hoke's division was on the way from Drewry's Bluff. . . . Then all along the line . . . the order was given 'to hold on at all hazards.' It was obeyed with the resolute fortitude of veterans, though many of the troops engaged . . . had hardly been under fire before."

Through the morning and afternoon, the bitter but sporadic fighting continued. Smith, a capable general but a bon vivant who commonly served champagne at his camp dinners, exhibited no sense of exigency. Perhaps, with the slaughter of Cold Harbor fresh in his mind, he wanted no part of a frontal assault on cannon. Much of his day was spent in reconnoitering and probing. "Wise's single brigade, with a part of Dearing's dismounted, had to be stretched out nearly three miles to face the enemy's three divisions," said Porter Alexander. "But they & the artillery kept up a sharp fire on the enemy's efforts to reconnoiter & deploy, & usually broke them up and drove them back. . . . At last, however, their very thin musketry fire disclosed to Gen. Smith that they were little more than a skirmish line." By 6 P.M. Wise was falling back from the breastworks, his men were in disarray, and Smith was readying an all-out attack. "Had he gone ahead at that hour," said Alexander, "the chances are that he would have gotten Petersburg. But his chief of artillery had taken all the artillery horses to water, & he lost another hour, during which both night and Hoke's Division were drawing near."[1]

Smith at this point decided to wait for morning before renewing the attack, giving Beauregard time to rush Hoke into the works. The latter's division now consisted of Johnson Hagood's South Carolinians, Alfred Colquitt's Georgians and Thomas Clingman's and James Martin's North Carolinians. Hagood, Colquitt and Clingman we have met before. Martin, a West Pointer who had lost an arm in the Mexican War, had until recently been responsible for the training of all North Carolina units. Moving on the double-quick through the city's streets, the troops found its residents in shock.

"Too late! Too late!" cried one old man. "General Wise was defeated, and there have been no armed soldiers between Grant's army and this city since sun-down."

"We marched on," stated a North Carolinian, "and there was no sound except the soldiers' tramping, and the wail of the women who wept."

Beauregard here made a second move. Needing every man he could get, he ordered Bushrod Johnson's division to Petersburg from Bermuda Hundred, leaving the lines there undefended. This decision exposed the railroad and the highway between Petersburg and the capital to Butler's raids, severing the two cities. "I had previously . . . asked the War Department to elect between the Bermuda Hundred line and Petersburg," said Beauregard, "as, under the present circumstances, I could no longer hold both. The War Department had given me no answer, clearly intending that I should assume the responsibility of the measure. . . ." During the battle at Drewry's Bluff in May, Johnson had led his brigade of Tennesseans in Hoke's division. Now he had his own division, which was comprised of Archibald Gracie's Alabamians, Matt Ransom's North Carolinians and Stephen Elliott's South Carolinians. Elliott, the son of an Episcopal bishop, was a wealthy and socially prominent planter.[2]

By June 16 Beauregard's force had grown to 10,000. But with three of the five Federal corps in place the enemy totaled 66,000, and Beauregard must have known, or at least thought probable, that Grant's whole army was assailing Petersburg. Yet he did not so inform Lee, instead continually badgering the War Department for reinforcements, which of course would have to be detached from Lee's army. In effect Beauregard wanted the troops without the commander. Perhaps, in his jealousy of Lee and his determination to pursue his own strategy, he thought that Davis might put him in command of the whole eastern Virginia theater of operations. In any event, his need to be on center stage was so intense that it justified, in his eyes, his dissembling. "I do not know the position of Grant's army and cannot strip north bank of James River," Lee asked him on June 16 at 10.30 A.M. "Have you not force sufficient?" Again Lee inquired at 4 P.M.: "Has Grant been seen crossing James River?" To which Beauregard replied with a carefully worded evasion, ignoring the obvious: "No *information* [emphasis added] yet received of Grant's crossing James River. Hancock's and Smith's Corps are however in our front."

Meanwhile Lee, belatedly learning that Beauregard had vacated the Bermuda line, hurried Richard Heron Anderson and two divisions of the First Corps, those of Charles Field and George Pickett, to restore it. In spirited fighting they pushed the enemy back, reopening communications between the two cities. This put some 23,000 troops south of the James. Remaining north of the river was Kershaw's division (not yet detached to the Shenandoah) and most of the cavalry, together with Powell Hill's Third Corps—21,000 men in all.[3]

Fortunately the Federals dallied once again before Petersburg, with no serious assault occurring until 5 P.M. Preceded by a heavy cannonade, thousands of Bluecoats then charged the works but made little progress. "About dark a feeble effort . . . was made upon my center," said Johnson Hagood, "none getting nearer than seventy-five yards to our line. It was kept up for an hour or more. . . ." Beauregard thus far had not paid for his willfulness, largely due to enemy sluggishness. However, by the next day, June 17, the Union army totaled some 90,000 men while Beauregard had the same 10,000. Under repeated and crushing attacks the Creole, who admittedly was conducting an adroit defense, now directly called upon Lee for help, still not telling him that he was facing Grant's whole army: "We greatly need reinforcements to resist such large odds against us. The enemy must be dislodged or the city will fall." To which Lee at 4:30 P.M. replied: "Have no information of Grant's crossing James River, but upon your report have ordered troops up to Chaffin's Bluff." These were the men of Powell Hill's division and from this point, opposite Drewry's Bluff, his troops could quickly cross the river and proceed to Petersburg.[4]

This confusing and convoluted situation resolved itself the night of June 17–18, when Rooney Lee, who had been reconnoitering in force, reported to Lee from Wilcox Landing that he had found the enemy's pontoon bridge. Even as this revealing dispatch came in, so did others from Beauregard, allowing in circumspect terms what he should have stated all along: Grant was south of the James. Now Lee took prompt action. Reads the First Corps record: "At 3 A.M. Kershaw moves for Petersburg, followed by Field, Pickett occupying the whole [Bermuda Hundred] line. We arrive at Petersburg and Kershaw relieves Bushrod Johnson's Division, Field taking position on Kershaw's right." The old men, women and children greeted them in the early morning, red battle flags waving in the breeze, with shouts and huzzahs. When Powell Hill subsequently came up with the divisions of Henry Heth, Cadmus Wilcox and Billy Mahone, the cheering intensified. "What regiment should come first but our own gallant 12th Virginia," one woman would say of a regiment in David Weisiger's brigade, Mahone's division, "—but oh! so worn with travel and fighting, so dusty and ragged, their faces so thin and drawn by privation that we scarcely knew them."

Greeting Lee, whose sentiments are unrecorded but must have been restrained, Beauregard was at his bland and self-congratulatory best. "My welcome to General Lee," he wrote, "was most cordial. He was at last where I had, for the past three days, so anxiously hoped to see him—within the limits of Petersburg!" Ignoring not only the odds—the Confederates totaled some 44,000 in and around the city, their opponents now more than 100,000—but the extreme weariness of the troops, the Creole urged going on the attack. Lee thought not, saying the men needed rest. Beauregard would object, claiming that the Federal troops were just as exhausted and not yet entrenched.

"But," he modestly concluded, "I was then only second in command, and my views did not prevail."[5]

Later on June 18, the Federals made one more attempt to breach the Petersburg lines. George Meade issued orders to all corps commanders to push forward at noon, but instead of a coordinated attack, the movements were piecemeal and easily repulsed by combined cannon and musket fire. Meade nonetheless persisted, with wicked results. The most painful of these was experienced by the 900-man 1st Maine Heavy Artillery, who suffered some 630 casualties—the largest loss in a single action of any regiment in the war. From June 15 to June 18 Grant incurred some 10,000 casualties; Confederate losses were 4,000.[6]

Temporarily giving up on storming Petersburg, Grant and Meade now resolved to extend their lines in a semicircle to the southwest of the city, cutting off the railroad supply lines or at least tearing up as much track as possible. On June 21–22, James Wilson with two cavalry divisions was dispatched in a wide arc against the Richmond & Danville and Southside Railroads, while Hancock's Second Corps, under David Birney, and Wright's Sixth Corps moved across the Jerusalem Pike Road to the Petersburg and Weldon Railroad. (Hancock, who had suffered a groin wound at Gettysburg that refused to heal, had been forced to take sick leave.) Lee sent his own cavalry to challenge Wilson, while the task of containing the Union infantry fell to Powell Hill, occupying the works south of the city with the divisions of Heth, Wilcox and Billy Mahone.

The tiny Mahone, whose dyspepsia confined him to a diet of milk and eggs, was emerging as one of the army's premiere combat officers. Late on the 22nd, when Lee noticed that Birney and Wright had halted in a heavily forested area to await further orders, he resolved to go on the offensive. Mahone, who knew the area well from the time he had surveyed it while building the Norfolk & Petersburg Railroad, proposed taking the enemy on their left flank, proceeding through a ravine that would screen three of his brigades—those of David Weisiger, Rans Wright and John Calhoun Sanders—from sight. Lee gave his assent, and Hill personally accompanied Mahone in the 5 P.M. advance.

The Federals were unsuspecting. "Suddenly and swiftly, with a wild yell which rang out shrill and fierce in the gloomy pines," said W. Gordon McCabe, an aide to artillerist Willie Pegram, "Mahone's men burst upon the flank—a peaking volley, which roared along the whole front—a stream of wasting fire, under which the adverse left fell as one man—and the bronzed veterans swept forward, shriveling up [Francis] Barlow's division as lightning shrivels the dead leaves of autumn; then cleaving a fiery path diagonally across the enemy's front, spreading dismay and destruction, rolled up [Gershom] Mott's division in turn, and without check, the woods still reverberating with their clamor, stormed and carried [John] Gibbon's entrenchments and seized his guns."[7]

In what Grant subsequently labeled "a stampede," Mahone before he withdrew routed Birney's three divisions, inflicted 3,000 casualties, captured four guns and eight regimental flags—with minimum loss in his own ranks. The next day, when the Federals gingerly reoccupied their positions, Mahone struck again, sending out Joseph Finegan's Florida brigade on a similar mission. Finegan likewise bloodied the foe, capturing 600 in the process, but, reported Hill: ". . . it was so hot, the undergrowth so thick, and the enemy retiring all this time, our men did not press forward." This was understandable: Mahone's men had been without sleep for 48 hours.[8]

James Wilson meanwhile would have his own problems. His cavalrymen initially had been successful in their destructive foray farther west against the railroads, but when he sought to withdraw he found a vengeful Fitzhugh nipping at his heels. "Lee hung upon [Wilson's] rear with an exasperating tenacity which brought delay and redoubled his difficulties," said McCabe. "At every step indeed the peril thickened, for Hampton, who had crossed the James, now came to Lee's help with a strong body of horse, and attacking the enemy on Tuesday evening (June 28) at Sappony Church drove him until dark . . . and sent him helter-skelter." Wilson the next day galloped toward Reams's Station on the Weldon Railroad, ten miles south of Petersburg, which he thought the Federals held. There he blundered into two of Mahone's brigades—Sanders's and Finegan's—which Lee had ordered out from the works to block his way. At this point Wilson was all but surrounded. "In a twinkling, as it seemed," continued McCabe, "the rattling fire of the carbines told us that [Lunsford] Lomax was hotly engaged, and on the instant the movement in front began—the infantry under Mahone advancing swiftly. . . . For a brief space the confused combat, ever receding, went on—shouts of triumph mingling with the dismal cries of stricken men, ringing pistol shots, the chattering fire of cavalry carbines, the dull roar of the guns. . . ."[9]

So furious was Mahone's attack that Wilson was soon overwhelmed. He spiked what guns and burned what wagons he could, then led his men in cutting their way out. When this first action at Reams's Station ended the Confederates had killed and wounded hundreds, and taken 1,000 prisoners, thirteen cannon, many wagonloads of small arms and ordnance and hundreds of badly needed horses. For the third time in one week, Mahone had shown his mettle. So taken were the Federals with his performance that they thereafter tried to guess where his division was in the lines—with an eye toward avoiding it. Complained Meade to Grant about the conflicting reports he was receiving: "Mahone's Division . . . has now been positively placed on our front, on our left and rear, and on its way to Pennsylvania." Mahone's fellow officers were equally impressed. "Whenever Mahone moves out," commented Brigadier Henry Wise, "somebody is apt to be hurt."[10]

With the stalemate continuing through July, even as Early was having his successes at Monocacy and Kernstown in the Valley, stories began to appear in the Northern newspapers that Grant wanted Lee to come out from the breastworks and fight. This was a challenge that chafed Lee. "There is nothing I desire now more than a 'fair field fight,' " he said after reading one such piece. "If Grant will meet me on equal grounds, I will give him two to one odds." Reflected Willie Pegram, who idolized Lee: "That was very strong for the old General." In truth Lee detested the present situation. Throughout the war he had relied on maneuvering to offset the enemy's superior numbers, and for the first time this strength had been taken from him. His stretched-out lines not only protected Petersburg, but ran up through Bermuda Hundred and Drewry's Heights, then crossed the James to end northeast of Richmond—a distance of 35 miles. When on July 26 Grant sent Birney's Second Corps and two divisions of Sheridan's cavalry north to the capital in a diversion, Lee had little choice but to send in pursuit Kershaw and Field of Anderson's corps, Heth and Wilcox of Hill's, as well as cavalry, to counter the move. This left the entire Petersburg works with only three divisions of infantry, perhaps 15,000 men: Mahone's, Hoke's and Bushrod Johnson's.[11]

For some weeks meanwhile the Federals had been excavating a 511-foot underground shaft from their lines to the east of Petersburg, then extending it laterally some 80 feet under the so-called Elliott Salient (named for Stephen Elliott, whose South Carolina troops were stationed there), and eventually packing it with 8,000 pounds of gunpowder. Doing the digging was the 48th Pennsylvania, a regiment composed mostly of coal miners and commanded by Lieutenant Colonel Henry Pleasants. Grant and Meade intended to blow a huge gap in the works, which were defended there only by four guns and two regiments, and then hurl two of Burnside's divisions—some 15,000 men—into the breach. The first of these would be white troops under Brigadier James Ledlie. The second would be black, mostly former slaves fighting under Brigadier Edward Ferrero. While blacks filled the ranks of some 160 Union regiments, this was the only such division in the Army of the Potomac.

Porter Alexander in retrospect could not help but admire the Yankee ingenuity that went into the tunnel, especially how the shaft was ventilated: "The entrance to the gallery was through an air-tight bulkhead. . . . A little way inside a fireplace was excavated on the side with a chimney up through the hill. A long air box or ventilating flue ran . . . along on the floor to the far end of the gallery. Now, a little fire being kindled in the fireplace, the chimney will begin to draw. Air will flow . . . to supply this draft, & thus fresh air is always being delivered to the far end of the gallery, whence it flows back to the fireplace."

On July 30 at 4:30 A.M. the Battle of the Crater began. "A slight tremor of the earth for a second," said artillerist McCabe, "then the rocking as of an earthquake, and with a tremendous burst that rent the sleeping hills beyond, a vast column of earth and smoke shoots upward to a great height, its dark sides flashing out sparks of fire, hangs poised for a moment in midair, and then hurtling downward with a roaring sound [and] showers of stones, broken timbers and blackened human limbs, subsides. . . ." The blast killed 256 of Elliott's men, and created a jagged crater 135 feet long, almost 100 feet wide and at least 30 feet deep. Trying to rally his troops, Elliott received a severe wound. "The dread upheaval has rent in twain Elliott's Brigade, and the men to the right and left of the huge abyss recoil in terror. Nor shall we censure them, for so terrible was the explosion that even the assaulting column shrank back aghast."

Then a storm of Federal cannon fire erupted, jolting the troops into motion. Fortunately for the rebels, the enemy was badly led. Neither Ledlie nor Ferrero would put themselves in harm's way, leaving the assault to their subordinates. The first wave of attackers, "uttering a mechanical cheer, slowly mounts the crest, passes unmolested across the intervening space, and . . . plunges in the crater, courting the friendly shelter of its crumbling sides. . . . Silence still reigned along the Confederate lines, yet Ledlie's men did not advance [from the crater], and now the supporting brigade of the same division was running forward over the crest, and with an incredible folly crowding in upon their comrades . . . all regimental and company organization was lost, and the men speedily passed from control."[12]

Here 23-year-old Confederate Major John Cheves Haskell, who had lost an arm at Gaines's Mill, was positioned with his sixteen-gun battalion some 600 yards behind the lines. Seeing that only cannon at this point barred the enemy's way to Petersburg he quickly galloped to the front, followed by two light batteries. Continued McCabe: ". . . having disposed these pieces along the [Jerusalem] Plank Road, and opened [Henry] Flanner's guns from the Gee House, [Haskell] passed to his left to speak a word of cheery commendation to [James] Lamkin of his battalion, who was already annoying the swarming masses of the enemy with his Virginia battery of eight-inch mortars." Encouraged by Haskell's example, all units held their ground under the incoming barrage. "The officers of one battery, indeed, misbehaved," said McCabe, "but these were promptly spurned aside, and the very spot of their deflection made glorious by the heroic conduct of Hampton Gibbes of the artillery and Sam Preston of Wise's Brigade, both of whom fell desperately wounded—while spurring hard from the hospital, with the fever still upon him, came Hampden Chamberlayne, a young officer of Hill's Corps, who so handled these abandoned guns that from that day the battery bore his name."[13]

Never was the Confederate artillery more effective than in the frenzied aftermath of the explosion. Lieutenant Colonel Frank Huger, pitching in as a loader at his heated Napoleons, worked with joyous zeal. Samuel Wright with his Halifax Battery, hidden by a concealing grove of pines, likewise opened up a withering fire. Soon eight-inch and ten-inch mortars from the rear joined in the response to the Federal assault. Shells rained down on both the crater itself and the approaches leading to it, further befuddling the enemy, who persisted in traipsing lemminglike into the huge pit, where they milled about without direction.

By 6 A.M. Meade was beside himself with frustration, wondering why the advance was stalling. "Our chance is now," he told Burnside. "Push your men forward at all hazards, white and black, and don't lose time in making formations, but rush for the crest." Such was not to be. The troops were becoming a leaderless mass and the crater would be a death trap. Soon Mahone rushed to the scene with David Weisiger's Virginians and Rans Wright's Georgians. "I stood where I could keep one eye on the adversary whilst I directed my own command," he said, "which every moment was in peril if the enemy should advance while the two brigades were moving. . . . A survey of the situation impressed me with the belief, so crowded were the enemy and his flags—eleven flags in less than one hundred yards—that he was greatly disordered but present in large force." He called up Sanders's Alabama brigade, then conferred with his officers. "The line of men which we have here," he said, "is the only barrier to the enemy occupying Petersburg. . . . We must carry his position immediately by assaulting it. If we don't carry it by the first attack we shall renew the attack as long as there is a man of us left."[14]

Despite the decline in Southern fortunes since Gettysburg, the esprit de corps of Mahone's troops remained high. "Mahone, cool, courageous and able, was by nature fitted for generalship as few men are," a comrade would say, "and none knew this better than the men of his command . . . they always felt a moral certainty that they were properly being led or placed, either to inflict the most damage on the enemy or to have the enemy inflict the least damage on them." On the morning of the charge at the crater then, "there was not a man in the brigade, knowing that General Mahone was present, who did not feel we . . . would be put in when and where the most effective service could be rendered."[15]

Not until 9 A.M. were the Federals able to sort out their units sufficiently to establish a ragtag front and surmount the far crest of the crater. Just at this moment Mahone hurled his troops forward from a protective ravine, with Colonel Weisiger leading the onslaught. "The whole line sprang along the crest," said McCabe, "and there burst from more than eight hundred warlike voices the fierce yell which no man has yet heard unmoved. . . . Storms of case shot from the right mingled with the tempest of bullets which smote upon them from the front, yet there was no answering volley for these were veterans . . . and even in the tumult the men did not forget their orders." Then one volley crashed from the whole line, the enemy fell back and the work of the bayonet began. "How long it lasted none may say with certainty, for in those moments no man heeded time, no man asked [nor] gave quarter, but in an incredibly

brief space . . . the whole of the advanced line north of the crater was retaken." In the pit below, the Federals, white and black, were all but helpless.
"From the great mortars to the right and left huge missiles, describing graceful
curves, fell with dreadful accuracy and burst among the masses . . . and often
times the very air seemed darkened by flying human limbs." From the crest
Weisiger's Virginians added their musket fire to the debacle.

In the wake of the charge, a watching Lee remarked: "That must have been
Mahone's old brigade." Told that it was, he smiled and said, "I thought so."[16]

The Confederates now held the ground north and west of the crater but
the area to the south, as well as the pit itself, was still in enemy hands. At 10
A.M. and again an hour later Mahone sent Wright's brigade forward, only to
see the Georgians after furious charges repulsed on both occasions. Pinned
down though they were, the enemy remained dangerous.

What was it like in the crater? A Union lieutenant takes up the story: "[The
Confederates] around the crest were loading and firing as fast as they could,
and the men were dropping thick and fast, most shot through the head. Every
man that was shot rolled down the steep sides to the bottom and in places
they were piled up four and five deep. . . . The cries of the wounded were
piteous in the extreme. An enfilading fire was coming through the traverse
down which we had retreated. General [William] Bartlett ordered the colored
troops to build a breastworks across it. . . . Someone called out, 'Put in the
dead men,' and acting on this suggestion a large number of dead, white and
black, were piled into the trench. This made a partial shelter."

About 1 P.M. Mahone put the eager Alabama brigade of 24-year-old Brigadier John Sanders into action. Sanders had been with the army since Seven
Pines, chiefly with the 11th Alabama, and was a seasoned fighter. His men
swept the enemy from the ground to the south, then with elements of Weisiger's and Wright's brigades rushed into the crater. What happened next,
though it lasted only minutes, was not one of the Army of Northern Virginia's
finest episodes. "It was the first time Lee's army had encountered negroes,"
said General Wise, "and their presence excited in the troops indignant malice
such as had characterized no former conflict. . . . Our men, inflamed to relentless vengeance, disregarded the rules of warfare. . . ." Wrote Willie Pegram
with understatement to his sister Virginia: "A few of our men were wounded
by the negroes, which exasperated them very much . . . as soon as we got to
them, they threw down their arms to surrender, but were not allowed to do
so." Remembered one Alabama soldier: "We tried to obey orders. Just before
the job was completed, General Mahone sent orders to us not to kill quite all
of them."

Not all the Rebels forgot their better instincts, of course. One officer of the
8th Alabama, standing in the middle of the clubbing and bayoneting, was
sickened by the bloodletting and tried to stop it.

"Why in hell don't you fellows surrender?" he shouted to a nearby white officer.

"Why the hell don't you let us?" came back the reply.[17]

For the Federals, regardless of race, the white flag soon went up and the carnage mercifully ended. "It was the saddest affair I have witnessed in this war," Grant told the War Department. "Such opportunity for carrying fortifications I have never seen and do not expect again to have." The Battle of the Crater cost him 5,000 casualties, including some 1,500 prisoners. Lee's losses were 1,500. Three battlefield promotions resulted: Mahone to major general, Weisiger to brigadier and young Victor Girardey of "Rans" Wright's brigade from captain to brigadier. Wright had been in failing health, and the brilliant Girardey, an emigrant from France, had been essential in helping Mahone launch the division's counterattack. His promotion to brigadier was the highest such jump in the army's history. Within two weeks, however, he would be killed in skirmishing north of the James.[18]

On August 18 Grant moved west once more and took possession of the upper stretch of the Weldon Railroad, advancing some 10,000 men of Warren's Fifth Corps to Globe Tavern. Not immediately grasping the extent of the threat, Powell Hill sent Heth's division out from Petersburg to oust them. Considering his far fewer numbers, Heth behaved with distinction, throwing back the Federal van and taking 150 prisoners before prudently withdrawing. The next day the Confederates came out in greater strength. Heth pushed straight down the Halifax Road while Mahone's division on his left, supported by Willie Pegram's batteries, moved through some woods to turn the enemy flank. About 4 P.M. he hit the Federal front just as Mahone struck from the left. "With a cheer the Confederate troops bounded forward and swept over all obstruction," a Petersburg newspaper reported, "pressing the Yankees back with severe loss into their second line; and, charging forward, forced them thence with an equal lack of ceremony." For the men in the field, the action was far more confusing. "Front and rear seemed to be on all sides," one of Mahone's soldiers said. "The bullets came from every direction."

Though the engagement was a tactical success, with Heth and Mahone taking 2,700 prisoners, the Federals retained control of the upper Weldon Railroad. Now supplies would be unloaded from freight cars 20 miles south of Petersburg and brought into the city by wagon. Burnside's Ninth Corps under John G. Parke (Burnside had in effect been relieved for the bungling at the Battle of the Crater) had reinforced Warren, and the enemy could not be budged. Hill made one last attempt, on August 21, but to no avail. On this occasion John Calhoun Sanders of Mahone's command was killed. Grant's losses overall totaled some 4,500 out of 20,000 engaged; Southern losses, 1,600 out of 14,000 engaged.[19]

Three days later Hancock's Second Corps was dispatched to Reams's Station on the Weldon line, four and one-half miles below Globe Tavern, with orders to tear up more track. They were busily going about this work when, on August 25, they were assailed by Wade Hampton's 5,000-man cavalry and Powell Hill's three divisions—those of Heth, Mahone and Wilcox. Lee had seen that Hancock, who was back from sick leave, lacked strong defensive works and was cut off from the Federals farther north, and he intended to take advantage of his weakness. "Do all in your power to punish the enemy," he told his officers. Though Hill would direct the attack, his prostatitis had flared up anew, forcing him to give Heth field command. By 5 P.M. the battle reached a crescendo. Here Pegram's gunners were particularly effective. Their barrage "scattered our breastworks like kindling wood," said one Union soldier, "and cut off the trees about us as if they were pipe-stems." The three North Carolina brigades of Jim Lane, John Cooke and William MacRae at this juncture struck the Federal front, even as Hampton's troopers swung around and turned its left flank. Panicking under the assault and the hand-to-hand fighting that ensued, Hancock's men surrendered in droves, driving him into a rage. "I pray God I may never leave the field!" he ranted.

Of 2,700 Federal casualties, at least 2,100 were prisoners. "I thought we had captured their whole army," said Mahone's ordnance officer, "for I had never seen so many prisoners in a battle before." Confederate losses were some 700. But the success at Reams's Station did not recover the railroad, and Lee was under no illusions that his dwindling numbers could continue to keep the enemy off balance indefinitely. Most divisions were now the size of brigades, and brigades the size of regiments. "Without some increase of strength," he had told Secretary of War James Seddon, "I cannot see how we can escape the natural military consequences of . . . numerical superiority."[20]

Grant meanwhile, his casualties continually replaced by new recruits, kept up the pressure on his adversaries, shuttling his forces back and forth across the James almost at will. On the foggy morning of September 29, just ten days after Early's defeat at Winchester in the Shenandoah, two Federal corps from Benjamin Butler's Army of the James moved out of their works at Bermuda Hundred, crossed the river and made a two-pronged attack on Richmond from the south. The column on the right, David Birney's Tenth Corps, headed for New Market Heights. The column on the left, Edward Ord's Eighteenth Corps, marched toward Forts Harrison and Gilmer, two redoubts in the capital's outer defenses. (Baldy Smith, like Burnside, had drawn Grant's wrath; he had been relieved from duty as head of the Eighteenth Corps for his hesitant advance on Petersburg June 15–16 and replaced with Ord.)

Birney's corps of the Army of the James, led on the march by Brigadier Charles Paine's black division, consisted of some 13,000 troops. Opposing them on the heights was John Gregg's much-depleted Texas Brigade—the 1st, 4th and 5th Texas—and the 3rd Arkansas, together with Brigadier Martin

Gary's dismounted cavalry, perhaps 1,800 men. The veteran Texans, stretched out in a single line each man six feet apart, fired volley after volley at the oncoming black soldiers, inflicting a fearsome toll. Fighting through abatis and riddled by enfilading fire, the Federals nonetheless came on. When one wave was repulsed, a second—ten ranks deep—took its place. With the fog lifting, the black soldiers made even more vulnerable targets. Still they persisted. By 8 A.M., minutes after Gregg fell back to reinforce Fort Gilmer, they took the summit. The Federals suffered 850 casualties; the Confederates, only 50.

Fourteen blacks and two white officers received the Medal of Honor for their heroism during the battle. One such soldier was Corporal James Miles of the 36th U.S. Colored Volunteers. Read the citation: "Having had his arm mutilated, making immediate amputation necessary, he loaded and discharged his piece with one hand and urged his men forward; this within thirty yards of the enemy's works." Wrote a reporter for the *New York Herald*: "The behavior of the negro troops . . . was of the most gallant character. Who dare say, after this, that negroes will not fight?" Added the *Philadelphia Press*: Paine's division "has covered itself with glory." Southern onlookers minimized the withdrawal. "Birney's whole corps . . . was so severely handled," wrote one letter-writer to the *Columbia Daily South Carolinian*, "that when the order came for us to fall back, it permitted our thin line . . . to retire in order and without injury."[21]

To the east of New Market Heights Edward Ord's Eighteenth Corps took undermanned Fort Harrison with ease, though Ord was severely wounded in the attack, but subsequently the Federals were driven back at Fort Gilmer. "The assault was made at precisely 2 P.M.," said the *Herald* of the latter action, "the men giving a cheer and starting forward on the run. They were met with a most murderous fire of grape and cannister, and unceasing volleys of musketry that worked terrible havoc in their ranks." Stated the *New York Times*: the "colored troops again distinguished themselves here. . . . At least twenty of them climbed up on the parapet of the fort, and were shot dead, tumbling back upon their comrades. The rest, it is said, were slaughtered by the enemy with shells thrown among them by hand."

Though the Confederate lines around Richmond overall were holding, the loss of Fort Harrison threatened the rear of the fortifications at Chaffin's Bluff and the river approaches to the capital. On September 30, therefore, Lee made a major effort to retake the redoubt. Charles Field's and Robert Hoke's divisions composed the bulk of the attacking troops, some 16,000 men against 21,000 of the enemy. With considerable misgivings, the men advanced about 1 P.M. Field and Hoke would have to double-quick across 200 yards of open ground, break through massed and well-protected skirmishers armed with repeating carbines and then scale the redoubt's baleful walls. "The enemy was now thoroughly protected & well prepared, & his trenches full of men," admitted Porter Alexander, who would be touching off the artillery barrage before the charge. Robert Hoke, standing next to him, was edgy. "I had rather you would not fire a shot from your guns, sir!" he told Alexander. "You will demoralize my men more by your shells falling short . . . than you will inflict damage on the enemy! If you will bring your guns up to the line and charge with my troops you may do some good. . . ."

"But my horses will get killed!" Alexander objected.

"Yes, and my men are going to be killed!" replied Hoke. "Are your horses of more value than the lives of my soldiers?"[22]

Regardless of Hoke's remonstrance, the thirty-minute barrage nonetheless went off on schedule, with Field sending forth in its wake "Tige" Anderson's Georgians, John Bratton's South Carolinas and the wounded Evander Law's Alabamians under William Perry. The uncoordinated movement, which Hoke was late in supporting, was doomed to failure. Met by a hail of fire Field's men made no headway. "The noise sounded like the magnified roar of a thousand kettle guns," said one officer in Bratton's brigade. Now Hoke belatedly gave the command to advance. Pushing forward were Colquitt's Georgia brigade and Thomas Clingman's North Carolina brigade under Hector McKethan—Clingman having been wounded during the fighting around the Weldon Railroad. "By the time we got [within] seventy yards of their works," said a captain in the 31st North Carolina, "our line was entirely broken, not from falling back, but literally from the men being cut down in piles." One private in the 27th Georgia put it more succinctly: "It was as bad a place as I was ever in."[23]

Here Lee came on the field, waving his hat and urging the men on as he had in the Wilderness and at the Mule Shoe. While his appearance had the desired effect, inspiring the rebels to make two more haphazard charges, the results were equally grim. All the brigades suffered terrible losses, but Clingman's were the greatest. Of 911 men whom McKethan put into action, only 383 answered roll call that night. Three out of four regimental and 27 out of 40 company commanders were among the casualties. "The brigade is literally cut to pieces," said the only surviving officer of the 31st North Carolina; "another such a fight will certainly wipe us out." Confederate losses in the engagement totaled some 2,200; Federal, 3,300.

Fort Harrison never would be recovered from the enemy, forcing the Confederates to redraw their lines. Lee seemed stunned by the outcome, with one of McKethan's officers saying he had "a face on him as long as gun barrel." Porter Alexander agreed: "General Lee was more worried by this failure than I have ever seen him. . . ."[24]

One more major action occurred outside of Richmond before winter set in, that of Lee's movement down the Darbytown Road on October 7 to retake some of the city's outer defensive lines. The plan called for Martin Gary's cavalry with Perry's Alabamians to turn the Federal right flank, then for Field to advance upon the center. Hoke was in reserve, poised to add his weight when needed. Gary and Field ably coordinated their attacks and were at first successful, driving in the enemy and capturing sixteen cannon. But when the time came for Hoke to join in the assault on the Federal breastworks, he did not commit. "My gallant fellows, led by the brigade commanders on foot," said Field, "rushed forward and penetrated to the abatis, facing a most terrific fire. . . . Hoke, for some unexplained cause, did not move forward. The consequence was that the whole fire was concentrated on [us]. We were repulsed with heavy loss." Here John Gregg of the Texas Brigade was shot dead through the neck and John Bratton, leading his South Carolinians, wounded in the shoulder.

Coming on the heels of his conduct at Fort Harrison, Hoke's failure to commit raised his fellow officers' eyebrows. While they did not question his courage, his critics wondered aloud about his willingness to cooperate. Johnson Hagood, one of his brigadiers, would defend Hoke, pointing out that Lee was at his side all during the assault. Lee must have kept him out of the fight, Hagood speculated, to make sure his troops stayed between the enemy and Richmond.[25]

While these engagements were going on north of the James, Grant continued to extend his lines westward outside of Petersburg, advancing Warren and Parke with twenty-four cannon on September 30 toward Poplar Springs Church. Here they were challenged again by Powell Hill, who sent elements of Heth's and Wilcox's commands, likewise supported by twenty-four guns, out of the city to meet them. "Thunder and fire and smoke," said a South Carolinian, "issued from the opposing hilltops in roaring volumes that rent the air and shook the earth, while shot and shell swept across the field hissing and screaming and crashing into the ranks of the opposing columns." Flanking the enemy right, Hill took hundreds of prisoners that day and the next, but then wisely fell back to Petersburg. The Federals were just too strong. Explained Willie Pegram: Hill had little choice "because of the disparity in numbers. The enemy had one corps & part of another. We had four small infantry brigades besides the cavalry."[26]

On a rainy October 27, eight days after Early's decisive defeat at Cedar Creek, Grant's next movement was still farther west to Hatcher's Run. Three corps under Parke, Hancock and Warren—some 43,000 men—pushed their way forward, their eventual goal the Southside Railroad, but swampland and ignorance of the terrain impeded and confused their progress. Though his prostate problems were keeping Hill from field command, he instinctively went on the attack, sending Heth, Wilcox and Mahone, together with Hampton, against the incursion. Finding a gap on the right between Hancock and Warren, the indomitable Mahone rushed into the opening, ripping the Federal lines asunder. "But," wrote Pegram to his mother, "it was like one man getting in between four. After making a brilliant dash, capturing a small number of prisoners, killing many and utterly disorganizing the enemy, Gen. Mahone became surrounded, but cut his way out in a very handsome manner."

Hampton's dismounted cavalry on the left double-quicked into the battle and added to the chaos, forcing Hancock on the defensive. Calbraith Butler's South Carolinians had so often fought on foot they were like seasoned infantry. Rooney Lee's troopers now galloped up, lending their sabers to the attack. In the midst of the melee was the brawny Hampton. This scion of a South Carolina planter dynasty had been newly named as Stuart's successor, and this day his two sons were under his command. "Preston Hampton rode recklessly into the hottest fire," Mary Chestnut would write subsequently. "His father sent his brother Wade to bring him back. Wade saw [Preston] reel in the saddle and galloped up to him. General Hampton followed." Just as young Wade reached his brother, he himself was wounded. "Preston recognized his father but died without speaking a word.... The general took his dead son in his arms, kissed him, and handed his body . . . to his friends . . . [bade] them take care of Wade . . . then rode back to his post." With tears in his eyes Hampton directed the inconclusive fight for the rest of the day. "Until night he did not know young Wade's fate," continued Mrs. Chestnut. "He might be dead, too."[27]

With winter coming on, this affair at Hatcher's Run effectively brought an end to the engagements around Petersburg and Richmond. Lee would use the weeks before the New Year to bring some order to his riddled command. The troublesome Beauregard had already been transferred to the West, supervising the departments headed by Richard Taylor and John Bell Hood. Longstreet, recovered from his wound, in late October was put in charge north of the James, permitting Lee for the most part to remain in Petersburg. Though Old Pete's arm was permanently impaired, he remained a resolute fighter. To make room for him, the increasingly less aggressive Dick Anderson was shifted to a minicommand, the division of Bushrod Johnson—Elliott's, Gracie's, Matt Ransom's and Wise's brigades. Toward year's end, too, the less-than-cooperative Hoke was transferred with his division to North Carolina.

Changes in the First Corps were relatively minimal. In Charles Field's division lawyer and legislator Colonel Robert Powell, who had been with the 5th Texas since 1861, replaced Gregg as head of the Texas Brigade. Educator William Flake Perry stayed with the Alabama brigade of the wounded Evander Law, who would go to the Carolinas. "Tige" Anderson and "Rock" Benning continued to head their Georgians and John Bratton his South Carolinians. Kershaw, once he returned from the Valley after the debacle of Cedar Creek, remained a tower of strength. In his division the experienced John D. Kennedy led Kershaw's old South Carolina brigade. There were new commanders of the Georgia brigades: Goode Bryan, forced to resign because of poor health, and William Wofford, recalled to Georgia by the governor, were replaced respectively by James Simms and Dudley DuBose. Reliable Benjamin Humphreys led his Mississippi brigade. Pickett's division contained the Virginia units of Monty Corse, Eppa Hunton, William R. Terry and George Steuart. Terry commanded the brigade of James Kemper, now free from imprisonment after Gettysburg but no longer fit for field duty; Steuart, returning to duty following his capture at the Mule Shoe, headed Lew Armistead's old command.

The bloodied Second Corps, back from the Shenandoah in December, now was led by John Brown Gordon. His former division, headed by Clement Evans, was comprised of Evans's old Georgia brigade under Colonel John Lowe, plus the tattered Virginians and Louisianans of William Terry and Zebulon York. The latter were under the devout and dogged Eugene Waggaman (York had been severely wounded in the Valley and would see no further action). In Bryan Grimes's division (which had been Rodes's) William Cox led his North Carolinians and Philip Cook his Georgians but colonels now headed the Alabamians and North Carolinians, respectively, of the impaired Cullen Battle and Grimes. Heading Gordon's third division was John Pegram, older brother of Willie. His brigades, those of Robert Johnston, William Lewis and John Hoffman were even weaker, at this juncture led by comparatively junior officers.

Powell Hill's Third Corps's strength was somewhere between that of Longstreet's and Gordon's. In Harry Heth's division, the brigades were comprised of the Mississippians of Joseph Davis, the president's nephew; the North Carolinians of John Rogers Cooke, Stuart's brother-in-law, and civil engineer William MacRae (replacing William Kirkland, transferred to North Carolina); and the Tennesseans of William McComb (stepping in for James Archer, who died in late October, his health broken by his stay in a Union prison). Wilcox's division included Edward Thomas's Georgians, Samuel McGowan's South Carolinians and Jim Lane's and Alfred Scales's North Carolinians. Lane had recovered from his wound at Cold Harbor. Colonel Joseph Hyman led the disabled Scales's brigade. In Mahone's division, three of the five brigades remained under stable leadership: David Weisiger's Virginians, Nathaniel Harris's Mississippians and Joseph Finegan's Floridians. William Forney, who had been badly crippled at Gettysburg, would lead the slain John Sanders's Alabamians. Mahone's fifth brigade, that of the ill-fated Victor Girardey's Georgians, was entrusted to Moxley Sorrel, the longtime Longstreet aide who had led the impromptu flanking attack at the Wilderness.

The cavalry under Hampton were comprised of three divisions: Fitz Lee's, Calbraith Butler's and Rooney Lee's. Fitz Lee's brigades were the Virginians of Tom Munford (replacing Williams Wickham, who resigned to join the Confederate Congress) and William Payne, plus Martin Gary's mixed command. Butler's were the South Carolinians of John Dunovant (who had been killed at Fort Harrison), the Georgians of Pierce Young and the Virginians of Tom Rosser. Rooney Lee commanded the North Carolina brigades of Rufus Barringer and 23-year-old William Roberts, and the Virginians of the slain John Chambliss under Richard Beale. In the artillery, the commanders were familiar names: Porter Alexander with the First Corps, Armistead Long with the Second, Lindsay Walker with the Third, and Preston Chew with the horse artillery.

In the late fall came very bad news indeed, at least for those Confederates who still thought there could be a negotiated peace. Abraham Lincoln running on the Republican ticket was reelected on November 8 as president of the United States. He received 2.3 million votes, compared to the conciliatory former General George McClellan—yes, that George McClellan—running on the Democratic ticket, who was named on 1.8 million ballots. Meantime the courageous but reckless John Bell Hood, who following his defeat at Atlanta had failed at Franklin, Tennessee, and would do so again at Nashville, would wreck the Army of Tennessee, exposing the underbelly of the South. Sherman would move, all but unopposed, through Georgia to the sea. Davis's and Lee's hopes of reinforcements from the Deep South now were dashed.

# 1865

ONE

\* \* \* \*

# THE STRONGHOLDS FALL

In the long semicircle of Confederate entrenchments protecting Richmond and Petersburg in the winter of 1865—from the Chickahominy River in the northeast across the James and Appomattox Rivers to Hatcher's Run in the southwest, misery was the lot of the common soldier. So meager were the rations that men grew faint if forced to dig longer than a half-hour in the excavations. "Now we experienced a greater suffering for food and clothing than we had ever known before," said one of McGowan's South Carolinians, Hill's corps. "The ration of food professed to be a pound of cornmeal and a third of a pound of bacon. But we received scarcely the full weight of the former, and the latter we had frequently to do without entirely . . . We had no meat for a whole week, once . . . Canned beef, imported from England (!), was issued a few times, and . . . small bits of poor, blue beef were doled out. Sometimes we had coffee, and now and then a spoonful of sugar. Tobacco, of the worst quality, was issued every month, at the rate of a fourth of a pound to each man." Proper clothing and blankets were rarely to be found. "I do not remember the issue of a single overcoat, and but a few blankets. Shoes were scarce. More than once a soldier left a bloody foot print on the frozen picket line." Firewood was equally in short supply. "The growth about the camp, never heavy, was soon consumed by the troops; and for the last two months of our stay we were obliged to carry logs on our shoulders for the distance of a mile or more . . ."[1]

Far more pressing for the soldiers than these problems, however, were the piteous entreaties from loved ones at home. Stated one of Pegram's can-

noneers: "From the cotton lands of Georgia and the rice fields of Carolina
came borne . . . the despairing cry which wives and little ones raised to win-
try skies . . . and men, with bated breath and cheeks flushing through their
bronze, whispered the dread word, 'desertion.' " For husbands of women
with young children, the strain that winter was intense, and the desertion
rate soared. "Ask any Confederate officer who commanded troops in the
latter part of the war and who was loved and trusted by his men," said
Lee's onetime aide Robert Stiles, now serving in the artillery. "He will tell
you of letters . . . [that] could not be read without tears—letters in which a
wife and mother, crazed by her starving children's cries for bread, required a
husband . . . to choose between his God-imposed obligations to her and to
them and his allegiance to his country."[2]

Despite these harsh realities, some units somehow kept up their spirits.
"The battalion had been reduced to about 100 men," said a private in the 1st
Maryland, "and yet we were expected to do the work of a full command. So
numerous have been the desertions in our brigade that it is necessary to keep
us almost constantly on picket; for as sure as this duty is entrusted to some
regiments in the brigade, just so sure were the posts found deserted in the
morning." The weather was bitter cold, he remarked, and his uniform was in
tatters. "I have the waist of my pantaloons left, and my only pair of cotton
drawers are not of the thickest material. However, as long as my blanket holds
out I am all right, for I wear it wrapped around me day and night. I often
wonder what my little Baltimore girl would say if she saw me in this plight.
Guess she'd look for some other fellow."

Days later the Marylander had a visitor while on picket. "Soon after day
broke I could hardly believe my eyes when I saw a Yank crawl out of a rifle
pit about 200 yards in our front, and walk deliberately toward us. There were
three of us in our pit and I told the boys he must be a deserter. He had no
gun."

"Don't shoot," the Yank yelled when he got within speaking distance. "I
only want to have a few words with you!" Then he pulled two bags from his
pockets.

"I thought maybe you Rebs would like to have a little coffee," he went on,
"and my mess in that pit over there just clubbed in and sent you this."

"Coffee!" remembered the Marylander. "Why, I hadn't had smell of it for
months. We invited the Yank into our parlor, made him sit down, and then
we filled his pipe, and that made his eyes sparkle. He had coffee and we had
tobacco . . . and when that Yank returned to his chums he carried some with
him. It's pretty tough to shoot such good fellows. There are a good many of
us who believe this shooting match has been carried on long enough."[3]

Life progressed in other ways as well. On January 19 the marriage of Brigadier John Pegram of Richmond to Hetty Cary of Baltimore was a notable so-

cial event in the capital. Enthused Kyd Douglas: "One of the handsomest and most lovable men I ever knew wed to the handsomest woman in the Southland—with her classic face, her pure complexion, her auburn hair, her perfect figure and her carriage, altogether the most beautiful woman I ever saw in any land." Ill omens attended the marriage. "President and Mrs. Davis sent their carriage and horses—the only private turnout, I fancy, in Richmond—to take the happy pair to the church. The horses balked, became unruly and threatened a smashup. The bride's dress was rent going into the church, and the veil nearly torn from her face as she approached the altar. A superstitious murmur passed through the immense congregation." On February 2, while Hetty was visiting her husband in Petersburg, Pegram's division passed in review before the bride—John Brown Gordon relinquishing the privilege in her favor. With Lee on her right, and the other generals and their ladies nearby, she could not have been happier. "Her rich color emblazoned her face, a rare light illumined her eyes and her soul was on fire with the triumph of the moment, the horrors of war forgotten."

Four days later, in skirmishing near Hatcher's Run, John Pegram was killed when a minie ball took him full in the chest. He and Hetty had been engaged for three years and married less than three weeks. While the bride went into seclusion Willie Pegram soldiered on, barely able to contain his emotions. "Whenever I meet anyone of Brother's friends . . . my grief breaks out afresh," he wrote his sister Mary.[4]

Lee's officers and men found themselves hunkering down, waiting for spring and trying to make the best of a grim situation. Longstreet held the works north of the James and at Bermuda Hundred; Gordon defended east and south of Petersburg as far as Fort Gregg on the Boydton Plank Road; Hill's works extended from Fort Gregg southwest to the headwaters of Hatcher's Run. With the distance between the picket lines so close, sharpshooters became a constant hazard. "To expose one's head an inch above the works was the risk of a hole in it," said Kyd Douglas, now Gordon's adjutant. "The rifle pits were made into apartments and the approaches to them were covered for protection against mortar shells, etc. It was a dreadful line to hold. Petersburg was virtually surrounded; daily the inevitable was staring us closer in the face, but we never 'let on.' We held the lines, slept little, ate less, and at night went about the town calling and making visits with incredible gaiety. We were waiting for something to explode, killing time, for time was killing us."

Dr. John Claiborne, director of the army's hospitals in the city, likewise thought the situation incongruous. "During the winter of 1864–65," he said, "amidst the sorrow and the suffering, which can hardly be exaggerated, gaiety among the young people was rife. There were parties, starvation parties as they were called, on account of the absence of refreshments impossible to be obtained; ball followed ball, and the soldier met and danced with his lady at night, and on the morrow danced the dance of death in the deadly trenches out on the line. . . ."[5]

In February, with the Confederate cause in near ruin, Davis was pressured by Congress into naming Lee general-in-chief. Had the president done this years earlier the judicious Lee might have been able to create more cohesion among the Confederate armies in Mississippi, Tennessee and Virginia, and less friction within them. Now the appointment was all but meaningless. With Savannah, Georgia, in Sherman's hands and the Federals turning north to Charleston, Lee earlier had been required to send to South Carolina's aid a single brigade under Colonel John Kennedy, plus Wade Hampton's and Calbraith Butler's cavalry. Even this commitment taxed his resources, but Charleston fell on February 18 and Wilmington, North Carolina, a few days later. To lend some semblance of organization to the remnants of Hood's Army of Tennessee, which continued to nip at Sherman's flanks, Lee within weeks restored the much-traveled Joseph Johnston to command. Whatever Johnston's weaknesses, he was a professional who could—defensively at least—handle large bodies of troops. Then in March Lee learned that Jubal Early, left in the Shenandoah with a token force, had been overwhelmed. This was not unexpected, but it added to the flood of bad news.

To Lee it had been obvious for some time that staying in the Richmond-Petersburg lines made defeat inevitable. His only hope—admittedly a slim one—was abandoning the cities and regaining his maneuverability. Grant and Meade had opened the siege with some 120,000 men against his 60,000, and though both armies subsequently suffered heavy casualties, the Federal two-to-one advantage remained intact. "I felt that the situation of the Confederate army was such that they would try to make an escape at the earliest practicable moment," Grant said, "and I was afraid, every morning, that I would awake from my sleep to hear that Lee had gone, and that nothing was left but a picket line. . . . I knew that he could move much more lightly and rapidly than I, and that, if he got the start, he would leave me behind. . . ." Grant's concern was that Lee, getting the lead on him, would push into North Carolina to join with Johnston in defeating Sherman, then quickly turn back on him.[6]

That evacuating the lines was Lee's preferred stratagem became apparent in early March when in the middle of the night he summoned Gordon to his quarters. "General Longstreet and General Ewell were both twenty miles away on their lines in front of Richmond," said Gordon, "A.P. Hill, who for weeks had been in delicate health, was absent on furlough, and I found myself alone with the obviously depressed commander." Lee described to Gordon the plight, not only of the Army of Northern Virginia but of Johnston's command at length, then asked what action he recommended. Not yet 33 years old, unique in the fact he was heading a corps despite having no prior military experience, Gordon hesitated. He regarded Lee "as almost infallible in such a crisis," and had no wish to muddy the waters. Finally he replied, saying there were only three courses of action, and naming them in the order they should be tried:

"First, make terms with the enemy, the best we can get.

"Second, if that is not practicable, the best thing to do is retreat—abandon Richmond and Petersburg, unite by rapid marches with General Johnston in North Carolina, and strike Sherman before Grant can join him. . . .

"Lastly we must fight, and without delay."

In the growing silence that ensued, an anxious Gordon wondered what Lee was thinking. "Is that your opinion?" he blurted.

"I agree with you fully," Lee answered.

Two days later the two men met again. In the interim Lee had journeyed to Richmond, met with Davis to propose either suing for peace or quitting the cities and been rebuffed. "Of President Davis he spoke in terms of strong eulogy: of the strength of his convictions, of his devotedness, in his remarkable faith in the possibility of still winning our independence. . . . The nearest approach to complaint or criticism were the words which I can never forget: 'You know that the President is very pertinacious in opinion and purpose.' President Davis did not believe we could secure such terms as we could afford to accept. . . . Neither were the authorities ready to evacuate the capital and abandon our lines of defense, though every railroad except the Southside was already broken." What then was to be done? Gordon asked.

"[Lee] replied that there seemed to be but one thing that we could do—fight. To stand still was death."[7]

In the weeks that followed, Gordon under Lee's direction meticulously planned what would be the last desperate assault on Grant's lines at Petersburg. The night attack would focus on Fort Stedman, a redoubt with four cannon less than 300 yards from the Confederate lines east of Petersburg. Protected by abatis—piles of felled trees—and fraises—breast-high, sharpened, angled logs bound together with wire—as well as supporting positions known as Batteries X, XI and XII, Stedman appeared quite formidable. But Gordon's plans for taking it covered every contingency. First, picked men would open up passages in the Confederate lines through which his 11,500-man force would advance. These were the Second Corps divisions of Clement Evans, Bryan Grimes and James A. Walker (replacing the slain John Pegram), as well as elements of Bushrod Johnson's division. Before this main assault, however, squads wearing white armbands would rush the 150 yards across no-man's land in the darkness, crush the enemy pickets and act as guides through the abatis. Behind them would be fifty men with axes to chop down the fraises. Next three columns of 100 men apiece would storm Stedman and Batteries X, XI and XII, breaching the Federal lines and enabling the massed infantry, following close behind, to fan out in the works.

Last, three more columns of 100 men apiece, led by locals who knew the country, were to push past Stedman and take three smaller redoubts in the fort's rear that Gordon believed constituted Grant's secondary line. This was critical if his master plan was to succeed. He intended to turn the guns he captured there on the enemy, expecting that such enfilading fire would discourage reinforcements and demoralize the foe. "The purpose of the movement," he said, "was not simply the capture of Fort Stedman and the breastworks flanking it. . . . Prisoners and guns we might thus capture would not justify the peril of the undertaking. The tremendous possibility was the disintegration of the whole left wing of the Federal army, or at least the dealing of such a staggering blow upon it as would disable it temporarily. . . ."[8] If Gordon were successful, Lee would rush up more divisions to exploit the gap and assail Grant's rear.

Shortly before 4 A.M. on March 25, even while the Confederates were removing the last of the obstructions in their lines, a Union picket grew alarmed.

"What are you doing over there, Johnny?" he called out. "What is that noise? Answer quick or I'll shoot."

"Never mind, Yank!" came the quick reply from a private at Gordon's side, a man accustomed to such nighttime repartee. ". . . We are just gathering a little corn. You know rations are mighty short over here."

"All right, Johnny; go ahead and get your corn. I'll not shoot at you while you are drawing your rations."

Within minutes the passages were cleared and the time had come to rush the pickets. Gordon ordered the private to signal for the attack. "He pointed his rifle upward, with his finger on the trigger, but hesitated," Gordon said. "His conscience seemed to get hold of him. He was going into the fearful charge, and he evidently did not feel disposed to go into eternity with the lie on his lips. . . . His hesitation surprised me, and I again ordered, 'Fire your gun, sir.' "

Fair play called for sounding a warning. "Hello, Yank! Wake up; we are going to shell the woods," the private shouted. "Look out; we are coming." His conscience satisfied, he fired his piece and double-quicked into the darkness.[9]

Gordon's tactics initially worked to perfection. Leading off the assault Eugene Waggaman's Louisiana Tigers of Clement Evans's division swept through the night, scaled Stedman's walls and fell with devastating effect among the sleeping foe—clawing and scratching, said one Tiger, "as if they had drank two quarts of brandy." By 4:45 A.M., with an hour remaining until full daylight, both the fort and Batteries X, XI and XII were in Confederate hands and the enemy seemed cowed and confused. "It was a complete surprise," said one North Carolinian. "Many were killed coming out of their tents by our men, using their guns as clubs." Some twenty guns and 1,000 prisoners were taken, including a Federal brigadier, all with minimal casualties.

Then the plan just as quickly unraveled. In the ongoing melee, the columns assigned to take the three redoubts behind Fort Stedman lost their guides and became disoriented. While the minutes ticked away, all chance of occupying these secondary positions and turning captured guns on the enemy was lost. (There is some doubt, in fact, that these Federal redoubts existed; Gordon may have confused them with the remains of Confederate works lost the year before.) "By the time the sun was above the horizon," said Walker, the one-time cadet at V.M.I. who had drawn Jackson's wrath, "the enemy had poured forth from their camps in rear, and filled the forts and breastworks of the second line with troops, both infantry and artillery." From these vantage points they delivered a withering fire on Fort Stedman, making Gordon's position untenable. Mourned Walker: "We had failed to carry the second line by surprise; [now] it was manned by four times our numbers, and the task was hopeless."[10]

Seeing that Gordon could not make further headway, Lee about 7 A.M. cancelled plans to reinforce him and ordered a withdrawal. "This was not easily accomplished," Gordon said. "Foiled by the failure of the guides, deprived of the great bodies of infantry which Lee [had] ordered to my support, I had stretched out my corps to occupy the entrenchments which we had captured. . . . Other troops were expected to arrive and join in the general advance. . . . The non-arrival of these heavy supports left me to battle alone. . . . A consuming fire on both flanks and front during this withdrawal caused a heavy loss to my command." Men who made it back across no-man's land to the Petersburg lines never forgot the experience. "Good God what a time!" marveled Henry Chambers. "It seemed as if the enemy's artillery opened with redoubled vigor and the minie balls came in showers." Wrote Henry London to his father: "I . . . only escaped capture by running as hard as I could a quarter of a mile through an open field swept by their fire, expecting every moment to be knocked over, as the dead lay in a long line. . . ." Explained Robert Graham: "The enemy . . . regretting their neglect to turn out in time to meet us more handsomely in the early morning, were now doing all in their power to make the procession more interesting as we returned."

Federal losses during the Fort Stedman operation were some 2,100. Confederate casualties were more than 4,000, almost half of them prisoners. "We were overwhelmed and driven from the enemy's enclosure by a galling fire," conceded Kyd Douglas, "and many surrendered rather than be shot." In truth, the fact that most soldiers did choose to fight their way out is testimony to the hold Lee still retained on his devoted but dwindling veterans.[11]

Within days Grant again moved to the southwest, sending Phil Sheridan's 10,000 sabers around the far Confederate right, where Hill's Third Corps held the lines in front of Hatcher's Run, in one more attempt to cut the Southside Railroad. To meet him Lee hurriedly assembled a five-brigade contingent under the star-crossed George Pickett, he of the long, perfumed ringlets, together with Fitz Lee's cavalry and Willie Pegram's artillery—some 10,600 men. When the two forces met on March 31 just north of Dinwiddie Courthouse, the Confederates in brisk skirmishing initially pushed the Federals back. Grant responded to Sheridan's call for help by sending him Warren's 12,000-man Fifth Corps. Outnumbered, Pickett withdrew at daybreak on April 1 to Five Forks, a vital crossroads some four miles west of Hill's breastworks. There he dug in and awaited the Federal assault. "Hold Five Forks at all hazards," Lee had wired. "Protect road to Ford's Depot and prevent Union forces from striking the Southside Railroad." Pickett had seen little action since Gettysburg. His postings had been to North Carolina and southeastern Virginia and, it must be acknowledged, in neither place had he distinguished himself.

On April 1, the two-mile-long Confederate order of battle at Five Forks looked like this: William Roberts's and Tom Munford's cavalry held the left flank, Rooney Lee's the right. Between them, from left to right, were the North Carolinians of Matt Ransom, the South Carolinians of William Wallace, the Virginians of George Steuart, Robert Mayo (replacing the wounded William R. Terry) and Monty Corse. Backing up the infantry were Pegram's six guns. Pickett's thin lines were particularly weak on his left, where his horsemen had only a tenuous connection with Hill and the Confederate right. Despite Lee's admonition, he and Fitz Lee—the senior officers on the field—seemed curiously indifferent to their danger. Perhaps Grant's relentless pressure had benumbed them. "Hearing nothing more of the [Federal] infantry's move, which we heard of the night before," Fitz Lee conceded, "I thought that the movements just there, for the time being, were suspended, and we were not expecting any attack that afternoon. . . ." Then he added: "Our throwing up works and taking position were simply matters of military precaution."

This explains, to some degree, Tom Rosser's infamous shadbake. Temporarily out of action with a flesh wound, cavalryman Rosser had caught and cooked many large shad, which were making their run in a nearby stream. Now about noon he invited Pickett and Fitz Lee to the feast. Hungry though the two men were, it is difficult to understand how they could neglect their duties and accept. But they did, leaving the lines without telling their officers where they were going and riding two miles to the rear. There they ate copiously and perhaps drank in moderation for several hours, oblivious to the fact that Sheridan and Warren were advancing on Five Forks. Reconnoitering on the left, the diligent Tom Munford saw the enemy moving up and sent repeated couriers to Pickett and Lee, but they could not be found. "All this time," he said, "Warren's swarming blue lines were plainly visible from the road, forming into line and preparing to assault Pickett's left; Merritt's dismounted cavalry was keeping up a sharp continuous fire along the whole of our infantry front, as if preparing to attack our right, and Custer's mounted Division was demonstrating . . . and I was still without orders."[12]

The Federals made their feint against Pickett's right flank around 3 P.M. There they were repulsed by Rooney Lee and Corse's Virginians. One hour later Sheridan struck in earnest, this time against the vulnerable left, shattering Roberts's troopers and rolling up Ransom and Wallace. Colonel Willie Pegram rode up and down the lines, urging on his gunners as the enemy threatened to engulf them.

"Fire your canister low, men!" he shouted, while his cannon delivered round after round of double canister at short range. Suddenly he reeled and fell from his horse, hit by a minie ball in the side.

"Gordon," he moaned, calling out to his friend and aide Gordon McCabe, "I'm mortally wounded; take me from the field." On his way to the rear in the jolting ambulance, Pegram's thoughts were of God and family. "If it is God's will to take me, I am perfectly resigned," he whispered to McCabe at one point. Later he added: "Give my love to mother and both sisters and tell them I thought of them in my last moments."

"Willie," sobbed McCabe, "I never knew how much I loved you until now."

"But I did," answered Pegram, reaching out and taking McCabe's hand.

Twenty-three-year-old Willie Pegram died the next day. In four years of artillery service, he had never lost a gun to the foe.[13]

Pickett first realized the seriousness of the 4 P.M. attack when a wave of blue-clad figures materialized out of the woods and interrupted the shadbake. He leaped on his horse and somehow made it back to his lines, although by then the damage had been done. (Fitz Lee never did get through, the Yankees having gotten between him and his command.) The entire Confederate left and now center was in disarray, with Steuart's and Mayo's Virginians—those proud brigades once headed by Lew Armistead and James Kemper—thoroughly humbled. "Charge after charge of the enemy was repulsed," Pickett would say defensively, "but they still kept pouring up division after division, and pressing around our left."

Only the stubborn resistance of Rooney Lee and Monty Corse on the right, providing a makeshift shield behind which the rest of Pickett's men could rally, kept the disaster from being worse. The Confederates nonetheless suffered some 4,500 casualties, almost all of them prisoners; the Federals, 820. Just as devastating was the loss of the Southside, the last supply line into Petersburg. One fellow officer, seeing Pickett soon after the battle, was dismayed, describing him as "hopeless, demoralized and prostrated. He did not look like Pickett, but like an old and broken man."[14]

Powell Hill had barely returned from sick leave on April 1, still burdened with fever and fatigue, when from the west he heard the sound of battle at Five Forks. Preparing for the worst, he checked the length of his works, riding the dozen or so miles from Fort Gregg to Burgess's Mill and back to ensure that all was well. Toward dark, after learning of Pickett's defeat, he redoubled his precautions. It was not until after 10 P.M. that he returned to the house he shared with Dolly and two of their three young daughters. Even then, tired and pain-wracked, he could not sleep. It was obvious now that the lines soon would be breached, and Richmond and Petersburg would fall.

If Hill could not sleep, neither could his men. "The night was extremely dark and still, so that we could see the flashes of musketry for a great distance, and could hear the roar that rang along the line for miles," said an officer in McGowan's brigade, Wilcox's division. The Federals were probing—first cannonading, then charging in one place and then repeating the process elsewhere. Morning, the soldiers knew, would bring a massive attack. "Hundreds of men in our army had predicted . . . that Grant would continue to stretch," the officer continued, "until he forced us to draw out our line as thin as a skirmish, and then storm some point with massed columns. . . . The end was drawing near."[15]

By 4 A.M. on Sunday April 2 a dutiful but downcast Hill was at Lee's headquarters, conferring with him about how best to evacuate the cities. Before leaving Dolly he had unaccountably put on, not one of his red battle shirts, but a white linen blouse she had recently made him. Suddenly Colonel Charles Venable, one of Lee's aides, burst in with unwelcome news. The Third Corps lines had been broken in front of Nathaniel Harris's Mississippi brigade, Mahone's division, and Yankee skirmishers were fanning out behind the works. Within minutes Hill, summoning up his old dash, was riding toward the Confederate right, intent on rallying his troops. Concerned about his safety, Lee sent Venable galloping after him, urging caution.

"The general requests that you not expose yourself," he told Hill.

"I thank General Lee for his consideration," Little Powell answered. "I am only trying to get in communication with the right."

What Hill did not know that was that the Federals had become as disorganized as their foes. There was no unbroken order of battle on either side. Skirmishing lines were improvised; stragglers were everywhere. Hill was riding not in front of but behind the lead elements of the Union assault. Spotting William Poague's artillery battalion on a nearby hill and seeing it needed direction, he dispatched Venable to position the guns. Then he rode on, still searching for his officers and their commands, escorted only by two couriers—Sergeant George Tucker and Private William Jenkins. Now he encountered two enemy soldiers. "Jenkins and myself," said Tucker, "who up to this time rode immediately behind the general, were instantly upon them." The Federals promptly laid down their arms and surrendered.

"Jenkins," Hill ordered, "take them to General Lee."

Hill with only Sergeant Tucker by his side pressed on. Noting some troops in the distance, the courier asked: "General, what troops are those?" Hill peered for a moment through his field glass.

"The enemy's," he replied.

Tucker was becoming worried. "Please excuse me, General," he said, "but where are you going?"

"Sergeant, I must go to the right as quickly as possible. We will go up this side of the branch to the woods, which will cover us until reaching the field in rear of General Heth's quarters. I hope to find the road clear at General Heth's."

From this moment on Tucker rode slightly ahead of Hill, keeping a drawn Colt revolver in his hand. It was then Hill told him: "Sergeant, should anything happen to me, you must go back to General Lee and report it."

Coming out of the woods opposite Heth's line, the two men found massed Union infantry blocking their way. "Which way now, General?" Tucker asked. "We must keep to the right," Hill answered, pointing to another clump of woods.

They had covered two-thirds of the distance when they came upon a half-dozen Yankees, two of whom were much in advance of the others. Hill now drew his own Colt. "We must take them," he said.

"Stay here; I will take them," Tucker replied.

No more than twenty yards separated them from the Federals. "Then General Hill was at my side, calling, 'Surrender,' " continued Tucker. Crouched behind a tree with muskets were two members of the 138th Pennsylvania. "I cannot see it," Corporal John Mauck said of the surrender demand to his comrade, Private Daniel Wolford. "Let us shoot them." Wolford's ball missed Tucker, but Mauck's struck Hill in the pistol hand and then pierced his heart, killing him instantly and throwing him from his horse. Remembering Hill's orders, Tucker had no choice but to gallop off and give Lee the dreadful tidings, leaving Hill sprawled on the ground.

Within the hour members of the 5th Alabama rushed to the scene to recover the body. By then the enemy had gone. "He is now at rest," said a tearful Lee of one of his favorite warriors, "and we who are left are the ones to suffer." The moralist who had rebelled at his mother's strict Baptist tenets, the dashing officer who had courted Miss Nellie, the prickly aristocrat who had feuded with Jackson, the fighting general beloved by his men who on many a field had saved the day—was dead. Dolly, seven months pregnant with their fourth child, screamed when she heard the news. Returning to her family home in Kentucky, she seldom spoke of the war again.[16]

For the rest of April 2 the shattered Confederate right managed to fall back and hold off the enemy, consolidating their defenses around Fort Gregg. Meanwhile Lee ordered the army to evacuate Richmond and Petersburg as soon as darkness permitted, hoping somehow to unite with Johnston. "There was no sleeping in Petersburg that night," said Kyd Douglas. "It was all commotion and bustle . . . Before we got away, shells were bursting at places over the town, and the air was now and then illumined by the baleful light of mortars." One of the last people he spoke to was Mary Bolling, the woman who would become the widowed Rooney Lee's second wife. "She uttered not a word of fear or complaint: the infinite sadness of her silence was pathetic beyond words." Nor for once could Fannie Gordon stay with her husband. "General John B. Gordon . . . marched off at the head of his command, leaving . . . his beautiful and heroic wife, to whom just twenty-four hours before a son had been born."

With the last days of the Confederacy at hand Jefferson Davis, still dedicated to continuing the struggle, led a refugee government out of the capital to Danville, Virginia. Officially, nobody as yet was willing to admit the obvious. "We discussed the comparative strategic merits of the line we had left," said one soldier leaving Richmond, "and the new one we hoped to make on the Roanoke River, and we wondered where the new seat of government would be, but not one word was said about a probable or personal surrender."[17]

# TWO

\* \* \* \*

# RETREAT TO APPOMATTOX

Lee's scattered and bloodied forces moved west on three principal but converging routes on April 3, leaving two burning and chaotic cities behind them. Their destination was Amelia Courthouse, a town on the Richmond & Danville Railroad some 39 miles from the capital and a few miles less from Petersburg. There Lee expected rations to be delivered by railcar to his hungry men. Dick Ewell, who had been in charge of the Richmond defense force, was northernmost. With him were the garrison troops and heavy artillery of Lee's oldest son, Custis, who had spent the war in the capital, and the First Corps division of dependable Joseph Kershaw. In the center was Mahone's Third Corps division, fresh from leaving the lines at Bermuda Hundred. Southernmost were Longstreet, Gordon and Dick Anderson, all evacuating the works at Petersburg. Longstreet led the other two First Corps divisions—Field's and the remnants of Pickett's. Following him were two of the slain Hill's Third Corps units—those of Heth and Wilcox. Gordon's Second Corps consisted of Clement Evans's, Bryan Grimes's and James A. Walker's divisions. Dick Anderson led a newly created mini Fourth Corps, comprised solely of Bushrod Johnson's command.

Problems at the bridges spanning the Appomattox caused a number of delays during the retreat, adding to the army's gloom. "There were not many words spoken," said one of McGowan's South Carolinians. "An indescribable sadness weighed upon us. The men were very gentle with each other—very liberal in bestowing the little of food that remained to them. I remember that one soldier shared his last scrap of bacon with me . . . and would have shared his bread, but I refused that. I had lost my pipe. He gave me his, and told me to keep it."

Lee and his top commanders, and well as their staffs, meantime maintained a resolute front. Invited during the march to sup at Clover Hill, the home of Judge James Cox, Lee was received by Kate Virginia Cox, the daughter of the house. "General Lee," she insisted, "we shall gain our cause, you will join General Johnston, and together you will be victorious."

"Whatever happens," he answered, "know this, that no men ever fought better than those who have stood by me."

Years later she would still remember Lee's reply, writing in a memoir: "No more, no less, and his words showed that his thoughts were with those ragged veterans, one mile away, resting by the roadside."[1]

By nightfall of April 4, the last of the Confederates—Ewell's command—were across the upper Appomattox and trudging toward Amelia Courthouse. Lee with the van of the army had already arrived there, only to find that due to poor staff work the promised rations were not awaiting him. With Grant and Meade at his heels and Sheridan on his flanks he was forced to halt for twenty-four hours to scour the countryside in a largely futile search for food. "The delay was fatal," he said, "and could not be retrieved."

On April 5, pushing on farther west to Jetersville, Lee predictably found his way blocked by Federal troops. With much of his army literally starving, he ordered an arduous night march around the enemy to Rice's Station on the Lynchburg Railroad and nearby Farmville, where he knew he could obtain rations. Longstreet with the two strongest divisions—those of Field and Mahone—led the way, followed by Heth's and Wilcox's commands. Dick Anderson was in the center with Bushrod Johnson and Pickett, then Ewell with Kershaw and Custis Lee. Gordon with the Second Corps acted as the rear guard, while Fitz Lee's cavalry guarded the van and flanks. "It was now a race of life or death," said one soldier of the quest for food. Even for the indefatigable Gordon the march was a nightmare: "On and on, hour after hour, from hilltop to hilltop, the lines were alternately forming, fighting and retreating, making one almost continuous shifting battle."[2]

By daylight on April 6 the column was strung out for ten miles. Elements of Longstreet's command were nearing Rice's Station but Anderson and Ewell, encumbered by supply and ordnance wagons in both front and rear, lagged far behind. Meanwhile the soldiers with every passing hour were succumbing to exhaustion and hunger. Small detachments, wrote Major McHenry Howard, were dispatched "to bring in whatever they could lay their hands on, if only a pig, a chicken, or a quart of meal," but usually to no avail. One lucky group, coming upon a small ox, promptly slaughtered the beast and ate it raw. "It was, perhaps, the only instance in my experience during the war," Howard said, "when the plea of . . . human necessity overruled all consideration due to private property and military discipline."[3]

Sheridan's cavalry was a constant irritant. At one juncture the enemy captured half of Porter Alexander's old battalion of artillery, now under Colonel Frank Huger. Stated Alexander: ". . . the two leading guns had reached the top of a long ascent of bad road, when Custer's Brigade . . . [charged] down upon them. Those two guns quickly unlimbered & fired two rounds each of cannister, when Custer's men were in between them, cutting & shooting." Huger blasted one noncom from his horse, and with another bullet laid open the cheek of a major. "But another fellow rode up & held a carbine to his head & said, 'Surrender, damn you!' . . . Custer & Huger had been great friends and classmates [at West Point], & Custer made him ride along all day . . . & sleep with him that night, & treated him very nicely." Even the officer Huger had wounded came to see him, "with his face sewed up and bandaged, & expressed his sincere thanks for the glorious furlough he was about to enjoy."

So bold were these raids that at 11 A.M. Anderson and Ewell halted to repulse them, then waited a while longer to let the rearmost wagons go past that were separating them from Gordon. Unfortunately, this opened up a gap between Mahone's rear and Anderson's front that Sheridan took full advantage of, rushing his troopers into the opening and at 2 P.M. setting up a roadblock. Compounding the problem, Ewell sent the wagons on a northerly route at a fork in the road without telling Gordon, who followed them, leaving Anderson and Ewell without support. With the Federals close behind, they found themselves in a trap.

The two generals hastily conferred. "General Anderson informed me that at least two divisions of cavalry were in his front," Ewell said, "and suggested two modes of escape, either to unite our forces and break through, or to move to the right through the woods and try to strike a road that ran toward Farmville. I recommended the latter, but as he knew the ground and I did not . . . I left the dispositions up to him." While they were talking Horatio Wright's Sixth Corps assailed Ewell's rear, making the decision moot. "General Anderson informed me he would make the attack in front, if I would hold in check those in the rear. . . . I had no artillery, all being with the trains."[4]

Desperate and confused fighting began about 5 P.M. On Ewell's front his 3,600 Confederates under Custis Lee and Kershaw were dug in along Little Sailor's Creek, a tributary of the Appomattox, facing 10,000 of the enemy. Lee's troops were largely untested militia and the heavy artillery battalions from Richmond. Kershaw's three brigades consisted of Dudley DuBose's and James Simms's Georgians and Benjamin Humphreys's Mississippians, the units once commanded by Tom Cobb, Paul Semmes and William Barksdale.

Finding their adversaries had no cannon, the Federals advanced within 800 yards and opened a withering fire. "The expression of the men's faces indicated clearly enough its effect upon them," said Major Robert Stiles, serving under Custis Lee. "They did not appear to be hopelessly demoralized, but they did look blanched and haggard." Then Wright's infantry moved to the attack. "The enemy was coming on and everything was still as the grave," remembered Stiles. "The Federal officers, knowing as I supposed that we were surrounded and appreciating the fearful havoc their artillery had wrought, evidently expected us to surrender and had their white handkerchiefs in their hands, waving them toward us as if suggesting this course. . . ." Instead the Confederates leveled their muskets as one and delivered a deadly volley. "The enemy seemed to have been totally unprepared for it. . . . The earth appeared to have swallowed up the first line of the Federal force in our front," marveled Stiles. "There was a rattling supplement to the volley and the second line wavered and broke. . . . On the instant every man in my battalion sprang to his feet and, without orders, rushed bareheaded and with unloaded muskets down the slope after the retreating Federals."[5]

The triumph was short-lived. By the time Stiles got his troops back to their lines they were assailed, in front and rear, by overwhelming numbers. "Quicker than I can tell it, the battle degenerated into a butchery. . . . I saw numbers of men kill each other with bayonets and the butts of muskets, and even bite each other's throats and ears and noses, rolling on the ground like wild beasts. I saw one of my officers and a Federal officer fighting with swords over the battalion colors, which we had brought back with us, each having his left hand upon the staff. . . ."[6]

One mile to the southwest Anderson's 6,300 men were faring just as badly against Sheridan's 10,000. "The troops seemed to be wholly broken down and disheartened," said the enigmatic Anderson by way of explanation. "After a feeble effort to advance they gave way. . . ." Now the Yankees seized the initiative. Exulted one trooper: "The bugles sounded the advance, and forward up the face of that ridge swept that grand cavalry command with a irresistible force . . . the Rebels rose and fired a terrific volley, but they fired too quickly and too high, and before they could reload the most of our brigade had leaped the works and were among them. . . ." In short order Anderson lost 2,600 of his men, most of whom surrendered. He himself, with Bushrod Johnson and Pickett, managed to escape through the woods, but Monty Corse and Eppa Hunton—serving under Pickett—were captured.[7]

Henry Wise, the 59-year-old former governor of Virginia leading a brigade in Johnson's division, was openly critical of some of his comrades. He initially had been successful in the attempted breakthrough, pushing back the Federals in his front from a plantation house and outbuildings, but got little support from Pickett's men on his left. Then the tide turned and he was ordered to retreat. "We had hardly formed and begun to move in [Pickett's] rear," he said bitterly, "before his whole command stampeded, leaving their artillery in the enemy's hands." Wise found himself surrounded but gave no thought to surrendering. "We pressed up a hill . . . halted behind a worm fence on the crest, fired three volleys to the rear . . . poured three volleys obliquely to the left and front, broke the enemy and got out." For good measure he sent three volleys into the woods where William Wallace's South Carolinians had taken refuge, sending them a strong signal that he expected them to withdraw rather than give up. Wallace's brigade, he reported with satisfaction, "raised a white flag and came out to us . . . and marched with us safely off the field."[8]

Once Ewell realized that Anderson's attack had failed, his first thought was to rally his own troops and likewise retreat through the woods, but he was too late. "On riding past my left," he said, "I came suddenly upon a strong line of the enemy's skirmishers advancing upon my left rear. This closed the only avenue of escape, as shells and even bullets were crossing each other from front and rear over my troops, and my right was completely enveloped. I surrendered myself and my staff to a cavalry officer who came in on the same road General Anderson had gone out on. At my request he sent a messenger to General G. W. C. Lee, who was nearest, with a note from me telling him he was surrounded. . . . I had surrendered, and he had better do so too, to prevent useless loss of life. . . ." Declared Kershaw: "Both in Lee's front and my own, [the enemy] were repulsed with loss on every advance, but pressed us constantly with fresh troops, extending all the while to our left. . . . On no battlefield of the war have I felt a [greater] pride in the conduct of my command." Ewell's defeat was even worse than Anderson's, costing the army in effect his entire force. Some 3,400 of his 3,600 men were lost, 3,000 of whom surrendered. Like the enfeebled Ewell, Custis Lee and Joseph Kershaw ended up prisoners, as did Seth Barton, Dudley DuBose and James Simms.[9]

The third of the firefights this April 6 involved John Brown Gordon, who with his 7,000-man corps had taken the right fork in the road and followed Ewell's wagons. Though pushed hard by Andrew Humpreys's 16,500-man Second Corps, he had been successful until dusk in defending the train, pausing now and again to drive the Federals off with cannon. When the wagons broke down in the marshland where Little and Big Sailor's Creeks converged, however, Gordon found himself beleaguered. "Many of these wagons, loaded with ammunition, mired so deep in the mud that they had to be abandoned," he said. "It was necessary to charge and force back the Union lines in order to rescue my men. . . ." Only darkness permitted him to escape, leaving behind some 200 wagons. His casualties were 1,700.[10]

Overall Sailor's Creek cost the Confederates some 7,700 men; the Federals, 1,150. Learning of the debacles, Lee rode back toward the battlefield with Mahone, where from the crest of a hill the two generals stared down on the chaos. (Longstreet during this time remained near Rice's Station, guarding the bridges across the Appomattox.) Here Mahone takes up the tale: ". . . The disaster which had overtaken our army was in full view, and the scene beggars description—hurrying teamsters with their teams and dangling traces (no wagons), retreating infantry without guns, many without hats, a harmless mob, with the massive columns of the enemy moving orderly on. At this spectacle General Lee straightened himself in his saddle, and, looking more the soldier than ever, exclaimed, as if taking to himself, 'My God! Has the army dissolved?' As quickly as I could control my voice I replied, 'No, general, here are troops willing to do their duty'; when, in a mellowed voice he replied, 'Yes, general, there are some true men left. Will you please keep those people back?' " While his division was moving into position, Mahone galloped back to Lee, who was holding a Confederate battle flag, and took it from him.

Planting the flag in the midst of his lines Mahone was true to his word, setting up a stout buffer where the fleeing units could re-form. Lee next asked him for his opinion on how best to continue the retreat. Mahone advised recrossing the Appomattox in an effort to keep the river between the two armies.

"Let General Longstreet move by the river road to Farmville," he said, "and cross the river there, and I will go through the woods to the High Bridge and cross there."[11]

Lee agreed. Longstreet with Field, Heth and Wilcox would move directly to Farmville, where rations awaited the famished men. Mahone with Gordon and the shreds of Anderson's command would cross a few miles below and then rejoin the rest of the army in the vicinity of the town.

One of the officers marching into Farmville the morning of April 7 was the hard-fighting politician Henry Wise. His face was streaked with red clay—the result of washing in a muddy pool—and instead of a lost uniform jacket he wore a blanket around his shoulders. When he reported to Lee with the two brigades he had withdrawn from Sailor's Creek he noticed that his division commander Bushrod Johnson, for whom he had scant respect, was nearby. "The latter had fled from Sailor's Creek and reported me killed and the whole division cut to pieces and dispersed," Wise explained. Then he saw that Lee was trying to suppress a smile. "He was right; I was savage and looked like an Indian, and waited not to be accosted, when I exclaimed with an oath: 'General Lee, these men shall not move another inch unless they have something more to eat than parched corn taken from starving mules!' "

"They deserve something to eat, sir," Lee replied, pointing to an area where food was being distributed. "And you, General Wise, will pause here a moment with me."

Once the brigades had passed Lee, who had a keen appreciation of the ex-governor's mettle if not his tact, came to the point. "You, sir, will take command of all these forces," he said, referring to the dazed men of Anderson's mini Corps.

Wise looked around him. There were no organized troops in the immediate vicinity but the brigades he had marched in, "only thousands of disorganized troops in all directions. . . . I protested that I could not take such a command."

Lee persisted: "You must obey your order, sir."

"I will, sir, or die a trying," Wise answered, "but I must first understand it. It is not the *men* who are deserting the ranks, but the *officers* who are *deserting the men* who are disorganizing your army." Then he added, looking pointedly at Bushrod Johnson: "Do you mean to say, General Lee, that I must take command *of all men of all ranks?*"

Then Lee, recounted Wise, "turned his head . . . [and] said: 'Do your duty, sir.' And I first went to breakfast and then to the work."[12] At this late date, Johnson had been found wanting. With Dick Anderson and Pickett, his fellow discouraged escapees from Sailor's Creek—he would be relieved from command.

What the army needed desperately at this point was time to rest and eat. Such was not to be. Mahone, trying to destroy High Bridge in the wake of his crossing, had fired the span too late. Grant's relentless pursuers had extinguished the flames and now the Federals were closing in on both sides of the river. Once more the army fell back, heading toward Appomattox Courthouse. "We reached Farmville on Friday the 7th at 9 A.M.," recalled artilleryman William Poague. "Here we got some bacon and corn meal, and going on beyond the town towards Cumberland Church I was directed to halt and cook rations. While this was going on an urgent order was received to hurry the battalion forward to Cumberland Church, where the enemy was threatening our trains. Hastily the partly cooked food was seized by all hands, men and officers, and devoured as we marched." Poague was one of the lucky ones. With the Yankees at their heels, many men in the rear units got no food at all.

Lee temporarily stopped his retreating column three miles north of Farmville, near Cumberland Church, to repulse Hancock's Second Corps, now under Andrew Humpreys. There he saw his men win their last victory. Helped by Poague's cannon Mahone again blunted a Federal assault, drawing up his division at right angles to the march to ensure the passage of the wagons. "This performance of Mahone's men was as fine a piece of work as ever I saw," said Poague. "His skirmishers deployed at a run and moved forward like a lot of sportsmen flushing partridges and old hares among the broomsedge and scrub pines. The enemy made no further demonstrations." Humpreys lost some 600 men, including two generals—one mortally wounded and one captured.

Later Poague visited Mahone to congratulate him. "I found him sheltering himself under a poplar tree from a passing thunder shower and in a towering passion abusing and swearing at the Yankees, who he had just learned had . . . captured his headquarters wagon and his cow, saying it was a most serious loss, for he was not able, in the delicate condition of his health, to eat anything but tea and crackers and fresh milk."[13]

About 8 P.M. that night Lee received a message from Grant. "The events of the last week," it read, "must convince you of the hopelessness of further resistance. . . . I feel that it is so, & regard it as my duty to shift from myself the responsibility of any further effusion of blood. . . ." Then he asked for Lee's surrender. The general-in-chief passed the note on to Longstreet, who read it and said, "Not yet." Sometime after midnight Grant received Lee's reply, which denied that his army's situation was hopeless, but asked "the terms you will offer on condition of its surrender."

April 8 was the first quiet day of the march since leaving Amelia. "Until now the sound of musketry and the boom of occasional guns could always be heard in some direction," said Porter Alexander. "But today's march was free from any flank attack, & we had such a head start of the II Corps under General Humpreys . . . that there was but little heard from the rear." Around noon Lee's close friend General William Pendleton, still mourning for his son Sandie killed the previous fall in the Shenandoah, informed Longstreet that he and other principal generals felt that the time had come to ask for terms. He asked him to so inform Lee. Longstreet bristled. "As Pendleton told it to me," said Alexander, "Longstreet said his corps were still able to whip four times their number, & as that as long as that was so he should never suggest a surrender. That he was there to back Lee up, not to pull him down." Pendleton then went directly to Lee. The general-in-chief rejected his plea, saying that there were too many men with arms in their hands to think of laying them down. "From [Pendleton's] report of the conversation," continued Alexander, "he had met a decided snub, and was plainly embarrassed in telling of it."[14]

Shortly thereafter Lee received a second message from Grant, this one referring to terms of surrender. "I would say that, peace being my great desire," it read, "that there is but one condition I would insist upon—namely, that the men and officers surrendered should be disqualified from taking up arms against the Government of the United States. . . ." Grant went on to suggest a meeting.

Lee responded immediately, but made a semantic distinction. "I did not intend to propose the surrender of the [army]," he wrote, "but to ask the terms of your proposition . . . as the restoration of peace should be the sole object of all, I desire to know whether your proposals would lead to that end. . . ." He proposed a 10 A.M. meeting the next morning. So the matter rested.

By dark the Confederate column with Gordon in the van was halted a mile from Appomattox Courthouse. Next were the wagons and artillery. In the rear was Longstreet, some five miles from Appomattox. Then from in front came the sound of cannon. Lindsay Walker, who had been sent ahead with guns, was coming under attack from Sheridan and Custer. Once again the rebels found their way blocked. Lee called his last council of war. There were no tents, tables, chairs or even campstools, only blankets on the ground around a low-burning fire. "No tongue or pen," said Gordon, "will ever be able to describe the anguish of Lee's commanders as they looked into the clouded face of their beloved leader. . . . We knew by our own breaking hearts that his was breaking. Yet he . . . stood calmly facing and discussing the long-dreaded inevitable." The final battle plan was simple: Gordon and Fitz Lee would attempt a breakthrough at 5 A.M. If they succeeded, Longstreet would follow close behind.[15] Opposing them were Sheridan's cavalry plus elements of John Gibbon's Twenty-fourth Corps, some 20,000 men.

Despite the odds, the Confederate assault on Palm Sunday, April 9, began promisingly enough. Lee's 2,400-man cavalry—Rooney Lee, Rosser and Munford—swept around the Union works while Gordon's 1,600-man infantry assailed the front, driving off Sheridan's dismounted troopers and capturing two guns. For brief minutes the road to Lynchburg was clear. Then the Federal numbers began to tell. "I discovered a heavy column of Union infantry coming from the right and upon my rear," said Gordon. "I gathered around me my sharpshooters . . . and directed Colonel Thomas H. Carter of the artillery to turn all his guns upon the advancing column. It was held at bay by his shrapnel, grape and cannister." Meanwhile Longstreet came under attack. "He was so pressed," said Gordon, "that he could not join, as contemplated, in the effort to break the cordon of men and metal around us. At this critical juncture, a column of Union cavalry appeared on the hills on my left, headed for the broad space between Longstreet's command and mine. In a few minutes that body . . . would not only have seized the trains but cut off all communications. . . . I therefore detached a brigade to double-quick and intercept [it]."

Colonel Venable of Lee's staff about 8 A.M. galloped up to ask how the battle was going. "Tell General Lee I have been fought to a frazzle," Gordon said, "and unless Longstreet can unite in the movement . . . I cannot long go forward."

This message dashed Lee's last slim hopes. "There is nothing left me but to go see General Grant," he said, "and I had rather die a thousand deaths."[16]

Presently he called for Longstreet. "He was dressed in a suit of new uniform," Longstreet said, "sword and sash, handsomely embroidered belt, boots, and a pair of gold spurs. At first approach his compact figure appeared as a man in the flush vigor of forty summers, but as I drew near, the handsome apparel and brave bearing failed to conceal his profound depression."

What, Lee wanted to know, did Longstreet think he should do?

"I asked," Longstreet said, "if the bloody sacrifice of his army could help the cause in other quarters." Lee said he thought not. "Then," replied Longstreet, "your situation speaks for itself." Mahone, called up next, voiced the same opinion.

Lee was riding to the meeting he had requested the night before when he got Grant's answer. "The meeting proposed for 10 A.M. today could lead to no good," the note read. ". . . The terms under which peace can be had are well understood. By the South laying down their arms, they would hasten that most desirable event. . . ." Semantics now discarded, Lee promptly replied that he was suing for surrender. Grant did not receive this note until noon, with the result that the two generals did not meet in Appomattox until perhaps 1:30 P.M. The only good news of the early morning was that Fitz Lee's cavalry had broken through the enemy's lines and escaped the trap.

In the interim, even though the Confederates were asking for a truce, Union officers in the field were not sure they should grant one. When Humpreys advanced with the Second Corps about 11 A.M. on Field's lines in the rebel rear, closely followed by Wright's Sixth Corps—together some 30,000 men against 3,000—he at first ignored the entreaties of one of Lee's aides, saying he had no authority to agree to a cease-fire. Fortunately Meade arrived on the scene and overruled him.

Gordon in the Confederate front, hearing that Lee was suing for peace, ordered forward Colonel Green Peyton, one of his aides, likewise to request a cessation. Peyton protested that the Second Corps had no flag of truce.

"Well," said Gordon, "take your handkerchief, tie it on a stick, and go!"

"General, I have no handkerchief."

"Then tear your shirt, sir, and tie that to a stick."

"General, I have on a flannel shirt, and I see you have [too]. I don't believe there is a white shirt in the army."

"Get something, sir; get something and go!"[17]

Colonel Peyton galloped toward the enemy lines, then returned with Brigadier George Custer, whose long blond hair, red scarf and immense gold shoulder straps made him a conspicuous figure.

"I am General Custer," he told Gordon, "and bear a message to you from General Sheridan. The general desires me . . . to demand the immediate and unconditional surrender of all the troops under your command. . . . He directs me to say to you, general, if there is any hesitation . . . he has you surrounded and can annihilate you within an hour."

Gordon coolly replied that if Major General Sheridan decided to continue the fighting the responsibility for the bloodshed would be his.

Soon another white flag approached. "Under it was Philip Sheridan," said Gordon, "accompanied by a mounted escort almost as large as one of Fitz Lee's regiments. Sheridan was mounted on an enormous horse, a very handsome animal. . . . Around me at the time were my faithful sharpshooters, and as General Sheridan and his escort came within easy range of the rifles, a halfwitted fellow raised his gun as if to fire. I ordered him to lower his gun. . . . He did not obey my order cheerfully. . . . In fact, he was again in the act of raising his gun to fire at Sheridan when I caught [it] and said, with emphasis, that he must not shoot men under flag of truce."

"Well, general, let him stay on his own side," the man protested.

Sheridan after a brief discussion agreed to a cease-fire while Lee and Grant were conferring. Dismounting, he then made some small talk. "We have met before, I believe," he told Gordon, "at Winchester and Cedar Creek in the Valley."

Gordon replied that he had been in the Valley. "I had the pleasure of receiving some artillery from your government," Sheridan went on, "consigned to me by your commander, General Early."

"That is true; and I have this morning received from your government artillery consigned to me through General Sheridan," Gordon could not resist answering, referring to the two guns captured that morning.

While this banter was going on, the 25-year-old Custer encountered Longstreet. "I have come to demand your instant surrender!" he called out. "We are in a position to crush you, and unless you surrender at once, we will destroy you!"

Longstreet began to lose his temper. "By what authority do you come in our lines? General Lee is in communication with General Grant. We will certainly not recognize any subordinate."

"Oh, Sheridan and I are independent of Grant today," Custer answered, "and we will destroy you if you don't surrender. . . ."

Longstreet became enraged: "I suppose you . . . have violated the decencies of military procedure because you know no better, but it will not save you if you do so again. Now go and act as you and Sheridan choose and I will teach you a lesson you won't forget! Now go!" Custer said little more.[18]

Later on April 9, before Lee went off to his conference, Longstreet assured him that his old friend Grant would not be vindictive. Lee remained pensive. Longstreet's last words to him were defiant: "General, unless he gives us honorable terms, come back and let us fight it out!"[19]

The two generals-in-chief met in the two-story brick house of Wilmer McLean, the largest of the half-dozen or so residences at Appomattox Courthouse. Only one aide, Colonel Charles Marshall, accompanied Lee. Ten officers were in Grant's retinue. "We walked in softly and arranged ourselves quietly about the sides of the room," said Horace Porter, one of Grant's aides, "very much as people enter a sick chamber when they expect to find the patient dangerously ill." Lee sat at a small oval table near a window, Grant at a marble-topped table in the center. The contrast between them was striking. Lee was 58 and erect, his thick hair and well-cut beard silver gray, his uniform, boots and sword of impeccable quality. Grant was nearly sixteen years younger and stooped, his hair and beard nut-brown, his uniform rumpled and his boots splattered with mud. He wore no sword and only his shoulder straps designated his rank.

Grant led off the conversation. "I met you once before, General Lee, while we were serving in Mexico, when you came over from General Scott's head-quarters to visit [John] Garland's brigade, to which I them belonged. . . . I think I should have recognized you anywhere."

"Yes," replied Lee, who while courteous would be reserved throughout the talks, "I know I met you on that occasion, and I have often thought of it, and tried to recollect how you looked, but I could not recall a single feature."

Soon Lee steered the talk toward the subject at hand, inquiring about the specific terms of surrender. "The terms I propose," said Grant, "are those stated substantially in my letter of yesterday . . . the officers and men surren-dered to be paroled and disqualified from taking up arms again . . . and all arms, ammunition and supplies to be delivered up as captured property." He went on to voice the hope that now hostilities would cease throughout the South. (Davis would not be captured, and most of the last organized Confed-erate forces disbanded, for another month.) Lee nodded in assent, and Grant began to write out the terms, ending with the sentence, "Each officer and man will be allowed to return to his home, not to be disturbed by the United States authorities so long as they observe their paroles, and the laws in force where they may reside." Later he would say that he realized it would be a needless humiliation to deprive the officers of their weapons. Without Lee's asking he therefore inserted the words that the delivering up of arms "will not embrace the side-arms of the officers, nor their private horses or baggage."[20]

Lee put on a pair of steel-rimmed spectacles and carefully read the agree-ment. When he came to the reference to officers' side arms and horses, he obviously was pleased.

"This will have a very happy effect upon my army," he said.

"Unless you have some suggestions . . . I will have a copy of the letter made in ink and sign it," Grant replied.

Lee paused. "There is one thing I would like to mention," he said. "The cavalrymen and artillerists own their own horses in our army. Its organization in this respect differs from that of the United States. . . . I would like to un-derstand whether these men will be permitted to retain their horses?"

"You will find the terms as written do not allow this," said Grant.

Lee read the agreement again. "No, I see the terms do not; that is clear," he said. His face showed he hoped for the concession, but could not bring himself to ask for it.

Here Grant proved as much the gentleman as Lee. "Well, the subject is quite new to me," he said. "Of course I did not know that any private soldiers owned their animals. . . . I take it that most of the men in the ranks are small farmers, and as the country has been so raided by the two armies, it is doubt-ful whether they will be able to put in a crop to carry themselves and their families through the next winter without the aid of the horses. . . . I will not change the terms as now written but I will instruct the officers I shall appoint to receive the paroles to let all the men who claim to own a horse or mule take the animals home with them. . . ."

Lee was relieved. He knew that many an infantryman, in the days to come, would claim cavalry affiliation and go home with a mule to raise a crop. "This will have the best possible effect upon the men," he said. "It will . . . do much toward conciliating our people."

While the document was being copied, Lee obliquely made a point about his army's need for rations. "I have a thousand or more of your men as prisoners, General Grant," he said, ". . . I shall be glad to send them into your lines as soon as it can be arranged, for I have no provisions for them. I have, indeed, nothing for my own men."

Here Grant showed his generosity once again, saying he would take steps at once to supply the Confederates with rations. "Of about how many men does your present force consist?"

"Indeed, I am not able to say. My losses in killed and wounded have been exceedingly heavy and, besides, there have been many stragglers and some deserters."

"Suppose I send over 25,000 rations. Do you think that will be a sufficient supply?"

"I think it will be ample," answered Lee, "and it will be a great relief, I assure you."[21]

The meeting broke up about 4 P.M. Lee strode onto the porch and waited for his horse. "He smote his hands together a number of times in an absent sort of way," said Porter, "seemed not to see the group of Union officers in the yard who rose respectfully at his approach, and appeared unconscious of everything about him. All appreciated the sadness that overwhelmed him. . . ." General Grant saluted him by raising his hat, as did all the Union officers. Lee raised his hat in turn and rode off.

Then the souvenir hunting began. Sheridan paid Wilmer McLean $20 in gold for the table at which Lee had sat, later giving it to Mrs. Custer. Major General Edward Ord, now commanding the Army of the James, paid $40 for the table Grant had used, subsequently presenting it to Mrs. Grant, who declined and insisted it should go to Mrs. Ord. "Bargains were at once struck for everything in the room," said Porter, "and it even said that some mementos were carried off for which no coin of the realm was ever exchanged."[22]

Toward sundown of April 9 Lee, mounted on his dapple-gray horse Traveler, started back to his headquarters one mile in the rear. His army was encamped all along the road. "When they saw the well-known figure of General Lee approaching," said William Blackford, now of the engineers, "there was a general rush . . . to greet him as he passed, and two solid walls of men were formed along the whole distance. Their officers followed . . . awaiting his coming. . . . As soon as he entered this avenue of old soldiers, the flower of his army, the men who had stood to their duty through thick and thin . . . wild heartfelt cheers arose which so touched General Lee that tears filled his eyes and trickled down his cheeks. . . ." Then the cheers died down, replaced by an eerie silence punctuated with choking sobs, while the troops doffed their hats as he passed. "Grim bearded men . . . covered their faces with their hands and wept like children. Officers of all ranks . . . sat on their horses and cried."

When the troops did learn of Grant's concessions, their relief was palpable. Many had feared they would be sent to prisons in the North. "The favorable and entirely unexpected terms restored our souls," said Ned Moore of the Rockbridge Artillery, "and at once plans, first for returning to our homes and then for starting life anew, afforded ample interest."[23]

In truth the Yankees could not have been more conciliatory. "I am forced to admit," said Major James Caldwell of McGowan's brigade, "that the Federal officers and troops conducted themselves with singular propriety. We could hear, within their lines, an occasional cheer and the music of bands; but they did not approach us, or even give any indication of malicious triumph. . . . A few of the general officers came within our lines, either on official errands or to visit their acquaintances among us; but they came without parade. . . ."

The West Pointers, both North and South, acted more like friends at a reunion than men who for four years had been doing their best to kill each other. Working out the details of the surrender for the Federals were Major Generals John Gibbon and Charles Griffin, commanding the Twenty-fourth and Fifth Corps respectively, and Wesley Merritt, Sheridan's deputy. The Confederate team consisted of Longstreet and Gordon, their disputes with Custer put aside, and William Pendleton. Though no West Pointer, Gordon fit right in, his battlefield exploits earning him entrée. Among these professional soldiers, possibly the most popular officer was Cadmus Wilcox, who had been best man at Grant's wedding. Wilcox had ridden up to Appomattox Courthouse on a bony horse, incongruously wearing a thick overcoat. This prompted Gibbon, his classmate at the academy, to ask him if he was sick.

"It's all I have," Wilcox answered, opening the coat and showing his underclothes. Then he turned to Sheridan with mock wrath: "You have captured all of the balance, and you can't have that until you capture me!"

Wilcox was that anomaly in the Confederate ranks, an officer who had never been killed, wounded or impaired by illness. Of the six lieutenant generals who had been corps commanders during the war under Lee—Longstreet, Jackson, Powell Hill, Ewell, Dick Anderson and Early—only Longstreet remained at Appomattox. Of forty-seven major generals seven were left, admittedly some transferred. Brigadiers at one juncture totaled 146; perhaps 22 now stood with the infantry. Of several hundred colonels at best 85, many recently commissioned, remained.[24]

On April 10 Lee met with Grant once more, then issued General Order

No. 9. "After four years of arduous service marked by unsurpassed courage and fortitude," he wrote, "the Army of Northern Virginia has been compelled to yield to overwhelming numbers and resources. . . . I need not tell the brave survivors . . . that I have consented to this result from no distrust of them, but feeling that valor and devotion could accomplish nothing. . . . I determined to avoid the useless sacrifice of those whose past services have endeared them to their countrymen. . . . With an unceasing admiration for your constancy and devotion . . . I bid you all an affectionate farewell." The armed and organized troops who read this message totaled no more 7,900, though the addition of prisoners, the weaponless and the ill would swell the list of parolees to some 28,000.

Lee remained in camp until April 12, but took no part that day in the official ceremony involving the stacking of arms and surrendering of battle flags. Leading the troops in the army's last march was John Brown Gordon of Georgia with the old Second Corps. Given the honor of reviewing the column was Brigadier Joshua Chamberlain of Maine, the man whose inspired defense of Little Round Top the second day of Gettysburg was arguably the turning point of the war.

Chamberlain left us an unsurpassed portrait of the scene. "The dusky swarms forge forward into gray columns of march," he said. "On they come, with the old swinging route step and swaying battle-flags. In the van, the proud Confederate ensign—the great field of white with canton of star-strewn cross of blue on a field of red, the regimental battle flags with the same escutcheon following on, crowded so thick, by thinning out of men, that the whole column seemed crowned with red."

The occasion affected him deeply, and he resolved to mark it with a salute of arms. "Before us in proud humiliation stood the embodiment of manhood: men whom neither toils and sufferings, nor the fact of death, nor disaster, nor hopelessness could bend from their resolve . . . was not such manhood to be welcomed back into a Union so tested and assured?"

When the head of each Confederate division came opposite, Chamberlain ordered a bugle call and instantly the Federal line from right to left, regiment by regiment in succession, snapped from "order arms" to "carry arms"—the marching salute. "Gordon at the head of the column . . . catches the sound of shifting arms, looks up and, taking the meaning, wheels superbly, making with himself and his horse one uplifted figure . . . as he drops the point of his sword to the boot toe; then facing to his own command, gives word to his successive brigades to pass us with the same position . . . honor answering honor. . . ."

In the Second Corps the Stonewall Brigade led the way, its ranks numbering some 200 men. Then came the other riddled units of Jackson's old command—troops once headed by Richard Taylor and Harry Hays and Leroy Stafford, by Sam Garland and Isaac Trimble, by Robert Rodes and Dodson Ramseur. Next swung by Dick Anderson's ill-fated Fourth Corps, with Bushrod Johnson's division led by Henry Wise. "Now makes its last front A.P. Hill's old (3rd) Corps, [Henry] Heth at the head, since Hill had gone too far forward ever to return." Fallen on the battlefield, too, were Lawrence Branch and Maxcy Gregg, William Pender and Abner Perrin. "Now the sad great pageant—Longstreet and his men! What shall we give them for greeting that has not already been spoken in volleys of thunder . . . on all the river-banks of Virginia?" Marching with the First Corps in spirit were Tom Cobb, William Barksdale and Paul Semmes; Lew Armistead, Richard Garnett and Micah Jenkins; John Bell Hood, Jerome Robertson and John Gregg.

Each Confederate unit halted at a predetermined place, dressed its ranks and faced the line of Federals across the road from them at a distance of perhaps 12 feet. "They fix bayonets, stack arms; then, hesitatingly remove cartridge boxes. . . . Lastly—reluctantly, with agony of expression—they tenderly fold their flags, battle-worn and torn, blood-stained, heart-holding colors, and lay them down; some . . . clinging to them, pressing them to their lips with burning tears." Finally, exulted Chamberlain: ". . . only the Flag of the Union greets the sky."[25]

For the Army of Northern Virginia, the war was done. Four years to the day had passed since the shelling of Fort Sumter had opened hostilities.

# THREE

\* \* \* \*

# THE SURVIVORS

Even as the officers and men of the army were streaming toward their homes, the news of Abraham Lincoln's assassination on April 14 shocked and dismayed the nation. His views had been far more moderate on how best to deal with the prostrate South than the radical Republicans who came to dominate the Reconstruction Era, and probably would have been more productive. With the passage of the 13th and 14th Amendments in 1865 and 1866, blacks won their freedom and the rights of citizenship, but changing the prevailing culture would be more difficult. Trying to do this the radical Republicans treated the South as a vassal state, carving it into five military districts and occupying it under martial law. Soon Northern carpetbaggers and Southern scalawags, running as Republicans and backed by Federal troops, captured state and local offices and made their fortunes amid the social upheaval. By 1871, however, Democrats were turning the tide, recapturing the political machinery in Tennessee, Virginia, North Carolina and Georgia. Now the North was tiring of imposing its will. By 1877 the last Federal troops would leave the South. Recounting how some survivors of the Army of Northern Virginia fared in this postwar period will make our story complete.

*Robert E. Lee* in the fall of 1865 accepted the presidency of Washington College, then a small provincial school in Lexington, Virginia, at the southern end of the Shenandoah Valley. There he was joined by his invalid wife, Mary, his daughters Mildred, Mary and Agnes and, for a time, his youngest son, Rob. Over the next few years he built up the school academically, instilled a gentleman's code of conduct ("the promotion of the happiness and welfare of others") and enjoyed daily rides on Traveler. In November of 1867, still the icon of the South, he traveled to Petersburg for Rooney's marriage to Mary Tabb Bolling. Meanwhile he and most Southern leaders advised their people to accept their defeat and be good citizens in a reunited land.

By 1870, Lee was plainly in failing health, the result of heart problems. Now he unburdened himself of some thoughts on the war to his cousin and boyhood friend Cassius Lee. Who was the best Union general? "McClellan by all odds." Why did he cross the Potomac and precipitate the Sharpsburg campaign? "Because my men had nothing to eat. I went to Maryland to feed my army." What factor most accounted for the defeat at Gettysburg? Ruminated Lee: If Jackson instead of Ewell had been commanding the Second Corps Cemetery Hill would have been taken, Meade could not have dug in on Cemetery Ridge, and the South would have won.

In late September Lee suffered a stroke and for the next two weeks drifted in and out of coma. During his delirium, just as Jackson had, he called out for Powell Hill: "Tell Hill he must come up." His last words were: "Strike the tent."[1] Following his death, Washington College was renamed Washington and Lee.

*Jefferson Davis*, the army's commander-in-chief, was captured on May 10, 1865, in Abbeville, Georgia, together with his wife and children. "Please don't shoot him," Varina said to the Union private accosting him. "Let him shoot," said Davis. "I may as well die here as anywhere." Stated one Pennsylvania officer of the Confederate president: he was "a very distinguished-looking man . . . who would be noted among a thousand for his striking personality."

Though his family would be allowed to go to Savannah, Davis was taken to Fort Monroe, where he spent the next two years under harsh prison conditions, at one point being shackled. Said he: "God's will be done." Taken to Richmond for trial in 1867, he was released on $100,000 bail—the money being put up by such New Yorkers as Horace Greeley, Cornelius Vanderbilt and Augustus Schell, who thought his treatment inhumane. No trial ever ensued.

For the next dozen years Davis endured considerable financial hardship, then took residence in a comfortable Biloxi, Mississippi, estate provided by a lifelong friend. There during the 1880s he produced his memoirs on the war. On a personal as well as public level, his life was marked with tragedy, with his four sons dying before him. He died in 1889, survived by Varina and two daughters.[2]

*Joseph Johnston*, perhaps Davis's least favorite general, surrendered the Army of Tennessee to Sherman on April 26 in North Carolina. How much the war might have been shortened had he not been wounded at Seven Pines and replaced by Lee is the source of much conjecture. He had none of Lee's audacity and might have been routed by McClellan during the Seven Days. For fourteen years after the war he worked as a railroad president and regulator. Later he served one term in the U.S. House of Representatives from Virginia. He died in 1891.

Johnston's First Manassas rival, *Pierre Gustav Toutant Beauregard*, who made a cameo appearance at Drewry's Bluff and the early days of the Petersburg siege, surrendered with him in North Carolina. He too prospered after the war, using his engineering skills to advantage over the next decade as a railroad executive. In 1877 he and Jubal Early began serving, at impressive salaries, as supervisors of the notorious Louisiana Lottery, which was reeling from charges of fraud. From 1879 to 1888, he also commanded the Louisiana militia. He died in 1893.

*James Longstreet* first settled with Louise and their children in New Orleans, where he became a successful businessman and investor. His evolution from Southern hero to villain began in 1867, when he wrote a letter to the *New Orleans Times* advocating cooperation with the radical Republicans. "It will ruin you, son, if you publish it," his Uncle Augustus had warned him.[3] But publish it he did, with predictable results. It was one thing, Southern believers in the Lost Cause felt, to be on good terms with the occupying Union troops—they had been worthy adversaries—quite another to embrace the hated abolitionists. Though ostracized by the Southern elite, Longstreet did not suffer financially for his principles, soon joining the Republican Party. In 1868 he endorsed his friend Grant for the presidency, and the next year Grant named him surveyor of the port of New Orleans, the first of numerous political plums he would receive from Republican hands. In the mid-1870s, now ensconced in Gainesville, Georgia, he published articles in *McClure's* magazine defending his own conduct at Gettysburg and criticizing Lee's decisions there, further enraging his detractors. Later during the 1880s he wrote similar pieces for the *Century* magazine, extending his criticism to Jackson. His last lucrative political appointment, that of U.S. commissioner of railroads, came from William McKinley in 1897. He died at age 82 in 1904.

Leading the attacks on Longstreet was *Jubal Early*, who had endured three years of self-imposed and impecunious exile in Canada following the end of the war rather than give his parole. With the granting of a general amnesty in December 1868, he subsequently settled in Lynchburg, Virginia, where he opened a none-too-successful law practice. When Beauregard in 1877 invited him to be co-supervisor of the Louisiana Lottery, a position that required attending a handful of drawings annually, Early gratefully accepted. He held this sinecure for the next fifteen years.

Meanwhile throughout the 1870s and 1880s he was a leading figure in the Southern Historical Society, which in its periodicals espoused the idea of the Lost Cause. Trying to explain how a righteous God could have let the South lose, this doctrine espoused Lee as a leader without peer, made Longstreet responsible for the defeat at Gettysburg and insisted that only Union numerical and industrial superiority had carried the day. While these points have merit, they were preached with messianic fervor by some Southerners. "The enlightened world," wrote Early, "does not accept as an infallible maxim that success is the only criterion of merit." Union Major General John Crook, visiting Lynchburg in 1890 when Early was 73, sat up late one night with him over drinks. "He is much stooped and enfeebled," Crook recorded, "but as bitter and violent as an adder. . . . Boasts of his being unreconstructed . . . [He] is living entirely in the past." Early died in 1894.[4]

*Daniel Harvey Hill*, the Jackson brother-in-law so brave in battle and contumacious in camp, also surrendered with Johnston in North Carolina. He returned to Charlotte, where the former college professor published from 1866 to 1869 a monthly magazine, *The Land We Love* ("The Organ of the Late Confederate Army"), and then in the 1870s a weekly paper, *The Southern Home*. In these pages he celebrated both his old comrades and Southern literature. He accepted defeat as God's will, but abhorred radical Republican rule. His "great sin," he admitted, was "hatred of the Yankees."

Lee respected Hill's gallantry on the field but never warmed to him, and Hill felt much the same way about his commander. "My impression of Genl Lee is not so enthusiastic as that of most men who served under him," he wrote Longstreet during the postwar years. In 1877 he returned to academia as president, first of Arkansas Industrial University (the future University of Arkansas) from 1877 to 1884, and then of Georgia Military and Agricultural College in Milledgeville from 1885 to 1889, the year he died. He and Isabella and their five grown children were a close and happy family, and the waspishness he often showed others did not mar their relationship. "Father . . . never does anything except with all his might," said one of the Hill children admiringly.[5]

Following his capture at Sailor's Creek, *Richard Ewell* was transported to dank and gloomy Fort Warren in Boston Harbor, where he spent the next three months. Though President Andrew Johnson issued a blanket amnesty May 29, 1865, freeing field grade prisoners, Ewell and the others as general officers were excluded. Each man would have to apply individually for his release. Meanwhile the headstrong Lizinka was in Nashville, trying to regain control of her extensive Tennessee properties. Finding her home occupied by Mrs. Johnson, she sent her a pert note, asking to use "one or two rooms in my own house." Mrs. Johnson made no answer, and it would not be until July 1 that the president allowed Lizinka to begin court proceedings to repossess her holdings. Later she visited Ewell at Fort Warren, only to be shocked at his appearance. "I have seen my husband . . . haggard from three months confinement in stone cells," she wrote Johnson, ". . . if Richard dies in Fort Warren how I will hate you, wicked as it is to hate anyone." On July 19 the president finally authorized Ewell's release.

By December 1865 he and Lizinka were in Tennessee, moving into 3,300-acre Spring Hill Farm, 30 miles south of Nashville. For the next six years Ewell actively managed that property and others in Mississippi, restoring them to profitability. On January 8, 1872, he came down with chills and fever while riding around Spring Hill doing farm chores in inclement weather. Two weeks later, while tending him, Lizinka came down with fever herself. She died on January 22, he three days later.[6]

*Richard Taylor*, Jackson's urbane subordinate in the Valley Campaign, was a lieutenant general at war's end, assigned to the Department of Alabama, Mississippi and East Louisiana. He surrendered on May 4, 1865. When he refused to ask for a pardon because he believed his decision to fight for the Confederacy an honorable one, his extensive Louisiana land holdings were confiscated. Nonetheless Taylor continued to have strong connections in Washington, D.C. "When the Whig Party dissolved," he said, "most of its Northern members joined the Republicans . . . and I had consorted with them when my father was President and afterward." Through the 1860s and 1870s he made his home in New Orleans, where he was active in Democratic politics, and mingled freely with the elite, both North and South. In 1879, he died while visiting friends in New York.[7]

*Richard Heron Anderson*, the hero of Spotsylvania and the goat of Sailor's Creek, proved unable to adjust to postwar life. The genteel, pipe-smoking South Carolinian failed as a planter, then in dire need went to Charleston to work as a laborer for the railroad. Eventually this "most silent and discreet of men" found a low-level state job as inspector of phosphates, a post he held until his death in 1879.[8]

Brilliant as a division head with the Army of Northern Virginia, a disaster as the commander of the Army of Tennessee, *John Bell Hood* soon decided to settle in New Orleans. There in 1867 he entered the insurance business—perhaps with the help of Longstreet—becoming president of the Louisiana and Texas branch of the Life Insurance Association of America. Hood never did marry Buck Preston but in 1868 he took as his bride Anna Marie Hennen, the only child of a prominent and wealthy Catholic family. Over the eleven years of their marriage she gave him eleven children, including three sets of twins, even as they divided their time between a plantation at Hammond, Louisiana, and a well-appointed apartment in New Orleans. The family, naturally enough, became known as Hood's Brigade.

During the 1870s Hood became sensitive about criticism of his wartime leadership in Tennessee. "They charge me with having made Franklin a slaughter pen," he told a veterans' group, "but, as I understand it, war means fight and fight means kill." In August 1879 a yellow fever epidemic hit New Orleans, killing Anna and their eldest child. Hood succumbed several days later. Mary Chestnut's words of 1863 about Hood: ". . . his sad Quixote face, the face of an old crusader who believed in his cause . . ." remained true to the end.[9]

*Lafayette McLaws*, who for so long led a potent division in the First Corps before Longstreet relieved him for disloyalty following the contretemps with

Bragg at Chickamauga, spent the rest of the war in Savannah. His career thereafter was long but not especially productive, consisting of jobs in the insurance business in Augusta, Georgia, then with the Internal Revenue Service and Post Office departments in Savannah. In 1886, he admitted, "I am without means." He died the next year.

*Alexander Lawton*, the brother-in-law of Porter Alexander, whose crack Georgia troops had done so well in the Seven Days, Second Manassas and Sharpsburg, had closed out his service in the thankless job of quartermaster-general, a post he at first vehemently rejected. After the surrender he was for decades an influential figure in Georgia politics, then president of the American Bar Association and, in 1887, ambassador to Austria. He died in 1896.

With Fanny and their children, *John Brown Gordon* returned to Georgia, where in 1868 he began simultaneous careers with the Southern Life Insurance Co. and the University Publishing Co., both of which flourished over the next five years under his direction. But the Democratic Party would be his real passion. In 1873 he was elected to the U.S. Senate, where he played a key role in deciding the disputed presidential election of 1876. (Republican Samuel Tilden had carried the popular vote, but Democrat Rutherford B. Hayes won by one electoral vote. Working behind the scenes, Gordon helped ensure that disputed Southern electoral votes remained in Hayes's column. In return he received assurances that the last Federal troops would be withdrawn from the South.) Reelected to the U.S. Senate in 1879, he soon resigned for financial reasons to become president of the Louisville & Nashville Railroad, a move that at the time brought charges of political chicanery. From 1886 to 1890 he returned to public life, serving as governor of Georgia. In 1891, on the occasion of his and Fanny's 37th wedding anniversary, the stern and unbending soldier composed a poem in her honor that ended:

> Still beauty's seal is on thy brow,
> No brighter, nobler, then than now,
> And love's still warm, as 'twas when you
> Were seventeen, I twenty-two.

Gordon was the commander-in-chief of the United Confederate Veterans from its inception in 1890 to his death in 1904.[10]

The division heads who surrendered at Appomattox followed various paths. In the First Corps *Charles W. Field*, who had shared a fateful dream with his wife, Nimmie, after his wounding at Second Manassas, pursued business interests for many years in Maryland and Georgia. In 1875 he accepted a commission as inspector general of the Egyptian army, then returned to the U.S. to serve as doorkeeper of the U.S. House of Representatives from 1878 to 1881. Competent, affable, unpretentious, he remained in government employ until his death in 1892.

Forceful and assured *Joseph Kershaw*, who had been with Longstreet that day in the Wilderness when he was wounded and Micah Jenkins killed, returned to his law practice in Camden, South Carolina. Subsequently he was a legislator and judge. He died in 1894.

*George Pickett* remained an enigma to the last. For ten years after the war he earned a meager living first as a farmer and then as an insurance agent in Norfolk, Virginia. One day in 1870 he bumped into Lee in a Richmond hotel. Cavalryman John Mosby, who witnessed the strained encounter, recalled that Lee was capable of "freezing out a man he did not like." When Lee departed, Pickett said to Mosby: "He had my division massacred at Gettysburg." Mosby, clearly no friend of Pickett, made a sharp retort: "Well, it made you immortal."[11] Pickett died in 1875 at age 50. His young widow, LaSalle Corbett Pickett, spent the rest of her life enshrining his memory in books, magazine articles and public appearances. She did not die until 1931.

*Clement Evans*, *Bryan Grimes* and *James A. Walker* headed the tattered Second Corps divisions. Evans, who had taken over Gordon's old command and whose wife, Allie, incredible as it seems, was captured unhurt as she drove her carriage in the melee at Sailor's Creek, returned to Georgia after the war. There he kept a promise he had made at Fredericksburg, becoming a Methodist minister in 1866 and beginning a thirty-year vocation. "The first thing I did, darling, after reading your letter," Allie said at the time, "was to go to myself and get on my knees and thank God if you were to be a minister of the Gospel. . . ." Evans died in 1911 in Atlanta. Bryan Grimes, a true believer in the superiority of Southern culture and a reckless fighter, returned to his North Carolina plantation and resumed farming. In 1880 an unknown assassin murdered him. Lawyer James A. Walker, the onetime commander of the Stonewall Brigade whom Jackson had expelled from V.M.I., took a seat in the Virginia legislature in 1871, then was elected lieutenant governor in 1877. A falling-out with fellow Democrats caused the short-tempered Walker to switch parties, and he later served two terms in the U.S. Congress. Crippled in a gunfight following a contested election, he died in 1901.[12]

The Third Corps commanders at Appomattox were *Henry Heth*, *Cadmus Marcellus Wilcox* and *William Mahone*. Heth, the close friend and look-alike of Lee who brought on the fight at Gettysburg with his search for shoes, lost his extensive land holdings near Richmond and, like so many other officers, was forced into the insurance business. Later he held a series of engineering jobs with the Federal government. Much esteemed in Virginia, he died in 1899. Wilcox, a genial bachelor, settled in Washington, D.C., with his widowed sister-in-law and several nieces and nephews. There he held a series of Federal posts, achieving financial security only in 1886, when President Grover Cleveland named him to a top position in the General Land Office. He died in 1890. At his funeral service four Confederate and four Union officers bore his casket, bearing testimony to friendships that survived seces-

sion. The self-reliant William Mahone returned to Norfolk with his wife, Otelia, and resumed the presidency of the Norfolk & Petersburg Railroad, then
simultaneously began to run the Southside Railroad. By 1867 he took over a
third line, creating an early conglomerate known as the Atlantic, Mississippi
& Ohio and paying himself a $25,000 salary. Detractors, jealous of his suc-
cess, sneered that the initials stood for All Mine and Otelia's. Forced out of
the AM&O in the panic of 1873, he entered politics. In 1881 he was elected
as a Democrat to the U.S. Senate but thereafter switched parties. By 1889,
when he ran unsuccessfully for governor, his politics had alienated many
friends. "General Mahone . . . was just as brave and just as gallant as he could
be," said one Southern woman. "It was such a pity he became a Republican."
He died in 1895.[13]

*Bushrod Johnson*, who fought so well in Tennessee and at Petersburg, may
have been unfairly judged at Sailor's Creek, where overwhelming numbers
caught up with Dick Anderson's dispirited mini Corps. Following the war
Johnson went back to Tennessee and served as chancellor of the University
of Nashville. When the school failed in 1874 he retired in ill health to a farm
in Illinois. He died in 1880. *Henry Wise*, the crusty ex-governor of Virginia
who was Johnson's principal critic, resumed his law practice. He died in Richmond in 1876.

*Fitzhugh Lee*, the commanding general's convivial nephew, surrendered soon
after his breakthrough at Appomattox. For the next two decades he farmed
at Richlands, his inherited estate in Stafford County, Virginia. Then he turned
to politics, serving as the Democratic governor of Virginia from 1885 to 1889.
He was named consul general to Cuba in 1896 and, when the Spanish-
American War broke out, was commissioned a major general in command of
the U.S. Seventh Corps in Cuba, though he saw no combat. He died in 1905.
*William Henry Fitzhugh "Rooney" Lee*—Robert's strapping six-foot-two
middle son—returned to White House, the Custis estate he had inherited on
the Pamunkey River. There he restored the plantation and embarked on a
farming career, becoming president of the Virginia Agricultural Society. He
served as a state senator from 1875 to 1878 and as a U.S. congressman from
1886 to 1891, the year he died.

*Wade Hampton* surrendered with Joe Johnston in North Carolina. With
much of his vast South Carolina land holdings confiscated and the rest in
ruins, he resolutely set about planting crops and rebuilding his life. Meanwhile
he pursued various business enterprises, including the co-founding of the
Southern Life Insurance Co., and worked behind the scenes to strengthen the
Democratic Party and oust the radical Republicans. John Quincy Adams II of
Massachusetts, invited by Hampton to speak in Charleston during this period,
praised his political restraint. "If he is a rebel," he said, pointing at Hampton,
"he is just such a rebel as I am and no more." The 58-year-old Hampton

moved into the public sector in 1876, winning the governorship just as the carpetbagger era was ending, and was reelected in 1878. He resigned to take a seat in the U.S. Senate, where he served from 1879 to 1891. He was named by Grover Cleveland as commissioner of railroads in 1893, and died in 1902.[14]

Cavalrymen *Thomas Rosser* and *Thomas Munford*, who served together in the Valley and at Five Forks, never did have much use for each other. Rosser initially went West, where he was chief engineer on a railroad being built through the Indian Territory. There Custer was deployed to protect the construction and the two men resumed their friendship. Later Rosser returned to Virginia and became a gentleman farmer. He died in 1910. Colonel Munford, who never did get his brigadier's wreath, settled in Uniontown, Alabama, where he raised cotton. He died in 1918, shy of his 87th birthday.

Lieutenant Colonel *William Blackford*, a key Stuart aide during the first three years of the war, first took a job as chief engineer of the Lynchburg & Danville railroad. Two years later he went to Louisiana with his family to develop a sugar plantation given him by his father-in-law. In 1874 a flood wiped out the fruits of many years' labor and Blackford returned to Virginia to accept a professorship at V.M.I. Subsequently he returned to railroad engineering. In 1890, at age 60, he bought a farm in Princess Anne County and became an oyster farmer. He died in 1905.

Twenty-four-year-old *Henry Kyd Douglas*, who served as an aide to Stonewall Jackson until his death and then several other commanders in the Second Corps—giving us intimate portraits of them—practiced law for many years at Hagerstown, Maryland. He became prominent in legal and political circles and sat on the bench of the 4th Judicial Circuit in Maryland. He died in 1903.

Brigadier *Edward Porter Alexander*, the army's most notable artillerist and the man who witnessed and recorded so many dramatic scenes—including Longstreet's vacillation the third day at Gettysburg, for several years taught mathematics and engineering at the University of South Carolina. Well-connected across the political spectrum—from the Republican Longstreet to the Democrat Gordon—Alexander in 1872 next took a series of senior railroad jobs that he would hold for the next twenty years. From 1865 to 1900 U.S. rail mileage would expand fourfold, and Alexander would be a key performer in making it happen. In 1892 he retired from railroading and took up plantation life. He died in 1910.

Colonel *William Poague*, a lawyer who rose through the ranks to command the Rockbridge Artillery, returned to Virginia. There he established and ran several secondary schools, served in the legislature from 1871 to 1873 and was treasurer of V.M.I. from 1885 to 1913. He died one year later.

Sixty-three-year-old *Isaac Trimble*, who lost a leg and was captured in the aftermath of Pickett's Charge at Gettysburg, went back to Baltimore, where he was a consulting engineer. *Edward "Allegheny" Johnson,* the loud and burly officer who spent many an evening wooing the ladies in Mary Chestnut's salon and later was captured in the Bloody Angle at Spotsylvania, became a Virginia farmer. He never married. *Alfred Colquitt*, the Princeton-educated lawyer who had been dilatory at Chancellorsville but fought with the army through Petersburg, proved an able postwar politician. He was twice elected governor of Georgia and in 1883 was named to the U.S. Senate, where he served until 1894, the year of his death. *Raleigh Colston*, the unlucky division head who lost all four of his brigadiers at Chancellorsville, first established a military school in North Carolina, then became a colonel in the Egyptian army. Paralyzed from the waist down as a result of a fall in the Sudan, he returned to the U.S. in 1879. Impoverished and crippled he subsequently took a series of low-level jobs. *Francis Nicholls*, who led the 2nd Louisiana until losing a foot at Chancellorsville, was twice elected governor of his state and, from 1892 to 1904, chief justice of the Louisiana Supreme Court. *Harry Hays*, severely wounded at Spotsylvania while commanding the 1st Louisiana, served for a time as sheriff of New Orleans Parish and thereafter practiced law.

Bad health forced *Ambrose Ransom "Rans" Wright* to finish the war in Georgia. He resumed his law practice, then became the successful and influential editor of the *Augusta Chronicle and Sentinel*. Illness likewise plagued *Robert Ransom* and forced him from Early's Shenandoah Campaign. He pursued an engineering career in North Carolina. His older brother *Matt*, who surrendered at Appomattox, went into law and politics. From 1872 to 1895 he served as U.S. senator from North Carolina, then minister to Mexico.

*Jerome Robertson*, exiled from the Texas Brigade because of Longstreet's displeasure, continued to practice medicine but also was active in railroad building in West Texas. *Evander McIvor Law*, who likewise ran afoul of Longstreet in his rivalry with Micah Jenkins, surrendered with Johnston. He first resided in South Carolina, where he was active in education and business, then established a military college in Florida. He did not die until 1920, at age 84. *George "Maryland" Steuart*, who fought in many actions but is best remembered as the pedant who refused an order from Jackson at Winchester because it had not come through channels, farmed in Maryland and became state commander of the United Confederate Veterans. *Benjamin Humphreys*, who took over Barksdale's brigade until a severe wound during Early's Valley Campaign sidelined him, was elected governor of Mississippi in 1865 despite the fact that President Johnson had not pardoned him. Soon removed from office by the Union military commander, he went into farming and the insurance business. *Nathaniel Harris*, another hard fighting Mississippian who had distinguished himself at Spotsylvania, practiced law and ran a railroad. He died in 1900 while on a business trip to England.

Wounded and captured at Gettysburg in Pickett's Charge, *James Kemper* after his exchange was unfit for field duty. In the postwar years he practiced law and pursued business interests in Madison County, was active in politics and, in 1873, was elected governor of Virginia. *Montgomery Corse*, captured at Sailor's Creek, resumed his banking career in Alexandria, Virginia. *Eppa Hunton*, likewise taken at Sailor's Creek, practiced law in Richmond and served four terms in the U.S. Congress.

*Cullen Battle*, whose war came to an end at Cedar Creek, went into law and politics in Alabama. In 1868 he was elected to Congress but never served, refusing to take the oath demanded of officeholders by radical Republicans. The last commander of the depleted Stonewall Brigade, *William Terry*, practiced law in Wytheville, Virginia, and served two terms in Congress. He drowned in 1888 while attempting to cross a rain-swollen creek near his home. *William R. Terry*, who took command of Kemper's brigade at Gettysburg, returned to Bedford, Virginia, was elected to four terms in the state legislature and then held several jobs in the public sector. *Robert Hoke* of North Carolina, boyhood friend of the slain Dorsey Pender, surrendered under Johnston. He went back to Lincolnton, ran several successful family businesses that included an ironworks and a cotton mill and sat on the board of the North Carolina Railroad Co.

*Samuel McGowan*, who took over Maxcy Gregg's South Carolina Brigade, returned to Abbeville and practiced law. Though elected to the U.S. Congress in 1865, he was denied his seat. In 1879 he was elected to the state supreme court. Dependable *George Thomas "Tige" Anderson* settled in Georgia and Alabama and held several posts with local government, most notably police chief of Atlanta. *Edward Thomas*, his close friend, went back to his Georgia plantation, where he farmed for twenty years. In the 1880s he was appointed by Grover Cleveland to posts in the Land and Indian Departments. Part Cherokee *Henry Lewis "Rock" Benning* resumed his law career in Columbus, Georgia, and became a leader of the community. *Philip Cook*, who replaced the slain George Doles, likewise practiced law—but in Americus, Georgia. He served in Congress from 1873 to 1883 and as Georgia secretary of state in 1890. *John Rogers Cook*, Stuart's brother-in-law who led his North Carolinians so long and so well, became a prominent Richmond businessman and a power in the Democratic Party. *James Lane* of North Carolina, who took over Lawrence Branch's brigade, turned his talents to academia. He taught at Virginia Polytechnic Institute and the Missouri School of Mines, then at Alabama Polytechnic Institute.

What better way to close this list than with the name of Colonel *William Calvin Oates*, who commanded the 15th Alabama in the futile assault against Chamberlain's 20th Maine at Little Round Top? Oates later served in the legislature, the U.S. Congress and as governor of his state. On his tombstone his epitaph reads in part: "He accepted the result of the war without a murmur."[15] Most of his comrades echoed this sentiment. The fighting was done, and honor had been served.

# NOTES

## 1861

### 1. THE SOUTHERN COMMANDERS

1. Shelby Foote, *The Civil War*, v. 1, Random House, 1958, p. 4.
2. Abraham Lincoln, *Speeches & Writings*, 1859–1865, Library of America, 1989, p. 224.
3. Carl Sandburg, *Abraham Lincoln, The War Years*, v. 1, Harcourt, 1939, p. 223.
4. Ibid., p. 523.
5. Douglas Southall Freeman, *Lee*, v. 1, Scribner's, 1934–36, p. 437.
6. Ibid., p. 437.
7. Ibid., p. 442.
8. Clifford Dowdey, *Lee*, Little, Brown, 1965, p. 41.
9. Ibid., p. 46.
10. Ibid., p. 85.
11. Ibid., p. 101.
12. J. B. Hood, *Advance and Retreat*, New Orleans, 1880, p. 7.
13. Dowdey, p. 111.
14. Freeman, *Lee*, v. 1, p. 470.
15. Walter H. Taylor, *Four Years with General Lee*, Indiana University Press, 1996, p. 13.
16. Freeman, *Lee*, v. 1, p. 529.
17. Lynda Crist et al., eds., *The Papers of Jefferson Davis*, v. 8, Louisiana State University Press, 1971–97, p. 100.
18. Foote, v. 1, p. 7.
19. Varina Davis, *Jefferson Davis, a Memoir by His Wife*, v. 1, New York, 1890, p. 191.

20. Foote, v. 1, p. 11.

21. Ibid., p. 12.

22. Ibid., p. 5.

23. Ibid., p. 17.

24. *Mary Chestnut's Civil War*, C. Vann Woodward, ed., Yale University Press, 1981, p. 90.

25. John L. Manning to his wife, July 7, 1861, Williams-Chesnut-Manning Papers, University of South Carolina.

26. William C. Davis, *Battle at Bull Run*, Doubleday, 1977, p. 82.

27. Alfred Roman, *Military Operations of General Beauregard*, v. 1, New York, 1884, p. 77.

28. Ibid., p. 82.

29. Chestnut, p. 352.

## 2. FIRST MANASSAS AND ITS AFTERMATH

1. Russell H. Beattie, Jr., *Road to Manassas*, New York, 1961, p. 104.

2. G. F. R. Henderson, *Stonewall Jackson and the American Civil War*, v. 1, London, 1898, p. 46.

3. A. P. Aldrich to Mattie Aldrich, June 23, 1861, Bonham Papers, University of South Carolina.

4. Douglas Southall Freeman, *Lee's Lieutenants*, v. 1, Scribner's, 1942, p. 87.

5. Charles Dufour, *Gentle Tiger*, Baton Rouge, 1957, pgs. 7–120.

6. E. P. Alexander, *Fighting for the Confederacy*, Gary Gallagher, ed., North Carolina Press, 1989, p. 49.

7. *War of the Rebellion, A Compilation of the Official Records of the Union and Confederate Armies*, 128 vols., Washington, D.C., 1880–1901, (henceforth known as O.R.), v. 2, p. 559; all citations are from Series I unless otherwise noted.

8. Alexander, p. 50.

9. Thomas Pelot to Lalla Pelot, Sept. 15, 1861, Lalla Pelot Papers, Duke University.

10. *Southern Historical Society Papers*, 52 vols., Richmond 1876–1959, (henceforth known as SHSP), v. 17, p. 54.

11. *Charleston Mercury*, July 25, 1861, p. 1, col. 1.

12. *Battles and Leaders of the Civil War*, 4 vols., New York, 1887–88, (henceforth known as B&L), v. 1, p. 236.

13. Henry Kyd Douglas, *I Rode with Stonewall*, North Carolina Press, 1940, p. 10.

14. W. W. Blackford, *War Years with Jeb Stuart*, Louisiana State University Press, 1993, p. 29.

15. John O. Casler, *Four Years in the Stonewall Brigade*, Morningside, 1982, p. 27.

16. Jubal A. Early, *Narrative of the War Between the States*, Da Capo, 1989, p. 37.

17. B&L, v. 1, p. 191.

18. Mary Anna Jackson, *Memoirs of Stonewall Jackson*, New York, 1892, pgs. 178, 180.

19. Raleigh Colston Papers, Southern Historical Collection, University of North Carolina.

20. Anna Jackson to Robert Dabney, 1863, Box 20, Dabney, Southern Historical Collection, University of North Carolina.

21. Douglas, p. 15.

22. Ibid., p. 16.

23. Roman, v. 1, p. 121.

24. Journal, Confederate States Congress, v. 1, p. 305, as cited in Freeman, *Lee's Lieutenants*, v. 1, p. 100.

25. O.R., v. 5, p. 904.

26. O.R., v. 5, p. 903.

27. *Richmond Whig*, Nov. 7, reprinted in *Richmond Dispatch*, Nov. 8, 1861.

28. O.R., Series IV, v. 1, p. 605.

29. O.R., Series IV, v. 1, p. 611.

30. Richard Taylor, *Destruction and Reconstruction*, New York, 1879, p. 44.

31. SHSP, v. 26, p. 150.

32. Freeman, *Lee*, v. 1, p. 552.

33. Taylor, p. 30.

34. Ibid., p. 33.

35. Dowdey and Manarin, *Wartime Papers of R. E. Lee*, Little, Brown, 1961, p. 95.

36. Freeman, Lee, v. 2, p. 557.

## 3. OFFICERS TO WATCH

1. H. J. Eckenrode and Bryan Conrad, *James Longstreet*, North Carolina Press, 1936, p. 3.

2. G. Moxley Sorrel, *Recollections of a Confederate Staff Officer*, New York, 1905, p. 26.

3. Ibid., p. 23.

4. The Thomas Jewitt Goree Letters, v. 1, p. 110, Bryan, Texas: Family History Foundation.

5. Blackford, p. 47.

6. Sorrel, p. 35.

7. Sorrel, p. 37.

8. Hill to wife, Jan. 26, Oct. 4, 1862, Hill Family Papers, as cited in Hal Bridges, *Lee's Maverick General*, University of Nebraska Press, 1961, pgs. 16–17.

9. D. H. Hill Mexican War Diary, Sept. 14, 1847, Southern Historical Collection, University of North Carolina; Bridges, p. 21.

10. Hill Diary, Sept. 10, 1847; Bridges, p. 20.

11. William Couper, *One Hundred Years at V. M. I.*, v. 1, Richmond 1939, p. 189.

12. O.R., v. 2, p. 95.

13. Hill Family Papers, June 11 and June 20, 1861; Bridges, pgs. 29, 32–33.

14. Ibid., March 19, 1862.

15. Ibid., Dec. 14, 1861.

16. Ibid., Feb. 3, 1862.

17. Ibid., Feb. 21, 1862.

18. Hill to family, January and February, 1848, Hill Papers, North Carolina Archives and Virginia Historical Society, as cited in James I. Robertson, Jr., *General A. P. Hill*, Random House, 1987, pgs. 17, 20–21.

19. Hill Diary, October 1849–May 1850, Hill Papers.

20. R. B. Marcy to daughter, May 28, 1856, George B. McClellan Papers, Library of Congress; Robertson, *General A. P. Hill*, pgs. 27–29.

21. *General A. P. Hill* to R. B. Marcy, 1856, McClellan Papers.

22. G. B. McClellan to Mrs. R. B. Marcy, July 22, 1856, McClellan Papers.

23. *Richmond Times Dispatch*, November 4, 1934; Robertson, *General A. P. Hill*, pgs. 30–31.

24. Hill to McClellan, June 18, 1859, McClellan Papers.

25. *Confederate Veteran*, I, p. 233.

26. Randoph H. McKim, *A Soldier's Recollections*, New York, 1910, p. 53.

27. SHSP, v. 1, p. 100.

28. Ibid., p. 100.

29. Stuart to J. M. Davis, January 25, 1851, Stuart Papers, Virginia Historical Society.

30. Stuart to wife, July 30, 1857, as cited in H. B. McClellan, *The Campaigns of Stuart's Cavalry*, Boston and New York, 1885, p. 21.

31. Stuart to mother, January, 1860; McClellan, p. 29.

32. John Thomason, *Jeb Stuart*, Scribner's, 1930, p. 84.

33. Blackford, p. 32.

34. Ibid., p. 32.

35. Early, as cited in McClellan, pgs. 36–39.

36. O.R., v. 5, p. 777.

37. Stuart to wife, November 24 and December 11, 1861, in Bingham Duncan ed., *Letters*, pgs. 19 and 25; Stuart to Cooke, January 18, 1862, Cooke

Papers, Virginia Historical Society; as cited in Emory M. Thomas, *Bold Dragoon*, Harper, 1986, p. 95.

38. Stuart to wife, December 12, 1861, and January 16, 1862, in Duncan, p. 27, and Stuart Papers, Virginia Historical Society; Thomas, p. 96.

# 1862

## 1. LINCOLN AND MCCLELLAN

1. Sandburg, *Lincoln, The War Years*, v. 1, p. 418.
2. Ibid., p. 419.
3. Ibid., p. 388; Foote, v. 1, p. 241.
4. Sandburg, *The War Years*, v. 1, p. 420.
5. Letter to McClellan, February 3, 1862, Lincoln, *Speeches & Writings, 1859–1865*, p. 304.
6. Sandburg, *The War Years*, v. 1, p. 457.
7. Foote, v. 1, p. 252.
8 Sandburg, *The War Years*, v. 1, p. 480.
9. Ibid., p. 485.
10. William C. Davis, *Duel Between the First Ironclads*, New York, 1975, p. 35.
11. Ibid., p. 120.
12. Ibid., p. 149.
13. McClellan to Samuel Barlow, March 16, 1861, McClellan, Civil War Papers, as cited in Stephen W. Sears, *To the Gates of Richmond*, Ticknor & Fields, 1992, p. 23.
14. Sandburg, *Lincoln, The Prairie Years*, v. 1, Harcourt, 1926, p. 303.
15. Foote, v. 1, p. 20.
16. Sandburg, *The Prairie Years*, v. 1, p. 428.
17. Lincoln, *Speeches & Writings, 1832–1856*, p. 742.
18. Sandburg, *The Prairie Years*, v. 2, p. 374.
19. William H. Russell, *My Diary North and South*, Gloucester, Massachusetts, 1969, p. 240.
20. Elizabeth McClellan to George McClellan, April 15, 1854, McClellan Papers, Library of Congress; W. Eugene Hollon, *Beyond the Cross Timbers*, p. 172; McClellan to Mary Marcy, August 27, 1854, Papers, Library of Congress.
21. McClellan to Ellen Marcy, March 17, 1859, Papers.
22. McClellan to Ellen Marcy, September 17, 1859, Papers.
23. McClellan, *Civil War Papers*, Stephen Sears, ed., Ticknor & Fields, 1989, p. 33.

24. B&L, v. 1, p. 135.

25. McClellan, *Civil War Papers*, p. 70.

26. Ibid., p. 85.

27. John Nicolay and John Hay, *Abraham Lincoln*, v. 4, New York, 1886–90, p. 469.

28. Edmund Ruffin, *Diary*, v. 2, Louisiana State University Press, 1976, p. 269.

29. Sandburg, *The War Years*, v. 1, p. 474.

30. Ibid., p. 474.

31. Robert H. Miller to uncle, April 27, 1862, *Virginia Magazine of History and Biography*, 70:1 (Jan. 1962) p. 82; James H. McMath Diary, Alabama Dept. of Archives and History; as cited in Sears, *To the Gates of Richmond*, p. 37.

32. SHSP, v. 12, p. 106.

33. McClellan to Louis Goldsborough, April 5, 1862, McClellan, *Civil War Papers*, p. 167.

34. Chestnut, p. 401.

35. Comte de Paris, *History of the Civil War in America*, v. 2, Philadelphia, 1876, pgs. 8–9.

## 2. ON THE DEFENSIVE

1. Davis, February 18, 1865, *Davis Papers*, Dunbar Rowland, ed., v. 6, p. 494, as cited in Freeman, *Lee's Lieutenants*, v. 1, p. 135.

2. O.R., v. 5, p. 1079.

3. Ibid., p. 1087.

4. Ibid., p. 1089.

5. Ibid., p. 527.

6. Dowdey and Manarin, *Wartime Papers*, p. 127.

7. Ibid., p. 127.

8. Freeman, *Lee*, v. 2, p. 19.

9. Dowdey and Manarin, pgs. 155, 157, 163.

10. Robert Stiles, *Four Years Under Marse Robert*, Bellum, Marietta, Georgia, 1995, p. 75.

11. James Longstreet, *From Manassas to Appomattox*, Philadelphia, 1895, p. 66.

12. Jefferson Davis, *The Rise and Fall of the Confederate Government*, v. 2, New York, 1881, p. 88.

13. Joseph Johnston, *Narrative of Military Operations*, New York, 1874, p. 116.

14. O.R., 11:3, pgs. 456, 461, 473.

15. SHSP, v. 17, p. 418.

16. SHSP, v. 8, p. 291.

17. O.R., 11:1, p. 211.

18. O.R., 11:1, pgs. 568, 565.

19. Hood, *Advance and Retreat*, p. 21.

20. B&L, v. 2, p. 276.

21. Davis to wife, May 13, *Davis Papers*, Rowland, ed.

22. O.R., 11:3, p. 530.

## 3. SEVEN PINES

1. Porter, *Fighting for the Confederacy*, pgs. 84–85.

2. SHSP, v. 7, p. 113.

3. Torrence to mother, June 8, as cited in Sears, *To the Gates of Richmond*, p. 132.

4. John B. Gordon, *Reminiscences of the Civil War*, Scribner's, 1903, p. 56.

5. B&L, v. 2, p. 231.

6. Bridges, p. 47.

7. Ibid., p. 58.

8. O.R., 11:1, p. 989 postscript.

9. B&L, v. 2, p. 236.

10. James K. Swisher, *Prince of Edisto*, Berryville, Virginia, 1996, p. 49.

11. B&L, v. 2, p. 237.

12. B&L, v. 2, p. 245.

13. Alexander, *Fighting*, p. 88.

14. Sears, *To the Gates*, p. 137.

15. J. L. Brent, *Memoirs of the War Between the States*, New Orleans, 1940, p. 144.

16. O.R., 11:1, p. 945.

17. Evander M. Law, "The Fight for Richmond," *Southern Bivouac*, II (April 1867), p. 649.

18. Gordon, p. 4.

19. Ibid., p. 59.

20. SHSP, v. 25, p. 311.

21. Brent, *Memoirs*, p. 147.

22. Porter, *Fighting for the Confederacy*, p. 88.

23. O.R., 11:3, p. 685.

24. John Cheves Haskell, *Memoirs*, New York, 1960, p. 16, as cited in Richard McMurry, *John Bell Hood*, University of Nebraska Press, 1982.

25. O.R., 11:1, p. 940.

26. O.R., 11:1, p. 935.

27. B&L, v. 2, p. 229.

28. Ibid., p. 228.

29. Ibid., p. 241.

30. Ibid., p. 243.

## 4. JACKSON'S VALLEY CAMPAIGN

1. B&L, v. 2, p. 420.

2. O.R., v. 5, p. 1053.

3. G. F. R. Henderson, *Stonewall Jackson*, v. 1, London, 1898, p. 199.

4. O.R., v. 5, p. 1053.

5. Henderson, v. 1, p. 205.

6. O.R., v. 5, p. 1063.

7. R. L. Dabney, *Life and Campaigns of Lieut.-Gen. T. J. Jackson*, Richmond, 1866, p. 281.

8. Douglas, p. 234.

9. Ibid., p. 235.

10. Ibid., p. 237.

11. Henderson, v. 1, p. 224.

12. Thomas Ashby, *Life of Turner Ashby*, p. 14, as cited in Dufour, p. 44.

13. Clarence Thomas, *General Turner Ashby*, Winchester, 1907, p. 141; Dufour, p. 54.

14. William Thomas Poague, *Gunner with Stonewall*, Wilmington, 1987, p. 14.

15. John H. Worsham, *One of Jackson's Foot Cavalry*, New York, 1902, p. 68.

16. Dabney, p. 325.

17. John O. Casler, p. 66.

18. Henderson, v. 1, p. 247.

19. Ibid., p. 257.

20. Winder Diary, August 15 and September 16, 1861, as cited in James I. Robertson, Jr., *Stonewall Jackson*, p. 351.

21. Hill to Dabney, March 26, 1862; ibid., p. 353.

22. T. C. Johnson, *Robert Lewis Dabney*, Richmond, 1903, pgs. 262, 270.

23. Jedediah Hotchkiss, *Make Me a Map of the Valley*, Southern Methodist University Press, 1973, p. 10.

24. Wilder Dwight, *Life and Letters of . . .* , p. 236, as cited in Robertson, *Stonewall Jackson*, p. 357.

25. Ashby to A. R. Boteler, April 25, 1862, as cited in Robertson, p. 362.

26. O.R., 12:3, p. 880.

27. Edward A. Moore, *The Story of a Cannoneer Under Stonewall Jackson*, New York, 1907, p. 44.

28. Chestnut, p. 444.

29. William Allen, *History of the Campaign of Gen. T. J. (Stonewall) Jackson in the Shenandoah Valley of Virginia*, Philadelphia, 1880, Da Capo Edition, 1995, p. 76.

30. Hotchkiss, p. 40.

31. B&L, v. 2, p. 288.

32. Judith McGuire, *Diary of a Southern Refugee*, New York, 1867, p. 112.

33. SHSP, v. 9, p. 362.

34. SHSP, v. 7, p. 523.

35. Donald C. Pfanz, *Richard S. Ewell*, University of North Carolina Press, 1998, p. 11.

36. Taylor, p. 37.

37. Pfanz, *Ewell*, p. 82.

38. Ibid., p. 148.

39. Bingham Duncan, ed., *Letters of General J. E. B. Stuart to His Wife*, Emory University Press, 1943, p. 25.

40. O.R., 12:3, p. 892.

41. Dabney, p. 359.

42. O.R., 12:3, p. 897.

43. Casler, p. 76.

44. O.R., 12:3, p. 898.

45. Taylor, p. 40.

46. Ibid., p. 47.

47. Ibid., p. 17.

48. Ibid., p. 49.

49. Valentine Southall to mother, June 14, 1862, as cited in Robertson, *Jackson*, p. 449.

50. Randoph H. McKim, *A Soldier's Recollections*, New York, 1910, p. 97.

51. Dabney, p. 365.

52. Ibid., p. 368.

53. Taylor, p. 54.

54. Jennings Cropper Wise, *The Long Arm of Lee*, v. 1, Bison Books, 1988, p. 166.

55. O.R., 12:1, p. 703.

56. Dabney, p. 373.

57. Moore, p. 54.

58. Taylor, p. 56.

59. Poague, p. 23.

60. Taylor, p. 57.

61. Worsham, p. 86.

62. Dabney, p. 381.

63. Henderson, v. 1, p. 351.

64. Taylor, pgs. 61–65.

65. Mary Anna Jackson, *Memoirs of Stonewall Jackson*, New York, 1892, p. 269.

66. Munford Manuscript, as cited in Pfanz, *Ewell*, p. 204.

67. *Confederate Military History*, Clement Evans, ed., Atlanta, 1899, v. 2, p. 78.

68. Dabney, p. 400.

69. O.R., 12:1, p. 712.

70. Poague, p. 26.

71. Moore, p. 69; Allen, *History of the Campaign*, p. 150.

72. Dabney, p. 413.

73. SHSP, v. 25, p. 95.

74. Pfanz, *Ewell*, p. 211.

75. McKim, p. 111.

76. Allen, *History of the Campaign*, p. 153.

77. Dabney, p. 418.

78. O.R., 12:1, p. 798.

79. SHSP, v. 7, p. 530.

80. Worsham, p. 92.

81. Winder Diary, June 9, 1862.

82. George N. Neese, *Three Years in the Confederate Horse Artillery*, New York, 1911, p. 74, as cited in Dufour, p. 21.

83. Taylor, p. 74.

84. Hotchkiss, p. 55.

85. Samuel D. Buck, *With the Old Confeds*, Baltimore, 1925, p. 38.

86. Taylor, p. 75.

87. Douglas, p. 91.

88. SHSP, v. 7, p. 530.

## 5. LEE ASSUMES COMMAND

1. Dowdey and Manarin, p. 192.

2. John Esten Cooke, *Wearing of the Gray*, New York, 1867, pgs. 169, 174.

3. Heros von Borcke, *Memoirs of the Confederate War*, New York, 1938, v. 1, p. 43.

4. H.-B. McClellan, *The Campaigns of Stuart's Cavalry*, Blue and Gray Press, 1993, p. 65.

5. Cooke, pgs. 186, 180.

6. B&L, v. 2, p. 348.

7. Ibid.

8. Dowdey and Manarin, p. 198.

9. O.R., 11:2, p. 174.

10. Dabney, p. 440.

11. O.R., 11:2, p. 835.

12. William Allan, *The Army of Northern Virginia in 1862*, Boston, 1892, Da Capo Edition, 1995, p. 80.

13. Dabney to Hotchkiss, April 6, 1896, as cited in Robertson, *Jackson*, p. 473.

14. O.R., 11:2, p. 841.

15. SHSP, v. 14, p. 12.

16. Ibid., v. 29, p. 350.

17. O.R., 11:2, p. 835.

18. John Hinsdale Diary, June 26, 1862, as cited in Sears, *To the Gates*, p. 206.

19. Edgar Allan Jackson to mother, July 1, 1862; ibid., p. 207.

20. Richard Wheeler, *Sword over Richmond*, p. 300.

21. B&L, v. 2, p. 352.

22. Benson Memoir, as cited in Sears, *To the Gates*, p. 224.

23. O.R., 11:2, p. 836.

24. Ibid., p. 757.

25. Dabney, p. 443; Freeman, *Lee's Lieutenants*, v. 1, p. 524; Robertson, *Jackson*, p. 477; Sears, *To the Gates*, p. 227.

26. O.R., 11:2, p. 615; Freeman, *Lee's Lieutenants*, v. 1, p. 525.

27. SHSP, v. 17, p. 57; Terry L. Jones, *Lee's Tigers*, Louisiana State University Press, 1887, pgs. 102, 104.

28. O.R., 11:2, p. 606.

29. Cooke, *Outlines from the Outpost*, p. 50.

30. Cooke, *Life of General Robert E. Lee*, New York, 1863, p. 84.

31. B&L, v. 2, p. 359.

32. George H. Lester, *This They Remember*, Washington, Georgia, 1985, p. 103.

33. Sears, *To the Gates*, p. 238.

34. J. B. Polley, *Hood's Texas Brigade*, New York, 1910, p. 42.

35. B&L, v. 2, p. 363.

36. Polley, p. 59.

37. McClellan, *Civil War Papers*, p. 322.

38. B&L, v. 2, p. 360.

39. Polley, p. 71.

40. Dabney, p. 460.

41. D. Augustus Dickert, *History of Kershaw's Brigade*, Newbury, South Carolina, 1899, p. 128.

42. John Wood to father, July 4, 1862, as cited in Sears, *To the Gates*, p. 272.

43. B&L, v. 2, p. 390.

44. Freeman, *Lee's Lieutenants*, v. 1, p. 568.

45. McHenry Howard, *Recollections of a Maryland Confederate Soldier*, Baltimore, 1914, p. 149.

46. B&L, v. 2, p. 389.

47. Henderson, v. 2, p. 57.

48. Dabney, p. 466.

49. Mary Anna Jackson, p. 302.

50. Harold R. Woodward, Jr., *The Confederacy's Forgotten Son*, Rockbridge, 1993, p. 60.

51. Edmund D. Patterson, *Yankee Rebel*, University of North Carolina Press, 1966, p. 48, as cited in Sears, *To the Gates*, p. 296.

52. Porter, *Fighting for the Confederacy*, p. 118.

53. *One of Lee's Best Men*, ed. William Woods Hassler, p. 161; Sears, *Richmond*, p. 305.

54. B&L, v. 2, p. 388.

55. *Richmond Times-Dispatch*, Oct. 28, 1934; William G. Morris to wife, July 21, 1862; as cited in Robertson, *General A. P. Hill*, p. 92.

56. B&L, v. 2, p. 390.

57. Ibid., p. 392.

58. O.R., 11:2, p. 790.

59. Brent, p. 212.

60. Sears, *To the Gates*, p. 324.

61. O.R., 11:2, pgs. 643, 634, 650.

62. B&L, v. 2, p. 394.

63. Freeman, *Lee*, v. 2, p. 218.

64. McClellan, *Civil War Papers*, p. 349.

65. Mark M. Boatner III, *Civil War Dictionary*, Vintage 1991, p. 659.

66. O.R., 11:2, p. 497.

## 6. CEDAR MOUNTAIN AND SECOND MANASSAS

1. Dowdey and Manarin, p. 239.

2. Susan Blackford, ed., *Letters from Lee's Army*, Scribner's, 1947, p. 97.

3. SHSP, v. 10, p. 83.

4. Mary Anna Jackson, p. 324.

5. Ewell to Elizabeth Stoddert, July 20, 1862, Library of Congress.

6. Benjamin S. Ewell, *Jackson and Ewell*, p. 32, as cited in Pfanz, *Ewell*, p. 238.

7. Porter, *Fighting for the Confederacy*, p. 127.

8. Moore, p. 95.

9. Casler, p. 104.

10. Howard, *Recollections*, p. 170.

11. Henderson, *Jackson*, v. 2, p. 94.

12. Dabney, p. 501.

13. Susan Blackford, p. 104.

14. Early, *Narrative*, p. 99.

15. Douglas, p. 124.

16. John B. Lindsley, *The Military Annals of Tennessee*, p. 234, as cited in Robertson, *General A. P. Hill*, p. 107.

17. SHSP, v. 10, p. 89.

18. James Binford, August 13, 1862, Charles Gwathmey Papers, Virginia Historical Society, as cited in Robertson, *Jackson*, p. 537.

19. Early, *Narrative*, p. 102.

20. W. W. Blackford, pgs. 89, 90.

21. Ibid., p. 97.

22. Ibid., p. 103.

23. Ibid., pgs. 104, 107.

24. Douglas, p. 134.

25. B&L, v. 2, p. 532.

26. Dabney, p. 517.

27. Henry W. Thomas, *History of the Doles-Cook Brigade*, Atlanta, 1903, p. 352.

28. Walter Clark, ed., *History of the Several Regiments and Battalions from North Carolina in the Great War*, v. 2, Raleigh 1901, p. 153; O.R., 12:2, p. 720.

29. B&L, v. 2, p. 504.

30. Casler, p. 107; Worsham, p. 121; Freeman, *Lee's Lieutenants*, v. 2, p. 100; Douglas, p. 136.

31. Moore, p. 106.

32. W. W. Blackford, pgs. 118, 120.

33. B&L, v. 2, p. 510.

34. Casler, p. 109.

35. W. W. Blackford, p. 123.

36. J. F. J. Caldwell, *The History of a Brigade of South Carolinians, Known First as Gregg's, and Subsequently as McGowan's Brigade*, Philadelphia, 1866, p. 62.

37. Douglas, p. 138.

38. SHSP, v. 13, p. 32.

39. Douglas, p. 138.

40. Henderson, *Jackson*, v. 2, p. 163; B&L, v. 2, p. 519.

41. B&L, v. 2, p. 523.

42. Ibid., p. 528.

43. Polley, *Hood's Texas Brigade*, p. 80.

44. Alexander, *Fighting*, p. 134.

45. Casler, p. 112.

46. *Confederate Veteran*, 22 (1914): 231; Robertson, *Jackson*, p. 572.

47. Ibid.

48. John J. Hennessy, *Return to Bull Run*, Simon & Schuster, 1993, pgs. 356, 357.

49. O.R. 12:2, p. 557; Robertson, *General A. P. Hill*, p. 124.

50. Cooke, *Life of Stonewall Jackson*, p. 297.

51. Polley, p. 103, p. 94.

52. Dowdey and Manarin, p. 268.

53. Douglas, p. 142.

54. Alexander, *Fighting*, p. 135.

## 7. STANDOFF IN MARYLAND

1. *Lincoln and the Civil War in the Diaries and Letters of John Hay*, Tyler Dennert, ed., New York, 1939, p. 47; George B. McClellan, *McClellan's Own Story*, New York, 1887, p. 535.

2. B&L, v. 2, p. 490.

3. Dowdey and Manarin, p. 293.

4. Alexander, *Fighting*, p. 139.

5. B&L, v. 2, p. 605.

6. Robertson, *General A. P. Hill*, p. 130; Robertson, *Jackson*, p. 585; Douglas, p. 146; Freeman, *Lee's Lieutenants*, v. 2, p. 147.

7. Alexander, *Fighting*, p. 141.

8. Hood, *Advance and Retreat*, p. 38.

9. Douglas, p. 149.

10. W. W. Blackford, p. 141.

11. B&L, v. 2, p. 606.

12. Douglas, p. 158.

13. B&L, v. 2, p. 610.

14. Poague, p. 43; James Robertson, *The Stonewall Brigade*, Louisiana State University Press, 1963, p. 155.

15. Douglas, p. 162.

16. Robertson, *The Stonewall Brigade*, p. 155.

17. O.R., 19:1, p. 951.

18. Mary Anna Jackson, p. 338.

19. Caldwell, p. 72.

20. B&L, v. 2, p. 559.

21. Ibid., p. 563.

22. Stephen W. Sears, *Landscape Turned Red*, p. 131.

23. B&L, v. 2, p. 566, 569.

24. Polley, *Texas Brigade*, p. 114; James V. Murfin, *The Gleam of Bayonets*, Bonanza, 1965, p. 176.

25. Polley, ibid.

26. Chestnut, p. 441.

27. Sears, *Landscape*, p. 142.

28. B&L, v. 2, p. 570.

29. Murfin, p. 183.

30. Sears, *Landscape*, p. 148.

31. Freeman, *Lee's Lieutenants*, v. 2, p. 191; von Borcke, v. 1, p. 217.

32. O.R., 18:1, p. 855.

33. *Encyclopedia of the Confederacy*, Simon & Schuster, 1993, v. 3, p. 974.

34. O.R., 19:1, p. 951.

35. Porter, *Fighting for the Confederacy*, p. 149.

36. Murfin, *Gleam*, p. 211.

37. Jones, *Lee's Tigers*, p. 129.

38. Henderson, *Stonewall Jackson*, v. 2, p. 245, p. 246.

39. Early, *Narrative*, p. 142.

40. Hood, *Advance*, p. 44.

41. Polley, p. 125.

42. Bridges, p. 117.

43. Sears, *Landscape*, p. 207.

44. SHSP, v. 8, p. 528.

45. Jennings Cropper Wise, *Long Arm*, v. 1, p. 301.

46. SHSP, v. 8, p. 528.

47. Polley, p. 135.

48. Early, *Narrative*, p. 146.

49. Sears, *Landscape*, p. 226, p. 225; Henderson, *Jackson*, v. 2, p. 253; B&L, v. 2, p. 597.

50. Poague, p. 48.

51. Gordon, *Reminiscences*, p. 84.

52. B&L, v. 2, p. 671.

53. Gordon, p. 87.

54. Ibid., p. 89.

55. O.R., 19:1, p. 1037.

56. B&L, v. 2, p. 669.

57. O.R., 19: 1, p. 1024.

58. Sorrel, *Recollections*, p. 113.

59. Gordon, p. 91.

60. SHSP, v. 14, p. 392; Garry Gallagher, ed., *The Antietam Campaign*, University of North Carolina Press, 1999, p. 236.

61. Freeman, *Lee's Lieutenants*, v. 2, p. 218.

62. B&L, v. 2, p. 650.

63. Ibid., p. 650.

64. Sorrel, *Recollections*, p. 115.

65. Sears, *Landscape*, pgs. 284, 285; Robertson, *General A. P. Hill*, p. 143.

66. Freeman, *Lee's Lieutenants*, v. 2, p. 224; Robertson, *General A. P. Hill*, p. 146.

67. Clark, ed., *North Carolina Regiments*, v. 2, p. 537.

68. O.R., 19:1, p. 891.

69. Dowdey and Manarin, p. 311.

70. Stephen D. Lee letter, as cited in Henderson, v. 2, p. 262.

71. G. G. Chamberlayne, ed., *Ham Chamberlayne—Virginian: Letters and Papers*, Richmond, 1932, p. 134.

72. O.R., 19:1, p. 833; Douglas, p. 184.

73. Susan P. Lee, *Memoirs of William Nelson Pendleton*, Philadelphia, 1893, p. 214; Emily Mason, *Popular Life of R. E. Lee*, p. 151, as cited in Freeman, *Lee's Lieutenants*, v. 2, p. 232.

74. D. H. Hill to Robert Dabney, July 19, 1864, as cited in Gallagher, ed., *The Antietam Campaign*, p. 273; Douglas, p. 184; O.R., 19:1, p. 982; William Hassler, ed., *One of Lee's Best Men*, University of North Carolina Press, 1965, p. 176.

75. O.R., 19:1, p. 834; O.R., 19:1, p. 151; G.G. Chamberlayne, *Ham Chamberlayne*, p. 118.

## 8. FREDERICKSBURG

1. Sorrel, p. 116.

2. Jackson Mss., as cited in Freeman, *Lee's Lieutenants*, vol. 2, p. 244; Hotchkiss, p. 87.

3. O.R., 19:2, p. 643.

4. Sorrel, p. 99.

5. Blackford, p. 165.

6. O.R., 19:2, p. 53; *Encyclopedia of the Confederacy*, p. 1556.

7. Blackford, p. 176.

8. Lincoln, *Speeches & Writings*, p. 379.

9. Mrs. Jackson, p. 360 ff.

10. Taylor, p. 76.

11. Dowdey and Manarin, p. 357.

12. Alexander, *Fighting*, p. 59; Douglas, p. 324; Hassler, *One of Lee's Best Men*, p. 165.

13. Alexander, *Fighting*, pgs. 5, 4.

14. Ibid., p. 21.

15. Ibid., pgs. 23, 25; Sorrel, pgs. 76, 127.

16. Dufour, p. 315.

17. Early, *Narrative*, p. xvii; Charles C. Osborne, *Jubal*, Algonquin, 1992, p. 17.

18. Early, *Narrative*, p. xxiii.

19. Ibid., p. xxiv.

20. Clark, ed., *North Carolina Regiments*, v. 1, p. 351.

21. Hassler, *One of Lee's*, pgs. 43, 45.

22. Ibid., pgs. 160, 169, 175.

23. Fitz-John Porter had been relieved of command and would soon be cashiered, charged by John Pope with "wilful failure" to attack Jackson's flank at Second Manassas. Two decades later he would be exonerated, a board of inquiry finding that Pope had given an order impossible to carry out.

24. Dabney, p. 595.

25. SHSP, v. 36, p. 20.

26. W. M. Owen, *In Camp and Battle with the Washington Artillery*, Boston, 1885, p. 180.

27. SHSP, v. 36, p. 22.

28. Dabney, p. 611.

29. SHSP, v. 43, p. 29.

30. von Borcke, v. 2, p. 117.

31. Freeman, *R. E. Lee*, v. 2, p. 457.

32. John Esten Cooke, *Wearing of the Gray*, p. 137.

33. SHSP, v. 40, p. 210.

34. B&L, v. 3, p. 140.

35. SHSP, v. 40, p. 211.

36. Moore, p. 162.

37. Hassler, *One of Lee's*, p. 194.

38. B&L, v. 3, p. 91.

39. Ibid., p. 79.

40. Ibid., p. 98.

41. SHSP, v. 28, p. 300.

42. B&L, v. 3, p. 98.

43. Edward J. Stackpole, *The Fredericksburg Campaign*, Bonanza, 1957, p. 206.

44. B&L, v. 3, p. 81.

45. William B. Pettit to wife, December 16, 1862, Pettit Papers, University of North Carolina, as cited in William G. Piston, *Lee's Tarnished Lieutenant*, University of Georgia Press, 1987, p. 33.

46. O.R., v. 21, p. 589.

47. B&L, v. 3, p. 81.

48. Alexander, *Fighting*, p. 178.

49. Ibid., p. 178.

50. Stackpole, p. 218.

51. SHSP, v. 8, p. 187.

52. Dowdey and Manarin, p. 365.

# 1863

## 1. THE ARMY RESTS

1. O.R., v. 21, p. 1098; O.R., 25:2, p. 730.

2. Henderson, *Jackson*, v. 2, p. 348.

3. Worsham, p. 138.

4. Carlton McCarthy, *Detailed Minutiae*, Richmond, 1882, p. 44.

5. James I. Robertson, Jr., *Soldiers Blue and Gray*, Warner Edition, 1991, p. 68.

6. McCarthy, p. 65.

7. Casler, p. 79; Alexander Hunter, *Johnny Reb and Billy Yank*, New York, 1905, p. 44; Robertson, *Soldiers*, p. 74.

8. Worsham, p. 160.

9. Robert Stiles, *Four Years*, p. 135.

10. Jacob Haas to brother, January 3, 1863, Fredericksburg National Military Park Library; *The New York Times*, December 19 and 23, 1862; as cited in Gary Gallagher, ed., *The Fredericksburg Campaign*, University of North Carolina Press, 1995, p. 172.

11. Gallagher, ed., *Fredericksburg*, p. 177.

12. Samuel Partridge to brother, January 25, 1863, FNMP Library; Williams to daughter, January 24, Alpheus S. Williams, *From the Cannon's Mouth*, Wayne State University Press, 1959, p. 159, as cited in Sears, *Chancellorsville*, p. 20; Gallagher, ed., *Fredericksburg*, pgs. 201, 202.

13. Lincoln, *Speeches & Writings*, p. 433.

14. Hill replaced Gustavus Smith, he who suffered the breakdown at Seven Pines just before Lee assumed command. Smith briefly took over the Richmond defenses, then soon resigned from the service.

15. P. G. Hamlin, ed., *The Making of a Soldier*, Richmond, 1935, p. 115; Trimble to Cooper, December 22, 1862; as cited in Freeman, *Lee's Lieutenants*, v. 2. pgs. 415, 416.

16. McClellan, *Stuart's Cavalry*, p. 211.

17. O.R., 25:1, p. 62.

18. Blackford, p. 201; O.R., 25:2, p. 675; Thomason, *Stuart*, p. 360.

19. R. B. Hudgens to uncle, T. F. Boatwright Papers, University of North Carolina, as cited in Bell Irvin Wiley, *Life of Johnny Reb*, Louisiana State University Press, 1943, p. 180; J. W. Jones, *Christ in the Camp*, Richmond, 1888, p. 468.

20. Robertson, *Soldiers*, p. 173.

21. McKim, p. 219.

22. J. G. Paxton, ed., *Elisha Franklin Paxton: Memoir*, New York, 1907, p. 92; *Confederate Veteran*, v. 13, p. 459; as cited in Freeman, *Lee's Lieutenants*, v. 2, p. 431.

23. O.R., v. 18, pgs. 189, 943, 961.

24. Samuel G. French, *Two Wars*, p. 160; O.R., 51:2, p. 697; O.R., v. 18, p. 1031; Dowdey and Manarin, p. 442.

25. H. J. Eckenrode and Bryan Conrad, *Longstreet*, University of North Carolina Press, 1936, p. 166.

26. Hassler, *One of Lee's*, pgs. 221–22; Cooke Mss., February 28, 1863.

27. O.R., 19:2, p. 732; Jackson Mss., April 24, 1863; as cited in Freeman, *Lee's Lieutenants*, v. 2, p. 514.

## 2. CHANCELLORSVILLE

1. Alexander, *Fighting*, p. 195.

2. Dowdey and Manarin, p. 438; O.R., 25:2, p. 759; O.R., 25:1, p. 850.

3. SHSP, v. 7, p. 562.

4. Alexander, *Fighting*, p. 196; John Wood to aunt, May 10, 1863, as cited in Sears, *Chancellorsville*, p. 206; O.R., 25:1, p. 833.

5. Alexander, *Fighting*, p. 197; B&L, v. 3, pgs. 159-60.

6. SHSP, v. 7, p. 567; SHSP, v. 34, p. 9.

7. SHSP, v. 34, p. 5.

8. Mrs. Jackson, p. 294; Thomas Munford to John Bigelow, December 24, 1908, Library of Congress.

9. Alexander, *Fighting*, p. 201; SHSP, v. 25, p. 110.

10. Harrison Griffith, *Variosa*, p. 67, as cited in Sears, *Chancellorsville*, p. 241; SHSP, v. 7, p. 572.

11. SHSP, ibid.; B&L, v. 3, p. 206.

12. O.R., 25:1, p. 940.

13. B&L, v. 3, p. 208.

14. Alexander, *Fighting*, p. 203; O.R., 25:1, p. 941.

15. Alexander, p. 204.

16. SHSP, v. 8, p. 489; Caldwell, p. 113.

17. W. G. Bean, *Stonewall's Man*, p. 115; Clark, ed., *North Carolina Regiments*, v. 5, p. 99.

18. Hotchkiss, p. 115; SHSP, v. 6, p. 261; Robertson, *General A. P. Hill*, p. 188; Robertson, *Jackson*, p. 731.

19. William Clegg to Mary Collins, May 8, 1863, as cited in Sears, *Chancellorsville*, p. 298; Jones, *Lee's Tigers*, p. 146; years later the maimed Nicholls would be elected governor of Louisiana, his supporters claimed in jest that he could not be elected a judge because he would be "too one-sided."

20. SHSP, v. 2, p. 166.

21. Alexander, *Fighting*, p. 208.

22. O.R., 25:1, p. 887.

23. Caldwell, p. 116.

24. Douglas, p. 224.

25. James Melhorn, May 3, 1863, Stanford Library, as cited in Sears, *Chancellorsville*, p. 329.

26. H. B. McClellan, p. 251.

27. *Confederate Veteran*, v. 5, no. 6, p. 288; Hassler, *One of*, p. 235.

28. O.R., 25:1, p. 996; Bryan Grimes, *Letters of*, p. 32; *North Carolina (Raleigh) Standard*, May 19, 1863, as cited in Gallagher, *Ramseur*, p. 63.

29. Early, *Narrative*, p. 200.

30. SHSP, v. 14, p. 416.

31. Ibid., p. 423; Freeman, *Lee's Lieutenants*, v. 2, p. 618.

32. O.R., 25:1, pgs. 854–57.

33. John Wood to aunt, May 10, 1863, Georgia Department of Archives; John Evans to wife, May 8, 1863, Duke University; as cited in Sears, *Chancellorsville*, p. 382.

34. William McClellan to father, May 10, 1863, Buchanan-McClellan Papers, University of North Carolina; Edmund Patterson Journal, May 3, 1863; Wilcox to sister, May 16, 1863, Library of Congress; as cited in Sears, pgs. 383–84.

35. SHSP, v. 14, p. 425.

36. Early, *Narrative*, p. 222; Gordon, p. 100.

37. Alexander, *Fighting*, p. 213.

38. Henry Handerson to father, May 13, 1863, and Henry Walker to J. J. Johnston, May 7, as cited in Sears, pgs. 415–16; O.R., 25:1, p. 828.

39. J. Hotchkiss to G. F. R. Henderson, Hotchkiss Papers, Library of Congress; Dowdey and Manarin, p. 457.

40. Casler, p. 151.

41. Dowdey and Manarin, p. 458.

42. Dabney, p. 702.

43. Ibid., p. 709, p. 713.

44. Dabney, p. 715; Hunter McGuire and George Christian, *The Confederate Cause and Conduct in the War Between the States*, p. 227; Dabney, p. 719; Freeman, *Lee's Lieutenants*, v. 2, p. 671, p. 676; Douglas, p. 228; McGuire, p. 228, p. 229.

45. Douglas, p. 228, p. 38.

46. Freeman, *Lee*, v. 2, p. 524.

## 3. LEE HEADS NORTH

1. Pfanz, *Ewell*, pgs. 265, 275; Gordon, p. 158.

2. O.R., 25:2, p. 810; O.R., 25:1, p. 1003.

3. Chestnut, p. 444.

4. Ibid., p. 444; O.R., 25:2, p. 789.

5. O.R., 25:1, p. 1007; O.R., 25:2, p. 810.

6. Dowdey and Manarin, p. 508.

7. Blackford, p. 212.

8. McClellan, *Campaigns*, p. 266.

9. Ibid., p. 268.

10. Freeman, *Lee's Lieutenants*, v. 3, p. 9.

11. H. B. McClellan, pgs. 270, 277.

12. Ibid., p. 282.

13. Ibid., p. 290.

14. Ibid., p. 292.

15. Ibid., p. 294.

16. *Richmond Sentinel*, June 12, 1863; Hassler, *One of Lee's*, p. 246.

17. Blackford, p. 218.

18. Jones, *Lee's Tigers*, pgs. 160–61; Pfanz, *Ewell*, p. 286.

19. Casler, p. 167; Percy G. Hamlin, *Old Bald Head*, Shenandoah Publishing, 1940, p. 140; Hotchkiss, p. 153; Freeman, *Lee's Lieutenants*, v. 3, p. 26.

20. Dowdey and Manarin, p. 524; Hotchkiss, p. 155.

21. Stiles, *Four Years*, p. 206.

22. Early, *Narrative*, p. 255; Stiles, p. 203.

23. SHSP, v. 4, p. 156; Sorrel, *Recollections*, p. 164.

24. Hotchkiss, p. 156.

25. O.R., 27:3, p. 913; Freeman, *Lee's Lieutenants*, v. 3, p. 66; Thomason, p. 440.

## 4. GETTYSBURG

1. SHSP, v. 4, p. 157.

2. Edward B. Coddington, *The Gettysburg Campaign*, Scribner's, 1968, p. 269; Robertson, *General A. P. Hill*, p. 208; O.R., 27:2, p. 638.

3. SHSP, v. 2, p. 146.

4. SHSP, v. 4, p. 158.

5. Gordon, p. 151; Stiles, p. 211.

6. Clark, ed., *North Carolina Regiments*, v. 2, p. 351.

7. Caldwell, p. 138; Freeman, *Lee's Lieutenants*, v. 3, p. 88; Robertson, *Hill*, p. 212.

8. *Annals of the War*, Philadelphia, 1879, Blue and Gray Press Edition, 1996, p. 420.

9. Gordon, p. 151.

10. Douglas, p. 247; Gordon, p. 155.

11. Douglas, p. 247; SHSP, v. 33, p. 144.

12. SHSP, v. 26, p. 123; Freeman, *Lee's Lieutenants*, v. 3, p. 95.

13. Taylor, p. 95; SHSP, v. 33, p. 145.

14. O.R., 27:2, p. 318.

15. SHSP, v. 33, p. 145.

16. SHSP, v. 4, p. 273.

17. Alexander, *Fighting*, p. 234.

18. SHSP, v. 4, p. 274; SHSP, v. 33, p. 146.

19. SHSP, v. 39, p. 110.

20. SHSP, v. 39, p. 111; SHSP, v. 33, p. 147.

21. *Hood*, p. 57; SHSP, v. 7, p. 68.

22. Freeman, *Lee's Lieutenants*, v. 3, p. 113; *Hood*, p. 57; *Annals*, p. 422.

23. SHSP, v. 7, p. 69.

24. Polley, p. 160; B&L, v. 3, p. 322.

25. SHSP, v. 7, p. 75.

26. Polley, pgs. 163, 169.

27. Ibid., p. 172.

28. Ibid., p. 173.

29. Ibid., p. 174.

30. B&L, v. 3, p. 324.

31. William Oates, *The War Between the Union and the Confederacy*, Neale, 1905; Morningside Edition with Robert K. Krick Introduction, 1974.

32. Ibid., p. 218, p. 755, p. 688, p. 674, p. 226; Harry W. Pfanz, *Gettysburg, The Second Day*, University of North Carolina Press, 1987, p. 231ff.; J. Gary Laine and Morris M. Penny, *Law's Alabama Brigade*, White Mane Publishing, 1996, p. 101ff.

33. SHSP, v. 6, p. 175; O.R., 27:1, p. 178.

34. *Montgomery Advertiser*, January 6, 1864, as cited in Laine and Penny, p. 111.

35. SHSP, v. 7, p. 72.

36. Coddington, p. 406.

37. Dickert, p. 238.

38. SHSP, v. 7, p. 74; B&L, v. 3, p. 360.

39. Wright to Mrs. Wright, July 7, 1863, as cited in Freeman, *Lee's Lieutenants*, v. 3, p. 125.

40. O.R., 27:2, p. 658; Hassler, *One of Lee's*, p. 254, p. 260; O.R., 27:2, p. 608; Caldwell, p. 143.

41. SHSP, v. 26, p. 125; Harry W. Pfanz, *Gettysburg, Culp's Hill and Cemetery Hill*, University of North Carolina Press, 1993, p. 179.

42. Pfanz, *Culp's Hill*, p. 168; Wise, *Long Arm*, v. 2, p. 652.

43. Pfanz, *Culp's Hill*, p. 185; Stiles, *Four Years*, p. 217; Wise, *Long Arm*, v. 2, p. 654.

44. McKim, p. 195.

45. Pfanz, *Culp's Hill*, p. 259; Jones, *Terry L.*, p. 172.

46. SHSP, v. 4, p. 280; Stiles, p. 189.

47. O.R., 27:2, p. 320; Alexander, *Fighting*, p. 244; Coddington, p. 455.

48. O.R., 27:2, p. 320; *Annals*, p. 430.

49. *Annals*, p. 429.

50. McKim, pgs. 201, 203; William Goldsborough, *The Maryland Line*, New York, 1972, p. 153.

51. Coddington, p. 459.

52. Lesley J. Gordon, *General George Pickett in Life & Legend*, University of North Carolina Press, 1998, p. 98; Sorrel, *Recollections*, p. 153.

53. Kemper Papers, University of Virginia, Mrs. Belfield Cave letter, as cited in Woodward, *Confederacy's Forgotten Son*, p. 67.

54. SHSP, v. 37, p. 147.

55. Alexander, *Fighting*, p. 250, p. 254.

56. Ibid., p. 257, p. 260.

57. SHSP, v. 34, p. 333.

58. SHSP, v. 32, p. 186, v. 37, p. 148; v. 32, p. 190; v. 37, p. 149.

59. SHSP, v. 37, p. 149, p. 150.

60. SHSP, v. 7, p. 92; v. 31, p. 355.

61. SHSP, v. 5, p. 44.

62. O.R., 27:2, p. 620.

63. B&L, v. 3, pgs. 404, 405.

64. George Stewart, *Pickett's Charge*, Houghton Mifflin, 1959, p. 230; SHSP, v. 38, p. 312; O.R., 27:3, p. 1075; Gordon, *General George E. Pickett*, p. 123.

65. Dowdey and Manarin, p. 589; Henry Steele Commager, *The Blue and the Gray*, v. 2, Fairfax, 1991, p. 642.

66. SHSP, v. 7, p. 84; p. 90.

67. B&L, v. 3, p. 421; Alexander, *Fighting*, p. 281, p. 283.

68. LaSalle Corbett Pickett, *McClure's* Magazine, May 1908, as cited in Gabor S. Boritt, ed., *The Gettysburg Nobody Knows*, Oxford University Press, 1997, p. 122.

## 5. LONGSTREET IN TENNESSEE

1. Stanley F. Horn, *The Army of Tennessee*, p. 220, as cited in Freeman, *Lee's Lieutenants*, v. 3, p. 220.

2. SHSP, v. 14, p. 221 (quotation marks added).

3. Longstreet, *From Manassas to Appomattox*, p. 437; Sorrel, p. 186.

4. Chestnut, pgs. 430, 443, 516.

5. Sorrel, p. 187.

6. Dickert, p. 265.

7. Alexander, *Fighting*, p. 288.

8. Polley, p. 201; Sorrel, p. 192.

9. Sorrel, p. 200; Alexander, *Fighting*, p. 289.

10. B&L, v. 3, p. 653; Alexander, *Fighting*, p. 290.

11. B&L, v. 3, p. 655, p. 663; Peter Cozzens, *This Terrible Sound*, University of Illinois Press, 1992, p. 411.

12. Polley, p. 202; Sorrel, p. 203.

13. Eckenrode and Conrad, p. 235.

14. B&L, v. 3, p. 659, p. 661.

15. Sorrel, p. 196; B&L, v. 3, p. 662.

16. O.R., 30:4, p. 705.

17. Longstreet, pgs. 465, 466; Thomas L. Connelly, *Autumn of Glory: The Army of Tennessee*, Louisiana State University Press, 1971, p. 244.

18. O.R., 31:1, p. 218; Swisher, *Prince of Edisto*, pgs. 113, 114.

19. Eckenrode and Conrad, pgs. 250, 255.

20. O.R., 31:1, p. 459.

21. B&L, v. 3, p. 722, p. 725.

22. Commager, *The Blue and the Gray*, v. 2, p. 913.

23. Alexander, *Fighting*, p. 326; O.R., 31:3, p. 757.

24. O.R., 31:1, p. 491, p. 494.

25. B&L, v. 3, p. 748.

26. Chestnut, p. 509.

27. Longstreet, p. 521; McLaws to Lizzie Ewell, February 24, 1864, as cited in Freeman, *Lee's Lieutenants*, v. 3, p. 300.

28. O.R., 31:1, p. 470.

29. O.R., 31:1, p. 471.

## 6. BRISTOE STATION TO MINE RUN

1. Caldwell, p. 157; Robertson, *General A. P. Hill*, p. 231.

2. Ibid., p. 157; ibid., p. 231, p. 230.

3. Clark, ed., *North Carolina Regiments*, v. 1, p. 545.

4. Ibid., v. 2, p. 441.

5. Robertson, *General A. P. Hill*, p. 238.

6. O.R., 29:1, p. 427, p. 428.

7. Freeman, *Lee*, v. 3, p. 183; Robertson, *General A. P. Hill*, p. 239.

8. Blackford, p. 238.

9. Ibid., p. 241.

10. SHSP, v. 8, p. 352.

11. Jones, *Lee's Tigers*, p. 183.

12. Early, *Narrative*, p. 314.

13. Ibid., p. 315; Jones, p. 185.

14. Early, *Narrative*, p. 316.

15. Osborne, *Jubal*, p. 209.

16. Pfanz, *Ewell*, p. 345.

17. Early, *Narrative*, p. 320.

18. Worsham, p. 187, p. 188; G. M. G. Stafford, *General Leroy Augustus Stafford*, p. 42, as cited in Jones, *Lee's Tigers*, p. 188.

19. Early, *Narrative*, pgs. 321, 323.

20. Walter Taylor, *Four Years*, p. 121; Moore, p. 212.

21. Freeman, *Lee*, v. 3, p. 202; *Richmond Daily Dispatch*, December 8, 1863, as cited in Robertson, *General A. P. Hill*, p. 244.

# 1864

## 1. THE ARMY IN LIMBO

1. Chestnut, p. 519.

2. Henry Halleck would be demoted, in effect becoming chief of staff.

3. Bruce Catton, *A Stillness at Appomattox*, Fairfax Press 3-vol. Edition, 1984, p. 482.

4. Stanton P. Allen, *Down in Dixie*, Boston, 1888, p. 180.

5. Horace Porter, *Campaigning with Grant*, New York, 1907, p. 46; Catton, *Stillness*, p. 483 (quotes added to last line).

6. Chestnut, pgs. 551, 559, 561, 804, 567.

7. Gary W. Gallagher, *Stephen Dodson Ramseur*, pgs. 6, 12.

8. Ibid., p. 21.

9. Ibid., pgs. 37, 40, 48, 50, 72, 76.

10. Ibid., pgs. 86, 95.

11. *Confederate Veteran*, vol. XI, no. 6, p. 271, as cited in Dufour, *Nine Men*, p. 162; Stiles, p. 110.

12. Dufour, p. 167; SHSP, vol. 14, p. 12; O.R., 11:2, p. 843.

13. Pegram to sister, August 14, 1862, Pegram-Johnson-McIntosh Papers, Virginia Historical Society; Pegram to mother, September 7, 1862, ibid.; O.R., 25:1, p. 937; Munford to Sallie Munford, June 12, 1863, Munford-Ellis Papers, Duke University.

14. Pegram to sister, February 11, 1864, Pegram-Johnson-McIntosh Papers, as cited in Dufour, p. 189.

15. Dufour, p. 234.

16. J. W. Ratchford manuscript, p. 20, North Carolina Department of Archives, Raleigh.

17. Dufour, p. 231.

18. Freeman, *Lee's Lieutenants*, v. 3, p. XXXVIII.

19. Daniel W. Barefoot, *General Robert F. Hoke*, John F. Blair 1996, p. 70.
20. Ibid., p. 72; Clark, ed., *North Carolina Regiments*, vol. 2, p. 135.
21. Barefoot, p. 85.
22. Clark, ed., *North Carolina Regiments*, vol. 3, p. 340; Barefoot, p. 143; Clark, vol. 3, p. 345; O.R., 51:2, p. 874; O.R., 33, p. 1321.


## 2. THE WILDERNESS TO SPOTSYLVANIA

1. Stiles, p. 245.
2. Noah Andre Trudeau, *Bloody Roads South*, Little, Brown, 1989, p. 57; Gordon, *Reminiscences*, p. 239; O.R., 36:1, p. 1077; Worsham, p. 228; Pfanz, *Ewell*, p. 367.
3. Alexander, *Fighting*, p. 353.
4. Clark, ed., *North Carolina Regiments*, v. 2, p. 665; Charles Page, *Letters of a War Correspondent*, Boston 1899, p. 50; Robertson, *General A. P. Hill*, p. 258.
5. *Annals*, p. 272; Caldwell, p. 176.
6. Clark, ed., *North Carolina Regiments*, v. 3, p. 75, p. 305; Robertson, *General A. P. Hill*, p. 260.
7. Henry Heth, *Memoirs*, Greenwood Press 1974, p. 184.
8. Robertson, *General A. P. Hill*, p. 265; Caldwell, p. 181; Alexander, *Military Memoirs of a Confederate*, Scribner's, 1912, p. 503.
9. Robertson, *General A. P. Hill*, p. 265; Dickert, p. 347.
10. Polley, p. 231.
11. Sorrel, p. 241.
12. O.R., 36:1, p. 1055; Longstreet, *Memoirs*, p. 563.
13. Sorrel, p. 243; Swisher, *Prince of Edisto*, p. 147; Freeman, *Lee's Lieutenants*, v. 3, p. 366; SHSP, v. 14, p. 545.
14. Stiles, p. 247.
15. Gordon, p. 244, p. 255; Ulysses S. Grant, *Memoirs and Selected Letters*, Library of America 1990, p. 529.
16. Gordon, p. 258.
17. O.R., 36:1, p. 1078.
18. Sorrel, p. 248.
19. Alexander, *Fighting*, pgs. 365, 366.
20. Dickert, p. 357.
21. Pfanz, *Ewell*, p. 378.
22. B&L, v. 4, p. 175.
23. Gordon C. Rhea, *The Battles for Spotsylvania Court House and the Road to Yellow Tavern*, Louisiana State University Press, 1997, pgs. 135–37.
24. Polley, p. 237; Rhea, *Spotsylvania*, p. 146.

25. Rhea, *Spotsylvania*, pgs. 169, 171.

26. Terry L. Jones, ed., *The Civil War Memoirs of Captain William J. Seymour*, Louisiana State University Press, 1991, p. 123; Alexander, *Fighting*, p. 376.

27. SHSP, v. 21, p. 235; Casler, p. 212; SHSP, v. 23, p. 338; Rhea, *Spotsylvania*, p. 237; Jones, *Lee's Tigers*, p. 206.

28. Rhea, *Spotsylvania*, p. 238; O.R., 36:1, p. 359.

29. SHSP, v. 14, p. 529; Gordon, p. 277, p. 279.

30. SHSP, v. 21, p. 247; v. 32, p. 204.

31. Robert Grier Stephens, Jr., ed., *Intrepid Warrior, Clement Anslem Evans*, Morningside, 1992, p. 393; Gallagher, *Ramseur*, p. 110; Pfanz, *Ewell*, p. 386.

32. Rhea, *Spotsylvania*, pgs. 268, 270, 271; SHSP, v. 8, p. 104.

33. Caldwell, p. 191; Stiles, p. 264.

34. Freeman, *Lee's Lieutenants*, v. 3, p. 407; Gordon, p. 284; Caldwell, p. 192.

35. Caldwell, p. 195.

36. H. B. McClellan, p. 411; Gallagher, ed., *The Spotsylvania Campaign*, p. 142; Emory M. Thomas, *Bold Dragoon*, Harper & Row, 1986, p. 291.

37. Gallagher, *Spotsylvania*, p. 143.

38. H. B. McClellan, p. 413; B&L, v. 4, p. 194; *Confederate Veteran*, v. 19, p. 531; SHSP, v. 1, p. 102.

39. H. B. McClellan, pgs. 415, 416; Freeman, *Lee's Lieutenants*, v. 3, pgs. 427, 432; SHSP, v. 37, p. 68.

40. SHSP, v. 33, p. 332; George Mead, ed., *The Life and Letters of George Gordon Meade*, v. 2, New York, 1913, p. 197; Gordon, p. 292.

41. O.R., 36:1, p. 1082.

## 8. DREWRY'S BLUFF AND NEW MARKET

1. B&L, v. 4, p. 198; SHSP, v. 25, p. 207.

2. O.R., 36:2, p. 1024.

3. Ibid., p. 200; Boatner, p. 318.

4. Barefoot, p. 182; O.R. 36:2, p. 202.

5. O.R., 36:2, p. 202; B&L, v. 4, p. 203.

6. O.R., 36:2, p. 211, p. 258; Freeman, *Lee's Lieutenants*, v. 3, p. 491.

7. William C. Davis, *Battle of New Market*, Doubleday, 1975, p. 15.

8. Ibid., p. 91; B&L, v. 4, p. 483.

9. Davis, *New Market*, p. 116.

10. Ibid., p. 119.

11. Ibid., pgs. 125, 133.

12. B&L, v. 4, p. 484, p. 485.

## 4. NORTH ANNA TO COLD HARBOR

1. Dowdey and Manarin, p. 747; Francis Johnson, Jr. to Emily Hutchings, University of Georgia, and Joseph D. Joyner to mother, University of North Carolina, as cited in Gordon C. Rhea, *To the North Anna River*, Louisiana State University Press, 2000, p. 287.

2. *Confederate Military History*, v. 3, p. 460; Alexander, *Fighting*, p. 389.

3. B&L, v. 4, p. 244.

4. Ewell to wife, Brown-Ewell family papers, as cited in Pfanz, *Ewell*, p. 396.

5. John Esten Cooke, *Wearing of the Gray*, p. 67; F. M. Meyers, *The Comanches, A History of White's Battalion, Virginia Cavalry*, Baltimore, 1871, p. 291.

6. Trudeau, *Bloody Roads South*, p. 256; Early, *Narrative*, p. 362.

7. Alfred Roman, *Military Operations of General Beauregard*, v. 2, p. 563; Dowdey and Manarin, p. 579.

8. Stiles, p. 289.

9. B&L, v. 4, p. 217.

10. Dickert, p. 372.

11. B&L, v. 4, p. 141.

12. Barefoot, p. 195.

13. William Dame, *From the Rapidan to Richmond*, Green-Lucas 1920, p. 203; John Esten Cooke, *Life of R. E. Lee*, New York, 1871, p. 406, as cited in Robertson, *Hill*, p. 279.

14. Grant, *Memoirs*, p. 588; William Swinton, *Army of the Potomac*, New York, 1866, p. 487.

15. Pfanz, *Ewell*, p. 398.

16. Ibid., p. 399; Ewell reported the conversation to Lizinka, who wrote of it to his older brother Benjamin June 8, 1864 (Hamlin, *The Making of a Soldier*, p. 126).

17. Grant, *Memoirs*, p. 586; Trudeau, *Bloody Roads South*, p. 302; Commager, *The Blue and the Gray*, v. 2, p. 10001.

18. Alexander, *Fighting*, pgs. 409, 411.

## 5. EARLY'S VALLEY CAMPAIGN

1. Early, *Narrative*, p. 376.

2. Ibid., p. 378, p. 380.

3. Douglas, p. 292; Worsham, p. 231; Douglas, p. 293.

4. Early, *Narrative*, p. 387; Stephens, *Intrepid Warrior*, p. 425.

5. Worsham, p. 237.

6. Gordon, p. 311; Worsham, p. 239.

7. Worsham, p. 239.

8. Stephens, p. 426.

9. Early, *Narrative*, p. 390; Douglas, pgs. 295, 296.

10. Gallagher, *Ramseur*, pgs. 133, 135.

11. Early, *Narrative*, p. 399.

12. SHSP, v. 31, p. 268; Early, *Narrative*, p. 404.

13. O.R., 43:1, p. 994; Early, *Narrative*, p. 405.

14. Osborne, p. 313.

15. Early, *Narrative*, p. 415; Grimes to wife, August 12, 1864, Southern Historical Collection, University of North Carolina.

16. Early, ibid.; Gallagher, *Ramseur*, p. 141; Douglas, p. 309.

17. Gordon, p. 319.

18. Osborne, p. 336; SHSP, v. 2, p. 26; Gordon, p. 321.

19. Gordon, pgs. 322, 323; Jeffry D. Wert, *From Winchester to Cedar Creek*, South Mountain Press, 1987, pgs. 95, 96.

20. O.R. 43:2, pgs. 894, 895, 897, 880, 892.

21. Ibid., 43:1, p. 612.

22. SHSP, v. 13, p. 134; some quotation marks have been added, but the import is clear.

23. Gordon, p. 335.

24. Ibid., p. 336; Freeman, *Lee's Lieutenants*, v. 3, p. 599; Gallagher, *Ramseur*, p. 155.

25. Gordon, p. 339.

26. Gallagher, *Ramseur*, p. 158; Douglas, p. 317; Wert, p. 190: Thomas A. Lewis, *The Guns of Cedar Creek*, Harper & Row, 1988, pgs. 205, 211; Osborne, p. 361.

27. Gordon, p. 341.

28. O.R., 43:1, pgs. 562, 563; Worsham, p. 276.

29. Stephens, *Intrepid Warrior*, p. 482; Gordon, p. 361.

30. Wert, p. 222; Osborne, p. 372.

31. Wert, p. 223; Lewis, *Guns of*, p. 255.

32. Gordon, pgs. 346, 347.

33. Ibid., p. 348; Dickert, p. 452; O.R., 43:1, p. 562.

34. Douglas, p. 319; Gallagher, *Ramseur*, p. 165.

## 6. PETERSBURG AND RICHMOND BESIEGED

1. B&L, v. 4, p. 540; Alexander, *Fighting*, p. 426.

2. Barefoot, *Hoke*, p. 204; B&L, v. 4, p. 541.

3. Dowdey and Manarin, p. 743, p. 784; Dowdey, *Lee's Last Campaign*, p. 339.

4. Barefoot, p. 205; O.R., 51:2, p. 1079; Dowdey and Manarin, p. 789.

5. O.R., 40:1, p. 761; Freeman, *Lee's Lieutenants*, v. 3, p. 537; B&L, v. 4, p. 544.

6. Trudeau, *The Last Citadel*, Little, Brown, 1991, p. 55.

7. SHSP, v. 2, p. 273.

8. Robertson, *General A. P. Hill*, p. 287; O.R., 51:2, p. 1027.

9. SHSP, v. 2, p. 275.

10. O.R., 40:3, p. 179; John S. Wise, *The End of an Era*, Boston, 1899, p. 319; Dufour, p. 251.

11. Pegram to Virginia Pegram, August 7, 1864, Pegram-Johnson-McIntosh Papers: Robertson, *General A. P. Hill*, p. 289.

12. Alexander, *Fighting*, p. 498; SHSP, v. 2, p. 283.

13. SHSP, v. 2, p. 285.

14. Ibid., p. 287; George S. Bernard, ed., *War Talks of Confederates*, p. 213, as cited in Dufour, p. 256.

15. SHSP, v. 18, p. 37.

16. SHSP, v. 2, p. 291; Wise, *The End of*, p. 364.

17. SHSP, v. 18, p. 17; Wise, p. 365; Pegram, August 7, 1864, Pegram-Johnson-McIntosh Papers; *Confederate Veteran*, v. 15, no. 11, p. 480; SHSP, v. 25, p. 85; Dufour, p. 258; Robertson, *Hill*, p. 293.

18. Grant, *Memoirs*, p. 1063.

19. *Richmond Daily Dispatch*, August 22, 1864; Trudeau, *The Last Citadel*, p. 168; E. B. Long with Barbara Long, *The Civil War Day by Day*, Da Capo, 1971, p. 558.

20. Dowdey and Manarin, p. 845; Robertson, *Hill*, p. 299, p. 300; O.R., 42:2, p. 1199.

21. Francis H. Kennedy, ed., *The Civil War Battlefield Guide*, Houghton Mifflin, 1990, p. 267; Trudeau, *Last Citadel*, p. 209.

22. Trudeau, *Last Citadel*, p. 210; Alexander, *Fighting*, p. 478; Clark, ed., *North Carolina Regiments*, v. 4, p. 496.

23. Barefoot, p. 225; Richard J. Sommers, *Richmond Redeemed*, Doubleday, 1981, p. 146.

24. Sommers, p. 148.

25. SHSP, v. 14, p. 558; Barefoot, p. 229.

26. Robertson, *General A. P. Hill*, p. 304.

27. Pegram to mother, October 28, 1864, Pegram-Johnson-McIntosh Papers; Chestnut, p. 665.

# 1865

## 1. THE STRONGHOLDS FALL

1. Caldwell, p. 254.

2. SHSP, v. 2, p. 299; Stiles, p. 350.

3. SHSP, v. 29, p. 289.

4. Douglas, pgs. 325, 326; Pegram to sister Mary, March 14, 1865, Pegram-Johnson-McIntosh Papers.

5. Douglas, p. 328; Trudeau, *The Last Citadel*, p. 259.

6. Grant, *Memoirs*, p. 687.

7. Gordon, pgs. 386, 389, 393.

8. Ibid., p. 403.

9. Ibid., p. 408.

10. Jones, *Lee's Tigers*, p. 223; Trudeau, *Last Citadel*, p. 340; SHSP, v. 31, p. 28.

11. Gordon, p. 411; Trudeau, *Last Citadel*, p. 348; Douglas, p. 329.

12. Freeman, *Lee's Lieutenants*, v. 3, pgs. 661, 664, 671.

13. SHSP, v. 14, p. 19; Chamberlayne, *Ham Chamberlayne*, p. 317; Dufour, p. 195.

14. LaSalle Pickett, *Pickett and His Men*, Atlanta, 1899, p. 395; Gordon, *General George E. Pickett*, p. 154; a curious irony of the battle at Five Forks is that it was not Pickett who was relieved of command but Gouverneur Warren; Sheridan felt that he had not been sufficiently aggressive and removed him that night.

15. Caldwell, p. 279.

16. Robertson, *General A. P. Hill*, p. 314, p. 316; SHSP, v. 12, p. 184 (quotation marks added); SHSP, v. 27, pgs. 30, 33; SHSP, v. 11, p. 566.

17. Douglas, p. 330; Freeman, *Lee's Lieutenants*, v. 3, p. 686.

## 2. RETREAT TO APPOMATTOX

1. Caldwell, p. 289; Freeman, *Lee's Lieutenants*, v. 3, p. 687.

2. O.R., 46:1, p. 1276; William Owen, *In Camp and Battle with the Washington Artillery of New Orleans*, Boston, 1885, p. 376; Gordon, p. 423.

3. Howard, *Recollections*, p. 376.

4. Alexander, *Fighting*, p. 522; SHSP, v. 13, p. 250.

5. Stiles, p. 330; we are using the spelling Sailor's Creek, although the original spelling is Sayler's Creek.

6. Ibid., p. 333.

7. Freeman, *Lee's Lieutenants*, v. 3, p. 706; Trudeau, *Out of the Storm*, p. 111.

8. SHSP, v. 25, p. 18; Burke Davis, *To Appomattox*, New York, 1959, p. 257.

9. SHSP, v. 13, pgs. 251, 253.

10. Gordon, p. 430.

11. Longstreet, *From Manassas*, p. 615.

12. SHSP, v. 25, p. 19.

13. Poague, p. 117.

14. Alexander, *Fighting*, pgs. 527, 528; Longstreet, p. 619; Alexander, *Military Memoirs of a Confederate*, Scribner's, 1907, p. 600.

15. Alexander, *Fighting*, p. 529; Gordon, p. 436.

16. Gordon, p. 437.

17. Eckenrode and Conrad, p. 354; Alexander, *Fighting*, p. 534; Gordon, p. 438.

18. Gordon, pgs. 439, 440, 442; Freeman, *Lee's Lieutenants*, v. 3, p. 730; Alexander, *Fighting*, p. 537.

19. Alexander, *Fighting*, p. 538.

20. B&L, v. 4, pgs. 737, 738.

21. Ibid., pgs. 740, 741.

22. Ibid., p. 743.

23. Blackford, p. 294; Moore, p. 290.

24. Caldwell, p. 308; John C. Waugh, *The Class of 1846*, Warner Books, 1994, p. 499; Freeman, *Lee's Lieutenants*, v. 3, p. 743.

25. Freeman, *Lee's Lieutenants*, v. 3, p. 752; Joshua L. Chamberlain, *The Passing of the Armies*, New York, 1915, p. 258.

## 3. THE SURVIVORS

1. All sources in this chapter come from standard reference works unless otherwise indicated; Lee's quotes are taken from Clifford Dowdey, *Lee*, pgs. 729, 733.

2. Trudeau, *Out of the Storm*, p. 294.

3. Piston, p. 105.

4. Osborne, p. 435, p. 469.

5. Bridges, p. 276.

6. Pfanz, pgs. 462, 465.

7. Taylor, p. 239.

8. Chestnut, p. 445.

9. Richard M. McMurry, *Hood*, p. 201; Chestnut, p. 441.

10. Ralph Lowell Eckert, *John Brown Gordon*, Louisiana State University Press, 1989, p. 318.

11. Lesley Gordon, *General Pickett*, p. 163.

12. Evans, *Intrepid Warrior*, p. 126.

13. Dufour, *Nine Men*, p. 266.

14. Manly Wade Wellman, *Giant in Gray*, Morningside, 1988, p. 226.

15. Laine and Penny, p. 343.

# INDEX